östberg™

Library of Design Management

Praise for the

ALMANAC *of* ARCHITECTURE & DESIGN

"The reader who uses this book well will come away with a richer sense of the texture of the profession and of the architecture it produces."
–Paul Goldberger
Pulitzer Prize-winning architecture critic, *The New Yorker*

"The essential and definitive tool for architecture and design facts. Very well done and valuable."
–William Stout Architectural Books

"Indispensable for any public library, any design firm, and any school of architecture, landscape architecture, or interior design...solid, reliable, and remarkably complete."
–Robert Campbell
Pulitzer Prize-winning architecture critic, *The Boston Globe*

"The only source book of its kind, this almanac is the design professional's definitive resource."
–MSN.com

"A goldmine of facts."
–HOK

"It won't tell you when the high tide will be next June 28 or who won the 1976 World Series, but the *Almanac of Architecture & Design* does fill you in on the field's best and little known facts...Where else can you find one book that lists the world's tallest buildings, average salaries for your region, and Ralph Adam Cram's birthday?"
–*Architecture* magazine

"A valuable and impressive resource."
–Industrial Designers Society of America

"Very useful."
–Art Institute of Chicago

"No comparable resource exists."
–Library Journal

"The Almanac is more than a mere compilation of numbers and words and charts and graphs...It is about ideas as well as information."
–Blair Kamin
Pulitzer Prize-winning architecture critic, *Chicago Tribune*

"Need a list of the world's 100 tallest buildings, or the fellows of the American Society of Landscape Architects, or the properties on the World Heritage List? This annual publication is a cornucopia of information about architecture and design award winners, professional organizations, records and rankings, leading firms, degree programs, preservation efforts, obituaries, and more. "
–Booklist

"...a core reference title for personal, professional, and academic reference collections."
–Midwest Book Review

Greenway's

ALMANAC *of* ARCHITECTURE & DESIGN 2004/FIFTH EDITION

Greenway's

ALMANAC *of* ARCHITECTURE & DESIGN 2004/FIFTH EDITION

Editors
James P. Cramer
Jennifer Evans Yankopolus

Foreword
Robert Ivy

The Greenway Group, Inc.

DesignIntelligence™

Editors: James P. Cramer and Jennifer Evans Yankopolus
Associate Editor: Lee Cuthbert
Editorial and Research Staff: Lisa Ashmore, Deanne Brown, Austin Cramer, Corinne Cramer, Doug Parker, Mary Pereboom
Consulting Architectural Historian: Jane Wolford
Layout: Jennie Monahan
Index: Kay Wosewick, Pathways Indexing

Greenway Communications,
a division of The Greenway Group
30 Technology Parkway South, Suite 200
Atlanta, GA 30092
(800) 726-8603
www.greenwayconsulting.com

Publisher's Cataloging-in-Publication

Almanac of architecture & design / James P. Cramer and Jennifer Evans Yankopolus, editors; foreword by Robert Ivy.
2004 ed.
p. cm.
Almanac of architecture and design
Includes bibliographical references and index.
ISBN: 0-9675477-7-6
ISSN: 1526-4017

1. Architecture–Directories. 2. Architectural design. 3. Architecture–United States. I. Title: Almanac of architecture and design

NA9.A27 2004 720

Cover: The Milwaukee Art Museum's Quadracci Pavilion. *Photo by William Lemke,* lemkephotography.com.

Distributed in North America by
National Book Network
(800) 462-6420
www.nbnbooks.com

Contents

Contents

4 RECORDS, RANKINGS & ACHIEVEMENTS

5 SUSTAINABLE/GREEN DESIGN

6 DESIGN & HISTORIC PRESERVATION

Contents

10 OBITUARIES

I INDEX

Foreword

What an extraordinary period for architecture. After years of feeling ignored or sidelined, suddenly architecture found itself at the center of national debate. Although propelled by the tragic events following the attacks on the World Trade Center in 2001, subsequent planning and design work, conducted squarely in the public eye, propelled architecture to prominence. Newspaper covers, interviews with architects in the media, critical columns, and public opinion polls: in them all, architecture served as the focus for a national dialogue on healing.

At the same time that the world sought new vision, it hunkered down. Hardly a week passed without seminars on beefing up security in public and private buildings; all clients struggled to balance easy access with adequate safety. Public bodies, such as the General Services Administration, held public forums to discuss how to justify a newfound transparency in public structures with the harsher realities of a terrorist-inflected world. The question on everyone's mind seemed to be, does every new building require stone walls and blast-resistant glass?

Ironically, while powerful political and economic interests envisioned multi-billion dollar projects for New York City, most of the nation struggled through the last days of a recession, which hovered like a bad cold, evaporating markets in a serious of hiccups. Schools and medical facilities remained active, however, encouraging a rush toward expertise in those two fields. In searching for sources for capital and commissions, architects looked east as the prospectors had once looked toward the American West, specifically toward China which seemed to contain boundless construction. Despite the lockdowns at the nation's airports, airplanes were still functioning and new airports were opening around the world.

International architects hopped planes to the United States, associating with American architects for high-profile commissions. Tadao Ando, for example, made Fort Worth, Tx., a regular stopping-off point, where he constructed a sanctuary for modern art in the prairie, all set on a reflective pond. But aircraft fly out as well as in. U.S. architects entered competitions alongside their international peers, chasing dollars and work. Not just the larger firms like Kohn Pederson Fox or Perkins & Will, either. Asymptote, a smallish group in New York, regularly bumped into Eric Moss who saw Steven Holl on his way to the same interview as Richard Meier.

Simultaneously as the economy was sliding toward its mushy nadir, designers coined a new form of wealth. Ironically, the recent past months have witnessed a robust flowering of innovation in building materials and systems. Magazine pages routinely reported on technological wonders, from digital media to new structural and glazing systems. As an example, every European architect seemed to have found new treatments for glass, which they etched, fritted, doubled or tripled in thickness,

Foreword

suspended or encased in window walls. Some architects like Steven Kieran and James Timberlake even began to rethink the structure of construction, a fundamental change for the entire industry.

While Ground Zero dominated the domestic media, other cities used architecture as an anchor for further urban advancement. Routinely, architects produced work of imagination and power; the greatest of the lot managed to wrest sculpturally expressive, individualistic works of art from mundane elements. Cultural landmarks grabbed most of the headlines. Frank Gehry, for instance, finally witnessed the opening of his Disney Concert Hall in Los Angeles, a masterwork by one of our greatest architects, originally conceived and designed before his Bilbao triumph. In Cincinnati, a museum by Zaha Hadid, the British architect, drew critical raves.

All was not Oz and the Emerald City. Left unchecked, despite all our concern, was the proliferation of sprawl, which continued to gobble up the American landscape at an alarming rate, including valuable agricultural land. Too many downtowns languished, even while yupsters headed back downtown for the amenities and the cultural mix. And housing deserved, though it failed to receive, its full measure of attention. Large architectural firms continued their assimilation of the marketplace at the same time that single practitioners' numbers increased, leaving the medium-sized firm struggling for air. The northeast went dark when the grid inexplicably frittzed.

Still, this was architecture's moment. Newspapers increased their coverage to include diverse points of view about the World Trade Center. Ordinary folk developed and argued their points of view about New York's plans, with some apparent spillover into their home communities. This marvelous three-dimensional medium, the language within which we live our lives, rose in all our consciousness beyond the esoteric or the realm of a consecrated priesthood to something that affects contemporary life–one positive development arising from tragic beginnings.

This almanac, filled with resources, can help all those involved in the building arts to better fulfill this unusual moment's potential.

Robert Ivy
Vice President, Editor in Chief
Architectural Record

Introduction: Architects and Designers Create Freedom and Flexibility

The cover of this 2004 Edition of our *Almanac on Architecture & Design* features the new Quadracci Pavilion at the Milwaukee Museum of Art designed by architect Santiago Calatrava. We believe that this museum is one of the most significant new museums built in the world in the last ten years. The Milwaukee Museum of Art inspired our new section featuring 100 American Art Museum and their Architects (see page 343). Thanks to this significant contribution in Milwaukee, the city's economy (and that of the museum itself) has soared. The economic importance of architecture and design is increasingly becoming a strategic imperative for institutions, corporations, and cities wishing to enhance their competitive appeal as a place to visit and as a quality of life enhancement for long time residents.

Not too long ago we also visited Dallas. Another museum there has brought significant attention. Just before this Almanac went to press, the Design Futures Council held a think-tank session in Dallas. We were fortunate to receive a preview tour of the Nasher Sculpture Center, designed by Renzo Piano, just days before it opened. The building is an elegant structure that works exceptionally well with its next-door neighbor, the Dallas Museum of Art, a national treasure nestled among the city's skyscrapers. The time we spent at the Dallas Museum of Art, in its garden courts, patios, and top-lit galleries, provided us with a metaphor for issues of cycles, changes, and growth in the design professions.

There are three entrances to the Dallas Museum of Art, which allow different areas to be opened or closed independently. A gently sloping hallway runs the length of the building, connecting the entrances and serving as the circulation spine. As the level of the museum's galleries change with the slope of the site, so does the hallway. The museum shop is prominent to all traffic inside the museum and is accountable to both visual arts education and enterprise itself. There is a steady line at the checkout counters where "architecture and design books are our top sellers," according to the manager. At the top of one of the longest stairways is the museum's gourmet restaurant–a classic design that is especially appealing for social and business appointments and even boasts an award-winning wine list. The Design Futures Council used this venue to celebrate two of its newest senior fellows: Ray Anderson, chairman of Interface and a leader in sustainable design, and Phil Bernstein, the leader of Autodesk's technology innovation program for the design professions. Following these presentations, we walked through the museum's exceptional galleries. The galleries are arranged on three levels, each giving coherence to the diverse collections, allowing visitors to progress in either direction from the bottom up or chronologically from the top down. The Founders Boardroom has a fireplace on one side and an open terrace looking out toward the city on the other.

Introduction

Significantly, the museum's spaces appear relevant today and yet flexible for tomorrow. In fact, the museum seems to be in control and, yet, free to change. It got us thinking about current changes in professional firms and organizations during these cyclical and sometimes turbulent days.

The survival of today's design organizations relies heavily on nimble management that can respond to and keep ahead of change. J.P. Morgan, the American financier and banker, testified before a committee of the U.S. Congress around the turn of the nineteenth-century where he was asked what the stock market would do next. Morgan paused for a moment, and then answered solemnly, "It will fluctuate." His reply is of course, just as relevant to architects and designers today. The economy will change. Certain segments will be stronger and others will lose their vibrancy. But just like the Nasher Museum and the Dallas Museum of Art, design firms that are in control are also free to change with these fluctuations.

We're hearing some stories of firms who are experiencing "reverse metamorphosis," turning from a frog to a tadpole. However, other firms are instead successfully managing the process of change toward new relevancy and new professional satisfaction.

Edward Larrabee Barnes, with John M.Y. Lee, Architects and Pratt Box Henderson and Partners, designed the Museum's spaces in 1984 to be flexible, agile, resilient, and anticipatory. Thus, this museum offers a visual reminder of structure, anticipation of future use, cycles, and of change management. The Nasher Sculpture Center by Piano, with design support and construction from the Beck Group, builds on the theme of flexibility where the curtain wall opens to the outdoors and an auditorium becomes a surprise amphitheater. Both museums anticipate the future.

There are methods and processes used to manage change, but fundamentally and most importantly it takes an attitude and structure that is open, flexible, and free. This structure allows natural movement toward renewal and creation of effective, relevant, strong, and nimble organizations. The Dallas Museum of Art and the new Nasher Museum remind us that value lives where there is flexibility to change. As we work in the context of 2004, we have come to appreciate the attitudes, strategies, and tactics of transformation. Best-in-class buildings and their designers can be our daily inspiration and remind us of new opportunities and relevance just ahead. In 2004 it will be our leaders in architecture and design who will create this better and more flexible world. We'll keep the records and keep the score. For the latest updates, track our progress at *www.di.net/almanac.*

James P. Cramer, Editor
jcramer@greenwayconsulting.com

Jennifer Evans Yankopolus, Editor
jyank@greenwayconsulting.com

1 Speeches & Essays

This year's contributors include speeches from Paul Goldberger, The New Yorker's architecture critic; urban planning authority Léon Krier, and AIA President Thom Penney as well as award-winning essays from design students. Also available are the 2003 Pritzker Prize acceptance speech and a discussion of sustainable design values, among many others.

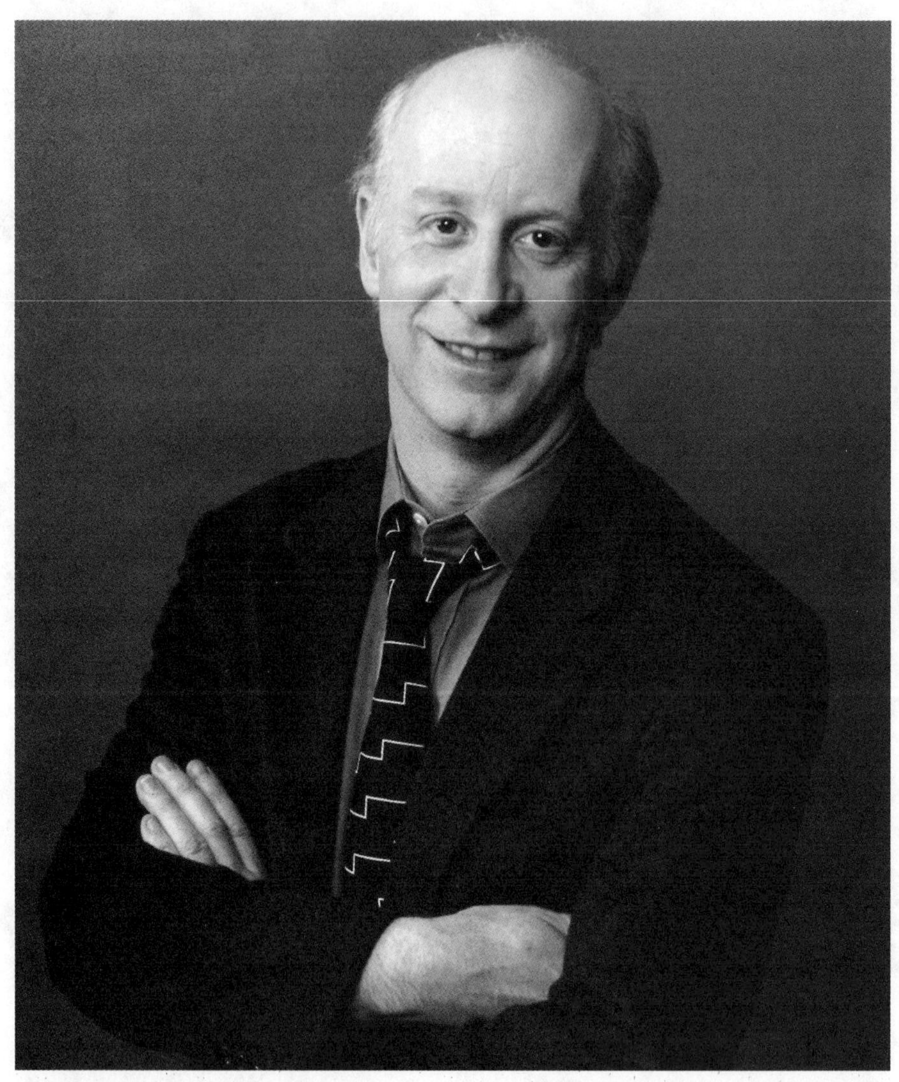

Paul Goldberger. *Photo: Gaspar Tringale*/The New Yorker.

The Case for Architecture

Paul Goldberger

The following comments were presented by Paul Goldberger, architecture critic for The New Yorker*, at the 14th annual Accent on Architecture Gala held at the National Building Museum on March 8, 2003.*

I'm honored and delighted to be here, not only to follow two such extraordinary awardees as that favorite building of mine in Cambridge and one of the great firms from the Northwest. It's also wonderful just to be here again in this space, which in and of itself makes the case so much better than words can about why architecture matters and how it can affect our lives. You know, lawyers often use a Latin phrase, "Res ipsa liquator" which means, "The thing speaks for itself," and I think that's what we can say about this extraordinary hall, that it speaks for itself.

That simply to be here in this space makes the case for architecture is clear. But, of course, not everyone is lucky enough to be here or in some other great architectural space. And I think we can't allow the case for architecture, if we're going to call it that, to rest solely on the experience of being in remarkable and wonderful buildings, those places that, as the great architectural critic Lewis Mumford once said, "Take your breath away with the experience of seeing form and space joyfully mastered."

Those are the great moments of architecture, those moments that take the breath away. And they are the most important ones, the ones that make civilization our cathedrals, both literally and figuratively, the works of architecture that add to our culture, the way Beethoven or Matisse add to our culture. Now at times like these, of course, when we face the possibility of American bombs dropping around the world, it is easy to put aside the significance of these moments, to think, as we are on the brink of war, that these experiences do not matter, that the joys of architecture are a luxury to be enjoyed in times of peace, not an essential part of our lives.

Well, sort of. But only sort of. Of course, architecture is not life or death. It is not as important as enlightened public policy or a healthy economy. It doesn't solve AIDS or cure cancer. It is not bread on the table or justice in the courtroom. It is always important to remember that a great court does not guarantee just and fair laws, just as a great religious edifice does not in itself assure the purity of the soul. But does that mean that great architecture cannot in its own way have a profound and subtle effect on the quality of life?

The Case for Architecture

Now these aren't easy questions in part because they invite such easy responses. The truth is that there's no way to tangibly measure the effect of architecture in our lives. There's no way even to be certain that it can make a demonstrable impact on the nature of a community. Don't think I'm going to follow up what I just said with some platitudes and homilies about how wonderfully architecture improves the quality of life, because the fact of the matter is I'm not always sure it always does.

I'll leave the absolute certainty on that subject to Frank Lloyd Wright. But I'm afraid that we can't necessarily count on architecture always to do all this wonderful stuff however much we may want it to. And even if we have experienced it ourselves, as so many of us in this room surely have either as clients or as users or as–better still–creators of spaces that do change lives, we know that sometimes architecture really does deliver in the way we want it to and change lives for the better.

But at the same time, we have to recognize that lots of the time it doesn't change lives and doesn't even provide for everyone the transcendent lift of brilliance that a great aesthetic experience can bring. But the point I want to make now is a little bit different. I don't want to think of architecture as only a luxury that we fight to protect, as an aesthetic experience like art and music but a thing we can't afford in times of stress and difficulty. I think that architecture is more essential, not less essential, in times of difficulty, that it can rise to its greatest potential and give us a symbol of what we want and what we aspire to as so few other things can.

It is not for nothing that Abraham Lincoln insisted that the building of the great dome of the Capitol continue during the Civil War, even though manpower was scarce and money was scarcer still. He knew that a rising dome was a symbol of the nation coming together and that no words could have the same affect on the psyche of the country that the physical reality of that building could. Lincoln knew, I suspect, that even the most eloquent words would not be present in front of people all the time the way the building could be.

And Lincoln knew also that there was value in making new symbols as well as in preserving older ones, and that building new was a way of affirming a belief in the future. Architecture is an effect of culture as much as a cause. It reflects and reinforces our values at least as much as it creates them. We've seen this more powerfully than ever in our lifetimes in these last 18 months, since September 11th, as the debate about what to do on the site of the World Trade Center has played itself out.

I'll come back to that in a moment, but first let me say that even before September 11th we were in a period of unprecedented interest in architecture, living through a time when the connection between architecture and the public took on a whole different dimension, a whole different meaning that it has in any of our lifetimes, or perhaps ever. I think this phenomenon is the result of several things, and one of them is closely connected to the national and international crisis we find ourselves in now. I want to try in the next few minutes to explain why.

But first, let me say that I think everyone knows that for a while people cared about architecture in a way that they did not before. You may not think this is so if you're an architect sitting around in your office in this down economy wondering why your phone doesn't ring more often with new clients. But that's not what I'm talking about. That's about economic cycles and I'm talking about cultural cycles. We are in the age of architecture and that is not going to change in the short term whatever the Dow Jones is doing.

There are several reasons for this and the first ones have nothing to do at all with world affairs and political crisis or war. In this very room when Frank Gehry received the Gold Medal just a few years ago, people talked at least implicitly about the Bilbao effect, about the way his extraordinary museum in Spain led to a rebirth of excitement about great buildings and their potential to awaken people to experience architecture in a broader way. Of course, Gehry's building, transforming event though it was, did not emerge all by itself with no connection to the culture.

It represented a kind of culmination of years of moving toward an increased willingness to see architecture as the basis for emotional experience, an increased willingness to celebrate expression and invention, not to mention creative power and the possibilities inherent in new technologies. Gehry summed up all these forces and put them together into a work that, like with all great art, we could say made the world a little bit different from the way it had been before.

But Bilbao and the buildings that preceded it and followed it in what we might call "new high visibility architecture with emotional impact"–not a very catchy name for a style, but it's all right; I'm not trying to name a style right now. Anyway, Bilbao and so many of the buildings like it have captured the public imagination, and they came about in part not only because of their architects and not only because we were living for a while in some pretty lush economic times (though that helped), we also had and still have a generation of clients who were better educated and more visually literate than the previous generation.

They have eyes. They look and they care about what they see. And that leads them to demand architecture that will excite them. And the more of that that gets built, the more the constituency for architecture grows. The age of architecture, if we can call it that, comes about in part because of architecture itself. The more it is a presence, the more there is a demand for it. I've always been very interested in the points of intersection between architecture and the rest of our culture, and I think today we have more of those points of intersection than ever before.

The Case for Architecture

But let me talk about another aspect of the current age of architecture...and try to connect it to this moment in history, a moment that, of course feels very different from Bilbao, a time that's defined more by the destruction of the World Trade Center than the construction of Gehry's museum. The question of rebuilding the World Trade Center put architecture on the front page quite literally as it has never been before. In fact, indeed, for a lot of my career as an architecture critic, I think I felt sort of like a sports reporter who covers lacrosse or something like that, and then suddenly I felt like I was writing about the World Series.

Architecture is Topic A as never before, written about in almost every newspaper in the world in the past year. We have to believe that this is fundamentally a good thing, whatever the problems it may bring along with it. If we thought there was a lot of public interest in architecture after Bilbao, that was nothing compared to what has happened since the World Trade Center. This is not the place to tell the long saga of rebuilding on this site and it's a saga without a clear end yet in any event.

But I would like to think for a moment about why it is that this has so captured the public imagination and what this can mean. The first reason, of course, is how it began. The city is not supposed to be subject to cataclysmic change. When something on the skyline is removed, the expected order of things is that it would be replaced relatively slowly, probably by something bigger. We may not like this Darwinism, but on some level I think we've nonetheless counted on the notion that the skyline did operate with a kind of predictable Darwinian order to it.

The survival of the fittest, the bigger things on the skyline would drive out the smaller ones. And while we didn't always believe it was, it would mean that things were getting better, we tended to accept this as the natural order of things. But on September 11th, of course, we experienced something else. Cataclysmic instantaneous change in the biggest things suddenly became the most vulnerable. It turned the entire order of this organic skyline upside down. Economics and aesthetics didn't matter. Only politics, and politics of the most horrific sort.

I'm talking about the skyline because it's become very clear to me over the last 18 months that while the horrendous loss of life is, of course, first and foremost in people's minds, the affection that people had for the skyline turns out to be pretty close behind. If you had asked me two years ago, I would have said only people like those of us in this room cared about the skyline as an object. But it turns out that almost everybody saw it as a public possession, as a shared work of public art.

I'm struck further by the paradox that the hugeness of the Trade Center Towers, which in the 1970s seemed to represent the utter destruction of the skyline, became what people missed most of all. What was demonized is now what is mourned. Some of this, of course, is the result of the terrible and tragic circumstances. These are our first skyscraper martyrs, and that changes everything about how they are perceived. We're not accustomed to thinking of buildings as martyrs.

But the World Trade Center is now inexplicably bound up in a whole set of other values that martyrdom embraces. If you doubt it, look at the sidewalk vendors all over New York who are still, 18 months later, selling pictures of the Twin Towers the way they used to sell pictures of Malcolm X or John F. Kennedy. All of this has put this building essentially out of the range of architectural criticism. Martyrs, after all, are beyond criticism. I suspect that Joan of Arc may not have been a very nice lady, but you will never hear anyone say that.

And no one dare say anymore that the World Trade Center was not a very nice building. But I should point out, if I can go off on one more quick tangent, that the World Trade Center, both for the terrorists who attacked it and for the people who mourn it, symbolized modernity. The Trade Center advertised the promise of modernity to the world. The fact that many of us thought there might have been a better advertisement for that idea is beside the point. To most of the world, the Towers represented the modernist idea in its most perfect, fully realized form.

And since to the attackers modernity was an evil that had to be abolished, the Towers were the ultimate target. Now these new associations have to change the way in which we now think of modernity. It is now, more than ever before, American. It has come to stand for the life we want to protect, as much as the Capitol and the Pentagon and the Lincoln Memorial. Modern architecture has never been intimately tied to the identity of this country, but it is now.

The terrorists have managed to do what no architect, nor architecture critic has ever been able to do, which is make this country cherish a piece of modern architecture and think of it as embodying the national ideals. Now modernity takes on a new aspect, that of cultural symbol, perhaps even more of a cultural symbol than the modernists had ever intended it to be. So we have now an extraordinary situation–modern skyscrapers as national symbols, as national martyrs coming in the context of a whole period, a decade or more, of rising architectural interests.

I guess, then, it should be no surprise that people were impassioned about the question of what should replace the World Trade Center, and that this became like no other land use question in American history. It has been a mess, highly politicized in the extreme, but is slouching toward resolution, and in a way that I have to say now is encouraging in spite of itself. There was a very bad start last summer when the Lower Manhattan Development Corporation, the state agency in charge of rebuilding, released six schemes for Ground Zero that were really more like six variations on a single

The Case for Architecture

scheme, every one of them looking pretty much like a bunch of medium-sized office towers around a dinky, little memorial park.

And it was not much of a surprise that they were roundly denounced by the public. In New York we have spent most of the last 15 months holding forums and public hearings and symposiums and panels, and some of them have been useful, some of them just blowing off steam. But one of these events turned out to be incredible, so much so that I would be tempted to call it a turning point in the story not only of the World Trade Center, but of American planning in general.

It was something called "Listening to the City" held in mid-July. And on a hot, July Saturday, when you would think people would have wanted to go to the beach, nearly 5,000 people came to the Javitz Convention Center to express their views, all done with modern, interactive technology, and it was a stunning moment. Thousands and thousands of people talking seriously about urban design is something I never thought I would see. And having them exercise this kind of judgment, demanding more vision, more boldness, something more special and less banal and less like business as usual, for that was how you could sum up the message of the day, that was pretty incredible.

Here you had citizens telling public officials that they were not showing enough boldness, that they were too cautious in what they had planned. You know, we've become, I think, so reactive and not proactive in our planning, so defensive, so hesitant to think boldly. And here were citizens saying it was time to think boldly again. That's what I mean when I say that the last few years in architecture really have had an effect on the culture and a positive one.

We are used to people saying "No" to big projects, but here they were saying, "Yes." They were responding not only to Bilbao and its progeny, but also to those same feelings that motivated Lincoln when he kept building the Capitol dome. Anyway, out of this little mess last summer came the idea of having the Lower Manhattan Development Corporation invite leading architects from all over the world to propose ideas for Ground Zero. They ended up choosing from 407 submissions seven teams.

Among them, as now everyone knows, Daniel Libeskind; Norman Foster; Skidmore, Owings and Merrill; a team including Charles Gwathmey, Richard Meier, Steven Holl, and Peter Eisenman; another team involving several of the most admired young architects from around the world like Greg Lynn, Ben Van Berkel, Kevin Kennon, and Jesse Reiser; another team with Rafael Viñoly, Fred Schwartz, and Shigeru Ban. When they presented their plans at a news conference a week before Christmas, you could see that something extraordinary was happening.

The Winter Garden at Battery Park City filled to the brim with television cameras and public officials, sitting still for three hours, three solid hours of serious presentations by serious architects, also televised live. Did you ever think that you would see the day? This was not an audience of architecture students coming to lectures, an audience of New York's power brokers. And then followed an exhibition of these designs that brought in tens of thousands of people and their display on a Web site that got literally millions of hits.

This was architecture's moment. It was not really designed to be a competition, but it kind of turned out that way. And the winner, as everyone in this room by now surely knows, was Daniel Libeskind. Libeskind calls his project "Memory Foundations" and it's based on the idea that the enormous concrete slurry wall that kept the Hudson River out of the World Trade Center foundation and which survived the attack should be retained as the heart of a below-ground memorial, which would surround the footprints of the Twin Towers.

In Libeskind's plan, a portion of the excavation at Ground Zero would always remain opened and exposed, and visitors would journey down into it. There would also be a museum structure and the eastern portion of the site would have taller commercial and cultural buildings and a new transit station. But the tallest structure of all would be largely symbolic, a 1776-foot tall broadcast tower attached to an office building at the northwest corner of the site.

Libeskind has an occasional tendency toward somewhat cloying, sentimental rhetoric, but he also has a great gift for the subtle interweaving of simple, commemorative concepts and abstract architectural ideas. In fact, there's no one alive who can do this better. His buildings are crisp and sharp and not nearly as sentimental as his words can sometimes be. He is both practical and visionary, and his ideas for this site resonate for meaning–with meaning, both for those who were directly affected by the attacks and for those who were not but who have also joined in the crusade to be sure that we do not settle for the ordinary here.

A few months ago I would never have imagined that the plan for Ground Zero would be designed by one of the world's most innovative and serious architects. Now the challenge is not to get a good plan, but to preserve it through the political process which has many hurdles still ahead. But we and all of you in this room have another challenge, too, and this is the one that has meaning for us right now. It is to take this extraordinary outpouring of public passion and make sure it is not lost, to make sure that we are able to harness the energy and emotion of this architectural moment and put it to good use as we move forward.

What we were seeing at Ground Zero is the recognition on the part of citizens that Lincoln was right. That buildings do have meanings and symbols, and that having lost one we need another, and that it should represent the best and the highest thing that we

The Case for Architecture

are capable of. Right now society is leading us. It is demanding imagination, boldness and vision in the public realm. That is the lesson of the Ground Zero planning process, as it is the lesson of the last generation of great buildings.

The problem today is not getting the public to care about architecture as it was for so long. Now everybody cares. The problem is making sure that architecture can live up to the public's hopes for it. Those hopes may sometimes be unrealistically high, but that is a glorious challenge for you as architects to face. The public wants architecture to inspire. And while that can be a hard thing to have to deliver, there can be no greater vote of confidence in this profession than the fact that the public looks to architecture now as something that will stand for all that this nation represents and enrich the life we live. Thank you.

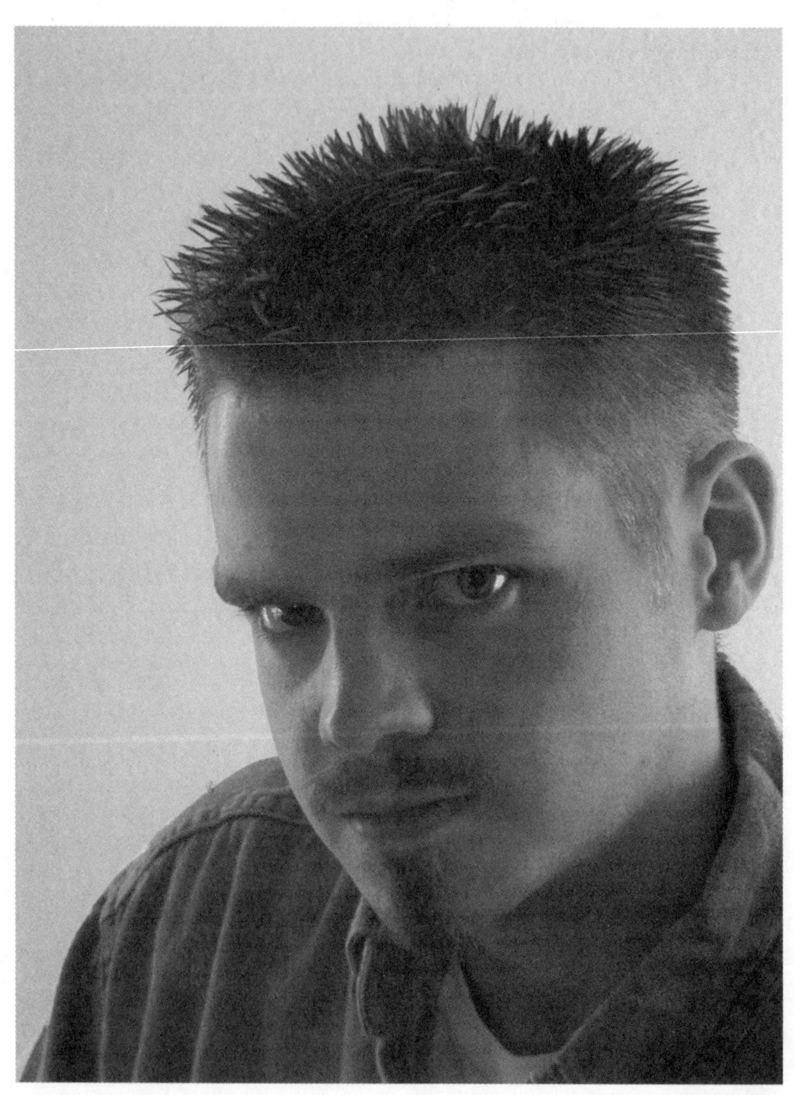

J. Brantley Hightower

Circles for a Living

J. Brantley Hightower

J. Brantley Hightower's essay "Circles for a Living" is the first prize recipient in the 2003 ArchVoices Essay Competition (refer to page 508), where entrants were asked to reflect on their career aspirations and values. Brantley Hightower is currently an intern architect working at Lake/Flato Architects, Inc. in San Antonio, Tx. He earned both a Bachelor of Architecture and Bachelor of Arts Degree from the University of Texas at Austin in 2000.

After graduating in May of 2000, I set out for the city of Chicago to become an architect. My heart was filled with a great optimism that the city and the work it surely offered held for me unbound promise. In time, I was able to land a job at a reputable Big Firm. I respected the work of the office, and it also offered me a good insurance and retirement plan. Keep in mind that in those heady, carefree days, people still wanted to place a portion of their hard-earned salaries in 401k plans–especially ones that invested heavily in high technology Internet stocks. It sounds crazy now, but I guess you had to have been there.

So with the innocent, idealistic optimism that only a six-year-old and a recent college graduate can possess, I began my professional architectural career. I was ready to do professionally what I had been training to do academically. I was ready to design.

And yet, for my first several months in Chicago, my primary task at the Big Firm was the creation of bubble diagrams. I also colored building elevations and floor plans. And so after five long years of arduous toil in architecture school, I realized I was coloring and drawing circles for a living.

Of course I knew that fresh out of school I would be starting at the bottom of the proverbial totem pole. Still, I was hoping that the transition from my education as a student to my education as an intern would be a harmonious one. It is not news to state that there is a substantial divide between the academic and the practical sides of architecture, but what I wasn't expecting was to lose the inspiration that I so loved about "doing" architecture. In school we are taught that architecture is not simply a job. It is a lifestyle. It is a way of looking at the world. It is a verb. It is a constant exploration where one looks for and finds inspiration in the world around them, and then applies that inspiration to create something completely new. And that thing we create is beautiful and makes a difference in the world.

And though in school we may slave away on hypothetical projects that will never be built, we can rationalize that it is all done in preparation for that first "real" job. But in

Circles for a Living

those first few months of that first real job, interns often find themselves as far away from architecture as ever. Instead of creating beauty, we find ourselves staring at colored circles on a 13-inch computer monitor, trying to remember at what point things had gone so horribly wrong.

To say I was unfulfilled would be an understatement. I sat in a large room full of men and women clicking and typing away furiously on their computers. I wondered if this was my lot in professional life.

As I sat in that room moving colored circles about on my screen, I couldn't help but wonder if every intern goes through the same bouts of depression and doubt. Most of my friends from architecture school seemed to be suffering a similar fate, but what about the Big Names that came before us? Had Le Corbusier ever questioned his career choice? Had Mies ever pondered a switch to professional polka dancing? Did Wright ever doubt if it was all worthwhile?

I decided to find out. I checked out Wright's autobiography from the library to see what it was like when he was an intern. As with his personality in general, Wright's *An Autobiography* is filled with plenty of self-serving prose and bombastic exposition. In his descriptions of his early career, he refers to himself in the third person more often than most and seems strangely immune to the humiliation and failure that are so much a part of most other early careers. Still, by reading through the text, I found that Wright's experience was not all that unlike what interns face today.

In 1887, Frank Lloyd Wright left architecture school in Wisconsin and, like me, set out for Chicago. He interviewed at several offices, and eventually found someone who would hire him. Joseph Lyman Silsbee, not Louis Henri Sullivan, was Wright's first employer. Wright was most likely hired because Silsbee had a professional relationship with Wright's uncle. While initially grateful for the job, Wright felt he was underpaid and that his non-work "experience" was undervalued.[1] Wright only worked in Silsbee's office for a year, but while he was there he was able to develop his drawing skills enough to impress Sullivan when he eventually went to him for a job.[2]

In 1888 Wright joined the firm of Adler and Sullivan. In the beginning, he was hired specifically to draw renderings of already executed designs. Wright apparently did this for some time. Over the course of many months, Wright and Sullivan developed a close working relationship, and Wright quickly rose to a position of prominence in the office. To be sure, Wright was talented, but he also seems to have acted as something of a "yes-man" to Sullivan. Other employees in the office took to calling him "Sullivan's Toady," which from time to time would cause Wright to become involved in rather violent brawls in the office. On one occasion, he knocked a co-worker unconscious with a T-square.[3] I must admit that there have been times when I would have liked to knock a co-worker or two unconscious with a T-square, but the opportunity has yet to present itself to me.

Regardless of if Wright was a kiss-up or not, he seems to have truly admired and respected his employer. Sullivan is the only architect Wright ever admitted to having been a direct influence on his work. And in addition to providing him with challenging work and a steady paycheck, Wright would listen eagerly as Sullivan described his matured views on the art and practice of architecture.[4] In other words, Wright positioned himself to be both professionally and academically educated by Sullivan.

Whether because he wanted more freedom to execute projects in the manner he saw fit, or because he needed the cash, Wright began to "moonlight" by taking on projects outside his regular job. For whatever the reason, Wright eventually left Sullivan's office and started a firm of his own.

I mention all of this not to try to impress people with my knowledge of Wright's early career, but rather to illustrate the point that becoming a good architect, like designing a good building, has apparently always been a slow, inefficient process. Wright's skill was a culmination of his year at Silsbee's office, his seven years at Sullivan's office, and everything else he read, saw, and did in between.

And so I kept Wright's story in mind when I headed back to work. As unfulfilling as the circle diagrams were, I tried, like Wright, to be patient with my initial task. I also started working on competitions in the evenings and on weekends. More important than the prospect of winning, these design exercises kept my creative gears lubricated in a way that work was initially not able to do. Competitions and travel also kept me inspired and reminded me of the excitement that architecture could possess. If I was not able to be inspired at work, there was nothing that prevented me from being inspired on my own time.

Eventually, because of my great skill at creating bubble diagrams, I was added to a team that was programming a school in Indiana. Over the next several months I traveled to a small town in that state and assisted in gathering information for the school's design. While I hadn't moved to Chicago to do programming, I found the process and the people I was working with intriguing. With them I was able to witness first hand how an infant building is formed. And while I was still drawing bubble diagrams, the circles now had a context and a meaning.

The time spent programming in Indiana would prove valuable in another way as well. When the programming was complete and the project turned over to the Lead Design Guy at the Big Firm, I made the case that I should be part of the design team. The people in charge agreed. This was no doubt because of my prior knowledge of the project, but I like to think my particular talent for drawing circles played a part as well.

Circles for a Living

The Lead Design Guy was an interesting fellow. While maybe not as influential as Wright's Sullivan, he was "my" Sullivan, and he was extremely good at what he did. As an intern, I was able to learn a great deal by working under him. I did not become the Lead Design Guy's Toady, for that was someone else's job, but by observing how he worked and how he made decisions, I feel I was able to grow as an intern.

Over the course of the next year, I averaged around 60 hours a week and worked most weekends. There was an unwritten rule at the Big Firm that if a person worked with the Lead Design Guy, that person was expected to stay extra hours. I was lucky in that I was at a point in my life where I had few outside commitments, and so I was able to maintain this lifestyle. And while I may have had less time to enter competitions and travel, I was being inspired more by what I was doing at work.

Ultimately, my experience at the Big Firm was a good one. I was able to see a project develop from the schematic design phase through the creation of construction documents. I had made friends and had experiences that would no doubt stay with me for the rest of my life. I had also steadily contributed to 401k plan that was now completely worthless, but that's another story altogether.

As I neared the end of my second year at the Big Firm, I began to sense my growth as an intern was beginning to plateau. Wright knew when it was time to leave Silsbee's office, and I knew when it was time to leave the Big Firm. And so after two years, I did.

In comparing my experience to that of Mr. Wright, I do not mean to imply that I am as talented as Frank and I certainly do not mean to imply that I dress as well, although I do intend to begin wearing a cape at some point. Having had the opportunity to experience many of his buildings first-hand while living in the Midwest, I feel strongly that he was truly a genius and that his work is worthy of respect even if some of his life choices are not. Still, Wright and I do share a few significant characteristics. Namely, we both can be categorized as white Anglo-Saxon Protestant males.

To be sure, the profession's playing field is considerably more level at the turn of this century than at the turn of the last one, but it would be overly optimistic to say that true equality yet exists. In speaking with friends, I have heard of many disturbing stories that confirm that glass ceilings and prejudiced views still exist in the profession. Interns have more than enough difficulty to overcome to begin with–they do not need more.

But there is reason to hope. The current crop of interns has grown up in an integrated global society and has graduated from architecture schools that now have a more evenly split gender ratio. We have studied with individuals from all over the world, and thanks to email, we are often able to stay in contact with those individuals. And unlike some of our employers, we have learned that the drafting board is blind to color and gender. And we, the interns of today, are the ones who will be running the profession in a few short decades.

* * *

After Chicago, I worked for a few months at a wonderfully Small Firm in Dallas with no computers and no bubble diagrams. And then, in the fall, I came to San Antonio, Texas, where I am currently employed at a Medium-Sized Firm. To be honest, I can't say which firm type is best for an intern. In the Small Firm I was able to keep up with everything that was going on at all times, but the scale and number of projects were limited, and so too was job security. The Medium-Sized Firm has a healthy range of projects, but I don't get dental insurance. I had great medical, dental and death and dismemberment coverage at The Big Firm, but the scale of the projects and the number of people in the office were so large that it was often overwhelming. I have yet to find an office type with a reliable fax machine.

The fact is each office offered opportunities for me to learn and, in time, things to get excited about. Sometimes the lessons were unclear and sometimes the opportunities were not the ones I wanted, but they all have contributed to a greater understanding of how buildings get built.

In addition, I have learned to not expect everything from my job. As easy as it is to blame employers for the frustrating situation recent graduates face, it may very well be that it is on our shoulders, as interns, to create the experiences we need to make ourselves better architects. To be sure, interns are in many ways at the mercy of our employers, but it seems to be much more empowering to believe that we and not they are ultimately in control. While we may have relatively little authority over what we are assigned to do at work, that is not the only place where we can learn. If someone else controls our destiny between 8 a.m. and 5 p.m., we owe it to ourselves to assert our autonomy in other places. Whether it is by volunteering for Habitat for Humanity or by taking home a copy of the International Building Code and learning all there is to know about dead end corridors, there are plenty of ways to learn outside of the office. This kind of "extracurricular" enrichment may not always be fun, but this sort of study was what we did all the time when we were students. If we are truly interested in learning, we should be no less inclined to study now.

In the end, we can find some comfort in knowing that even Frank Lloyd Wright was an intern once and endured experiences similar to those we face today. Times may have changed, but much has remained the same. We are all still in the business of creating architecture. We are all still in the business of creating beauty. And in order to do that, someone has to draw the circles for the bubble diagrams.

Circles for a Living

References

[1] Wright, Frank Lloyd. *An Autobiography*. New York: Duell, Sloan and Pearce, 1962. p. 68.

[2] Williamson, Roxanne Kuter. *American Architects and the Mechanics of Fame*. Austin: University of Texas, 1991. p. 41.

[3] Wright. p. 101.

[4] Wright. p. 108.

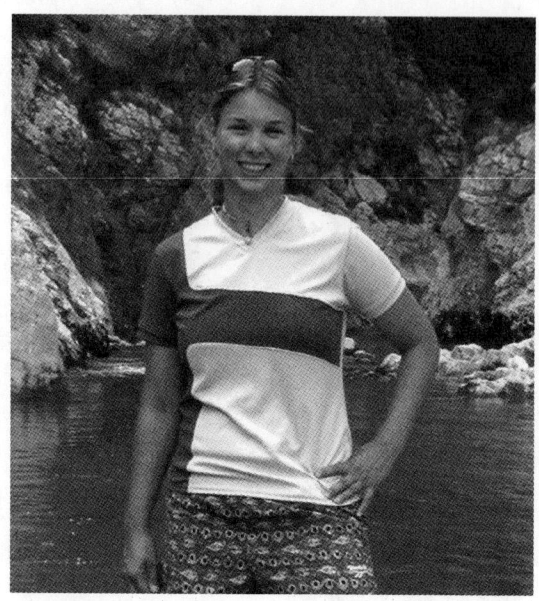

Emily Dow

Evolving Design Education: A Necessity for the Future

Emily Dow

Each year the Almanac of Architecture & Design *asks a recent graduate from our top-ranked school for interior design (see page 554 for this year's complete list) to contribute his or her thoughts on design education and the future of the profession. This year's essayist, Emily Dow, graduated magna cum laude from the University of Cincinnati with a Bachelors of Science of Interior Design. She is currently working for the Walt Disney Company in Los Angeles as an Imagineer.*

With ever-increasing fossil fuel prices, a scarcity of natural resources, and an unstable global economy, the future of the design profession stands undetermined. During the past decades of economic and social expansion, many architects and designers have failed to take responsibility for their buildings beyond their vellum drawings and compositions. As society slowly shifts from an old model based on individualism to a new philosophy based upon collective goals, architecture must complement this shift by challenging the field to rethink its ideology. Design has been based upon artistic expression and exhibitions of personal interpretations of society. The design of this new century must change the framework of its education and profession by taking responsibility for social issues, environmental concerns, and global problems. Ian McHarg challenges designers and architects to take initiative in their field and to "be leaders in this paradigm shift–not like we deserve to be, but no other group is sitting around with T-squares in sight."

The metamorphosis of the field of design rests upon the ability of colleges and universities to rethink educational practices and standards. To create the most valued design professionals, design education must acknowledge the evolving complexity of the world's problems. Instead of creating designers to feed the existing infrastructure, design curricula must prepare their leaders for unprecedented challenges. By infusing curricula with interdisciplinary opportunities and enriching studio projects with real-world experiences, students will learn the critical thinking and creative leadership necessary to facilitate change in the profession and world.

Universities are ideal forums for students to engage in interdisciplinary learning since experts from a variety of fields are in such close proximity. If studio projects were focused on integrated solutions instead of pure formalism and theories, students would grow into designers equipped with broader perspectives, enhancing innovation and solving multidimensional problems. Since changes in the field of architecture and

Evolving Design Education: A Necessity for the Future

interior design arrive slowly, it is essential that students study other fields so that they can anticipate changes in their profession. A solid education in business and economics would demonstrate to students that designs are only ideas unless accompanied by sound marketing strategies. Additionally, business education would enable designers to carefully define their target market to create economic solutions that satisfy the client's needs. Learning from educators of human physiology, psychology, sociology, and cultural anthropology would motivate design students to create projects that are both formally intriguing and contextually specific. Knowledge of geology, biology, and physics would help students understand technology and scientific principles that are the foundations of their design. Creating studio projects that engage different levels of students and faculty in diverse university programs would encourage an interdisciplinary approach and help students learn to work in team situations in design firms.

As students learn to work with many different professionals on projects, they will become design professionals who can fluently facilitate ideas between diverse fields, since as many as twenty-five specialists may be required for a single building. Traditional architecture and design firms currently function on a linear design process where certain specialties are involved at different stages of the project. Complex buildings and efficient designs require understanding by all parties for correct implementation. Cost estimators, contractors, mechanical engineers, structural specialists, landscape designers, interior designers, and architects working together in an initial meeting will heighten efficiency by communicating concerns early in the process. When Lewis Mumford was asked why he stopped writing about architecture he stated, "Because the real problems of civilization aren't solvable by the architect or by any one group of people." Integration of disciplines will allow each group to contribute their exclusive information toward a common goal.

The most important aspect of design education is its direct relationship with the profession. By supplementing theoretical projects with real-world experience, students begin to understand the necessity of the strong communication of ideas and interpretation of information. Internship and cooperative educational programs are a transcendent way to provide students a practical application for their theoretical knowledge. This is a necessary component of every professional curriculum. As students work alongside designers, they apply the knowledge gained through their coursework to actual design problems. This process allows a shift to occur from the explicit learning of the university to the implicit understanding of a professional career.

Students can further understand the profession by participating in studio projects that engage community members as clients, enabling students to gain authentic experiences while enhancing the surrounding community. In order to create a building that better suits the users' needs, a strong dialogue must exist between the architect and the client. By working with stakeholders in a charrette process, issues can be addressed in order to create the most appropriate solution. This procedure does not presume that every person possesses the building expertise of a designer or engineer, but it validates the idea that individuals have the fundamental design literacy that allows them to participate in the shaping of their places. As students learn to develop a project with the client's input, they will become diplomatic professionals who can facilitate interactions between different viewpoints in the design process. Students spend a great deal of time formulating thoughtful design solutions for fictional clients when the time could be better spent learning valuable professional skills and enhancing the lives of local clienteles.

When developing a curriculum, it is vital for universities to realize that they not only teach students to be designers, but can actually change the definition of the design profession. With the diverse learning opportunities students experience in a competitive design program they will become innovative professionals and visionaries within their firm. By teaching students a variety of approaches to design and allowing them to apply their newfound knowledge to actual situations, universities will create a generation of design students who will revolutionize the future.

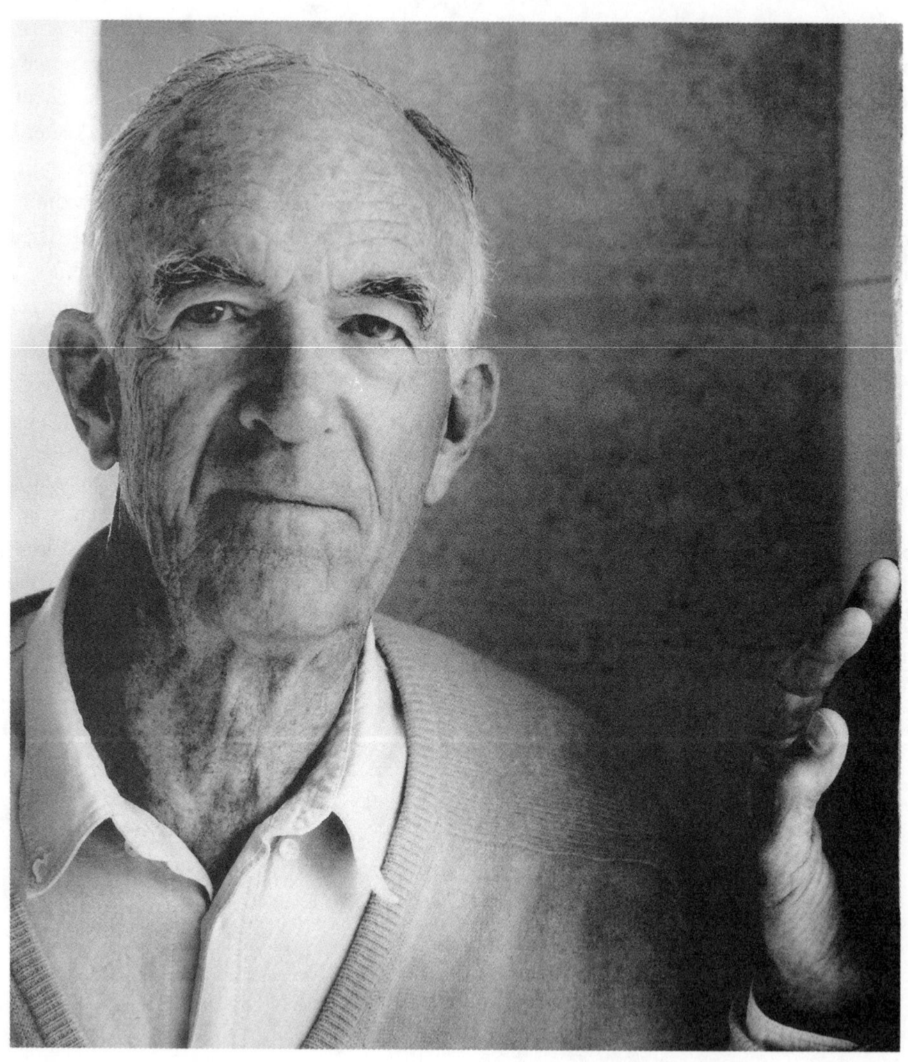

Jørn Utzon. *Photo courtesy of the Hyatt Foundation.*

Jørn Utzon: the 2003 Pritzker Prize Laureate

Jørn Utzon was awarded the Pritzker Prize at the Royal Academy of Fine Arts of San Fernando in Madrid, Spain on May 20, 2003. His son and partner, Jan Utzon, spoke on his behalf.

Your Majesty, your Royal Highness, we are greatly honored by your presence here. I want, in the name of my father, Jørn Utzon, to apologize for his absence. It is for reasons completely independent of his own wish that unfortunately he cannot come here today. I thank you all for your wonderful and kind words to him and about my father. Words I'll convey to him, words he will cherish as part of the prize.

It is with great joy I stand here today receiving the Pritzker Prize for Architecture on my father's behalf. My father has asked me to express his happiness and his gratitude to the Pritzker family and to the members of the Pritzker jury for honoring him this way.

As his son for nearly 60 years and his professional associate for more than 30 years, I feel deeply grateful to represent him, as some of the honor of the Pritzker Prize also rubs off on the past and present staff in our office and myself.

When my father was in his final year in school, after a not terribly successful time in that institution, he told one of his teachers that he might want to try to become an architect. The teacher responded that she thought that that was possibly the only profession he might be able to cope with.

However, as he entered The Royal Academy of Fine Arts in Copenhagen he entered a whole new world. Suddenly he found himself surrounded by like minds and subjects that he was able to soak up like intellectual nourishment after the boring school years.

His career is indebted to many things: other architects, artists, nature, diversity of cultures and, of course, his parents who infused him with a healthy outlook on life. He would also be the first to point to my mother, Lis, his wife for more than 60 years, as the one person who has supported him throughout his whole career enabling him to pursue his profession with the intensity needed to achieve the results we can all enjoy today.

It is indeed my father's good fortune that enables me to stand here today. When he commenced practicing architecture in the early post-war years in Denmark, the country's economy was at an all-time low and work was hard to come by. He therefore participated in a lot of architectural competitions, and winning the competition for the new Sydney Opera House was a major turning point in his career. From practicing in a small Nordic country with little possibility of working outside Denmark, even though inspired by a multitude of other persons and cultures, his experience of the world suddenly opened to him in a way unheard of at the time.

Jørn Utzon: the 2003 Pritzker Prize Laureate

This project has been the stepping stone, admittedly a large one, for an international practice which has brought him and us as a family in contact with a multitude of opportunities around the world.

My father has always been very inspiring for people around him and for us, his children. His joy over other people and peoples, over beautiful places, over nature, color, light, etc. spills over onto those surrounding him. The enthusiasm he always expresses over things that he likes or admires has had a very positive effect upon the rest of us. I often hear from former employees how positive an influence in their lives it has been to have worked with my father.

But when you grow up in such an environment you hardly recognize the situation as a special one. And it was not until we approached Sydney that I began to realize that my childhood environment was unique. From then on our lives were filled with a succession of wonderful experiences only temporarily to be interrupted by the unfortunate termination of my father's work in Sydney. It is therefore a great joy for my father to have been asked back to Sydney to act as a consulting architect in the planning of the future of the Sydney Opera House.

When I hear him speak of the then Premier of New South Wales, Joe Cahill, with great fondness and when I think of how his love for Australia and the many wonderful people he encountered while we were living there, it makes me very happy on his behalf that he is again involved in this most important work in his life. As his son and his associate it has been a great privilege working with him for all these years and it is my great fortune to be involved in the continued development of the Sydney Opera House as his partner.

After our family left Sydney, my father worked in Denmark, in Switzerland, and the United States. Following some years teaching at the School of Architecture in Honolulu, he won a competition for a new parliament building in Kuwait. Around this time my parents decided to build their first home in the beautiful island of Mallorca. This was first to be a holiday home but it soon turned out to be the permanent residence. My father loved working with the local craftsmen among whom he found a parallel to the many craftsmen he knew from his boyhood in Denmark.

When my father appeared at the building site with some bottles of wine, the craftsmen knew that he had new ideas during the night and that some of the work already done would have to be changed. And the mild climate, the generous people, the nature and culture of Mallorca and Spain became an integral part of my parents' lives. And after living in this wonderful place for about 25 years they can think of no other place they would rather be. So I would like to end this speech by reading to you my father's own words of thanks for the Pritzker Prize.

"This is indeed a wonderful day. I am deeply grateful and happy for the recognition of my work I have received via The Pritzker Prize. The prize means so much to me because the group of architects who received the Pritzker Prize before me are all architects I admire very much and whose works are so important for the future of architecture. My two sons and my daughter with whom I work, my wife Lis, the architects with whom I work in our office, and my good clients are all very happy. We see our work in a new light and we feel that the Pritzker Prize heightens people's awareness to the importance of architecture, and that it creates a benchmark of excellence in architecture.

The Pritzker family and the Pritzker Prize jury are the strongest exponents for the highest standards of architecture. I thank you with all my heart and send you all my best wishes for the future success of the Pritzker Prize."

Courtesy of the Hyatt Foundation

Tom Johnson. *Photo courtesy of the Design Resource Institute.*

Old and New Value in Eco Design

Tom Johnson

Tom Johnson, the co-founder of the International Design Resource Awards Competition (IDRA), gave a speech on the idea of Design with Memory™ and sustainable design at the IDRA seminar held in Kanagawa, Japan, in December 2002. A portion of that speech is excerpted below. A description of the program and a list of current winners can be found on page 409, with more detailed information available online at www.designresource.org.

In 1994 the International Design Resource Awards Competition was begun with the goal of encouraging the development of the new concept of sustainable design in products and architecture. Washington State has an interesting history which contributed to the formation of the Competition. Historically, the Pacific Northwest has been a place of great natural abundance around which many communities and businesses sprang up to harvest the trees and fish. As time passed, Seattle and Portland developed into major metropolitan areas with new industries centered around information technology, trade, transportation and biotechnology. As this evolution was occurring, citizens as well as business owners and the government were becoming aware that our long term survival is linked to maintaining a healthy eco-system. With modern technology coupled with increased consumer demand, the rate of harvesting of these natural resources began to accelerate rapidly. Eventually these resources would no longer renew themselves and were on the verge of exhaustion. This situation led to many conflicts between groups dependent on harvesting the resources and those committed to helping preserve them for the future. These conflicts reached a climax in the early 1990s with many lawsuits halting traditional industries and many communities finding their economies devastated.

At the same time efforts were being made to develop recycling systems in the urban areas to help reduce the quantity of materials going into landfills as waste. The Competition was founded with the idea that these "new," post-consumer recycled materials, being gathered primarily from urban centers, could become new raw materials that would fuel the development of products and businesses to help rejuvenate the economy. At the same time these new businesses would help the environment by lessening the demand for traditionally sourced raw materials–doing well by doing good. The goal was for the Competition to serve as a focal point where designers could explore the potential of these new materials and design strategies by

Old and New Value in Eco Design

drawing attention to winning designs through awards and exhibitions. Manufacturers, marketing people and the general public could then find a place to look for new sustainably designed products and this would help launch new business activity.

Criteria for the jurors to make their selections were determined early on and included: 1. Do the projects contain a high degree of used, post-consumer recycled, or sustainably harvested materials? The more the better. 2. Do the projects demonstrate the ability to add value to these new materials and to increase their usage? 3. Will the work be suitable for commercial production?

In addition to these questions, the jurors also wanted to know if the project could be reused or easily disassembled for reuse and recycling, and what was the relative amount of energy used to produce the work. Finally, the jurors were also interested to know if there were any toxic material issues, and, if so, how was that dealt with. It was also recognized that sustainable design is inherently complex, so it was important that we have jurors from different backgrounds select the best work. Typically there are six jurors with materials science, marketing, manufacturing, education, architecture and product design backgrounds.

Since the time the Competition began we have seen the development of two important new concepts in the field of sustainable design. The first is called "Life Cycle Assessment" or LCA. Sometimes known as cradle to grave analysis, this process analyzes the entire "life cycle" of a product, from procurement of the raw materials, through its use, to its eventual disposal and the possible reuse or recycling of its components. With this new tool, updated with information from around the globe, designers can now make increasingly better environmental choices when choosing materials and creating products.

The second concept is called "Biomimicry." This is the title of a book by Janine Benyrus and serves as a reminder that in this life all we are learning about is nature and that the more we learn, the more we will tend to imitate nature when making products and buildings for our society. This is inherently a positive message because we can recognize that in nature there is no waste, and it is waste that has created some of the most difficult environmental challenges for us today. We have become very good at gathering materials from the earth and refining them and manufacturing products for use, but we have forgotten what happens while the person is using the product or building and what will happen next after its useful life is past. Increasingly, more designers are remembering to include these ideas as part of the design process.

Thinking about the projects that have come through the Competition over the years gives me the opportunity to see the differences between old and new values in eco-design. An "old" value in eco-design can be seen in an ancient Japanese tea ceremony cup that was broken and carefully repaired. This care and attention gives the cup an added value as it becomes a cultural icon. "Old" values in eco-design might also refer to products that have a long life, and to the fact that prior to the twentieth century, most materials were not "synthetic" and therefore would decay and return back to the earth if the product had a short life.

The "old" idea of returning materials to the earth is no less valuable today. Evidence of this is found in the recent book *Cradle to Cradle* by William McDonough in which he advocates for the idea of creating products and buildings where the natural and technological materials can be recycled separately. This way the natural materials can return back to the earth and the technological materials can be reprocessed and reused again.

It is important to think about products and buildings as part of a bigger system of relationships between ourselves and nature. Designing in this way gives products and buildings an added value which is derived from the respect these projects have for the environment and the well being of humankind. For example, these added values could come from the elimination of waste or from improving our eco-system. It is vitally important that these added values also translate to added commercial value so that this new way of designing can grow and prosper. In our "new" world of mass communication and mass production, we are in the process of developing these new values for eco-design.

Over the last three years we have used the phrase "Design with Memory™" as a theme for the Competition and for the traveling exhibits. At first the phrase was created to remind us that with sustainable design it is necessary to think about where a material comes from and how it is used and where can it be useful again in the future. Through interaction with the entrants and jurors this phrase has grown to include additional complementary levels of meaning. For example, Design with Memory could mean adding value to a design by employing the memory of the material's previous use in the new work. It could also mean adding value to the project by actively employing the memory of the user or, perhaps, the memory of the material or product itself in the new work. These are all new strategies to create a design aesthetic that will add value to the works and delight the customer while working to design in harmony with nature.

The following 2002 winning International Design Resource Awards projects, and their photos on pages 32, 34) illustrate some of the "new" values in eco-design:

Adding Value to Reprocessed Recyled Materials

NIKE Park: The jurors awarded this project to salute NIKE's efforts to create a new sportmat material, which they use in their NIKE Parks, by regrinding the soles of used

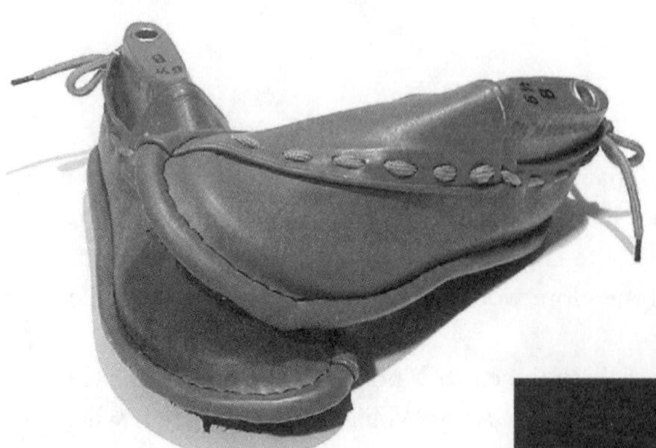

Top, OURO; *right*, NIKE Park; *bottom*, Sycamore Fan. *Photos courtesy of the Design Resource Institute."*

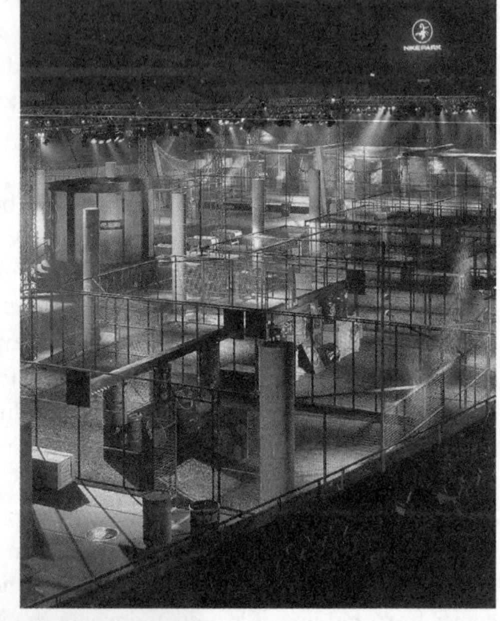

shoes. These parks provide an environment where it is hip to be into re-use and recycling and strengthens the link in the participant's recycling and health and exercise.

Design for Composting

OURO: This award-winning shoe design uses many new strategies including the use of recycled rubber from tires in the soles, but I think what particularly caught the jurors attention was the research undertaken to locate leather tanned without using chrome so that the uppers of the shoe could be composted back to the earth, the fact that the shoes are stitched, not glued, and the insoles are made from reprocessed recycled leather.

Biomimicry

The Sycamore Fan: Have you ever watched a maple seed spin as it falls to the ground? If you hold the seed stationary and spin it on its axis then air should circulate–and it does! This designer learned from nature. The fan is made from rotationally molded recycled PET plastic and should be available commercially in the spring of 2004.

New High Value Uses with Traditional Materials

Charcoal Hanger: The hanger is molded from waste pieces of wood and then carbonized in a furnace. The hanger takes advantage of the humidity control and anti-odor effect of charcoal. Washing the charcoal eliminates any staining of clothing from the hanger. After us, the hanger can be used as a soil nutrient or water purifier.

Design with Memory of the Previous Material Use

Bags from Bags products: This project is a great example of a high value product made with materials that are commonly thrown away (used plastic shopping bags) and which incorporates the good qualities of these materials. Here the waterproof and colorful aspects of the material are emphasized, and the Memory of the original product is very evident.

Design with the Memory of the User

Radio: This project has had perhaps the most influence on my thinking about sustainable design. This project was created in a remote village in Indonesia–the product of a commune which is developing business initiatives to keep the young people in the village from leaving, and provide an alternative to harvesting the natural resources surrounding the village. The Radio was designed to be made from pallet lumber from the local airstrip. A notable feature of the design is the lack of graphic information, which is quite intentional. The idea is that you must develop a relationship and

Top left, Bags from Bags; *right*, Radio; *bottom*, Charcoal Hanger. *Photos courtesy of the Design Resource Institute.*

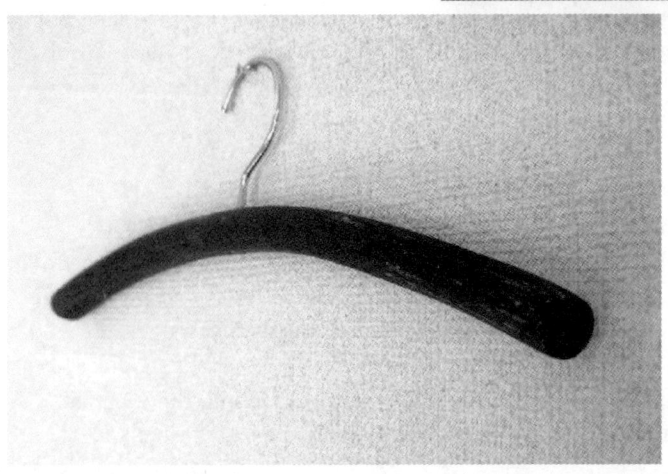

familiarity with the Radio to use it, and that this will lead the user to develop a strong bond to the product and thus keep the Radio for a long time. This is a strategy to reduce consumerism by developing a feeling of companionship between the product and user.

This is a wonderful time to be a designer. There has perhaps never been a time when these talents are more needed to invent methods by which we can grow and transition from our current forms of social and economic interaction to a more sustainable future. With the outpouring of creativity we have seen in hosting the Competition, I am very much looking forward to seeing these new materials and forms of design expression in new products and architecture. It has been said that the past century has been the age of the individual, but this new century will be the age of relationships. Buckminster Fuller observed that humans are constantly inventing means of communication, and this will mean that it is inevitable that we will all get to know each other around the globe. We need to learn how to manage relationships for the benefits of this event to be realized. Sustainable design is the mirror to this social trend in the economic world. We are learning to "design with memory" now and to remember where materials come from, how to use and re-use them and to think about where will they go next–back into the eco-system or into another product–as we create the buildings and products for the future.

Source: Design Resource Institute

Top to bottom: Robert Hull, Dave Miller. *Photos courtesy of The Miller/Hull Partnership*.

Pacific Northwest Regionalism: Miller/Hull, 2003 Firm of the Year

Robert Hull and David Miller, partners in The Miller Hull Partnership, the 2003 AIA Architecture Firm of the Year, delivered the following acceptance speech at the 14th annual Accent on Architecture Gala at the National Building Museum in Washington, D.C., on March 8, 2003.

(Bob Hull begins…)

Thank you, Thom. Dear AIA Board Members, dear friends and clients, ladies and gentlemen, thank you for so many things. Thank you for your uncompromising commitment to architecture. Thank you for choosing us for this incredible award, which we were longing and hoping to get. Thank you to our nominator, Bruce Blackmer, FAIA, with your wise counsel and encouragement we are standing here tonight. Thank you to my partners, principals and associates, all who are here tonight. We have worked together for many years with an unbelievable commitment to design quality and our community. And finally, thank you for recognizing The Miller/Hull Partnership for this incredible honor.

In 1977, Dave Miller and I opened our office in Seattle. In school Dave and I had a lot in common, and it seemed like a natural evolution to practice together–it has been a remarkable partnership, one of trust, love and *desperation.* When we started the firm, we didn't have a clear vision for where we were going and certainly no clients. But we had our mutual faith in creating the best architecture for each of our clients. This is still true. We hold design on the highest pedestal of our ambitions, everything follows from that. Over the past 25 years, Miller/Hull has slowly evolved into a balanced culture of design collaboration and risk taking. We have been joined along the way by our partners, Norm Strong, our fearless leader, and Craig Curtis who is doing some great design work and giving the firm his boundless energy. We never would have received this honor without the amazing collaborative spirit the four of us share and our faith in the strength of the Firm's position on the humanistic and environmental considerations in architecture. So what is this position?

(David Miller continues…)

Architects are the inventors of much of our environmental fabric and have the responsibility to confront a difficult world. We should design by example; our architecture should reflect our vision of an ideal world. Although Miller/Hull's houses

Pacific Northwest Regionalism: Miller/Hull, 2003 Firm of the Year

have received most of the press, our public institutional work has had the greatest effect on people. Public architecture by definition has an obligation to impart meaning and symbolism for people. Meanings are contained in the essence of form. We must liberate architecture from the confused meanings of form and create responsible cultural representation. The public architecture of Miller/Hull expresses clarity of form–form and program evoke one another. Our city halls invite the public in, our recreation centers strengthen communities, our college buildings teach students and faculty about space and structure and our park structures connect people to the land.

As all four partners grew up in the Northwest, we love the land. Miller/Hull has been described as a leader in Pacific Northwest Regionalism. What is regionalism? It is certainly an understanding of place. It involves having an awareness of local vernacular structures, of climate, building traditions, and the qualities of a region's landscape. We feel that sustainable design and regionalism are intricately tied together. All significant lessons in sustainable architecture come from the vernacular. We seek to use local materials and crafts in an endeavor to produce a modern architecture out of regional building traditions. We attempt to build small, even with our large and complex programs, in that social sustainability and ecological design are closely related. As we design more outside the Northwest, as our reputation grows and as a result of this award, we hope to employ a regional approach to these new environments.

Our architecture has been the result of a creative and energetic studio of architects, working with fantastic clients, some with very modest budgets but with a high level of trust in us and with great expectations. Miller/Hull is united in the belief that architecture can create positive change in our communities.

In closing, being included with the remarkable firms that have received this honor will push us to continue to produce authentic and beautiful architecture for our environment. It has been a fantastic adventure and we look forward to the possibilities ahead.

Thank you from all of us at Miller/Hull.

Courtesy of The Miller/Hull Partnership.

Thompson E. Penney

Pursuing the "Proof" of Design: New AIA President Takes the Reigns

Thompson E. Penney was inaugurated as the 2003 AIA president on December 6, 2002, at a ceremony held at Union Station in Washington, D.C. The following remarks were excerpted from his acceptance speech.

Every AIA member who occupies the office set aside for the president at Institute headquarters brings something from his or her home to personalize the space. If you stop by the president's office next year, you'll find photos of my lovely family. You'll also see a wonderful painting by the renowned Charleston artist Betty Anglin Smith.

Over the years, Betty has become a friend, so when I was selecting those things that touch my heart and would remind me of home, I immediately thought of her colorful, impressionistic landscapes.

I had in mind one of her marsh scenes of South Carolina. It would serve as a substitute for the view from my home that I would not be seeing much next year. But as I walked into her studio, I was immediately taken by the first painting I saw. It wasn't a marsh scene. Yet it struck me as not only a reminder of my home state, but as a metaphor. It was a painting of a barn.

The barn is a classic icon of functional beauty. However, its beauty goes beyond its marvelous craftsmanship. The soul of its beauty dwells in how it was built–not by formal contracts and reams of paperwork–but rather, by a community.

A community that works together collaboratively–eyes fixed not on the inevitable flaws and imperfections along the way but on the energy and sheer *joy* of moving forward together, shoulder-to-shoulder urging one another on. The barn itself is merely a sign of a human miracle that has taken place.

I've come to realize that the great work of design is not the solitary pursuit of novelty. The great work of design is its creative engagement with human needs. It's a job you can't do well unless you have empathy...unless you can put yourself in someone else's shoes; listening patiently and carefully and humbly to their hopes, their aspirations, their dreams. You have to care about people, care deeply. You have to believe people matter. That means caring for the children and the teachers in the classrooms you design; caring for the elderly and sick in our hospitals and nursing homes; caring for the janitors, the plumbers, and window washers who maintain the physical fabric.

We have an opportunity–unique in my professional life–to reach out. To make the connection in the public's mind between their growing hunger for value and what we architects actually do. We have an opportunity not only to celebrate the *poetry* of our

Pursuing the "Proof" of Design: New AIA President Takes the Reigns

work, in other words, what elevates the human spirit; we also have an opportunity, and I would say the responsibility to offer *proof* about how design enriches human life.

"Design"–the product *and* the process–is at the heart of how well we lead our lives and the choices we make; it is at the soul of how faithfully we carry out our role–not to own the earth, but to be of it. It's about discovery, integration, application and the sharing of knowledge about the consequences of our work. It's called "predictive knowledge." With such knowledge we could predict the effects of our decisions. We could design education into our schools, curing into our hospitals, and dignity into our low-income housing.

We know in our hearts that's what design is all about. However, the tools we have to objectively measure the impact of architecture are few and crude. So it is not at all surprising that when we talk with the public and our clients, we architects are used to discussing our work in terms of what the eye sees. But we impoverish our conversation with the public when we position ourselves primarily as form givers.

Until there is a broad understanding of how design works and what it does, neither the public nor our clients will truly appreciate the value of design and our unique role in the design process. But being a knowledge-driven profession will not be enough. To pursue the "proof" of design, we must become a profession distinguished by a Culture of Sharing.

Many of us developed in school and perfected in our practices a mentality of drawing with one hand while using the other to hide the work from our colleagues. It's time to stop holding our professional cards close to our chest. A profession is a *community*, not a jungle.

Nearly 150 years ago, a group of visionary architects freed themselves and our profession from the tyranny of "every man for himself." They turned their backs on the jungle that characterized contemporary practice. Instead, they pooled their resources. They pledged to work for the common good, convinced a rising professional tide would lift the fortunes of every individual member of their community.

The great idea that became the American Institute of Architects 150 years ago was forged in the face of incredible economic, political, and professional adversity. Just imagine what we, their heirs, can accomplish now! Clues as to what is possible are on all sides of us, seated at these tables and reflected in the very fabric of this great space.

I would like to think that Daniel Burnham, himself a former AIA president and the great architect who imagined this wonderful space, would be pleased tonight–would be pleased to see that after nearly 100 years, this gift to the City of Washington and to the nation is still a thing of beauty and utility. A century ago, his words, "make no little plans," became the inspiration for a wave of optimism that beautified and ennobled cities from coast to coast. His words inspired great things 100 years ago; they continue to challenge and inspire us today.

We know there is much work before us to meet society's yearning for integrity, trust, and value. The greater prize for us and our clients will not be the objects of our hands. It will be the vital community of lives intertwined, lives enriched, lives made more hopeful by pursuing together the poetry and proof of design.

Thank you for allowing me to serve as your seventy-ninth president, and thank you for being here to share this very special evening.

Reprinted with permission of the author.

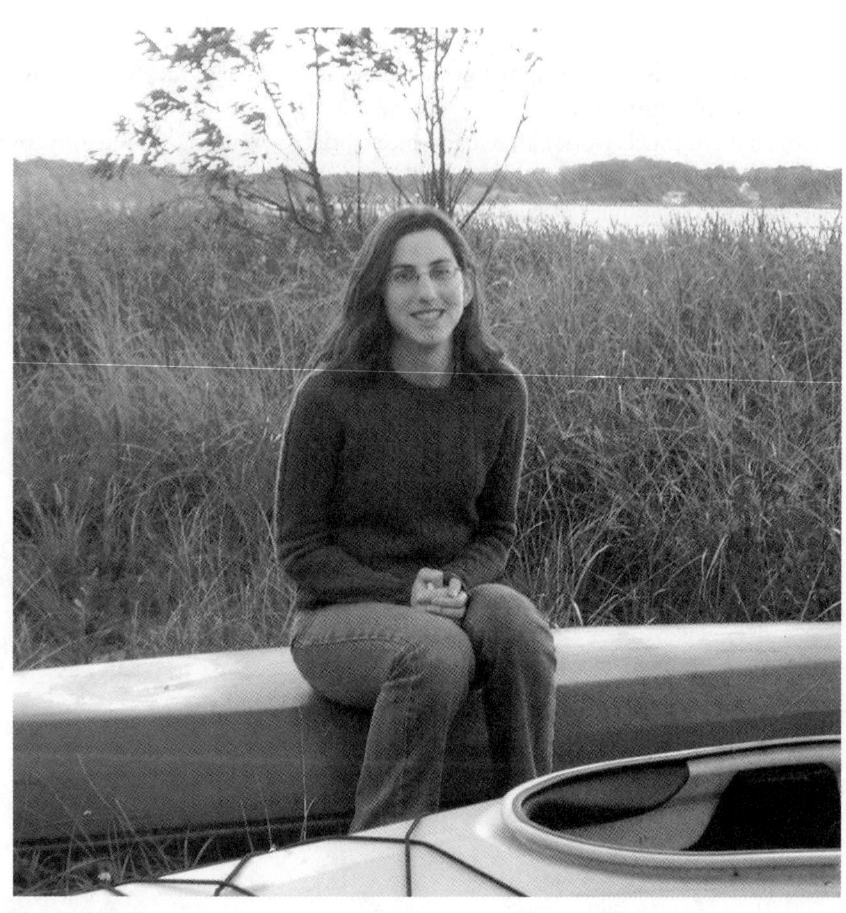

Karen Weise

Troublemakers

Karen Weise

*Karen Weise's essay "Troublemakers," won second place in the 2003 Berkeley Prize Essay Competition (**see page 513**) in which entrants responded to the question:* When architects strive to create lasting monuments, some become part of the significant cultural heritage of our age. These successes seem to embody the most socially important values of a city, region, country, or even the world. Other attempts are only the reflection of the vanity of the designer or client and pass into oblivion. Worse, they become a permanent blight on the environment. As an architect, specifically, how can your work simultaneously embody the social values of one place, a particular culture, and universal human concerns?

A May 2003, graduate of Yale University, Karen majored in both Architecture and an interdisciplinary program called Ethnicity, Race and Migration. In addition to learning how to "make trouble," Karen has spent her summers: as an intern in the department of architecture and design at the Museum of Modern Art in New York, in Azerbaijan researching her senior thesis on humanitarian building projects funded by oil companies, riding her bike 4000 miles across the U.S. to raise money for Habitat for Humanity, and in the fall 2004, sketching architecture and learning Turkish in Istanbul. *She can be reached at* karen.weise@aya.yale.edu.

I think Tibor Kalman had it right. "Good designers (and writers and artists) make trouble," the maverick graphic designer once wrote. A designer should not just make a pack of cigarettes look cool or make Nike shoes into a necessity. Designers must use their power of communication toward lasting, meaningful explorations and challenges. They must provoke and anger, dismay, and entice. These imperatives lay at the center of Kalman's work. He challenged the branding of consumer goods, the ethics of his viewers, and the values of his field.

Such grand ideas these all seem. But can (and do) these play out in reality? Or are they forever to remain in the realm of hopes, pushed aside by the seductive lure of corporate headquarters and fancy homes?

Bit by bit, I have come to think that a growing number of designers (and writers and artists) are finding the time and opportunity to use the power of their spatial, visual and literary languages to "make trouble." These little moments of protest and actions started calling my attention, challenging me as a viewer and designer. Browsing a newsstand and noticing a copy of *Adbusters* magazine, listening in art history lectures to tales of the Gorilla Girls and Gran Fury, or driving by a small temporary kiosk built to provide shade for migrant day laborers in Southern California.

Troublemakers

Many architecture offices find time amidst designing custom homes for the wealthy and office-park headquarters for companies to build non-profit projects–schools, museums, and parks. These municipal projects are immanently important as cities and spaces are increasingly shaped by corporate rather than public forces. Local communities deserve the same right to intelligent, coherent, and beautiful space as any wealthy client, if not more so. Architecture firms that undertake these projects balance a wide range of community concerns while working off a limited and often fluctuating budget. With the exception of the recent smattering of flashy museums, these non-profit projects often go unnoticed by the press.

While these projects carry great social importance, the projects that Kalman admires depart from them in one key way: they are deliberately incendiary. They are intrusions in our daily landscape that demand viewers to come face to face with potent questions of power and politics. They challenge systems of race and gender, of class and capitalism. Though the projects may be temporary, their permanence resides in the conversations they ignite, in the people they anger, and in the memories they burn on the minds of their audience. To make these statements–these spatial disruptions–designers and architects buck the standard operations of design practice. They put their time, energy and money toward designing projects without individual recognition, without a clear "client," and often without funding.

These incendiary projects gained my admiration immediately, though they still seemed like far off ideals promoted by a brave few. Yet, I finally came to believe that rebellious design is a viable movement in the design world when I interned at an architecture firm in Los Angeles a few summers back. At the very beginning of my interview, I learned of an installation piece that the firm built four years before to protest the closure of a local park. At a cost of over $25,000, the city gated the park to keep out homeless people who turned the benches into beds at night. The designers at the firm were dismayed by the use of public funds to lock out citizens rather than meeting their basic needs. And the park closure marked a loss of public space in a city that already had the lowest ratio of public space per capita of any city in the United States. So these artists, builders and architects constructed a day-glo orange staircase over the seven-foot fence, reclaiming access to the local open space. It took the city almost a month to solder off this architectural rebellion. This anonymous group of artists, architects, and builders took action, and I loved it. Little did I know at the time that I would end up spending my summer planning the next installation.

At the core of our project laid an abstract goal: we wanted to ignite debate about transportation and politics in Los Angeles. In our giant metropolis, like in most cities, the politics of transportation fundamentally shaped the daily experience of inhabitants.

Angelenos spend hours commuting on freeways, breathe smog-filled air, and rarely interact with anyone not in a neighboring zip code. Yet it was not always so; for years the redline cable cars in the city composed the most extensive intraurban transit system in the country, until it was systematically dismantled by a ghost consortium of automotive industry corporations. With that vibrant system long gone from the daily patterns of the city, wealthy homeowner groups consistently wield the power to stop a proposed transit line dead in its tracks and in doing so squash the opportunity for the social and economic integration that comes from healthy transit systems. On the opposite side of the political spectrum, the progressive Bus Riders Union often fights fiercely to stop subway proposals because subway expenditures are often funded from bus fare increases, which disproportionately effect low-income residents of the city. With all of these forces swimming around the political spheres of the MTA, transit systems were essentially a dead issue in Los Angeles, a victim of brutal politics of space.

And so we dreamed up our own transit system, creating "The Aqua Line." We designed a fictional subway line crossing the Westside of Los Angeles, connecting the beach in Santa Monica to the subway system downtown, providing access for the entire area to many of the city's cultural resources and connecting areas of different races and income levels. Mimicking the bureaucratic design of the Metropolitan Transit Authority, we designed eight-foot signs to be installed at seven locations along our "line." Each sign proudly announced that the subway line was "coming soon" and depicted a "route map" of this ideal transit rightaway. And on the morning one day before the Democratic Convention 2000, disguised as construction workers in trucks and hardhats, we successfully installed seven "Future Station Location" signs for the "Metro Aqua Line."

It took no time for our "information hotline" to receive messages from neighbors (who were quite concerned), local newspapers (who were quite intrigued), and MTA officials (who were quite confused). We sent copies of our "manifesto" to press outlets and people who called our hotline in order to provide an explanation of our motivations for the action, a political history of transit in the city, and a vision of the possibilities for transit in our future. Over the following weeks, talk of the Aqua Line buzzed around LA: in *Los Angeles Times* articles and letters to the editor, in coffee bar and yoga class conversation, and in over 200 calls to our hotline. Initial conversations questioned what exactly the Aqua Line was, but once our message got out to the wider population through the press and individual letters, people began to directly address the politics of our action. "What are you trying to do," questioned one enraged homeowner on our hotline, "ignite class warfare?" While the signs were taken down by week's end, we had indeed ignited a debate about politics and transportation. One transit advocate was

Troublemakers

quoted in the *Los Angeles Times* saying, "They raised public awareness in such a way. It has been bubbling under the surface. It has captured the imagination of the people."

Before this experience, small moments of design interventions into the politics of space existed in an outside, idealized world for me. They were impactful when I saw them, but never lay within my reach. From afar, I admired these acts of "trouble," as Kalman would say, though I never gave serious consideration to the process of creating them. Yet with the Aqua Line, I learned of intricate planning and secrecy tactics, of display design and manifesto writing, and of effective presentations and group facilitation. No longer did I have to take a leap of faith to believe Kalman's words. I knew architects and designers could "make trouble" because I had become a trouble maker.

Left to right: Léon Krier, Richard H. Driehaus.
Photo courtesy of the University of Notre Dame School of Architecture.

Why I Practice Classical Architecture and Traditional Urbanism

Léon Krier

Léon Krier is the first recipient of the Richard H. Driehaus Prize for Classical Architecture (see page 175) from the University of Notre Dame School of Architecture and Richard H. Driehaus, chairman of Driehaus Capital Management in Chicago. He presented this speech at the University of Notre Dame School of Architecture on November 3, 2003 and is scheduled to deliver it at the School's Rome Studies Center in spring 2004. It is also published in The Richard H. Driehaus Prize 2003, *which commemorates this inaugural event.*

I grew up in an environment which, despite two recent world wars, was unblemished by modernist architecture and planning. Until the mid-1960s, Luxembourg was a miracle of traditional architecture, a small capital city of 70,000 souls, embedded in manicured agricultural and horticultural landscapes and lofty beach forests. We lived on a tree-lined corniche, overlooking a deep valley and one of the most accomplished townscapes in Europe. My father's tailoring workshop occupied the ground floor of the townhouse, and for my primary education, I hopped across the street when hearing the school bells chime from our garden. I had most of my secondary education in the baroque abbey of Echternach, a small medieval town, which together with its four-towered Romanesque Basilica had in less than 10 years been beautifully reconstructed in a 100 percent artisan way after a near total destruction during the 1944 Rundstedt offensive.

My mother's piano playing filled the house and during holidays my parents took us four children to Switzerland, France and Italy to visit places of beauty. Neighboring Germany was avoided for obvious reasons and in front of the Jungfrau, the panorama of Florence or the lakefront of Lugano, we all experienced an aesthetic communion of awe and admiration. The family concord shattered with a bang when for once I had chosen a destination and taken my parents in the summer of 1963 to see Le Corbusier's "Cite Radieuse." Though I didn't realize it immediately, my life's orientation became defined by that visit.

Until then, I had, via my brother, become acquainted with modernism merely through books of Le Corbusier, Giedion and Gropius. The formidable promises expressed there had swollen my sails. In a Sunday high Mass, our parish priest had spoken of Ronchamp as the "ship of concrete, which had given body to our religion of love and hope," no less.

Why I Practice Classical Architecture and Traditional Urbanism

Le Corbusier had become for me a second messiah, and, as a result, I imagined modernist architecture to be something superior to all the beautiful buildings I had seen and grown up with so far. I fantasized of white Cubist volumes adorning my favorite places and mile-long inhabited walls, ploughing across Luxembourg's historic city center, bridging its valley and digging into its forested hillsides, radiant visions of an unearthly splendor. Before the ill-fated visit, we camped in an uncle's olive grove in the Provence, enjoying perfectly intact beaches, towns, and landscapes. The timeless perfection of a nearby Cistercian monastery, the picturesque charm of the surrounding farms and hill towns, and not least our bloated expectations for the impending Marseille visit had indeed ill-prepared us for the tawdry reality of the cite "Radieuse." We were all speechless with shock, wondering at first whether we were at the right address. Nobody, including myself, could quite believe that this was what I had been eulogizing for years.

Next thing, and for weeks and months, trying desperately to overcome my unavowable disappointment, I found myself for the first time in my life justifying to my parents, something which I profoundly felt to be socially unacceptable and aesthetically inferior to all we had commonly admired so far. The relentless modernist devastation of Luxembourg, which started in full a few years later, not only alienated me from my cherished birthplace, but more radically from modernism, the intellectual homeland in which I had sought temporary refuge from a provincial upbringing.

It was this double exile that paradoxically opened my eyes and gave sense and direction to my life. The rape of my beloved childhood places became for me what genocide is for a persecuted people–a life-threatening menace. I took it totally personally and decided to fight back, not clearly knowing who the enemy was.

My resources being very limited, I had to calculate from early on how to spend them. Unable to find a master, a school or a doctrine which could teach me how to stop the holocaust and learn my craft, I felt I had no choice but to learn from buildings, towns and landscapes, which I and my family had experienced and loved. I decided to abandon university, not to have kids, not to engage in building, but rather to think, to draw and generally find out what was so wrong with contemporary architecture and urbanism and how to right it...not because I had a special gift in that direction but because of an absurd realization that nobody else, not even those I most esteemed, seemed inclined to do what I imperatively felt had to be done.

It soon dawned on me that the "critical theory," of the "Frankfurt school," which in its pessimistic and utopian forms so enchanted my generation, offered only consolatory delusions, was not a cure but part of a near-all engulfing confusion. Instead, the incredibly fast and beautiful traditional reconstruction of Luxembourg's war-ravaged small towns, villages and farms, which I had witnessed as a child, became for me, on reflection, a model of civilized and generally-accepted modernity.

Indeed the various brands of post-modernism, which the critical theory of the Frankfurt School continues to inspire, are but futile attempts to escape from the debilitating tenets of modernism itself. Their experimentalism condemns them to very short life spans, to technological and cultural irrelevance, to broad social rejection. Not only have they proved incapable of replacing the technological and artistic heritage of traditional urbanism and classical architecture, but the colossal human cost of these failed experiments seems to me mostly but sterile diversions from an inevitable return to common sense. Furthermore, how can the modernist and post-modernist errant ways be redeemed by a cult and culture of masterworks, when the masters themselves lack technical mastery, artistic maturity, and, more profoundly, philosophy?

To me the worst consequences of modernism lie not only in the worldwide degeneration of the general building activity through the loss of traditional building skills but more tragically in the intellectual corruption of their forms of transmission and theoretical foundations. Modernism's historicization of traditional architectures, i.e. the ideologically-motivated reduction of a timeless building technology to a mere collection of obsolete styles and crafts, has blinded several generations to the continuing modernity and irreplaceable value of classical architecture and traditional practices. That is why I am primarily not interested in the "history" of traditional architectures and urbanisms but in their technology in their modern practice.

The question of modernity can therefore no longer be one of period and style but one of persistent utility and quality. Practicing traditional architecture today is then not a refuge in past styles or history but a return to mature and experienced forms of environment building and management.

Be it in democratic or totalitarianism countries the reign of modernism has been so complete for the last half century that few people wonder why the great awards have for two score years solely recompensed architects who practice exclusively modernist styles, ranging from Bauhaus to deconstruction, from so-called "high-tech" to "critical regionalism."

The ideological monopoly has extended to architectural teaching, competitions, publishing, and above all, to public commissions. The creation of the Richard H. Driehaus Prize for Classical Architecture breaks this untenable sectarian deadlock and announces the long-awaited democratization of architecture, a sea-change in the official architectural culture of today.

Source: The Richard H. Driehaus Prize 2003 and the University of Notre Dame.

2

Awards & Honors

Approximately 100 major national and international design awards programs–both project and individual recognition awards–are included in this chapter with information about their scope, purpose, and winners. Other award programs related to sustainable/green design (pg. 397) historic preservation (pg. 427), and design education (pg. 493) can be found in their respective chapters.

Aga Khan Award for Architecture

Granted once every three years, the Aga Khan Trust for Culture's Aga Khan Award for Architecture recognizes outstanding contributions to the built environment in the Muslim world. The diversity of winning projects includes individual buildings, restoration and reuse schemes, large-scale community developments, and environmental projects. In addition to the physical, economic, and social needs of a region, this award seeks to emphasize the importance of the cultural and spiritual aspects of a project. The steering committee, comprised of internationally distinguished architects and scholars, governs this complex three-year process of nominations and technical review as well as the selection of the master jury, which chooses the final winning entries. Eligible projects must have been completed within the past twenty-five years and in use for a minimum of two years. An award of $500,000 is apportioned between each cycle's winners.

For more information about this award and photographs, drawings and descriptions of the winning projects, visit the Aga Khan Award for Architecture's Web site at *www.akdn.org.*

The Eighth Award Cycle, 1999-2001, Recipients

New Life for Old Structures
Various locations, Iran
Urban Development and Revitalization Corporation and Iranian Cultural Heritage Organization (Iran)

Aït Iktel
Abadou, Morocco
Aït Iktel de Développement (Morocco)

Barefoot Architects
Tilonia, India
Barefoot Architects of Tilonia (India)

Kahere Eila Poultry Farming School
Koliagbe, Guinea
Heikkinen-Komonen Architects (Finland)

Nubian Museum
Aswan, Egypt
Mahmoud El-Hakim (Egypt)

SOS Children's Village
Aqaba, Jordan
Jafar Tukan & Partners (Jordon)

Olbia Social Centre
Antalya, Turkey
Cengiz Bektas (Turkey)

Bagh-e-Ferdowsi
Tehran, Iran
Baft-e-Shahr Consulting Architects and Urban Planners (Iran)

Datai Hotel
Pulau Langkawi, Malaysia
Kerry Hill Architects (Australia)

Steering Committee

His Highness The Aga Khan (Chair)
Selma al-Radi, archaeologist (Iraq)
Charles Correa, architect (India)
Kenneth Frampton, architect and architectural historian (US)
Frank O. Gehry, architect (US)
Zaha Hadid, architect (UK)
Luis Monreal, historian and archaeologist (Spain)
Azim Nanji, professor (UK)
Ali Shuaibi, architect (Saudi Arabia)

Aga Khan Award for Architecture

Master Jury
Abdou Filali-Ansari, philosopher (Morocco)
Darab Diba, architect (Iran)
Dogan Hasol, architect and publisher (Turkey)
Zahi Hawass, archaeologist (Egypt)
Mona Hatoum, artist (UK)
Ricardo Legorreta, architect (Mexico)
Glenn Murcutt, architect (Australia)
Norani Othman, sociologist (Malaysia)
Raj Rewal, architect (India)

Chairman's Awards

On three occasions the Chairman's Award has been granted. It was established to honor individuals who have made considerable lifetime achievements to Muslim architecture but whose work was not within the scope of the Master Jury's mandate.

1980 Hassan Fathy (Egypt)
1986 Rifat Chadirji (Iraq)
2001 Geoffrey Bawa (Sri Lanka)

Source: The Aga Khan Trust for Culture

Architecture cannot be explained: it must be experienced directly. It could be understood only in its own terms.

Geoffrey Bawa

AIA Gold Medal

The Gold Medal is The American Institute of Architects' highest award. Eligibility is open to architects or non-architects, living or dead, whose contribution to the field of architecture has made a lasting impact. The AIA's Board of Directors, with rare exception, grants no more than one Gold Medal each year, occasionally granting none.

For more information, contact the AIA's Honor and Awards Department at (202) 626-7586 or visit their Web site at *www.aia.org*.

1907	Sir Aston Webb (UK)
1909	Charles Follen McKim (US)
1911	George Browne Post (US)
1914	Jean Louis Pascal (France)
1922	Victor Laloux (France)
1923	Henry Bacon (US)
1925	Sir Edwin Landseer Lutyens (UK)
1925	Bertram Grosvenor Goodhue (US)
1927	Howard Van Doren Shaw (US)
1929	Milton Bennett Medary (US)
1933	Ragnar Östberg (Sweden)
1938	Paul Philippe Cret (France)
1944	Louis Henry Sullivan (US)
1947	Eliel Saarinen (Finland)
1948	Charles Donagh Maginnis (US)
1949	Frank Lloyd Wright (US)
1950	Sir Patrick Abercrombie (UK)
1951	Bernard Ralph Maybeck (US)
1952	Auguste Perret (France)
1953	William Adams Delano (US)
1955	William Marinus Dudok (The Netherlands)
1956	Clarence S. Stein (US)
1957	Ralph Walker (US)
1957	Louis Skidmore (US)
1958	John Wellborn Root II (US)
1959	Walter Adolph Gropius (Germany)
1960	Ludwig Mies van der Rohe (Germany)
1961	Le Corbusier (Charles Édouard Jeanneret) (Switzerland)
1962	Eero Saarinen* (US)
1963	Alvar Aalto (Finland)
1964	Pier Luigi Nervi (Italy)
1966	Kenzo Tange (Japan)
1967	Wallace Kirkman Harrison (US)
1968	Marcel Lajos Breuer (Germany)
1969	William Wilson Wurster (US)
1970	Richard Buckminster Fuller (US)
1971	Louis I. Kahn (US)
1972	Pietro Belluschi (US)
1977	Richard Joseph Neutra* (Germany)
1978	Philip Cortelyou Johnson (US)
1979	Ieoh Ming Pei (US)
1981	Joseph Lluis Sert (Spain)
1982	Romaldo Giurgola (US)
1983	Nathaniel Alexander Owings (US)
1985	William Wayne Caudill* (US)
1986	Arthur Charles Erickson (Canada)
1989	Joseph Esherick (US)
1990	E. Fay Jones (US)
1991	Charles W. Moore (US)
1992	Benjamin Thompson (US)
1993	Thomas Jefferson* (US)
1993	Kevin Roche (US)
1994	Sir Norman Foster (UK)
1995	Cesar Pelli (US)
1997	Richard Meier (US)
1999	Frank Gehry (US)
2000	Ricardo Legorreta (Mexico)
2001	Michael Graves (US)
2002	Tadao Ando (Japan)

* Honored posthumously

Source: The American Institute of Architects

AIA Honor Awards

The American Institute of Architects' (AIA) Honor Awards celebrate outstanding design in three areas: architecture, interior architecture, and regional and urban design. Juries of designers and executives present separate awards in each category.

Additional information and entry forms may be obtained by contacting the AIA Honors and Awards Department at (202) 626-7586 or by visiting their Web site at *www.aia.org*.

2003 Honor Awards for Architecture

Concert Hall and Exhibition Complex
Rouen, France
Bernard Tschumi Architects

American Folk Art Museum
New York, NY
Tod Williams Billie Tsien Architects

Howard House
Nova Scotia, Canada
Brian MacKay-Lyons Architecture Urban Design

Heritage Health & Housing
New York, NY
Caples Jefferson Architects

Will Rogers World Airport Snow Barn
Oklahoma City, OK
Elliott + Associates Architects

Federal Building and United States Courthouse
Central Islip, NY
Richard Meier & Partners

Boston Public Library
Allston, MA
Machado and Silvetti Associates, Inc

Diamond Ranch High School
Pomona, CA
Morphosis

3rd & Benton/7th & Grandview Primary Centers
Los Angeles, CA
Rios Associates, Inc.

Simmons Hall, MIT
Cambridge, MA
Steven Holl Architects

New Academic Complex, Baruch College CUNY
New York, NY
Kohn Pedersen Fox Associates PC

BoO1 "Tango" Housing
Malmö, Sweden
Moore Ruble Yudell Architects & Planners

Colorado Court
Santa Monica, CA
Pugh Scarpa Kodama

Lever House Curtain Wall Replacement
New York, NY
Skidmore, Owings & Merrill LLP

Hypo Alpe-Adria-Center
Klagenfurt, Austria
Morphosis

Architecture Jury

Jack Hartray, Nagle Hartray Danker Kagan McKay Architects Planners Ltd. (chair)
Paul Byard, Platt Byard Dovell Architects
Merrill Elam, Mack Scogin Merrill Elam Architects
Mary Griffin, Turnbull Griffin Haesloop Architects
Vincent James, Vincent James Associates Inc.
Michael D. Perry, W.P. Hickman Systems
Barton Phelps
Ryan Sullivan
Thomas J. Trenolone, RTKL Associates Inc.

"Tango," a building containing 27 rental units, was commissioned as part of the Bo01 housing exhibition in Malmö, Sweden, a bi-annual exhibition program based on the themes of environmental sustainability and information technology. No two apartments are alike, and tenants can further alter their layout with a moveable modular wall. *Photos by Werner Huthmacher, courtesy of Moore Ruble Yudell Architects & Planners.*

AIA Honor Awards

2003 Honor Awards for Outstanding Interiors

Kate and Laurance Eustis Chapel
New Orleans, LA
Eskew+Dumez+Ripple

Central Synagogue
New York, NY
Hardy Holzman Pfeiffer Associates, LLP

Craft
New York, NY
Bentel & Bentel, Architects/Planners, LLP

Lutece
Las Vegas, NV
Morphosis

Collins Gallery
West Hollywood, CA
Patrick J. Tighe

Gardner-James Residence
New York, NY
Valerio Dewalt Train Associates

Martin Shocket Residence
Chevy Chase, MD
McInturff Architects

Global Crossing Corporate Headquarters
New York, NY
Lee H. Skolnick Architecture

ImageNet
Oklahoma City, OK
Elliott + Associates Architects

South Court, The New York Public Library
New York, NY
Davis Brody Bond, LLP

The Architecture of R.M. Schindler Exhibit at MOCA
Los Angeles, CA
Chu + Gooding Architects

Interior Architecture Jury

Lawrence Scarpa, Pugh + Scarpa (chair)
Sara E. Caples, Caples Jefferson Architects
Olvia Demetriou, Adamstein and Demetriou
Debbra A.K. Johnson, Dupont Safety & Protection
Juan Miró, Miró Rivera Architects

2003 Honor Awards for Outstanding Regional and Urban Design

Schuylkill Gateway
Philadelphia, PA
Sasaki Associates, Inc.

Interstate MAX Station Area Revitalization Strategy
Portland, OR
Crandall Arambula, PC

Howard University: LeDroit Park Revitalization Initiative
Washington, DC
Sorg and Associates, PC

Charlottesville Commercial Corridor Plan
Charlottesville, VA
Torti Gallas and Partners-CHK, Inc.

East Baltimore Comprehensive Physical Redevelopment Plan
Baltimore, MD
Urban Design Associates

AIA Honor Awards

Regional and Urban Design Jury

Martha Welborne, Grand Avenue Committee (chair)
William Holloway, Bernandon Haber Holloway Architects Inc.
Steven Hurtt, University of Maryland School of Architecture
Robert Kroin, Boston Redevelopment Authority
Diane Legge Kemp, DLK Architecture Inc.

Source: The American Institute of Architects

In the last 10 years, the following firms won the most AIA Honor Awards:

Skidmore, Owings & Merrill, LLP—19
Hardy Holzman Pfeiffer Associates—8
Elliott + Associates Architects—7
Herbert Lewis Kruse Blunck—7
Polshek Partnership Architects, LLP—7
Richard Meier & Partners—6
Davis Brody Bond, LLP—5
Morphosis—5
Shelton, Mindel & Associates—5
William Rawn Associates, Architects Inc.—5
HOK Sports Facilities Group—4
Kallmann, McKinnell & Wood Architects, Inc.—4
Studio E Architects—4
Tod Williams Billie Tsien and Associates—4
Torti Gallas and Partners—4

AIA Honors for Collaborative Achievement

The American Institute of Architects (AIA) biennially presents their Honors for Collaborative Achievement award to recognize achievements in influencing or advancing the architectural profession. Recipients may be individuals or groups. Nominees must be living at the time of their nomination and may have been active in any number of areas, including administration, art, collaborative achievement, construction, industrial design, information science, professions allied with architecture, public policy, research, education, recording, illustration, and writing and scholarship.

For more information, refer to the AIA's Web site at *www.aia.org* or contact the AIA's Honors and Awards Department at (202) 626-7586.

1976

Edmund N. Bacon
Charles A. Blessing
Wendell J. Campbell
Gordon Cullen
James Marston Fitch
The Institute for Architecture and Urban Studies
New York City Planning Commission and New York City Landmarks Preservation Committee
Saul Steinberg
Vincent J. Scully Jr.
Robert Le Ricolais

1977

Claes Oldenburg
Louise Nevelson
Historic American Buildings Survey
Arthur Drexler
G. Holmes Perkins
The Baroness Jackson of Lodsworth DBE (Barbara Ward)
Walker Art Center
City of Boston
Pittsburgh History & Landmarks Foundation
Montreal Metro System

1978

Frederick Gutheim
Richard Haas
Dr. August Komendant
David A. Macaulay
National Trust for Historic Preservation
Stanislawa Nowicki
John C. Portman Jr.
Robert Royston
Nicholas N. Solovioff
Robert Venturi

1979

Douglas Haskell
Barry Commoner
John D. Entenza
Bernard Rudofsky
Steen Eiler Rasmussen
National Endowment for the Arts
Christo
Bedford-Stuyvesant Restoration
Charles E. Peters
Arthur S. Siegel*

1980

Cyril M. Harris
Sol LeWitt
Robert Campbell
Committee for the Preservation of Architectural Records
Progressive Architecture Awards Program
The Rouse Company for Faneuil Hall Marketplace
John Benson
M. Paul Friedberg
Jack E. Boucher
Mrs. Lyndon B. Johnson

AIA Honors for Collaborative Achievement

1981
Kenneth Snelson
Paul Goldberger
Sir Nikolaus Pevsner
Herman Miller, Inc.
Edison Price
Colin Rowe
Reynolds Metals Company
Smithsonian Associates

1982
"Oppositions" (Institute for Architecture & Urban Studies)
Historic New Harmony, Inc.
The MIT Press
Jean Dubuffet
Sir John Summerson
The Plan of St. Gall
The Washington Metropolitan Area Transit Authority
William H. Whyte

1983
The Honorable Christopher S. Bond, Governor of Missouri
Donald Canty
Fazlur Khan*
Knoll International
Christian Norberg-Schulz
Paul Stevenson Oles

1984
Reyner Banham
Bolt, Beranek & Newman
Cooper-Hewitt Museum
Inner Harbor Development of the City of Baltimore
His Highness the Aga Khan
T.Y. Lin
Steve Rosenthal
San Antonio River Walk
Bruno Zevi

1985
Ward Bennett
Kenneth Frampton
Esther McCoy
Norman McGrath
The Hon. John F. Seiberling
Weidlinger Associates
Nick Wheeler
Games of the XXIII Olympiad
Cranbrook Academy of Art
Central Park

1986
Cathedral Church of St. John the Divine
Antoinette Forrester Downing
David H. Geiger
Gladding, McBean & Company
William H. Jordy
Master Plan for the United States Capitol
Adolf Kurt Placzek
Cervin Robinson
Rudolf Wittkower*

1987
James S. Ackerman
Jennifer Bartlett
Steven Brooke
The Chicago Architecture Foundation
Jules Fisher & Paul Marantz, Inc.
Charles Guggenheim
John B. Jackson
Mesa Verde National Park
Rizzoli International Publications, Inc.
Carter Wiseman

1988
Spiro Kostof
Loeb Fellowship in Advanced Environmental Studies, Harvard University
Robert Smithson*
Society for the Preservation of New England Antiquities

AIA Honors for Collaborative Achievement

Sussman/Prejza & Company, Inc.
Robert Wilson

1989

Battery Park City Authority
American Academy in Rome
Eduard Sekler
Leslie E. Robertson
Niels Diffrient
David S. Haviland
V'Soske

1990

The Association for the Preservation of Virginia Antiquities
Corning Incorporated
Jackie Ferrara
Timothy Hursley
Marvin Mass
Mary Miss
Peter G. Rolland
Joseph Santeramo
Taos Pueblo
Emmet L. Wemple

1991

James Fraser Carpenter
Danish Design Centre
Foundation for Architecture, Philadelphia
The J.M. Kaplan Fund
Maguire Thomas Partners
Native American Architecture (Robert Easton and Peter Nabokov)
Princeton Architectural Press
Seaside, Florida
Allan Temko
Lebbeus Woods

1992

Siah Armajani
Canadian Centre for Architecture
Stephen Coyle
Milton Glaser
The Mayors' Institute on City Design
The Municipal Art Society of New York
John Julius Norwich
Ove Arup & Partners Consulting Engineers PC
Peter Vanderwarker
Peter Walker

1993

ADPSR (Architects/Designers/Planners for Social Responsibility)
Michael Blackwood
The Conservation Trust of Puerto Rico
Benjamin Forgey
The Gamble House
Philadelphia Zoological Society
The Princeton University Board of Trustees, Officers and the Office of Physical Planning
Jane Thompson
Sally B. Woodbridge
World Monuments Fund

1994

Joseph H. Baum
Beth Dunlop
Mildred Friedman
Historic Savannah Foundation
Rhode Island Historical Preservation Commission
Salvadori Educational Center on the Built Environment
Gordon H. Smith
The Stuart Collection
Sunset magazine
Judith Turner

1995

The Art Institute of Chicago, Dept. of Arch.
ASAP (The American Society of Architectural Perspectivists)
Friends of Post Office Square
The University of Virginia, Curator and Architect for the Academical Village/ The Rotunda
Albert Paley

AIA Honors for Collaborative Achievement

UrbanArts, Inc.
Dr. Yoichi Ando

1996

Boston by Foot, Inc.
William S. Donnell
Haley & Aldrich, Inc.
Toshio Nakamura
Joseph Passonneau
Preservation Society of Charleston
Earl Walls Associates
Paul Warchol Photography, Inc.

1997

Architecture Resource Center

1998

Lian Hurst Mann
SOM Foundation
William Morgan

1999

Howard Brandston
Jeff Goldberg
Ann E. Gray
Blair Kamin
Ronald McKay
Miami-Dade Art in Public Places
Monacelli Press
New York Landmarks Conservancy

2000

The Aga Khan Award for Architecture
Douglas Cooper
Dr. Christopher Jaffe
Donald Kaufman and Taffy Dahl
William Lam
San Antonio Conservation Society
F. Michael Wong

2001

Vernon L. Mays Jr.
John R. Stilgoe

2003

Kathryn H. Anthony
Herve Descottes
Gilbert Gorski
Jane Merkel
J. Irwin Miller
New York, New Visions
Joan Ockman
Martin Puryear
The Robin Hood Foundation

* Awarded posthumously

Source: The American Institute of Architects

AIA Housing Awards

The Housing Professional Interest Area (PIA) of The American Institute of Architects (AIA) established the Housing Awards to recognize the importance of good housing as a necessity of life, a sanctuary for the human spirit, and a valuable national resource. AIA-member architects licensed in the United States are eligible to enter U.S.-built projects. Winning projects are published in *Architectural Record* and displayed at the annual AIA National Convention and Expo.

For additional information, contact the AIA Honors and Awards department at (202) 626-7563 or visit them on the Internet at *www.aia.org*.

2003 Recipients

Single Family—Custom

Calvert Street Residence
Washington, DC
Robert M. Gurney

Cyronak House
Block Island, RI
Estes/Twombly Architects, Inc.

Single Family—Market

Chiricahua Villas
Scottsdale, AZ
B3 Architects, a Berkus Design Studio

Multifamily Housing

Gateway Lofts
Charlotte, NC
David Furman Architecture

MONTAGE
Palo Alto, CA
Seidel/Holzman

Edward T. Lewis Quadrangle Residence Hall
St. Mary's City, MD
Muse Architects

Colorado Court
Santa Monica, CA
Pugh Scarpa Kodama

1310 East Union Live/Work Lofts
Seattle, WA
Miller/Hull Partnership

Community Design

Monterey Place HOPE VI
New Haven, CT
Fletcher-Thompson, Inc.

Jury

John Klockeman, Blumentals/Architecture, Inc. (chair)
Carol Burns, Taylor & Burns Architects
Jane Kolleeny, *Architectural Record*
J. Carson Looney, Looney Ricks Kiss Architects
Michael Pyatok, Pyatok Associates

Source: The American Institute of Architects

> Doing a house is so much harder than doing a skyscraper.
>
> **Philip Johnson**

AIA/HUD Secretary's Housing and Community Design Award

Innovative, affordable and accessible building designs are honored by the HUD Secretary's Housing and Community Design Award, presented jointly by The American Institute of Architects (AIA) and the U.S. Department of Housing and Urban Development (HUD). The AIA's Center for Livable Communities and the AIA Housing Professional Interest Area, in partnership with HUD, created this biennial award program to recognize the best in residential and community design. Categories include Mixed-Use/Mixed Income Development, for projects that revitalize neighborhoods through a combination of residential and non-residential uses; Community Building by Design, to honor projects that rebuild poor neighborhoods; and the Alan J. Rothman Housing Accessibility Award, named in honor of the late HUD senior policy analyst, an expert on disability issues.

Additional information can be found on the AIA's Web site at *www.aia.org*.

2003 Winners

Residential Design

101 San Fernando
San Jose, CA
Solomon E.T.C., A WRT Company
Togawa and Smith Inc.

Community Design

Outdoor Classroom at Eib's Pond Park
Staten Island, NY
Marpillero Pollak Architects

Alan J. Rothman Award for Housing Accessibility

Independent Communities
Decatur, GA
Smith Dalia Architects LLC

Jury

Suman Sorg, Sorg & Associates (chair)
Lawrence "Murphy" Antoine, Torti Gallas and Partners-CHK, Inc.
Carlos Martin, U.S. Dept. of Housing and Urban Development and Research
Marina L. Myhre, U.S. Dept. of Housing and Urban Development and Research

Source: The American Institute of Architects

> A home is not a mere transient shelter; its essence lies in its permanence...in its quality of representing in all its details, the personalities of the people who live in it.
>
> **H.L. Mencken**

Alice Davis Hitchcock Book Award

The Alice Davis Hitchcock book award has been granted annually by the Society of Architectural Historians (SAH) since 1949. It is given to a publication by a North American scholar, published within the preceding two years, that demonstrates a high level of scholarly distinction in the field of the history of architecture.

For more information contact the SAH at (312) 573-1365 or visit their Web site at *www.sah.org*.

1949
Colonial Architecture and Sculpture in Peru by Harold Wethey (Harvard University Press)

1950
Architecture of the Old Northwest Territory by Rexford Newcomb (University of Chicago Press)

1951
Architecture and Town Planning in Colonial Connecticut by Anthony Garvan (Yale University Press)

1952
The Architectural History of Newport by Antoinette Downing and Vincent Scully (Harvard University Press)

1953
Charles Rennie Mackintosh and the Modern Movement by Thomas Howarth (Routledge and K. Paul)

1954
Early Victorian Architecture in Britain by Henry Russell Hitchcock (Da Capo Press, Inc.)

1955
Benjamin H. Latrobe by Talbot Hamlin (Oxford University Press)

1956
The Railroad Station: An Architectural History by Carroll L. V. Meeks (Yale University Press)

1957
The Early Architecture of Georgia by Frederick D. Nichols (University of N.C. Press)

1958
The Public Buildings of Williamsburg by Marcus Whiffen (Colonial Williamsburg)

1959
Carolingian and Romanesque Architecture, 800 to 1200 by Kenneth J. Conant (Yale University Press)

1960
The Villa d'Este at Tivoli by David Coffin (Princeton University Press)

1961
The Architecture of Michelangelo by James S. Ackerman (University of Chicago Press)

1962
The Art and Architecture of Ancient America by George Kubler (Yale University Press)

1963
La Cathédrale de Bourges et sa Place dans l'Architecture Gothique by Robert Branner (Tardy)

1964
Images of American Living, Four Centuries of Architecture and Furniture as Cultural Expression by Alan Gowans (Lippincott)

1965
The Open-Air Churches of Sixteenth Century Mexico by John McAndrew (Harvard University Press)

1966
Early Christian and Byzantine Architecture by Richard Krautheimer (Penguin Books)

1967
Eighteenth-Century Architecture in Piedmont: the open structures of Juvarra, Alfieri & Vittone by Richard Pommer (New York University Press)

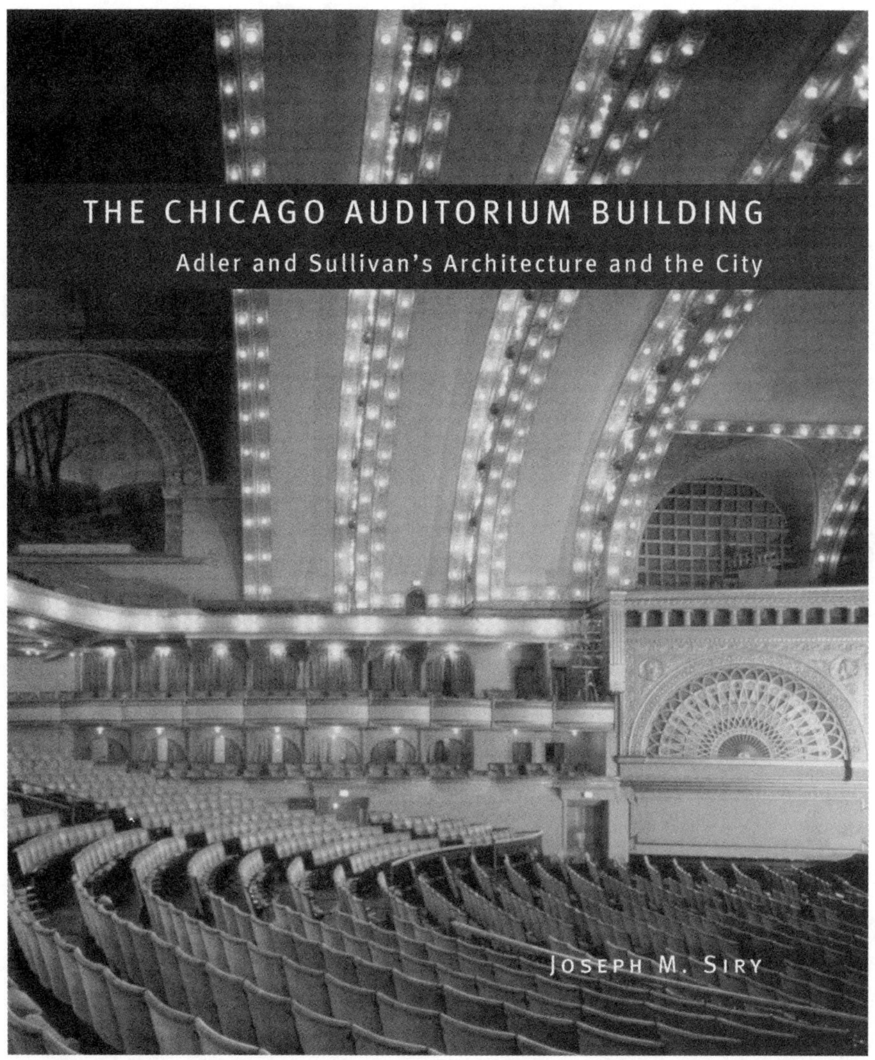

THE CHICAGO AUDITORIUM BUILDING
Adler and Sullivan's Architecture and the City
JOSEPH M. SIRY

In this lavishly illustrated book, Joseph M. Siry explores the architectural history of Chicago's Auditorium Building, one of the earliest multipurpose civic centers in the United States, housing a 4,200-seat theater, 400-room hotel, offices, and stores. The building's many technical and aesthetic innovations launched the national reputations of architects Dankmar Adler and Louis Sullivan. *Image courtesy of the University of Chicago Press.*

Alice Davis Hitchcock Book Award

1968
Architecture and Politics in Germany, 1918-1945 by Barbara Miller Lane (Harvard University Press)

1969
Samothrace, Volume III: The Hieron by Phyllis Williams Lehmann (Princeton University Press)

1970
The Church of Notre Dame in Montreal by Franklin Toker (McGill-Queen's University Press)

1971
No award granted

1972
The Prairie School; Frank Lloyd Wright and his Midwest Contemporaries by H. Allen Brooks (University of Toronto Press)

The Early Churches of Constantinople: Architecture and Liturgy by Thomas F. Mathews (Pennsylvania State University Press)

1973
The Campanile of Florence Cathedral: "Giotto's Tower" by Marvin Trachtenberg (New York University Press)

1974
FLO, A Biography of Frederick Law Olmstead by Laura Wood Roper (Johns Hopkins University Press)

1975
Gothic vs. Classic, Architectural Projects in Seventeenth-Century Italy by Rudolf Wittkower (G. Braziller)

1976
No award granted

1977
The Esplanade Ridge (Vol.V in The New Orleans Architecture Series) by Mary Louise Christovich, Sally Kitredge Evans, Betsy Swanson, and Roulhac Toledano (Pelican Publishing Company)

1978
Sebastiano Serlio on Domestic Architecture by Myra Nan Rosenfeld (Architectural History Foundation)

1979
The Framed Houses of Massachusetts Bay, 1625-1725 by Abbott Lowell Cummings (Belknap Press)

Paris: A Century of Change, 1878-1978 by Norma Evenson (Yale University Press)

1980
Rome: Profile of a City, 312-1308 by Richard Krautheimer (Princeton University Press)

1981
Gardens of Illusion: The Genius of Andre LeNotre by Franklin Hamilton Hazelhurst (Vanderbilt University Press)

1982
Indian Summer: Luytens, Baker and Imperial Delhi by Robert Grant Irving (Yale Univ. Press)

1983
Architecture and the Crisis of Modern Science by Alberto Pérez-Goméz (MIT Press)

1984
Campus: An American Planning Tradition by Paul Venable Turner (MIT Press)

1985
The Law Courts: The Architecture of George Edmund Street by David Brownlee (MIT Press)

1986
The Architecture of the Roman Empire: An Urban Appraisal by William L. MacDonald (Yale University Press)

1987
Holy Things and Profane: Anglican Parish Churches in Colonial Virginia by Dell Upton (MIT Press)

Alice Davis Hitchcock Book Award

1988

Designing Paris: The Architecture of Duban, Labrouste, Duc and Vaudoyer by David Van Zanten (MIT Press)

1989

Florentine New Towns: Urban Design in the Late Middle Ages by David Friedman (MIT Press)

1990

Claude-Nicolas Ledoux: Architecture and Social Reform at the End of the Ancient Régime by Anthony Vidler (MIT Press)

1991

The Paris of Henri IV: Architecture and Urbanism by Hilary Ballon (MIT Press)

Seventeenth-Century Roman Palaces: Use and the Art of the Plan by Patricia Waddy (MIT Press)

1992

Modernism in Italian Architecture, 1890-1940 by Richard Etlin (MIT Press)

1994*

Baths and Bathing in Classical Antiquity by Fikret Yegul (MIT Press)

1995

The Politics of the German Gothic Revival: August Reichensperger by Michael J. Lewis (MIT Press)

1996

Hadrian's Villa and Its Legacy by William J. MacDonald and John Pinto (Yale University Press)

1997

Gottfried Semper: Architect of the Nineteenth Century by Harry Francis Mallgrave (Yale University Press)

1998

The Dancing Column: On Order in Architecture by Joseph Rykwert (MIT Press)

1999

Dominion of the Eye: Urbanism, Art & Power in Early Modern Florence by Marvin Trachtenberg (Cambridge University Press)

2000

The Architectural Treatise in the Renaissance by Alina A. Payne (Cambridge University Press)

2001

The Architecture of Red Vienna, 1919-1934 by Eve Blau (MIT Press)

2002

Modernism and Nation-Building: Turkish Architectural Culture in the Early Republic by Sibel Bozdogan (University of Washington Press)

Marcel Breuer: The Career and the Buildings by Isabelle Hyman (Harry N. Abrams)

2003

The Chicago Auditorium Building: Adler and Sullivan's Architecture and the City by Joseph Siry (University of Chicago Press)

* At this time the SAH altered their award schedule to coincide with their annual meeting, and no award for 1993 was granted.

Source: Society of Architectural Historians

American Academy of Arts and Letters Academy Awards for Architecture

The American Academy of Arts and Letters grants their annual Academy Awards for Architecture to an American architect(s) whose work is characterized by a strong personal direction. The prize consists of a $7500 cash award. Recipients must be citizens of the United States. Members of the Academy are not eligible.

For more information, contact the American Academy of Arts and Letters at (212) 368-5900.

1991	Rodolfo Machado and Jorge Silvetti
1992	Thom Mayne and Michael Rotondi, Morphosis
1993	Franklin D. Israel
1994	Craig Hodgetts and Hsin-Ming Fung
1995	Mack Scogin and Merrill Elam
1996	Maya Lin
1997	Daniel Libeskind
1998	Laurie Olin
1999	Eric Owen Moss
2000	Will Bruder
	Jesse Reiser and Nanako Umemoto
2001	Vincent James
	SHoP/Sharples Holden Pasquarelli
2002	Rick Joy
	Office dA/Mónica Ponce de León with Nader Tehrani
2003	Greg Lynn
	Guy Nordensen
	Andrew Zago

Source: American Academy of Arts and Letters

Did you know...

In 2003 Maya Lin was named the recipient of Denmark's first Finn Juhl Architectural Award for addressing "complex historical and social issues" in her work.

American Academy of Arts and Letters Gold Medal for Architecture

The American Academy of Arts and Letters annually grants a gold medal in the arts, rotating among painting, music, sculpture, poetry and architecture. The entire work of the architect is weighed when being considered for the award. Only citizens of the United States are eligible.

For more information contact the American Academy of Arts and Letters at (212) 368-5900.

1912	William Rutherford Mead
1921	Cass Gilbert
1930	Charles Adams Platt
1940	William Adams Delano
1949	Frederick Law Olmsted
1953	Frank Lloyd Wright
1958	Henry R. Shepley
1963	Ludwig Mies van der Rohe
1968	R. Buckminster Fuller
1973	Louis I. Kahn
1979	I. M. Pei
1984	Gordon Bunshaft
1990	Kevin Roche
1996	Philip Johnson
2002	Frank Gehry

Source: American Academy of Arts and Letters

Annual Interiors Awards

The Annual Interiors Awards, one of the industry's most prestigious awards competition, recognizes interior design excellence in multiple commercial categories. A jury of design professionals selects winning projects based on aesthetics, design creativity, function, and achievement of client objectives, which are published in *Contract* magazine. Winners are also honored at the Annual Awards Breakfast at the Waldorf-Astoria Hotel in New York.

For more information, visit *Contract*'s Web site at *www.contractmagazine.com.*

2003 Recipients

Education
Fashion Institute of Design & Merchandising
Los Angeles, CA
Clive Wilkinson Architects

Retail
Apple Soho Store
Berkeley, CA
Bohlin Cywinski Jackson

Restoration
O'Keefe Elevator Company
Omaha, NE
Avant Architects

Spa/Fitness
Clear Spa
Toronto, ON, Canada
burdiilek

Small Office
ImageNet
Oklahoma City, OK
Elliott + Associates

Public Space
York Event Theatre
Toronto, ON, Canada
II BY IV Design Associates

Restaurant
Holt's Cafe
Toronto, ON, Canada
II BY IV Design Associates

Showroom/Exhibit
DuPont Antron Corporate Resource Center
Chicago, IL
Perkins & Will/Eva Maddox Branded Environments

Student/Conceptual Work
Swell
Shadow Hills, CA
Devanee Frazier

Large Office
Korea Development Bank
Los Angeles, CA
DMJM Design
DMJM/Rottet

Jury
David Brininstool, Brininstool + Lynch
Emanuela Frattini Magnusson, EFM Design
Glenn Pushelberg, Yabu Pushelberg
Rysia Suchecka, NBBJ
Charles Thanhauser, Thanhauser Esterson Kapell Architects

Source: Contract *magazine*

APA Journalism Awards

The American Planning Association (APA) honors outstanding newspaper coverage of city and regional planning issues each year with its Journalism Awards. These honors are presented to daily or weekly newspapers in each of three classes: circulation below 50,000; circulation of 50,000 to 100,000; and circulation above 100,000. Papers in the United States and Canada are eligible; nominations may be made by an editor, publisher, or the readers themselves. Winning articles must render outstanding public service in their coverage, perspective, interpretation and impact.

Additional information is available on the Internet at *www.planning.org* or by contacting Sylvia Lewis at *slewis@planning.org*.

2003 Recipients

Large Newspaper (circulation 100,000+)

"The View from Schley Mountain: A Case Study in How We Use Our Land"
The Star-Ledger (Newark, NJ)
Steve Chambers

"Code Red"
The Denver Post (Denver, CO)
Marsha Austin

Medium Newspaper (circulation 50,000-100,000)

No recipients

Small Newspaper (under 50,000)

"Route 100: Road to Riches or Ruin?"
The Mercury (Pottstown, PA)
Newspaper's staff led by editor Nancy March and staff writer Margaret Fitzcharles

Source: American Planning Association

> True involvement comes when the community and the designer turn the process of planning the city into a work of art.
>
> **Edmund N. Bacon**

Architectural Photography Competition

The American Institute of Architects' (AIA) St. Louis chapter sponsors the Architectural Photography Competition each year. Winners are awarded a cash prize. In addition, all entrants are eligible to be selected for the American Architectural Foundation's yearly Engagement Calendar. All architects, AIA associate members and American Institute of Architecture Students (AIAS) members in the United States are eligible to enter. The subject matter must have an architectural theme or contain some element of the man-made environment.

Winning photos can be seen on the AIA St. Louis chapter's Web site at *www.aia-stlouis.org*.

2003 Winners

First Place
Moorish Detail
Granada, Spain
Scott R. Bonney

Second Place
"O" – Rock
Berkeley, CA
Takane Eshima

Third Place
Purple Haze
Seattle, WA
Jeffrey Allen Wierenga

Louise Bethune Award
Yellow Storage
Oakland, CA
Takane Eshima

Digital Category
Lahaina in Silhouette # 2
Lahaina, Maui, Hawaii
Chad M. Okinaka

Judges Special Commendation Awards
Rural Boulevard
Red Lodge, MT
Henry E. Sorenson Jr.

Log Cabin Door Handle
Stockholm, Sweden
Neil A. Larson

Dinner and a Show
Galway, Ireland
Andrew Goldman

Trees & White Wall
Folegandros, Greece
Robert L. Cassway

New York Parking Lot
New York, NY
Tamar Kisilevitz

Olympic Stadium II
Athens, Greece
Thomas V.S. Cullins

Oil Tanks A – Rustin
West Texas
James R. Lewis

Tobacco Barn
Caswell County, NC
Dwayne Poovey

Shadows
San Juan Chamula, Mexico
Steven House

Architectural Photography Competition

An Urn's Life / Bellefontaine Cemetery
St. Louis, MO
Peter B. Smith

Jury
Steven Strassburg, AIA Iowa Magazine
Kiku Obata, Kiku Obata & Company
Michael Eastman, photographer

Source: AIA St. Louis

> There is something about a building which is akin to the quality we refer to in humans as "personality." We even use the same words for them —buildings are noble, mysterious, friendly or forbidding. No great architecture can exist without emotion. When architecture is reduced to a mere intellectual exercise, it is sterile.
>
> **Ralph Tubbs**

Architecture Firm Award

The American Institute of Architects (AIA) grants its Architecture Firm Award, the highest honor the AIA can bestow on a firm, annually to an architecture firm for "consistently producing distinguished architecture." Eligible firms must claim collaboration within the practice as a hallmark of their methodology and must have been producing work as an entity for at least 10 years.

For more information, visit the AIA on the Internet at *www.aia.org* or contact the AIA Honors and Awards Department at (202) 626-7586.

1962	Skidmore, Owings & Merrill
1964	The Architects Collaborative
1965	Wurster, Bernardi & Emmons
1967	Hugh Stubbins & Associates
1968	I.M. Pei & Partners
1969	Jones & Emmons
1970	Ernest J. Kump Associates
1971	Albert Kahn Associates, Inc.
1972	Caudill Rowlett Scott
1973	Shepley Bulfinch Richardson Abbott
1974	Kevin Roche John Dinkeloo & Associates
1975	Davis, Brody & Associates
1976	Mitchell/Giurgola Architects
1977	Sert, Jackson and Associates
1978	Harry Weese & Associates
1979	Geddes Brecher Qualls Cunningham
1980	Edward Larrabee Barnes Associates
1981	Hardy Holzman Pfeiffer Associates
1982	Gwathmey Siegel & Associates, Architects
1983	Holabird & Root, Architects, Engineers & Planners
1984	Kallmann, McKinnell & Wood, Architects
1985	Venturi, Rauch and Scott Brown
1986	Esherick Homsey Dodge & Davis
1987	Benjamin Thompson & Associates
1988	Hartman-Cox Architects
1989	Cesar Pelli & Associates
1990	Kohn Pedersen Fox Associates
1991	Zimmer Gunsul Frasca Partnership
1992	James Stewart Polshek and Partners
1993	Cambridge Seven Associates Inc.
1994	Bohlin Cywinski Jackson
1995	Beyer Blinder Belle
1996	Skidmore, Owings & Merrill
1997	R. M. Kliment & Frances Halsband Architects
1998	Centerbrook Architects and Planners
1999	Perkins & Will
2000	Gensler
2001	Herbert Lewis Kruse Blunck
2002	Thompson, Ventulett, Stainback & Associates
2003	The Miller/Hull Partnership

Source: The American Institute of Architects

ar+d award

The ar+d award for emerging architecture is an international annual competition open to architects and designers age 45 and under, which is intended to bring wider recognition to a talented new generation of architects and designers. Encompassing the full range of design activity, entries can be made for any building, interior, landscape, urban, or product design as long as it is a completed work. Each year the jury selects the award categories and chooses any number of winners and highly commended entries. A total of £10,000 in prize money is awarded. Sponsored by the British periodical *The Architectural Review*, d line™ international, a Danish architectural firm, and Buro Happold, a European engineering firm, the ar+d award was inaugurated in 1999.

Additional information and an entry form can be found on the ar+d award Web site, *www.arplusd.com.*

2002 Winners

HoneyHouse
Cashiers, NC
Marlon Blackwell (US)

Peninsula House
Victoria, Australia
Sean Godsell Architects (Australia)

Cemetery for the Unknown
Mirasaka Sousa, Hiroshima, Japan
Archipro Architects (Japan)

Stylepark Lounge, UIA Congress 2002
Berlin, Germany
J. Mayer H. Architects (Germany)

Memorial Bridge
Rijeka, Croatia
3LHD (Croatia)

2002 Commendations

Congress Centre
Murcia, Spain
Paredes Pedrosa Arquitectos (Spain)

Installation for Summer Festival, Academy of Fine Arts
Munich, Germany
Munich Architecture Class, Academy of Fine Arts (Germany)

Experimental 'Tree' Housing
Addis Ababa, Ethiopia
Ahadu Abaineh (Ethiopia)

Float-Tea Lantern
Vancouver, BC, Canada
Forsythe + MacAllen Design Associates (Canada)

Single family house
Musashino, Toyko, Japan
Yumi Kori + Toshiya Endo (Japan)

De la Warr Pavilion Bandstand
Bexhill, UK
Niall McLaughlin Architects (UK)

Car Park
Offenburg, Germany
Ingenhoven Overdiek & Partner (Germany)

The Memorial Bridge in Rijek, Croatia serves a functional purpose as a pedestrian walkway as well as plays an aesthetic and cultural role as a memorial to the victims of the Balkan wars. Its straightforward composition in aluminum and glass stands apart from the surrounding classical buildings, although it complements the city's public spaces. At night, the bridge is illuminated by blue LED lights under the handrails. *Photo courtesy of 3LHD.*

ar+d award

Office Building
Ljubljana, Slovenia
Andrej Kalamar (Slovenia)

Women's Centre
Rufisque, Senegal
Helena Sandman, Jenni Reuter, Saija Hollmén (Finland)

Church
Mortensrud, Oslo, Norway
Jensen & Skodvin (Norway)

Indoor Swimming Pool
Pontedeume, Spain
Quintáns + Raya + Crespo (Spain)

School Shapel
Bogota, Colombia
Daniel Bonilla Arquitectos (Columbia)

Place for Meditation
Malacca, Malaysia
SCDA Architects (Singapore)

Adjustable Urban Light
Hong Kong
Edge (HK) Ltd. (Hong Kong)

Art Installation, Friends of the Australian Chamber Orchestra
Brisbane, Australia
Alice Hampson, Sarah Foley, Sheona Thomson, Sebastian di Mauro (Australia)

Millennium Bridge
Gateshead, Newcastle, UK
Wilkinson Eyre Architects (UK)

Camp Dining Hall
Dorset, ON, Canada
Shim-Sutcliffe Architects (Canada)

Underground Metro Stations
Copenhagen, Denmark
KHR AS Architects (Denmark)

Clinic and Pharmacy
Kyoto, Japan
Tatsuo Kawanishi Architects (Japan)

Elementary and Junior High Schools
Nan Tou, Taiwan
Jou Min Lin (Taiwan)

Fruit Warehouse
Calera de Tango, Chile
Felipe Assadi (Chile)

Jury

Stefan Behnisch, Behnisch, Behnisch & Partner (Germany)
Margrét Hardardottir, Studio Granda (Iceland)
Rick Joy, architect (US)
Carme Pinós, (Spain)
Hin L. Tan, Hin Tan Associates (Malaysia)
Peter Davey, *The Architectural Review* (UK)

Source: The ar+d award

Arnold W. Brunner Memorial Prize

The American Academy of Arts and Letters annually recognizes an architect who has contributed to architecture as an art with the Arnold W. Brunner Memorial Prize. A prize of $5000 is granted to each recipient. Eligibility is open to architects of any nationality.

For more information contact the American Academy of Arts and Letters at 212-368-5900.

1955	Gordon Bunshaft (US)
	Minoru Yamasaki (US), *Honorable Mention*
1956	John Yeon (US)
1957	John Carl Warnecke (US)
1958	Paul Rudolph (US)
1959	Edward Larrabee Barnes (US)
1960	Louis I. Kahn (US)
1961	I. M. Pei (US)
1962	Ulrich Franzen (US)
1963	Edward Charles Basset (US)
1964	Harry Weese (US)
1965	Kevin Roche (US)
1966	Romaldo Giurgola (US)
1968	John M. Johansen (US)
1969	Noel Michael McKinnell (US)
1970	Charles Gwathmey and Richard Henderson (US)
1971	John Andrews (Australia)
1972	Richard Meier (US)
1973	Robert Venturi (US)
1974	Hugh Hardy with Norman Pfeiffer and Malcolm Holzman (US)
1975	Lewis Davis and Samuel Brody (US)
1976	James Stirling (UK)
1977	Henry N. Cobb (US)
1978	Cesar Pelli (US)
1979	Charles W. Moore (US)
1980	Michael Graves (US)
1981	Gunnar Birkerts (US)
1982	Helmut Jahn (US)
1983	Frank O. Gehry (US)
1984	Peter K. Eisenman (US)
1985	William Pederson and Arthur May (US)
1986	John Hejduk (US)
1987	James Ingo Freed (US)
1988	Arata Isozaki (Japan)
1989	Richard Rogers (UK)
1990	Steven Holl (US)
1991	Tadao Ando (Japan)
1992	Sir Norman Foster (UK)
1993	Jose Rafael Moneo (Spain)
1994	Renzo Piano (Italy)
1995	Daniel Urban Kiley (US)
1996	Tod Williams and Billie Tsien (US)
1997	Henri Ciriani (France)
1998	Alvaro Siza (Portugal)
1999	Fumihiko Maki (Japan)
2000	Toyo Ito (Japan)
2001	Henry Smith-Miller and Laurie Hawkinson (US)
2002	Kazuyo Sejima + Ryue Nishizawa (Japan)
2003	Elizabeth Diller and Ricardo Scofidio

Source: American Academy of Arts and Letters

Left to right: Ricardo Scofidio, Elizabeth Diller.
Photo courtesy of the architects.

ASLA Design Medal

In 2003, the American Society of Landscape Architects (ASLA) added the ASLA Design Medal to its award program. The Design Medal recognizes an individual landscape architect who has produced a body of exceptional design work at a sustained level for a period of at least 10 years. Medals are conferred by the board of trustees of the ASLA, and are presented during the ASLA annual meeting.

For additional information, visit the ASLA on the Web at *www.alsa.org* or call (202) 898-2444.

2003 Lawrence Halprin

Source: American Society of Landscape Architects

> What differentiates our art is that it is multidimensional, based as it is on the physical experience of moving through the landscape. As we move, all of our senses are engaged: we become aware of colors, smells, sounds, and the feel of earth and stone underfoot. The emotional impact of water in pools, streams, and waterfalls tugs at us consciously and subconsciously. No other art form designs with so many elements of nature, whose experiences are often extremely ephemeral. The enjoyment of landscapes is primarily experiential.
>
> **Lawrence Halprin**

Among Lawrence Halprin's many notable works are the master plan for the Seattle Center, the Seattle World's Fair, Sea Ranch, Ghirardelli Square, Yerba Buena Gardens, and portions of the BART System in San Francisco. He has also won wide acclaim for the FDR Memorial in Washington, D.C. He is currently working with the National Park Service on redesigning the approach to Yosemite Falls in Yosemite National Park. *Photo by Ernest Braun, courtesy of the American Society of Landscape Architects.*

ASLA Firm Award

New in 2003, the American Society of Landscape Architects (ASLA) presents its ASLA Firm Award annually to landscape architecture firms that have produced bodies of distinguished work influencing professional practice for a sustained period of at least 10 years. It is the highest award the ASLA may bestow on a landscape architecture firm. The winning firm is selected by the organization's Board of Trustees on the following criteria: the firm's influence on the profession of landscape architecture; the collaborative environment of the firm; and the consistent quality of the firm's work and its recognition by fellow practitioners, teachers of landscape architecture, members of allied professions and the general public.

For more information, contact the ASLA online at *www.asla.org* or (202) 898-2444.

2003 Jones & Jones

Source: American Society of Landscape Architects

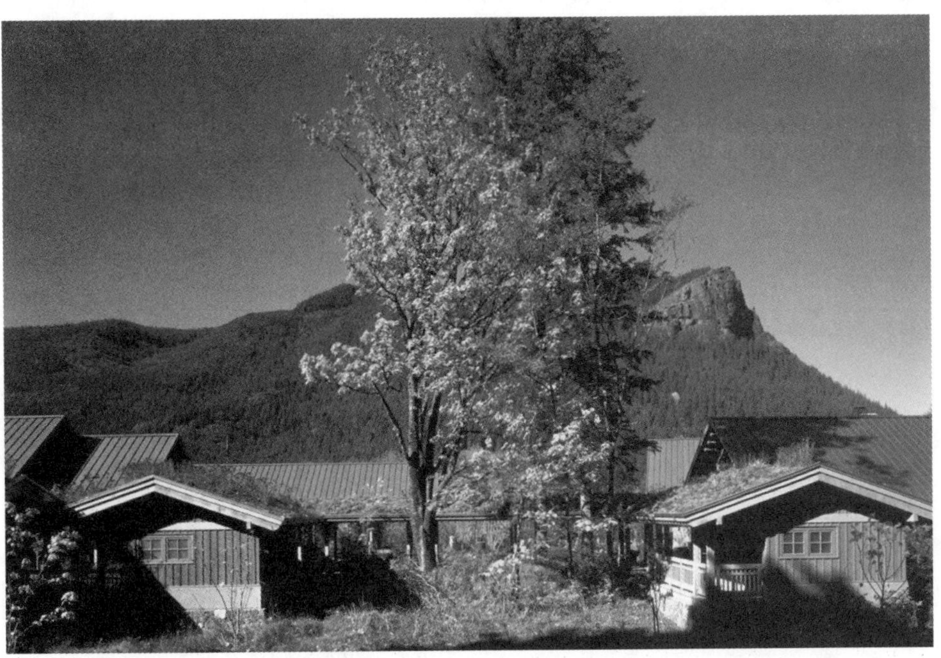

Above, Jones & Jones' design for the Cedar River Watershed Education Center in Cedar Falls, Wash. Principals Grant Jones and Ilze Jones formed Jones & Jones in 1969 to practice landscape architecture, environmental planning, architecture, and urban design as a fully integrated collaborative. Some of their signature projects include: Seattle's Pioneer Square Historic District, the Portland International Airport Parkway, the San Diego Zoo, the Singapore Botanic Gardens, the North Carolina Botanic Gardens, the Jerusalem Zoo, Disney's Wild Kingdom in Orlando, and the Smithsonian National Museum of the American Indian. *Photo by Lara Swimmer, courtesy of the American Society of Landscape Architects.*

ASLA Medal

Every year the American Society of Landscape Architects (ASLA) awards its highest honor, the ASLA Medal, to an individual who has made a significant contribution to the field of landscape architecture. The following individuals were chosen for their unique and lasting impact through their work in landscape design, planning, writing and/or public service. Eligibility is open to ASLA members and non-members of any nationality.

For more information, contact the ASLA at (202) 898-2444 or visit their Web site at *www.asla.org*.

1971	Hideo Sasaki
1972	Conrad L. Wirth
1973	John C. Simonds
1974	Campbell E. Miller
1975	Garrett Eckbo
1976	Thomas Church
1977	Hubert Owens
1978	Lawrence Halprin
1979	Norman T. Newton
1980	William G. Swain
1981	Sir Geoffrey Jellicoe
1982	Charles W. Eliot II
1983	Theodore O. Osmundson
1984	Ian McHarg
1985	Roberto Burle Marx
1986	William J. Johnson
1987	Phillip H. Lewis Jr.
1988	Dame Sylvia Crowe
1989	Robert N. Royston
1990	Ray Freeman
1991	Meade Palmer
1992	Robert S. "Doc" Reich
1993	A. E. "Ed" Bye Jr.
1994	Edward D. Stone Jr.
1995	Dr. Ervin Zube
1996	John Lyle
1997	Julius Fabos
1998	Carol R. Johnson
1999	Stuart C. Dawson
2000	Carl D. Johnson
2001	Robert E. Marvin
2002	Morgan "Bill" Evans
2003	Richard Haag

Source: American Society of Landscape Architects

> I have all my life been considering distant effects and always sacrificing immediate success and applause to that of the future.
>
> **Frederick Law Olmsted**

Richard Haag has had a distinguished career as both a teacher and professional practitioner, with more than 500 projects to his credit, including Seattle's Gas Works Park and the Bloedel Reserve on Bainbridge Island, Wash. In 1960 he founded the Department of Landscape Architecture and Building Construction at the University of Washington, which became the Department of Landscape Architecture under his chairmanship in 1964. He continues to teach and lecture internationally. *Photo courtesy of the American Society of Landscape Architects.*

ASLA Professional Awards

The American Society of Landscape Architects' (ASLA) annual Professional Awards program is intended to encourage the profession of landscape architecture by rewarding works of distinction and to generate increased visibility for the winners and the profession in general. Entries are accepted for placement in one of four areas: design, analysis & planning, research, and communication. Eligibility is open to any landscape architect or, in the case of research and communication, any individual or group. Juries for each category are comprised of landscape professionals and appointed by the ASLA's Professional Awards Committee.

For additional information, visit the ASLA's Web site at *www.asla.org* or contact them at (202) 898-2444.

2003 Design Award Recipients

Excellence Award

Westlake Corporate Campus, Circle T Ranch
Westlake, TX
SWA Group

Honor Awards

Hither Lane
East Hampton, NY
Reed Hilderbrand Associates, Inc.

J. Paul Getty Center
Los Angeles, CA
Olin Partnership

Merit Awards

560 Mission Street
San Francisco, CA
Hart Howerton and Christian Lemon

Arthur Ross Terrace of the Rose and Priest Center for Earth and Space at the American Museum of Natural History
New York, NY
Charles Anderson Landscape Architecture

Christian Science Center Seasonal Plantings
Boston, MA
Reed Hilderbrand Associates, Inc.

Conference Center for the Church of Jesus Christ of Latter-Day Saints
Salt Lake City, UT
Olin Partnership

Emerson Residence
Los Angeles, CA
R. Michael Schneider

Jinji Lake Public Open Space, Park, and Landscape
Suzhou, China
EDAW, Inc.

Lewis Avenue Corridor
Las Vegas, NV
SWA Group

Maple Avenue
Cambridge, MA
Reed Hilderbrand Associates, Inc.

Michigan Avenue Streetscape
Chicago, IL
Douglas Hoerr Landscape Architecture, Inc.

Pennswood Village Regional Storm Water Quality and Management System Middletown Township, Bucks County, PA
Wells Appel Land Strategies

Above, The plaza at the Jinji Lake Park in Suzhou, China, contains a representation of the solar system. Over-scaled planets are carved out of solid granite and narrow stainless steel "rings" inlaid into the granite flooring indicate the planets' orbiting paths. The granite columns delineate the neighborhood's gathering space overlooking the lake. *Photo by Dixi Carrillo, courtesy of the American Society of Landscape Architects.*
Below, For their master planning and landscape architecture work at the Foreign Studies Campus at Tokyo University, SWA Group's strong geometrical design is interwoven among existing, mature trees. *Photo by Tom Fox, courtesy of the American Society of Landscape Architects.*

ASLA Professional Awards

Robert F. Wagner Jr. Park
New York, NY
Olin Partnership

Tide Point
Baltimore, MD
W Architecture & Landscape Architecture, LLC

Tokyo University Foreign Studies Campus
Fuchu, Japan
SWA Group

Watercolor Cerulean Park
Watercolor, Walton County, FL
Nelson-Byrd Landscape Architects

2003 Analysis & Planning Award Recipients

Honor Awards

Highbrook Business Park
Auckland, New Zealand
Peter Walker and Partners

The Blue Ring: Seattle's Center City Open Space Strategy
Seattle, WA
Mithun Architectects + Designers + Planners

Merit Awards

A Vision for the Menomonee River Valley
Milwaukee, WI
Wenk Associates, Inc.

Masterplan for Buffalo Bayou and Beyond
Houston, TX
Dodson Associates, Inc.

The Presidio Trust Management Plan
San Francisco, CA
Sasaki Associates, Inc.

The Tidal Schuylkill River Master Plan
Philadelphia, PA
EDAW, Inc.

University of Virginia Carr's Hill Master Plan and Landscape Design for the New Arts Precinct and Art Museum
Charlottesville, VA
Olin Partnership

Wetland Mitigation at the Santa Lucia Preserve
Carmel, CA
Wetlands Research Associates, Inc.

2003 Research Award Recipients

Merit Awards

Restoring the Earth: Reconstructing the Post-mining Environment
Jon Bryan Burley, ASLA, Michigan State University, Perrinton, MI

ASLA Professional Awards

2003 Communications Award Recipients

Honor Awards

Inventing the Charles River
Charles River Conservancy, Newton, MA

National Capital Memorials and Museums Master Plan
Leo A Daly; EDAW, Inc.

Merit Awards

Garden History Reference Encyclopedia CD
Tom Turner, University of Greenwich, London, UK

Dreaming Gardens: Landscape Architecture and the Making of Modern Israel
Kenneth Helphand, University of Oregon, Eugene, OR
Center for American Places
University of Virginia Press
Israeli Association of Landscape Architects

The City in a Garden: A Photographic History of Chicago's Parks
Julia Sniderman Bachrach, Chicago Park District of Planning and Development

Jury

J. Brooks Breeden, Ohio State Univerity
Benjamin Forgey, *The Washington Post*
John Jackson III, Jackson Person & Associates, Inc.
Joseph J. Lalli, EDSA
Carol Mayer-Reed, Mayer/Reed
Witold Rybczynski, University of Pennsylvania
Frederick R. Steiner, University of Texas at Austin
Ramiro Cillalvazo, USDA Forest Service
Joan H. Woodward, California State Polytechnic University

Source: American Society of Landscape Architects

Auguste Perret Prize

The International Union of Architects (UIA) grants the triennial Auguste Perret Prize to an internationally renowned architect or architects for their work in applied technology in architecture.

For more information, visit the UIA's Web site at *www.uia-architectes.org*.

1961

Felix Candela (Mexico)

Honorary Mention: the architects of the British Ministry for Education office and the architects of the office for the study of industrial and agricultural buildings of Hungary

1963

Kunio Mayekawa (Japan)

Jean Prouvé (France)

1965

Hans Scharoun (GFR)

Honorary Mention: Heikki and Kaija Siren (Finland)

1967

Frei Otto and Rolf Gutbrod (GFR)

1969

Karel Hubacek (Czechoslovakia)

1972

E. Pinez Pinero (Spain)

1975

Arthur C. Erickson and team (Canada)

Honorary Mention: J. Cardoso (Brazil)

1978

Kiyonori Kitutake (Japan)

Piano & Rogers (Italy/UK)

1981

Günter Behnisch (GFR)

Honorary Mention: Jacques Rougerie (France)

1984

Joao Baptista Vilanova Artigas (Brazil)

1987

Santiago Calatrava (Spain)

Honorary Mention: Clorindo Testa (Argentina)

1990

Adien Fainsilber (France)

1993

KHR AS Arkitekten (Denmark)

1996

Thomas Herzog (Germany)

1999

Ken Yeang (Malaysia)

2002

Sir Norman Foster (UK)

Source: International Union of Architects

Austrian Frederick Kiesler Prize for Architecture and the Arts

The biennial Austrian Frederick Kiesler Prize for Architecture and the Arts is presented for extraordinary achievements in architecture and the arts as that achievement relates to the work and philosophy of the award's namesake, Frederick Kiesler. A native of Vienna, Kiesler worked as a theatrical producer, architect, painter and sculptor, among other things, and was a prolific author. His non-traditional ideas about the 'correlated arts' were both visionary and theoretical. This award honors that spirit. The award is organized by the Austrian Frederick and Lillian Kiesler Private Foundation and presented alternately by the Republic of Austria and the City of Vienna.

Additional information is available at *www.kiesler.org*.

1998 Frank O. Gehry (US)
2000 Judith Barry (US)
2002 Cedric Price (UK)

Source: Austrian Frederick and Lillian Kiesler Private Foundation

> Architects are the greatest whores in town. They talk in platitudes about improving the quality of life, and then get out drawings of the prison they're working on.
>
> **Cedric Price**

Best in American Living Award

Each year the National Association of Home Builders (NAHB) and *Professional Builder* magazine jointly present the Best in American Living Award for residential housing. The judges' criteria includes not only appearance but the interior floor plans, how the project related to its local market, and construction techniques and materials. The competition is open to builders, developers, architects, land planners, and designers nationwide who may enter their designs in one of 22 categories including smart growth communities and the HUD Secretary's Award for Excellence. Awards are presented at platinum, gold, and silver levels in addition to regional winners.

For a complete list of all winners with photos and floor plans or an entry form, visit the Best in American Living Award page on the Internet at *www.housingzone.com/design/bala02/* or by phone at (630) 288-8184.

2002 Home of the Year

The Sentinels – Plan 1
San Diego, CA
Scheurer Architects

2002 Platinum Winners

Best One-of-a-Kind Custom Home
6,501 Square Feet and Over
Private residence
Scottsdale, AZ
H&S International

Best Single-Family Detached Home
2,401-3,000 Square Feet
The Sentinels – Plan 1
San Diego, CA
Scheurer Architects

Best Rental Development
Casa del Maestro
Santa Clara, CA
KTGY Group Inc.

Best Single-Family Detached Home
1,801-2,400 Square Feet
Liberty on the Lake – Pioneer Model
Stillwater, MN
Senn & Youngdahl Inc.

Best Single-Family Detached Home
3,001-4,000 Square Feet
Clifton Heights – Plan 2
Ladera Ranch, CA
Bassenian Lagoni Architects

Best Single-Family Detached Home
3,001-4,000 Square Feet
Villas at The Bridges – Plan 1
Rancho Santa Fe, CA
Bassenian Lagoni Architects

Best Single-Family Detached Home
4,001 Square Feet and Over
Palmilla – Ironwood
La Quinta, CA
Downing, Thorpe & James

Best Single-Family Detached Home
4,001 Square Feet and Over
Homearama Entry – The Enchantment
Solon, OH
RSA Architects Inc.

Best in American Living Award

Best Attached Home

To and Including 8 Units per Acre
Palmilla – Ocotillo
La Quinta, CA
Downing, Thorpe & James

Best Attached Home

20 Units and Over
Viejo Carmel – Plan E (The Carmel)
Carmel-by-the-Sea, CA
McLarand Vasquez Emsiek & Partners Inc.

Best Smart-Growth Community

151 Units and Over
Ohlone Chynoweth Commons
San Jose, CA
Chris Lamen and Associates

Source: Professional Builder *magazine*

Best of Seniors' Housing Awards

The National Council on Seniors' Housing (NCOSH), a council established by the National Association of Home Builders (NAHB) in 1989, annually presents the Best of Seniors' Housing Awards. Winning projects are chosen for their ability to meet the demands and needs of the ever-changing seniors' housing market, including the constraints of seniors' housing in marketability, budget, density and programs. Gold and silver awards are presented in a range of categories based on project type and size.

For a complete list of all winners, including photos and full project credits, visit NCOSH online at *www.nahb.org/seniors.*

2003 Gold Recipients

Large Active Adult Community
Sun City Center Fort Myers
Fort Myers, FL
WCI Communities Inc.

Midsize Active Adult Community
Grand Haven
Romeoville, IL
Bloodgood Sharp Buster

Small Active Adult Community
Carriage Hill
Southborough, MA
Bloodgood Sharp Buster

Vistoso Village
Oro Valley, AZ
Richardson Associates Architects

Community Center for Midsize Active Adult Community
Dunbarton
Bristow, VA
Devereaux & Associates

Grand Haven
Romeoville, IL
Bloodgood Sharp Buster

Community Center for Small Active Adult Community
Vistoso Village
Oro Valley, AZ
Richardson Associates Architects

Community Center Interior Design for Midsize Active Adult Community
Grand Haven
Romeoville, IL
Bloodgood Sharp Buster

Community Center Interior Design for Small Active Adult Community
Carriage Hill
Southborough, MA
Bloodgood Sharp Buster

Active Adult Home Design Over 2,100 Square Feet
Village of Five Parks – Somerville Model
Arvada, CO
Bloodgood Sharp Buster

Active Adult Home Design 1,500-2,100 Square Feet
Regency at Monroe – Bayhill Model
Monroe, NJ
Toll Architecture

Active Adult Home Design Up To 1,500 Square Feet
Crofton Park – Canterbury Model
Broomfield, CO
Bloodgood Sharp Buster

Active Adult Model Merchandising Over 2,100 Square Feet
Carriage Hill – Berkeley Model
Southborough, MA
Bloodgood Sharp Buster

The Fran & Ray Stark Assisted Living Villa in Woodland Hills, Calif., is home to aging members of the motion picture and television industry. Indoor and outdoor spaces encourage residents' interaction, helping them remain physically active and socially engaged. The entire facility echoes the design of a traditional home, allowing the villa to support socialization, privacy, and independence. *Photos by Tom Bonner (above) and John Edward Linden (below), courtesy of SmithGroup, Inc.*

Best of Seniors' Housing Awards

Sun City Center Fort Myers – D'Angelo Model
Fort Myers, FL
WCI Communities Inc.

Active Adult Model Merchandising 1,500-2,100 Square Feet

The Villas at Shady Brook – The Willow Model
Langhorne, PA
Feinberg & Associates

Active Adult Model Merchandising Up To 1,500 Square Feet

Crofton Park – Canterbury Model
Broomfield, CO
Bloodgood Sharp Buster

Canterbury Woods
Williamsville, NY
EGA P.C.

Sun City Takatsuki
Takatsuki, Japan
Perkins Eastman Architects PC

Small & Midsize Continuing Care Retirement Community and Congregate Care Community

Fuller Village
Milton, MA
DiMella Shaffer

Large Assisted Living Housing

Motion Picture & Television Fund – Fran & Ray Stark Villa
Woodland Hills, CA
SmithGroup Inc.

Small Assisted Living Housing

Sunrise Assisted Living of Pacific Palisades
Pacific Palisades, CA
Hill Partnership Inc.

Common Area Interior Design for Service-Enriched Housing

The Fountains at La Cholla
Tucson, AZ
Barg Meeks Group Inc.

Renovated Service-Enriched Housing

The Essex and Sussex
Spring Lake, NJ
Kanalstein Danton Associates P.A.

On the Boards Service-Enriched Housing

Burbank Senior Artists Colony
Burbank, CA
Scheurer Architects

Senior Apartments

The Manor at Yorktown
Doylestown, PA
Perkins Eastman Architects PC

Affordable Seniors Apartments

Las Cascada II
Phoenix, AZ
Todd & Associates Inc.

North Richmond Senior Housing
Richmond, CA
Pyatok Architects Inc.

Jurors' Innovation Award

Motion Picture & Television Fund – Fran & Ray Stark Villa
Woodland Hills, CA
SmithGroup Inc.

Best of Seniors' Housing Awards

Jury
Lolita A. Dirks, Lita Dirks & Co, LLC
Scott Glaus, Centex Homes
Quincy R. Johnson III, Quincy Johnson Architects
Kenneth J. Rohde, KTGY Group, Inc.
William T. Slenker, Slenker Land Corp.
Kimberly M. Kenney, Orchards Group
Mary Morrow Bax, Seniors Marketing Services
Kevin Glover, Erickson Retirement Communities
Richard Rosen, JSA Architects
Barry Rosengarten, Rosengarten Companies
Mary Russell, Builders' Design & Leasing
Stephen Wattenbarger, Wattenbarger Architects

Source: National Council on Seniors' Housing, National Association of Home Builders

All architecture is shelter; all great architecture is the design of space that contains, cuddles, exalts or stimulates the persons in that space.

Philip Johnson

Business Week/Architectural Record Awards

The *Business Week/Architectural Record* Awards are given annually to organizations that prove "good design is good business." Sponsored by The American Institute of Architects, in conjunction with *Architectural Record* and *Business Week* magazines, the award's special focus is on collaboration and the achievement of business goals through architecture. Eligible projects must have been completed within the past three years and submitted jointly by the architect and the client. Projects may be located anywhere in the world.

For additional information, call (202) 682-3205 or visit the AIA on the Internet at *www.aia.org*.

2002 Winners

Allsteel Headquarters
Muscatine, IA
Gensler

Gateshead Millennium Bridge
Gateshead, UK
Wilkinson Eyre Architects

Abercrombie & Fitch Headquarters
New Albany, OH
Anderson Architects

Toys "R" Us
New York, New York
Gensler

Paul Brown Stadium
Cincinnati, OH
NBBJ

University of Pennsylvania Dept. of Facilities and Real Estate Services
Philadelphia, PA
MGA Partners

Valeo Electrical Systems
San Luis Potosi, Mexico
Davis Brody Bond

Trumpf Customer and Technology Center
Farmington, CT
Barkow Leibinger Architects

Dominion Funds Multi-Use Centre
Albany, New Zealand
JASMAX Limited

Texas Children's Hospital Clinical Care Center
Houston, TX
FKP Architects

Cellular Operations Headquarters
Swindon, UK
Richard Hywel Evans Architecture

Jury

Lawrence L. Edge, World Development Federation
Steven M. Goldberg, Mitchell/Giurgola Architects, LLP
Dr. Michael Hammer, Hammer and Company, Inc.
Jon Adams Jerde, The Jerde Partnership, Inc.
Toshiko Mori, Harvard University Graduate School of Design
Timothy J. O'Brien, Ford Motor Company
Chee Pearlman, design consultant
Cathy J. Simon, Simon Martin-Vegue Winkelstein Moris
David A. Thurm, The New York Times Company
Robert W. Vanech, AMP5, LLC

Source: Business Week/Architectural Record

Charter Awards

Presented annually by the Congress for the New Urbanism (CNU), the Charter Awards honor projects that best comply with the Charter of the New Urbanism. The Charter provides principles for development at three levels: the region; the neighborhood, district and corridor; and the block, street and building. Dedicated to improving and restoring the quality of life in urban neighborhoods as well as to preserving the built environment, the CNU's Charter Awards specifically address how plans and projects respond to and integrate with their environment and, consequently, how they improve the human experience of blocks, neighborhoods, and regions. All architects, urban designers, planners, landscape architects, transportation planners, and civil engineers are eligible to enter the awards program, as are developers, institutions, government agencies, and the owners of the submitted projects.

For additional information as well as entry materials, visit the CNU on the Web at *www.cnu.org*.

2002 Winners

The Region

UrbanRiver Visions
Massachusetts
Goody, Clancy & Associates

Sarasota 2050
Sarasota, FL
Glatting Jackson Kercher Anglin Lopez Rinehart, Inc.

Smart Growth Strategy/Regional Livability Footprint Project
San Francisco Bay Area, CA
California Design Community & Environment and The Association of Bay Area Governments

The Neighborhood, District, and Corridor

Doña Ana Plaza Reconstruction
Doña Ana, NM
Moule & Polyzoides Architects and Urbanists with University of New Mexico Design & Planning Assistance Center

I'on
Mount Pleasant, SC
Civitas, Inc.

East Baltimore Comprehensive Physical Redevelopment Plan
Baltimore, MD
Urban Design Associates

Glenwood Park
Atlanta, GA
Tunnell-Spangler-Walsh

Memphis Ballpark Neighborhood
Memphis, TN
Looney Ricks Kiss Architects, Inc.

The Commons
Denver, CO
Design Workshop, Inc.

Park East Redevelopment Plan
Milwaukee, WI
Planning & Design Institute, Inc.

The Block, Street, and Building

Soleil Court
San Diego, CA
Kelley-Markham Architecture and Planning

The Soleil Court townhouses provide this historic San Diego neighborhood with attractive, low-rise housing and home office space. The central courtyard plan, rather than back and side yards, allows for higher density and provides semi-public spaces and easier parking. The street facade supports the pedestrian experience with the courtyard and home office entrances, while providing privacy for residents. *Photo by Tim Crowson and Jim Kelley-Markham, courtesy of the Congress for New Urbanism.*

Charter Awards

Quartier am Tacheles
Berlin, Germany
Duany Plater-Zyberk & Company

15th & Pearl Parking Structure
Boulder, CO
RNL Design

The Corner at Eastern Market
Washington, DC
Stanton Development Corporation

Del Mar Station Transit Village
Pasadena, CA
Moule & Polyzoides, Architects and Urbanists

Jury

Daniel Solomon, Solomon E.T.C. (chair)
Larry Beasley, City of Vancouver Planning Department
Ellen Dunham-Jones, Georgia Institute of Technology
Robert Fishman, University of Michigan
Peter Katz, CNU
Hans Stimmann, Berline Urban Planning Department
John Torti, Torti-Gallas and Partners

Source: Congress for the New Urbanism

> A city should be a garden for growing people.
>
> **James Rouse**

Design for Humanity Award

Every year the American Society of Interior Designers (ASID) grants the Design for Humanity Award to an individual or institution that has made a significant contribution toward improving the quality of the human environment through design related activities that have had a universal and far-reaching effect. A committee appointed by the ASID Board reviews the nominations. The award is presented at ASID's annual national convention.

For additional information about the Design for Humanity Award, contact the ASID at (202) 546-3480 or on the Internet at *www.asid.org*.

1990 The Scavenger Hotline
1991 E.I. Du Pont de Nemours & Company
1992 The Preservation Resource Center
1993 Neighborhood Design Center
1994 Elizabeth Paepcke & The International Design Conference in Aspen
1995 Cranbrook Academy of Art
1996 Wayne Ruga and the Center for Health Design
1997 Barbara J. Campbell, *Accessibility Guidebook For Washington, D.C.*
1998 William L. Wilkoff, District Design
1999 AlliedSignal, Inc.-Polymers Division
2000 Victoria Schomer
2001 ASID Tennessee Chapter, Chattanooga
2002 Cynthia Leibrock

Source: American Society of Interior Designers

Designer of Distinction Award

The Designer of Distinction Award is granted by the American Society of Interior Designers (ASID) to an ASID interior designer whose professional achievements have demonstrated design excellence. Eligibility is open to members in good standing who have practiced within the preceding 10 years. Nominations are accepted by ASID's general membership body and reviewed by a jury selected by the national president. This is a merit based award and, thus, is not always granted annually.

For more information, visit the ASID on the Internet at *www.asid.org* or contact them at (202) 546-3480.

1979	William Pahlman
1980	Everett Brown
1981	Barbara D'Arcy
1982	Edward J. Wormley
1983	Edward J. Perrault
1984	Michael Taylor
1985	Norman DeHaan
1986	Rita St. Clair
1987	James Merricksmith
1988	Louis Tregre
1994	Charles D. Gandy
1995	Andre Staffelbach
1996	Joseph Minton
1997	Phyllis Martin-Vegue
1998	Janet Schirn
1999	Gary E. Wheeler
2000	Paul Vincent Wiseman
2001	William Hodgins
2002	Hugh Latta
	Margaret McCurry

Source: American Society of Interior Designers

> The main purpose of my work is to provoke people into using their imagination.
>
> **Verner Panton**

Edward C. Kemper Award

Edward C. Kemper served as Executive Director of The American Institute of Architects (AIA) for nearly 35 years, from 1914 to 1948. The Edward C. Kemper Award honors an architect member of the AIA who has similarly served as an outstanding member of the Institute.

For more information, visit the AIA on the Internet at *www.aia.org* or contact the AIA Honors and Awards Department at (202) 626-7586.

1950	William Perkins
1951	Marshall Shaffer
1952	William Stanley Parker
1953	Gerrit J. De Gelleke
1954	Henry H. Saylor
1955	Turpin C. Bannister
1956	Theodore Irving Coe
1957	David C. Baer
1958	Edmund R. Purves
1959	Bradley P. Kidder
1960	Philip D. Creer
1961	Earl H. Reed
1962	Harry D. Payne
1963	Samuel E. Lunden
1964	Daniel Schwartzman
1965	Joseph Watterson
1966	William W. Eshbach
1967	Robert H. Levison
1968	E. James Gambaro
1969	Philip J. Meathe
1970	Ulysses Floyd Rible
1971	Gerald McCue
1972	David N. Yerkes
1973	Bernard B. Rothschild
1974	Jack D. Train
1975	F. Carter Williams
1976	Leo A. Daly
1977	Ronald A. Straka
1978	Carl L. Bradley
1979	Herbert E. Duncan Jr.
1980	Herbert Epstein
1981	Robert L. Durham
1982	Leslie N. Boney Jr.
1983	Jules Gregory
1984	Dean F. Hilfinger
1985	Charles Redmon
1986	Harry Harmon
1987	Joseph Monticciolo
1988	David Lewis
1989	Jean P. Carlhian
1990	Henry W. Schirmer
1991	John F. Hartray Jr.
1992	Betty Lou Custer*
1993	Theodore F. Mariani
1994	Harry C. Hallenbeck
1995	Paul R. Neel
1996	Sylvester Damianos
1997	Harold L. Adams
1998	Norman L. Koonce
1999	James R. Franklin
2000	James A. Scheeler
2001	Charles F. Harper
2002	*No award granted*
2003	C. James Lawler Jr.

* Honored posthumously

Source: The American Institute of Architects

Left to right: Jim and Cindy Lawler. 2003 TOPAZ Medallion recipient Marvin Malecha said of Jim Lawler, "At every opportunity he inspires others to become involved and to make a commitment to the advancement of the profession. I have yet to witness a single moment of reticence on Jim's part when it involves acting on behalf of the AIA."

Engineering Excellence Awards

The American Council of Engineering Companies' (ACEC) annual Engineering Excellence Awards begin at the state level, with finalists moving to the national competition. Each year one project receives the "Grand Conceptor" Award, and up to 23 other projects receive either Grand or Honor Awards. Projects are judged by a panel of 20–25 engineers and infrastructure experts on the basis of uniqueness and originality, technical value to the engineering profession, social and economic considerations, complexity, and how successfully the project met the needs of the client. Projects must be entered in one of nine categories: studies, research and consulting engineering services, building support systems; structural systems; surveying and mapping; environmental; water and wastewater; water resources; transportation; and special projects. Any firm engaged in the private practice, consulting engineering, or surveying is eligible to participate. Entries must be submitted to an ACEC member organization.

For more information and winning project descriptions, visit *www.acec.org* on the Internet.

2003 Winners

Grand Conceptor Award

Removable Spillway Weir
Snake River, Washington State
Jacobs Civil Inc.

Grand Awards

Keys Carrying Capacity Study
Florida Keys, FL
URS Corporation

Milwaukee Art Museum Addition
Milwaukee, WI
Graef, Anhalt, Schloemer and Associates

Seahawks Stadium
Seattle, WA
Magnusson Klemencic Associates

World Trade Center Disaster Response
New York, NY
The Thornton-Tomasetti Group

Leonard P. Zakim Bunker Hill Bridge
Boston, MA
HNTB Corporation

McNamara Terminal/Northwest World Gateway
Detroit, MI
SmithGroup, Inc.

The Alameda Corridor
Los Angeles – Long Beach, CA
Alameda Corridor Engineering Team

Honor Awards

Diamondback Bridge
Tucson, AZ
T.Y. Lin International

Reliant Stadium
Houston, TX
Walter P. Moore, Inc.

Fallingwater Structural Retrofit
Mill Run, PA
Robert Silman Associates, P.C.

William H. Natcher Bridge
Owensboro, KY
Parsons Brinckerhoff Quade & Douglas

Engineering Excellence Awards

Cheju Stadium
Cheju, Korea
Weidlinger Associates

"World Trade Center Report"
Greenhorne & O'Mara

Austrian Cultural Forum
New York, NY
Arup

"Charting a Clear Course," Inland Electronic Navigational Charts
Photo Science, Inc.

Horizontal Interceptor Well at the University of Minnesota
Minneapolis, MN
Peer Engineering, Inc.

Owens Dry Lake Project, Phase 1
California
Boyle Engineering Corporation

Eastern North Carolina Flood Mapping
North Carolina
Hayes, Seay, Mattern & Mattern, Inc.

Dallas Area Rapid Transit, Phase 1 – Light Rail Transit Build-Out
Dallas, TX
Lockwood, Andrews, & Newnam
STV Inc.
Chiang Patel & Yerby

The Phoenix Project
Washington, DC
KCE Structural Engineers, P.C.

Interstate 40 Arkansas River Bridge
Webber's Falls, OK
Cobb Engineering Company
Poe & Associates Engineering
White Engineering

East Bay Municipal Utility District, Southern Loop Pipeline
Alameda and Contra Costa counties, CA
Kennedy/Jenks Consultants

Stormwater/Deicer System
Wilmington, OH
Malcolm Pirnie, Inc.

Source: American Council of Engineering Companies

Did you know...
Graef, Anhalt, Schloemer & Associates, engineers for the Milwaukee Art Museum's Quadracci Pavilion (designed by Santiago Calatrava and Kahler Slater Architects) was awarded the 2003 Outstanding Civil Engineering Achievement Award from the American Society of Civil Engineers.

Excellence on the Waterfront Awards

Awarding projects that convert abandoned or outmoded waterfront spaces into those for constructive use in the public interest, the Excellence on the Waterfront Awards are presented annually by the non-profit Waterfront Center. Any built project on any body of water, new or old, is eligible to win. Judging criteria include the design's sensitivity to the water, quality and harmony, civic contribution, environmental impact, and educational components. The group also presents a Clearwater Citizens Award that recognizes outstanding grassroots efforts.

Additional information about the awards are available on the Waterfront Center's Web site at *www.waterfrontcenter.org*.

2003 Top Honor Award—Project

Making Waves–Principles for Building Toronto's Waterfront
Toronto, ON, Canada
City Planning Division, City of Toronto
Community Planning South District, City of Toronto

2003 Top Honor Award—Plan

Herring's House Park
Seattle, WA
J.A. Brennan Associates, PLLC

Waterfront Geelong
Geelong, Victoria, Australia
Taylor Cullity Lethlean

2003 Honor Awards by Category

Artistic, Cultural, Educational

The Scientific Center
Kuwait City, Kuwait
Cambridge Seven Associates, Inc.

Commercial and Mixed Use

Bishop's Landing
Halifax, NS, Canada
Andy Lynch

Park/Walkway/Recreation

The Liffey Boardwalk
Dublin, Ireland
Dublin City Council City Architects Division
McGarry Ni Eanaigh Architects

Riverwalk and Western Canal Walk
Lowell, MA
Pressley Associates, Inc.

Bayshore
Vancouver, BC, Canada
Durante Kreuk Ltd.

Stuyvesant Cove Waterfront
New York, NY
Donna Walcavage Landscape Architecture and Urban Design

Excellence on the Waterfront Awards

Plans

Master Plan for the Buffalo Bayou and Beyond
Houston, TX
Thompson Design Group Inc.

Oceanfront Asbury
Asbury Park, NJ
Clarke Caton Hintz Architects
Ehrenkrantz Eckstut and Kuhn Architects

Bo01 "Tango" Housing
Malmö, Sweden
Moore Ruble Yudell Architect and Planners
FFN Architects AB

2003 Clearwater Citizens Awards

Sylvia McLaughlin, Berkeley, CA
Bandra Bandstand and Carter Road Waterfront Development, Mumbai, India

Jury

Larry Beasley, City of Vancouver Planning Department (chair)
Ed Freer, SmithGroup JJR
Tom McInally, McInally Associates
John Mateyko, architect
Zari Santner, Portland Parks and Recreation Department

Source: Waterfront Center

Did You Know...
Asbury Park, NJ, was developed by James Bradley in 1873 as a shore resort community with a religious orientation. It featured an open space plan including three Oceanside lakes that facilitated the movement of sea breezes into the city and increased the views of the ocean.

Exhibition of School Architecture Awards

As part of the juried Exhibition of School Architecture, outstanding school design and educational environments are honored each year with two awards: the Walter Taylor and Shirley Cooper awards, named in honor of the original organizers of the School Architecture Exhibit. Additional citations may be presented at the discretion of the jury. Sponsored by the American Association of School Administrators (AASA), The American Institute of Architects and the Council of Education Facility Planners International, the Exhibition is open to registered architects and landscape architects.

For more information, contact the AASA at (703) 528-0070 or visit them on the Internet at *www.aasa.org*.

2003 Recipients

Walter Taylor Award

The Academy of Irving ISD
Irving, TX
Powell/PSP

Shirley Cooper Award

Carlin Springs Elementary School
Arlington, VA
Grimm + Parker Architects

Citation Honorees

Century High School, Carroll County Public Schools
Westminster, MD
SHW Group, Inc.

Rio del Norte Elementary School
El Rio, CA
Dougherty + Dougherty Architects

Rome Free Academy
Rome, NY
SBLM Architects, PC
Fanning Howey Associates, Inc

Sac & Fox Settlement School – Phase I
Tama, IA
Leo A. Daly Architects

Woodland Regional High School
Prospect, CT
Jeter, Cook and Jepson Architects, Inc.

Zach Elementary School
Fort Collins, CO
RB+B Architects, Inc.

Source: American Association of School Administrators

Gold Key Awards for Excellence in Hospitality Design

For over 20 years the Gold Key Awards for Excellence in Hospitality Design have honored hospitality designers for excellence in multiple categories. In addition, the "Best of Show" Award is chosen from among the award winners as the project that exhibits the most ingenious design. The awards are presented by the International Hotel/Motel & Restaurant Show and sponsored by *Hospitality Design* and *Hotel & Motel Management* magazines.

For a description of eligibility requirements and an entry form, visit *www.ihmrs.com.*

2002 Recipients

Best of Show" Award
Blue Fin at the W Times Square Hotel
New York, NY
Yabu Pushelberg

Guest Rooms
Le Touessrok Hotel & Spa
Trou D'Eau Douce, Mauritius
Hirsch Bedner Associates

Lobby/Reception Area
Hotel Monaco
New Orleans, LA
Cheryl Rowley Design

Restaurants—Seating To 110
Basilico
Woodbridge, ON, Canada
Burdifilek

Restaurants—Seating Over 110
Blue Fin at the W Times Square Hotel
New York, NY
Yabu Pushelberg

Senior Living Facility
Sun City Takatsuki
Takatsuki, Japan
Perkins Eastman Architects

Spa/Resort
Boca Raton Resort & Club Spa
Boca Raton, FL
RTKL Associates

Suites
Disney's Grand Californian Hotel
Anaheim, CA
Brayton + Hughes and Walt Disney Imagineering

Jury
Raymond Bickson, The Mark
Wing Chao, Walt Disney Imagineering
Suzanne Couture, Ian Schrager Hotels
Stephen Hanson, BR Guest, Inc.
Colum McCartan, MCCARTAN

Source: Hospitality Design *magazine and the International Hotel/Motel & Restaurant Show*

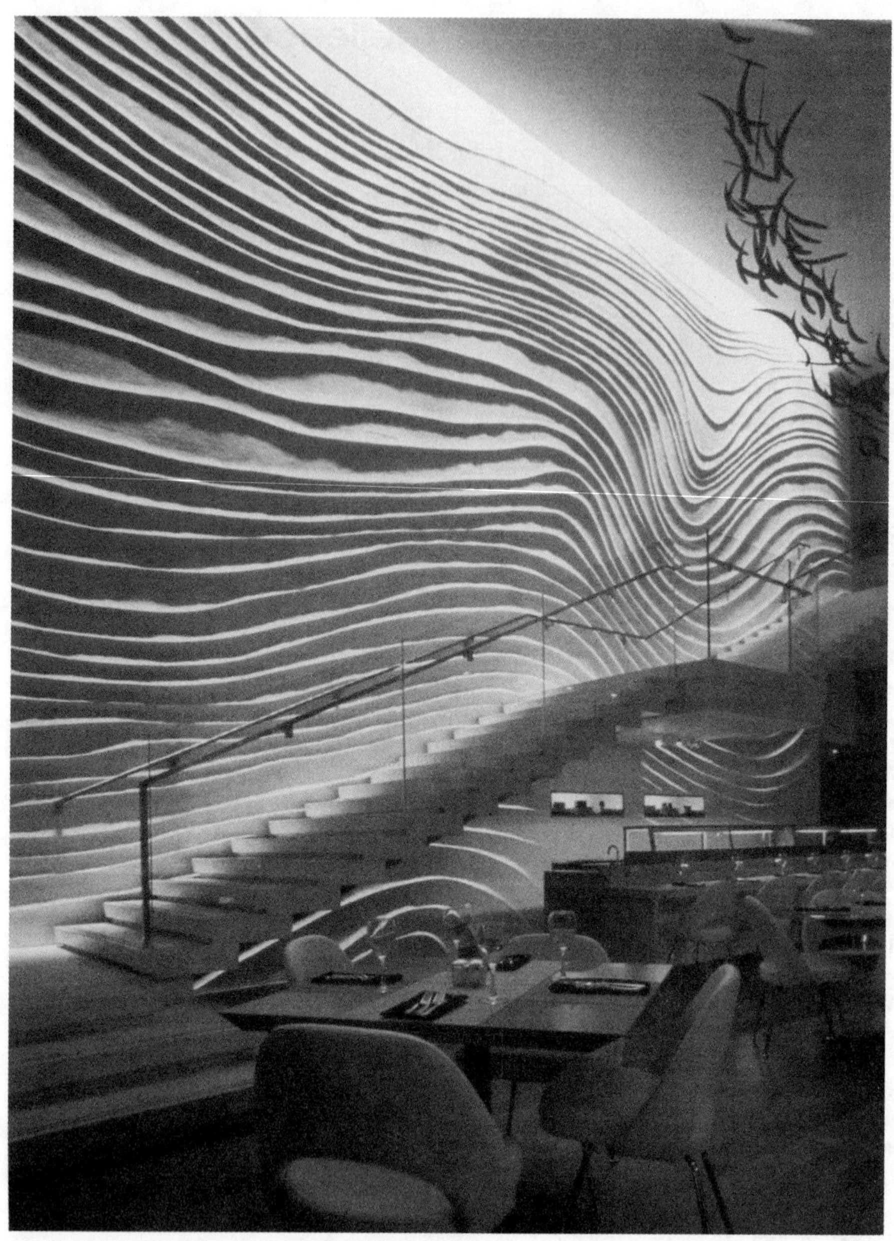

The floating terrazzo staircase in the Gold Key-winning W Times Square Hotel's BlueFin restaurant looks out over a school of decorative black fish suspended from the ceiling by fishing line. The lighted white plaster wall along the staircase appears to have been sculpted by the ebb and flow of the ocean. *Photo courtesy of the International Hotel/Motel & Restaurant Show and GLM Shows.*

GSA Design Awards

The U.S. General Services Administration (GSA) presents its biennial Design Awards as part of its Design Excellence Program, which seeks the best in design, construction, and restoration for all Federal building projects. The Design Awards were developed to encourage and recognize innovative design in Federal buildings and to honor noteworthy achievements in the preservation and renovation of historic structures.

For additional information about the GSA Design Awards or to view photographs and descriptions of the winners, visit GSA's Web site at *www.gsa.gov*.

2002 Honor Award Recipients

Workplace Environment
Office of the Chief Architect, GSA
Washington, DC
Lehman-Smith McLeish

Graphic Design
GSA Design Excellence Monograph Series
Washington, DC
Chermayeff & Geismar, Inc.

Interior Design
Poste Restaurant, Hotel Monaco
Washington, DC
Adamstein & Demetriou Architects

Historic Preservation, Restoration, Renovation
José V. Toledo U.S. Post Office and Courthouse
Old San Juan, Puerto Rico
Finegold Alexander + Associates, Inc.

Construction Excellence
Wallace F. Bennett Federal Building
Salt Lake City, UT
Big-D Construction Corporation, Inc.

Ariel Rios Federal Building Modernization, Phase II
Washington, DC
Grunley Construction Company, Inc.

James H. Quillen U.S. Courthouse
Greeneville, TN
Caddell Construction Company, Inc.

2002 Citation Award Recipients

Architecture
Harvey W. Wiley Federal Building, Center for Food Safety and Nutrition
College Park, MD
Kallmann McKinnell & Wood Architects, Inc. with HDR Inc.

Pacific Highway U. S. Port of Entry
Blaine, WA
Thomas Hacker Architects, Inc.

On the Boards
U.S. Courthouse
Eugene, OR
Morphosis with DLR Group

Census Bureau Headquarters
Suitland, MD
Skidmore, Owings & Merrill, LLP

Temecula Border Patrol Station
Murietta, CA
Garrison Architects

GSA Design Awards

National Oceanic and Atmospheric Administration Satellite Operations Facility
Suitland, MD
Morphosis in joint venture with Einhorn Yaffee Prescott Architecture & Engineering

Art Conservation
"State Pride" and "Justice" by Leo Friedlander
Nashville, TN
Art Conservation Associates

Engineering/Technology
Wallace F. Bennett Federal Building
Salt Lake City, UT
Reaveley Engineers & Associates, Inc.

First Impressions
James A. Byrne U.S. Courthouse
Philadelphia, PA
MGA Partners

Martinsburg Federal Building and U.S. Courthouse
Martinsburg, WV
Lehman-Smith McLeish

Graphic Design
GSA Historic Building Poster Series
Washington, DC
Cox & Associates, Inc.

Jacob Weinberger U.S. Courthouse Booklet
San Diego, CA
Rightside Imaging

Sandra Day O'Connor U.S. Courthouse Tenant Guide
Phoenix, AZ
Ray Vote Graphics

Sustainability
U.S. Environmental Protection Agency Research and Administration Facility
Research Triangle Park, NC
Hellmuth, Obata + Kassabaum, Inc.

Historic Preservation, Restoration, Renovation
U.S. Courthouse
Camden, NJ
MGA Partners; Art Conservation Associates

Ariel Rios Federal Building Façade Completion
Washington, DC
Karn Charuhas Chapman & Twohey

Harry S. Truman Presidential Library and Museum
Independence, MO
Gould Evans Goodman Associates

Jury
Moshie Safdie (chair)
Gerald Anderson
Deborah Berke
Richard Brayton
Susan Child
Wendy Feuer
Tracy Hart
Ralph Johnson
Ethel Kessler
Raymond Messer
Elizabeth Moule
Mary Oehrlein
William Stanley
Joe Valerio

Source: U.S. General Services Administration

Did you know...

By 2001, historic buildings comprised almost 25 percent of the General Services Administration's federally-owned space.

Healthcare Environment Award

Since 1989 the annual Healthcare Environment Awards have recognized innovative, life-enhancing design that contributes to the quality of healthcare. The award is sponsored by The Center for Health Design, *Contract* magazine, and The American Institute of Architecture Students. The competition is open to architects, interior designers, healthcare executives, and students. Winners are presented an award at the annual Symposium on Healthcare. First-place winners also receive two complimentary registrations to the Symposium and their projects are published in *Contract* magazine.

For additional information, contact The Center for Health Design on the Web at *www.healthdesign.org*.

2003 Professional Awards

Acute (Inpatient) Care Facilities

Edward Heart Center
Naperville, IL
Matthei & Colin Associates

Honorable Mention

Aurora Women's Pavilion
West Allis, WI
Kahler Slater Architects

Ambulatory (Outpatient) Care Facilities

Mt. Zion Outpatient Cancer Center
San Francisco, CA
SmithGroup

Honorable Mention

Group Health Cooperative Downtown Medical Center
Seattle, WA
Clark/Kjos Architects

Detroit Medical Center, Lawrence & Idell Weisberg Cancer Center
Farmington Hills, MI
Cannon Design; TMP Architecture

Long-Term Care/Assisted Living Facilities

Sun City Kashiwa II
Kashiwa City, Chiba Prefecture, Japan
Perkins Eastman; Barry Design Associates

Honorable Mention

The State Veterans Home at Fitzsimons
Aurora, CO
Boulder Associates, Inc.

Health and Fitness Facilities

No awards granted

2003 Student Awards

Honorable Mention

"Designing Unique Restorative Healthcare Facility Landscapes for Dissimilar Patient Populations: An Independent Study Addressing the Differing Needs of Ambulatory Care and Cancer Patients at UM/JMH"
William Speidel, State University of New York, College of Environmental Science and Forestry

"The Importance of Play in Healing: A Children's Clinic for Scott's Run, West Virginia"
Lina Liu, School of Architecture, Carnegie Mellon University

Healthcare Environment Award

Jury

Jennifer Thiele Busch, *Contract* magazine
David Bynum, Ewing Cole Cherry Brott
Rosalyn Cama, CAMA Inc.
James R. Fair, AHSC Architects, P.C.
Jeanine Gunderson, American Institute of Architecture Students
Pam R. Rosenberg, Loebl Schlossman & Hackl

Source: The Center for Health Design

A day spent without the sight or sound of beauty, the contemplation of mystery, or the search for truth and perfection is a poverty-stricken day; and a succession of such days is fatal to human life.

Lewis Mumford

Henry C. Turner Prize for Innovation in Construction Technology

Newly established in 2002, the Henry C. Turner Prize for Innovation in Construction Technology is presented jointly by the National Building Museum and Turner Construction Company for notable advances and high achievement in the process of construction. The Henry C. Turner Prize is named for the founder of Turner Construction Company, which began operation in New York City in 1902. It recognizes invention, innovative methodologies and/or exceptional leadership by an individual or team in construction technology. At the discretion of the jury, the Turner Prize and its $25,000 cash award is presented annually.

For additional information about this award, contact the National Building Museum at (202) 272-2448 or visit them online at *www.nbm.org*.

2002 Leslie E. Robertson
2003 I.M. Pei

Source: National Building Museum

Did you know...
I.M Pei's design for the Bank of China Tower (1990) in Hong Kong, required engineers to devise the first space truss frame for a tall building.

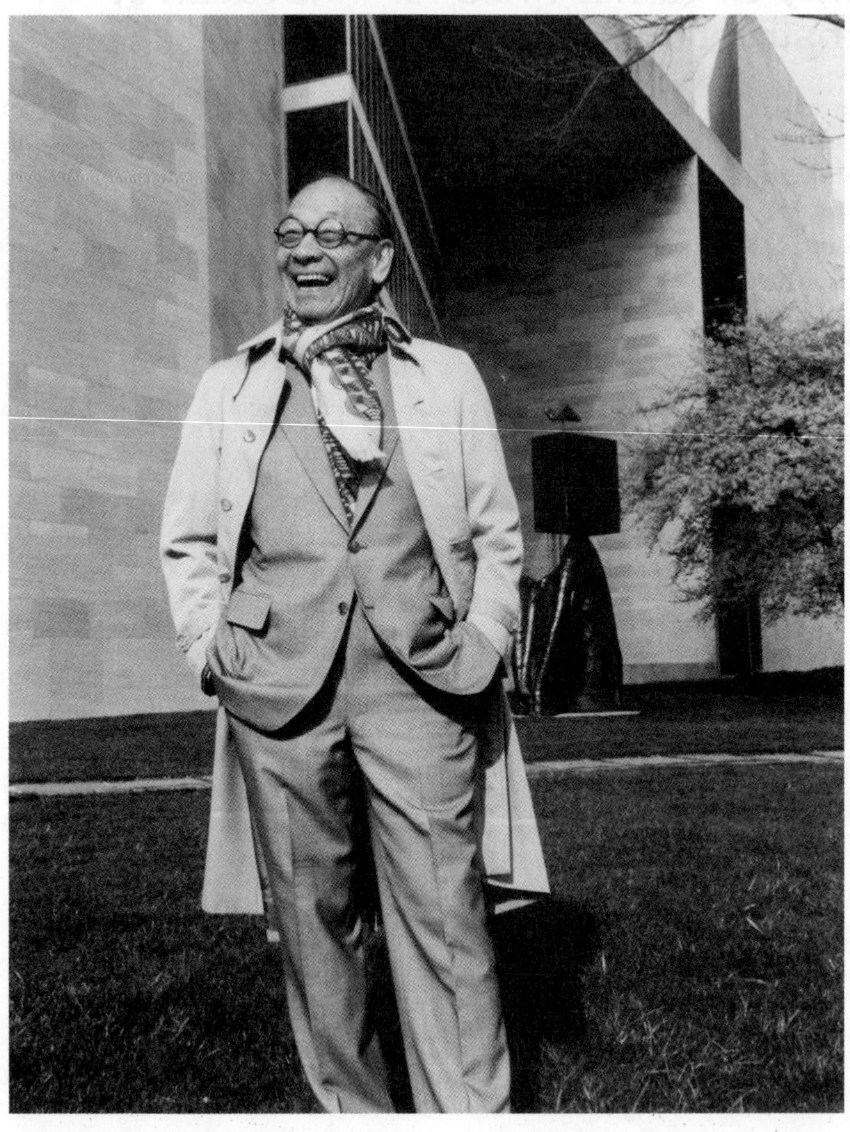

Henry Turner Prize recipient I.M. Pei at the East Wing of the National Gallery of Art. *Image from the film* First Person Singular: I.M. Pei, *courtesy Peter Rosen Productions and the National Building Museum.*

Hugh Ferriss Memorial Prize

The Hugh Ferriss Memorial Prize is awarded annually by the American Society of Architectural Illustrators(ASAI) to recognize excellence in architectural illustration. This international awards program is open to all current members of the Society. A traveling exhibition, *Architecture in Perspective*, co-sponsored by the Otis Elevator Company, highlights the winners and selected entries and raises awareness of the field.

To see the winning drawings, visit the ASAIP's Web site at *www.asai.ws.*

1986
Lee Dunnette and James Record

1987
One Montvale Avenue
Richard Lovelace

1988
Proposed Arts and Cultural Center
Thomas Wells Schaller

1989
Edgar Allen Poe Memorial (detail)
Daniel Willis

1990
The Interior of the Basilica Ulpia
Gilbert Gorski

1991
Affordable Housing Now!
Luis Blanc

1992
BMC Real Properties Buildings
Douglas E. Jamieson

1993
Additions and Renovations to Tuckerton Marine Research Field Station
David Sylvester

1994
3rd Government Center Competition
Rael D. Slutsky

1995
The Pyramid at Le Grand Louvre
Lee Dunnette

1996
Hines France Office Tower
Paul Stevenson Oles

1997
World War II Memorial
Advanced Media Design

1998
Baker Library Addition, Dartmouth College
Wei Li

1999
Five Star Deluxe Beach Hotel
Serge Zaleski

2000
1000 Wilshire Blvd.
Thomas W. Schaller

2001
The Royal Ascot, Finishing Post
Michael McCann

2002
Chicago 2020
Gilbert Gorski

2003
Edge City
Ronald Love

Source: American Society of Architectural Illustrators

I.D. Annual Design Review

I.D. magazine's Annual Design Review began in 1954 and today is considered America's largest and most prestigious industrial design competition. Entries are placed in one of seven separate categories (consumer products, graphics, packaging, environments, furniture, equipment, concepts and student work) and reviewed by juries of leading practitioners. Within each category, projects are awarded on three levels: Best of Category, Design Distinction, and Honorable Mention. Winning entries are published in a special July/August issue of *I.D.* magazine.

For additional information about the Annual Design Review, contact *I.D.* magazine at (212) 447-1400.

2003 Best of Category Winners

Consumer Products

Supercrosse Lacrosse Glove
Kyle Lamson

Environments

Memorial Bridge
Rijeka, Croatia
3LHD

Equipment

Sony VPL-CX5/CS5 LCD Front Projector
Sony Corp.

Furniture

Allsteel's #19 Chair
Marcus Curtis Design

Graphics

One Hundred Years of Idiocy
ASYL Design Inc.

Packaging

Nike Portable Sport Audio
Nike Techlab Audio Team

Concepts

24110
Michael Simonian

Jury

Valerie Aurilio, Landor Associates
Gadi Amit, newdealdesign
Johnson Chou, Johnson Chou Inc.
Stuart Constantine, Core77
Janet Dedonato, Methodologie
Richard Holbrook, Holbrook Design
Dana Lytle, Planet Propaganda
Michael Manfredi, Weiss/Manfredi Architects
Will Miller, Deskey Integrated Branding
Robert Probst, University of Cincinnati
Duane Smith, Vessel
Janet Villano, Ancona 2
Michael Wiklund, American Institutes for Research
Karen Wolf, Topdeq Corp.

Source: I.D. *Magazine*

IDSA Personal Recognition Award

The Industrial Designers Society of America (IDSA) presents a Personal Recognition Award to an individual whose involvement in, and support of, design makes him or her a special friend of the profession and a major contributor to its long-term welfare and importance. Nominees are chosen for final consideration by a nominating committee, and IDSA officers select the final winners.

Nomination forms and additional information can be found on the IDSA Web site at *www.idsa.org*, or contact the IDSA by phone at (703) 707-6000.

1968	Dave Chapman
1969	John Vassos
1978	Raymond Loewy
1980	William Goldsmith
1981	George Nelson
1982	Jay Doblin
1985	Deane Richardson
1986	Carroll Gantz
1991	Budd Steinhilber
1992	Cooper Woodring
	Ellen Manderfield
1993	Ray Spilman
	Brooks Stevens
1994	Belle Kogan
1995	David B. Smith
1996	Jane Thompson
1997	Eva Zeisel
1998	Donald Dohner
1999	Victor Papanek
2000	Robert Schwartz
2001	William Stumpf
2002	Viktor Schreckengost
2003	Sam Farber

Source: Industrial Designers Society of America

Never leave well enough alone.

Raymond Loewy

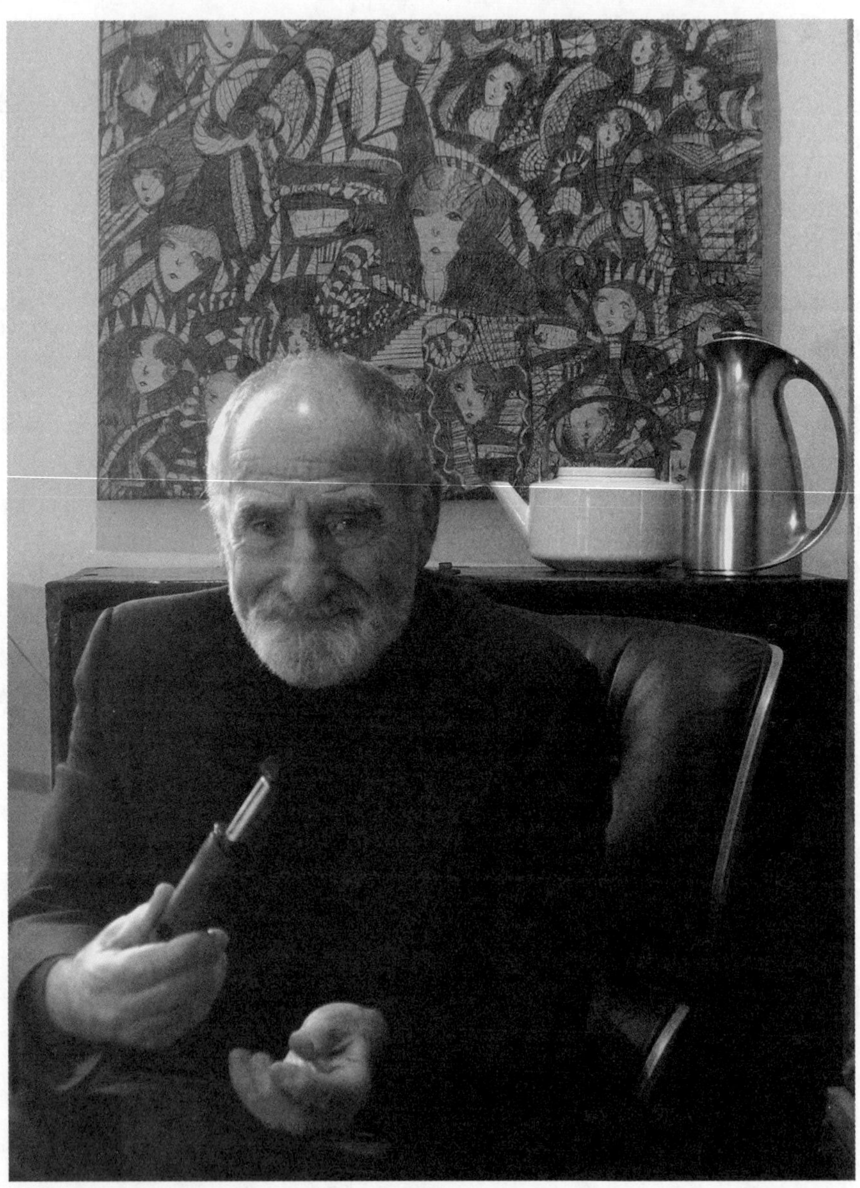

IDSA Personal Recognition Award recipient Sam Farber is a pioneer of affordable kitchen tools that are easily used by people of all ages and abilities. Now a leader in the manufacture of kitchen tools with innovative user-centered designs, he founded OXO International in 1989 after watching his arthritic wife struggle with a can opener. He is currently creating thoughtfully designed products for the home with his company WOVO, which he cofounded with his son John. *Photo courtesy of Sam Farber.*

Industrial Design Excellence Awards

The Industrial Design Excellence Awards (IDEA), co-sponsored by *Business Week* magazine and the Industrial Designers Society of America (IDSA), are presented annually to honor industrial design worldwide. Any U.S. or non-U.S. designer whose product is distributed in North America may enter their designs in one of nine categories. Each year a jury of business executives and design professionals issue as many awards as they deem necessary, evaluating over 1,000 entries on the following criteria: design innovation, benefit to the user, benefit to the client/business, ecological responsibility, and appropriate aesthetics and appeal. Gold, silver, and bronze level citations are granted.

For detailed descriptions, photographs, and contact information for all Gold, Silver, and Bronze winners, visit the IDSA on the Internet at *www.idsa.org*.

IDEA 2003 Gold Award Winners

Business & Industrial Products

FC4000 Series Sit-down Counterbalanced Electric Lift Truck
Crown Equipment Corp.

Wharton Lectern
Aaron DeJule and KI

WARN Works® Utility Winches
ZIBA Design Team

Pandora Pogle Evolution
PDD Ltd.

Computer Equipment

Palm™ Zire™ Handheld Computer
newdealdesign, LLC and Palm, Inc.

PowerBook G4 (12 and 17 inch)
Apple Computer, Inc.

Consumer Products

Watercone®
Augustin Product Development

Robertshaw LP Tank Monitoring System
Herbst LaZar Bell, Inc. and Robertshaw Co.

17" Wide LCD Personal TV (LT17E3)
Samsung Electronics Co., Ltd

Birkenstock Footprints: The Architect Collection
fuseproject, inc.

Duet Fabric Care System and Dreamspace
Whirlpool Corp.

STX: Fuse Lacrosse Stick
Priority Designs and STX

Logitech Pocket Digital Camera
IDEO, MOTO Development Group and Logitech, Inc.

Windsurfing Sail Collection
meyerhoffer and Neil Pryde Int.

Logitech® Mobile Cordless and FlexLoop TM Headsets
ZIBA Design

Neurosmith Musini
RKS Design Team

First Years Comfort Care Baby Products
Herbst LaZar Bell, Inc.

Motorola V.70
Motorola Consumer Experience Design

Industrial Design Excellence Awards

Design Exploration
Microsoft Center for Information Work
Microsoft Office Design Team

Survival Pod
Euforia Design

Bombardier EMBRIO/2025
Bombardier Design Group

ThinkPad Exploration
IBM Corp

WARN Works® Utility Winches Strategy
ZIBA Design Team

Gyrus Diego Powered Dissector
IDEO and Gyrus ENT. LLC

Digital Media & Interfaces
@radical.media Website (www.radicalmedia.com)
@radical.media

Zinio Reader
IDEO and Zinio

Environmental Designs
TopCon Trade Show Exhibit
fuseproject, inc. and volumesf

The Art of Car Design
BMW AG and Designwork

Rewarding Lives: An Exhibition for American Express
The Moderns LTD

Furniture
No award granted

Graphics & Packaging
Dutch Boy Twist & Pour Paint Delivery System
Nottingham-Spirk Design Assoc.

100% Generosity Bag
@radical.media

Schroeder Milk Package
Capsule

Medical & Scientific Products
HeartStart Home Defibrillator
Philips Medical Systems

Isolite™ Dryfield Illuminator
Desmar Product Design and Barker Design Group

Joey Clamp and Cutter
Design Edge, Inc. and Maternus, Inc.

Student Design
Modular Hinge Sandal
Arvind Gupta, San Francisco State University

Sustainable Design
Brian Carter, University of Kansas

In the past five years, the following design firms won the most IDEA Awards:

IDEO—50
ZIBA Design—23
Lunar Design—15
Smart Design—15
Design Continuum—14
Pentagram—14
Herbst Lazar Bell—12
frog design-10
Hauser—8
Ralph Applebaum—8

Source: **Industrial Designers Society of America**

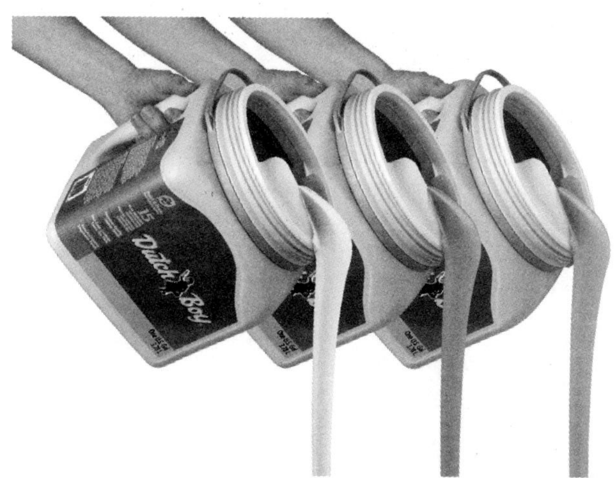

Top: Dutch Boy's new Twist and Pour Paint System replaces the standard metal paint can with a plastic container with a screw off top, ergonomic side handle, and "lug" lip for drip-free pouring. *Middle*: Schroeder Milk's new packaging emphasizes the fat content, which research has shown is of greater interest to the consumer than the specific brand. *Bottom*: The Watercone® is a solar water still that makes distilled water from salty/brackish water, yielding 1 to 1.4 liters per day. *Photos courtesy of the Industrial Designers Society of America.*

Industrial Design Excellence Awards

Transportation
BMW Mini Cooper S
BMW AG

Jury
Naomi Gornick, Brunel University (chair)
Charles Burnette, consultant
Carol Catalano, Catalano Design
Jim Couch, industrial designer
Tom R. Hardy, design strategist
Julie Heard, Mixer* Group
Lorraine Justice, Georgia Institute of Technology
Michael Laude, Bose Design Center
Tom Matano, Academy of Art College
Brian J. Matt, Altitude, Inc.
Louis Nelson, Louis Nelson Associates
Duncan Paul, Procter & Gamble
Elizabeth Sanders, SonicRim
Mark Steiner, Steiner Design Associates
Craig M. Vogel, Carnegie Mellon University School of Design

Source: Industrial Designers Society of America

In the past five years, the following corporations won the most IDEA Awards:

Apple Computer—19
Samsung Electronics—18
IBM—15
Hewlett-Packard—12
Microsoft—11
Nike—10
OXO International—10
Steelcase—10
Fisher-Price—9
BMW—8
Logitech—8
Motorola—8
Philips Design—8
Target—8

***Source:* Industrial Designers Society of America**

Interior Design Competition

The Interior Design Competition is presented jointly each year by the International Interior Design Association (IIDA) and *Interior Design* magazine. The Competition was established in 1973 to recognize outstanding interior design and to foster new interior design ideas and techniques. Winning projects appear in *Interior Design* magazine, and the "Best of Competition" winner receives a $5,000 cash prize.

For more information, contact IIDA at (888) 799-IIDA or visit their Web site at *www.iida.org*.

2003 Recipients

Best of Competition
Williamsburg Community Center
Brooklyn, NY
Pasanella+Klein Stolzman+Berg Architects, P.C.

Award Winners
SEVEN
Toronto, ON, Canada
BY IV Design Associates Inc.

Zola
Washington, DC
Adamstein & Demetriou Architects

Zaytinya
Washington, DC
Adamstein & Demetriou Architects

Tip Top Lofts Sales Centre
Toronto, ON, Canada
burdifilek

Oni One
Toronto, ON, Canada
Cecconi Simone Inc.

Safady Residence
Austin, TX
Dick Clark Architecture

New Phoenix Children's Hospital
Phoenix, AZ
Karlsberger Companies

Jury
Shashi Caan, Shashi Caan Collective
Eva Maddox, Perkins & Will / Eva Maddox Branded Environments
Frank Nuovo, Nokia Design
Michael Vanderbyl, Vanderbyl Design

Source: International Interior Design Association

James Beard Foundation Restaurant Design Award

Since 1995 the James Beard Foundation has awarded the James Beard Restaurant Design Award to the project executed in the United States or Canada that most demonstrates excellence in restaurant design or renovation. Architects and interior designers are eligible to enter restaurant projects that have been completed within the proceeding three years. The award is presented at the annual Beard Birthday Fortnight celebration.

Entry forms and additional information can be found at *www.jamesbeard.org* or by calling the Awards office at (212) 627-2090.

1995
Fifty Seven Fifty Seven
New York, NY
Chhada Siembieda and Partners

1996
Bar 89
New York, NY
Ogawa/Depardon Architects

1997
Paci Restaurant
Westport, CT
Ferris Architects

1998
Monsoon
Toronto, ON, Canada
Yabu Pushelberg

1999
MC Squared
San Francisco, CA
Mark Cavagnero Associates

2000
Brasserie
New York, NY
Diller & Scofidio

2001
Russian Tea Room
New York, NY
Leroy Adventures

2002
Blackbird Restaurant
Chicago, IL
Thomas Schlesser & Demian Repucci

2003
L'Impero Restaurant
New York, NY
Vicente Wolf Associates

Source: James Beard Foundation

Arranging the table for dinner is a great artistic opportunity.

Frank Lloyd Wright

Vicente Wolf has been designing commercial, residential, and retail interiors for 28 years. He also designs furniture, lighting and housewares. *Photo by Tom Kirkman, courtesy of the James Beard Foundation.*

J.C. Nichols Prize for Visionary Urban Development

The Urban Land Institute (ULI) created the J.C. Nichols Prize for Visionary Urban Development to honor an individual or an institution who has made a commitment to responsible urban community development. As a founding member of the Urban Land Institute and whose work as a visionary developer includes the Country Club Plaza in Kansas City (Mo.), the award's namesake, J.C. Nichols, embodied the ULI's commitment to fostering responsible land use and reputable development. Nominees can be drawn from a wide range of disciplines, including, but not limited to, architects, researchers, developers, journalists, public officials, and academics, and must be U.S. or Canadian citizens. A jury of urban experts, each representing diverse backgrounds and experiences, reviews the nominations. Recipients receive a $100,000 honorarium.

For additional information, visit the Prize on the Web at *www.nicholsprize.org* or contact them at (202) 624-7000.

2000	Joseph P. Riley Jr.
2001	Daniel Patrick Moynihan
2002	Gerald D. Hines
2003	Vincent Scully

Source: Urban Land Institute

Do not be afraid to dream...and then set out to make it happen.

J.C. Nichols

Jean Tschumi Prize

The Jean Tschumi Prize is awarded by the International Union of Architects (UIA) to individuals for a significant contribution to architectural criticism or architectural education.

For more information, visit the UIA's web site at *www.uia-architectes.org*.

1967
Jean-Pierre Vouga (Switzerland)

1969
I. Nikolaev (USSR)
Pedro Ramirez Vazquez (Mexico)

1972
João Batista Vilanova Artigas (Brazil)

1975
Reyner Banham (UK)

1978
Rectory and Faculty of Architecture of the University of Lima (Peru)

1981
Neville Quarry (Australia)
Honorary Mention: Jorge Glusberg (Argentina) and Tadeusz Barucki (Poland)

1984
Julius Posener (GDR)

1987
Christian Norberg-Schultz (Norway)
Ada Louise Huxtable (US)

1990
Eduard Franz Sekler (Austria)
Honorary Mention: Dennis Sharp (UK) and Claude Parent (France)

1993
Eric Kumchew Lye (Malaysia)

1996
Peter Cook (UK)
Liangyong Wu (P.R. of China)
Honorary Mention: Toshio Nakamura and the Mexican editor COMEX

1999
Juhani Pallasmaa (Finland)
Honorary Mention: Jennifer Taylor (Australia)

2002
Manuel Tainha (Portugal)
Elias Zenghelis (Greece)
Honorary Mention: The authors of the collection of books: *World Architecture: A Critical Mosaic* (P.R. of China)

Source: International Union of Architects

Kenneth F. Brown Asia Pacific Culture & Architecture Design Award

Every two years the School of Architecture at the University of Hawai'i at Manoa and the Architects Regional Council of Asia (ARCASIA) sponsor the Kenneth F. Brown Asia Pacific Culture & Architecture Design Award program. The award recognizes outstanding examples of contemporary architecture in Asia and the Pacific Rim that successfully balance spiritual and material aspects and demonstrate a harmony with the natural and cultural settings. Through this award program the sponsors hope to promote the development of humane environments within the multicultural Asia Pacific region as well as inspire a more culturally, socially, and environmentally appropriate approach to architecture. In order to be eligible, projects must have been completed within the previous 10 years and be located in Asia or countries that touch the Pacific Ocean. Winners receive a $25,000 cash prize and are invited to speak at the International Symposium on Asia Pacific Architecture.

For additional information or to view photographs and descriptions of winning projects, visit *www2.hawaii.edu/~kbda/* on the Internet.

2002 Recipients

Award Winner

SPRINGTECTURE B
Higashiasai-gun, Shiga, Japan
Shuhei Endo (Japan)

Second Prize

Jinji Lake Open Space
Suzhou Industrial Park, Suzhou, Jiangsu, China
EDAW Earthasia Ltd. (Hong Kong)

Honorable Mentions

National Museum of Australia
Canberra, Australia
Ashton Raggatt McDougall Pty Ltd. (Australia)

Leek House
Machida-shi, Tokyo, Japan
I.I.S. University of Tokyo (Japan)

Gathawudu Community Housing, Marika Alderton House
Yirrkala Northern Territory, Australia
Glenn Murcutt (Australia)

Lee Treehouse
Singapore
Joseph Lim Ee Man (Singapore)

The Lalu
Sun Moon Lake, Nantou, Taiwan, R.O.C.
Kerry Hill Architects (Singapore)

Federation Square
Melbourne, Australia
Lab Architecture Studio with Bates Smart (Australia)

Benjamin House
Bangalore, India
Mathew & Ghosh Architects (India)

SLOWTECTURE S
Maihara, Shiga, Japan
Shuhei Endo (Japan)

Shuhei Endo's small house addition in Tokyo, SPRINGTECTURE B, contains a highly imaginative use of corrugated metal and juxtaposition of interlocking and continuously folded spaces. The jurors also found the home to evoke elements of traditional Japanese domestic architecture, which they especially noted in the undulating ridge and profile of the eaves to be reminiscent of a traditional tile roof. *Photos courtesy of the University of Hawai'i at Manoa, School of Architecture.*

Kenneth F. Brown Asia Pacific Culture & Architecture Design Award

Jury

Kenneth Brown, chair (US)
Gregory Burgess (Australia)
Balkrishna Doshi (India)
Kenneth Frampton (US)
William Lim (Singapore)

Source: University of Hawaii at Manoa, School of Architecture

Did You Know...

Tadao Ando received the 2002 Kyoto Prize for Arts and Philosophy for his lifetime achievements, joining Isamu Noguchi and Renzo Piano as the award's only architecture and design laureates.

Keystone Award

Created by the American Architectural Foundation (AAF) in 1999, the Keystone Award honors individuals who have furthered the Foundation's vision "of a society that participates in shaping its environment through an understanding of the power of architecture to elevate and enrich the human experience." The award's objective is to recognize and encourage leadership that results in citizen participation in the design process, and advances communication with key decision-makers about how design issues affect a community's quality of life. Nominees may include, but are not limited to, patrons, advocates, critics, activists, clients, government representatives, and educational leaders. The award selection committee is comprised of experts in the fields of community development, communication, design, preservation, and government. Presentation of the award is made at the annual Accent on Architecture Gala in Washington, D.C.

For additional information, contact the AAF at (202) 626-7500 or on the Web at *www.archfoundation.org*.

1999 Richard M. Daley
2000 Rick Lowe
2002 Joseph P. Riley Jr.

Source: American Architectural Foundation

> The experience of space is not a privilege of the gifted few, but a biological function.
>
> **Laszio Moholy-Nagy**

Lewis Mumford Prize

Every two years the Society for American City and Regional Planning History (SACRPH) grants the Lewis Mumford Prize to the best book on American city and regional history. Winners are chosen based on originality, depth of research, quality of writing, and the degree to which the book contributes to a greater understanding of the rich history of American city or regional planning. The presentation of a plaque and $500 cash prize is made at the Society's biennial conference.

For additional information, visit the Society on the Internet at *www.urban.uiuc.edu/sacrph/*.

1991-93

The New York Approach: Robert Moses, Urban Liberals, and Redevelopment of the Inner City by Joel Schwartz (Ohio State University Press)

1993-95

The City of Collective Memory: Its Historical Imagery and Architectural Entertainments by M. Christine Boyer (MIT Press)

1995-97

City Center to Regional Mall: Architecture, the Automobile, and Retailing in Los Angeles, 1920-1950 by Richard Longstreth (MIT Press)

1997-99

Boston's Changeful Times: Origins of Preservation and Planning in America by Michael Holleran (Johns Hopkins University Press)

Honorable Mention

Remaking Chicago: The Political Origins of Urban Industrial Change by Joel Rast (Northern Illinois University Press)

1999-01

Downtown: Its Rise and Fall, 1880-1950 by Robert Fogelson (Yale University Press)

2001-03

The Bulldozer in the Countryside: Suburban Sprawl and the Rise of American Environmentalism by Adam Rome (Cambridge University Press)

Source: Society for American City and Regional Planning History

Did you know...

Tadao Ando received the 2002 Kyoto Prize for Arts and Philosophy for his lifetime achievements, joining Isamu Noguchi and Renzo Piano as the award's only architecture and design laureates.

Library Buildings Awards

The American Institute of Architects (AIA) and the American Library Association (ALA) present the biennial Library Buildings Awards to encourage excellence in the architectural design and planning of libraries. Architects licensed in the United States are eligible to enter any public or private library project from around the world, whether a renovation, addition, conversion, interior project or new construction. The jury consists of three architects and three librarians with extensive library building experience.

Additional information is available on the American Library Association Web site at *www.ala.org* or by contacting the AIA Awards Office at (202) 626-7586.

2003 Winners

Lee B. Philmon Branch Library
Riverdale, GA
Mack Scogin Merrill Elam Architects

The Jefferson Library at Monticello
Charlottesville, VA
Hartman-Cox Architects

Suzzallo Library, University of Washington
Seattle, WA
Mahlun Architects
Cardwell Architects, associate architect

Seattle Public Temporary Central Library
Seattle, WA
LMN Architects

South Court, New York Public Library
New York City, NY
Davis Brody Bond, LLP

The Hockaday School Upper and Lower School Library
Dallas, TX
Overland Partners Architects
Good Fulton & Farrell Architects, associate architect

Shady Hill School Library
Cambridge, MA
Kennedy and Violich Architecture Ltd.

Jury

Henry Myerberg, (chair)
Mary Werner DeNadai
David Milling
Kay Johnson
Barbara Norland
Rich Rosenthal

Source: The American Institute of Architects

Did you know...

The Seattle Public Temporary Central Library was built to house the main library during construction of Rem Koolhaas' $152.4 million new central library building, designed in conjunction with Seattle-based LMN Architecture and scheduled to open in early 2004.

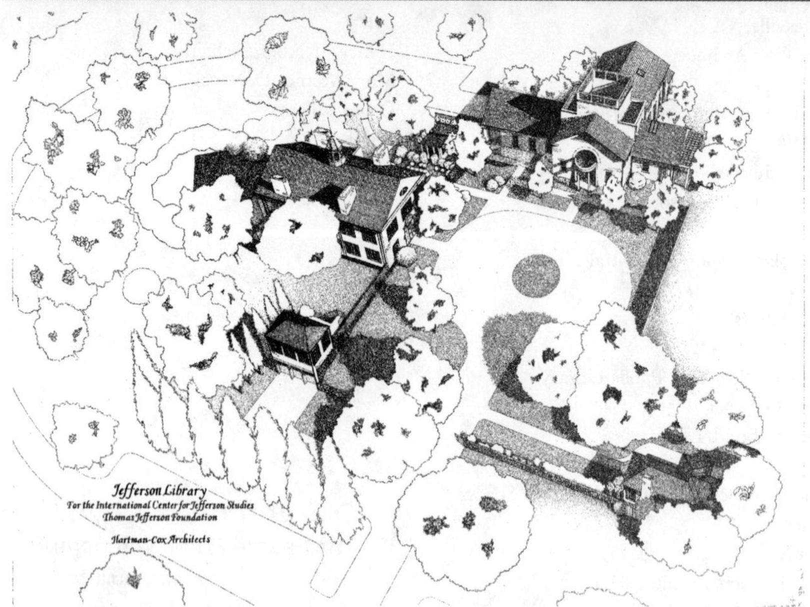
Jefferson Library
For the International Center for Jefferson Studies
Thomas Jefferson Foundation
Hartman-Cox Architects

Hartman-Cox disguised the true size of their 2003 Library Buildings Award-winning project, the Thomas Jefferson Library at Monticello, by placing its bulk at the rear and down the hill. The library sits adjacent to the Center for International Jefferson Studies, located in the Colonial Revival Kenwood house, and incorporates complimentary architectural features: the angularity of the roofs, rectangular planning, and exterior materials. *Photo by Robert Lautman, perspective plan by Justin Kilman. Images courtesy of Hartman-Cox Architects.*

Lighting Design Awards

Presented for lighting installations that couple aesthetic achievement with technical expertise, the Lighting Design Awards are bestowed annually by the International Association of Lighting Designers (IALD) and *Architectural Lighting* magazine. The Awards emphasize design with attention to energy usage, economics, and sustainable design. Projects are judged individually, not in competition with each other. The Radiance Award recognizes the finest example of lighting design excellence among all submissions. Awards of Excellence and Merit are awarded at the jury's discretion.

For additional information, visit the IALD on the Internet at *www.iald.org*.

2003 Recipients

Radiance Award

MIT Building 7
Cambridge, MA
Available Light

Award of Excellence

Solar Pipe Light (SLP)
Washington, DC
Carpenter/Norris Consulting

Chung-Tai Chan Temple
Pu-Li, Na-Tou County, Taiwan
CWI Lighting Design

School of the International Center of Photography
New York, NY
Cline Bettridge Bernstein Lighting Design, Inc.

Awards of Merit

M39/40
Taipei, Taiwan
Architectural Lighting Design Inc.

ERCO P3 Warehouse
Nordrhein Westfalen, Germany
Belzner Holmes Architektur Licht Bühne

Façade/Show Illumination of the Golden Moon Hotel/Casino
Philadelphia, MS
Brilliant Lighting Design

Korean Development Bank
Seoul, South Korea
Fisher Marantz Stone

Deutsch Inc.
Los Angeles, CA
Arc Light Design

Country Music Hall of Fame and Museum
Nashville, TN
Brandston Partnership, Inc.

South Court of the New York Public Library
New York, NY
Fisher Marantz Stone

Magna Science Adventure Centre
Templeborough, Rotherham, UK
Speirs and Major Associates

The Modern Art Museum of Fort Worth
Fort Worth, TX
George Sexton Associates

First Presbyterian Church
Evanston, IL
Schuler & Shook, Inc.

Minneapolis Convention Center Expansion
Minneapolis, MN
Schuler & Shook, Inc.

Top: The design for the Modern Art Museum of Fort Worth seamlessly integrates natural daylight and electric lighting. Diffused and reflected natural light is transmitted through skylight and clerestory systems to illuminate the galleries. Fluorescent luminaires supplement the natural lighting by backlighting the stretched fabric ceiling. *Photo: ©David Woo, 2003, courtesy of the International Association of Lighting Designers.* *Bottom*: At the Country Music Hall of Fame, lighting harmonizes with the architecture and exhibits to create a backstage atmosphere where the public images of artists are recaptured and the cherished memorabilia are presented to the fans. Symbolic elements of this American musical artform grace the architecture, such as the piano-key windows on the prominent curved wall and the steeple-like rendition of the famous WSM radio tower. *Photo courtesy of the International Association of Lighting Designers.*

Lighting Design Awards

Special Citation for Energy Efficiency
Symantec
Springfield, OR
Benya Lighting Design

Jury
Helen Diemer, The Lighting Practice
Raymond Grenald, Grenald Waldron Associates
Samantha Hollomon LaFleur, Hayden McKay Lighting Design
John Marstellar, TSLEAG–The Spatial Light Environments
Gene Watanabe, Gensler and Associates/Architects
Graham Wyatt, Robert A. M. Stern Associates
Galina Zbrizher, Total Lighting Solutions/Welch Zbrizher Associates

Source: International Association of Lighting Designers

> Light is the beautifier of the building.
>
> **Frank Lloyd Wright**

Mies van der Rohe Award for European Architecture

Established in 1987 by the European Commission, the European Parliament, and the Mies van der Rohe Foundation, the Mies van der Rohe Award for European Architecture seeks to highlight notable projects within the context of contemporary European architecture. Works by European architects that are constructed in the member states of the European Union and associated European states within the two years following the granting of the previous award are eligible for the program. Winning projects are chosen for their innovative character and excellence in design and execution by an international panel of experts in the field of architecture and architectural criticism. The Award consists of a cash prize of 50,000 Euros and a sculpture by Xavier Corberó, a design inspired by the Mies van der Rohe Pavilion in Barcelona.

For more information, visit the Mies van der Rohe Foundation's Web site at *www.miesbcn.com*.

1988

Borges e Irmão Bank
Vila do Conde, Portugal
Alvaro Siza (Portugal)

1990

New Terminal Development
Stansted Airport, London, England
Norman Foster & Partners (UK)

1992

Municipal Sports Stadium
Badalona, Barcelona, Spain
Esteve Bonell and Francesc Rius (Spain)

1994

Waterloo International Station
London, England
Nicholas Grimshaw & Partners (UK)

1996

Bibliotèque Nationale de France
Paris, France
Dominique Perrault (France)

1999

Art Museum in Bregenz
Bregenz, Austria
Peter Zumthor (Switzerland)

2001

Kursaal Congress Centre
San Sebastian, Spain
Rafael Moneo (Spain)

Emerging Architect Special Mention

Kaufmann Holz Distribution Centre
Bobingen, Germany
Florian Nagler, Florian Nagler Architekt (Germany)

2003

Car Park & Terminal Hoenheim North
Strasbourg, France
Zaha Hadid (UK)

Emerging Architect Special Mention

Scharnhauser Park Town Hall
Ostfildern, Germany
Jürgen Mayer (Germany)

Source: Mies van der Rohe Foundation

Did you know...

When it opened on May 31, 2003, the Contemporary Arts Center in Cincinnati became Zaha Hadid's first American building as well as the first American art museum designed by a woman.

Mies van der Rohe Award for Latin American Architecture

A sister award to the Mies van der Rohe Award for European Architecture, this biennial program recognizes projects in Mexico, Central America, South America, Cuba, and the Dominican Republic. The Foundation created the award in 1997 to bring greater attention to contemporary Latin American architecture by honoring works of considerable conceptual, aesthetic, technical, and construction solutions. In order to be eligible, projects must have been completed within the two years following the granting of the previous award and be located in a member country. The award itself is identical to that of the European award, a cash prize of 50,000 Euros and a sculpture by Xavier Corberó inspired by the pillars of the Mies van der Rohe Pavilion in Barcelona.

For more information, visit the Mies van der Rohe Foundation's Web site at *www.miesbcn.com.*

1998

Televisa Headquarters
Mexico City, Mexico
TEN Arquitectos (Mexico)

2000

São Paulo State Picture Library Building, restoration and adaptation
São Paulo, Brazil
Paulo A. Mendes da Rocha Arquitectos Associados (Brazil)

Source: Mies van der Rohe Foundation

Modern Healthcare/AIA Design Awards

Each year, registered architects are invited to enter the *Modern Healthcare*/AIA Design Awards competition, which recognize excellence in the design and planning of new and remodeled healthcare facilities. Sponsored by *Modern Healthcare* magazine and The American Institute of Architects' Academy of Architecture for Health (AAH), all types and sizes of patient care-related facilities are eligible for submission. Winners are recognized in an issue of *Modern Healthcare* magazine and at the annual AAH convention.

Details are available on the Internet at *www.modernhealthcare.com.*

2002 Recipients

Awards of Excellence

Swedish Cancer Institute
Seattle, WA
NBBJ

Honorable Mention

Long Island Jewish Medical Center, Ambulatory Chemotherapy Transfusion Unit
New Hyde Park, NY
Larsen Shein Ginsberg Snyder

Center for Advance Medicine/Siteman Cancer Center
St. Louis, MO
Hellmuth, Obata + Kassabaum

Crozer-Chester Regional Cancer Center
Upland, PA
Ellerbe Becket

The Motion Picture and Television Fund - Fran and Ray Stark Villa
Woodland Hills, CA
SmithGroup

University of California San Francisco, Mount Zion Comprehensive Cancer Center
San Francisco, CA
SmithGroup

Citation

Outside In
Portland, OR
Clark/Kjos Architects

Planned Parenthood Eastmont Mall
Oakland, CA
Fougeron Architecture

Honorable Mention—Unbuilt Projects

Memorial Sloan-Kettering Cancer Center, Pediatric Day Hospital and Inpatient Unit
New York, NY
Granary Associates

Citation—Unbuilt Projects

University of New Mexico Children's Hospital and Critical Care Pavilion
Albuquerque, NM
Perkins & Will

Jury

Annie Coull, Anshen+Allen
Samuel Daniel, M.D., North General Hospital
Peter Ellis, Skidmore, Owings & Merrill
Gerald Oudens, Oudens+Knoop Architects
Charles Redmon, Cambridge Seven Associates
Michael Schroeder, Langdon Wilson Architecture
John Shelton, Baptist Health System
Matthew Van Vranken, Brigham and Women's Hospital
Scott Wing, Ratcliff
Joan Saba, SLAM Collaborative

Source: Modern Healthcare *magazine*

This new flagship for all Swedish Cancer Institute facilities takes a different approach to cancer treatment and care. The design strikes a balance between the human and natural environments that is essential to health and healing. Links to nature and the outdoors, such as open spaces and natural light, are located on all levels of the structure. *Photo © Assassi Productions, courtesy of NBBJ.*

National Building Museum Honor Award

Since 1986 the National Building Museum has honored individuals and organizations that have made an exceptional contribution to America's built history. The award is presented each year at an elegant gala held in the Museum's Great Hall, which has often been the site of the Presidential Inaugural Ball since 1885.

For more information, contact the National Building Museum at (202) 272-2448 or visit their Web site at *www.nbm.org*.

1986	J. Irwin Miller
1988	James W. Rouse
1989	Senator Daniel Patrick Moynihan
1990	IBM
1991	The Rockefeller Family
1992	The Civic Leadership of Greater Pittsburgh
1993	J. Carter Brown
1994	James A. Johnson and Fannie Mae
1995	Lady Bird Johnson
1996	Cindy and Jay Pritzker
1997	Morris Cafritz, Charles E. Smith, Charles A. Horsky and Oliver T. Carr Jr.
1998	Riley P. Bechtel and Stephen D. Bechtel Jr. of the Bechtel Group
1999	Harold and Terry McGraw and The McGraw-Hill Companies
2000	Gerald D. Hines
2001	Michael D. Eisner and The Walt Disney Company
2002	DuPont
2003	National Football League and Major League Baseball

Source: National Building Museum

> I try to make buildings which belong in the place they are, which are rooted in the earth, which give one the feeling that they always have been and always will be.
>
> **Christopher Day**

National Design Awards

Each year the Smithsonian Institution's Cooper-Hewitt, National Design Museum honors American designers with its National Design Awards. Presented in seven categories for excellence, innovation, and enhancement of the quality of life, awards are bestowed for a body of work and not a specific project. Journalists, designers, filmmakers, architects, authors and other professionals are invited by the Smithsonian Institution to make nominations for the awards.

Complete information is available from the award's Web site, *www.si.edu/ndm/.*

2002 Recipients

Lifetime Achievement
Dan Kiley

Architectural Design
Steven Holl

Corporate Achievement
Whirlpool Corporation

Special Commendation for Corporate Achievement
New York City Housing Authority

American Original
Geoffrey Beene

Environment Design
James Carpenter

Product Design
Niels Diffrient

Communications Design
Lucille Tenazas

Design Patron
Andre Balazs

Jury
Rob Forbes, Design Within Reach
Richard Gluckman, Gluckman Mayner Architects
Walter Hood, University of California, Berkeley
Reed Krakoff, Coach
Sheila Levrant de Bretteville, Yale University
Frank Nuovo, Vertu
Robyn Waters, Target

Source: Smithsonian Institution, Cooper-Hewitt, National Design Museum

Clockwise from top left, the 2002 National Design Award winners: Dan Kiley (*Photo: Aaron Kiley*); Steven Holl (*Photo: © Nelson-Atkins Museum*); Lucille Tenazas (*Photo: David Peterson*); Niels Diffrient (*Photo courtesy of Niels Diffrient*). *All photos courtesy of Cooper-Hewitt, National Design Museum.*

National Design-Build Awards

Every year the Design-Build Institute of America (DBIA) honors exemplary design-build projects through its National Design-Build Awards. The DBIA's goal with this award program is to promote the design-build process as an effective project delivery method through the recognition of outstanding design-build projects. Submitted entries in each category are evaluated on their overall success in fulfilling the owner's project goals. The projects' achievement within the design-build approach of efficiency, performance, architecture, risk management, and problem solving and the design team's use of innovation to add value are also considerations. Projects completed within the last five years that met the criteria of a qualified design-build contract are eligible. When merited, the jury may choose to grant the Design-Build Excellence Award to those projects which were outstanding but fell short of the National Design-Build Award.

For additional information and a complete list of all the National Design-Build and the Design-Build Excellence Award winners, visit DBIA's Web site at *www.dbia.org* or contact them at (202)682-0110.

2002 National Design-Build Award Recipients

Private Project Over $15 Million
Paramount Tower
San Francisco, CA
Charles Pankow Builders, Ltd.

Private Project Under $15 Million
Congregation of Sisters of St. Agnes Motherhouse
Fond du Lac, WI
Hoffman Corporation

Public Project Over $15 Million
University of Texas San Jacinto Residence Hall
Austin, TX
Hensel Phelps Construction Company

Public Project Under $15 Million
The Korte Recreation Center
Highland, IL
The Korte Company

Rehabilitation/Renovation/Restoration
Design-Build Flood Control Ecological Restoration on Lincoln Creek
Milwaukee, WI
Edgerton Contractors and HNTB Corporation

Civil Project Over $15 Million
I-15 Corridor Reconstruction
Salt Lake City, UT
Wasatch Constructors

Civil Project Under $15 Million
FDOT - SR60/Peace Creek Bridge
Bartow, Polk County, FL
Johnson Bros. Corporation

Project Under $5 Million
Lavazza Coffee Drive-Thru
Villa Park, IL
Kullman Industries, Inc.

Industrial/Process Project Over $25 Million
Strategic Computing Complex
Los Alamos, NM
Hensel Phelps Construction Co.

Industrial/Process Project Under $25 Million
BreathSavers Relocation
Memphis, TN
AVCA/Alberici Joint Venture

National Design-Build Awards

Developer Design-Build

Providence Public Safety Complex
Providence, RI
O. Ahlborg & Sons, Inc.

Jury

Patrick Klein, PCL Construction Services
William Angelo, *Design-Build* magazine/*ENR*
Judy Passwaters, Dupont
Sheryl Kolasinski, Smithsonian Institution
Charles Linn, *Architectural Record*
Philip McCurdy, Gensler
Arthur Cotton Moore, Arthur Cotton Moore/Associates PC
Richard C. Viohl, Naval Facilities Engineering Command
Sue Anderson, General Mills

Source: Design-Build Institute of America

Did you know...

According to the *National Real Estate Investor*, design-build is used by more than a third of all commercial construction clients, up from less than 10 percent a decade ago.

National Medal of Arts

The National Medal of Arts was established by Congress in 1984 to honor individuals and organizations "who in the President's judgement are deserving of special recognition by reason of their outstanding contributions to the excellence, growth, support and availability of the arts in the United States." All categories of the arts are represented; although awards are not always granted in each category every year. No more than 12 medals may be awarded per year. Individuals and organizations nationwide may make nominations to the National Endowment for the Arts (NEA). The National Council on the Arts reviews these nominations and makes recommendations to the President of the United States for final selection of the annual medal. The following individuals received this honor for their work in the design profession.

Visit the NEA's Web site at *www.arts.endow.gov* for additional information or nomination forms.

1987	Isamu Noguchi
1988	I.M. Pei
1989	Leopold Adler
1990	Ian McHarg
1991	Pietro Belluschi
1992	Robert Venturi
	Denise Scott Brown
1995	James Ingo Freed
1997	Daniel Urban Kiley
1998	Frank Gehry
1999	Michael Graves
2003	Florence Knoll Basset +
	Lawrence Halprin

Source: National Endowment for the Arts

Outstanding Planning Awards

The American Planning Association's annual Outstanding Planning Awards honor group achievement and planning excellence. Winners may be a planning agency, planning team or firm, community group, or local authority, and are judged on criteria ranging from project originality to public participation to community acceptance. Four Outstanding Planning Awards may be presented each year: Outstanding Planning Award for a Plan, which may include housing plans, historic conservation plans, economic development plans and other types; Outstanding Planning Award for a Project/Program/Tool, for a project, program or tool that is a significant advancement to specific elements of planning; Outstanding Planning Award for a Special Community Initiative, and Outstanding Planning Award for Implementation, for an effort that shows significant achievement in accomplishing positive change.

For additional information about the Outstanding Planning Awards, call the American Planning Association at (202) 872-0611, or visit the group's Web site at *www.planning.org*.

2003 Winners

Outstanding Planning Award for a Plan

Destination 2003, Metropolitan Transportation Plan for the Central Puget Sound Region (Oregon)

Outstanding Planning Award for Implementation

The Southside Development Plan, Greensboro, North Carolina

Outstanding Planning Award for a Project/Program/Tool

Philadelphia City (Pennsylvania) Planning Commission's Community Heritage Preservation Project

Outstanding Planning Award for a Special Community Initiative

The Eau Gallie Improvement Project, Melbourne, Florida

Source: American Planning Association

> We know that where community exists it confers upon its members identity, a sense of belonging, and a measure of security. It is in communities that the attributes that distinguish humans as social creatures are nourished.
>
> **John W. Gardner**

P/A Awards

The P/A Awards were first granted in 1954 by *Progressive Architecture* magazine and are now presented annually by *Architecture* magazine. The awards recognize design excellence in unbuilt projects. A jury of designers and architects selects the winners.

For more information, call (212) 536-6221 or visit the magazine on the Internet at *www.architecturemag.com.*

2003 Recipients

Palenque at Centro JVC
Guadalajara, Mexico
Morphosis

Omaha Cultural and Interpretive Center
Macy, NE
Vincent Snyder, Architect

Scoville-Turgel Residence
Los Angeles, CA
Michael Maltzan Architecture

City of Culture Galicia
Santiago de Compostela, Spain
Eisenman Architects

2003 Citations

Dalki Theme Park
Seoul, Korea
Cho Slade Architecture/Ga.A Architects

Eyebeam Museum of Art and Technology
New York, NY
Diller + Scofidio

Witte Arts Building
Green Bay, WI
Office dA

Mayo Plan #1
Rochester, MN
Coen + Partners

Jury

Jane Cee (chair), Holt Hinshaw Pfau Jones
Ángel Fernández Alba, Ángel Fernández Alba Architects
Louisa Hutton, Sauerbruch Hutton Architects
Greg Lynn, Greg Lynn FORM
Mary-Ann Ray, Studio Works
Eddie Jones, Jones Studio

Source: Architecture *magazine*

Did you know...
In its 30-year history, Shane Coen, of Coen + Partners, is only one of three landscape architects to have won a P/A Award.

Philip Johnson Award

With its Philip Johnson Award, the Society of Architectural Historians (SAH) annually recognizes an outstanding architectural exhibition catalogue. In order to be eligible, the catalogue must have been published within the preceding two years.

For more information contact the SAH at (312) 573-1365 or visit their Web site at *www.sah.org*.

1990
Los Angeles Blueprints for Modern Living: History and Legacy of the Case Study Houses by Elizabeth A.T. Smith (The Museum of Contemporary Art and MIT Press)

1991
Architecture and Its Image: Four Centuries of Architectural Representation, Works from the Collection of the Canadian Centre for Architecture by Eve Blau and Edward Kaufman, eds. (The Canadian Centre for Architecture and MIT Press)

1992
No award granted

1993
The Making of Virginia Architecture by Charles Brownell (Virginia Museum of Fine Arts and the University Press of Virginia)

Louis Kahn: In the Realm of Architecture by David Brownlee (The Museum of Contemporary Art and Rizzoli International)

1994
Chicago Architecture and Design 1923-1993: Reconfiguration of an American Metropolis by John Zukowsky (Prestel and Art Institute of Chicago)

1995
The Palladian Revival: Lord Burlington, His Villa and Garden in Chiswick by John Harris (Yale University Press)

1996
The Perspective of Anglo-American Architecture by James F. O'Gorman (The Athenaeum of Philadelphia)

An Everyday Modernism: The Houses of William Wurster by Marc Treib (San Francisco Museum of Modern Art and the University of California Press)

1997
Sacred Realm: The Emergence of the Synagogue in the Ancient World by Steven Fine (Yeshiva University Museum and Oxford University Press)

1998
Building for Air Travel: Architecture and Design for Commercial Aviation by John Zukowsky (Art Institute of Chicago and Prestel)

1999
The Work of Charles and Ray Eames: a Legacy of Invention by Donald Albrecht (The Library of Congress, Vitra Design Museum, and Abrams Publishing)

2000
E.W. Godwin: Aesthetic Movement Architect and Designer by Susan Weber Soros (Yale University Press)

2001
Mapping Boston by Alex Krieger and David Cobb, editors (MIT Press)

2002
Mies in Berlin by Terry Riley, Barry Bergdoll, and the Museum of Modern Art (Harry N. Abrams)

2003
Richard Neutra's Windshield House by Dietrich Neumann, ed. (Yale University)

Source: Society of Architectural Historians

RICHARD NEUTRA'S WINDSHIELD HOUSE
EDITED BY DIETRICH NEUMANN

Completed in 1938, Windshield was a watershed design for Richard Neutra and was his only home built on the East Coast. Named for its large expanses of glass, it was a striking example of International Style architecture; the house was destroyed by fire in 1975. The monograph also contains J. Carter Brown's personal recollections about growing up in the house. *Image courtesy of the Yale University Press.*

Praemium Imperiale

The Praemium Imperiale is awarded by the Japan Art Association, Japan's premier cultural institution, for lifetime achievement in the fields of painting, sculpture, music, architecture, and theater/film. The following individuals received this honor for architecture, which includes a commemorative medal and 15,000,000 yen (U.S. $140,000) honorarium.

For more information visit the Japan Art Association's Web site at *www.praemium imperiale.org*.

1989	I. M. Pei (US)
1990	James Stirling (UK)
1991	Gae Aulenti (Italy)
1992	Frank Gehry (US)
1993	Kenzo Tange (Japan)
1994	Charles Correa (India)
1995	Renzo Piano (Italy)
1996	Tadao Ando (Japan)
1997	Richard Meier (US)
1998	Alvaro Siza (Portugal)
1999	Fumihiko Maki (Japan)
2000	Richard Rogers (UK)
2001	Jean Nouvel (France)
2002	Sir Norman Foster (UK)
2003	Rem Koolhaas (The Netherlands)

Source: Japan Art Association

Architectural space creates consciousness, an awareness of a larger universal rhythm and balance.

Tadao Ando

Presidential Design Awards

Established by President Ronald Reagan in 1983, the Presidential Design Awards recognize outstanding contributions to federal design by government agencies, government employees and private-sector designers in the categories of architecture, engineering, graphic design, historic preservation, interior design, landscape architecture, industrial and product design, and urban design and planning. The Presidential Design Awards are administered by the National Endowment for the Arts (NEA) and are presented every four years. Projects are judged based on their purpose, leadership, cost, aesthetics and performance.

For a detailed description of the winners from both award programs and photographs of the projects listed below, visit the NEA's Web site at *www.arts.endow.gov.*

2000 Recipients

U.S. Census Bureau National Data Processing Center
Bowie, MD
General Services Administration, National Capital Region; Department of Commerce, U.S. Census Bureau; Davis Brody Bond; Tobey + Davis

U.S. Port of Entry
Calexico, CA
General Services Administration, Pacific Rim Region; Dworsky Associates

Grand Central Terminal
New York, NY
Department of Transportation, Federal Transit Administration, Region 2; Metropolitan Transportation Authority; Metro-North Railroad; GCT Venture; Beyer Blinder Belle Architects & Planners LLP; Harry Weese & Associates; STV/Seelye Stevenson, Value & Knecht; Fisher Marantaz Renfro Stone, Inc.; The Rockwell Group

Mars Pathfinder Mission
National Aeronautics and Space Administration, Office for Space Science for the Mars Pathfinder Mission and the Jet Propulsion Laboratory

Interstate 70
Glenwood Canyon, CO
Department of Transportation, Federal Highway Administration, Colorado Division; Colorado Department of Transportation, Division of Highways; Gruen Associates; Nelson Haley Patterson and Quirk; DMJM Phillips Reister; Joseph Passonneau & Partners; Leigh Whitehead Associates; DeLeuw, Cather & Co.; Citizens Advisory Committee for Glenwood Canyon

Franklin Delano Roosevelt Memorial
Washington, D.C.
Department of the Interior, National Park Service, Denver Service Center, National Capital Region, and National Capital Parks-Central; Office of Lawrence Halprin; Leonard Baskin; Neil Estern; Robert Graham; Tom Hardy; George Segal; John Benson

National Park Service Park Cultural Landscapes Program
Department of the Interior, National Park Service, Cultural Resource Stewardship and Partnerships

Presidential Design Awards

Westside MAX Light Rail
Portland, OR
Department of Transportation, Federal Transit Administration, Region 10; Tri-County Metropolitan Transportation District of Oregon; Zimmer, Gunsul, Frasca Partnership; Otak, Inc.; Parsons Brinckerhoff Quade & Douglas, Inc.; BRW, Inc.

The Mayors' Institute on City Design
National Endowment for the Arts, Design Program; Joseph P. Riley, Jr.; Jaquelin T. Robertson; Adele Chatfield-Taylor; Joan Abrahamson

Jury

Vincent Scully, Yale University (Chair)
James Stewart Polshek, Polshek Partners Architects
David P. Billington, Princeton University
April Greiman, Greimanski Labs
George Hargreaves, Hargreaves Associates
David DeLong, University of Pennsylvania
Karal Ann Marling, University of Minnesota
Noel Mayo, The Ohio State University
Elizabeth Smith, The Museum of Contemporary Art
Adele Chatfield-Taylor, American Academy in Rome

Source: U.S. General Services Administration and the National Endowment for the Arts

Pritzker Architecture Prize

In 1979, Jay and Cindy Pritzker, through the Hyatt Foundation, established the Pritzker Architecture Prize to inspire greater creativity among the architectural profession and to generate a heightened public awareness about architecture. Today, it is revered as one of the highest honors in the field of architecture. The Prize is awarded each year to a living architect whose body of work represents a longstanding, significant contribution to the built environment. Nominations are accepted every January from any interested party. Architects from all nations are eligible. Laureates of the Pritzker Prize receive a $100,000 grant, citation certificate, and a bronze medallion.

For additional information, visit their Web site at *www.pritzkerprize.com.*

1979	Philip Johnson (US)
1980	Luis Barragan (Mexico)
1981	James Stirling (UK)
1982	Kevin Roche (US)
1983	Ieoh Ming Pei (US)
1984	Richard Meier (US)
1985	Hans Hollein (Austria)
1986	Gottfried Boehm (Germany)
1987	Kenzo Tange (Japan)
1988	Gordon Bunshaft (US)
	Oscar Niemeyer (Brazil)
1989	Frank O. Gehry (US)
1990	Aldo Rossi (Italy)
1991	Robert Venturi (US)
1992	Alvaro Siza (Portugal)
1993	Fumihiko Maki (Japan)
1994	Christian de Portzamparc (France)
1995	Tadao Ando (Japan)
1996	Rafael Moneo (Spain)
1997	Sverre Fehn (Norway)
1998	Renzo Piano (Italy)
1999	Sir Norman Foster (UK)
2000	Rem Koolhaas (The Netherlands)
2001	Jacques Herzog and Pierre de Meuron (Switzerland)
2002	Glenn Murcutt (Australia)
2003	Jørn Utzon (Denmark)

Source: The Pritzker Architecture Prize

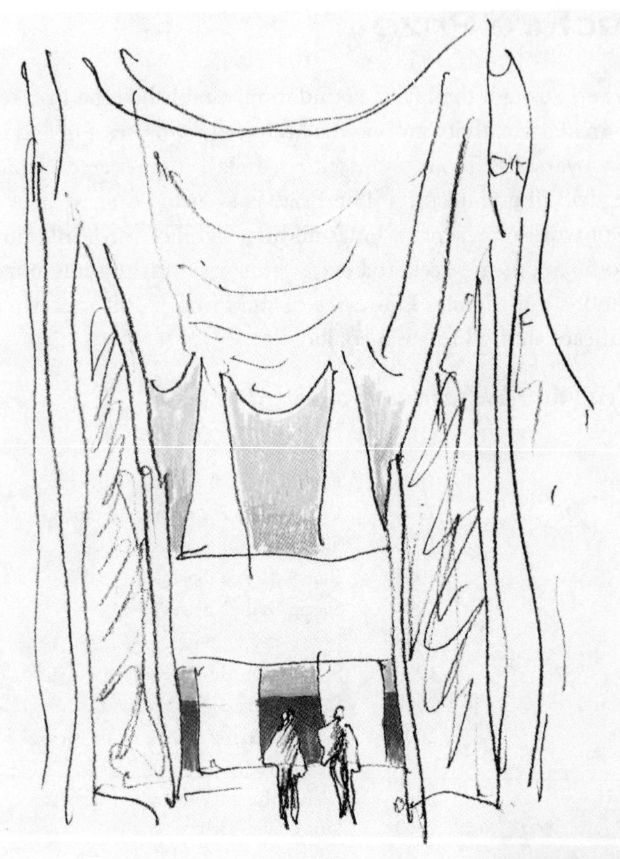

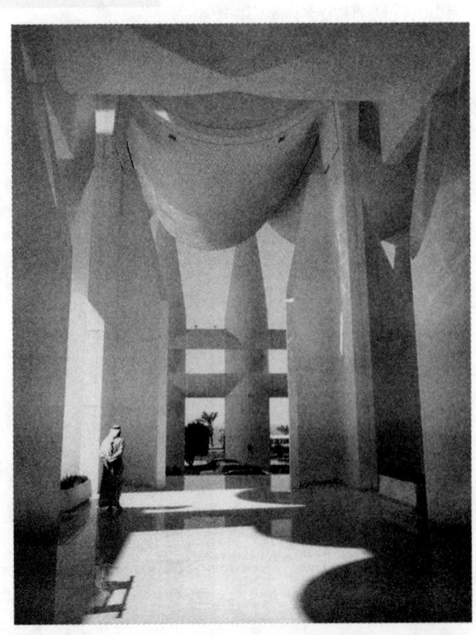

Top, One of Pritzker Prize-winning Jørn Utzon's sketches for the 1982 Kuwait National Assembly (*pictured below*). *Sketch by Jørn Utzon, photo by Carsten Do Anderson. All images courtesy of the Hyatt Foundation.*

Pulitzer Prize for Architectural Criticism

As one of the many lasting contributions he made to the field of journalism, Joseph Pulitzer established the Pulitzer Prize as an incentive to excellence in journalism, music, and letters. Over the years, the scope of the award has been expanded from its original 1917 configuration. Since 1970, the Pulitzer Prize Board has awarded a prize for distinguished journalistic criticism. In the past this category has included winners in the arts, culture, and literary fields. The following individuals received this honor for their work in architectural criticism.

Visit the Pulitzer Prize's Web site at *www.pulitzer.org* for a detailed history, chronology, and archive of past winners.

1970 Ada Louise Huxtable
The New York Times

1979 Paul Gapp
Chicago Tribune

1984 Paul Goldberger
The New York Times

1990 Allan Temko
San Francisco Chronicle

1996 Robert Campbell
The Boston Globe

1999 Blair Kamin
Chicago Tribune

Since 1980, the Pulitzer Prize Board has also acknowledged two finalists in each category. The following individuals were finalists for their work in architectural criticism.

1981 Allan Temko
San Francisco Chronicle

1983 Beth Dunlop
The Miami Herald

1988 Allan Temko
San Francisco Chronicle

1997 Herbert Muschamp
The New York Times

2002 John King
San Francisco Chronicle

2003 John King
San Francisco Chronicle

Nicolai Ouroussoff
Los Angeles Times

Source: The Pulitzer Prize Board

> Beauty or beast, the skyscraper is a major force with a strong magnetic field. It draws into its physical being all the factors that propel and characterize modern civilization.
>
> **Ada Louise Huxtable**

RAIA Gold Medal

The Gold Medal is the highest honor bestowed by the Royal Australian Institute of Architects (RAIA). It is presented annually to recognize distinguished service by architects who have designed or executed buildings of high merit or have advanced the architecture profession. Gold medallists are nominated by their peers in confidence, and a jury comprised of past medallists and the national president make the final selection. Since 1970, the Gold Medallist traditionally delivers the A.S. Hook Address, named in memory of the early RAIA promoter Alfred Samuel Hook, that provides insight into the life, work, and principles of the Gold Medallist and the state of the profession at the time.

For additional information about the Gold Medal or to read past A.S. Hook Addresses, visit the RAIA on the Internet at *www.architecture.com.au.*

1960	Leslie Wilkinson
1961	Louis Layborne-Smith
1962	Joseph Charles Fowell
1963	Sir Arthur Stephenson
1964	Cobden Parkes
1965	Sir Osborn McCutcheon
1966	William Rae Laurie
1967	William Purves Race Godfrey
1968	Sir Roy Grounds
1969	Robin Boyd
1970	Jack Hobbs McConnell
1971	Frederick Bruce Lucas
1972	Edward Herbert Farmer
1973	Jørn Utzon
1974	Raymond Berg
1975	Sydney Edward Ancher
1976	Harry Seidler
1977	Ronald Andrew Gilling
1978	Mervyn Henry Parry
1979	Harold Bryce Mortlock
1980	John Hamilton Andrews
1981	Colin Frederick Madigan
1982	Sir John Wallace Overall
1983	Gilbert Ridgway Nicol and Ross Kingsley Chisholm
1984	Philip Sutton Cox
1985	Richard Norman Johnson
1986	Richard Butterworth
1987	Daryl Sanders Jackson
1988	Romaldo Giurgola
1989	Robin Findlay Gibson
1990	Peter McIntyre
1991	Donald Campbell Rupert Bailey
1992	Glenn Marcus Murcutt
1993	Kenneth Frank Woolley
1994	Neville Quarry
1995	*No award granted*
1996	Denton Corker Marshall
1997	Roy Simpson
1998	Gabriel Poole
1999	Richard Leplastrier
2000	John Morphett
2001	Keith Cottier
2002	Brit Andresen
2003	Peter Corrigan

Source: Royal Australian Institute of Architects

RAIC Gold Medal

The Royal Architectural Institute of Canada (RAIC) began their Gold Medal program in 1967 to recognize the achievement of an architect or individual related to the field and their contribution to Canada's built environment. As the RAIC Gold Medal is merit based, awards are not always granted yearly.

For more information contact the RAIC at (613) 241-3600 or visit their Web site at *www.raic.org*.

1967	Mayor Jean Drapeau (Canada)
1968	The Right Honorable Vincent Massey (Canada)
1970	Eric R. Arthur (Canada)
	The Late John A. Russell (Canada)
1973	Serge Chermayeff (Georgia)
1976	Constantinos Doxiadis (Greece)
1979	John C. Parkin (Canada)
1981	Jane Jacobs (Canada)
1982	Ralph Erskine (Sweden)
1984	Arthur Erickson (Canada)
1985	John Bland (Canada)
1986	Eberhard Zeidler (Canada)
1989	Raymond T. Affleck (Canada)
1991	Phyllis Lambert (Canada)
1992	Doug Shadbolt (Canada)
1994	Barton Myers (Canada)
1995	Moshe Safdie (Israel)
1997	Raymond Moriyama (Canada)
1998	Frank O. Gehry (US)
1999	Douglas Cardinal (Canada)
2001	A.J. "Jack" Diamond (Canada)

Source: Royal Architectural Institute of Canada

Did you know...

On June 15, 2003, Canadian-born Frank Gehry was invested as a Companion of the Order of Canada, the country's highest honor.

Religious Art & Architecture Design Awards

The annual Religious Art & Architecture Design Awards, co-sponsored by *Faith & FORM* magazine and the Interfaith Forum on Religion, Art and Architecture (IFRAA), a Professional Interest Area (PIA) of The American Institute of Architects, acknowledge the highest standards in architecture, liturgical design, and art for religious spaces. Awards are presented for religious architecture in three categories: New Facilities Awards, Renovation Awards, and Restorations Awards. Additionally, awards are presented for Liturgical/Interior Design and Religious Art, including visual arts, liturgical consultants and ceremonial objects. The awards are open to architects, liturgical consultants and interior designers in the United States, Canada, and Mexico. Winning projects are featured in *Faith & FORM* magazine.

For additional information and entry forms, visit *www.aia.org* on the Internet or contact *Faith & FORM* magazine at (919) 489-3359.

2002 Winners

New Facility

The Pope John Paul II Cultural Center
Washington, DC
Leo A Daly

Quaker Meetinghouse
Houston, TX
Leslie Elkins Architecture

St. Boniface Episcopal Church
Mequon, WI
Hammel, Green and Abrahamson, Inc.

Episcopal House of Prayer Oratory
Collegeville, MN
Cuningham Group

Phoenix First Assembly/Early Childhood Education Center/Youth Pavilion
Phoenix, AZ
DeBartolo Architects Ltd.

Saint Therese Catholic Church
Sioux Falls, SD
RDG Schutte Wilscam Birge, Inc.

Renovation

The Cathedral of St. John the Evangelist
Milwaukee, WI
Hammel, Green and Abrahamson, Inc.

St. Patrick Catholic Church
Gretna, NE
Zenon Beringer Mabrey Partners, Inc., Architects

Embassy Center Apostolic Church
Bremerton, WA
McClellan Architects

Restoration

Tao Fong Shan Christian Centre
New Territories, Hong Kong, China
Nelson Chen Architects Ltd.

Liturgical/Interior Design

Congregation Beth Israel
San Diego, CA
Austin Veum Robbins Parshalle

Kate and Laurance Eustis Chapel at the Ochsner Clinic Foundation
New Orleans, LA
Eskew + Dumez + Ripple

The bold and contemporary design of the Pope John Paul II Cultural Center in Washington, D.C. is a marked departure from traditional religious architecture. The building serves as a scholarly study center and interactive museum for religion and contemporary cultural issues. The complex is integrated into the site's natural landscape and uses traditional materials–limestone, copper, granite, and glass. *Photos by Maxwell MacKenzie, courtesy of Leo A Daly.*

Religious Art & Architecture Design Awards

St. Joseph Abbey Church Renovation
St. Benedict, LA
Rafferty Rafferty Tollefson Architects, Inc.

Religious Arts/Visual Arts

Ten Commandments at Main Sanctuary, Peninsula Temple Beth El
San Mateo, CA
Herman & Coliver

"Stand 1," "Stand 2," "Aramesque IV," "How Words Work" at Andover Newton Theological School
Newton Centre, MA
Hope Liturgical Works

Jury

Douglas Hoffman (chair)
Lawrence Cook
Rev. Hope Eakins
Kenneth J. Griesemer
David Wilson

Source: Faith & FORM *magazine*

> The Gothic cathedral is a blossoming in stone subdued by the insatiable demand of harmony in man.
>
> **Ralph Waldo Emerson**

residential architect Design Awards

In 2000, *residential architect* magazine established a design award program to honor the best in American housing. Projects may be submitted in one of eight categories, though judges may eliminate, add or combine categories–bestowing as many awards or none–as they see fit. In addition, the jury, comprised of top residential architects, selects the Best Residential Project of the Year from among the winning entries. Winning projects are published in *residential architect* magazine.

For photographs and descriptions of all the winning projects, visit *www.residential architect.com* on the Internet.

2003 Best Residential Project of the Year

Blue Ridge Farmhouse Addition
Washington, VA
Robert M. Gurney

2003 Grand Prize Winners

Custom Home

Less than 2,000 sq. ft.

Tower House
Chicago, IL
Frederick Phillips and Associates, Architects

Private Residence
St. Helena, CA
Turnbull Griffin Haesloop

Custom Home

2,000 to 3,500 sq. ft.

Estes House
Jamestown, RI
Estes/Twombly Architects

Custom Homes

More than 3,500 sq. ft.

Pacitti House
Warwick, RI
Estes/Twombly Architects

Multifamily

Venice Beach Lofts
Venice, CA
Steven Ehrlich Architects

Single Family Production, detached

Copeland Hill Cottages at the Greenbrier Resort
White Sulfur Springs, WV
Ferguson Shamamian & Rattner Architects

Single Family Production, attached

Phillips Row
Washington, DC
Sorg and Associates, P.C.

Affordable Housing

Waterloo Heights Apartments
Los Angeles, CA
Koning Eizenberg Architecture

2003 Merit Winners

Custom Home

2,000 to 3,500 sq. ft.

Van Sweden Residence
Sherwood, MD
Sorg and Associates, P.C.

Goline Residence
Seattle, WA
Bohlin Cywinski Jackson

residential architect Design Awards

Custom Home

More than 3,500 sq. ft.

Georgian Bay Retreat
Cedar Ridge, ON, Canada
Bohlin Cywinski Jackson

Private Residence
Napa, CA
Turnbull Griffin Haesloop

Renovation

Rappahannock Bend
King George, VA
McInturff Architects

Martin Shocket Residence
Chevy Case, MD
McInturff Architects

Pool House at Little Falls
McLean, VA
Randall Mars Architects

Multifamily

Logan Heights Development
Washington, DC
Division One, Inc.

Box & One Lofts
Portland, OR
Fletcher Farr Ayotte

Radford Court
Seattle, WA
Mithun Architects + Designers + Planners

Loyola Village
San Francisco, CA
Seidel/Holzman

Affordable Housing

The Wellington Neighborhood
Breckenridge, CO
Wolff Lyon Architects

Kitchen

Private Residence
Washington, DC
Cunningham + Quill Architects

Bath

Fiate Lux "Let the Light Flow"
Del Mar, CA
Smyer Architecture

Architectural Detail

Belvedere Lagoon Residence
Belvedere, CA
Sutton Suzuki Architects

P + D House
Omaha, NE
Randy Brown Architects

2003 Judges' Award

Tick Hall Reconstruction
Montauk, NY
Wank Adams Slavin Associates

McKinley Bathroom
Omaha, NE
Randy Brown Architects

Jury

David Baker, David Baker + Partners Architects
Harry Teague, Harry Teague Architects
Heather McKinney, McKinney Architects
Mark Hutker, Mark Hutker & Associates
Rick Emsiek, McLarand Vasquez & Partners
D. Graham Davidson, Hartman-Cox Architects

Source: residential architecture *magazine*

RIBA Royal Gold Medal

The Royal Institute of British Architects' (RIBA) Royal Gold Medal was inaugurated by Queen Victoria in 1848. It is conferred by the Sovereign annually on a distinguished architect, person, or firm "whose work has promoted, either directly or indirectly, the advancement of architecture."

For additional information, visit the RIBA on the Internet at *www.riba.org*.

1848	Charles Robert Cockerell (UK)
1849	Luigi Canina (Italy)
1850	Sir Charles Barry (UK)
1851	Thomas L. Donaldson (UK)
1852	Leo von Klenze (Germany)
1853	Sir Robert Smirke (UK)
1854	Philip Hardwick (UK)
1855	Jacques Ignace Hittorff (France)
1856	Sir William Tite (UK)
1857	Owen Jones (UK)
1858	Friedrich August Stuler (Germany)
1859	Sir G. Gilbert Scott (UK)
1860	Sydney Smirke (UK)
1861	Jean-Baptiste Cicéron Lesueur (France)
1862	Rev. Robert Willis (UK)
1863	Anthony Salvin (UK)
1864	Eugène Emmanuel Violett-le-Duc (France)
1865	Sir James Pennethorne (UK)
1866	Sir Matthew Digby Wyatt (UK)
1867	Charles Texier (France)
1868	Sir Henry Layard (UK)
1869	C.R. Lepsius (Germany)
1870	Benjamin Ferrey (UK)
1871	James Fergusson (UK)
1872	Baron von Schmidt (Austria)
1873	Thomas Henry Wyatt (UK)
1874	George Edmund Street (UK)
1875	Edmund Sharpe (UK)
1876	Joseph Louis Duc (France)
1877	Charles Barry Jr. (UK)
1878	Alfred Waterhouse (UK)
1879	Marquis de Vogue (France)
1880	John L. Pearson (UK)
1881	George Godwin (UK)
1882	Baron von Ferstel (Austria)
1883	Francis Cranmer Penrose (UK)
1884	William Butterfield (UK)
1885	H. Schliemann (Germany)
1886	Charles Garnier (France)
1887	Ewan Christian (UK)
1888	Baron von Hansen (Austria)
1889	Sir Charles T. Newton (UK)
1890	John Gibson (UK)
1891	Sir Arthur Blomfield (UK)
1892	Cesar Daly (France)
1893	Richard Morris Hunt (US)
1894	Lord Leighton (UK)
1895	James Brooks (UK)
1896	Sir Ernest George (UK)
1897	Petrus Josephus Hubertus Cuypers (The Netherlands)
1898	George Aitchison (UK)
1899	George Frederick Bodley (UK)
1900	Rodolfo Amadeo Lanciani (Italy)
1901	*No award granted due to death of Queen Victoria*
1902	Thomas Edward Collcutt (UK)
1903	Charles F. McKim (US)
1904	Auguste Choisy (France)
1905	Sir Aston Webb (UK)
1906	Sir Lawrence Alma-Tadema (UK)
1907	John Belcher (UK)
1908	Honore Daumet (France)
1909	Sir Arthur John Evans (UK)
1910	Sir Thomas Graham Jackson (UK)
1911	Wilhelm Dorpfeld (Germany)
1912	Basil Champneys (UK)
1913	Sir Reginald Blomfield (UK)
1914	Jean Louis Pascal (France)
1915	Frank Darling (Canada)
1916	Sir Robert Rowand Anderson (UK)
1917	Henri Paul Nenot (France)
1918	Ernest Newton (UK)
1919	Leonard Stokes (UK)
1920	Charles Louis Girault (France)
1921	Sir Edwin Landseer Lutyens (UK)

In the citation celebrating Rafael Moneo as the 2003 RIBA Royal Gold Medal recipient, Mohsen Mostafavi said of him: "He is the closest embodiment we have of the idea of the renaissance architect–practitioner, teacher, theorist, critic, deeply knowledgeable on the arts. His work does not just delight the eye, but always provokes thinking." *Photo courtesy of the Royal Institute of British Architects.*

RIBA Royal Gold Medal

1922	Thomas Hastings (US)
1923	Sir John James Burnet (UK)
1924	*No award granted*
1925	Sir Giles Gilbert Scott (UK)
1926	Ragnar Östberg (Sweden)
1927	Sir Herbert Baker (US)
1928	Sir Guy Dawber (US)
1929	Victor Alexandre Frederic Laloux (France)
1930	Sir Percy Scott Worthington (UK)
1931	Sir Edwin Cooper (US0
1932	Hendrik Petrus Berlage (The Netherlands)
1933	Sir Charles Reed Peers (UK)
1934	Henry Vaughan Lanchester (UK)
1935	Willem Marinus Dudok (The Netherlands)
1936	Charles Henry Holden (UK)
1937	Sir Raymond Unwin (UK)
1938	Ivar Tengbom (Sweden)
1939	Sir Percy Thomas (UK)
1940	Charles Francis Annesley Voysey (UK)
1941	Frank Lloyd Wright (US)
1942	William Curtis Green (UK)
1943	Sir Charles Herbert Reilly (UK)
1944	Sir Edward Maufe (UK)
1945	Victor Vesnin (USSR)
1946	Sir Patrick Abercrombie (UK)
1947	Sir Albert Edward Richardson (UK)
1948	Auguste Perret (France)
1949	Sir Howard Robertson (UK)
1950	Eleil Saarinen (Finland)
1951	Emanuel Vincent Harris (UK)
1952	George Grey Wornum (UK)
1953	Le Corbusier (C.E. Jeanneret-Gris) (Switzerland)
1954	Sir Arthur George Stephenson (Australia)
1955	John Murray Easton (UK)
1956	Walter Adolf Gropius (Germany)
1957	Hugo Alvar Henrik Aalto (Finland)
1958	Robert Schofield Morris (Italy)
1959	Ludwig Mies van der Rohe (Germany)
1960	Pier Luigi Nervi (Italy)
1961	Lewis Mumford (US)
1962	Sven Gottfrid Markeluis (Sweden)
1963	The Lord Holford (UK)
1964	E. Maxwell Fry (UK)
1965	Kenzo Tange (Japan)
1966	Ove Arup (UK)
1967	Sir Nikolaus Pevsner (UK)
1968	Richard Buckminster Fuller (US)
1969	Jack Antonio Coia (UK)
1970	Sir Robert Matthew (UK)
1971	Hubert de Cronin Hastings (UK)
1972	Louis I. Kahn (US)
1973	Sir Leslie Martin (UK)
1974	Powell & Moya (UK)
1975	Michael Scott (Ireland)
1976	Sir John Summerson (UK)
1977	Sir Denys Lasdun (UK)
1978	Jørn Utzon (Denmark)
1979	The Office of Charles and Ray Eames (US)
1980	James Stirling (UK)
1981	Sir Philip Dowson (UK)
1982	Berthold Lubetkin (Georgia)
1983	Sir Norman Foster (UK)
1984	Charles Correa (India)
1985	Sir Richard Rogers (UK)
1986	Arata Isozaki (Japan)
1987	Ralph Erskine (Sweden)
1988	Richard Meier (UK)
1989	Renzo Piano (Italy)
1990	Aldo van Eyck (The Netherlands)
1991	Sir Colin Stansfield Smith (UK)
1992	Peter Rice (UK)
1993	Giancarlo de Carlo (Italy)
1994	Sir Michael and Patty Hopkins (UK)
1995	Colin Rowe (UK)
1996	Harry Seidler (Australia)
1997	Tadao Ando (Japan)
1998	Oscar Niemeyer (Brazil)
1999	Barcelona, Spain
2000	Frank Gehry (US)
2001	Jean Nouvel (France)
2002	Archigram (UK)
2003	Rafael Moneo (Spain)

Source: Royal Institute of British Architects

Richard H. Driehaus Prize for Classical Architecture

The Richard H. Driehaus Prize for Classical Architecture was established, endowed and named for the founder of Chicago's Driehaus Capital Management Company and presented by the University of Notre Dame's School of Architecture. The annual award honors a major contributor in the field of traditional and classical architecture or historic preservation. Each year a panel of educators and leading architects selects one recipient of the Prize. Winners receive $100,000 and a bronze and stone model of the Choregic Monument of Lysikrates in Athens, Greece.

For additional information about the Driehaus Prize, visit the Notre Dame School of Architecture on the Web at *www.nd.edu/~arch/*.

2003 Léon Krier

Source: University of Notre Dame, School of Architecture

Did you know...
The Choregic Monument of Lysikrates (334 B.C.) in Athens, Greece, is best known as the first use of the Corinthian Order on a building's exterior.

Rudy Bruner Award for Urban Excellence

The biennial Rudy Bruner Award for Urban Excellence is awarded to projects which approach urban problems with creative inclusion of often competing political, community, environmental, and formal considerations. Established in 1987, the Award recognizes one Gold Medal and four Silver Medal winners. Any project which fosters urban excellence is eligible to apply. A multi-disciplinary selection committee performs an on-site evaluation of each finalist before final selections are made.

For photographs and project descriptions, visit the Bruner Foundation on the Internet at *www.brunerfoundation.org* or contact them at (617) 876-8404.

2003 Winners

Gold Medal
Camino Nuevo Charter Academy
Los Angeles, CA

Silver Medal
Bridgemarket
New York, NY

Colorado Court
Santa Monica, CA

Providence River Relocation
Providence, RI

Red Hook Community Justice Center
Brooklyn, NY

Selection Committee
Alicia Mazur Berg, City of Chicago Planning and Development Department
Kofi S. Bonner, Cleveland Browns
Gary Hack, University of Pennsylvania
Maurice Lim Miller, The Family Independence Initiative
Thomas M. Menino, Mayor of Boston
Gail L. Thompson, Performing Arts Center of Greater Miami

Source: The Bruner Foundation

Camino Nuevo Charter Academy, the 2003 Rudy Bruner Gold Medal recipient, is a new elementary school located in a formerly vacant mini-mall in inner-city Los Angeles. Built by a community development corporation working with the Los Angeles Unified School District to create a new model for a community-based school, Camino Nuevo exemplifies the reuse of a commonplace urban resource and serves as a model for public-private partnerships. *Photo courtesy of the Bruner Foundation.*

Russel Wright Award

Established by Manitoga, The Russel Wright Center in Garrison, New York, the Russel Wright Award honors individuals who are working in the tradition of the mid-twentieth century design pioneer Russel Wright (1904-1976) to provide outstanding design to the general public. Russel Wright was a well-known home furnishings designer in the 1930s through the 1950s who throughout his career maintained the importance of making well-designed objects accessible to the public. The 75-acre wooded landscape he sculpted, Manitoga, is on the National Register of Historic Places and includes Dragon Rock, the home he designed, which exemplifies his philosophy that architecture should enhance rather than dominate its surroundings.

For additional information about the Russel Wright Award, contact Manitoga at (845) 424-3812 or *www.russelwrightcenter.org*.

2000

Michael Graves

2001

Lella and Massimo Vignelli
William T. Golden
Copper-Hewitt National Design Museum, Smithsonian Institution

2002

Murray Moss
Frances S. Reese
Eva Zeisel

2003

Jack Lenor Larsen
Harvey Keyes Flad
Rob Forbes

Source: Manitoga, The Russel Wright Center

Did you know...

Russel Wright designed his American Modern dinnerware in 1937 and spent the next two years trying to convince a manufacturer to produce it. Between 1939 and 1959 it sold over 80 million pieces, making it the most popular ceramic pattern sold in the United States. In the mid-1950s the Ideal Toy company even produced miniature plastic replicas for children to play with.

SADI Awards

The Superior Achievement in Design and Imaging (SADI) Awards are presented each year by *Retail Traffic* Magazine, formerly *Shopping Center World* magazine, for retail design achievement and trendsetting. Award categories range from restaurants to renovated shopping centers, plus a "best-in-show" Grand SADI Award, and honorable mentions at the judges' discretion. The jury is comprised of leading retail architects and designers from across the United States who score projects based on such criteria as construction problem solving, general aesthetics, image-building and implementation. The competition is open to any architectural or design firm, retailer or developer responsible for the design of a new or renovated retail store, shopping center or restaurant.

For additional information, visit *Retail Traffic* magazine's Web site at *www.retailtrafficmag.com.*

2003 Grand Award

Lladró store
Tokyo, Japan
Walker Group/CNI

2003 Winners

New Retail Store
Less than 5,000 sq. ft.
Schedoni
Coral Gables, FL
Pavlik Design Team

New Retail Store
5,000 sq. ft or more
Lladró store
Tokyo, Japan
Walker Group/CNI

New Centers
400,000 sq. ft. – 1 million sq. ft.
The Grove
Los Angeles, CA
Elkus/Manfredi Architects

New Centers
More than 1 million sq. ft.
The Streets at Southpoint
Durham, NC
RTKL Associates, Inc.

New Restaurants
El Palacio de Hierro
Puebla, Mexico
Pavlik Design Team

Renovated Centers
Tabor Center
Denver, CO
Anthony Bellusch/OWP/P Architects

SADI Awards

2003 Honorable Mention

New Retail Store
Less than 5,000 sq. ft.
JR Dunn Jewelers
Fort Lauderdale, FL
Pavlik Design Team

New Retail Store
5,000 sq. ft or more
El Palacio de Hierro
Puebla, Mexico
Pavlik Design Team

New Centers
More than 1 million sq. ft.
The Mall at Millenia
Orlando, FL
JPRA Architects

New Restaurants
Brasserie Vert, Hollywood & Highland Center
Beverly Hills, CA
Engstrom Design Group

Renovated Centers
Grand Avenue
Milwaukee, WI
Urban Design Group

Renovated Retail Stores
The Disney Store – Champs Elysees
Paris, France
The Disney Store

Jury
Barbara Ashley, Retail Ventures
Frankie J. Campione, CREATE Architecture Planning & Design
Kevin McCarthy, Paul Davril Inc.
Mark Carter, Thompson, Ventulett, Stainback & Associates Inc.
Gaylon Melton, The Mills Corp.
Russell Sway, R. Sway Associates
Greg Moe, Carter & Burgess Inc.
Dawn Clark, Callison Architecture Inc.
Thomas M. Morbitzer, Cowan & Associates Inc.
Darrell Pattison, KA Inc. Architecture
Angelo Carusi, Cooper Carry
Brendan Cotter, Alexander Gorlin Architect

Source: Retail Traffic *magazine*

> I think of the users of a building as including the people who drive or walk by it every day but never set foot in it. Somehow that building has an impact on their landscape.
>
> **Robert Ryan**

SCUP/AIA-CAE Excellence in Planning Awards

The Society for College and University Planning (SCUP) and The American Institute of Architects' Committee on Architecture for Education (AIA-CAE) jointly present the annual Excellence in Planning Awards to honor planning and design that recognizes excellence in higher education environments. The jury considers the quality of the physical environment as well as the comprehensiveness of the planning process. The award is open to any professional who has prepared plans for higher education institutions and the institutions themselves and is presented to all members of the project team.

Additional information can be found at the SCUP Web site, *www.scup.org*, or by calling (734) 998-6595.

2003 Recipients

Honor Awards

New Campus, Capital Community College
Hartford, CT
The S/L/A/M Collaborative

Merit Awards

Co-located Campus for University of Washington Bothell/Cascadia Community College
Bothell, WA
NBBJ

Science Precinct Plan and New Science Center, Oberlin College
Oberlin, OH
Payette Associates

Central Campus Planning Study, The University of Michigan
Ann Arbor, MI
SmithGroup/JJR

Jury

Pamela Delphenich, Yale University
Richard Dober, Dober Lidsky & Craig
Thomas F. Fortier, BOORA Architects
Pam Loeffelman, Perkins Eastman
Richard Macias, San Jose State University
Philip Parsons, Parsons Consulting Group
Barbara White, Rice University
Pablo Campos, University of Madrid

Source: Society for College and University Planning and the American Institute of Architects' Committee on Architecture for Education

The New Science Center at Oberlin College (Ohio) reconnects the once isolated science precinct to the rest of the campus with a series of interconnected buildings consistent in scale, proportion, and materials to neighboring structures. *Photo: Jeff Goldberg/Esto, courtesy of Payette Associates.*

SEGD Design Awards

The Society for Environmental Graphic Design's (SEGD) Design Awards recognize the best in environmental design–the planning, design, and specifying of graphic elements in the built and natural environment. Eligible projects include signage, wayfinding systems, mapping, exhibit design, themed environments, retail spaces, sports facilities and campus design. A jury of professionals reviews the entries to determine which projects best help to identify, direct, inform, interpret, and visually enhance our surroundings. Three levels of awards are granted–Honor Awards, Merit Awards, and the Juror Award. Winners are announced at SEGD's annual conference each spring and are honored in an annual exhibition and bi-annual publication.

For a list of all winning entries, visit SEGD's Web site at *www.segd.org*.

2002 Honor Awards

Sony Playstation 2002 E3 Exhibit
Los Angeles Convention Center, Los Angeles, CA
Mauk Design

Wayfinding System for New York and New Jersey Airports
New York and New Jersey
Bureau Mijksenaar
Chermayeff & Geismar

Scorpion Knockout @NikePark
Tokyo, Seoul, Beijing, Berlin, London, Los Angeles, Madrid, Mexico City, Paris, Rome, Rotterdam, and São Paulo
Nike Brand Design

The NPS UniGuide Program: Identity, Wayfinding and Visitor Information for the National Park Service
Nationwide
Meeker & Associates, Inc.

San Francisco International Terminal Building Food and Retail Signage Program
San Francisco, CA
Mayer/Reed

Rewarding Lives
American Express Lobby, World Financial Center, New York, NY
The Moderns

Family Voices/Austin
Chicago, IL
BJ Krivanek Art+Design

Gaudi in Barcelona
Parsons School of Design, New York, NY
Jihea Kim

Jury

Kate Keating, Kate Keating Associates, Inc. (chair)
Stuart Ash, Gottschalk+Ash International
Ken D. Carbone, Carbone Smolan Agency
Patrick J. Gallagher, Gallagher & Associates
Jacinta M. McCann, EDAW Inc.
Katherine McCoy, Illinois Institute of Technology's Institute of Design
Rebecca M. Nolan, SmithGroup California

Source: Society for Environmental Graphic Design

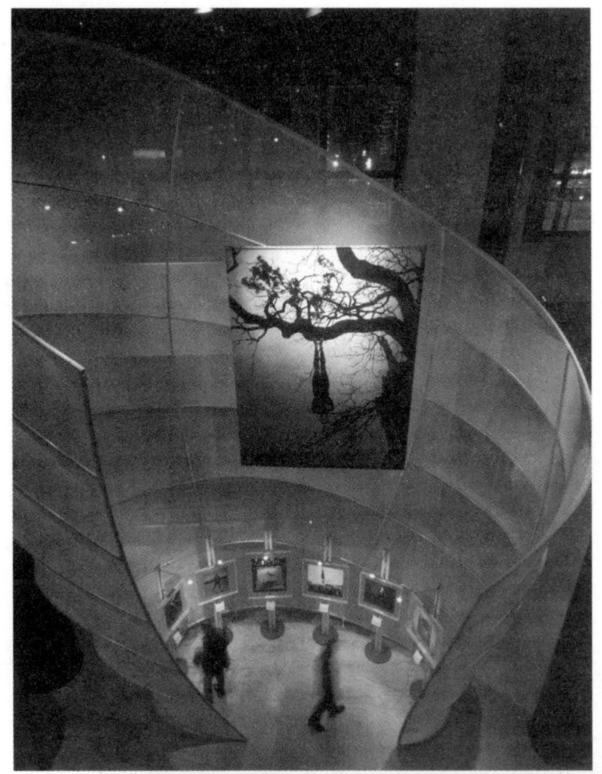

The Rewarding Lives exhibit, which features more than 80 portraits by Annie Lebowitz, was intended to bring an uplifting, memorable experience to the lobby of the newly re-opened American Express Headquarters in the World Financial Center, which was nearly destroyed on September 11. The jury said of the exhibit: "In an attempt to provide models for inspiration and reflect on the positive aspect of life, the designers have created an exhibit which, in theme and execution, exceeds the objective. The combination of beautiful diaphanous forms acting as a soft and delicate backdrop to the photos is deftly done. The forms are engaging from a distance and reduce the scale of an immense corporate lobby to one that is intimate and graceful. All aspects of this exhibit are beautifully detailed, controlled, and elegant." *Photo © Paul Warchol, courtesy of The Moderns.*

Sir Patrick Abercrombie Prize

The International Union of Architects (UIA) grants this triennial award to an internationally renowned architect or architects for significant work in town planning and territorial development.

For more information visit the UIA's Web site at *www.uia-architectes.org*.

1961
Town Planning Service of the City of Stockholm (Sven Markelius and G. Onblahd, Sweden)

1963
Constantinos Dioxiadis (Greece)

1965
Colin Buchanan and team (UK)
T. Farkas and team (Hungary)

1967
Giancarlo De Carlo (Italy)

1969
H. Bennet and team (UK)
Honorary Mention: Belaunde Terry (Peru)

1972
Centre for Experimentation, Research and Training (Morocco)

1975
Iosif Bronislavovitch Orlov and Nilolai Ivanovitch Simonov (USSR)

1978
The City of Louvain la Neuve (Belgium)

1981
Warsaw architects (Poland) for the reconstruction of their capital
Honorary Mention: M. Balderiotte and team (Argentina)

1984
Hans Blumenfeld (Canada) and Lucio Costa (Brazil)

1987
AIA Regional/Urban Design Assistance Team (R/UDAT) (US)
Honorary Mention: Eduardo Leira (Spain); L. Bortenreuter, K. Griebel, H.G. Tiedt for the remodeling of the city center of Gera (GDR)

1990
Edmund N. Bacon (US)

1993
Jan Gehl (Denmark)

1996
Juan Gil Elizondo (Mexico)

1999
Karl Ganser (Germany)
Honorary Mention: Master plan of the city of Shenzhen (People's Republic of China)

2002
Group 91 Architects for the Temple Bar district in Dublin (Ireland)

Source: International Union of Architects

> Above all we need, particularly as children, the reassuring presence of a visible community, an intimate group that enfolds us with understanding and love, and that becomes an object of our spontaneous loyalty, as a criterion and point of reference for the rest of the human race.
>
> **Lewis Mumford**

Sir Robert Matthew Prize

The International Union of Architects (UIA) awards the Sir Robert Matthew Prize triennially to an internationally renowned architect or architects whose work has improved the quality of human settlements.

For more information, visit the UIA's Web site at *www.uia-architectes.org*.

1978
John F.C. Turner (UK)

1981
Hassan Fathy (Egypt)
Honorary Mention: Rod Hackney (UK) and Hardt Walther Hamer (GFR)

1984
Charles Correa (India)

1987
Housing Reconstruction Program for the City of Mexico (Mexico)

1990
Department of Architecture of the Singapore Housing & Development Board (Singapore)

1993
Laurie Baker (UK)

1996
Giancarlo De Carlo (Italy)
Jury Citation: Oberste Baubehörde (the German team under the guidance of architect Benno Brugger and led by Hans Jörg Nussberger)

1999
Martin Treberspurg (Austria)
Honorary Mention: Development & Construction Branch of the Hong Kong Housing Department

2002
Justin Kilcullen (Ireland)
Jaime Lerner (Brazil)
Honorary Mention: Kooperation GdW-BDA-DST (Germany)

Source: International Union of Architects

Spiro Kostof Book Award

The Society of Architectural Historians (SAH) grants the annual Spiro Kostof Award to a work that has made the greatest contribution to understanding the historical development of the change in urbanism and architecture.

For more information, contact the SAH at (312) 573-1365 or visit their Web site at *www.sah.org.*

1994

Architecture Power and National Identity by Lawrence J. Vale (Yale University Press)

1995

In the Theatre of Criminal Justice: The Palais de Justice in Second Empire Paris by Katherine Fischer Taylor (Princeton University Press)

1996

The Topkapi Scroll: Geometry and Ornament in Islamic Architecture by Gülru Necipoglu (Getty Center for the History of Art and Humanities)

1997

The Projective Cast: Architecture and Its Three Geometries by Robin Evans (MIT Press)

Auschwitz: 1270 to the Present by Debórah Dwork and Robert Jan van Pelt (Norton)

1998

The Architects and the City by Robert Bruegmann (University of Chicago Press)

Magnetic Los Angeles by Gregory Hise (Johns Hopkins Press)

1999

City Center to Regional Mall: Architecture, the Automobile and Retailing in Los Angeles, 1920-1950 by Richard Longstreth (MIT Press)

Housing Design and Society in Amsterdam: Reconfiguring Urban Order and Identity, 1900-1920 by Nancy Stieber (University of Chicago Press)

2000

The Architecture of Red Vienna 1919-1934 by Eve Blau (MIT Press)

2001

The Creative Destruction of Manhattan, 1900-1940 by Max Page (The University of Chicago Press)

2002

Buildings on Ruins: The Rediscovery of Rome and English Architecture by Frank Salmon (Ashgate Publishing Company)

2003

Architecture in the Age of Printing: Orality, Writing, Typography and Printed Images in the History of Architectural Theory by Mario Carpo (MIT Press)

Concrete and Clay: Reworking Nature in New York City by Matthew Gandy (MIT Press)

Source: Society of Architectural Historians

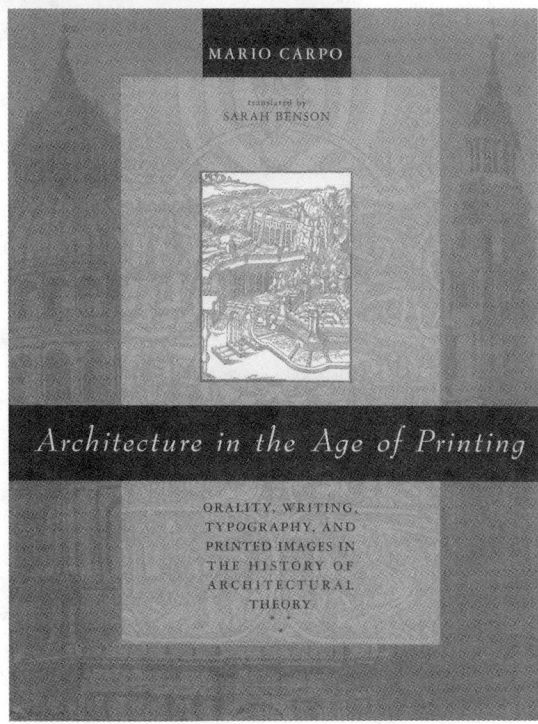

Above: *In Concrete and Clay*, Matthew Gandy traces five broad developments in New York City's environmental history: the expansion and redefinition of public space, the construction of landscaped highways, the creation of a modern water supply system, the radical environmental politics of the barrio in the late 1960s and early 1970s, and the contemporary politics of the environmental justice movement. *Below*: In his book *Architecture in the Age of Printing*, Mario Carpo investigates how different forms of communication have influenced Western architectural thinking, from classical antiquity to the twentieth-century, including the effect of the current shift to digital media on architecture. *Images courtesy of the MIT Press.*

Star Award

Through its Star Award, the International Interior Design Association (IIDA) recognizes individuals who have made an outstanding contribution to the interior design profession. No more than one award is granted each year. However, as this is merit based, awards are not always given annually. Although non-members are eligible for the Star Award, the IIDA board of directors, the selection body, only accepts nominations from IIDA fellows, chapter presidents, and directors.

For more information about the Star Award, visit IIDA's Web site at *www.iida.org* or contact them at (888) 799-4432.

1985	Lester Dundes
1986	William Sullivan
1987	Orlando Diaz-Azcuy
1988	Paul Brayton
1989	Florence Knoll Bassett
1990	Beverly Russell
1991	Stanley Abercrombie
1992	M. Arthur Gensler Jr.
1993	Sivon C. Reznikoff
1994	Michael Kroelinger
1995	Douglas R. Parker
1997	Michael Wirtz
1998	Charles and Ray Eames
1999	Michael Brill
2000	Eva L. Maddox
2001	Andrée Putman
2002	Karim Rashid
2003	Ray Anderson

Source: International Interior Designers Association

Design is rooted in everyday life, every tap you turn, every doorknob you touch.

Karim Rashid

IIDA president Anita Barnett said of Ray Anderson's selection for the Star Award: "While Interface is noted in its industry for its commitment to high quality design and innovation, under Ray's leadership the company is fast gaining a reputation as a corporation carrying the banner for the environment." *Photo courtesy of Interface.*

Tau Sigma Delta Gold Medal

Presented annually by Tau Sigma Delta, the honor society of architecture and the allied arts, the Gold Medal honors an individual who has made outstanding contributions in the fields of architecture, landscape architecture or an allied profession.

More information about the Medal can be found online at *www.ttu.edu/~tsd.*

1970	Norman Fletcher
1971	Gunnar Birkerts
1972	O'Neil Ford
1973	Arthur Erickson
1974	Ian McHarg
1975	Hugh Stubbins
1976	Vincent G. Kling
1977	Harry Weese
1978	William Wayne Caudill
1979	Edmond Bacon
1980	Alexander Girard
1981	Charles Moore
1982	Moshe Safdie
1983	Ricardo Legorreta
1984	E. Fay Jones
1985	Pietro Belluschi
1986	Walter A. Netsch
1987	Lawrence Halprin
1988	Kenneth Frampton
1989	Richard Meier
1990	Joseph Esherick
1991	Denise Scott Brown
1992	Charles Moore (repeat)
1993	Harold L. Adams
1994	Harvey B. Gantt
1995	Peter Eisenman
1996	Vincent Scully
1997	Cesar Pelli
1998	William Pedersen
1999	William Curtis
2000	Pierre Koenig
2001	Malcolm Holzman
2002	Cynthia Weese
2003	Michael Graves

Source: Tau Sigma Delta

> The dreams which accompany all human actions should be nurtured by the places in which people live.
>
> **Charles W. Moore**

Thomas Jefferson Award for Public Architecture

The Thomas Jefferson Award for Public Architecture is presented by The American Institute of Architects (AIA) to recognize and foster the importance of design excellence in government and infrastructure projects. Awards are presented in three categories: private sector architects who have amassed a portfolio of accomplished and distinguished public facilities, public sector architects who produce quality projects within their agencies, and public officials or others who have been strong advocates for design excellence.

For more information, visit the AIA on the Internet at *www.aia.org* or contact the AIA Honors and Awards Department at (202) 626-7586.

1992
James Ingo Freed
George M. White
Patrick J. Moynihan

1993
Jack Brooks

1994
Richard Dattner
M.J. "Jay" Brodie
Joseph P. Riley Jr.

1995
Herbert S. Newman
Edward A. Feiner
Henry G. Cisneros

1996
Thomas R. Aidala
Douglas P. Woodlock

1997
John Tarantino
Richard A. Kahan
Hunter Morrison

1998
Arthur Rosenblatt

1999
Lewis Davis
Robert Kroin

2000
Charles Emil Peterson
Jay Chatterjee

2001
Terrel M. Emmons
J. Stroud Watson

2003*
Edmund W. Ong
Susan Williams

* At this time the AIA altered the schedule for this award from annual to biennial.

Source: The American Institute of Architects

The 2003 Thomas Jefferson Award recipients: *top*, Edmund W. Ong; *bottom*, Susan Williams. *Photos courtesy of the architects.*

Twenty-Five Year Award

Awarded annually by The American Institute of Architects (AIA), the Twenty-Five Year Award is presented to buildings which excel under the test of time. Projects must have been completed 25 to 35 years ago by an architect licensed in the United States, though the buildings may be located anywhere in the world. To be eligible, submissions must still be carrying out their original program and demonstrate a continued viability in their function and form.

For more information, visit the AIA on the Internet at *www.aia.org* or contact the AIA Honors and Awards Department at (202) 626-7586.

1969

Rockefeller Center
New York, NY, 1931-40
Reinhard & Hofmeister with Corbett, Harrison & MacMurray and Hood & Fouilhoux

1971

The Crow Island School
Winnetka, IL, 1939
Perkins, Wheeler & Will and Eliel and Eero Saarinen

1972

Baldwin Hills Village
Los Angeles, CA, 1941
Reginald D. Johnson with Wilson, Merrill & Alexander and Clarence S. Stein

1973

Taliesin West
Paradise Valley, AZ, 1938
Frank Lloyd Wright

1974

Johnson and Son Administration Building
Racine, WI, 1936-39
Frank Lloyd Wright

1975

Philip Johnson Residence ("The Glass House")
New Canaan, CT, 1949
Philip Johnson

1976

860-880 North Lakeshore Drive Apartments
Chicago, IL, 1948-51
Ludwig Mies van der Rohe

1977

Christ Lutheran Church
Minneapolis, MN, 1948-51
Saarinen, Saarinen & Associates with Hills, Gilbertson & Hays

1978

The Eames House
Pacific Palisades, CA, 1949
Charles and Ray Eames

1979

Yale University Art Gallery
New Haven, CT, 1954
Louis I. Kahn with Douglas Orr

1980

Lever House
New York, NY, 1952
Skidmore, Owings & Merrill

1981

Farnsworth House
Plano, IL, 1950
Ludwig Mies van der Rohe

1982

Equitable Savings and Loan Building
Portland, OR, 1948
Pietro Belluschi

Twenty-Five Year Award

1983
Price Tower
Bartlesville, OK, 1956
Frank Lloyd Wright

1984
Seagram Building
New York, NY, 1957
Ludwig Mies van der Rohe

1985
General Motors Technical Center
Warren, MI, 1951
Eero Saarinen & Associates with Smith, Hinchman & Grylls Associates

1986
Solomon R. Guggenheim Museum
New York, NY, 1959
Frank Lloyd Wright

1987
Bavinger House
Norman, OK, 1953
Bruce Goff

1988
Dulles International Airport Terminal Building
Chantilly, VA, 1962
Eero Saarinen & Associates

1989
Vanna Venturi House
Chestnut Hill, PA, 1964
Robert Venturi

1990
The Gateway Arch
St. Louis, MO, 1965
Eero Saarinen & Associates

1991
Sea Ranch Condominium I
The Sea Ranch, CA, 1965
Moore Lyndon Turnbull Whitaker

1992
The Salk Institute for Biological Studies
La Jolla, CA, 1966
Louis I. Kahn

1993
Deere & Company Administrative Center
Moline, IL, 1963
Eero Saarinen & Associates

1994
The Haystack Mountain School of Crafts
Deer Isle, ME, 1962
Edward Larrabee Barnes

1995
The Ford Foundation Headquarters
New York, NY, 1968
Kevin Roche John Dinkeloo and Associates

1996
The Air Force Academy Cadet Chapel
Colorado Springs, CO, 1962
Skidmore, Owings & Merrill

1997
Phillips Exeter Academy Library
Exeter, NH, 1972
Louis I. Kahn

1998
Kimbell Art Museum
Fort Worth, TX, 1972
Louis I. Kahn

1999
The John Hancock Center
Chicago, IL, 1969
Skidmore, Owings & Merrill

2000
The Smith House
Darien, CT, 1967
Richard Meier & Partners

Twenty-Five Year Award

2001

Weyerhaeuser Headquarters
Tacoma, WA, 1971
Skidmore, Owings & Merrill

2002

Fundació Joan Miró
Barcelona, Spain, 1975
Sert Jackson and Associates

2003

Design Research Headquarters Building
Cambridge, MA, 1969
BTA Architects Inc.

Source: The American Institute of Architects

UIA Gold Medal

Every three years at its World Congress, the International Union of Architects (UIA), awards its Gold Medal to a living architect who has made an outstanding achievement to the field of architecture. This honor recognizes the recipients' lifetime of distinguished practice, contribution to the enrichment of mankind, and the promotion of the art of architecture.

For more information, visit the UIA Web site at *www.uia-architectes.org*.

1984	Hassan Fathy (Egypt)
1987	Reima Pietila (Finland)
1990	Charles Correa (India)
1993	Fumihiko Maki (Japan)
1996	Rafael Moneo (Spain)
1999	Ricardo Legorreta (Mexico)
2002	Renzo Piano (Italy)

Source: International Union of Architects

Tradition among the peasants is the only safeguard of their culture. They cannot discriminate between unfamiliar styles, and if they run off the rails of tradition they will inevitably meet disaster. Willfully to break a tradition in a basically traditional society, like a peasant one, is a kind of cultural murder, and the architect must respect the tradition he is invading.

Hassan Fathy

Urban Land Institute Awards for Excellence

The Urban Land Institute Awards for Excellence follow the organization's mission "to provide responsible leadership in the use of land in order to enhance the environment." Considered by many the most prestigious award within the development community, the Urban Land Institute has recognized outstanding land development projects throughout the world since 1979. Submissions are accepted from developers in the United States and Canada (except for the International Prize which is worldwide in scope) and judged by a panel of experts. Winning entries represent superior design, improve the quality of the built environment, exhibit a sensitivity to the community, display financial viability, and demonstrate relevance to contemporary issues.

For more information about the awards, contact the Urban Land Institute at (800) 321-5011 or visit their Web site at *www.uli.org*.

2002 Recipients

Large-Scale, Office

One Raffles Link
Singapore
Hongkong Land Property Company, Ltd., owner/developer
Kohn Pedersen Fox Associates PC, architect
LPT Architects, associate architect
Gammon Pte. Ltd., general contractor/construction organization
Meinhardt (Singapore) Ptd. Ltd., cvil/structural/electrical/mechanical engineers
Aspinwall Clouston Pte. Ltd., landscape architect

Large-Scale, Recreational

Station Mont Tremblant
Quebec, Canada
Intrawest Corporation, Mont-Tremblant, owner/developer
Desmarais and Associates, architect
Cote, Leahy and Associates, architect
Le groupe ARCOP, architect
Gross, Kaplin Coviensky, architect
Cogela, builder
Les constructions Devlor, builder
Les enterprises du Bon Conseil Ltee, builder
Eldon Beck and Associates, planner
Daniel Arbour and Associates, planner

Large-Scale, Mixed-Use

CityPlace
West Palm Beach, FL
CityPlace Retail LLC/CityPlace Residential LLC, owner
The Palladium Company, developer
Elkus/Manfredi Architects, architect
Wolfberg Alvarez and Partners, architect
Roger Fry AIA, architect
Whiting-Turner Contracting Company, construction manager

Small-Scale, Mixed-Use

Bethesda Row
Bethesda, MD
Federal Realty Investment Trust, owner/developer
Cooper Carry, architect
Street-Works, key consultants

Urban Land Institute Awards for Excellence

New Community
Summerlin North
Las Vegas, NV
The Howard Hughes Corporation, owner/developer
McLarand, Vasquez and Partners, Inc., architects
G.C. Wallace, Inc., engineers
Davies Associates, graphic design
David Jensen Associates, land planners
Design Workshop, land planners
P.B.R., land planners
Design Workshop, landscape architects
Glanville Associates, landscape architects
IDEA, Inc., landscape architects

Small-Scale Rehabilitation
Recreational Equipment, Inc. (REI) Denver Flagship Store
Denver, CO
Mithun Architects + Designers + Planners, architect/designer
Otten, Johnson, Robinson, Neff and Ragonetti, PC, consultant
Semple Brown Design, consultant
Wenk Associates, Inc., consultant

Small-Scale Rehabilitation
Hotel Burnham at the Reliance Building
Chicago, IL
Antunovich Associates, architect
McClier, restoration architect

Public
Homan Square Community Center Campus
Chicago, IL
The Shaw Company, developer
Homan Square Community Center Foundation, owner
Booth Hansen Associates, architect
Pepper Construction, general contractor

Special
Envision Utah
Salt Lake City, UT
Coalition for Utah's Future, owner
The William and Flora Hewlett Foundation, consultant
Fregonese Calthorpe Associates, consultant

Memphis Ballpark District
Memphis, TN
Looney Ricks Kiss, architect
HOK Sport + Venue + Event, architect
Beers Inman, Joint Venture, contractor
CF Jordan Residential, contractor
Jameson-Gibson Construction Company, Inc., contractor
Flintco, Inc., contractor

Jury
Wayne Ratkovich, The Ratkovich Company (chair)
Robert A. Alleborn, Robert A. Alleborn Properties, Inc.
J. Brad Griffith, Griffith Properties LLC
Helen D. Hatch, Thompson Ventulett Stainback and Associates, Inc.
Richard E. Heapes, Street Works
Pamela J. Herbst, Direct Investments Group, AEW Capital Management
Daniel T. McCaffery, McCaffery Interests, Inc.
Laurin McCracken, Looney Ricks Kiss
James F. Porter, Altoon + Porter Architects, LLP
James A. Ratner, Forest City Commercial Group
Michael Spies, Tishman Speyer Properties
Frank P. Stanek, Universal Studios Recreation Group

Source: Urban Land Institute

What is the city but the people?

William Shakespeare, *Coriolanus*, Act III

Veronica Rudge Green Prize in Urban Design

Established by Harvard University in 1986, the Veronica Rudge Green Prize in Urban Design recognizes excellence in urban design with an emphasis on projects that contribute to the public spaces and improve the quality of urban life. The Prize is awarded biennially by a jury of experts in the field of architecture and urban design. Nominations are made to Harvard's Graduate School of Design by a panel of critics, academics, and practitioners in the field of architecture, landscape architecture, and urban design. Eligible projects must be larger in scope than a single building and must have been constructed within the last 10 years. Winners receive a monetary award and certificate.

Additional information about the award can be found on the Internet at *www.gsd.harvard.edu.*

1988

Byker Redevelopment
Newcastle upon Tyne, UK
Ralph Erskine (Sweden)

Malagueira Quarter Housing Project
Evora, Portugal
Alvaro Siza (Portugal)

1990

Urban Public Spaces of Barcelona
Barcelona, Spain
The City of Barcelona

1993

Hillside Terrace Complex
Tokyo, Japan
Fumihiko Maki (Japan)

Master Plan and Public Buildings
Monte Carasso, Switzerland
Luigi Snozzi (Switzerland)

1996

Restoration of the Historic Center of Mexico City and Ecological Restoration of the District of Xochimilco
Mexico City, Mexico

1998

Subway System
Bilbao, Spain
Sir Norman Foster and Foster and Partners (UK)

Development of Carré d'Art Plaza
Nîmes, France
Sir Norman Foster and Foster and Partners (UK)

2000

Favela-Bairro Project
Rio de Janeiro, Brazil
Jorge Mario Jáuregui and Jorge Mario Jáuregui Architects (Brazil)

2002

Borneo-Sporenburg Housing Project
Amsterdam, The Netherlands
Adriaan Geuze and West 8 Landscape Architects (The Netherlands)

Source: Harvard Graduate School of Design/School of Architecture

Vincent J. Scully Prize

The National Building Museum founded the Vincent J. Scully Prize to recognize practice, scholarship, and criticism in the design professions–architecture, landscape architecture, historic preservation, city planning, and urban design. By naming the prize after Vincent J. Scully, America's renowned architectural scholar, mentor, and critic whose lifetime of work made a tremendous impact on the profession, the Museum hopes to celebrate others who have yielded a significant contribution to the betterment of our world. The award carries a $25,000 honorarium, and the recipient is invited to present a lecture at the Museum.

For more information about the Vincent J. Scully Prize, contact the National Building Museum at (202) 272-2448 or visit them on the Internet at *www.nbm.org*.

1999	Vincent J. Scully
2000	Jane Jacobs
2001	Elizabeth Plater-Zyberk
	Andrés Duany
2002	Robert Venturi
	Denise Scott Brown

Source: National Building Museum

Exceptions ought to be exceptional.

Robert Venturi

Whitney M. Young Jr. Award

The American Institute of Architects (AIA) bestows the Whitney M. Young Jr. Award annually upon an architect or architecturally oriented organization that makes a significant contribution toward meeting the challenge set forth by Mr. Young to architects: to assume a professional responsibility toward current social issues. These issues are ever present and flexible and include such things as housing the homeless, affordable housing, minority and women participation in the profession, disability issues, and literacy.

For more information, visit the AIA on the Internet at *www.aia.org* or contact the AIA Honors and Awards Department at (202) 626-7586.

1972	Robert J. Nash
1973	Architects Workshop of Philadelphia
1974	Stephen Cram*
1975	Van B. Bruner Jr.
1976	Wendell J. Campbell
1980	Leroy M. Campbell*
1981	Robert T. Coles
1982	John S. Chase
1983	Howard Hamilton Mackey Sr.
1984	John Louis Wilson
1985	Milton V. Bergstedt
1986	The Rev. Richard McClure Prosse*
1987	J. Max Bond Jr.
1988	Habitat for Humanity
1989	John H. Spencer
1990	Harry G. Robinson III
1991	Robert Kennard
1992	Curtis J. Moody
1993	David Castro-Blanco
1994	Ki Suh Park
1995	William J. Stanley III
1996	John L. Wilson
1997	Alan Y. Taniguchi
1998	Leon Bridges
1999	Charles F. McAfee
2000	Louis L. Weller
2001	Cecil A. Alexander Jr.
2002	Robert P. Madison
2003	Hispanic American Construction Industry Association (HACIA)

* Honored posthumously

Source: The American Institute of Architects

Wolf Prize for Architecture

Dr. Ricardo Wolf established the Wolf Foundation in 1976 in order to "promote science and arts for the benefit of mankind." In this vein, the Wolf prize is awarded annually to outstanding living scientists and artists in the fields of agriculture, chemistry, mathematics, medicine, physics, and the arts. The awards, an honorarium of $100,000 and a diploma, are presented each year in Jerusalem's Chagall Hall. In the arts category, the Wolf Prize rotates annually between architecture, music, painting, and sculpture. The following individuals received this honor for their contribution to the field of architecture.

For more information about the Wolf Prize, contact the Wolf Foundation at +972 (9) 955 7120 or visit their Web site at *www.aquanet.co.il/wolf*.

1983

Ralph Erskine (Sweden)

1988

Fumihiko Maki (Japan)
Giancarlo de Carlo (Italy)

1992

Frank O. Gehry (US)
Jørn Utzon (Denmark)
Sir Denys Lasdun (UK)

1996

Frei Otto (Germany)
Aldo van Eyck (Holland)

2001

Alvaro Siza (Portugal)

Source: Wolf Foundation

Wood Design Awards

The Wood Design Awards annually recognize excellence in wood architecture in the United States and Canada. Judging criteria includes the creative, distinctive and appropriate use of wood materials, though buildings do not need to be constructed entirely of wood. Entries may include residential and non-residential buildings, new construction, or renovation. Honor, merit and citation awards may be given in each category, at the discretion of the jury. Special awards issues of *Wood Design & Building* (U.S.) and *Wood Le Bois* (Canada) magazines feature winning projects.

For project descriptions and photos, visit *www.woodmags.com/wda* on the Internet.

2003 Recipients

Honor Awards

Minneapolis Rowing Club Boathouse
Minneapolis, MN
Vincent James Associates

Maison Goulet
Ste-Marguerite du Lac Masson, QC, Canada
Saia Barbarese Topouzanov architectes

Merit Awards

Riddell Residence
Wilson, WY
Will Bruder Architects, Ltd.

Messenger House II
Upper Kingsburg, NS, Canada
Brian MacKay-Lyons Architecture Urban Design

Milanville House
Milanville, PA
Joe Levine, Bone/Levine Architects

Emerson Sauna
Duluth, MN
Salmela Architect

Outdoor Classrooms at Eib's Pond Park
Staten Island and Roy Wilkins Park, Southern Queens, NY
Marpillero Pollak Architects

Citation Awards

Onominese Retreat
Leelanau Peninsula, MI
Betsy Williams with Cornelius Alig

Bunch Residence
Napa, CA
Turnbull Griffin Haesloop

Home Observatory
Ghent, NY
Wendy Evans Joseph Architecture

Bird Studies Canada Headquarters
Port Rowan, ON, Canada
Montgomery Sisam Architects Inc.

Ocean Education Center
Dana Point, CA
Bauer and Wiley Architects

Think Small
San Diego, CA
Steven Lombardi, Architect

Jury

Laura Hartman, Fernau & Hartman Architects, Inc.
Raymond Moriyama, Moriyama & Teshima Architects
Peter Bohlin, Bohlin Cywinski Jackson

Source: Wood Design & Building *magazine and* Wood Le Bois *magazine*

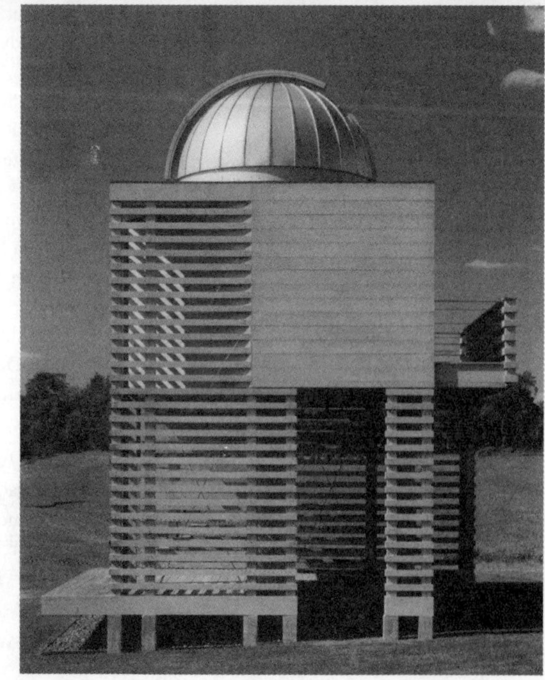

The jury said of this 2003 Wood Design Award-winning project, a home observatory located in Ghant, N.Y.: "The project takes the liberties of a traditional folly, however, its execution meets completely the specific program demands of an observatory. The wood details are clear and simple resulting in a lovely piece of sculpture." *Photo: © Photo by Pamela Cobb, courtesy of the Wood Design Awards.*

Young Architects Award

The Young Architects Award is presented annually by The American Institute of Architects (AIA) to an architect in the early stages of his or her career who has made significant contributions to the profession. The competition is open to AIA members who have been licensed to practice for less than 10 years. The term "young architect" has no reference to the age of nominees.

For additional information about the Young Architects Award visit the AIA online at *www.aia.org* or contact the AIA Honors and Awards Department at (202) 626-7586.

1993

Joan M. Soranno
Vicki L. Hooper
Thomas Somerville Howorth
Brett Keith Laurila

1995

William A. Blanski
Anne Tate

1996

Christopher W. Coe
George Thrush
Keith Moskow

1997

Robert S. Rothman
William J. Carpenter
Michael A. Fischer
Brad Simmons

1998

J. Windom Kimsey
Jose Luis Palacious
Karin M. Pitman
Charles Rose
Karl W. Stumpf
David Louis Swartz
Maryann Thompson
Randall C. Vaughn

1999

Father Terrence Curry
Victoria Tatna Jacobson
Michael Thomas Maltzan
David T. Nagahiro
Peter Steinbrueck

2000

Mary Katherine Lanzillotta
Andrew Travis Smith

2001

J. Scott Busby
P. Thomas M. Harboe
Jeffry Lee Kagermeier
Elizabeth Chu Richter
George A. Takoudes

2002

Randy G. Brown
Barbara Campagna
Mohammed Lawal
Joe Scott Sandlin

2003

Lisa M. Chronister
Paul D. Mankins
Paul Neuhaus
Ronald Todd Ray
Paul Woolford

Source: The American Institute of Architects

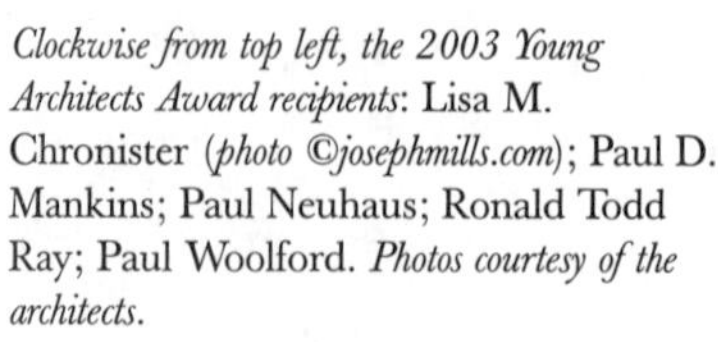

Clockwise from top left, the 2003 Young Architects Award recipients: Lisa M. Chronister (*photo ©josephmills.com*); Paul D. Mankins; Paul Neuhaus; Ronald Todd Ray; Paul Woolford. *Photos courtesy of the architects.*

3

Leadership In Design

Induction as a fellow, honorary member, or president of a professional organization is an honor that is commonly bestowed upon the industry's preeminent leaders. This chapter lists those noteworthy individuals; names in bold indicate new inductees for 2003.

Architecture Critics

Below is a listing of the major U.S. newspapers that regularly feature architectural writing and criticism. Some papers have a staff architecture critic while others an art critic or critic-at-large that routinely cover architecture stories for the paper.

Arizona Republic

John Carlos Billani
Art & Architecture Critic
200 East Van Buren Street
Phoenix, AZ 85004
Tel: (602) 444-8000
Internet: www.arizonarepublic.com

Atlanta Journal-Constitution

Catherine Fox
Architecture Critic
PO Box 4689
Atlanta, GA 30302
Tel: (404) 526-5151
Internet: www.ajc.com

Austin American-Statesman

Michael Barnes
Arts Critic
PO Box 670
Austin, TX 78767
Tel: (512) 445-3500
Internet: www.statesman.com

Baltimore Sun

Edward Gunts
Architecture Critic
501 N. Calvert Street
P.O. Box 1377
Baltimore, MD 21278
Tel: (410) 332-6000
Internet: www.baltimoresun.com

Bergen Record

John Zeaman
Art Critic
150 River Street
Hackensack, NJ 07601
Tel: (201) 646-4000
Internet: www.bergen.com

Boston Globe

Robert Campbell
Architecture Critic
135 Morrissey Blvd.
Boston, MA 02107
Tel: (617) 929-2000
Internet: www.boston.com

Boston Herald

David Eisen
Architecture Critic
One Herald Square
P.O. Box 2096
Boston, MA 02106
Tel: (617) 426-3000
Internet: www.bostonherald.com

Charleston Post and Courier

Robert Behre
Architecture & Preservation Critic
134 Columbus Street
Charleston, SC 29403-4800
Tel: (843) 577-7111
Internet: www.charleston.net

Charlotte Observer

Richard Maschal
Visual Arts Editor
600 S. Tryon Street
Charlotte, NC 28202
Tel: (704) 358-5000
Internet: www.charlotte.com

Chicago Tribune

Blair Kamin
Architecture Critic
435 N. Michigan Avenue
Chicago, IL 60611
Tel: (312) 222-3232
Internet: www.chicagotribune.com

Architecture Critics

Cleveland Plain Dealer
Steve Lit
Art & Architecture Critic
700 West St. Clair Avenue
Suite 414
Cleveland, OH 44113
Tel: (216) 515-2525
Internet: www.cleveland.com

Dallas Morning News
David Dillon
Architecture Critic
P.O. Box 655237
Dallas, TX 75265
Tel: (214) 977-8222
Internet: www.dallasnews.com

Dayton Daily News
Ron Rollins
Critic-at-Large
45 S. Ludlow Street
Dayton, OH 45402
Tel: (937) 225-2000
Internet: www.daytondailynews.com

Denver Post
Kyle MacMillan
Critic-at-Large
1560 Broadway
Denver, CO 80202
Tel: (303) 820-1201
Internet: www.denverpost.com

Detroit Free Press
John Gallagher
Architecture Critic
600 Fort
Detroit, MI 48226
Tel: (313) 222-6400
Internet: www.freep.com

Los Angeles Times
Nicolai Ouroussoff
Architecture Critic
202 West 1st Street
Los Angeles, CA 90012
Tel: (213) 237-5000
Internet: www.latimes.com

Louisville Courier-Journal
Diane Heilenman
Art Critic
525 W. Broadway
P.O. Box 740031
Louisville, KY 40201
Tel: (502) 582-4011
Internet: www.courier-journal.com

Milwaukee Journal Sentinel
Whitney Gould
Urban Landscape Writer
P.O. Box 661
Milwaukee, WI 53201
Tel: (414) 224-2358
Internet: www.jsonline.com

Minneapolis Star-Tribune
Linda Mack
Architecture Critic
425 Portland Avenue
Minneapolis, MN 55488
Tel: (612) 673-4000
Internet: www.startribune.com

New York Times
Herbert Muschamp
Architecture Critic
229 43rd Street
New York, NY 10036
Tel: (212) 556-1234
Internet: www.nytimes.com

Architecture Critics

New Yorker
Paul Goldberger
Architecture Critic
4 Times Square
New York, NY 10036
Tel: (212) 286-5400
Internet: www.newyorker.com

Newark Star-Ledger
Dan Bischoff
Art Critic
1 Star-Ledger Plaza
Newark, NJ 07102
Tel: (973) 392-4141
Internet: www.starledger.com

Newport News Daily Press
Mark Erickson
Critic-at-Large/Reporter
7505 Warwick Boulevard
Newport News, VA 23607
Tel: (757) 247-4800
Internet: www.dailypress.com

Philadelphia Inquirer
Inga Saffron
Architecture Critic
400 N. Broad Street
P.O. Box 8263
Philadelphia, PA 19101
Tel: (215) 854-2000
Internet: www.phillynews.com

Pittsburgh Post-Gazette
Patricia Lowry
Architecture Critic
34 Blvd. of the Allies
Pittsburgh, PA 15222
Tel: (412) 263-1100
Internet: www.post-gazette.com

Portland Oregonian
Randy Gragg
Architecture Critic
1320 SW Broadway
Portland, OR 97201
Tel: (503) 221-8327
Internet: www.oregonian.com

Providence Journal
Bill Van Siclen
Art Critic
75 Fountain Street
Providence, RI 02902
Tel: (401) 277-7000
Internet: www.projo.com

Raleigh News & Observer
Caitlin Cleary
Visual Arts Critic
215 S. McDowell Street
P.O. Box 191
Raleigh, NC 27601
Tel: (919) 829-4500
Internet: www.news-observer.com

Rocky Mountain News
Mary Voelz Chandler
Art & Architecture Critic
400 West Colfax Avenue
Denver, CO 80204
Tel: (303) 892-5000
Internet: www.rockymountainnews.com

San Antonio Express-News
Mike Greenberg
Arts & Entertainment Critic
Avenue E & 3rd Street
San Antonio, TX 78205
Tel: (210) 250-3000
Internet: www.mysanantonio.com

Architecture Critics

San Diego Union-Tribune
Ann Jarmusch
Architecture Critic
P.O. Box 120191
San Diego, CA 92112
Tel: (619) 299-3131
Internet: www.signonsandiego.com

San Francisco Chronicle
John King
Urban Design Writer
901 Mission Street
San Francisco, CA 94103
Tel: (415) 777-1111
Internet: www.sfgate.com

San Jose Mercury News
Alan Hess
Architecture Writer
750 Ridder Park Drive
San Jose, CA 95190
Tel: (408) 920-5000
Internet: www.bayarea.com

Seattle Post-Intelligencer
Sheri Olson
Architecture Columnist
P.O. Box 1909
Seattle, WA 98111-1909
Tel: (206) 448-8000
Internet: http://seattlepi.nwsource.com

Seattle Times
Linda Parrish
Home & Garden Critic
1120 John Street
Seattle, WA 98109
Tel: (206) 464-2111
Internet: www.seattletimes.nwsource.com

South Florida Sun-Sentinel
Matt Schudell
Art & Architecture Critic
200 E. Las Olas Blvd
Ft. Lauderdale, FL 33301
Tel: (954) 356-4000
Internet: www.sun-sentinel.com

St. Paul Pioneer Press
Don Effenberger
Architecture Critic
345 Cedar Street
St. Paul, MN 55101
Tel: (651) 222-1111
Internet: www.twincities.com

Wall Street Journal
Ada Louise Huxtable
Architecture Critic
200 Liberty Street
New York, NY 10281
Tel: (212) 416-2000
Internet: http://online.wsj.com

Washington Post
Ben Forgey
Architecture Critic
1150 15th Street NW
Washington, DC 20071
Tel: (202) 334-6000
Internet: www.washingtonpost.com

Source: Counsel House Research

Chancellors of The American Institute of Architects' College of Fellows

Since the founding of The American Institute of Architects' College of Fellows in 1952, the Chancellor is elected, now annually, by the Fellows to preside over the College's investiture ceremonies and business affairs.

1952-53	Ralph Thomas Walker
1954-55	Alexander C. Robinson III
1956	Edgar I. Williams
1957-60	Roy F. Larson
1961-62	Morris Ketchum
1963-64	Paul Thiry
1965-66	George Holmes Perkins
1967-68	Norman J. Schlossman
1969-70	John Noble Richards
1971-72	Jefferson Roy Carroll Jr.
1973	Ulysses Floyd Rible
1974	Albert S. Golemon
1975	Robert S. Hutchins
1976	William Bachman
1977	Philip J. Meathe
1978	George Edward Kassabaum
1979	David Arthur Pugh
1980	Robert L. Durham
1981	Leslie N. Boney Jr.
1982	William Robert Jarratt
1983	William C. Muchow
1984	Bernard B. Rothschild
1985	Donald L. Hardison
1986	Vladimir Ossipoff
1987	S. Scott Ferebee Jr.
1988	C. William Brubaker
1989	Preston Morgan Bolton
1990	William A. Rose Jr.
1991	Robert B. Marquis
1992	L. Jane Hastings
1993	John A. Busby Jr.
1994	Thomas H. Teasdale
1995	Robert T. Coles
1996	Ellis W. Bullock Jr.
1997	Jack DeBartolo Jr.
1998	Harold L. Adams
1999	Jimmy D. Tittle
2000	Robert A. Odermatt
2001	Harold Roth
2002	C. James Lawler
2003	Sylvester Damianos
2004	Betsey Olenick Dougherty

Source: The American Institute of Architects

Fellows of the American Academy in Rome

Every year the American Academy in Rome grants fellowships to study and work in Rome at the Academy's center for independent study, advanced research, and creative work. Also known as the Rome Prize, the fellowships are granted in a broad range of fields including design, music, literature, and archaeology. The following individuals have been the recipients of the Rome Prize for design related disciplines.

Architecture

Stanley Abercrombie, FAAR'83
Kimberly A. Ackert, FAAR'97
Rachel Allen, FAAR'03
Anthony Ames, FAAR'84
Joseph Amisano, FAAR'52
Amy Anderson, FAAR'81
Ross S. Anderson, FAAR'90
Richard W. Ayers, FAAR'38
Clarence Dale Badgeley, FAAR'29
Gregory S. Baldwin, FAAR'71
Marc Balet, FAAR'75
Richard Bartholomew, FAAR'72
Frederick Blehle, FAAR'87
James L. Bodnar, FAAR'80
Thomas L. Bosworth, FAAR'81
Charles G. Brickbauer, FAAR'57
Cecil C. Briggs, FAAR'31
Turner Brooks, FAAR'84
Andrea Clark Brown, FAAR'80
Theodore L. Brown, FAAR'88
William Bruder, FAAR'87
Marvin Buchanan, FAAR'76
Walker O. Cain, FAAR'48
Peter Carl, FAAR'76
Daniel Castor, FAAR'98
Judith Chafee, FAAR'77
Coleman Coker, FAAR'96
Caroline B. Constant, FAAR'79
Frederic S. Coolidge, FAAR'48
Roger Crowley, FAAR'85
Teddy Edwin Cruz, FAAR'92
Thomas V. Czarnowski, FAAR'68
Royston T. Daley, FAAR'62
Spero Daltas, FAAR'51
J. Yolande Daniels, FAAR'04
Douglas Darden, FAAR'89
Thomas L. Dawson, FAAR'52
Joseph De Pace, FAAR'85
Andrea O. Dean, FAAR'80
Kathryn Dean, FAAR'87
Judith Di Maio, FAAR'78
Ronald L. Dirsmith, FAAR'60
Robert Ward Evans, FAAR'73
James Favaro, FAAR'86
Ronald C. Filson, FAAR'70
Garrett S. Finney, FAAR'95
Mark M. Foster, FAAR'84
Robert M. Golder, FAAR'63
Michael L. Goorevich, FAAR'01
Alexander C. Gorlin, FAAR'84
Michael Graves, FAAR'62, RAAR'78
James A. Gresham, FAAR'56
Brand Norman Griffin, FAAR'74
Olindo Grossi, FAAR'36
Michael Gruber, FAAR'96
Michael Guran, FAAR'71
Steven Harby, FAAR'00
George E. Hartman, FAAR'78, RAAR'96
John D. Heimbaugh, Jr., FAAR'70
Margaret Helfand, FAAR'03
George A. Hinds, FAAR'84
Peter Hopprier, FAAR'77
Elizabeth Humstone, FAAR'86
Sanda D. Iliescu, FAAR'95
Franklin D. Israel, FAAR'75
Erling F. Iversen
David J. Jacob, FAAR'58, RAAR'71
Allan B. Jacobs, FAAR'86, RAAR'96
James R. Jarrett, FAAR'59
E. Fay Jones, FAAR'81
Wesley Jones, FAAR'86
Wendy Evans Joseph, FAAR'84
Henri V. Jova, FAAR'51

Fellows of the American Academy in Rome

Robert Kahn, FAAR'82
Spence Kass, FAAR'81
Stephen J. Kieran, FAAR'81
Alexander Kitchin, FAAR'02
Grace R. Kobayashi, FAAR'90
Johannes M.P. Knoops, FAAR'00
Peter Kommers, FAAR'76
Eugene Kupper, FAAR'83
James R. Lamantia, FAAR'49
James L. Lambeth, FAAR'79
Gary Larson, FAAR'83
Thomas N. Larson, FAAR'64
John Q. Lawson, FAAR'81
David L. Leavitt, FAAR'50
Celia Ledbetter, FAAR'83
Diane Lewis, FAAR'77
Paul Lewis, FAAR'99
Roy W. Lewis, FAAR'86
George T. Licht, FAAR'37
Theodore Liebman, FAAR'66
Robert S. Livesey, FAAR'75
John H. MacFadyen, FAAR'54
Robert Mangurian, FAAR'77
Tallie B. Maule, FAAR'52
Arthur May, FAAR'76
David Mayernik, FAAR'89
John J. McDonald, FAAR'83
William G. McMinn, FAAR'82
Cameron McNall, FAAR'92
D. Blake Middleton, FAAR'82
Henry D. Mirick, FAAR'33
Robert Mittelstadt, FAAR'66
Grover E. Mouton III, FAAR'73
Vincent Mulcahy, FAAR'77
Anne Munly, FAAR'96
Theodore J. Musho, FAAR'61
Robert Myers, FAAR'54
John Naughton, FAAR'85
Richard M. Olcott, FAAR'04
Stanley H. Pansky, FAAR'53
William Pedersen, FAAR'66
Charles O. Perry, FAAR'66
Warren A. Peterson, FAAR'55
Thomas M. Phifer, FAAR'96
Warren Platner, FAAR'56
Linda Pollak, FAAR'04
Kelly D. Powell, FAAR'02
Antoine S. Predock, FAAR'85
George L. Queral, FAAR'88
Patrick J. Quinn, FAAR'80
Jason H. Ramos, FAAR'91
William Reed, FAAR'68
Walter L. Reichardt, FAAR'33
Jesse Reiser, FAAR'85
Richard Rosa, FAAR'99
Peter Miller Schmitt, FAAR'72
Thomas L. Schumacher, FAAR'69, RAAR'91
J. Michael Schwarting, FAAR'70
Frederic D. Schwartz, FAAR'85
Daniel V. Scully, FAAR'70
Catherine Seavitt, FAAR'98
Werner Seligmann, FAAR'81
Thomas Silva, FAAR'89
Jorge Silvetti, FAAR'86
Thomas G. Smith, FAAR'80
Barbara Stauffacher Solomon, FAAR'83
Friedrich St. Florian, FAAR'85
Charles Stifter, FAAR'63
James S. Stokoe, FAAR'79
John J. Stonehill, FAAR'60
Richard Taransky, FAAR'01
Wayne Taylor, FAAR'62
Milo H. Thompson, FAAR'65
Duane Thorbeck, FAAR'64
Evelyn Tickle, FAAR'02
James Timberlake, FAAR'83
Robert H. Timme, FAAR'86
Fred Travisano, FAAR'82
William Turnbull, Jr., FAAR'80
James Velleco, FAAR'77
Robert Venturi, FAAR'56
Austris J. Vitols, FAAR'67
Peter D. Waldman, FAAR'00
Craig H. Walton, FAAR'82

Fellows of the American Academy in Rome

Robert A. Weppner, Jr., FAAR'36
Nichole Wiedemann, FAAR'97
Charles D. Wiley, FAAR'48
Tod Williams, FAAR'83
Andrew Zago, FAAR'03
Christian Zapatka, FAAR'91
Astra Zarina, FAAR'63

Landscape Architecture

Eric Armstrong, FAAR'61
E. Bruce Baetjer, FAAR'54
Julie Bargmann, FAAR'90
Cheryl Barton, FAAR'04
Richard C. Bell, FAAR'53, RAAR'75
Stephen F. Bochkor, FAAR'57
Elise Brewster, FAAR'98
Robert T. Buchanan, FAAR'59
Richard Burck, FAAR'82
Vincent C. Cerasi, FAAR'50
Henri E. Chabanne, FAAR'34
Linda J. Cook, FAAR'89
Joanna Dougherty, FAAR'86
F. W. Edmondson, FAAR'48
Jon S. Emerson, FAAR'67
Eric Reid Fulford, FAAR'92
Ralph E. Griswold, FAAR'23
Edgar C. Haag, FAAR'79
Robert Mitchell Hanna, FAAR'76
Stephen C. Haus, FAAR'79
Dale H. Hawkins, FAAR'52
Elizabeth Dean Hermann, FAAR'87
Gary R. Hilderbrand, FAAR'95
Walter Hood, FAAR'97
Alden Hopkins, FAAR'35
Dr. Frank D. James, FAAR'68
Dean A. Johnson, FAAR'66
Mary Margaret Jones, FAAR'98
Joel Katz, FAAR'03
John F. Kirkpatrick, FAAR'39
Robert S. Kitchen, FAAR'38
Mark Klopfer, FAAR'01
Albert R. Lamb, III, FAAR'70
Edward Lawson, FAAR'21
Tom Leader, FAAR'99
James M. Lister, FAAR'37
Alex S. MacLean, FAAR'04
Roger B. Martin, FAAR'64
Laurel McSherry, FAAR'00
Stuart M. Mertz, FAAR'40
David Meyer, FAAR'01
Stacy T. Moriarty, FAAR'84
Richard C. Murdock, FAAR'33
Norman T. Newton, FAAR'26, RAAR-67
Peter O'Shea, FAAR'96
Laurie D. Olin, FAAR'74, RAAR'90
Don H. Olson, FAAR'62
Peter Osler, FAAR'02
Thomas R. Oslund, FAAR'92
Nell H. Park, FAAR'33
George E. Patton, FAAR'51
Paul R. V. Pawlowski, FAAR'69
Peter M. Pollack, FAAR'71
Thomas D. Price, FAAR'32
Joseph Ragsdale, FAAR'04
Charles A. Rapp, FAAR'72
Michael Rapuano, FAAR'30
Peter G. Rolland, FAAR'78
Leslie A. Ryan, FAAR'95
Peter Lindsay Schaudt, FAAR'91
Terry Schnadelbach, FAAR'66
Seth H. Seablom, FAAR'68
Stephen Sears, FAAR'00
A. Paul Seck, FAAR'03
Charles Sullivan, FAAR'85
Jack Sullivan, FAAR'83
Charles R. Sutton, FAAR'32
Erik A. Svenson, FAAR'58
Andrew Thanh-Son Cao, FAAR'02
L. Azeo Torre, FAAR'76
Morris E. Trotter, FAAR'35
James R. Turner, FAAR'76
Daniel Tuttle, FAAR'88
Michael R. Van Valkenburgh, FAAR'88
E. Michael Vergason, FAAR'80

Fellows of the American Academy in Rome

Craig P. Verzone, FAAR'99
Richard K. Webel, FAAR'29, RAAR'63
James L. Wescoat Jr., FAAR'97
Brooks E. Wigginton, FAAR'50
Gall Wittwer, FAAR'96
John L. Wong, FAAR'81
Prof. Ervin H. Zube, FAAR'61

Historic Preservation and Conservation

Elmo Baca, FAAR'00
Charles A. Birnbaum, FAAR'04
Prof. Margaret Holben Ellis, FAAR'94
Shelley Fletcher, FAAR'98
Eric Gordon, FAAR'97
Eleanor Esser Gorski, FAAR'03
Randolph Langenbach, FAAR'03
Anne Frances Maheux, FAAR'96
T.K. McClintock, FAAR'04
Pablo Ojeda-O'Neill, FAAR'96
Alice Boccia Paterakis, FAAR'00
Leslie Rainer, FAAR'99
Bettina A. Raphael, FAAR'94
Elizabeth Riorden, FAAR'02
Thomas C. Roby, FAAR'95
Catherine Sease, FAAR'95
Ellen Phillips Soroka, FAAR'02
Prof. Frederick Steiner, FAAR'98
Jonathan Thorton, FAAR'99
Elizabeth Walmsley, FAAR'01
Dr. George Wheeler, FAAR'97
Deirdre Windsor, FAAR'01

Design Arts

William Adair, FAAR'92
Gerald D. Adams, FAAR'68
Donald Albrecht, FAAR'03
Thomas Angotti, FAAR'90
Donald Appleyard, FAAR'75
Joseph H. Aronson, FAAR'74
Morley Baer, FAAR'80
Gordon C. Baldwin, FAAR'78
Phillip R. Baldwin, FAAR'94
Karen Bausman, FAAR'95
Ellen Beasley, FAAR'89
Anna Campbell Bliss, FAAR'84
Robert W. Braunschweiger, FAAR'74
Paul M. Bray, FAAR'97
Steven Brooke, FAAR'91
Michael B. Cadwell, FAAR'99
Heather Carson, FAAR'99
John J. Casbarian, FAAR'86, FAIA
Adele Chatfield-Taylor, FAAR'84
Walter Chatham, FAAR'89
Morison S. Cousins, FAAR'85
Russell Rowe Culp, FAAR'80
Phoebe Cutler, FAAR'89
Joseph Paul D'Urso, FAAR'88
Paul Davis, FAAR'98
Robert S. Davis, FAAR'91
Robert De Fuccio, FAAR'76
Robert Regis Dvorak, FAAR'72
William H. Fain Jr., FAAR'02
Hsin-ming Fung, FAAR'92
Jeanne Giordano, FAAR'87
Miller Horns, FAAR'90
Robert Jensen, FAAR'76
June Meyer Jordan, FAAR'71
Wendy Kaplan, FAAR'00
J. Michael Kirkland, FAAR'70
Robert Kramer, FAAR'72
George Krause, FAAR'77, RAAR'80
Lisa Krohn, FAAR'01
Reed Kroloff, FAAR'04
Norman Krumholz, FAAR'87
Michael Lax, FAAR'78
Debra McCall, FAAR'89
R. Alan Melting, FAAR'70
Donald Oenslager
Michael Palladino, FAAR'01
Donald Peting, FAAR'78
William L. Plumb, FAAR'86
William Reed, FAAR'68
Julie Riefler, FAAR'87

Fellows of the American Academy in Rome

Mark Robbins, FAAR'97
Michael Rock, FAAR'00
Danny M. Samuels, FAAR'86
Mark Schimmenti, FAAR'98
Paul D. Schwartzman, FAAR'77
Paul Shaw, FAAR'02
William V. Shaw, FAAR'68
Alison Sky, FAAR'78
Paul L. Steinberg, FAAR'82
Joel Sternfeld, FAAR'91
Michelle Stone, FAAR'78
Marc Treib, FAAR'85
Kevin Walz, FAAR'95
Edward Weinberger, FAAR'03
Emily M. Whiteside, FAAR'82
Janet Zweig, FAAR'92

FAAR = Fellow of the American Academy in Rome
RAAR = Resident of the American Academy in Rome

Source: American Academy in Rome

Fellows of the American Academy of Arts and Sciences

Since its founding in 1780, the American Academy of Arts and Sciences has pursued its goal "To cultivate every art and science which may tend to advance the interest, honor, dignity, and happiness of a free, independent, and virtuous people." Throughout its history, the Academy's diverse membership has included the best from the arts, science, business, scholarship, and public affairs. Nominations for new members are taken from existing fellows and evaluated by panels from each discipline and the membership at large.

Design Professionals, Academics, and Writers

Christopher Alexander '96
U. of Calif., Berkeley

Edward Larrabee Barnes '78
Edward Larrabee Barnes/
John M. Y. Lee Architects, New York

Herbert Lawrence Block '59
Washington, D.C.

Robert Campbell '93
Cambridge, MA

Henry Nichols Cobb '84
Pei, Cobb, Freed & Partners, New York, NY

Peter D. Eisenman '00
Eisenman Architects, New York, NY

Kenneth Frampton '93
Columbia University

James Ingo Freed '94
Pei, Cobb, Freed & Partners, New York, NY

Frank Owen Gehry '91
Frank O. Gehry and Assoc., Santa Monica, CA

Lawrence Halprin '78
San Francisco, CA

Steven Holl '02
Steven Holl Architects, New York, NY

Robert S.F. Hughes '93
Time Magazine

Ada Louise Huxtable '74
New York, NY

Philip Johnson '77
Philip Johnson Architects, New York, NY

Gerhard Michael Kallmann '85
Kallmann, McKinnell and Wood, Architects, Inc., Boston, MA

(Noel) Michael McKinnell '85
Kallmann, McKinnell and Wood, Architects, Inc., Boston, MA

Richard Alan Meier '95
New York, NY

Henry Armand Millon '75
National Gallery of Art, Washington, D.C.

William Mitchell '97
Massachusetts Institute of Technology

I(eoh) M(ing) Pei '67
Pei, Cobb, Freed & Partners, New York, NY

James Polshek '02
Polshek Partnership Architects, LLP, New York, NY

Kevin Roche '94
Hamden, CT

Robert Rosenblum '84
New York University

Moshe Safdie '96
Moshe Safdie & Assoc., Sommerville, MA

Denise Scott Brown '93
Venturi Scott Brown & Assoc., Inc., Philadelphia

Vincent J. Scully '86
Yale University

Hugh Asher-Stubbins '57
Ocean Ridge, FL

Fellows of the American Academy of Arts and Sciences

Robert Venturi '84
Venturi Scott Brown & Assoc., Inc., Philadelphia

Foreign Honorary Members

Charles Correa '93
Bombay, India

Carl Theodor Dreyer '65
Copenhagen, Denmark

Norman Robert Foster '96
Foster and Associates, London

Phyllis Lambert '95
Center Canadien d'Architecture, Montreal, Quebec

Ricardo Legorreta '94
Mexico City, Mexico

Fumihiko Maki '96
Maki and Associates, Tokyo, Japan

J. Rafael Moneo '93
Harvard University

Oscar Niemeyer '49
Rio de Janeiro, Brazil

Renzo Piano '93
London, England

Alvaro Siza '92
Porto, Portugal

Kenzo Tange '67
Tokyo, Japan

Source: American Academy of Arts and Sciences

Fellows of the American Council of Engineering Companies

Fellowship in the American Council of Engineering Companies (ACEC) is open to any individual who has been a principal in a member firm for five or more years; has served ACEC as an officer, director or active committee member or has served a Member Organization as an officer or director; and has notably contributed to the advancement of consulting engineering in administrative leadership, design, science, by literature, in education, or by service to the profession.

Allen M. Acheson
A. George Adamson Jr.
William H. Addington
Frank E. Alderman
Harl P. Aldrich
Norman G. Almquist
Raymond G. Alvine
Al Anderson, WI
Al E. Anderson, CO
Harry G. Anderson
Stephen C. Anderson
Peter N. Andrews
C. Adrian Arnold
Frederick G. Aufiero
Quent Augspurger
Don Austin
John Baker
George Barnes
Michael Barrett
Robert T. Bates
Richard T. Baum
Clifton R. Baxter
Ralph W. Becker
James G. Bell
Theodore T. Bell
William I. Bigger
Wilson V. Binger
David K. Blake
Robert C. Bogart
Samuel A. Bogen
Ronald L. Bonar
Lewis A. Bosworth
Gary R. Bourne
Dwight A. Boyd
Erwin R. Breihan
Carlyle W. Briggs
Arthur N. Brooks
Jeffery M. Bross
Joseph L. Brown
Wayne H. Brown
Robert O. Bruton
Ross Bryan
Paul C. Bucknam Jr.
Dudley W. Budlong
Edmund Burke
Robert G. Burkhardt
Ion Caloger
R. Neal Campbell
Aubrey Caplan
James W. Carpenter
Charles D. Carr
Dominic B. Carrino
Daniel M. Carson
Hugh C. Carter
Robert J. Caton
M. Steve Cavanaugh Jr.
T. Z. Chastain
Fu Hua Chen
John H. Clark III
William A. Clevenger
James D. Cobb
Edward Cohen
William J. Collins Jr.
Paul E. Conrad
William H. Cooke Jr.
Philip M. Corlew
J. Richard Cottingham
Paul E. Cox
L. LeRoy Crandall
Ralph Crosby
John C. Crowser
Jeffrey M. Daggett

Fellows of the American Council of Engineering Companies

Henry Eugene Damon
David L. Davidson
Edward W. Davidson
G. Robert Davidson
Ansel L. Davis
Edward T. Davis
Ray H. Davis
Edwin K. Dedeaux
Kenneth L. Delap
Chris Demopulos
Daniel J. DeYoung
H. Boyd Dickenson
Harold Dombeck
Emery Domingue
Wallace L. Donley
Stephen E. Dore
Albert A. Dorman
J. Edward Doyle
Ronald J. Drnevich
James A. Duddlesten
James R. Duncan
Lamar Dunn
Howard C. Dutzi
Arthur A. Edwards
Carl Eiden
Stanley D. Elkerton
Clifford E. Evanson
Gilbert L. Faison
H. Ben Faulkner
John R. Fee
Harry R. Feldman
Dean R. Felton
James F. Finn
David E. Fleming
Eric L. Flicker
Harold E. Flight
Robert C. Flory
Michael E. Flynn
John H. Foster
Ronald D. Foster
William C. Freeman
E. M. Fucik
Lester Fukuda
David R. Fuller
Thomas D. Furman Jr.
Elliot H. Gage
E. B. 'Bas' Gaither
F. Vreeland George Jr.
Frank B. Gianotti III
Ralph W. Gilbert Jr.
Bruce L. Gilmore
Albert B. Gipe
William J. Glover Jr.
Stephen G. Goddard
E. Jackson Going
Donald T. Goldberg
Luther Graef
Anthony J. Grasso
Brian L. Gray
Robert F. Grimes
Paul D. Guertin
John J. Guth
Wilton N. Hammond
Philip M. Hampton
Richard E. Hangen
Brian L. Hanson
Walter E. Hanson
Joseph E. Hardee
Thomas B. Harrell Jr.
Michael J. Hartigan
Arthur F. Hartung
Eugene C. Harvey
James M. Hastings
Donald Hattery
Amy J. Haugerud
Steve M. Hays
George Heck
Alfred Hedefine
Paul L. Heineman
Joseph E. Heney
John F. Hennessy III
Marble J. Hensley Sr.
Richard J. Hesse
Robert E. Hickman
Lyle F. Hird
Robert E. Hogan
A. W. Holland
Darrel V. Holmquist
Stephen A. Holt
W. N. Holway

Fellows of the American Council of Engineering Companies

Donald E. Houser
William S. Howard
Linda L. Huff
Harold E. Hughes
Roger L. Jacobson
J. Edward Jenkins
Thomas L. Jester
Clifford W. Johnson
Derrell E. Johnson
Edmund G. Johnson
Melvin E. Jones
Ralph W. Junius Jr.
C. Hayden Kaiser Jr.
Dennis Kamber
John J. Kassner
Stanley K. Kawaguchi
Theodore S. Kawahigashi
Charles W. Keller
Chester C. Kelsey
David D. Kennedy
Todd J. Kenner
Frederick D. A. King Jr.
Edward B. Kinner
Jack Kinstlinger
George Kirgis
Gordon L. Kirjassoff
Robert C. Kirkpatrick
Donald F. Klebe
Donald H. Kline
Dag I. Knudsen
Kenneth J. Koch
James H. Konkel
Charles W. Kopplin
Emil Kordish
Michael E. Krannitz
Paul B. Krebs
James M. Kring
Donald R. LaRochelle
Calvin E. Levis
Raoul L. Levy
William D. Lewis
David H. Lillard
Frank L. Lincoln
Leon J. Lindbloom
Howard D. Linders
Joseph Lipscomb
John L. Littrell
Bruce Livingstone
C. Richard Lortz
LeRoy D. Loy
Ray Lundgren
J. L. MacFarlane
Cline L. Mansur
Paul W. Masten
Richard E. Masters
Michael P. Matsumoto
David R. Matthews
Aubrey D. May
William (Skip) H. McCombs
Kenneth A. McCord
H. Clay McEldowney
Robert McEldowney
James D. McFall
John C. McGlenn
Larry A. McKee
Robert W. McKenzie
Herbert P. McKim Jr.
Arthur W. McKinney
Raymond F. Messer
Charles A. Meyer
Vernon F. Meyer
William J. Mielke
Raymond T. Miller
Robert D. Mitchell
Thomas E. Mohler
Dayton Molzen
R. Duane Monical
Robert C. Moore
Frederick K. Mosher
W. A. Mossbarger
James (Bud) E. Moulder
Edward J. Mulcahy
Salim Najjar
Albert L. Nelson
Kenneth E. Nelson
James R. Nichols
Frank Nicoladis
E. N. Nicolaides
George K. Nishimura
Lennox K. Nishimura

Fellows of the American Council of Engineering Companies

Judith Nitsch
Jack Noblitt
David Novick
Satoshi Oishi
Stephen M. Olko
Pedro J. Ortiz-Santiago
Paul Ostergaard
R. Stanton Over
J. Hambleton Palmer
Ralph J. Palmer
Stewart R. Palmer
Joseph P. Paoluccio
S. G. Papadopoulos
Andrew J. Parker Jr.
Charles A. Parthum
J. L. Patton
Donald D. Paxton
E. J. Peltier
C. R. Pennoni
Leo F. Peters
Boyd W. Phelps
Emanuel Pisetzner
Richard Piske
Joe H. Pitts
William H. Plautz
Rex T. Pless
James M. Poché
Lester H. Poggemeyer
James W. Poirot
H. A. Pontier
Allen Poppino
Michael A. Postiglione
Richard Q. Praeger
Paul W. Prendiville
David G. Presnell Jr.
Richard E. Ragold
Stan L. Rankin
William R. Ratliff
Frederick Reusswig
Robert B. Richards
Theodore J. Richards
Louis W. Riggs
G. Michael Ritchie
Cathy S. Ritter
William J. Rizzo Jr.
Robert F. Robertson
T.B. Robinson
Elmer O. Rodes Jr.
Lawrence P. Rogoway
Sigmund Roos
Robert W. Rosene
Donald E. Ross
Donald K. Ross
David T. Rowe
Robert D. Rowland
George O. Sadler
Leo A. Santowasso
J. Gorman Schaffer
Charles E. Schaffner Jr.
Harold A. Schlenger
Paul G. Scott
James F. Shivler Jr.
William E. Short
Wayne F. Shuler
Devindar S. Sidhu
Donald J. Smally
Herman E. Smith
Lester H. Smith
Russell L. Smith Jr.
Scott S. Smith
E. Per Sorenson
William A. Sowers
James A. Speedie
Gerald E. Speitel
A J. Spiess
Gary J. Spinkelink
Paul F. Sprehe
Richard H. Stanley
David R. Stewart
Henry A. Stikes
Roger G. Stroud
Douglas F. Suess
Billy T. Sumner
Anne C. Symonds
A. J. Szabo
John P. Talerico
Russell C. Taylor
Thomas J. Terrell
James R. Thomas Jr.
Gregs G. Thomopulos

Fellows of the American Council of Engineering Companies

Donald E. Thompson
Everett S. Thompson
T. Curtiss Torrance
William A. Clevenger Torrance
Donald R. Trim
Taylor F. Turner Jr.
Jack K. Tuttle
J. Howard Van Boerum
J. E. Van Dell
Charles O. Velzy
Donald D. Vick
Carlos C. Villarrceal
Robert C. Wade
Sam H. Wainwright
Robert A. Waitkus
Richard O. Walker Jr.
F. Spencer Weber
William W. Webster
Vernon M. Wegerer
Victor Weidmann
Richard Weingardt
John P. Weir
Robert G. Werden
Robert D. Wesselink
Lewis H. West
Richard B. Wetzel
Brian R. Whiston
H. Kenneth White
Ronald R. White
Charles K. Whitescarver Jr.
Eugene R. Wilkinson
Jerald A. Williams
Richard L. Williams
Harry M. Wilson
Arnold L. Windman
Douglas G. Wolfangle
Riley D. Woodsen
Thomas D. Wosser
Kenneth R. Wright
Robert G. Wright
Theodore E. Wynne
L. Carl Yates

Source: American Council of Engineering Companies

Fellows of The American Institute of Architects

The College of Fellows of The American Institute of Architects (AIA) is composed of AIA members who have been elected to Fellowship by a jury of their peers. Fellowship is granted for significant contributions to architecture and society and for achieving a high standard of professional excellence. Architect members who have been in good standing for at least 10 years may be nominated for Fellowship. The following individuals are current active members of The American Institute of Architects' College of Fellows.

A

Carlton S. Abbott, Williamsburg, VA
J. C. Abbott Jr., Sarasota, FL
James Abell, Tempe, AZ
Jan M. Abell, Tampa, FL
Stephen N. Abend, Kansas City, MO
Bruce A. Abrahamson, Minneapolis, MN
Max Abramovitz, Pound Ridge, NY
Raymond C. Abst, Modesto, CA
Harold L. Adams, Baltimore, MD
William M. Adams, Venice, CA
William T. Adams, Dallas, TX
Michael Adlerstein, New York, NY
Antonin Aeck, Atlanta, GA
P. Aguirre Jr., Dallas, TX
Loren P. Ahles, Minneapolis, MN
Thomas R. Aidala, San Francisco, CA
Roula Alakiotou, Chicago, IL
Charles A Albanese, Tucson, AZ
Richard K. Albyn, Pisgah Forest, NC
N. Sue Alden, Seattle, WA
Iris S. Alex, New York, NY
Cecil A. Alexander Jr., Atlanta, GA
Earle S. Alexander Jr., Houston, TX
Henry C. Alexander Jr., Coral Gables, FL
James G. Alexander, Boston, MA
A. Notley Alford, Englewood, FL
Stanley N. Allan, Chicago, IL
Maurice B. Allen Jr., Bloomfield Hills, MI
Ralph G. Allen, Chicago, IL
Rex W. Allen, Sonoma, CA
Robert E. Allen, San Francisco, CA
Robert E. Allen, Longview, TX
Susan Allen, Morgantown, IN
Gerald L. Allison, Newport Beach, CA
James V. Allred, Reston, VA
Killis P. Almond Jr., San Antonio, TX
Alfred S. Alschuler, Highland Park, IL
Ronald A. Altoon, Los Angeles, CA
Jesus E. Amaral, San Juan, Puerto Rico
Joseph Amisano, Atlanta, GA
Gregg D. Ander, Irwindale, CA
Dorman D. Anderson, Seattle, WA
Harry F. Anderson, Oakbrook, IL
J. Timothy Anderson, Cambridge, MA
John D. Anderson, Denver, CO
Richard Anderson, Tucson, AZ
Ross S. Anderson, New York, NY
Samuel A. Anderson, Charlottesville, VA
William L. Anderson, Des Moines, IA
J. Philip Andrews, Pittsburgh, PA
Lavone D. Andrews, Houston, TX
Martha P. Andrews, Portland, OR
Charles Angyal, San Diego, CA
George Anselevicius, Albuquerque, NM
James H. Anstis, West Palm Beach, FL
Natalye Appel, Houston, TX
Richard M. Archer, San Antonio, TX
Peter F. Arfaa, Philadelphia, PA
Bruce P. Arneill, Glastonbury, CT
Chris Arnold, Palo Alto, CA
Christopher C. Arnold, Commerce Twp., MI
Robert V. Arrigoni, San Francisco, CA
J. Tom Ashley III, Lower Rio Grande, Mexico
Yvonne W. Asken, Portage, MI
Laurin B. Askew, Columbia, MD
Lee Hewlett Askew III, Memphis, TN
Neil L. Astle, Salt Lake City, UT
Louis D. Astorino, Pittsburgh, PA
Charles H. Atherton, Washington, DC
Tony Atkin, Philadelphia, PA
James B. Atkins, Dallas, TX
John L. Atkins, Research Triangle Park, NC
Eugene E. Aubry, Holmes Beach, FL
Seymour Auerbach, Chevy Chase, MD
Douglas H. Austin, San Diego, CA
Daniel Avchen, Minneapolis, MN
Donald C. Axon, Laguna Beach, CA
Alfred L. Aydelott, Carmel, CA

B

Howard J. Backen, Sausalito, CA
Edmund N. Bacon, Philadelphia, PA
David C. Baer, Houston, TX
Stuart Baesel, La Jolla, CA
Deon F. Bahr, Lincoln, NE

Fellows of The American Institute of Architects

Ray B. Bailey, Houston, TX
William J. Bain Jr., Seattle, WA
Royden Stanley Bair, Houston, TX
Louis J. Bakanowsky, Cambridge, MA
David Baker, San Francisco, CA
Isham O. Baker, Washington, DC
Jack Sherman Baker, Champaign, IL
James Barnes Baker, London, England
Josiah (Jay) Baker, Houston, TX
Gregory S. Baldwin, Portland, OR
Samuel T. Balen, Waldport, OR
Rex M. Ball, Tulsa, OK
Richard S. Banwell, Walnut Creek, CA
Shalom S. Baranes, Washington, DC
Robert A. Barclay, Cleveland, OH
Paul H. Barkley, Falls Church, VA
John M. Barley, II, Jacksonville, FL
Charles C. Barlow, Jackson, MS
William Lewis Barlow IV, Marblehead, MA
Edward L. Barnes, Cambridge, MA
Linda Barnes, Portland, OR
Rebecca Barnes, Boston, MA
Jay William Barnes Jr., Austin, TX
Jonathan Barnett, Washington, DC
Carol R. Barney, Chicago, IL
Howard R. Barr, Austin, TX
Raj Barr-Kumar, Washington, DC
Nolan E. Barrick, Lubbock, TX
Errol Barron, New Orleans, LA
Richard E. Barrow, Birmingham, AL
Richard W. Bartholomew, Philadelphia, PA
Armand Bartos, New York, NY
Edward C. Bassett, Mill Valley, CA
Fred Bassetti, Seattle, WA
Peter Batchelor, Raleigh, NC
Ronald J. Battaglia, Buffalo, NY
Jay S. Bauer, Newport Beach, CA
Edward Baum, Dallas, TX
Joseph D. Bavaro, Punta Gorda, FL
John Craig Beale, Dallas, TX
Burtch W. Beall Jr., Salt Lake City, UT
Leroy E. Bean, Petaluma, CA
Alan J. Beard, Portland, OR
Lee P. Bearsch, Binghamton, NY
William H. Beaty, Memphis, TN
William B. Bechhoefer, Bethesda, MD
Lee Becker, Washington, DC
Rex L. Becker, St. Louis, MO
Herbert Beckhard, New York, NY
Robert M. Beckley, Ann Arbor, MI
Michael Bednar, Charlottesville, VA
Carmi Bee, New York, NY
David W. Beer, New York, NY
Edgar C. Beery, Springfield, VA
Ann M. Beha, Boston, MA
Byron Bell, New York, NY
Frederic Bell, Long Island City, NY
M. Wayne Bell, Austin, TX
John Belle, New York, NY
Anthony Belluschi, Chicago, IL
Ralph C. Bender, San Antonio, TX
Barry Benepe, New York, NY
Daniel D. Bennett, Fayetteville, AR
David J. Bennett, Minneapolis, MN
Carol Rusche Bentel, Locust Valley, NY
Frederick R. Bentel, Locust Valley, NY
Maria A. Bentel, Locust Valley, NY
Paul Louis Bentel, Locust Valley, NY
Kenneth E. Bentsen, Houston, TX
Frederick J. Bentz, Minneapolis, MN
Karl A. Berg, Denver, CO
Richard R. Bergmann, New Canaan, CT
Lloyd F. Bergquist, Bloomington, MN
Robert J. Berkebile, Kansas City, MO
Marlene J. Berkoff, San Rafael, CA
Anthony N. Bernheim, San Francisco, CA
Phillip Bernstein, New Haven, CT
K. Norman Berry, Louisville, KY
Richard J. Bertman, Boston, MA
Ronald P. Bertone, Middletown, NJ
Frederic A. Bertram, Clearwater, FL
Hobart Betts, Sag Harbor, NY
William Bevins, Charleston, WV
John H. Beyer, New York, NY
William Beyer, Minneapolis, MN
John H. Bickel, Louisville, KY
Frederick C. Biebesheimer, III, Old Lyme, CT
T. J. Biggs, Jackson, MS
Rebecca L. Binder, Playa Del Rey, CA
James Binkley, Arlington, VA
Lance L. Bird, Pasadena, CA
John R. Birge, Omaha, NE
Gunnar Birkerts, Bloomfield Hills, MI
James A. Bishop, Bellville, TX
George Bissell, Newport Beach, CA
Georgia Bizios, Chapel Hill, NC
J. Sinclair Black, Austin, TX
Walter S. Blackburn, Indianapolis, IN
Leonard D. Blackford, Sacramento, CA
Bruce E. Blackmer, Spokane, WA
Jan Gaede Blackmon, Dallas, TX
Boyd A. Blackner, Salt Lake City, UT
Peter Blake, Riverdale, NY
Frederick A. Bland, New York, NY
Wilfred E. Blessing, Oak Harbor, WA
Richard L. Blinder, New York, NY
Richard L. Bliss, Kirkwood, MO
Robert L. Bliss, Salt Lake City, UT
Ronald B. Blitch, New Orleans, LA
Timothy Brent Blonkvist, San Antonio, TX

Fellows of The American Institute of Architects

John D. Bloodgood, Des Moines, IA
Martin Bloomenthal, Princeton, NJ
Sigmund F. Blum, Naples, FL
Susan Blumentals, Brooklyn Center, MN
H. M. Blumer, Paradise Valley, AZ
Kirk V. Blunck, Des Moines, IA
William A. Blunden, Cleveland, OH
William E. Blurock, Newport Beach, CA
William Bobenhausen, Norwalk, CT
L. Kirkpatrick Bobo, Memphis, TN
Michael L. Bobrow, Los Angeles, CA
Bruce T. Bockstael, Hartford, CT
William N. Bodouva, New York, NY
Joe Boehning, Albuquerque, NM
Robert J. Boerema, Gainesville, FL
Joseph Boggs, Annapolis, MD
Walter F. Bogner, Larchmont, NY
Peter Bohlin, Wilkes Barre, PA
Friedrich K.M. Bohm, Columbus, OH
Mario H. Boiardi, Washington, DC
Stanley G. Boles, Portland, OR
Michael E. Bolinger, Baltimore, MD
Robert D. Bolling, Torrance, CA
Antonio R. Bologna, Memphis, TN
Preston M. Bolton, Houston, TX
James R. Bonar, Los Angeles, CA
J. Max Bond Jr., New York, NY
Charles Hussey Boney, Wilmington, NC
Leslie N. Boney Jr., Wilmington, NC
Paul D. Boney, Wilmington, NC
Dwight M. Bonham, Wichita, KS
Daniel Boone, Abilene, TX
David C. Boone, Santa Cruz, CA
Laurence O. Booth, Chicago, IL
Bill C. Booziotis, Dallas, TX
L. G. Borget, Houston, TX
Bernard Bortnick, Dallas, TX
Thomas L. Bosworth, Seattle, WA
Elmer Botsai, Honolulu, HI
Gary A. Bowden, Baltimore, MD
David M. Bowen, Fishers, IN
Gary Bowen, Omaha, NE
Ronald Gene Bowen, Middleton, WI
John A. Bower Jr., Philadelphia, PA
Paul D. Bowers Jr., Grand Rapids, MI
William A. Bowersox, Saint Louis, MO
Chester Bowles Jr., San Francisco, CA
J. Donald Bowman, Bellevue, WA
John Harold Box, Austin, TX
Hugh A. Boyd, Montclair, NJ
Robert A. Boynton, Richmond, VA
John Bozalis, Oklahoma City, OK
James H. Bradburn, Denver, CO
David R. Braden, Dallas, TX
Richard H. Bradfield, Clearwater, FL
Thomas G. Bradley, Decatur, IL
Clyde A. Brady, III, Orlando, FL
Scott W. Braley, Atlanta, GA
Ronald M. Brame, Dallas, TX
Joel Brand, Houston, TX
Robert Brannen, Boston, MA
Charles S. Braun, Longwood, FL
Richard M. Brayton, San Francisco, CA
William E. Brazley Jr., Matteson, IL
Melvin Brecher, Broomhall, PA
William N. Breger, New York, NY
Simon Breines, Scarsdale, NY
John Michael Brendle, Denver, CO
Daniel R. Brents, Houston, TX
Adrienne G. Bresnan, New York, NY
Joseph Bresnan, New York, NY
Benjamin E. Brewer Jr., Houston, TX
Leon Bridges, Baltimore, MD
Stanford R. Britt, Washington, DC
Joseph M. Brocato Sr., Alexandria, LA
Myra M. Brocchini, Berkeley, CA
Ronald G. Brocchini, Berkeley, CA
Paul Broches, New York, NY
Raymond D. Brochstein, Houston, TX
William R. Brockway, Baton Rouge, LA
M. J. Brodie, Baltimore, MD
H. Gordon Brooks, II, Lafayette, LA
John W. Broome, Tualatin, OR
Robert C. Broshar, Clear Lake, IA
David J. Brotman, Los Angeles, CA
Charles E. Broudy, Philadelphia, PA
George D. Brown Jr., Peekskill, NY
Jennie Sue Brown, Seattle, WA
Kenneth F. Brown, Honolulu, HI
Lance Jay Brown, New York, NY
Paul B. Brown, Traverse City, MI
Peter Hoyt Brown, Houston, TX
Robert F. Brown Jr., Philadelphia, PA
Robert L. Brown Jr., Lithonia, GA
Terrance Brown, Albuquerque, NM
Woodlief Brown, Abilene, TX
C. William Brubaker, Chicago, IL
Barry B. Bruce, Bellaire, TX
Van B. Bruner Jr., Haddonfield, NJ
Harry A. Bruno, Walnut Creek, CA
Larry S. Bruton, Portland, OR
Harvey Bryan, Belmont, MA
John H. Bryant, Stillwater, OK
Algimantas V. Bublys, Birmingham, MI
Marvin H. Buchanan, Berkeley, CA
James W. Buckley, Greensboro, GA
Michael P. Buckley, New Haven, CT
Huber H. Buehrer, Maumee, OH
John B. Buenz, Chicago, IL

Fellows of The American Institute of Architects

Glenn A. Buff, Miami, FL
Henrik H. Bull, San Francisco, CA
Ellis W. Bullock Jr., Pensacola, FL
Thomas A. Bullock, Sr., Brenham, TX
W. Glenn Bullock, Knoxville, TN
Franklin S. Bunch, Sugar Land, TX
Richard S. Bundy, San Diego, CA
John H. Burgee, Montecito, CA
Charles E. Burgess, Houston, TX
J. Armand Burgun, Kitty Hawk, NC
Edward M. Burke, Austin, TX
James E. Burlage, Sausalito, CA
Robert Burley, Waitsfield, VT
Arthur L. Burns, Winter Haven, FL
John A. Burns, Alexandria, VA
Norma DeCamp Burns, Raleigh, NC
Robert P. Burns, Raleigh, NC
Rodger E. Burson, Wimberley, TX
John A. Busby Jr., Atlanta, GA
C. Joe Buskuhl, Dallas, TX
H. Kennard Bussard, Des Moines, IA
Jerome R. Butler, Chicago, IL
Theodore R. Butler, Minneapolis, MN
Fred W. Butner, Winston Salem, NC
Thomas K. Butt, Point Richmond, CA
Harold Buttrick, New York, NY
Paul S. Byard, New York, NY
Brent Byers, Austin, TX
Jeanne Byrne, Pacific Grove, CA
Arne Bystrom, Seattle, WA

C

Burns Cadwalader, Oakland, CA
Timothy G. Cahill, Kansas City, MO
Harold Calhoun, Houston, TX
C. Robert Campbell, Albuquerque, NM
Robert Campbell, Cambridge, MA
Wendell J. Campbell, Chicago, IL
Jaime Canaves, Miami, FL
H. F. Candela, Coral Gables, FL
Robert H. Canizaro, Jackson, MS
William T. Cannady, Houston, TX
Jamie Cannon, Town & Country, MO
Roger Cannon, Raleigh, NC
Marvin J. Cantor, Fairfax, VA
Horace S. Cantrell Jr., Indianapolis, IN
Richard Scott Carde, Santa Monica, CA
Kenneth Harvey Cardwell, Berkeley, CA
Jean P. Carlhian, Boston, MA
William A. Carlisle, Columbia, SC
DeVon M. Carlson, Boulder, CO
Donald Edwin Carlson, Seattle, WA
Clyde R. Carpenter, Lexington, KY
Jack A. Carpenter, San Diego, CA
William J. Carpenter, Atlanta, GA
Edwin Winford Carroll, El Paso, TX
M. E. Carroll, Chevy Chase, MD
Marley Carroll, Charlotte, NC
W. T. Carry, Atlanta, GA
Chris Carson, San Antonio, TX
Donald K. Carter, Pittsburgh, PA
Virgil R. Carter, Newtown Square, PA
David R. Cartnal, San Jose, CA
Timothy A. Casai, Bloomfield Hills, MI
John Casbarian, Houston, TX
A. Cascieri, Lexington, MA
Donald W. Caskey, Irvine, CA
Heather W. Cass, Washington, DC
Joseph W. Casserly, Chicago, IL
John J. Castellana, Bloomfield Hills, MI
Stephan Castellanos, Stockton, CA
Samuel J. Caudill, Aspen, CO
Giorgio Cavaglieri, New York, NY
W. Brooks Cavin Jr., Shelburne, VT
Lawrence Chaffin Jr., Koloa, HI
Ann R. Chaintreuil, Rochester, NY
Alfred V. Chaix, South Pasadena, CA
Michael Dale Chambers, Minneapolis, MN
Dean B. Chambliss, Denver, CO
Junius J. Champeaux, II, Lake Charles, LA
Lo-Yi Chan, Ashley Falls, MA
Wing T. Chao, Burbank, CA
L. William Chapin II, Alexandria, VA
Donald D. Chapman, Kula, HI
John S. Chase, Houston, TX
Walter F. Chatham, New York, NY
Peter Chermayeff, Boston, MA
Edith Cherry, Albuquerque, NM
Edward E. Cherry, Hamden, CT
Robert A. Chervenak, Mount Vernon, WA
Lugean L. Chilcote, Little Rock, AR
G. Cabell Childress, Castle Rock, CO
James C. Childress, Centerbrook, CT
David M. Childs, New York, NY
Maurice F. Childs, Boston, MA
Susan Chin, New York, NY
Robert E. Chisholm, Miami, FL
Gordon H. Chong, San Francisco, CA
Frederick L. Christensen, Salinas, CA
George W. Christensen, Scottsdale, AZ
James W. Christopher, Salt Lake City, UT
Daniel Chun, Honolulu, HI
Eric A. Chung, Radnor, PA
William C. Church, Portland, OR
Richard J. Chylinski, Los Angeles, CA
Mario J. Ciampi, Kentfield, CA
Robert L. Cioppa, New York, NY
Eugene D. Cizek, New Orleans, LA
George L. Claflen, Philadelphia, PA

Fellows of The American Institute of Architects

John M. Clancy, Boston, MA
James F. Clapp Jr., Cambridge, MA
Fred W. Clarke III, New Haven, CT
Gerald L. Clark, Havasu City, AZ
Roger H. Clark, Raleigh, NC
John P. Clarke, Trenton, NJ
Marshall F. Clarke, Greenville, SC
Charles Clary, Destin, FL
Thomas R. Clause, Des Moines, IA
Jerry L. Clement, St. Louis, MO
Glen E. Cline, Boise, ID
Elizabeth Close, St. Paul, MN
Robert K. Clough, Chicago, IL
James A Clutts, Dallas, TX
Henry N. Cobb, New York, NY
R. F. Coffee, Austin, TX
Daniel P. Coffey, Chicago, IL
Adrian O. Cohen, Los Angeles, CA
Andrew S. Cohen, Middlebury, CT
Jack C. Cohen, Bethesda, MD
Martin H. Cohen, Armonk, NY
Stuart Cohen, Evanston, IL
Doris Cole, Concord, MA
Robert Traynham Coles, Buffalo, NY
David S. Collins, Cincinnati, OH
Donald Comstock, Sacramento, CA
William T. Conklin, Washington, DC
Richard T. Conrad, Sacramento, CA
W. M. Conrad, Kansas City, MO
John Conron, Santa Fe, NM
J. J. Conroy, Chicago, IL
Eugene E. Cook, Roselle, IL
Lawrence D. Cook, Falls Church, VA
Richard B. Cook, Chicago, IL
William H. Cook, Sonoita, AZ
Alexander Cooper, New York, NY
Jerome M. Cooper, Atlanta, GA
W. Kent Cooper, Washington, DC
Christopher Coover, Phoenix, AZ
Gerald M. Cope, Philadelphia, PA
Lee G. Copeland, Seattle, WA
C. Jack Corgan, Dallas, TX
Jack M. Corgan, Dallas, TX
William Corlett, Berkeley, CA
Araldo A. Cossutta, New York, NY
Walter H. Costa, Lafayette, CA
Anthony J. Costello, Muncie, IN
Leland Cott, Cambridge, MA
John O. Cotton, Marina Del Rey, CA
W. Philip Cotton Jr., St. Louis, MO
C. H. Cowell, Houston, TX
Page Ayres Cowley, New York City, NY
Dan C. Cowling, Little Rock, AR
David C. Cox, Washington, DC
Frederic H Cox, Richmond, VA
Warren J. Cox, Washington, DC
Whitson W. Cox, Carmichael, CA
Bruce I. Crabtree Jr., Nashville, TN
Kirk R. Craig, Greenville, SC
Steade Craigo, Sacramento, CA
George M. Crandall, Portland, OR
David A. Crane, Tampa, FL
Steve H. Crane, Salt Lake City, UT
Ronald O. Crawford, Roanoke, VA
Martin W. Crennen, Helena, MT
Frank W. Crimp, Milton, MA
James H. Crissman, Watertown, MA
Edwin B. Crittenden, Anchorage, AK
K. C. Crocco, Chicago, IL
Charles B. Croft, Austin, TX
Edwin B. Cromwell, Little Rock, AR
Eason Cross Jr., Alexandria, VA
Samuel Crothers, III, Radnor, PA
S. Fiske Crowell Jr., Boston, MA
R. L. Crowther, Denver, CO
Randolph R. Croxton, New York, NY
Metcalf Crump, Memphis, TN
Evan D. Cruthers, Honolulu, HI
Beatriz del Cueto, Guaynabo, Puerto Rico
John W. Cuningham, Minneapolis, MN
Ben Cunningham, St. Petersburg, FL
Gary M. Cunningham, Dallas, TX
Warren W. Cunningham, Philadelphia, PA
James L. Cutler, Bainbridge Is, WA
Bernard J. Cywinski, Havertown, PA

D

Charles E. Dagit Jr., Philadelphia, PA
Fernand W. Dahan, Rockville, MD
David A. Daileda, Springfield, VA
Curt Dale, Denver, CO
Todd Dalland, New York, NY
J. E. Dalton, Kent, OH
Leo A. Daly III, Washington, DC
Paul Damaz, East Hampton, NY
Sylvester Damianos, Pittsburgh, PA
Robert Damora, Bedford, NY
George E. Danforth, Chicago, IL
Arthur C. Danielian, Irvine, CA
George N. Daniels, Salt Lake City, UT
Stanley L. Daniels, Atlanta, GA
Doris Andrews Danna, St. Louis, MO
Robert F. Darby, Jacksonville, FL
Samuel N. Darby, Rockford, IL
Edwin S. Darden, Fresno, CA
Ben R. Darmer, Atlanta, GA
Richard Dattner, New York, NY
Theoharis L. David, New York, NY
D. G. Davidson, Washington, DC
David S. Davidson, Great Falls, MT

Fellows of The American Institute of Architects

Robert I. Davidson, New York, NY
Albert J. Davis, Blacksburg, VA
Arthur Q. Davis, New Orleans, LA
Charles M. Davis, San Francisco, CA
Clark Davis, St. Louis, MO
Clark A. Davis, San Francisco, CA
Jerry A Davis, New York, NY
John M. Davis, Austin, TX
Lewis Davis, New York, NY
Nicholas Davis, Auburn, AL
Steven M. Davis, New York, NY
W. T. Davis, Greenville, SC
Clare Henry Day, Redlands, CA
Frederic L. Day Jr., Concord, MA
Natalie De Blois, San Antonio, TX
John Neff De Haas Jr., Bozeman, MT
Rey de la Reza, Houston, TX
Alfredo De Vido, New York, NY
Jack DeBartolo Jr., Phoenix, AZ
Rudolph V. DeChellis, Woodland Hills, CA
Vernon DeMars, Berkeley, CA
Kenneth DeMay, Watertown, MA
Louis DeMoll, Moylan, PA
Mary Werner DeNadai, Chadds Ford, PA
J. R. DeStefano, Chicago, IL
Panayotis E. DeVaris, South Orange, NJ
E. L. Deam, Highland Park, IL
Robert C. Dean, Boston, MA
C. M. Deasy, San Luis Obispo, CA
Howard S. Decker, Chicago, IL
Ward W. Deems, Solana Beach, CA
Allan J. Dehar, New Haven, CT
Jorge Del Rio, San Juan, Puerto Rico
Homer T. Delawie, San Diego, CA
Eugene A. Delmar, Olney, MD
Pamela J. Delphenich, New Haven, CT
Sidney L. Delson, East Hampton, NY
Olvia Demetriou, Washington, DC
William Deno, Boulder, CO
Jos. Robert Deshayes, Caldwell, TX
Gary L. Desmond, Denver, CO
John J. Desmond, Baton Rouge, LA
Gita Dev, Woodside, CA
Suzanne Di Geronimo, Paramus, NJ
Antonio Di Mambro, Boston, MA
A P. DiBenedetto, Portland, OR
Eugene L. DiLaura, Milan, MI
Robert Diamant, Longboat Key, FL
J. J. J. Diamond, Jacksonville, FL
Katherine Diamond, Los Angeles, CA
Horacio Diaz, San Juan, Puerto Rico
James R. Diaz, San Francisco, CA
David R. Dibner, McLean, VA
Bruce Dicker, Portsmouth, NH
Gerald G. Diehl, Dearborn, MI
Paul E. Dietrich, Cambridge, MA
Robert H. Dietz, Apache Junction, AZ
William M. Dikis, Des Moines, IA
Frank Dimster, Los Angeles, CA
Philip Dinsmore, Tucson, AZ
David D. Dixon, Boston, MA
F. Dail Dixon Jr., Chapel Hill, NC
John M. Dixon, Old Greenwich, CT
Michael A. Dixon, St. Charles, IL
Lawrence S. Doane, San Francisco, CA
Jim C. Doche, Amarillo, TX
Peter H. Dodge, San Francisco, CA
George S. Dolim, San Francisco, CA
Peter Hoyt Dominick Jr., Denver, CO
Milford W. Donaldson, San Diego, CA
Janet Donelson, Seattle, WA
Richard C. Donkervoet, Baltimore, MD
Paul J. Donnelly, St. Louis, MO
Kermit P. Dorius, Newport Bch, CA
Albert A. Dorman, Los Angeles, CA
Richard L. Dorman, Santa Fe, NM
Robert W. Dorsey, Cincinnati, OH
Darwin V. Doss, Salem, OR
Betsey O. Dougherty, Costa Mesa, CA
Brian P. Dougherty, Costa Mesa, CA
Frank F. Douglas, Houston, TX
John Douglas, Scottsdale , AZ
H. Robert Douglass, Missouri City, TX
C.R. George Dove, Washington, DC
Gerald A. Doyle, Phoenix, AZ
Peter G. Doyle, Houston, TX
Boris Dramov, San Francisco, CA
Helene Dreiling, Warrenton, VA
Roy M. Drew, San Diego, CA
Albert M. Dreyfuss, Sacramento, CA
Robert W. Drummond, Gainesville, FL
Andrés Duany, Miami, FL
Martin David Dubin, Highland Park, IL
George A. Dudley, Rensselaerville, NY
J. Paul Duffendack, Leawood, KS
Herbert E. Duncan, Kansas City, MO
Foster W. Dunwiddie, Henderson, NV
Eugene C. Dunwody, Macon, GA
William L. Duquette, Los Gatos, CA
Gabriel Durand-Hollis, San Antonio, TX
Almon J. Durkee, Traverse City, MI
William R. Dutcher, Berkeley, CA
Donald J. Dwore, Coral Gables, FL
Daniel L. Dworsky, Los Angeles, CA

E

Mary Jean Eastman, New York, NY
John P. Eberhard, Alexandria, VA
Jeremiah Eck, Boston, MA
Stanton Eckstut, New York, NY

Fellows of The American Institute of Architects

Robert N. Eddy, Bakersfield, CA
Judith Edelman, New York, NY
David J. Edwards Jr., Columbia, SC
Jared I. Edwards, Hartford, CT
Albert Efron, Staten Island, NY
David L. Eggers, West Palm Beach, FL
Ezra D. Ehrenkrantz, New York, NY
John P. Ehrig, Merritt Island, FL
Joseph Ehrlich, Menlo Park, CA
Steven D. Ehrlich, Culver City, CA
Thomas N. Eichbaum, Washington, DC
John A. Eifler, Chicago, IL
Steven L. Einhorn, Albany, NY
Peter D. Eisenman, New York, NY
Sidney H. Eisenshtat, Los Angeles, CA
Richard Karl Eisner, Oakland, CA
Barry P. Elbasani, Berkeley, CA
Joseph L. Eldredge, Vineyard Hvn, MA
Charles N. Eley, San Francisco, CA
James H. Eley, Jackson, MS
Howard F. Elkus, Boston, MA
Harry Ellenzweig, Cambridge, MA
Robin M. Ellerthorpe, Chicago, IL
Dale R. Ellickson, Great Falls, VA
Benjamin P. Elliott, Rockville, MD
Rand L. Elliott, Oklahoma City, OK
John M. Ellis, New York, NY
James E. Ellison, Washington, DC
Frank L. Elmer, Columbus, OH
James W. Elmore, Phoenix, AZ
Frederick E. Emmons, Bel Tiburon, CA
Terrel M. Emmons, Springfield, VA
William Eng, Champaign, IL
Douglas K. Engebretson, West Springfield, MA
Mark C. Engelbrecht, Des Moines, IA
Philip J. Enquist, Chicago, IL
William L. Ensign, Annapolis, MD
Lawrence Enyart, Phoenix, AZ
Herbert Epstein, Delray Beach, FL
Elizabeth S. Ericson, Boston, MA
Jerome R. Ernst, Seattle, WA
R. Allen Eskew, New Orleans, LA
Philip A. Esocoff, Washington, DC
Harold Lionel Esten, Silver Spring, MD
A. B. Etherington, Honolulu, HI
Deane M. Evans Jr., Arlington, VA
J. Handel Evans, Camarillo, CA
Ralph F. Evans, Salt Lake City, UT
Robert J. Evans, Marshall, CA
William S. Evans, Shreveport, LA
C. Richard Everett, Houston, TX
Gary Everton, Nashville, TN
Thomas J. Eyerman, Chicago, IL

F

Otto Reichert Facilides, Philadelphia, PA
William H. Fain Jr., Los Angeles, CA
James Falick, Houston, TX
Kristine K. Fallon, Chicago, IL
Jay David Farbstein, San Luis Obispo, CA
Michael Farewell, Princeton, NJ
Richard T. Faricy, Saint Paul, MN
Richard C. Farley, Denver, CO
Stephen J. Farneth, San Francisco, CA
Avery C. Faulkner, Delaplane, VA
Winthrop W. Faulkner, Chevy Chase, MD
James G. Fausett, Marietta, GA
Robert E. Fehlberg, Pleasanton, CA
Werner L. Feibes, Schenectady, NY
Daniel J. Feil, Washington, DC
Edward A. Feiner, Fairfax, VA
Jose Feito, Miami, FL
Curtis W. Fentress, Denver, CO
S. Scott Ferebee Jr., Charlotte, NC
Franklin T. Ferguson, Salt Lake City, UT
Richard E. Fernau, Berkeley, CA
Stephanie E. Ferrell, Tampa, FL
Miguel Ferrer, Santurce, Puerto Rico
Richard B. Ferrier, Arlington, TX
James D. Ferris, Michigan City, IN
Robert D. Ferris, San Diego, CA
M. L. Ferro, Weare, NH
Donald E. Ferry, Springfield, IL
Michael T. Fickel, Kansas City, MO
H. H. Field, Shirley, MA
John L. Field, San Francisco, CA
Robert A. Fielden, Las Vegas, NV
Michael M. Fieldman, New York, NY
Kenneth J. Filarski, Providence, RI
R. Jerome Filer, Miami, FL
Bob G. Fillpot, Norman, OK
Ronald C. Filson, New Orleans, LA
Curtis Finch, Lake Oswego, OR
James H. Finch, Alpharetta, GA
Robert A. Findlay, Ames, IA
Maurice N. Finegold, Boston, MA
Ira S. Fink, Berkeley, CA
Jerry V. Finrow, Seattle, WA
A. Robert Fisher, Belvedere, CA
Benjamin P. Fisher, San Francisco, CA
James Herschel Fisher, Dallas, TX
John L. Fisher, Marysville, CA
Laura A. Horstman Fisher, Chicago, IL
Hollye C. Fisk, Dallas, TX
Michael A. Fitts, Nolensville, TN
Darrell A. Fitzgerald, Atlanta, GA
James T. Fitzgerald, Cincinnati, OH
Joseph F. Fitzgerald, Chicago, IL

Fellows of The American Institute of Architects

Richard A. Fitzgerald, Houston, TX
Joseph H. Flad, Madison, WI
Earl Robert Flansburgh, Boston, MA
Ted Flato, San Antonio, TX
Joseph L. Fleischer, New York, NY
Richard J. Fleischman, Cleveland, OH
Norman C. Fletcher, Lexington, MA
David J. Flood, Santa Monica, CA
Colden R. Florance, Washington, DC
Luis Flores-Dumont, Santurce, Puerto Rico
J. Chadwick P. Floyd, Centerbrook, CT
Richard F. Floyd, Dallas, TX
W. Jeff Floyd Jr., Atlanta, GA
Ligon B. Flynn, Wilmington, NC
Michael Flynn, New York, NY
John W. Focke, Houston, TX
Bernd Foerster, Manhattan, KS
James Follett, Chicago, IL
Fred L. Foote, San Francisco, CA
Stephen M. Foote, Boston, MA
Peter Forbes, Boston, MA
Robert M. Ford, Starkville, MS
Russell Forester, La Jolla, CA
Bernardo Fort-Brescia, Miami, FL
James R. Foster, Fayetteville, AR
Richard Foster, Wilton, CT
Bruce S. Fowle, New York, NY
Bob J. Fowler, PE, CBO, Pasadena, CA
Marion L. Fowlkes, Nashville, TN
Sheldon Fox, Stamford, CT
Harrison Fraker, Berkeley, CA
Edward D. Francis, Detroit, MI
Jay E. Frank, Dallas, TX
Morton Frank, Redwood City, CA
Richard C. Frank, Gregory, MI
Neil P. Frankel, Chicago, IL
James R. Franklin, San Luis Obispo, CA
Gregory Franta, Boulder, CO
John P. Franzen, Southport, CT
Ulrich J. Franzen, New York, NY
Robert J. Frasca, Portland, OR
James I. Freed, New York, NY
Philip G. Freelon, Research Triangle Park, NC
Beverly L. Freeman, Charlotte, NC
William W. Freeman, Burlington, VT
Jeffrey S. French, Philadelphia, PA
Thomas K. Fridstein, Chicago, IL
Stephen Friedlaender, Cambridge, MA
Daniel S. Friedman, Cincinnati, OH
Hans A. Friedman, Evanston, IL
Rodney F. Friedman, Belvedere, CA
Edward Friedrichs, Santa Monica, CA
Louis E. Fry Jr., Washington, DC
Louis E. Fry, Washington, DC
Richard E. Fry, Ann Arbor, MI
Joseph Y. Fujikawa, Winnetka, IL
Randall K. Fujiki, Kailua, HI
Albert B. Fuller Jr., St. Louis, MO
Frank L. Fuller, IV, Oakland, CA
Duncan T. Fulton, Dallas, TX
David F. Furman, Charlotte, NC
James E. Furr, Houston, TX

G

Robert C. Gaede, Cleveland, OH
Fulton G. Gale III, Seattle, WA
Herbert K. Gallagher, Boston, MA
Leslie M. Gallery-Dilworth, Philadelphia, PA
Harvey B. Gantt, Charlotte, NC
Theodore Garduque, Honolulu, HI
Robert D. Garland Jr., El Paso, TX
Douglas A. Garofalo, Chicago, IL
Charles E. Garrison, Diamondhead, MS
Truitt B. Garrison, Granbury, TX
Alan G. Gass, Denver, CO
Fred C. Gast Jr., Portland, OR
Kirk A. Gastinger, Kansas City, MO
James A. Gatsch, Princeton, NJ
Martha M. Gates, Pittsford, NY
Robert F. Gatje, New York, NY
James B. Gatton, Houston, TX
F. E. Gaulden, Greenville, SC
John C. Gaunt, Lawrence, KS
Robert Geddes, Princeton, NJ
Barbara L. Geddis, Stamford, CT
William J. Geddis, Chestnut Hill, MA
Robert J. Geering, San Francisco, CA
Frank O. Gehry, Santa Monica, CA
Carolyn D. Geise, Seattle, WA
Martin B. Gelber, Los Angeles, CA
M. Arthur Gensler Jr., San Francisco, CA
David W. George, Southlake, TX
Frank Dan George, Stamford, CT
Reagan W. George, Willow City, TX
Robert S. George, San Bruno, CA
Stephen A. George, Pittsburgh, PA
Preston M. Geren, Fort Worth, TX
Thomas B. Gerfen, San Francisco, CA
Phillip H. Gerou, Evergreen, CO
Joe P. Giattina Jr., Birmingham, AL
James D. Gibans, Cleveland, OH
Dale L. Gibbs, Lincoln, NE
Donald H. Gibbs, Long Beach, CA
Randall C. Gideon, Fort Worth, TX
Sidney P. Gilbert, New York, NY
Victor C. Gilbertson, Minnetonka, MN
Wilmot G. Gilland, Eugene, OR
Norman M. Giller, Miami Beach, FL
W. Douglas Gilpin, Charlottesville, VA
James S. Gimpel, Chicago, IL

Fellows of The American Institute of Architects

Raymond L. Gindroz, Pittsburgh, PA
David L. Ginsberg, New York, NY
Raymond Girvigian, South Pasadena, CA
Joseph Carl Giuliani, Washington, DC
Romaldo Giurgola, Australia
Richard E. Glaser, Cincinnati, OH
William R. Glass, Oakland, CA
David Evan Glasser, Fayetteville, AR
E. A. Glendening, Cincinnati, OH
Val Glitsch, Houston, TX
Richard J. Gluckman, New York, NY
Harold D. Glucksman, Union, NJ
James M. Glymph, Santa Monica, CA
Ronald V. Gobbell, Nashville, TN
James Goettsch, Chicago, IL
Lewis J. Goetz, Washington, DC
Alan E. Goldberg, New Canaan, CT
Steven M. Goldberg, New York, NY
M. H. Goldfinger, New York, NY
Ron Goldman, Malibu, CA
Nicholas Goldsmith, New York, NY
Roger Neal Goldstein, Boston, MA
Stanley J. Goldstein, West Orange, NJ
Harmon H. Goldstone, New York, NY
Harry A. Golemon, Houston, TX
Bennie M. Gonzales, Nogales, AZ
Armando L. Gonzalez, Pasadena, CA
Donald W. Y. Goo, Honolulu, HI
R. L. Good, Dallas, TX
Wayne L. Good, Annapolis, MD
D. B. Goodhue, Monterey, CA
Cary C. Goodman, Kansas City, MO
John P. Goodman, Manlius, NY
Michael K. Goodwin, Phoenix, AZ
Warren N. Goodwin, Brentwood, TN
Joan E. Goody, Boston, MA
Ezra Gordon, Chicago, IL
Harry T. Gordon, Washington, DC
T.J. Gottesdiener, New York, NY
Amy L. Gould, Baltimore, MD
Robert E. Gould, Kansas City, MO
Ronald Gourley, Tucson, AZ
Brian Gracey, Knoxville, TN
Bernard J. Grad, Elberon, NJ
Bruce J. Graham, Hobe Sound, FL
Gary L. Graham, Boston, MA
Roy E. Graham, Washington, DC
Robert E. Gramann, Cincinnati, OH
Warren Wolf Gran, New York, NY
Charles P. Graves, Lexington, KY
Dean W. Graves, Kansas City, MO
Michael Graves, Princeton, NJ
Ann E. Gray, Los Angeles, CA
David Lawrence Gray, Santa Monica, CA
Thomas A. Gray, Little Rock, AR
Lyn E. Graziani, Miami, FL
Robert E. Greager, Pleasant Ridge, MI
Dennis W. Grebner, St. Paul, MN
Aaron G. Green, San Francisco, CA
Curtis H. Green, Shorewood, MN
Richard J. Green, Cambridge, MA
Thomas G. Green, Boston, MA
Aubrey J. Greenberg, Chicago, IL
James A. Greene, Oviedo, FL
Sanford R. Greenfield, Westfield, NJ
Susan Greenwald, Chicago, IL
John O. Greer, Bryan, TX
Glenn H. Gregg, New Haven, CT
Nonya Grenader, Houston, TX
Raymond Grenald, Narberth, PA
James A. Gresham, Tucson, AZ
William C. Gridley, Washington, DC
L. Duane Grieve, Knoxville, TN
James R. Grieves, Baltimore, MD
Donald I. Grinberg, Boston, MA
Edward A. Grochowiak, San Diego, CA
Olindo Grossi, Manhasset, NY
William H. Grover, Centerbrook, CT
J. C. Grube, Portland, OR
Ernest A. Grunsfeld, Chicago, IL
Jordan L. Gruzen, New York, NY
John C. Guenther, St. Louis, MO
Francis A. Guffey II, Charleston, WV
Paul J. Gumbinger, San Mateo, CA
Graham Gund, Cambridge, MA
Brooks R. Gunsul, Portland, OR
Gerald Gurland, West Orange, NJ
Robert M. Gurney, Alexandria, VA
William R. Gustafson, Philadelphia, PA
Dean L. Gustavson, Salt Lake City, UT
Cabell Gwathmey, Harwood, MD
Charles Gwathmey, New York, NY
Willard E. Gwilliam, Hayes, VA

H

E. Keith Haag, Cuyahoga Falls, OH
Lester C. Haas, Shreveport, LA
Wallace L. Haas Jr., Redding, CA
Donald J. Hackl, Chicago, IL
John B. Hackler, Charlotte, NC
Stephen R. Hagan, Washington, DC
L.R. Hahnfeld, Fort Worth, TX
Frank S. Haines, Honolulu, HI
William H. Haire, Stillwater, OK
Imre Halasz, Boston, MA
Gaines B. Hall, Downers Grove, IL
Mark W. Hall, Toronto, ON
William A. Hall, New York, NY
Harry C. Hallenbeck, Sacramento, CA
Stanley I. Hallet, Washington, DC

Fellows of The American Institute of Architects

Gerald Hallissy, Port Washington, NY
Anna M. Halpin, New York, NY
Frances Halsband, New York, NY
William Hamby, New York, NY
Robert L. Hamill Jr., Boise, ID
D.K. Hamilton, Bellaire, TX
E.G. Hamilton Jr., Dallas, TX
Robert P. Hammell, Arlington, VA
Theodore S. Hammer, New York, NY
Gerald S. Hammond, Cincinnati, OH
John Hyatt Hammond, Greensboro, NC
W. Easley Hamner, Cambridge, MA
Mark G. Hampton, Coconut Grove, FL
John Paul C. Hanbury, Norfolk, VA
Peter H. Hand, Atlanta, GA
J. Paul Hansen, Savannah, GA
Richard F. Hansen, Sanibel, FL
Robert E. Hansen, Hendersonville, NC
Alan M. Hantman, Washington, D.C.
Ernest H. Hara, Honolulu, HI
John M. Hara, Honolulu, HI
Dellas H. Harder, Columbus, OH
Donald L. Hardison, El Cerrito, CA
Hugh Hardy, New York, NY
John C. Harkness, Arlington, MA
Sarah P. Harkness, Lexington, MA
Frank Harmon, Raleigh, NC
Harry W. Harmon, Lake San Marcos, CA
John C. Haro, Scottsdale, AZ
Charles F. Harper, Wichita Falls, TX
David M. Harper, Coral Gables, FL
Robert L. Harper, Centerbrook, CT
James W. Harrell, Cincinnati, OH
David A. Harris, Washington, DC
Edwin F. Harris Jr., Raleigh, NC
James Martin Harris, Tacoma, WA
Robert S. Harris, Los Angeles, CA
Samuel Y. Harris, Philadelphia, PA
Robert V.M. Harrison, Jackson, MS
Roy P. Harrover, Memphis, TN
Craig W. Hartman, San Francisco, CA
Douglas C. Hartman, Dallas, TX
George E. Hartman, Washington, DC
Morton Hartman, Highland Park, IL
William E. Hartmann, Castine, ME
John F. Hartray Jr., Chicago, IL
Timothy Hartung, New York, NY
Wilbert R. Hasbrouck, Chicago, IL
Dennis E. Haskell, Seattle, WA
Albert L. Haskins Jr., Raleigh North, NC
Peter M. Hasselman, Orinda, CA
Sami Hassid, Pleasant Hill, CA
Herman A. Hassinger, Moorestown, NJ
George J. Hasslein, San Luis Obispo, CA
L. J. Hastings, Seattle, WA
Marvin Hatami, Denver, CO
Harold D. Hauf, Sun City, AZ
Robert O. Hausner, Santa Fe, NM
Daniel J. Havekost, Denver, CO
Perry A. Haviland, Oakland, CA
Velpeau E. Hawes Jr., Dallas, TX
H. Ralph Hawkins, Dallas, TX
Jasper Stillwell Hawkins, Phoenix, AZ
William J. Hawkins III, Portland, OR
William R. Hawley, E. Palo Alto, CA
Bruce A. Hawtin, Jackson, WY
Richard S. Hayden, New York, NY
J. F. Hayes, Cambridge, MA
John Freeman Hayes, Radnor, PA
Irving B. Haynes, Lincoln, RI
Edward H. Healey, Cedar Rapids, IA
Michael M. Hearn, San Francisco, CA
George T. Heery, Atlanta, GA
Clovis Heimsath, Austin, TX
Dan Heinfeld, Irvine, CA
John Hejduk, Bronx, NY
Margaret Helfand, New York, NY
Barbara Heller, Washington, D.C.
Jeffrey Heller, San Francisco, CA
Maxwell Boone Hellmann, Cardiff by the Sea, CA
George F. Hellmuth, St. Louis, MO
A. C. Helman, Maitland, FL
David P. Helpern, New York, NY
James C. Hemphill Jr., Charlotte, NC
Arn Henderson, Norman, OK
John D. Henderson, San Diego, CA
Philip C. Henderson, Dallas, TX
James L. Hendricks, Rockwall, TX
William R. Henry, Jackson, MS
Justin Henshell, Red Bank, NJ
Donald C. Hensman, Pasadena, CA
Charles Herbert, Des Moines, IA
Robert G. Herman, San Francisco, CA
William W. Herrin, Huntsville, AL
Ricardo C. Herring, Washington, D.C.
Robert G. Hershberger, Tucson, AZ
Paul A. Hesson, San Antonio, TX
Charles R. Heuer, Charlottesville, VA
D. M. Hewitt, Seattle, WA
Warren Cummings Heylman, Spokane, WA
Mason S. Hicks, Fayetteville, NC
Charles C. Hight, Charlotte, NC
Dean F. Hilfinger, Bloomington, IL
Eric Hill, Detroit, MI
John W. Hill, Baltimore, MD
J. Robert Hillier, Princeton, NJ
Mark Hinshaw, Seattle, WA
Kem G. Hinton, Nashville, TN
Don M. Hisaka, Berkeley, CA
Gregory O. Hnedak, Memphis, TN

Fellows of The American Institute of Architects

Paul S. Hoag, Bellevue, WA
Richard W. Hobbs, Washington, DC
Peter S. Hockaday, Seattle, WA
Murlin R. Hodgell, Norman, OK
Thomas H. Hodne, Minneapolis, MN
David C. Hoedemaker, Seattle, WA
August F. Hoenack, Bethesda, MD
David H. Hoffman, Evant, TX
David L. Hoffman, Wichita, KS
John J. Hoffmann, North Haven, CT
J. David Hoglund, Pittsburgh, PA
John A. Holabird, Chicago, IL
L. M. Holder, Austin, TX
Major L. Holland, Tuskegee, AL
Dwight E. Holmes, Tampa, FL
Jess Holmes, Henderson, NV
Nicholas H. Holmes Jr., Mobile, AL
Harry J. Holroyd, Columbus, OH
David A. Holtz, Potomac, MD
Malcolm Holzman, New York, NY
George W. Homsey, San Francisco, CA
Bobbie S. Hood, San Francisco, CA
Van D. Hooker, Albuquerque, NM
G. N. Hoover, Houston, TX
George Hoover, Denver, CO
Ray C. Hoover III, Atlanta, GA
Frank L. Hope Jr., San Diego, CA
Eugene Hopkins, Detroit, MI
Edward M. Hord, Baltimore, MD
Howard N. Horii, Newark, NJ
Gerald Horn, Chicago, IL
Patrick Horsbrugh, South Bend, IN
T. Horty, Minneapolis, MN
Reginald D. Hough, Larchmont, NY
Marvin C. Housworth, Atlanta, GA
David C. Hovey, Winnetka, IL
J. Murray Howard, Charlottesville, VA
John Howey, Tampa, FL
Thomas S. Howorth, Oxford, MS
Charles K. Hoyt, Old Lyme, CT
Michael M. Hricak Jr., Venice, CA
Robert Y. Hsiung, Boston, MA
Charles A. Hubbard, Cortez, CO
Jeffrey A. Huberman, Charlotte, NC
Daniel Huberty, Seattle, WA
Richard W. Huffman, Philadelphia, PA
Stanford Hughes, San Francisco, CA
Stephan S. Huh, Minneapolis, MN
Robert E. Hull, Seattle, WA
Charles F. Hummel, Boise, ID
Fred E. Hummel, Sacramento, CA
Harry J. Hunderman, Northbrook, IL
Gregory Hunt, Washington, DC
Frances P. Huppert, New York, NY
Sam T. Hurst, Montecito, CA
Syed V. Husain, Kensington, CA
Mary Alice Hutchins, Portland, OR
Remmert W. Huygens, Wayland, MA
Bryden B. Hyde, Jarretsville, MD
Fred J. Hynek, Parker, CO

I

Dean Illingworth, Indianapolis, IN
Elizabeth W. Ingraham, Colorado Springs, CO
William A. Isley, Bainbridge Island, WA
H. Curtis Ittner, St. Louis, MO
Robert A. Ivy Jr., New York, NY

J

Huson Jackson, Lexington, MA
Mike Jackson, Springfield, IL
R. G. Jackson, Houston, TX
Ralph T. Jackson, Boston, MA
Bernard Jacob, Minneapolis, MN
Harry M. Jacobs, Oakland, CA
Stephen B. Jacobs, New York, NY
Hugh N. Jacobsen, Washington, DC
Phillip L. Jacobson, Seattle, WA
J. P. Jacoby, Menomonee Falls, WI
Helmut Jahn, Chicago, IL
Timm Jamieson, Roanoke, VA
Henry A. Jandl, Richmond, VA
William R. Jarratt, Ann Arbor, MI
Lloyd Jary, San Antonio, TX
Peter Jefferson, Highlands, NC
Jordan O. Jelks, Macon, GA
J. J. Jennewein, Tampa, FL
Richard W. Jennings, Austin, TX
Bruce H. Jensen, Salt Lake City, UT
David Jepson, Hartford, CT
Jon Adams Jerde, Venice, CA
John W. Jickling, Birmingham, MI
John M. Johansen, New York, NY
Anthony N. Johns Jr., Mt. Irvine, Trinidad & Tobaga
Arthur D. Johnson, Omaha, NE
Danie Johnson, Asheville, NC
Edwin J. Johnson, Dallas, TX
Eric B. Johnson, Savannah, GA
Floyd E. Johnson, Scottsville, VA
James H. Johnson, Denver, CO
Jed V. Johnson, Wappingers Falls, NY
Mark Robert Johnson, Valley Forge, PA
Marvin R. Johnson, Raleigh, NC
Philip C. Johnson, New York, NY
Ralph E. Johnson, Chicago, IL
Scott Johnson, Los Angeles, CA
Walker C. Johnson, Chicago, IL
Yandell Johnson, Little Rock, AR
Norman J. Johnston, Seattle, WA
James O. Jonassen, Seattle, WA

Fellows of The American Institute of Architects

Arthur E. Jones, Houston, TX
Bernard I. Jones, Carbondale, IL
E. Fay Jones, Fayetteville, AR
J. Delaine Jones, Troy, NY
Jack B. Jones, Tamuning, Guam
Johnpaul Jones, Seattle, WA
Paul Duane Jones, Kailua, HI
Renis Jones, Montgomery, AL
Robert Lawton Jones, Tulsa, OK
Rudard Artaban Jones, Urbana, IL
Bendrew G. Jong, Orinda, CA
Joe J. Jordan, Philadelphia, PA
David A. Jordani, Minneapolis, MN
Roberta W. Jorgensen, Irvine, CA
Wendy Evans Joseph, New York, NY
Henri V. Jova, Atlanta, GA
Bruce D. Judd, San Francisco, CA
Yu Sing Jung, Boston, MA
Howard H. Juster, San Diego, CA

K

Carl F. Kaelber Jr., Pittsford, NY
Richard E. Kaeyer, Mt. Kisco, NY
Gerald Kagan, New Haven, CT
David T. Kahler, Milwaukee, WI
Charles H. Kahn, Chapel Hill, NC
Eino O. Kainlauri, Ames, IA
Harry Kale, Conshohocken, PA
Mark Kalin, Newton Center, MA
G. M. Kallmann, Boston, MA
Stephen H. Kanner, Los Angeles, CA
Gary Y. Kaplan, Red Bank, NJ
Richard H. Kaplan, Cleveland, OH
Raymond L. Kappe, Pacific Palisades, CA
Raymond John Kaskey, Washington, DC
Kirby M. Keahey, Houston, TX
Gustave R. Keane, Bradenton, FL
Jan Keane, New York, NY
Richard C. Keating, Marina Del Rey, CA
Allan Kehrt, Princeton, NJ
Douglas S. Kelbaugh, Ann Arbor, MI
Duane A. Kell, St. Paul, MN
John H. Kell, San Antonio, TX
Bernard Kellenyi, Red Bank, NJ
Larry J. Keller, Fairfax, VA
Frank S. Kelly, Houston, TX
F. L. Kelsey, Scottsdale, AZ
Diane Legge Kemp, Chicago, IL
William D. Kendall, Houston, TX
Robert N. Kennedy, Indianapolis, IN
Gertrude L. Kerbis, Chicago, IL
Thomas L. Kerns, Arlington, VA
William H. Kessler, Detroit, MI
Herbert A. Ketcham, Minneapolis, MN
Russell V. Keune, Arlington, VA
A.H. Keyes Jr., Washington, DC
Stephen J. Kieran, Philadelphia, PA
Leevi Kiil, New York, NY
Lee F. Kilbourn, Portland, OR
James R. Killebrew, Grapevine, TX
Edward A. Killingsworth, Long Beach, CA
Tai Soo Kim, Hartford, CT
Jong S. Kimm, APO
David R. H. King, Washington, DC
Dennis M. King, Huntington Woods, MI
Donald King, Seattle, WA
Gordon L. King, Sacramento, CA
J. Bertram King, Asheville, NC
Leland King, Bodega Bay, CA
Sol King, Palm Beach, FL
M. Ray Kingston, Salt Lake City, UT
Paul Kinnison Jr., San Antonio, TX
Ballard H. Kirk, Columbus, OH
D. W. Kirk Jr., Fort Worth, TX
Stephen J. Kirk, Grosse Pointe Pk, MI
John M. Kirksey, Houston, TX
Peyton E. Kirven, Westlake Village, CA
Robert S. Kitchen, Ocean Hills, CA
Henry Klein, Mount Vernon, WA
J. Arvid Klein, New York, NY
Robert M. Kliment, New York, NY
Stephen A. Kliment, New York, NY
Kenneth F. Klindtworth, Duck Key, FL
Lee B. Kline, Los Angeles, CA
Vincent G. Kling, Chester Springs, PA
James F. Knight, Gunnison, CO
Roy F. Knight, Tallahassee, FL
William H. Knight, Santa Rosa, CA
Stuart Knoop, Chevy Chase, MD
Charles M. Kober, Long Beach, CA
Carl Koch, Cambridge, MA
Steven Y. Kodama, San Francisco, CA
Edward J. Kodet Jr., Minneapolis, MN
Pierre F. Koenig, Los Angeles, CA
Alfred H. Koetter, Boston, MA
A. Eugene Kohn, New York, NY
Keith R. Kolb, Seattle, WA
Nathaniel K. Kolb Jr., Dallas, TX
Ronald Kolman, Savannah, GA
S. Richard Komatsu, El Cerrito, CA
Hendrik Koning, Santa Monica, CA
Norman L. Koonce, McLean, VA
James F. Kortan, Atlanta, GA
Panos G. Koulermos, La Crescenta, CA
Alexander Kouzmanoff, Rye Brook, NY
Gerhardt Kramer, Webster Groves, MO
Robert Kramer, Brookline, MA
Peter Krasnow, New York City, NY
M. Stanley Krause Jr., Newport News, VA
William Henry Kreager, Seattle, WA

Fellows of The American Institute of Architects

Eugene Kremer, Manhattan, KS
J. Richard Kremer, Louisville, KY
Jerrily R. Kress, Washington, DC
John L. Kriken, San Francisco, CA
Robert N. Kronewitter, Denver, CO
Kenneth C. Kruger, Santa Barbara, CA
James O. Kruhly, Philadelphia, PA
Rod Kruse, Des Moines, IA
Denis G. Kuhn, New York, NY
Julian E. Kulski, Orlean, VA
Ernest J. Kump, Zurich, Switzerland
Moritz Kundig, Spokane, WA
Theodore E. Kurz, Cleveland, OH
Peter Kuttner, Cambridge, MA
Sylvia P. Kwan, San Francisco, CA
Michael Kwartler, New York, NY

L

David N. LaBau, Bloomfield, CT
Ronald J. Labinski, Kansas City, MO
John W. Lackens Jr., Minneapolis, MN
Bill N. Lacy, Purchase, NY
Thomas Laging, Lincoln, NE
Henry J. Lagorio, Orinda, CA
Jerry Laiserin, Woodbury, NY
David C. Lake, San Antonio, TX
Charles E. Lamb, Annapolis, MD
James Lambeth, Fayetteville, AR
James I. Lammers, Chisago City, MN
Gregory W. Landahl, Chicago, IL
Peter H. Landon, Chicago, IL
D. E. Landry, Dallas, TX
Jane Landry, Dallas, TX
John M. Laping, West Amherst, NY
Arnold Les Larsen, Port Salerno, FL
Robert G. Larsen, New York City, NY
Dayl A. Larson, Denver, CO
William L. Larson, Omaha, NE
William N. Larson, Park Ridge, IL
Carroll J. Lawler, West Hartford, CT
Charles E. Lawrence, Houston, TX
Jerry Lawrence, Tacoma, WA
Robert M. Lawrence, Oklahoma City, OK
David E. Lawson, Madison, WI
Elizabeth Lawson, Charlottesville, VA
William R. Lawson, Reston, VA
Franklin D. Lawyer, Houston, TX
John C. Le Bey, Savannah, GA
William E. Leddy, San Francisco, CA
Robert LeMond, Fort Worth, TX
Glen S. LeRoy, Kansas City, MO
Benjamin B. Lee, Honolulu, HI
Donald R. Lee, Charlotte, NC
Elizabeth B. Lee, Lumberton, NC
John Lee, New York, NY
M. David Lee, Boston, MA
Gene Leedy, Winter Haven, FL
James M. Leefe, Sausalito, CA
Andrea P. Leers, Boston, MA
Gillet Lefferts, Darien, CT
Spencer A. Leineweber, Honolulu, HI
Lawrence J. Leis, Louisville, KY
Richard Leitch, South Laguna, CA
Herbert Lembcke, San Francisco, CA
James T. Lendrum, Phoenix, AZ
Peter A. Lendrum, Phoenix, AZ
Eason H. Leonard, Carmel, CA
Ralph Lerner, Princeton, NJ
Nicholas Lesko, Cleveland, OH
Francis D. Lethbridge, Nantucket, MA
Conrad Levenson, New York, NY
Jonathan Levi, Boston, MA
Brenda A. Levin, Los Angeles, CA
Richard D. Levin, Longboat Key, FL
Alan G. Levy, Philadelphia, PA
Eugene P. Levy, Little Rock, AR
Herbert W. Levy, Spring House, PA
Morton L. Levy, Houston, TX
Toby S. Levy, San Francisco, CA
Anne McCutcheon Lewis, Washington, DC
Calvin F. Lewis, Des Moines, IA
David Lewis, Homestead, PA
George B. Lewis, Oklahoma City, OK
Howarth Lewis, Jr., West Palm Beach, FL
Richard L. Lewis, Pebble Beach, CA
Roger K. Lewis, Washington, DC
Tom Lewis Jr., Kissimmee, FL
Walter H. Lewis, Champaign, IL
Alan C. Liddle, Lakewood, WA
Frederick Liebhardt, La Jolla, CA
Theodore Liebman, New York, NY
Bernard J. Liff, Pittsburgh, PA
John H. Lind, Iowa City, IA
David Lindsey, Seattle, WA
Gail A. Lindsey, Wake Forest, NC
Charles D. Linn, New York, NY
H. Mather Lippincott Jr., Moylan, PA
William H. Liskamm, San Rafael, CA
Robert A. Little, Cleveland, OH
Robert S. Livesey, Columbus, OH
Stanley C. Livingston, San Diego, CA
Thomas W. Livingston, Anchorage, AK
Walter R. Livingston Jr., Crum Lynne, PA
Peter Lizon, Knoxville, TN
W. Kirby Lockard, Tucson, AZ
James L. Loftis, Oklahoma City, OK
Vivian Loftness, Pittsburgh, PA
Donn Logan, Berkeley, CA
Dirk Lohan, Chicago, IL
Thomas E. Lollini, Berkeley, CA

Fellows of The American Institute of Architects

Jerrold E. Lomax, Carmel Valley, CA
J. Carson Looney, Memphis, TN
R. Nicholas Loope, Phoenix, AZ
Gabor Lorant, Phoenix, AZ
Larry Lord, Atlanta, GA
George H. Loschky, Seattle, WA
John C. Loss, Whitehall, MI
Rex Lotery, Montecito, CA
William C. Louie, New York, NY
William Love, Los Angeles, CA
Ivenue Love-Stanley, Atlanta, GA
Robert D. Loversidge Jr., Columbus, OH
Wendell H. Lovett, Seattle, WA
Frank E. Lucas, Charleston, SC
Thomas J. Lucas, Southfield, MI
Lenore M. Lucey, Washington, DC
Carl F. Luckenbach, Ann Arbor, MI
Lucinda Ludwig, Omaha, NE
Graham B. Luhn, Houston, TX
Anthony J. Lumsden, Los Angeles, CA
Frithjof Lunde, Center Valley, PA
Phillip Lundwall, Grand Rapids, MI
Victor A. Lundy, Bellaire, TX
Donald H. Lutes, Springfield, OR
Frederic P. Lyman, Sebeka, MN
Robert Dale Lynch, Pittsburgh, PA
Robert J. Lynch, Scottsdale, AZ
Donlyn Lyndon, Berkeley, CA
Maynard Lyndon, Kuessaberg, Germany

M

Michael Maas, W. Hampton Bch, NY
R. Doss Mabe, Los Angeles, CA
John E. MacAllister, San Francisco, CA
Donald MacDonald, San Francisco, CA
Virginia B. MacDonald, Kaneohe, HI
H. A. MacEwen, Tampa, FL
Ian MacKinlay, San Francisco, CA
Charles H. MacMahon, Deland, FL
Robert C. Mack, Minneapolis, MN
Eugene J. Mackey III, St. Louis, MO
John Macsai, Chicago, IL
Robert P. Madison, Cleveland, OH
Peter E. Madsen, Boston, MA
Theodore S. Maffitt Jr., Palestine, TX
Henry J. Magaziner, Philadelphia, PA
Gary Mahaffey, Minneapolis, MN
Victor C. Mahler, New York, NY
John E. Mahlum, Seattle, WA
C. R. Maiwald, Wilmington, NC
Marvin J. Malecha, Raleigh, NC
L. Vic Maloof, Atlanta, GA
Arthur E. Mann, Irvine, CA
Michael Mann, Los Angeles, CA
Carter H. Manny Jr., Chicago, IL
Clark D. Manus, San Francisco, CA
Virginia S. March, Fairhope, AL
Roger W. Margerum, Detroit, MI
Phillip T. Markwood, Columbus, OH
Harvey V. Marmon Jr., San Antonio, TX
Jud R. Marquardt, Seattle, WA
Clinton Marr Jr., Riverside, CA
Mortimer M. Marshall Jr., Reston, VA
Richard C. Marshall, San Francisco, CA
Albert C. Martin, Los Angeles, CA
Christopher C. Martin, Los Angeles, CA
David C. Martin, Los Angeles, CA
Robert E. Martin, Toledo, OH
W. Mike Martin, Berkeley, CA
Walter B. Martinez, Miami, FL
Thomas S. Marvel, San Juan, Puerto Rico
Joseph V. Marzella, Wallingford, PA
Ronald L. Mason, Denver, CO
George Matsumoto, Oakland, CA
Edward H. Matthei, Chicago, IL
Robert F. Mattox, Boston, MA
Frank J. Matzke, St. Augustine, FL
John M. Maudlin-Jeronimo, Bethesda, MD
Laurie M. Maurer, Brooklyn, NY
Susan A. Maxman, Philadelphia, PA
Murvan M. Maxwell, Metairie, LA
Arthur May, New York, NY
Kenneth D. Maynard, Anchorage, AK
Marsha Maytum, San Francisco, CA
Charles F. McAfee, Wichita, KS
Cheryl Lynn McAfee-Mitchell, Atlanta, GA
Charles McCafferty, Saint Clair Shores, MI
E. K. McCagg, II, Kirkland, WA
Joe M. McCall, Dallas, TX
Ann K. McCallum, Williamstown, MA
Michael A. McCarthy, New York, NY
John McCartney, Washington, DC
Bruce McCarty, Knoxville, TN
Harlan E. McClure, Pendleton, SC
Wesley A. McClure, Raleigh, NC
Richard E. McCommons, Falls Church, VA
Robert E. McConnell, Tucson, AZ
Edward D. McCrary, Hillsborough, CA
M. Allen McCree, Austin, TX
Gerald M. McCue, Cambridge, MA
Grant G. McCullagh, Chicago, IL
James McCullar, New York, NY
Margaret McCurry, Chicago, IL
William A. McDonough, Charlottesville, VA
Stephen A. McDowell, Kansas City, MO
Connie S. McFarland, Tulsa, OK
A. S. McGaughan, Washington, DC
John M. McGinty, Houston, TX
Milton B. McGinty, Houston, TX
Richard A. McGinty, Hilton Hd Island, SC

Fellows of The American Institute of Architects

John W. McGough, Spokane, WA
James R. McGranahan, Lacey, WA
Mark McInturff, Bethesda, MD
Herbert P. McKim, Wrightsville Beach, NC
David A. McKinley, Seattle, WA
Noel M. McKinnell, Boston, MA
Thomas L. McKittrick, College Station, TX
H. Roll McLaughlin, Carmel, IN
C. Andrew McLean, II, Atlanta, GA
James M. McManus, Glastonbury, CT
George A. McMath, Portland, OR
William G. McMinn, Coconut Grove, FL
E. Eean McNaughton Jr., New Orleans, LA
Carrell S. McNulty Jr., Cincinnati, OH
E. Keith McPheeters, Auburn, AL
John M. McRae, Starkville, MS
Charles B. McReynolds, Newport News, VA
Franklin Mead, Boston, MA
George C. Means Jr., Clemson, SC
Philip J. Meathe, Grosse Pte Farms, MI
David Meckel, San Francisco, CA
Henry G. Meier, Fishers, IN
Richard A. Meier, New York, NY
Carl R. Meinhardt, New York, NY
Lawrence P. Melillo, Louisville, KY
Roger C. Mellem, Port Republic, MD
R. A. Melting, New York, NY
Mark R. Mendell, Boston, MA
Francois de Menil, New York, NY
John O. Merrill, Tiburon, CA
William Dickey Merrill, Carmel, CA
James R. Merritt, Tacoma, WA
David R. Messersmith, Lubbock, TX
Robert C. Metcalf, Ann Arbor, MI
William H. Metcalf, McLean, VA
Andrew Metter, Evanston, IL
David Metzger, Washington, DC
C. Richard Meyer, Seattle, WA
James H. Meyer, Richardson, TX
John T. Meyer, Saginaw, MI
Kurt W. Meyer, Los Angeles, CA
Richard C. Meyer, Philadelphia, PA
Marshall D. Meyers, Pasadena, CA
Nancy A. Miao, New York, NY
Linda H. Michael, Charlottesville, VA
Constantine E. Michaelides, St. Louis, MO
Valerius Leo Michelson, Minneapolis, MN
Robert Miklos, Boston, MA
Arnold Mikon, Detroit, MI
Juanita M. Mildenberg, Bethesda, MD
Don C. Miles, Seattle, WA
Daniel R. Millen Jr., Cherry Hill, NJ
David E. Miller, Seattle, WA
Ewing H. Miller, Port Republic, MD
George H. Miller, New York, NY
Henry F. Miller, Orange, CT
Hugh C. Miller, Richmond, VA
James W. Miller, Madison, WI
John F. Miller, Cambridge, MA
Joseph Miller, Washington, DC
L. Kirk Miller, San Francisco, CA
Leroy B. Miller, Santa Monica, CA
Richard Miller, Nashville, TN
Robert L. Miller, Washington, DC
Steven Miller, Prague, Czechoslovakia
William C. Miller, Salt Lake City, UT
Edward I. Mills, New York, NY
Gordon E. Mills, Dubuque, IA
Michael Mills, Glen Ridge, NJ
Willis N. Mills Jr., Ponte Vedra Beach, FL
John D. Milner, Chadds Ford, PA
Lee Mindel, New York, NY
Adolfo E. Miralles, Altadena, CA
Henry D. Mirick, Fairless Hills, PA
Dan S. Mitchell, St. Louis, MO
Ehrman B. Mitchell Jr., Philadelphia, PA
Melvin L. Mitchell, Baltimore, MD
Richard R. Moger, Port Washington, NY
Ronald L. Moline, Bourbonnais, IL
Robert B. Molseed, Annandale, VA
Lynn H. Molzan, Indianapolis, IN
Frank Montana, Dade City, FL
Joseph D. Monticciolo, Woodbury, NY
Curtis J. Moody, Columbus, OH
Thomas B. Moon, Rancho Santa Margarita, CA
Arthur C. Moore, Washington, DC
Barry M. Moore, Houston, TX
Gerald L. Moorhead, Houston, TX
Jill K. Morelli, Columbus, OH
Jesse O. Morgan Jr., Shreveport, LA
Robert Lee Morgan, Port Townsend, WA
William N. Morgan, Jacksonville, FL
Howard H. Morgridge, Newport Beach, CA
Lamberto G. Moris, San Francisco, CA
Seth I. Morris, Houston, TX
Lionel Morrison, Dallas, TX
Murdo D. Morrison, Redwood City, CA
John Morse, Seattle, WA
James R. Morter, Vail, CO
Allen D. Moses, Kirkland, WA
Robert Mosher, La Jolla, CA
Samuel Z. Moskowitz, Naples, FL
Eric O. Moss, Culver City, CA
G. Michael Mostoller, Princeton, NJ
Kenneth L. Motley, Roanoke, VA
John K. Mott, Alexandria, VA
Edward A. Moulthrop, Atlanta, GA
Jennifer T. Moulton, Denver, CO
Frederic D. Moyer, Northbrook, IL
Frank R. Mudano, Clearwater, FL

Fellows of The American Institute of Architects

Theodore Mularz, Ashland, OR
Paul Muldawer, Atlanta, GA
Dale Mulfinger, Excelsior, MN
John W. Mullen III, Dallas, TX
Rosemary F. Muller, Oakland, CA
Harold C. Munger, Toledo, OH
Frank W. Munzer, Clinton Corners, NY
Charles F. Murphy, Mesa, AZ
Frank N. Murphy, Clayton, MO
David G. Murray, Tulsa, OK
Stephen A. Muse, Washington, DC
Robert C. Mutchler, Fargo, ND
John V. Mutlow, Los Angeles, CA
Donald B. Myer, Washington, DC
John R. Myer, Tamworth, NH
Barton Myers, Beverly Hills, CA
Ralph E. Myers, Prairie Village, KS

N

Daniel J. Nacht, Fair Oaks, CA
Barbara Nadel, Forest Hills, NY
Herbert N. Nadel, Los Angeles, CA
Chester Emil Nagel, Colorado Springs, CO
James L. Nagle, Chicago, IL
Louis Naidorf, Burbank, CA
Noboru Nakamura, Orinda, CA
C. S. Nakata, Colorado Springs, CO
Daniel H. Nall, Princeton, NJ
Robert J. Nash, Oxon Hill, MD
Eric Christopher Naslund, San Diego, CA
Thomas M. Nathan, Memphis, TN
Kenneth H. Natkin, Esq., San Francisco, CA
James A. Neal, Greenville, SC
Paul R. Neel, San Luis Obispo, CA
Ibsen Nelsen, Vashon, WA
Edward H. Nelson, Tucson, AZ
James Richard Nelson, Wilmington, DE
John H. Nelson, Chicago, IL
T. C. Nelson, Kansas City, MO
Ede I. Nemeti, Houston, TX
Donald E. Neptune, Newport Beach, CA
John F. Nesholm, Seattle, WA
Barbara Neski, New York, NY
Julian J. Neski, New York, NY
Walter A. Netsch, Chicago, IL
Perry King Neubauer, Cambridge, MA
Kurt Neubek, Houston, TX
Roger L. Neuenschwander, Atlanta, GA
J. Victor Neuhaus, III, Hunt, TX
William O. Neuhaus, III, Houston, TX
David J. Neuman, Palo Alto, CA
Hans Neumann, Las Vegas, NV
S. Kenneth Neumann, Beverly Hills, MI
Peter Newlin, Chestertown, MD
Herbert S. Newman, New Haven, CT
Michael Newman, Winston-Salem, NC
Robert L. Newsom, Los Angeles, CA
Chartier C. Newton, Austin, TX
Doreve Nicholaeff, Osterville, MA
Karen V. Nichols, Princeton, NJ
Michael H. Nicklas, Raleigh, NC
Robert Duncan Nicol, Oakland, CA
George Z. Nikolajevich, St. Louis, MO
Edward R. Niles, Malibu, CA
Christopher G. Nims, Denver, CO
Ivey L. Nix, Atlanta, GA
Robert J. Nixon, Port Angeles, WA
Douglas Noble, Los Angeles, CA
George M. Notter Jr., Washington, DC
John M. Novack, Dallas, TX
Frederick Noyes, Boston, MA
Jimmie R. Nunn, Flagstaff, AZ
John Nyfeler, Austin, TX

O

James W. O'Brien, Minneapolis, MN
W. L. O'Brien Jr., Research Triangle Park, NC
Thomas O'Connor, Detroit, MI
L. J. O'Donnell, Chicago, IL
Arthur F. O'Leary, County Louth, Ireland
Paul Murff O'Neal Jr., Shreveport, LA
Charles W. Oakley, Pacific Palisades, CA
Gyo Obata, Saint Louis, MO
Jeffrey K. Ochsner, Seattle, WA
Robert A. Odermatt, Berkeley, CA
Mary L. Oehrlein, Washington, DC
Rolf H. Ohlhausen, New York, NY
Richard M. Olcott, New York, NY
Edward A. Oldziey, Wyckoff, NJ
P. S. Oles, Newton, MA
H. B. Olin, Chicago, IL
Donald E. Olsen, Berkeley, CA
Carole J. Olshavsky, Columbus, OH
James W. Olson, Seattle, WA
Herbert B. Oppenheimer, New York, NY
Joseph K. Oppermann, Winston-Salem, NC
Edward L. Oremen, San Diego, CA
Robert E. Oringdulph, Portland, OR
Gordon D. Orr Jr., Madison, WI
David William Osler, Ann Arbor, MI
G. F. Oudens, Chevy Chase, MD
Raymond C. Ovresat, Wilmette, IL
Kenneth Owens Jr., Birmingham, AL

P

C. J. Paderewski III, San Diego, CA
Elizabeth Seward Padjen, Marblehead, MA
Gregory Palermo, Des Moines, IA
Joshua J. Pan, Taipei, Taiwan
Solomon Pan, Tucson, AZ

Fellows of The American Institute of Architects

Lester C. Pancoast, Miami, FL
John R. Pangrazio, Seattle, WA
Donald H. Panushka, Salt Lake City, UT
Dennis A. Paoletti, San Francisco, CA
Tician Papachristou, New York, NY
Laszlo Papp, New Canaan, CT
George C. Pappageorge, Chicago, IL
Constantine George Pappas, Troy, MI
Nicholas A. Pappas, Richmond, VA
Ted P. Pappas, Jacksonville, FL
Charles J. Parise, Grosse Pointe Woods, MI
Ki Suh Park, Los Angeles, CA
Sharon C. Park, Arlington, VA
Alfred B. Parker, Gainesville, FL
Derek Parker, San Francisco, CA
Howard C. Parker, Dallas, TX
Leonard S. Parker, Minneapolis, MN
R. C. Parrott, Knoxville, TN
Steven A. Parshall, Houston, TX
Giovanni Pasanella, New York, NY
C. H. Paseur, Houston, TX
Joseph Passonneau, Washington, DC
Piero Patri, San Francisco, CA
Allen L. Patrick, Columbus, OH
S. Glen Paulsen, Ann Arbor, MI
Sherida Elizabeth Paulsen, New York, NY
Charles Harrison Pawley, Coral Gables, FL
Thomas M. Payette, Boston, MA
H. Morse Payne, Lincoln, MA
Richard W. Payne, Houston, TX
George Clayton Pearl, Albuquerque, NM
Bryce Pearsall, Phoenix, AZ
Charles Almond Pearson Jr., Arlington, VA
J. Norman Pease Jr., Charlotte, NC
John G. Pecsok, Indianapolis, IN
William Pedersen Jr., New York, NY
Katherine N. Peele, Raleigh, NC
Gerard W. Peer, Charlotte, NC
William R. Peery, Clearwater, FL
I. M. Pei, New York, NY
Maris Peika, Toluca Lake, CA
Norbert A. Peiker, Mansfield, OH
John W. Peirce, Topsfield, MA
Cesar Pelli, New Haven, CT
William M. Pena, Houston, TX
Thompson E. Penney, Charleston, SC
David L. Perkins, Lafayette, LA
G. Holmes Perkins, Philadelphia, PA
L. Bradford Perkins, New York, NY
John Gray Perry, Portland, OR
Norman K. Perttula, Aurora, OH
Stuart K. Pertz, New York, NY
Robert W. Peters, Albuquerque, NM
Carolyn S. Peterson, San Antonio, TX
Charles E. Peterson, Philadelphia, PA
Guy W. Peterson, Sarasota, FL
Jesse Julius Peterson Jr., Wilmington, NC
Leonard A. Peterson, Chicago, IL
Edward G. Petrazio, Spanish Fort, AL
Eleanore Pettersen, Saddle River, NJ
Jay S. Pettitt Jr., Beulah, MI
Mark A. Pfaller, Elm Grove, WI
Norman Pfeiffer, Los Angeles, CA
J. D. Pfluger, Austin, TX
Barton Phelps, Los Angeles, CA
Frederick F. Phillips, Chicago, IL
W. Irving Phillips Jr., Houston, TX
J. Almont Pierce, Falls Church, VA
John Allen Pierce, Dallas, TX
Walter S. Pierce, Lexington, WA
Raymond A. Pigozzi, Evanston, IL
George J. Pillorge, Oxford, MD
Robert J. Piper, Winnetka, IL
Carl W. Pirscher, Windsor, Canada
John W. Pitman, Santa Barbara, CA
Peter A. Piven, Philadelphia, PA
Elizabeth Plater-Zyberk, Miami, FL
Charles A. Platt, New York, NY
Kalvin J. Platt, Sausalito, CA
G. Gray Plosser Jr., Birmingham, AL
Jan Hird Pokorny, New York, NY
Lee A. Polisano, London, England
William M. Polk, Seattle, WA
Richard N. Pollack, San Francisco, CA
Wilson Pollock, Cambridge, MA
James Stewart Polshek, New York, NY
Donald P. Polsky, Omaha, NE
Ralph Pomerance, New York, NY
Leason F. Pomeroy, III, Santa Ana, CA
Lee H. Pomeroy, New York, NY
Lynn S. Pomeroy, Sacramento, CA
Gerrard S. Pook, Bronx, NY
Samuel D. Popkin, West Bloomfield, MI
William L. Porter, Cambridge, MA
John C. Portman Jr., Atlanta, GA
Penny H. Posedly, Phoenix, AZ
Raymond G. Post Jr., Baton Rouge, LA
Boone Powell, San Antonio, TX
Peter Pran, Seattle, WA
James Pratt, Dallas, TX
Antoine Predock, Albuquerque, NM
Andy Pressman, Albuquerque, NM
William T. Priestley, Lake Forest, IL
Kathryn Tyler Prigmore, Washington, D.C.
Arnold J. Prima Jr., Washington, DC
Harold E. Prinz, Dallas, TX
Donald Prowler, Philadelphia, PA
Theodore H.M. Prudon, New York, NY
Homer L. Puderbaugh, Lincoln, NE
David A. Pugh, Portland, OR

Fellows of The American Institute of Architects

William L. Pulgram, Atlanta, GA
James G. Pulliam, Pasadena, CA
Joe T. Pursell, Jackson, MS
Michael Pyatok, Oakland, CA

Q

G. William Quatman, Kansas City, MO
Jerry L. Quebe, Chicago, IL
Robert W. Quigley, San Diego, CA
Marcel Quimby, Dallas, TX
Michael L. Quinn, Washington, DC
Richard W. Quinn, Avon, CT

R

Martin D. Raab, New York, NY
Bruce A. Race, Berkeley, CA
John A. Raeber, San Francisco, CA
Craig E. Rafferty, St. Paul, MN
George E. Rafferty, St. Paul, MN
Richard J. Rafferty, St. Paul, MN
Lemuel Ramos, Miami, FL
Linda M. Ramsay, Savannah, GA
Peter A. Rand, Minneapolis, MN
Terry Rankine, Cambridge, MA
Raymond R. Rapp, Galveston, TX
Ralph Rapson, Minneapolis, MN
Howard Terry Rasco, Little Rock, AR
Peter T. Rasmussen, Tacoma, WA
John K. Rauch Jr., Philadelphia, PA
John G. Rauma, Minneapolis, MN
William L. Rawn, Boston, MA
James T. Ream, San Francisco, CA
Suzane Reatig, Kensington, MD
Mark Reddington, Seattle, WA
Charles Redmon, Cambridge, MA
Daniel A. Redstone, Southfield, MI
Louis G. Redstone, Southfield, MI
Ronald Reed, Cleveland, OH
Vernon Reed, Liberty, MO
William R. Reed, Tacoma, WA
Henry S. Reeder Jr., Cambridge, MA
Frank Blair Reeves, Gainesville, FL
I. S. K. Reeves, V, Winter Park, FL
Roscoe Reeves Jr., Chevy Chase, MD
Victor A. Regnier, Los Angeles, CA
Patrick C. Rehse, Phoenix, AZ
Pierce K. Reibsamen, Los Angeles, CA
Jerry Reich, Chicago, IL
Johnstone Reid Jr., Orlando, FL
Leonard H. Reinke, Oshkosh, WI
Ilmar Reinvald, Tacoma, WA
John Rex, Carpinteria, CA
John S. Reynolds, Eugene, OR
M. Garland Reynolds Jr., Gainesville, GA
David A. Rhodes, Memphis, TN
James W. Rhodes, New York, NY
Kenneth Ricci, New York, NY
Paul J. Ricciuti, Youngstown, OH
David E. Rice, San Diego, CA
Richard L. Rice, Raleigh, NC
James W. Rich, Tulsa, OK
Lisle F. Richards, San Jose, CA
Heidi A. Richardson, Sausalito, CA
Walter J. Richardson, Newport Beach, CA
Charles H. Richter Jr., Baltimore, MD
David R. Richter, Corpus Christi, TX
Hans Riecke, Haiku, HI
James V. Righter, Boston, MA
Jorge Rigau, Rio Piedras, Puerto Rico
Jefferson B. Riley, Centerbrook, CT
Ronnette Riley, New York, NY
David N. Rinehart, La Jolla, CA
David Rinehart, Los Angeles, CA
M. Jack Rinehart Jr., Charlottesville, VA
Mark W. Rios, Los Angeles, CA
Darrel D. Rippeteau, Delray Beach, FL
Dahlen K. Ritchey, Bradfordwoods, PA
P. Richard Rittelmann, Butler, PA
James W. Ritter, Alexandria, VA
Richard E. Ritz, Portland, OR
I. L. Roark, Lawrence, KS
Jack Robbins, Berkeley, CA
Darryl Roberson, San Francisco, CA
Jaquelin T. Robertson, New York, NY
C. David Robinson, San Francisco, CA
Harry G. Robinson III, Washington, DC
J. W. Robinson, Atlanta, GA
Kevin Roche, Hamden, CT
Garth Rockcastle, Minneapolis, MN
George T. Rockrise, Glen Ellen, CA
Burton L. Rockwell, San Francisco, CA
Kenneth A. Rodrigues, San Jose, CA
Susan T. Rodriguez, New York, NY
Carl D. Roehling, Detroit, MI
Chester E. Roemer, St. Louis, MO
Ralph J. Roesling II, San Diego, CA
R. G. Roessner, Austin, TX
Archibald C. Rogers, Baltimore, MD
James G. Rogers III, New York, NY
John B. Rogers, Denver, CO
John D. Rogers, Asheville, NC
Craig W. Roland, Santa Rosa, CA
B. F. Romanowitz, Lexington, KY
James G. Rome, Corpus Christi, TX
Benjamin T. Rook, Charlotte, NC
Robert W. Root, Denver, CO
Richard M. Rosan, Washington, DC
William A. Rose Jr., White Plains, NY
Alan Rosen, Palm Desert, CA
Alan R. Rosen, Lake Forest, IL

Fellows of The American Institute of Architects

Manuel M. Rosen, La Jolla, CA
Arthur Rosenblatt, New York, NY
Norman Rosenfeld, New York, NY
Edgar B. Ross, Tiburon, CA
Ken L. Ross Jr., Houston, TX
James S. Rossant, New York, NY
Louis A. Rossetti, Birmingham, MI
Bill Rostenberg, San Francisco, CA
Harold Roth, New Haven, CT
Richard Roth Jr., Freeport,
Edward N. Rothe, Edison, NJ
Martha L. Rothman, Boston, MA
Richard Rothman, Rising Fawn, GA
Bernard B. Rothschild, Atlanta, GA
Bernard Rothzeid, New York, NY
Maurice Rotival, Paris, France
Michael Rotondi, Los Angeles, CA
Lauren L. Rottet, Los Angeles, CA
Judith L. Rowe, Oakland, CA
Daniel Rowen, New York, NY
Ralph T. Rowland, Cheshire, CT
Albert W. Rubeling Jr., Towson, MD
John Ruble, Santa Monica, CA
J. Ronald Rucker, Tyler, TX
J. W. Rudd, Knoxville, TN
Gordon E. Ruehl, Spokane, WA
Evett J. Ruffcorn, Seattle, WA
John A. Ruffo, San Francisco, CA
Herman O. Ruhnau, Riverside, CA
Peter L. Rumpel, Saint Augustine, FL
William W. Rupe, St. Louis, MO
T. T. Russell, Miami, FL
Walter A. Rutes, Scottsdale, AZ
H. Mark Ruth, Agana, Guam
Harry R. Rutledge, York, PA
Roger N. Ryan, N. Canton, OH
James E. Rydeen, Rio Verde, AZ
Donald P. Ryder, New Rochelle, NY

S

Werner Sabo, Chicago, IL
Harold G. Sadler, San Diego, CA
Moshe Safdie, Somerville, MA
Carol S. Sakata, Honolulu, HI
Raj Saksena, Bristol, RI
David D. Salmela, Duluth, MN
F. Cuthbert Salmon, Stillwater, OK
Nathaniel W. Sample, Madison, WI
Peter Samton, New York, NY
Danny Samuels, Houston, TX
Thomas Samuels, Chicago, IL
Gil A. Sanchez, Santa Cruz, CA
James J. Sanders, Seattle, WA
Kenneth D. Sanders, Portland, OR
Linda Sanders, Walnut, CA
Donald Sandy Jr., San Francisco, CA
Martin G. Santini, Englewood Cliffs, NJ
Adele N. Santos, San Francisco, CA
Carlos R. Sanz, Santurce, Puerto Rico
Charles M. Sappenfield, Sanibel, FL
Angel C. Saqui, Coral Gables, FL
Victor Saroki, Birmingham, MI
Louis Sauer, Pittsburgh, PA
Louis R. Saur, Clayton, MO
Robert W. Sawyer, Wilmington, NC
Peter M. Saylor, Philadelphia, PA
Sam Scaccia, Chicago, IL
Joseph J. Scalabrin, Columbus, OH
Mario L. Schack, Baltimore, MD
K. M. Schaefer, Kirkwood, MO
Robert J. Schaefer, Wichita, KS
Walter Schamu, Baltimore, MD
David Scheatzle, Tempe, AZ
James A. Scheeler, Reston, VA
Jeffrey Allen Scherer, Minneapolis, MN
David W. Schervish, Detroit, MI
G. G. Schierle, Los Angeles, CA
Arthur A. Schiller, Manhasset, NY
Don P. Schlegel, Albuquerque, NM
Frank Schlesinger, Washington, DC
Jon R. Schleuning, Portland, OR
Todd H. Schliemann, New York, NY
John I. Schlossman, Hubbard Woods, IL
Roger Schluntz, Albuquerque, NM
Mildred F. Schmertz, New York, NY
Fred C. Schmidt, Oklahoma City, OK

Did you know...
The States with the most AIA Fellows are:
California—411
New York—230
Texas—218
Illinois—133
Massachusetts—125
Florida—105
Washington—96
Pennsylvania—82
Virginia—74
D.C.—71
Michigan—70
North Carolina—66

Fellows of The American Institute of Architects

Wayne S. Schmidt, Indianapolis, IN
R. Christian Schmitt, Charleston, SC
Herbert W. Schneider, Scottsdale, AZ
Walter Scholer Jr., Fort Myers, FL
John P. Schooley, Columbus, OH
Barnett P. Schorr, Seattle, WA
Charles F. Schrader, San Rafael, CA
Douglas F. Schroeder, Chicago, IL
Kenneth A. Schroeder, Chicago, IL
John H. Schruben, North Bethesda, MD
George A. D. Schuett, Glendale, WI
Kenneth Schwartz, Charlottesville, VI
Kenneth E. Schwartz, San Luis Obispo, CA
Robert Schwartz, Washington, DC
Alan Schwartzman, Paris, France
Katherine L. Schwennsen, Ames, IA
Charles E. Schwing, Baton Rouge, LA
Alan D. Sclater, Seattle, WA
David M. Scott, Pullman, WA
William W. Scott, Taylors Falls, MN
Der Scutt, New York, NY
Jim W. Sealy, Dallas, TX
Linda Searl, Chicago, IL
Thomas J. Sedgewick, Clio, MI
Jonathan Segal, La Jolla, CA
Paul Segal, New York, NY
Lawrence P. Segrue, Visalia, CA
E. J. Seibert, Boca Grande, FL
Alexander Seidel, Belvedere, CA
Larry D. Self, St. Louis, MO
Theodore Seligson, Kansas City, MO
Bruce M. Sellery, Marina Del Rey, CA
Dale E. Selzer, Dallas, TX
John C. Senhauser, Cincinnati, OH
Ronald S. Senseman, Silver Spring, MD
Jerome M. Seracuse, Colorado Springs, CO
Diane Serber, Old Chatham, NY
Phillip K. Settecase, Salem, OR
Betty Lee Seydler-Hepworth, Franklin, MI
Richard S. Sharpe, Norwich, CT
John A. Sharratt, Boston, MA
James L. Shay, San Rafael, CA
Leo G. Shea, Leland, MI
John P. Sheehy, Mill Valley, CA
George C. Sheldon, Portland, OR
W. Overton Shelmire, Dallas, TX
Carol Shen, Berkeley, CA
John V. Sheoris, Grosse Pointe, MI
Herschel E. Shepard, Atlantic Beach, FL
Hugh Shepley, Manchester, MA
Patricia C. Sherman, Concord, NH
Takashi Shida, Santa Monica, CA
Roger D. Shiels, Portland, OR
Dan Sidney Shipley, Dallas, TX
Edward H. Shirley, Atlanta, GA
Philip A. Shive, Charlotte, NC
William C. Shopsin, New York City, NY
Evan H. Shu, Melrose, MA
George Whiteside Shupee, Arlington, TX
Jack T. Sidener, Shatin, New Territories, PRC
Paul G. Sieben, Toledo, OH
Lloyd H. Siegel, Washington, DC
Robert H. Siegel, New York, NY
Charles M. Sieger, Miami, FL
Henry N. Silvestri, Corona Del Mar, CA
Brad Simmons, St. Louis, MO
Cathy J. Simon, San Francisco, CA
Mark Simon, Centerbrook, CT
Lawrence L. Simons, Santa Rosa, CA
Donal R. Simpson, Dallas, TX
Robert T. Simpson Jr., Berkeley, CA
Scott Simpson, Cambridge, MA
Howard F. Sims, Detroit, MI
Jerome J. Sincoff, St. Louis, MO
Donald I. Singer, Fort Lauderdale, FL
E. Crichton Singleton, Kansas City, MO
Charles S. Sink, Denver, CO
Lorri D. Sipes, Ann Arbor, MI
William H. Sippel Jr., Allison Park, PA
Michael M. Sizemore, Atlanta, GA
Ronald L. Skaggs, Dallas, TX
Norma M. Sklarek, Pacific Palisades, CA
Gary Skog, Southfield, MI
Lee H. Skolnick, New York, NY
Murray A. Slama, Walnut Creek, CA
Clifton M. Smart Jr., Fayetteville, AR
Saul C. Smiley, Minnetonka, MN
Adrian D. Smith, Chicago, IL
Arthur Smith, Southfield, MI
Bill D. Smith, Dallas, TX
Bruce H. Smith, Pontiac, MI
Christopher J. Smith, Honolulu, HI
Cole Smith, Dallas, TX
Colin L. M. Smith, Cambridge, MA
Darrell L. Smith, Eugene, OR
Edward Smith, Salt Lake City, UT
Fleming W. Smith Jr., Nashville, TN
Frank Folsom Smith, Sarasota, FL
Hamilton P. Smith, Garden City, NY
Harwood K. Smith, Dallas, TX
Ivan H. Smith, Jacksonville, FL
John R. Smith, Ketchum, ID
Joseph N. Smith III, Atlanta, GA
Kenneth Smith, Jacksonville, FL
Macon S. Smith, Raleigh, NC
Michael E. Smith, Bellingham, WA
Stephen B. Smith, Salt Lake City, UT
T. Clayton Smith, Baton Rouge, LA
Tyler Smith, Hartford, CT
Whitney R. Smith, Sonoma, CA

Fellows of The American Institute of Architects

David I. Smotrich, New York, NY
Neil H. Smull, Boise, ID
Richard Snibbe, New York, NY
Sheila Snider, Indianapolis, IN
Julie V. Snow, Minneapolis, MN
Sam T. Snowdon, Jr., Laurinburg, NC
William E. Snyder, Henderson, NV
Walter H. Sobel, Chicago, IL
Daniel Solomon, San Francisco, CA
Richard J. Solomon, Chicago, IL
Stuart B. Solomon, Watertown, MA
James Hamilton Somes Jr., Portsmouth, NH
Hak Son, Santa Monica, CA
Suman Sorg, Washington, D.C.
John R. Sorrenti, Mineola, NY
Charles B. Soule, Montgomery Village, MD
Michael Southworth, Berkeley, CA
Edward A. Sovik, Northfield, MN
George S. Sowden, Fort Worth, TX
Marvin Sparn, Boulder, CO
Laurinda H. Spear, Miami, FL
Beverley Spears, Santa Fe, NM
Lawrence W. Speck, Austin, TX
Michael H. Spector, New Hyde Park, NY
John H. Spencer, Hampton, VA
Tomas H. Spiers Jr., Camp Hill, PA
Pat Y. Spillman, Dallas, TX
Robert A. Spillman, Bethlehem, PA
Donald E. Sporleder, South Bend, IN
Joseph G. Sprague, Dallas, TX
Kent Spreckelmeyer, Lawrence, KS
Paul D. Spreiregen, Washington, DC
Bernard P. Spring, Brookline, MA
Everett G. Spurling Jr., Bethesda, MD
Dennis W. Stacy, Dallas, TX
Alfred M. Staehli, Portland, OR
Richard P. Stahl, Springfield, MO
Raymond F. Stainback Jr., Atlanta, GA
Duffy B. Stanley, El Paso, TX
William J. Stanley, III, Atlanta, GA
Jane M. Stansfeld, Austin, TX
Michael J. Stanton, San Francisco, CA
Earl M. Starnes, Cedar Key, FL
Frank A. Stasiowski, Newton, MA
Donald J. Stastny, Portland, OR
Russell L. Stecker, Montpelier, VT
Mark W. Steele, La Jolla, CA
John E. Stefany, Tampa, FL
Peter Steffian, Boston, MA
Charles W. Steger Jr., Blacksburg, VA
Douglas Steidl, Akron, OH
Carl Stein, New York, NY
Morris A. Stein, Phoenix, AZ
Goodwin B. Steinberg, San Jose, CA
Robert T. Steinberg, San Jose, CA
Ralph Steinglass, New York, NY
Henry Steinhardt, Mercer Island, WA
Douglas E. Steinman Jr., Beaumont, TX
James A. Stenhouse, Charlotte, NC
Donald J. Stephens, Berlin, NY
Michael J. Stepner, San Diego, CA
Robert A. M. Stern, New York, NY
William F. Stern, Houston, TX
Preston Stevens Jr., Atlanta, GA
James M. Stevenson, Highland Park, IL
W. Cecil Steward, Lincoln, NE
R. K. Stewart, San Francisco, CA
William W. Stewart, Clayton, MO
Sherwood Stockwell, Wolcott, CO
Claude Stoller, Berkeley, CA
Randall Paul Stout, Los Angeles, CA
Neal P. Stowe Salt Lake City, UT
H. T. Stowell, Western Springs, IL
Neil E. Strack, Champaign, IL
Ronald A. Straka, Denver, CO
Michael J. Stransky, Salt Lake City, UT
Frank Straub, Troy, MI
Carl A. Strauss, Cincinnati, OH
John R. Street Jr., Marietta, GA
Arthur V. Strock, Santa Ana, CA
Hugh Asher Stubbins Jr., Cambridge, MA
Sidney W. Stubbs Jr., Mount Pleasant, SC
Donald L. Stull, Boston, MA
Robert S. Sturgis, Weston, MA
Erik Sueberkrop, San Francisco, CA
Marvin D. Suer, Willow Grove, PA
John W. Sugden, Park City, UT
Douglas R. Suisman, Santa Monica, CA
Edward Sullam, Honolulu, HI
John P. Sullivan, Valhalla, NY
Patrick M. Sullivan, Claremont, CA
Gene R. Summers, Cloverdale, CA
Alan R. Sumner, Saint Louis, MO
Richard P. Sundberg, Seattle, WA
Donald R. Sunshine, Blacksburg, VA
Eugene L. Surber, Atlanta, GA
Charles R. Sutton, Honolulu, HI
Sharon E. Sutton, Seattle, WA
George Suyama, Seattle, WA
Vernon D. Swaback, Scottsdale, AZ
Eugene C. Swager, Peoria, IL
Robert M. Swatt, San Francisco, CA
Earl Swensson, Nashville, TN
Richard Swett, Bow, NH
Stephen Swicegood, Decatur, GA
H. H. Swinburne, Philadelphia, PA
Don A. Swofford, Charlottesville, VA
John M. Syvertsen, Chicago, IL

Fellows of The American Institute of Architects

T

William B. Tabler, New York, NY
Edgar Tafel, Venice, FL
Marvin Taff, Beverly Hills, CA
Edward K. Takahashi, Santa Monica, CA
Ray Takata, Sacramento, CA
Francis T. Taliaferro, Santa Monica, CA
R. H. Tan, Spokane, WA
Ted Tokio Tanaka, Marina Del Rey, CA
Virginia W. Tanzmann, Pasadena, CA
Charles R. Tapley, Houston, TX
A. Anthony Tappe, Boston, MA
John Tarantino, New York City, NY
H. Harold Tarleton, Greenville, SC
D. Coder Taylor, Glenview, IL
Marilyn J. Taylor, New York, NY
Richard L. Taylor Jr., Atlanta, GA
Walter Q. Taylor, Jacksonville, FL
Thomas H. Teasdale, Kirkwood, MO
Jerry R. Tepe, Hopkinton, NH
Clinton C. Ternstrom, Los Angeles, CA
Roland Terry, Mt. Vernon, WA
Robert L. Tessier, Yarmouth Port, MA
B. C. Tharp, Montgomery, TX
Dorwin A. J. Thomas, Boston, MA
James B. Thomas, Houston, TX
James L. Thomas, Spartanburg, SC
Joseph F. Thomas, Pasadena, CA
Val Thomas, Seattle, WA
Benjamin Thompson, Cambridge, MA
David C. Thompson, San Diego, CA
Milo H. Thompson, Minneapolis, MN
Robert L. Thompson, Portland, OR
Warren D. Thompson, Fresno, CA
Charles B. Thomsen, Houston, TX
Duane Thorbeck, Minneapolis, MN
Karl Thorne, Gainesville, FL
Oswald H. Thorson, Marco, FL
John P. Tice Jr., Pensacola, FL
Stanley Tigerman, Chicago, IL
Patrick Tillett, Portland, OR
James H. Timberlake, Philadelphia, PA
Robert H. Timme, Los Angeles, CA
Leslie D. Tincknell, Saginaw, MI
Glen A. Tipton, Baltimore, MD
James D. Tittle, Abilene, TX
Philip E. Tobey, Reston, VA
Calvin J. Tobin, Highland Park, IL
Logic Tobola II, El Campo, TX
Anderson Todd, Houston, TX
David F. M. Todd, New York, NY
Thomas A. Todd, Jamestown, RI
Lee Tollefson, Saint Paul, MN
John Tomassi, Chicago, IL
James E. Tomblinson, Flint, MI
Frank Tomsick, San Francisco, CA
John Francis Torti, Silver Spring, MD
Mark Joseph Tortorich, Martinez, CA
Coulson Tough, The Woodlands, TX
Dennis T. Toyomura, Honolulu, HI
Jack Train, Chicago, IL
Karl E. Treffinger Sr., West Linn, OR
Kenneth Treister, Coconut Grove, FL
Michael Tribble, Charlotte, NC
David M. Trigiani, Jackson, MS
William H. Trogdon, Olga, WA
Leroy Troyer, Mishawaka, IN
William H. Truex Jr., Burlington, VT
Chiu Lin Tse-Chan, San Francisco, CA
Charles N. Tseckares, Boston, MA
Edward T. M. Tsoi, Arlington, MA
Seab A. Tuck, III, Nashville, TN
Jack R. Tucker Jr., Memphis, TN
Thomas B. Tucker, San Diego, CA
Richard L. Tully, Columbus, OH
Emanuel N. Turano, Boca Raton, FL
John Gordon Turnbull, San Francisco, CA
Thomas P. Turner Jr., Charlotte, NC
Wilbur H. Tusler Jr., Kentfield, CA
Ilene R. Tyler, Ann Arbor, MI
James L. Tyler, Pacific Palisades, CA
Robert Tyler, Tarzana, CA
Anne G. Tyng, Philadelphia, PA

U

Edward K. Uhlir, Chicago, IL
Kenneth A. Underwood, Philadelphia, PA
Dean F. Unger, Sacramento, CA
Roberta Marrano Unger, Atlanta, GA
Denorval Unthank Jr., Eugene, OR
Robert H. Uyeda, Los Angeles, CA

V

Joseph D. Vaccaro, Los Angeles, CA
Edward Vaivoda Jr., Portland, OR
William E. Valentine, San Francisco, CA
Joseph M. Valerio, Chicago, IL
William L. Van Alen, Wilmington, DE
Robert Van Deusen, Grand Junction, CO
Peter van Dijk, Cleveland, OH
George V. Van Fossen Schwab, Baltimore, MD
Thomas Van Housen, Minneapolis, MN
Harold F. VanDine Jr., Birmingham, MI
Johannes VanTilburg, Santa Monica, CA
Mitchell Vanbourg, Berkeley, CA
Harutun Vaporciyan, Huntington Woods, MI
Harold R. Varner, Berkley, MI
Andrew A. Vazzano, Detroit, MI
Leonard M. Veitzer, San Diego, CA

Fellows of The American Institute of Architects

Thomas W. Ventulett, Atlanta, GA
Robert Venturi, Philadelphia, PA
Shirley J. Vernon, Philadelphia, PA
Kathryn C. Vernon-McKeen, Hartford, CT
William R. Vick, Sacramento, CA
Robert L. Vickery, Charlottesville, VA
Wilmont Vickrey, Chicago, IL
Gregory D. Villanueva, Los Angeles, CA
John Vinci, Chicago, IL
Rafael Vinoly, New York, NY
Stephen Vogel, Detroit, MI
Leonard W. Volk II, Dallas, TX
A. R. Von Brock, Buchanan, VA
Robert J. Von Dohlen, W Hartford, CT
Richard L. Von Luhrte, Denver, CO
Thomas Vonier, Paris, France
Bartholome Voorsanger, New York, NY
R. Randall Vosbeck, Vail, CO
William F. Vosbeck, Alexandria, VA
Thomas R. Vreeland, Century City, CA
R. E. Vrooman, College Station, TX

W

Hobart D. Wagener, Coronado, CA
William J. Wagner, Dallas Center, IA
John G. Waite, Albany, NY
Lawrence G. Waldron, Mercer Island, WA
Bruce M. Walker, Spokane, WA
Kenneth H. Walker, New York, NY
David A. Wallace, Philadelphia, PA
David D. Wallace, Westport, MA
Donald Q. Wallace, Lexington, KY
Les Wallach, Seattle, WA
Charles G. Walsh, Los Angeles, CA
Lloyd G. Walter Jr., Winston Salem, NC
W. G. Wandelmaier, New York, NY
Sheldon D. Wander, New York, NY
R. J. Warburton, Coral Gables, FL
G. T. Ward, Fairfax, VA
Robertson Ward Jr., Boston, MA
C. E. Ware, Rockford, IL
John Carl Warnecke, San Francisco, CA
Charles H. Warner Jr., Nyack, NY
Clyde K. Warner Jr., Louisville, KY
William D. Warner, Exeter, RI
Sharon F. Washburn, Bethesda, MD
Robert E. Washington, Richmond, VA
Barry L. Wasserman, Sacramento, CA
Joseph Wasserman, Southfield, MA
David H. Watkins, Bellaire, TX
Donald R. Watson, Trumbull, CT
Raymond L. Watson, Newport Beach, CA
William J. Watson, LaJolla, CA
John L. Webb, Ponchatoula, LA
P. R. Webber, Rutland, VT
Arthur M. Weber, Aiea, HI
Frederick S. Webster, Cazenovia, NY
C. R. Wedding, St. Petersburg, FL
Benjamin H. Weese, Chicago, IL
Cynthia Weese, Chicago, IL
Gary K. Weeter, Dallas, TX
Wesley Wei, Philadelphia, PA
Bryce Adair Weigand, Dallas, TX
Joe Neal Weilenman, Pago Pago, American Samoa
Nicholas H. Weingarten, Chicago, IL
Amy Weinstein, Washington, DC
Edward Weinstein, Seattle, WA
Jane Weinzapfel, Boston, MA
Gerald G. Weisbach, San Francisco, CA
Sarelle T. Weisberg, New York, NY
Steven F. Weiss, Chicago, IL
Martha L. Welborne, Los Angeles, CA
Frank D. Welch, Dallas, TX
John A. Welch, Tuskegee, AL
Louis L. Weller, Albuquerque, NM
William P. Wenzler, Milwaukee, WI
Lester Wertheimer, Los Angeles, CA
Helge Westermann, Cambridge, MA
Merle T. Westlake, Lexington, MA
Paul E. Westlake Jr., Cleveland, OH
I. Donald Weston, Brooklyn, NY
Charles H. Wheatley, Charlotte, NC
C. Herbert Wheeler, State College, PA
Daniel H. Wheeler, Chicago, IL
James H. Wheeler Jr., Abilene, TX
Kenneth D. Wheeler, Lake Forest, IL
Richard H. Wheeler, Los Angeles, CA
Murray Whisnant, Charlotte, NC
Arthur B. White, Havertown, PA
George M. White, Bethesda, MD
Janet Rothberg White, Bethesda, MD
Norval C. White, Salisbury, CT
Samuel G. White, New York, NY
Stephen Q. Whitney, Detroit, MI
Ward B. Whitwam, Sioux Falls, SD
Leonard S. Wicklund, Long Grove, IL
Christopher Widener, Springfield, OH
Chester A. Widom, Santa Monica, CA
William Wiese, II, Shelburne, VT
E. D. Wilcox, Tyler, TX
Jerry Cooper Wilcox, Little Rock, AR
Gordon L. Wildermuth, Greeley, PA
James E. Wiley, Dallas, TX
Charles E. Wilkerson, Richmond, VA
Joseph A. Wilkes, Annapolis, MD
Michael B. Wilkes, San Diego, CA
Barbara E. Wilks, Baltimore, MD
Paul Willen, Yorktown Heights, NY
A. Richard Williams, Saint Ignace, MI

Fellows of The American Institute of Architects

Allison G. Williams, San Francisco, CA
Daniel E. Williams, Coconut Grove, FL
Donald L. Williams, Houston, TX
E. Stewart Williams, Palm Springs, CA
F. Carter Williams, Raleigh, NC
Frank Williams, New York, NY
George Thomas Williams, Kitty Hawk, NC
Harold L. Williams, Los Angeles, CA
Homer L. Williams, Riverside, MO
John G. Williams, Fayetteville, AR
Lorenzo D. Williams, Minneapolis, MN
Mark F. Williams, Ambler, PA
Roger B. Williams, Seattle, WA
Terrance R. Williams, Washington, DC
Tod C. Williams, New York, NY
W. Gene Williams, The Woodlands, TX
Wayne R. Williams, Harmony, CA
Beverly A. Willis, New York, NY
Michael E. Willis, San Francisco, CA
John C. Wilmot, Damascus, MD
Jeffrey Wilson, Anchorage, AK
John E. Wilson, Richmond, VA
John L. Wilson, Boston, MA
William D. Wilson, Bridgehampton, NY
Steven R. Winkel, Berkeley, CA
Jon Peter Winkelstein, San Francisco, CA
John H. Winkler, Verbank, NY
Paul D. Winslow, Phoenix, AZ
Arch R. Winter, Mobile, AL
Steven Winter, Norwalk, CT
Marjorie M. Wintermute, Lake Oswego, OR
Norman E. Wirkler, Denver, CO
Joseph J. Wisnewski, Alexandria, VA
Gayland B. Witherspoon, Pendleton, SC
Charles Witsell Jr., Little Rock, AR
Gordon G. Wittenberg, Little Rock, AR
Fritz Woehle, Birmingham, AL
Robert L. Wold, Hilton Head, SC
Harry C. Wolf, III, Malibu, CA
Martin F. Wolf, Wilmette, IL
Richard Wolf, San Mateo, CA
Gin D. Wong, Los Angeles, CA
Joseph O. Wong, San Diego, CA
Kellogg H. Wong, New York, NY
William Wong Jr., Taikooshing, PRC
Carolina Y. Woo, San Francisco, CA
George C. Woo, Dallas, TX
Kyu S. Woo, Cambridge, MA
H. A. Wood III, Boston, MA
John M. Woodbridge, Sonoma, CA
David Geoffrey Woodcock, College Station, TX
David Woodhouse, Chicago, IL
Robert S. Woodhurst III, Augusta, GA
Stanford Woodhurst Jr., Augusta, GA
Enrique Woodroffe, Tampa, FL
Thomas E. Woodward, Buena Vista, CO
David L. Wooley, Knoxville, TN
Evans Woollen, Indianapolis, IN
J. R. Wooten, Fort Worth, TX
John C. Worsley, Portland, OR
David H. Wright, Seattle, WA
George S. Wright, Fort Worth, TX
Henry L. Wright, Canby, OR
John L. Wright, Redmond, WA
Marcellus Wright Jr., Richmond, VA
Rodney H. Wright, Liberty, KY
Thomas W. D. Wright, Washington, DC
Hofu Wu, Pomona, CA
Cynthia Wuellner, Kansas City, MO
Scott W. Wyatt, Seattle, WA

Y

Jack R. Yardley, Dallas, TX
Barry David Yatt, Arlington, VA
John L. Yaw, Aspen, CO
Zeno Lanier Yeates, Memphis, TN
Raymond W. Yeh, Honolulu, HI
Ronald W. Yeo, Corona Del Mar, CA
David N. Yerkes, Washington, DC
William R. Yost, Portland, OR
Clayton Young, Seattle, WA
Joseph L. Young, Clemson, SC
Norbert Young Jr., New York, NY
Theodore J. Young, Greenwich, CT

Did you know...

The States with the least AIA Fellows are:

Wyoming—1
South Dakota—1
North Dakota—1
Maine—1
Delaware—2
West Virginia—2
Montana—3
Alaska—4
Nevada—4
Rhode Island—5
Idaho—5
New Hampshire—6
Vermont—7

Fellows of The American Institute of Architects

Linda Yowell, New York City, NY
Hachiro Yuasa, Orleans, CA
Robert J. Yudell, Santa Monica, CA

Z

James Zahn, Chicago, IL
Saul Zaik, Portland, OR
H. Alan Zeigel, Denver, CO
J. Zemanek, Houston, TX
Golden J. Zenon Jr., Omaha, NE
Robert L. Ziegelman, Birmingham, MI
Raymond Ziegler, Altadena, CA
Rick Zieve, Seattle, WA
Frank Zilm, Kansas City, MO
John J. Zils, Chicago, IL
Bernard B. Zimmerman, Los Angeles, CA
Gary V. Zimmerman, Milwaukee, WI
Thomas A. Zimmerman, Rochester, NY
Hugh M. Zimmers, Philadelphia, PA
Joel P. Zingeser, Rockville, MD
Peter Jay Zweig, Houston, TX

Source: The American Institute of Architects

Did you know...
At the Royal Australian Institute of Architects' national conference in May 2003, Thompson E. Penney, the 2003 AIA president, was inducted as an honorary fellow.

Fellows of the American Institute of Certified Planners

Election as a Fellow in the American Institute of Certified Planners (AICP) is one of the highest honors that the AICP can bestow upon a member. Fellowship is granted to planners who have been a member of AICP and have achieved excellence in professional practice, teaching and mentoring, research, public/community service and leadership.

David J. Allor
John E. Anderson
Richard T. Anderson
Uri P. Avin
Edmund Bacon
Robert S. Baldwin
Tridib K. Banerjee
Jonathan Barnett
Carol D. Barrett
Ernest R. Bartley
Peter Batchelor
Ralph E. Becker Jr.
Robert W. Becker
James R. Bell
Teree L. Bergman
Paul A. Bergmann
Richard C. Bernhardt
James Bertram
Dale F. Bertsch
Dave E. Bess
Eugenie Ladner Birch
Daniel Bird
Merle H. Bishop
Alan Black
Lachlan F. Blair
John A. Blayney
David Booher
Fred P. Bosselman
William W. Bowdy
Melville C. Branch
John E. Bridges
Jane S. Brooks
David J. Brower
Nancy Benziger Brown
Martin Bruno
Raymond Burby
Bob Burke
David Lee Callies
Paulette Carolin
Eugene E. Carr
Sam Casella
Anthony James Catanese
Robert A. Catlin
F. Stuart Chapin Jr.
George B. Chapman
Jay Chatterjee
Hyung C. Chung
Philip Hart Clark
Arnold Cogan
Fred Collignon
Brad Collins
Thomas Cooke
Connie B. Cooper
Bob Cornish
Linda R. Cox
Paul C. Crawford
Betty Croly
John F. (Jack) Crowley
Samuel J. Cullers
James W. (Bill) Curtis
Patrick J. Cusick, Jr.
Linda Lund Davis
Dennis E. Daye
Lillian Frost Dean
F. John Devaney
Tom Dinell
Boris Dramov
James B. Duncan
Wilmer C. Dutton Jr.
Michael V. Dyett

Fellows of the American Institute of Certified Planners

V. Gail Easley
Joseph T. Edmiston
Robert C. Einsweiler
Henry Eng
Leon S. Eplan
John W. Epling
Ernest Erber
Craig Farmer
Hermann Haviland Field
Frank Fish
David J. Forkenbrock
Laurence Conway Gerckens
David R. Godschalk
Carl Goldschmidt
Dennis Andrew Gordon
Sigurd Grava
Clifford W. Graves
Sherman Griselle
Albert Guttenburg
Dianne Guzman
Besim S. Hakim
Irving Hand
Angela N. Harper
Britton Harris
William M. Harris, Sr.
Michael S. Harrison
Roger K. Hedrick
Edward Helfeld
Mary Lou Henry
Vernon G. Henry
Albert Herson
Jesus H. Hinojosa
Mark L. Hinshaw
John E. Hirten
Allan A. Hodges
Stanley R. Hoffman
Edward A. Holden
Lewis D. Hopkins
Deborah A. Howe
Robert P. Huefner
Robert Hunter
Fred Hurand
Edward J. Hustoles
Morris. E. Johnson
Robert J. Juster
Vivian Kahn
Edward Kaiser
Jerome L. Kauffman
Barbara Kautz
Lloyd Keefe
John Keller
Eric Damian Kelly
Paul B. Kelman
Mary R. Kihl
Bruce A. Knight
Kenneth M. Kreutziger
Bruce M. Kriviskey
Donald A. Krueckeberg
Norman Krumholz
Glenn Kumekawa
Steven K. Kurtz
Richard T. Lai
Bruce Laing
William Lamont Jr.
Floyd Lapp
Glen S. LeRoy
Anthony Lettieri
Julius S. Levine
Constance Lieder
Helen M. Olson Lightle
Richard R. Lillie
Barbara Lukermann
Robert H. Lurcott
Dean L. Macris
Marjorie Macris
George G. Mader
Riad G. Mahayni
Alan Mallach
Lawrence Mann
George T. Marcou
Richard May, Jr.
Michael D. McAnelly

Fellows of the American Institute of Certified Planners

Heather McCartney
Bruce W. McClendon
Alan McClennen, Jr.
Ron McConnell
Mike McCormick
Margarita P. McCoy
Bruce D. McDowell
Dorn Charles McGrath Jr.
Stuart Meck
Joy Mee
Dwight Merriman
John Merrill
Darrell C. Meyer
Martin Meyerson
J. Laurence Mintier
Vijay Mital
Terry Moore
Harvey Moskowitz
Louis Bert Muhly
John R. Mullin
Norman Murdoch
Arthur C. Nelson
Dick Netzer
Thomas P. Niederkorn
Perry Norton
Ki Suh Park
Jacqueline A. Parnell
Carl V. Patton
James Paulmann
Robert J. Paternoster
Gene Pearson
Phillip D. Peters
Robert J. Piper
Norbert J. Pointner
Leslie S. Pollock
Douglas R. Porter
David J. Portman
Roy Wilson Potter
Steven A. Preston
David L. Pugh
Mary Joan Pugh
Ray Quay
George Raymond
Robert E. Reiman
H. Randal Roark
Thomas H. Roberts
Harold Robertson
Sergio Rodriguez
Wolfgang G. Roeseler
Joseph Lee Rodgers
Janet M. Ruggiero
Peter D. Salins
Gary Schoennauer
Sue Schwartz
Paul H. Sedway
Ann Meriweather Shafor
Sumner Sharpe
Ronald Shiffman
Ronald N. Short
Marshall D. Slagle
Herbert H. Smith
Myles Greene Smith
Frank So
Lester Solin
Jeff Soule
James A. Spencer
Marvin Springer
Earl M. Starnes
Donald J. Stastny
Stuart W. Stein
Michael J. Stepner
Susan Stoddard
Israel Stollman
Robert L. Sturdivant
Kenneth E. Sulzer
Vernon Dale Swaback
Robert B. Teska
Carol J. Thomas
June Manning Thomas
Sidney F. Thomas Jr.
Michael P.C. Tillett
Anthony R. Tomazinis

Fellows of the American Institute of Certified Planners

Kenneth C. Topping
Nohad A. Toulan
Frank F. Turner
Stuart Turner
Richard E. Tustian
Francis Violich
Alan M. Voorhees
Martin Wachs
Fritz Wagner
Robert Wagoner
Larry W. Watts
Robert Wegner Sr.
Frank B. Wein
Louis B. Wetmore
Sara Jane White
Ronald A. Williamson
J.D. Wingfield
Arch R. Winter
Benjamin Withers
Joel C. Wooldridge
Mark A. Wyckoff
Bruce T. Yoder
Paul Zucker

Source: American Institute of Certified Planners

Fellows of the American Society of Interior Designers

The American Society of Interior Designers (ASID) grants fellowship to those members who have made notable and substantial contributions to the profession and society. The following individuals are current, active fellows of the ASID.

Stanley Abercrombie
Dan Acito
Stephen W. Ackerman
Gail Adams
Joy E. Adcock
Michael Alin*
Estelle Alpert
Jerry R. Alsobrook
William F. Andrews
Ellen Angell
Robert H. Angle*
Robert A. Arehart
Warren G. Arnett
Anita Baltimore
David Barrett
Nancy Hoff Barsotti
Jeannine Bazer-Schwartz
Tamara A. Bazzle
Roy F. Beal
Marjorie A. Bedell
Frank Lee Berry
Hal F.B. Birchfield
Adriana Bitter
Edwin Bitter*
Joan Blutter
Daisy Houston Bond*
Penny Bonda
Joseph Daniel Bouligny
Blair S. Bowen
H. Don Bowden
William D. Bowden
Susan Bradford
Bruce J. Brigham
C. Dudley Brown
Everett Brown
R. Michael Brown
Walton E. Brown*
Mary A. Bryan
Eleanor Brydone
Joyce A. Burke-Jones
David M. Butler
Rosalyn Cama
Barbara J. Campbell
Orville V. Carr
Elizabeth M. Castleman
Juliana M. Catlin
Carl E. Clark
Brian Clay Collins
John P. Conron
Loverne C. Cordes
Herbert Cordier
Jini Costello
Virginia W. Courtenay
P.A. Dale
Hortense Davis
Robert John Dean
Ken Deck
Hon C. Doxiadis*
Dede Draper
Hilda M. East
H. Gerard Ebert
Barbara Ebstein
Garrett Eckbo*
Arlis Ede
Martin Elinoff
John Elmo
Joel M. Ergas
Sammye J. Erickson
Adele Faulkner
Jon J. Fields
Lyn Fontenot
John G. Ford

Fellows of the American Society of Interior Designers

Deborah Lloyd Forrest
Dorothy L. Fowles
Thomas Frank
Sandra C. Friend
Charles D. Gandy
Marion Gardiner
Francis J. Geck*
Alexander Girard*
Judy Girod
Milton Glaser
Diane Gote
Thomas C. Grabowski
Theodora Kim Graham
Stephen Greenberger
Jody Greenwald
Roberta S. Griffin
Olga Gueft*
Rita C. Guest
David W. Hall
Lawrence Halprin*
James M. Halverson
William D. Hamilton*
Shirley Hammond
A. Niolon Hampton
Marilyn Hansen
Buie Harwood*
Patricia Harvey
Dennis Haworth
Dorothy G. Helmer
Albert E. Herbert
Robert Herring*
Fred B. Hershey
Joseph P. Horan
Elizabeth B. Howard
Nina Hughes
Dorian Hunter
H. Cliff Ivester
Barbara L. Jacobs
Sarah B. Jenkins
Charlotte Jensen
Connie Johannes
Wallace R. Jonason
Richard W. Jones
Henry Jordan
Henri V. Jova
Franklin S. Judson*
Janet E. Kane
Mary V. Knackstedt
Binnie Kramer
Gayle Kreutzfeld
Karlyn Kuper
Anita M. Laird*
Hugh L. Latta
Drue Lawlor
Dennis W. Leczinski
Nila Leiserowitz
Robert S. Lindenthal
Boyd L. Loendorf
Michael Love
Joseph LoVecchio*
Odette Lueck
Ruth K. Lynford
William M. Manly
Helen Masoner
Terri Maurer
Sandra McGowen
James E. McIntosh
James Mezrano
John Richard Miller
Thomas H. Miller
Susan I. Mole
Kathy Ford Montgomery
Phyllis Moore
Mark Nelson
Roi C. Nevaril
Linda Newton
W. E. Noffke
Barbara Nugent
Douglas Parker*
Jan Parker
Suzanne Patterson
Lawrence Peabody

Fellows of the American Society of Interior Designers

Edward J. Perrault
BJ Peterson
H. Albert Phibbs
Dianne H. Pilgrim*
Norman Polsky*
Betty J. Purvis
Catharine G. Rawson
William Dunn Ray
Martha Garriott Rayle
Mary Jane Reeves
John Robinson
Pedro Rodriguez
Agnes H. Rogers
Wayne Ruga*
Jack G. Ruthazer
Chester F. Sagenkahn
Barbara A. Sauerbrey
Hollie Schick
Janet S. Schirn
Barbara Schlattman
Robin Schmidt
E. Williard Schurz
Irving D. Schwartz
Melinda K. Sechrist
Otho S. Shaw
Alan Siegel*
James L. Simpson
Theodore A. Simpson
Edna A. Smith
Fran Kellog Smith
James Merrick Smith
Linda Elliot Smith
Sandra H. Sober
Jerrold Sonet*
Michael Sorrentino*
Michael Souter
Beulah G. Spiers
Paul D. Spreiregen*
Edward H. Springs
Rita St.Clair
Russell M. Stanley
Ed Starr
Karl L. Steinhauser
Deborah Steinmetz
C. Eugene Stephenson
Blanche F. Strater
Ann Sullivan
Caroline Torley
Doris Nash Upshur
Judith André Verges
Bernard Vinick
Donna Vining
G.F. Weber
Maurice Weir
Vicki Wenger
Gary E. Wheeler
Miriam Whelan
Michael Wiener
William L. Wilkoff
Frances E. Wilson
Gail Casey Winkler
Michael Wirtz
John B. Wisner
D. C. Witte
Edmund D. Wood
Alene Workman
Diane B. Worth
Julie M. Wyatt

* Honorary Fellow

Source: American Society of Interior Designers

Fellows of the American Society of Landscape Architects

Fellows of the American Society of Landscape Architects (ASLA) are landscape architects of at least ten years standing as full members of the ASLA, elected to Fellowship in honor of their outstanding contributions to the profession. Categories of election are: works of landscape architecture, administrative work, knowledge, and service to the profession. The list below indicates current, active Fellows of the ASLA.

Howard G. Abel
Wm. Dwayne Adams Jr.
Marvin I. Adleman
Russell A. Adsit
Timothy M. Agness
John F. Ahern
J. Robert Anderson
Domenico Annese
Ellis L. Antuñez
David E. Arbegast
David S. Armbruster
Henry F. Arnold
Sadik C. Artunc
Roy O. Ashley
D. Lyle Aten
Donald B. Austin
Kenneth J. Backman
Ted Baker
William H. Baker
Harry J. Baldwin
Edward B. Ballard
Thomas Balsley
Alton A. Barnes Jr.
Milton Baron
Cheryl Barton
James H. Bassett
Kenneth E. Bassett
Anthony M. Bauer
Clarence W. Baughman
Howard R. Baumgarten
Eldon W. Beck
Yoshiro Befu
Arthur G. Beggs
William A. Behnke
James R. Bell
Richard C. Bell
Vincent Bellafiore
Armand Benedek
Claire R. Bennett
Shary Page Berg
Karl Berry
Charles A. Birnbaum
Calvin T. Bishop
David H. Blau
Kerry Blind
Lloyd M. Bond
Norman K. Booth
W. Frank Brandt
J. Brooks Breeden
Michael Wayne Breedlove
Theodore W. Brickman Jr.
Samuel W. Bridgers
Donald Carl Brinkerhoff
Mark K. Brinkley
Robert F. Bristol
Judy Byrd Brittenum
Joseph E. Brown
Jeffrey L. Bruce
Jackie Karl Bubenik
Alexander Budrevics
Robert S. Budz
Dennis R. Buettner
Wayne L. Buggenhagen
Frank Burggraf Jr.
William S. Burton
Russell L. Butler II
Arthur E. Bye Jr.
Willard C. Byrd
Raymond F. Cain
Robert A. Callans

Fellows of the American Society of Landscape Architects

William B. Callaway
Craig S. Campbell
Paschall Campbell
Dean Cardasis
Robert R. Cardoza
Charles Cares
Bryan D. Carlson
John Leslie Carman
Dennis B. Carmichael
Derr A. Carpenter
Jot D. Carpenter
David B. Carruth
Donald R. Carter
Eugene H. Carter
Anthony B. Casendino
Carlos J. Cashio
James E. Christman
Ann Christoph
Russell Y. J. Chung
Alan B. Clarke
Lewis J. Clarke
Roger D. Clemence
Franklin C. Clements
Jack R. Cochran
Jon Charles Coe
Beatriz de Winthuysen Coffin
Laurence E. Coffin Jr.
Donald C. Collins
John F. Collins
Dennis C. Colliton
Richard Conant
Max Z. Conrad
George Glenn Cook
Charles Douglas Coolman
Fred J. Correale
James Robert Cothran
Kenneth R. Coulter
Van L. Cox
H. Kenneth Crasco
George E. Creed
Samuel G. Crozier
Joseph H. Crystal
George W. Curry
Jack Curtis
John E. Cutler
Jack R. Daft
Peter Dangermond Jr.
Edward L. Daugherty
Stuart O. Dawson
Dennis J. Day
Francis H. Dean
Neil J. Dean
Roy H. DeBoer
Richard K. Dee
Robert B. Deering
Bruce Dees
C. Christopher Degenhardt
Roger DeWeese
P. Woodward Dike
F. Christopher Dimond
Nicholas T. Dines
Carlton T. Dodge
Dan W. Donelin
Thomas R. Dunbar
Robert W. Dyas
Robert P. Ealy
Garrett Eckbo
Allen R. Edmonson
Jon Stidger Emerson
Katherine G. Emery
Donald H. Ensign
Steve Estrada
James Matthew Evans
Morgan Evans
L. Susan Everett
Julius Gy. Fabos
Barbara Faga
Oliver M. Fanning
Damon Farber
David Fasser
Rudy J. Favretti
Barbara V. Fealy
Bruce K. Ferguson
Donald L. Ferlow

Fellows of the American Society of Landscape Architects

John J. Fernholz
Ian J.W. Firth
Charles Albert Flink
Phillip E. Flores
William L. Flournoy Jr.
Everett L. Fly
George E. Fogg
Donald Mark Fox
Kathleen M. Fox
Mark Francis
Carol L. Franklin
Daniel B. Franklin
Robert L. Frazer
Jere S. French
John W. Frey
M. Paul Friedberg
John F. Furlong
Emily J. Gabel-Luddy
Paul Gardescu
Harry L. Garnham
Benjamin W. Gary Jr.
George G. Gentile
Richard George Gibbons
James E. Glavin
D. Newton Glick
Donald H. Godi
James B. Godwin
Ellin Goetz
Robert E. Goetz
Susan M. Goltsman
Robert Wilson Good
Robert Gorman
J. Patrick Graham IV
Philip H. Graham Jr.
Leonard Grassli
James W. Gray Jr.
Bradford M. Greene
Isabelle Clara Greene
E. Robert Gregan
John N. Grissim
Clare A. Gunn
Anthony M. Guzzardo
Richard Haag
Frederick Edward Halback
John C. Hall
Lawrence Halprin
Calvin S. Hamilton
Asa Hanamoto
Byron R. Hanke
Karen C. Hanna
Robert M. Hanna
Becca Hanson
Richard E. Hanson
Nancy M. Hardesty
George Hargreaves
Terence G. Harkness
Charles W. Harris
Robert R. Harvey
Susan M. Hatchell
Richard G. Hautau
William H. Havens
Richard S. Hawks
Robert Graham Heilig
Kenneth I. Helphand
Edith H. Henderson
Glenn O. Hendrix
Glendon M. Herbert Jr.
Randolph T. Hester
Gary R. Hilderbrand
Donald F. Hilderbrandt
Arthur W. Hills
Allen W. Hixon Jr.
Leonard J. Hopper
Mark Elison Hoversten
Perry Howard
Donovan E. Hower
Joseph Hudak
Sam L. Huddleston
Mary V. Hughes
Mark B. Hunner
Lester Hikoji Inouye
Alice R. Ireys
Wayne D. Iverson
Ronald M. Izumita
H. Rowland Jackson
Bernard Jacobs

Fellows of the American Society of Landscape Architects

Peter D. A. Jacobs
Susan L.B. Jacobson
Dale G.M. Jaeger
Frederick D. Jarvis
Leerie T. Jenkins Jr.
David R. Jensen
Linda Lee Jewell
Carl D. Johnson
Carol R. Johnson
Dean A. Johnson
Mark W. Johnson
William J. Johnson
Grant R. Jones
Ilze Jones
Robert Trent Jones
Warren D. Jones
Dirk Jongejan
Gary E. Karner
Joseph P. Karr
Jean Stephans Kavanagh
Frank H. Kawasaki
James E. Keeter
Walter H. Kehm
J. Timothy Keller
Leslie A. Kerr
Gary B. Kesler
Sidney R. Kime, Jr.
Steven G. King
Masao Kinoshita
Charles L. Knight
Harold Kobayashi
Ken R. Krabbenhoft
Brian S. Kubota
William B. Kuhl
Bruce G. Kulik
Ray O. Kusche
Joseph J. Lalli
Joe W. Langran
Lucille Chenery Lanier
Mary Ann Lasch
Warren E. Lauesen
Michael M. Laurie
Dennis L. Law
Richard K. Law
Jack E. Leaman
Donald F. Lederer
Charles L. Leider
Donald W. Leslie
Aaron Levine
Philip H. Lewis Jr.
J. Roland Lieber
Mark S. Lindhult
Karl Linn
J. Mack Little
Susan P. Little
Earl R. Littlejohn
R. Burton Litton Jr.
Thomas A. Lockett
Nimrod W. E. Long III
David O. Lose
Eldridge Lovelace
Paul C. K. Lu
J. Douglas Macy
A. Catherine Mahan
Michael H. Malyn
Cameron R. J. Man
Lane L. Marshall
Richard K. Marshall
Edward C. Martin Jr.
Roger B. Martin
Steve Martino
Robert E. Marvin
Robert M. Mattson
Lewis T. May
Richard E. Mayer
Carol Mayer-Reed
Earl Byron McCulley
Phillip L. McDade
Vincent C. McDermott
Roger B. McErlane
Mark E. McFarland
Ian McHarg
Kathryn E. McKnight-Thalden
David A. McNeal
Gary W. Meisner
Robert Melnick

Fellows of the American Society of Landscape Architects

Dee S. Merriam
Vincent N. Merrill
Stuart M. Mertz
Elizabeth K. Meyer
Richard J. Meyers
Luciano Miceli
E. Lynn Miller
Patrick A. Miller
Ann Milovsoroff
Debra L. Mitchell
Michael T. Miyabara
Lawrence R. Moline
Donald J. Molnar
Lynn A. Moore
Patrick C. Moore
Richard A. Moore
Roger D. Moore
Paul F. Morris
Darrel G. Morrison
Mark K. Morrison
Baker H. Morrow
Robert H. Mortensen
Margaret Ann Mullins
Robert K. Murase
Thomas A. Musiak
Kenneth S. Nakaba
Kenichi Nakano
Joan I. Nassauer
Darwina L. Neal
John A. Nelson
William R. Nelson Jr.
Joseph N. Nevius
Signe Nielsen
Thomas J. Nieman
Satoru Nishita
Robert L. O'Boyle
Patricia M. O'Donnell
William A. O'Leary
Cornelia A. Oberlander
Warren J. Oblinger
Neil Odenwald
Wolfgang W. Oehme
Laurie D. Olin
Peter J. Olin
Edward J. Olinger
Don H. Olson
Brian Orland
Thomas R. Oslund
Theodore Osmundson
Dennis Y. Otsuji
J. Steve Ownby
Michael Painter
James F. Palmer
Meade Palmer
Thomas P. Papandrew
Cary M. Parker
John G. Parsons
Tito Patri
Gerald D. Patten
Courtland P. Paul
Merlyn J. Paulson
Gerald Phillip Pearson
Robert Perron
Robert C. Perry Jr.
Owen H. Peters
Karen A. Phillips
Robert W. Pierson
J. Edward Pinckney
Marjorie E. Pitz
Kenneth J. Polakowski
Peter M. Pollack
Harry W. Porter
Joe A. Porter
Neil H. Porterfield
Marion Pressley
William Pressley
Rae L. Price
Paul N. Procopio
Edward L. Pryce
Helen M. Quackenbush
Nicholas Quennell
F. Truitt Rabun Jr.
David C. Racker
John Rahenkamp
Geoffrey Lew Rausch
Robert S. Reich

Fellows of the American Society of Landscape Architects

Grant W. Reid
Robert G. Reimann
John J. Reynolds
John Paul Ribes
Artemas P. Richardson
Donald Richardson
Jane S. Ries
Robert B. Riley
Craig D. Ritland
James F. Ritzer
William H. Roberts
Gary O. Robinette
Jon Rodiek
Richard H. Rogers
Peter G. Rolland
Clarence Roy
Robert N. Royston
Harvey M. Rubenstein
Robert H. Rucker
Virginia Lockett Russell
Terry Warriner Ryan
Paul M. Saito
Charles S. Saladino II
Margaret Sand
William D. Sanders
Hideo Sasaki
George L. Sass
Terry W. Savage
William Scatchard
Herbert R. Schaal
Horst Schach
Janice C. Schach
Sally Schauman
Mario G. Schjetnan
Arno S. Schmid
Helmut Schmitz
Amy L. Schneckenburger
Gunter A. Schoch
Ollie Schrickel
Sunny Jung Scully
Bradford G. Sears
Jonathan G. Seymour
Bruce Sharky
Richard William Shaw
Juanita D. Shearer-Swink
Ruth P. Shellhorn
Dr. Hamid Shirvani
J. Kipp Shrack
Jeffrey L. Siegel
Kenneth B. Simmons Jr.
John Ormsbee Simonds
John B. Slater
Gerald L. Smith
Herrick H. Smith
Robert W. Smith
Jerrold Soesbe
Randy Sorensen
Stanley V. Specht
Burton S. Sperber
Andrew J. Spurlock
James C. Stansbury
Barry W. Starke
Richard G. Stauffer
Robert Steenhagen
Achva Benzinberg Stein
John Goddfrey Stoddart
Edward D. Stone Jr.
Edward H. Stone II
Allen D. Stovall
Jan Striefel
Steven Strom
Rosheen Marie Styczinski
Doris M. Sullivan
William G. Swain
Rodney L. Swink
Lolly Tai
Austin Paul Tao
D. Rodney Tapp
Leslee A. Temple
Christine Elizabeth Ten Eyck
Barry R. Thalden
Robert Thayer Jr.
Michael Theilacker
J. William Thompson
William H. Tishler
Donald H. Tompkins

Fellows of the American Society of Landscape Architects

L. Azeo Torre
Shavaun Towers
Roger T. Trancik
Howard E. Troller
Peter J. Trowbridge
Stephen J. Trudnak
James R. Turner
Jerry Mitchell Turner
Suzanne Louise Turner
Ronald W. Tuttle
Anthony Tyznik
Raymond L. Uecker
Takeo Uesugi
James R. Urban
James Van Sweden
Michael R. Van Valkenburgh
Albert R. Veri
Keith J. Villere
Karl Von Bieberstein
Mark J. Von Wodtke
John Wacker
Lawrence L. Walker
Peter E. Walker
Theodore D. Walker
Victor J. Walker
Larry D. Walling
Thomas H. Wallis
Ronald M. Walters
Thomas C. Wang
Barry J. Warner
Kent E. Watson
Dwight W. Weatherford
E. Neal Weatherly Jr.
Richard K. Webel
Scott S. Weinberg
V. Michael Weinmayr
Roger Wells
William E. Wenk
Robert A. Weygand
James K. Wheat
Morgan Dix Wheelock
Carol A. Whipple
Robert F. White
George W. Wickstead
Ron Wigginton
Sara Katherine Williams
Larry T. Wilson
Richard A. Wilson
William P. Winslow III
Theodore J. Wirth
Robert L. Woerner
J. Daniel Wojcik
David G. Wright
Patrick H. Wyss
Joseph Y. Yamada
Mark J. Zarillo
Floyd W. Zimmerman
Robert L. Zion
Robert W. Zolomij
Ervin H. Zube
Laurence W. Zuelke
Jack W. Zunino
K. Richard Zweifel

Source: American Society of Landscape Architects

Fellows of the Design Futures Council

Fellowship in the Design Futures Council (DFC) is annually granted to an outstanding individual(s) who has provided noteworthy leadership to the advancement of design, design solutions, and/or the design professions. Any person worldwide may nominate candidates. Final selection of the Fellows is made by the Senior Fellows Selection Committee.

Ray Anderson, Interface, Inc.
Rodrigo Arboleda, MIT Media Lab
Peter Beck, The BECK Group
Robert J. Berkebile, BNIM Architects
Phil Bernstein, Autodesk
John Seely Brown, Xerox Research PARC
Phil Enquist, Skidmore, Owings & Merrill
Richard Farson, Western Behavioral Sciences Institute
Edward Feiner, U.S. General Services Administration
Steve Fiskum, HGA
Jim Follett, Gensler
Harrison Fraker, University of California, Berkeley
Neil Frankel, Frankel + Coleman
R. Buckminster ("Bucky") Fuller*, engineer, inventor, educator, and architectural innovator
Art Gensler, Gensler
Paul Goldberger, The New Yorker
Jerry Hobbs, AC Neilson
Louis I. Kahn*, architect and educator
Norman Koonce, The American Institute of Architects
Janet Martin, Communications Arts
Sandra Mendler, HOK
Doug Parker, Steelcase
Alexander "Sandy" Pentland, MIT Media Lab
B. Joseph Pine II, Strategic Horizons LLP
Witold Rybczynski, University of Pennsylvania
Jonas Salk, founder, The Salk Institute, and architectural patron
Terrence J. Sejnowski, The Salk Institute
Scott Simpson, The Stubbins Associates
Karen Stephenson, UCLA and NetForm International
Cecil Steward, University of Nebraska and Joslyn Castle Institute
Sarah Susanka, architect and author
Richard Swett, architect, and former U.S. ambassador to Denmark
April Thornton, Armstrong World Industries
Alan Traugott, Flack + Kurtz Inc.
Robert Tucker, author
John Carl Warnecke, architect
Jon Westling, Boston University
Gary Wheeler, Perkins and Will
Arol Wolford, Construction Market Data Group

*Awarded posthumously

Source: Design Futures Council

Fellows of the Industrial Designers Society of America

Membership in the Industrial Designers Society of America's (IDSA) Academy of Fellows is conferred by a two-thirds majority vote of its Board of Directors. Fellows must be Society members in good standing who have earned the special respect and affection of the membership through distinguished service to the Society and to the profession as a whole. The following individuals are the current, active fellows of the IDSA.

James M. Alexander
Wallace H. Appel
Alfons Bach
Alexander Bally
Betty Baugh
George Beck
Nathaniel Becker
Arthur N. BecVar
Melvin H. Best
Robert I. Blaich
Alfred M. Blumenfeld
Eugene Bordinat
William Bullock
Peter Bressler
Joseph Carriero
Bruce Claxton
Arthur H. Crapsey
Donald E. Dailey
Thomas David
Niels Diffrient
Jay Doblin
H. Creston Doner
Henry Dreyfuss
Mark Dziersk
Arden Farey
Vincent M. Foote
James F. Fulton
Roger Funk
Walter Furlani
Carroll M. Gantz
Franceco Gianninoto
Henry P. Glass
William Goldsmith
John S. Griswold
Robert Gruen
Olle E. Haggstrom
James G. Hansen
Jon W. Hauser
Stephen G. Hauser
Richard Hollerith
Robert H. Hose
James L. Hvale
Charles Jones
Marnie Jones
Lorraine Justice
Ron Kemnitzer
Belle Kogan
George Kosmak
Rowena Reed Kostellow
Rudolph W. Krolopp
David Kusuma
LeRoy LaCelle
Richard S. Latham
Raymond Loewy
Peter E. Lowe
Paul MacAlister
Tucker P. Madawick
Pascal Malassigné
Joseph R. Mango
Katherine J. McCoy
Donald McFarland
Leon Gordon Miller
Pat Moore
Dana W. Mox
Peter Müller-Munk
C. Stowe Myers
George Nelson
Joseph M. Parriott

Fellows of the Industrial Designers Society of America

Lee Payne
Charles Pelly
Nancy Perkins
James J. Pirkl
William L. Plumb
Arthur J. Pulos
Robert E. Redmann
Jean Otis Reinecke
Harold Reynolds
Deane W. Richardson
James Ryan
Clair A. Samhammer
Kenneth Schory
F. Eugene Smith
Robert G. Smith
Paul B. Specht
Raymond Spilman
Darrell S. Staley
Budd Steinhilber
Brooks Stevens
Philip H. Stevens
Ernest L. Swarts
Sharyn Thompson
David D. Tompkins
Herbert H. Tyrnauer
John Vassos
Read Viemeister
Tucker Viemeister
Noland Vogt
Sandor Weisz
Steve Wilcox
Arnold Wolf
Peter Wooding
Cooper C. Woodring
Edward J. Zagorski

Source: Industrial Designers Society of America

Did you know...

Arne Jacobsen's most influential commission was the Scandinavian Airlines System Royal Hotel and Air Terminal in Copenhagen, Denmark, (1956–1960) which became an extraordinary showcase for Danish industrial design. Besides designing the building, Jacobsen also designed all the fixtures and furnishings, including rugs, curtains, beds, chairs, lighting fixtures, glassware, cutlery, and ceramic ashtrays, which were concurrently offered for sale to the public.

Fellows of the International Interior Design Association

Professional members of the International Interior Design Association (IIDA) are inducted into the College of Fellows by a two-thirds vote by their Board of Directors. This honor recognizes members who have demonstrated outstanding service to the IIDA, the community, and the interior design profession. The following individuals are current, active fellows of the IIDA.

Robin Klehr Avia
Laura Bailey
Jeanne Baldwin
Claude Berube
Charles Blumberg
Dan Bouligny
Michael Bourque
Bonnie Bruce
Rus Calder
Richard Carlson
Particia Gutierrez Castellanos
Amarjeet Chatrath
Susan Coleman
David Cooke
Eleanor Corkle
Christine Dandan
Eugene Daniels
Carol Disrud
Jacqueline Duncan
Cheryl Duvall
Hilda East
Marilyn Farrow
James Ferguson II
Dorothy Fowles
Neil Frankel
Angela Frey
Charles D. Gandy
Gerald Gelsomino
M. Arthur Gensler Jr.
Lewis Goetz
Carol S. Graham
Karen Guenther
Beth Harmon-Vaughan
Judith Hastings
Jo Heinz
Edna Henner
John Herron
Frederick Hutchirs
David Immenschuh
Cary D. Johnson
Christina Johnson
Carol Jones
Margo Jones
Robert Kennedy
Tessa Kennedy
Sooz Klinkhamer
Mary Knackstedt
Lili Kray
Marjorie Kriebel
Michael Kroelinger
Robert Ledingham
Fola Lerner-Miller
Jack Levin
Neville Lewis
Pamela Light
John A. Lijewski
Charles Littleton
Ronald Lubben
Hiroko Machida
Candace MacKenzie
Richard Mazzucotelli
Jose Medrano
Ruth Mellergaard
Kenneth Muller
Donald Parker
J. Derrell Parker
Janie Petkus
Paul Petrie

Fellows of the International Interior Design Association

Richard N. Pollack
Shirley Pritchard
Carole Price Shanis
Sandra Ragan
Charles Raymond
Patti Richards
Jane Rohde
Wayne Ruga
Joyce Saunders
Mitchell E. Sawasy
Allan Shaivitz
Donald Sherman
Rayne Sherman
Gail Shiel
Bernard Soep
Henrietta Spencer-Churchill
Andre Staffelbach
Andrew Stafford
William Stankiewicz
Janice Stevenor-Dale
Donald Thomas
Joann Thompson
Betty Treanor
Marcia Troyan
Robert Valentine
Margaret Velardo
Roen Viscovich
Allison Carll White
Ron Whitney-Whyte
Glenda Wilcox
Frances Wilson
M. Judith Wilson
D. Geary Winstead
Michael Wirtz
Susan Wood
Minoru Yokoyama
Janice Young

Source: International Interior Design Association

Fellows of the Society of Architectural Historians

Fellowship in the Society of Architectural Historians is granted for "exceptional and distinguished service to the Society."

H. Allen Brooks
Marian C. Donnelly
Alan W. Gowans
Richard W. Howland
Carol Herselle Krinsky
Elisabeth Blair MacDougall
Carter H. Manny
Henry A. Millon
Denys Peter Myers
Osmund Overby
Seymour H. Persky
Charles E. Peterson
William H. Pierson Jr.
Adolf K. Placzek
George B. Tatum

Source: Society of Architectural Historians

Existence does not follow a straight line. It has curves, voids, jumps, returns, breaks. If an architect designed the stage for the comedy/drama of existence, then this stage must also always be changing.

Ettore Sottsass

Honorary Fellows of The American Institute of Architects

The American Institute of Architects (AIA) grants Honorary Fellowship to non-members, both architects and non-architects, who have made substantial contributions to the field of architecture.

Kurt H.C. Ackermann, Munich, Germany
Gunnel Adlercreutz, Helsinki, Finland
O. J. Aguilar, Lima, Peru
Hisham Albakri, Kuala Lumpur, Malaysia
William A. Allen, London, England
Alfred V. Alvares, Vancouver, Canada
Jose Alvarez, Lima, Peru
Mario R. Alvarez, Buenos Aires, Argentina
Tadao Ando, Osaka, Japan
John H. Andrews, Australia
Carlos D. Arguelles, Manila, Philippines
Gordon R. Arnott, Regina, Canada
Carl Aubock, Austria
Carlo Aymonino, Venice, Italy
George G. Baines, England
Juan Navarro Baldeweg, Madrid, Spain
W. D. Baldwin, Sterling, Canada
W. K. Banadayga, Sterling, Canada
Essy Baniassad, Halifax, Canada
Nikolai B. Baranov, Moscow, Russia
Geoffrey M. Bawa, Columbo, Sri Lanka
Eugene Beaudouin, France
Gerard Benoit, Paris, France
Jai R. Bhalla, New Delhi, India
Jacob Blegvad, Aalborg, Denmark
Ricardo L. Bofill, Barcelona, Spain
Oriol Bohigas, Barcelona, Spain
Irving D. Boigon, Richmond Hill, Canada
Ferenc Callmeyer, Telki, Hungary
Santiago A. Calvo, Lima, Peru
Felix Candela, Raleigh, North Carolina
Rifat Chadirji, Surrey, England
Suk-Woong Chang, Seoul, Korea
Te L. Chang, Taipei, Taiwan
Jean Marie Charpentier, France
Bill Chomik, Calgary, Canada
Adolf Ciborowski, Warsaw, Poland
E. Gresley Cohen, Dalkeith, Australia
Charles M. Correa, Bombay, India
Philip S. Cox, Sydney, Australia
Charles H. Cullum, Newfoundland, Canada
Carlos E. Da Silva, Rizal, Philippines
John M. Davidson, Richmond, Australia
David Y. Davies, Surrey, England
Sara T. De Grinberg, Mexico
Rafael De La Hoz, Spain
S. D. De La Tour, Durville, France
Eduardo De Mello, Braga, Portugal
Costantin N. Decavalla, Greece
Ignacio M. Delmonte, Mexico City, Mexico
A. J. "Jack" Diamond, Toronto, Canada
Ignacio Diaz-Morales, Jalisco, Mexico
Balkrishna V. Doshi, Ahmedabad, India
Philip Dowson, London, England
Kiril Doytchev, Sofia, Bulgaria
G. M. Dubois, Toronto, Canada
Allan F. Duffus, Halifax, Canada
Werner Duttman, Lindenalle, Germany
David W. Edwards, Regina, Canada
Yehya M. Eid, Cairo, Egypt
Abdel W. El Wakil, Kent, England
Arthur C. Erickson, Vancouver, Canada
Lord Esher, England
Inger Exner, Denmark
Johannes Exner, Denmark
Tobias Faber, Copenhagen, Denmark
Francisco B. Fajardo, Philippines
Hassan Fathy, Egypt
Sverre Fehn, Oslo, Norway
Bernard M. Feilden, Norfolk, England
Ji Z. Feng, Shanghai, PRC

Honorary Fellows of The American Institute of Architects

Angelina Munoz Fernandez de Madrid, Sonora, Mexico
A. I. Ferrier, Red Hill, Australia
Jozsef Finta, Budapest, Hungary
Antonio F. Flores, Mexico
Cesar X. Flores, Mexico D.F., Mexico
Norman Foster, London, England
Charles A. Fowler, Canada
Massimiliano Fuksas, Rome, Italy
Jorge Gamboa de Buen, Mexico DF, Mexico
Juan Gonzalez, Spain
Roderick P. Hackney, Cheshire, England
Zaha Hadid, London, England
H. H. Hallen, Australia
Shoji Hayashi, Tokyo, Japan
Jacques Herzog, Switzerland
Tao Ho, North Point, Hong Kong
Barry J. Hobin, Ottawa, Canada
Hans Hollein, Vienna, Austria
Wilhelm Holzbauer, Vienna, Austria
Sir Michael Hopkins, London, England
Lady Patricia Hopkins, London, England
Thomas Howarth, Toronto, Canada
Nobuo Hozumi, Tokyo, Japan
Il-in Hwang, Korea
Arata Isozaki, Tokyo, Japan
Toyo Ito, Tokyo, Japan
Daryl Jackson, Melbourne, Australia
R. D. Jackson, Sydney, Australia
Alvaro Joaquim de Meio Siza, Porto, Portugal
Barry Johns, Edmonton, Canada
P. N. Johnson, Australia
Sumet Jumsai, Bangkok, Thailand
Achyut P. Kanvinde, New Dehli, India
Vladimir Karfik, Brno, Czech Republic
Kiyonori Kikutake, Tokyo, Japan
Reiichiro Kitadai, Tokyo, Japan
Azusa Kito, Tokyo, Japan
Josef P. Kleihues, Berlin, Germany
Rob Krier, Berlin, Germany
Dogan Kuban, Istanbul, Turkey
Alexandr P. Kudryavtsev, Moscow, Russia
Kisho Kurokawa, Tokyo, Japan
Colin Laird, Port of Spain, Trinidad and Tobago
Jean L. Lalonde, Canada
Phyllis Lambert, Canada
Henning Larsen, Denmark
Denys L. Lasdun, London, England
Kwang-Ro Lee, Seoul, Korea
Kyung-Hoi Lee, Seoul, Korea
Juha Ilmari Leiviskä, Helsinki, Finland
Sergio Lenci, Rome, Italy
Jaime Lerner, Parana, Brazil
Wu Liang Yong, Beijing, PRC
Kington Loo, Kuala Lumpur, Malaysia
Aldana E. Lorenzo, San Jeronimo, Mexico
Serapio P. Loza, Jalisco, Mexico
Kjell Lund, Oslo, Norway
Brian MacKay-Lyons, Halifax, Nova Scotia, Canada
Olufemi Majekodunmi, Gaborone, Botswana
Fumihiko Maki, Tokyo, Japan
Matti K. Makinen, Finland
Rutilo Malacara, Mexico D. F., Mexico
Motlatsi Peter Malefane, Johannesburg, South Africa
Albert Mangones, Port Au Prince, Haiti
Yendo Masayoshi, New York, New York
Peter McIntyre, Victoria, Australia
Rodrigo Mejia-Andrion, Panama
Hector Mestre, Mexico, D.F., Mexico
Pierre de Meuron, Switzerland
Wladimir Mitrofanoff, Paris, France
Jose Raphael Moneo, Madrid, Spain
Raymond Moriyama, Toronto, Canada
Padraig Murray, Dublin, Ireland
Toshio Nakamura, Tokyo, Japan
Nikola I. Nikolov, Sofia, Bulgaria
Juan Bassegoda Nonell, Barcelona, Spain
Rafael Norma, Mexico City, Mexico
Jean Nouvel, Paris, France
Carl J.A. Nyren, Stockholm, Sweden

Honorary Fellows of The American Institute of Architects

ShinIchi Okada, Tokyo, Japan
Oluwole O. Olumyiwa, Lagos, Nigeria
Georgui M. Orlov, Moscow, Russia
Juhani Pallasmaa, Helsinki, Finland
Gustav Peichl, Wein, Austria
Raili Pietila, Helsinki, Finland
Methodi A. Pissarski, Sofia, Bulgaria
Ernst A. Plischke, Wien, Austria
Paolo Portoghesi, Rome, Italy
Christian de Portzamparc, Paris, France
Ivor C. Prinsloo, Rondebosch, South Africa
Victor M. Prus, Montreal, Canada
Luis M. Quesada, Lima, Peru
Hector M. Restat, Santiago, Chile
Jose F. Reygadas, Mexico City, Mexico
Philippe Robert, Paris, France
Derry Menzies Robertson, Picton, Canada
Juan J. Rocco, Montevideo, Uruguay
Xavier Cortes Rocha, Coyoacan, Mexico
Aldo A. Rossi, Milano, Italy
Witold Rybczynski, Philadelphia, PA
Thomas J. Sanabria, Miami, FL
Alberto Sartoris, Cossonay Ville, Switzerland
Helmut C. Schulitz, Braunschweig, Germany
Michael Scott, Ireland
Harry Seidler, Australia
J. Francisco Serrano, Mexico City, Mexico
Hchioh Sang Seung, Seoul, Korea
Vassilis C. Sgoutas, Athens, Greece
Haigo T.H. Shen, Taipei, Taiwan
Peter F. Shepheard, Philadelphia, PA
Dr. Tsutomu Shigemura, Kobe, Japan
Zheng Shiling, Shanghai, China
Kazuo Shinohara, Yokohama, Japan
Brian Sim, Vancouver, Canada
Antonio S. Sindiong, Rizal, Philippines
Heikki Siren, Helsinki, Finland
Kaija Siren, Helsinki, Finland
Nils Slaatto, Oslo, Norway
Vladimir Slapeta, Praha, Czech Republic
Inette L. Smith, Cornwall, England
J. M. Smith, Cornwall, England
Gin Su, Bethesda, MD
Michio Sugawara, Tokyo, Japan
Timo Suomalainen, Espoo, Finland
Minoru Takeyama, Littleton, CO
Yoshio Taniguchi, Tokyo, Japan
German Tellez, Bogota, Colombia
Anders Tengbom, Sweden
Paul-André Tétreault, Montreal, Canada
Alexandros N. Tombazis, Athens, Greece
Luben N. Tonev, Bulgaria
Marion Tournon-Branly, Paris, France
Shozo Uchii, Tokyo, Japan
Lennart Uhlin, Stockholm, Sweden
Jørn Utzon, Denmark
Pierre Vago, Noisy, France
Gino Valle, Udine, Italy
Marcelo E. Vargas, Lima, Peru
Pedro R. Vasquez, Mexico City, Mexico
Eva Vecsei, Montreal, Canada
Jorge N. Verdugo, Mexico City, Mexico
Tomas R. Vicuna, Santiago, Chile
Jean-Paul Viguier, Paris, France
Ricardo L. Vilchis, Mexico City, Mexico
Eduardo O. Villacortaq, Lima, Peru
William Whitefield, London, England
Terence J. Williams, Victoria, Canada
Roy W. Willwerth, Halifax, Canada
C. A. Wnderlich, Guatemala City, Guatemala
Chung Soo Won, Seoul, Korea
Bernard Wood, Ottawa, Canada
Rutang Ye, Beijing, PRC
Richard Young, Sterling, Canada
Abraham Zabludovsky, Codesa, Mexico
Jose M. Zaragoza, Philippines
Eberhard Heinrich Zeidler, Toronto, Canada

Source: The American Institute of Architects

Honorary Members of The American Institute of Architects

The American Institute of Architects (AIA) grants honorary membership to individuals outside the architecture profession who are not otherwise eligible for membership in the Institute. They are chosen for their distinguished service to architecture or the allied arts and sciences. Nominations may be submitted by the national AIA Board of Directors, a component, or a PIA (Professional Interest Area). National and component staff with 10 years or more of service are also eligible for Honorary Membership.

Suzie Adams, Fort Worth, TX
Ava J. Abramowitz, Chevy Chase, MD
Joseph F. Addonizio, New Rochelle, NY
His Highness The Aga Khan
Joseph Ahearn, Littleton, CO
Michael L. Ainslie, New York, NY
R. Mayne Albright, Charlotte, NC
Barbara Allan, Seattle, WA
George A. Allen, CAE, Tallahassee, FL
Trudy Aron, Topeka, KS
Ludd Ashley, Washington, DC
Janice Axon, Laguna Niguel, CA
William M. Babcock, Madison, WI
Kermit Baker, Washington, DC
Mariana Barthold, Oklahoma City, OK
Augustus Baxter, Sr., Philadelphia, PA
Stephen M. Bennett, Columbus, OH
Leo L. Beranek, Cambridge, MA
Elaine Bergman, Tulsa, OK
James Biddle, Andalusia, PA
J. Bidwill, Chicago, IL
Sherry Birk, Washington, DC
The Honorable Sherwood L. Boehlert
Oriol Bohigas, Barcelona, Spain
Sara H. Boutelle, Santa Cruz, CA
A. S. Boyd, Washington, DC
Ann Marie Boyden, Arlington, VA
Eleanor K. Brassel, Bethesda, MD
John W. Braymer, Richmond, VA
David Brinkley, Chevy Chase, MD
Jack Brooks, Washington, DC
A. B. Brown, Providence, RI
Charlotte Vestal Brown, Raleigh, NC
J. N. Brown, Providence, RI
William A. Brown Sr., Washington, DC
William D. Browning, Snowmass, CO
John M. Bryan, Columbia, SC
Muriel Campaglia, Washington, DC
Donald Canty, Seattle, WA
Joan Capelin, New York, NY
Edward Carlough, Washington, DC
Charles M. Cawley, Wilmington, DE
Henry C. Chambers, Beaufort, SC
Mary Chapman-Smith, Mancelona, MI
William W. Chase, Alexandria, VA
Henry Cisneros, San Antonio, TX
F. J. Clark, Washington, DC
Grady Clay Jr., Louisville, KY
Ernest A. Connally, Alexandria, VA
S. B. Conroy, Washington, DC
Rolaine V. Copeland, Seattle, WA
Weld Coxe, Block Island, RI
Lois Craig, Cambridge, MA
James P. Cramer, Atlanta, GA
Alfonse M. D'Amato, Washington, DC
Kathleen L. Daileda, Washington, DC
Ann Davidson, North Canton, OH
Joan K. Davidson, New York, NY
Brent L. Davis, Tucson AZ
Mabel S. Day, Alexandria, VA
Fred R. Deluca, Washington, DC
Deborah Dietsch, Washington, DC
John A. DiNardo, Austin, TX
Carlos Diniz
Rae Dumke, Detroit, MI
M. Durning, Seattle, WA

Honorary Members of The American Institute of Architects

J. Sprigg Duvall, Washington, DC
Linda J. Ebitz, Oakland, PA
Judy A. Edwards, New Haven, CT
M. D. Egan, Anderson, SC
James R. Ellis, Seattle, WA
John D. Entenza, Santa Monica, CA
Marie L. Farrell, Belvedere, CA
Alan M. Fern, Chevy Chase, MD
Angelina Munoz Fernandez de Madrid, Sonora, Mexico
L. A. Ferre, San Juan, Puerto Rico
David W. Field, CAE, Columbus, OH
Harold B. Finger, Washington, DC
James M. Fitch, New York, NY
Louise H. "Polly" Flansburgh, Boston, MA
Terrance R. Flynn, Wilmington, DE
J. D. Forbes, Charlottesville, VA
William S. Fort, Eugene, OR
Arthur J. Fox Jr., New York, NY
Doris C. Freedman, New York, NY
Mildred Friedman, New York, NY
Patsy L. Frost, Columbus, OH
Ruth Fuller, Houston, TX
Paul Gapp, Chicago, IL
D. E. Gardner, Delaware, OH
Paul Genecki, Kensington, MD
C. D. Gibson, Ogden, UT
Brendan Gill, New York, NY
Jorge Glusberg, Buenos Aires, Argentina
Tina M. Gobbel, Phoenix, AZ
Alfred Goldberg, Belvedere Tiburo, CA
Howard G. Goldberg, Esq.
Paul Goldberger, New York, NY
Douglas E. Gordon, Washington, DC
H. B. Gores, Alpharetta, GA
D. R. Graham, Tallahassee, FL
Ginny W. Graves, Prairie Village, KS
Barbara Gray, Takoma Park, MD
Roberta Gratz
Cecil H. Green, Dallas, TX
Thomas Griffith, New York, NY
Roberta J. Guffey, Charleston, WV
Robert Gutman, Princeton, NJ
Richard Haag, Seattle, WA
Donald J. Hall, Kansas City, MO
William L. Hall, Eden Prairie, MN
Donalee Hallenbeck, Sacramento, CA
P. Hammer, Beverley Beach, MD
Marga Rose Hancock, Seattle, WA
Partrick K. Harrison, London, England
Dr. F. Otto Hass, Philadelphia, PA
Arthur A. Hart, Boise, ID
Dianne Hart, California
Beverly E. Hauschild-Baron, Minneapolis, MN
A. Hecksher, New York, NY
Andrew Heiskell, New York, NY
Brenda Henderson, Washington, DC
Amy Hershfang
Gerald D. Hines, Houston, TX
Charles L. Hite
William Houseman, Portland, ME
Thomas P. Hoving, New York, NY
Philip A. Hutchinson, Harwood, MD
Ada L. Huxtable, New York, NY
J. Michael Huey
Donald G. Iselin, Santa Barbara, CA
Kathy C. Jackson, CAE, Jackson, MS
J. B. Johnson, Watertown, NY
Dr. Joseph E. Johnson
Lady B. Johnson, Austin, TX
Gerre Jones, Albuquerque, NM
V. Jordan, Jr., New York, NY
H. A. Judd, Beaverton, OR
Lloyd Kaiser, Oakmont, PA
Shelly Kappe
Robert J. Kapsch, Gaithersburg, MD
Suzanne Keller, Princeton, NJ
Dorothy Kender
Roger G. Kennedy, Alexandria, VA
Jonathan King, Houston, TX
R. Lawrence Kirkegaard, Downers Grove, IL
Lee E. Koppelman, Stonybrook, NY

Honorary Members of The American Institute of Architects

Peter H. Kostmayer, Washington, DC
Mabel Krank, Oklahoma City, OK
Florence C. Ladd, Cambridge, MA
Anita M. Laird, Cape May, NJ
David P. Lancaster, Austin, TX
George Latimer, St. Paul, MN
Robin Lee, Washington, D.C.
William J. Le Messurier, Cambridge, MA
Barry B. LePatner
Aaron Levine, Menlo Park, CA
E. H. Levitas, Washington, DC
Lawrence Lewis Jr.
Weiming Lu, St. Paul, MN
Major General Eugene Lupia
Jane Maas, New York, NY
Diane Maddox, Washington, DC
Jon D. Magnusson, Seattle, WA
Randell Lee Makinson
Stanley Marcus, Dallas, TX
Louis L. Marines, Corte Madera, CA
Judy Marks, Washington, DC
Albert R. Marschall, Alexandria, VA
Maureen Marx, Springfield, VA
Mary Tyler Cheek McClenaham
F. M. McConihe, Potomac, MD
Dr. Robert McCoy
Terrence M. McDermott, Chicago, IL
Evelyn B. McGrath, Holiday, FL
Ian L. McHarg, Philadelphia, PA
Cheri C. Melillo, New York, NY
Paul Mellon, Upperville, VA
Betty H. Meyer
E. P. Mickel, Bethesda, MD
J. I. Miller, Columbus, IN
Martha P. Miller, Portland, OR
R. Miller, Sherman Oaks, CA
Richard B. Miller, Elmsford, NY
Roger Milliken, Spartanburg, SC
Hermine Mitchell, Philadelphia, PA
Richard Moe, Washington DC
Martha Barber Montgomery
William B. Moore Jr., Kilmarnock, VA
John W. Morris, Arlington, VA
Philip A. Morris, Birmingham, AL
Terry B. Morton, Chevy Chase, MD
Woolridge Brown Morton III
Jean G. Muntz, Omaha, NE
Martha Murphree, Houston, TX
Maria Murray, Kensington, MD
Betty J. Musselman, Accokeek, MD
Raymond D. Nasher
Doreen Nelson, Los Angeles, CA
Shirley J. Norvell, Springfield, IL
Laurie D. Olin, Philadelphia, PA
Mary E. Osman, Columbia, SC
Rep. Frank Pallone
Ronald J. Panciera, Bradenton, FL
R. B. Pease, Pittsburgh, PA
C. Ford Peatross, Washington, DC
Robert A. Peck, Esq, Washington, DC
Claiborne Pell, Washington, DC
David Perdue, Silver Spring, MD
Michael D. Perry, Virginia Beach, VA
G. E. Pettengill, Arlington, VA
Janet D. Pike, Lexington, KY
Philip W. Pillsbury Jr., Washington, DC
Walter F. Pritchard II, Costa Mesa, CA
Jay A. Pritzker, Chicago, IL
Jody Proppe, Portland, OR
Marvin Rand, Venice, CA
Sidney A. Rand, Minneapolis, MN
David P. Reynolds, Richmond, VA
William G. Reynolds Jr., Richmond, VA
Brenda Richards
Carolyn Richie
Raymond P. Rhinehart, Washington, DC
Joseph P. Riley, Charleston, SC
J. P. Robin, Pittsburgh, PA
Laurance Rockefeller, New York, NY
Barbara J. Rodriguez, Albany, NY
Gini Rountree, Sacramento, CA
Mario G. Salvadori, New York, NY

Honorary Members of The American Institute of Architects

Stephen P. Sands
Carl M. Sapers, Boston, MA
William D. Schaefer, Baltimore, MD
Martin Schaum, Garden City, NY
Paul Schell, Seattle, WA
Vincent C. Schoemehl Jr., Clayton, MO
Philip Schreiner, Washington, DC
Rosemary Schroeder, Dallas, TX
Robert H. Schuller, Garden Grove, CA
Susan E. Schur
Frederick D. Schwengel
Suzanne K. Schwengels, Des Moines, IA
Rex Scouten, Washington, DC
B. Sebastian, San Francisco, CA
James H. Semans, Durham, NC
Julian B. Serrill, Des Moines, IA
Elaine K. Sewell Jones, Los Angeles, CA
Polly E. Shackleton, Washington, DC
Julius Shulman, Los Angeles, CA
John R. Silber
Betty W. Silver, Raleigh, NC
Alice Sinkevitch, Chicago, IL
John B. Skilling, Seattle, WA
W. L. Slayton, Washington, DC
Eleanor McNamara Smith, Somerset, WI
Nancy Somerville, Washington, DC
S. Spencer, Washington, DC
Ann Stacy, Baltimore, MD
B. Carole Steadham
S. Steinborn, Seattle, WA
Saundra Stevens, Portland, OR
P. D. Stitt, Yreka, CA
Deborah Sussman, Culver City, CA
Anne J. Swager, Pittsburg, PA
Pipsan S. Swanson, Bloomfield, MI
G. B. Tatum, Chester, CT
Anne Taylor, Kansas City, MO
Richard Thevenot, Baton Rouge, LA
J. S. Thurmond, Washington, DC
Carolyn H. Toft, St. Louis, MO
Bernard Tomson, Voorheesville, NY
W. F. Traendly, Thetford Center, VT
R. E. Train, Washington, DC
Tallman Trask III, Durham, NC
Pierre Vago, Noisy, France
Mariana L. Verga, Edmond, OK
Wolf Von Eckardt, Washington, DC
Connie C. Wallace, CAE, Nashville, TN
Paul Weidlinger, New York, NY
Paul W. Welch, Jr. Sacramento, CA
Emmet L. Wemple, Los Angeles, CA
Katie Westby, Tulsa, OK
Frank J. Whalen Jr., Cheverly, MD
Richard Guy Wilson, Charlottesville, VA
Gloria Wise, Dallas, TX
Honorable Pete Wilson, Washington, DC
Arol Wolford, Norcross, GA
Marilyn Wood, Santa Fe, NM
Tony P. Wrenn, Fredricksburg, VA
Honorable Sidney Yates, Washington, DC
Jill D. Yeomans, Santa Barbara, CA
John Zukowsky, Chicago, IL

Source: The American Institute of Architects

Honorary Members of the American Society of Landscape Architects

Honorary Membership is granted by the American Society of Landscape Architects' (ASLA) Board of Directors, to persons, other than landscape architects, who have performed notable service to the profession of landscape architecture.

Edward H. Able Jr.
Philip J. Arnold
Hon. Douglas Bereuter
Randall Biallas
Earl Blumenauer
Nancy Callister Buley
Hon. Dale Bumpers
Pres. James Earl Carter Jr.
Clarence "Buck" Chaffee
Grady Clay
Richard M. Daley
Russell E. Dickenson
Walter L. Doty
Marvin Durning
Carolyn B. Etter
Don D. Etter
Albert Fein
Charles E. Fraser
Marshall M. Fredericks
Gwen Frostic
Mary L. Hanson
Donald M. Harris
George B. Hartzog Jr.
Vance R. Hood
Patrick Horsbrugh
Thomas Hylton
Pres. Lyndon B. Johnson
Dr. Harley Jolley
Genevieve Pace Keller
Hon. Edward M. Kennedy
Peter A. Kirsch
Balthazar Korab
Norbert Kraich
Prof. Walter H. Lewis
Dr. Binyi Liu
John A. Love
Lee MacDonald
Prof. E. Bruce MacDougall
Charles C. McLaughlin
Hugh C. Miller
Philip A. Morris
Frederick L. Noland
Gyo Obata
Ross D. Pallay
R. Max Peterson
William Phelps
Richard Pope, Sr.
Gen. Colin Powell
Peter H. Raven
Hon. Joseph P. Riley Jr.
L. S. Rockefeller
Martin J. Rosen
John Seiberling
Thomas D. Seifert
Ron Taven
Dr. Ralph J. Warburton

Source: American Society of Landscape Architects

Honorary Members of the Industrial Designers Society of America

The Board of Directors of the Industrial Designers Society of America (IDSA) grants honorary membership to individuals whose relationship to, involvement with, or special efforts on behalf of the design profession merit the recognition and gratitude of the Society. Honorary membership is awarded by a three-quarters majority vote by the Board of Directors.

1965	R. Buckminster Fuller
1965	Edgar Kaufmann Jr.
1981	Ray Eames
1982	Florence Knoll Bassett
1983	Ralph Caplan
1988	Brian J. Wynne
1998	Bruce Nussbaum

Source: Industrial Designers Society of America

> The relationship between object and user should be friendly so that you can play with it and interact as if it were a toy.
>
> **Achille Castiglioni**

Honorary Members of the International Interior Design Association

The International Interior Design Association (IIDA) grants honorary membership to individuals who, although they are not interior designers, have made substantial contributions to the interior design profession. The following individuals are current Honorary Members of the IIDA.

Stanley Abercrombie
Clarellen Adams
George Baer
Shirley Black
Charles Blumberg
Chilton Brown
Margaret Buckingham
Dennis Cahill
Len Corlin
Christine Cralle
James P. Cramer
Tom Cramer
Cheryl Durst
Lori Graham
Dianne Jackman
Cynthia Leibrock
Paul Leonard
Viscount David Linley
Chris McKellar
Doug Parker
Norman Polsky
Lois Powers
John Sample
Thomas Sutton Jr.
Dean Thompson
Jan Toft
Jill Vanderfleet-Scott
John West

Source: International Interior Design Association

Interior Design Hall of Fame

In 1985 *Interior Design* magazine established the Interior Design Hall of Fame to recognize individuals who have made significant contributions to the growth and prominence of the Interior Design profession. New inductees are presented every December at an awards ceremony at New York's Waldorf-Astoria Hotel. This event also serves as a fundraising effort for the non-profit Foundation for Interior Design Education Research (FIDER) and other charitable organizations supporting interior design educational initiatives.

Marvin. B Affrime
Kalef Alaton
Davis Allen
Stephen A. Apking
Pamela Babey
Benjamin Baldwin
Florence Knoll Bassett
Louis M.S. Beal
Ward Bennett
Maria Bergson
Deborah Berke
Barbara Berry
Bruce Bierman
Laura Bohn
Joseph Braswell
Robert Bray
Don Brinkmann
Tom Britt
R. Scott Bromley
Mario Buatta
Richard Carlson
Francois Catroux
Steve Chase
Antonio Citterio
Clodagh
Celeste Cooper
Robert Currie
Barbara D'Arcy
Joseph D'Urso
Thierry W. Despont
Orlando Diaz-Azcuy
Angelo Donghia
Jaime Drake
Jack Dunbar
Tony Duquette
Melvin Dwork
David Easton
Henry End
Mica Ertegun
Bernardo Fort-Brescia
Billy W. Francis
Neil Frankel
Michael Gabellini
Frank Gehry
Arthur Gensler
Richard Gluckman
Mariette Himes Gomez
Jacques Grange
Margo Grant
Michael Graves
Bruce Gregga
Charles Gwathmey
Albert Hadley
Anthony Hall
Mel Hamilton
Mark Hampton
Antony Harbour
Hugh Hardy
David Hicks
Edith Mansfield Hills
Richard Himmel
Howard Hirsch
William Hodgins
Malcolm Holzman
Franklin D. Israel
Carolyn Iu
Eva Jiricna
Jed Johnson

Interior Design Hall of Fame

Melanie Kahane
Ronette King
Robert Kleinschmidt
Ronald Krueck
Gary Lee
Sarah Tomerlin Lee
Naomi Leff
Debra Lehman-Smith
Joseph Lembo
Lawrence Lerner
Neville Lewis
Sally Sirkin Lewis
Christian Liaigre
Eva Maddox
Stephen Mallory
Peter Marino
Patrick McConnell
Margaret McCurry
Zack McKown
Kevin McNamara
Richard Meier
Robert Metzger
Lee Mindel
Juan Montoya
Frank Nicholson
James Northcurr
Mrs. Henry Parish II
John Pawson
Norman Pfeiffer
Charles Pfister
Warren Platner
Donald D. Powell
William Pulgram
Glenn Pushelberg
Andrée Putman
Chessy Rayner
David Rockwell
Lauren Rottet
Rita St. Clair
John F. Saladino
Michael Schaible
Denise Scott Brown
Peter Shelton
Berry Sherrill
Robert Siegel
Ethel Smith
Laurinda Spear
Jay Spectre
Andre Staffelbach
Philippe Starck
Robert A.M. Stern
Rysia Suchecka
Lou Switzer
Rose Tarlow
Michael Taylor
Stanley Tigerman
Adam Tihany
Calvin Tsao
Billie Tsien
Carleton Varney
Robert Venturi
Lella Vignelli
Massimo Vignelli
Kenneth H. Walker
Sally Walsh
Kevin Walz
Gary Wheeler
Bunny Williams
Tod Williams
Trisha Wilson
Vicente Wolf
George Yabu

Special Honorees

Robert O. Anderson
Jaime Ardiles-Arce
Stanley Barrows
Howard Brandston
Adele Chatfield-Taylor
John L. Dowling
Lester Dundes
Sherman R. Emery

Interior Design Hall of Fame

Karen Fisher
Arnold Friedmann
Alberto Paolo Gavasci
Jeremiah Goodman
Louis Oliver Gropp
Olga Gueft
Jack Hedrich
Benjamin D. Holloway
Philip E. Kelly
Kips Bay Decorator Show House
Jack Lenor Larsen
Santo Loquasto
Ruth K. Lynford
Gene Moore
Diantha Nype
Dianne Pilgrim
Paige Rense
Ian Schrager
Julius Shulman
Tony Walton
Winterthur Museum and Gardens

Source: Interior Design *magazine*

We have to replace beauty, which is a cultural concept, with goodness, which is a humanist concept.

Philippe Starck

Presidents of The American Council of Engineering Companies

1973-74 William N. Holway
1974-75 Malcolm M. Meurer
1975-76 Billy T. Sumner
1976-77 Richard H. Stanley
1977-78 William A. Clevenger
1978-79 R. Duane Monical
1979-80 George W. Barnes
1980-81 Everett S. Thompson
1981-82 William R. Ratliff
1982-83 Russell L. Smith Jr.
1983-84 Shelby K. Willis
1984-85 Clifford E. Evanson
1985-86 Arnold L. Windman
1986-87 Lester H. Poggemeyer
1987-88 Lester H. Smith Jr.
1988-89 Robert E. Hogan
1989-90 James W. Poirot
1990-91 William D. Lewis
1991-92 Andrew J. Parker Jr.
1992-93 John H. Foster
1993-94 Paul F. Sprehe
1994-95 J. Les MacFarlane
1995-96 Richard G. Weingardt
1996-97 Stanley K. Kawaguchi
1997-98 James R. Thomas Jr.
1998-99 Donald R. Trim
1999-00 Leo F. Peters
2000-01 Arlo J. Spiess
2001-02 Stephen G. Goddard
2002-03 Daniel J. DeYoung
2003-04 Eric L. Flicker
2004-05 William S. Howard

* In 2001, the title of President was changed to Chairman.

Source: The American Council of Engineering Companies

Presidents of The American Institute of Architects

1857-76	Richard Upjohn
1877-87	Thomas U. Walter
1888-91	Richard M. Hunt
1892-93	Edward H. Kendall
1894-95	Daniel H. Burnham
1896-98	George B. Post
1899	Henry Van Brunt
1900-01	Robert S. Peabody
1902-03	Charles F. McKim
1904-05	William S. Eames
1906-07	Frank M. Day
1908-09	Cass Gilbert
1910-11	Irving K. Pond
1912-13	Walter Cook
1914-15	R. Clipston Sturgis
1916-18	John L. Mauran
1919-20	Thomas R. Kimball
1921-22	Henry H. Kendall
1923-24	William B. Faville
1925-26	Dan E. Waid
1927-28	Milton B. Medary
1929-30	Charles H. Hammond
1931-32	Robert D. Kohn
1933-34	Earnest J. Russell
1935-36	Stephen F. Voorhees
1937-38	Charles D. Maginnis
1939-40	Edwin Bergstrom
1941-42	Richmond H. Shreve
1943-44	Raymond J. Ashton
1945-46	James R. Edmunds Jr.
1947-48	Douglas W. Orr
1949-50	Ralph T. Walker
1951-52	A. Glenn Stanton
1953-54	Clair W. Ditchy
1955-56	George B. Cummings
1957-58	Leon Chatelain Jr.
1959-60	John Noble Richards
1961-62	Philip Will Jr.
1963	Henry L. Wright
1964	J. Roy Carroll Jr.
1965	A. Gould Odell Jr.
1966	Morris Ketchum Jr.
1967	Charles M. Nes Jr.
1968	Robert L. Durham
1969	George E. Kassabaum
1970	Rex W. Allen
1971	Robert F. Hastings
1972	Max O. Urbahn
1973	S. Scott Ferebee Jr.
1974	Archibald C. Rogers
1975	William "Chick" Marshall Jr.
1976	Louis DeMoll
1977	John M. McGinty
1978	Elmer E. Botsai
1979	Ehrman B. Mitchell Jr.
1980	Charles E. Schwing
1981	R. Randall Vosbeck
1982	Robert M. Lawrence
1983	Robert C. Broshar
1984	George M. Notter Jr.
1985	R. Bruce Patty
1986	John A Busby Jr.
1987	Donald J. Hackl
1988	Ted P. Pappas
1989	Benjamin E. Brewer Jr.
1990	Sylvester Damianos
1991	C. James Lawler
1992	W. Cecil Steward
1993	Susan A. Maxman
1994	L. William Chapin Jr.
1995	Chester A. Widom
1996	Raymond G. "Skipper" Post Jr.
1997	Raj Barr-Kumar
1998	Ronald A. Altoon
1999	Michael J. Stanton
2000	Ronald Skaggs
2001	John D. Anderson
2002	Gordon Chong
2003	Thompson E. Penney
2004	Eugene Hopkins
2005	Douglas L. Steidl

Source: The American Institute of Architects

Presidents of the American Society of Interior Designers

1974-75 Norman DeHann
1974-76 Richard Jones
1977-78 H. Albert Phibbs
1978-79 Irving Schwartz
1979-80 Rita St. Clair
1980-81 Wallace Jonason
1981-82 Jack Lowery
1982-83 Martin Ellinoff
1984-85 William Richard Waley
1985-86 Gail Adams
1986-87 Janet Schirn
1987-88 Joy Adcock
1988-89 Charles Gandy
1989-90 Elizabeth Howard
1990-91 Robert John Dean
1991-92 Raymond Kennedy
1992-93 Martha G. Rayle
1993-94 B.J. Peterson
1994-95 Gary Wheeler
1995-96 Penny Bonda
1996-97 Kathy Ford Montgomery
1997-98 Joyce Burke-Jones
1998-99 Rosalyn Cama
1999-00 Juliana M. Catlin
2000-01 Terri Maurer
2001-02 Barbara Nugent
2002-03 H. Don Bowden
2003-04 Linda Elliot Smith
2004-05 Anita Baltimore

Source: American Society of Interior Designers

Design is one of the most forceful influences on behavior and is part of everything we human beings experience. I am not talking only of interior design, here, but of architecture, graphic, industrial, landscape, fashion, and product design. Brilliant or ordinary, awful or annoying, design evokes emotions in us. It's the principles of design—scale and proportions, color, texture and their appropriateness to each other—that are all contributing factors. It's the delight when something works well and the frustration when it's poorly designed... It's this connection between design, emotion, and behavior that gives design its power.

Penny Bonda

Presidents of the American Society of Landscape Architects

1899-01	John C. Olmsted*
1902	Samuel Parsons Jr.*
1903	Nathan F. Barrett*
1904-05	John C. Olmsted*
1906-07	Samuel Parsons Jr.*
1908-09	Frederick Law Olmsted Jr.*
1910-11	Charles N. Lowrie*
1912	Harold A. Caparn
1913	Ossian C. Simonds*
1914	Warren H. Manning*
1915-18	James Sturgis Pray
1919-22	Frederick Law Olmsted Jr.*
1923-27	James L. Greenleaf
1927-31	Arthur A. Shurcliff
1931-35	Henry Vincent Hubbard
1935-41	Albert D. Taylor
1941-45	S. Herbert Hare
1945-49	Markley Stevenson
1949-51	Gilmore D. Clarke
1951-53	Lawrence G. Linnard
1953-57	Leon Zach
1957-61	Norman T. Newton
1961-63	John I. Rogers
1963-65	John Ormsbee Simonds
1965-67	Hubert B. Owens
1967-69	Theodore Osmundson
1969-71	Campbell E. Miller
1971-73	Raymond L. Freeman
1973-74	William G. Swain
1974-75	Owen H. Peters
1975-76	Edward H. Stone II
1976-77	Benjamin W. Gary Jr.
1977-78	Lane L. Marshall
1978-79	Jot Carpenter
1979-80	Robert L. Woerner
1980-81	William A. Behnke
1981-82	Calvin T. Bishop
1982-83	Theodore J. Wirth
1983-84	Darwina L. Neal
1984-85	Robert H. Mortensen
1985-86	John Wacker
1986-87	Roger B. Martin
1987-88	Cheryl L. Barton
1988-89	Brian S. Kubota
1989-90	Gerald D. Patten
1990-91	Claire R. Bennett
1991-92	Cameron R.J. Man
1992-93	Debra L. Mitchell
1993-94	Thomas Papandrew
1994-95	Dennis Y. Otsuji
1995-96	Vincent Bellafiore
1996-97	Donald W. Leslie
1997-98	Thomas R. Dunbar
1998-99	Barry W. Starke
1999-00	Janice Cervelli Schach
2000-01	Leonard J. Hopper
2001-02	Rodney Swink
2002-03	Paul Morris
2003-04	Susan Jacobson
2004-05	Patrick A. Miller

*Charter Member

Source: American Society of Landscape Architects

Presidents of the Association of Collegiate Schools of Architecture

1912-21 Warren Laird
Univ. of Pennsylvania

1921-23 Emil Lorch
Univ. of Michigan

1923-25 William Emerson
Massachusetts Institute of Technology

1925-27 Francke Bosworth Jr.
Cornell Univ.

1927-29 Goldwin Goldsmith
Univ. of Kansas

1929-31 Everett Meeks
Yale Univ.

1931-34 Ellis Lawrence
Univ. of Oregon

1934-36 Roy Childs Jones
Univ. of Minnesota

1936-38 Sherely Morgan
Princeton Univ.

1938-40 George Young Jr.
Cornell Univ.

1940-42 Leopold Arnaud
Columbia Univ.

1942-45 Wells Bennett
Univ. of Michigan

1945-47 Loring Provine
Univ. of Illinois

1947-49 Paul Weigel
Kansas State College

1949-51 B. Kenneth Johnstone
Carnegie Institute

1951-53 Thomas FitzPatrick
Iowa State College

1953-55 Lawrence Anderson
Massachusetts Institute of Technology

1955-57 Elliott Whitaker
Ohio State Univ.

1957-59 Buford Pickens
Washington Univ.

1959-61 Harlan McClure
Clemson College

1961-63 Olindo Grossi
Pratt Institute

1963-65 Henry Kamphoefner
North Carolina St. College

1965-67 Walter Sanders
Univ. of Michigan

1967-69 Robert Bliss
Univ. of Utah

1969-71 Charles Burchard
Virginia Polytechnic

1971-72 Alan Taniguchi
Rice Univ. & Univ. of Texas, Austin

1972-73 Robert Harris
Univ. of Oregon

1973-74 Sanford Greenfield
Boston Arch. Center

1974-75 Don Schlegal
Univ. of New Mexico

1975-76 Bertram Berenson
Univ. of Illinois at Chicago

1976-77 Donlyn Lyndon
Massachusetts Institute of Technology

1977-78 Dwayne Nuzum
Univ. of Colorado, Boulder

1978-79 William Turner
Tulane Univ.

1979-80 Robert Burns
North Carolina State Univ.

1980-81 Richard Peters
Univ. of California, Berkeley

1981-82 Eugene Kremer
Kansas State Univ.

1982-83 O. Jack Mitchell
Rice Univ.

1983-84 Charles Hight
Univ. of North Carolina, Charlotte

1984-85 Wilmot Gilland
Univ. of Oregon

1985-86 George Anselevicius
Univ. of New Mexico

Presidents of the Association of Collegiate Schools of Architecture

1986-87	Blanche Lemco van Ginkel Univ. of Toronto
1987-88	J. Thomas Regan Univ. of Miami
1988-89	Robert Beckley Univ. of Michigan
1989-90	Marvin Malecha Cal. State Poly. Univ., Pomona
1990-91	John Meunier Arizona State Univ.
1991-92	Patrick Quinn Rensselaer Polytechnic Institute
1992-93	James Barker Clemson Univ.
1993-94	Kent Hubbell Cornell Univ.
1994-95	Diane Ghirardo Univ. of Southern California
1995-96	Robert Greenstreet Univ. of Wisconsin-Milwaukee
1996-97	Linda W. Sanders Calif. State Polytechnic Univ.
1997-98	John M. McRae Mississippi State Univ.
1998-99	R. Wayne Drummond Univ. of Florida
1999-00	Jerry Finrow Univ. of Washington
2000-01	Tony Schuman New Jersey Institute of Technology
2001-02	Frances Bronet Renssalaer Polytechnic Institute
2002-03	Bradford C. Grant Hampton University
2003-04	Geraldine Forbes Isais Woodbury University
2004-05	Rafael Longoria University of Houston

Source: Association of Collegiate Schools of Architecture

Presidents of the Industrial Designers Society of America

1965	Henry Dreyfuss
1966	Joseph M. Parriott
1967-68	Robert Hose
1969-70	Tucker Madawick
1971-72	William Goldsmith
1973-74	Arthur Pulos
1975-76	James Fulton
1977-78	Richard Hollerith
1979-80	Carroll M. Gantz
1981-82	Robert G. Smith
1983-84	Katherine J. McCoy
1985-86	Cooper C. Woodring
1987-88	Peter H. Wooding
1989-90	Peter W. Bressler
1991-92	Charles Pelly
1993-94	David Tompkins
1995-96	James Ryan
1997-98	Craig Vogel
1999-00	Mark Dziersk
2001-02	Betty Baugh
2003-04	Bruce Claxton

Source: Industrial Designers Society of America

It is easy to describe something which stands before you, but when you design you must start by describing something that does not exist.

Eva Zeisel

Presidents of the International Interior Design Association

1994-95	Marilyn Farrow
1995-96	Judith Hastings
1996-97	Beth Harmon-Vaughan
1997-98	Karen Guenther
1998-99	Neil Frankel
1999-00	Carol Jones
2000-01	Richard Pollack
2001-02	Cary D. Johnson
2002-03	Anita L. Barnett
2003-04	Lewis Goetz
2004-05	John Lijewski

Source: International Interior Design Association

Presidents of the International Union of Architects

1948-53 Sir Patrick Abercrombie (UK)
1953-57 Jean Tschumi (Switzerland)
1957-61 Hector Mardones-Restat Chili)
1961-65 Sir Robert Matthew (UK)
1965-69 Eugène Beaudouin (France)
1969-72 Ramon Corona Martin (Mexico)
1972-75 Georgui Orlov (Russia)
1975-78 Jai Rattan Bhalla (India)
1978-81 Louis DeMoll (UK)
1981-85 Rafael de la Hoz (Spain)
1985-87 Georgi Stoilov (Bulgaria)
1987-90 Rod Hackney (UK)
1990-93 Olufemi Majekodunmi (Nigeria)
1993-96 Jaime Duro Pifarré (Spain)
1996-99 Sara Topelson de Grinberg (Mexico)
1999-02 Vassilis Sgoutas (Greece)
2002-05 Jaime Lerner (Brazil)

Honorary Presidents

1948-53 Auguste Perret (France)
1953-57 Sir Patrick Abercrombie (UK)
1969-02 Pierre Vago (France)

Source: International Union of Architects

Presidents of the National Council of Architectural Registration Boards

1920-22	Emil Loch
1923-24	Arthur Peabody
1925	Miller I. Kast
1926-27	W.H. Lord
1928	George D. Mason
1929-30	Clarence W. Brazer
1931-32	James M. White
1933	A.L. Brockway
1933	A.M. Edelman
1934-35	Joseph W. Holman
1936	Charles Butler
1938-39	William Perkins
1940-41	Mellen C. Greeley
1942-44	Louis J. Gill
1945-46	Solis Seiferth
1947-49	Warren D. Miller
1950	Clinton H. Cowgill
1951	Roger C. Kirchoff
1952-52	Charles E. Firestone
1954-55	Fred L. Markham
1956-58	Edgar H. Berners
1959-60	Walter F. Martens
1961	A. Reinhold Melander
1962	Chandler C. Cohagen
1963	Paul W. Drake
1964	Ralph O. Mott
1965	C.J. "Pat" Paderewski
1966	Earl L. Mathes
1967	George F. Schatz
1968-69	Howard T. Blanchard
1970	Dean L. Gustavson
1971	William J. Geddis
1972	Daniel Boone
1973	Thomas J. Sedgewick
1974	E.G. Hamilton
1975	John (Mel) O'Brien Jr.
1976	William C. Muchow
1977	Charles A. Blondheim Jr.
1978	Paul H. Graven
1979	Lorenzo D. Williams
1980	John R. Ross
1981	Dwight M. Bonham
1982	Thomas H. Flesher Jr.
1983	Sid Frier
1984	Ballard H.T. Kirk
1985	Robert E. Oringdulph
1986	Theodore L. Mularz
1987	Robert L. Tessier
1988	Walter T. Carry
1989	George B. Terrien
1990	Herbert P. McKim
1991	Charles E. Garrison
1992	Robert H. Burke Jr.
1993	Harry G. Robinson III
	William Wiese II *Honorary Past President*
1994	Robert A. Fielden
1995	Homer L. Williams
1996	Richard W. Quinn
1997	Darrell L. Smith
1998	Ann R. Chaintreuil
1999	Susan May Allen
2000	Joseph P. Giattina Jr.
2001	William Bevins
2002	C. Robert Campbell
2003	Robert A. Boynton
2004	Frank M. Guillot

Source: National Council of Architectural Registration Boards

> Space is architectural when the evidence of how it is made is seen and comprehended.
>
> **Louis Kahn**

Presidents of the Royal Architectural Institute of Canada

1907-10 A.E. Dunlop
1910-12 E.S. Baker
1912-16 J.H.G. Russell
1916-18 J.P. Ouellet
1918-20 A. Frank Wickson
1920-22 David R. Brown
1922-24 Lewis H. Jordan
1924-26 John S. Archibald
1926-29 J.P. Hynes
1929-32 Percy E. Nobbs
1932-34 Gordon M. West
1934-36 W.S. Maxwell
1936-38 W.I. Somerville
1938-40 H.L. Fetherstonbaugh
1940-42 Burwell R. Coon
1942-44 Gordon McL. Pirts
1944-46 Forsey Page
1946-48 David Chas
1948-50 A.J. Hazelgrove
1950-52 J. Roxburgh Smith
1952-54 R. Scholfield Morris
1954-56 A.J.C. Paine
1956-58 D.F. Kertland
1958-60 Maurice Payette
1960-62 Harland Steele
1962-64 John I. Davies
1964-65 F. Bruce Brown
1965-66 Gérard Venne
1966-67 Charles A.E. Fowler
1967-68 James F. Searle
1968-69 Norman H. McMurrich
1969-70 Wm. G. Leithead
1970-71 Gordon R. Arnott
1971-72 Jean-Louis Lalonde
1972-73 C.F.T. Rounthwaite
1973-74 Allan F. Duffus
1974-75 Bernard Wood
1975-76 Fred T. Hollingsworth
1976-77 Charles H. Cullum
1977-78 W. Donald Baldwin
1978-79 Gilbert R. Beatson
1980-81 David H. Hambleton
1981-82 J. Douglass Miller
1982-83 G. Macy DuBois
1983-84 Patrick Blouin
1984-85 W. Kirk Banadyga
1985-86 Brian E. Eldred
1986-87 Rudy P. Ericsen
1987-88 Terence J. Williams
1988-89 Alfred C. Roberts
1989-90 Essy Baniassad
1990-91 Richard Young
1991-92 David W. Edwards
1992-93 Roy Willwerth
1993-94 J. Brian Sim
1994-95 Paul-André Tétreault
1995-97 Bill Chomik
1997-98 Barry J. Hobin
1998-99 Eva Matsuzaki
1999-00 Eliseo Temprano
2000-01 David Simpson
2001-02 Diarmuid Nash
2002-03 Ronald Keenberg
2003-04 Bonnie Maples

Source: Royal Architectural Institute of Canada

Presidents of the Royal Australian Institute of Architects

1929-30 Alfred Samuel Hook
1930-31 William Arthur Blackett
1931-32 Philip Rupert Claridge
1932-33 Lange Leopold Powell
1933-34 Charles Edward Serpell
1934-35 Arthur William Anderson
1935-36 Guy St. John Makin
1936-37 James Nangle
1937-38 Louis Laybourne-Smith
1938-39 Frederick Bruce Lucas
1939-40 Otto Abrecht Yuncken
1940-42 William Ronald Richardson
1942-44 John Francis Scarborough
1944-46 Roy Sharrington Smith
1946-48 William Rae Laurie
1948-50 Jack Denyer Cheesman
1950-52 Cobden Parkes
1952-54 Robert Snowden Demaine
1954-56 Edward James Weller
1956-57 William Purves Godfrey
1957-59 Wilfried Thomas Haslam
1959-60 Kenneth Charles Duncan
1960-61 Thomas Brenan Gargett
1961-62 Henry Ingham Ashworth
1962-63 James Campbell Irwin
1963-64 Max Ernest Collard
1964-65 Raymond Berg
1965-66 Gavin Walkley
1966-67 Mervyn Henry Parry
1967-68 Acheson Best Overend
1968-69 Jack Hobbs McConnell
1969-70 John David Fisher
1970-71 Ronald Andrew Gilling
1971-72 Kenneth William Shugg
1972-73 Henry Jardine Parkinson
1973-75 Peter McIntyre
1975-76 Harold Bryce Mortlock
1976-77 Blair Mansfield Wilson
1977-78 Eustace Gresley Cohen
1978-79 John Davidson
1979-80 Geoffrey Lawrence
1980-81 Alexander Ian Ferrier
1981-82 Michael Laurence Peck
1982-83 Richard Norman Johnson
1983-84 David Alan Nutter
1984-85 Richard Melville Young
1985-86 Roland David Jackson
1986-87 Graham Alan Hulme
1987-88 Robert Darwin Hall
1988-89 Dudley Keith Wilde
1989-90 Ronald Barrie Bodycoat
1990-91 Robert Lindsay Caufield
1991-92 Jamieson Sayer Allom
1992-93 Robert Cheesman
1993-94 James Taylor
1994-95 Virginia Louise Cox
1995-96 Peter Robertson Gargett
1996-97 John Stanley Castles
1997-98 Eric Graham Butt
1998-99 Graham Humphries
1999-00 Nigel Warren Shaw
2000-01 Edward Robert Haysom
2001-02 Graham Jahn
2002-03 Caroline Pidcock
2003-04 David Parken

Source: Royal Australian Institute of Architects

Presidents of the Royal Institute of British Architects

1835-59 Earl de Grey
1860 Charles Robert Cockerell
1861-63 Sir William Tite
1863-65 Thomas L. Donaldson
1865-67 A.J.B. Beresford Hope
1867-70 Sir William Tite
1870-73 Thomas Henry Wyatt
1873-76 Sir Gilbert G. Scott
1876-79 Charles Barry Jr.
1879-81 John Whichcord
1881 George Edmund Street
1882-84 Sir Horace Jones
1884-86 Ewan Christian
1886-87 Edward l'Anson
1888-91 Alfred Watershouse
1891-94 J. Macvicar Anderson
1884-96 Francis C. Penrose
1896-99 George Aitchison
1899-02 Sir William Emerson
1902-04 Sir Aston Webb
1904-06 John Belcher
1906-08 Thomas Edward Collcutt
1908-10 Sir Ernest George
1910-12 Leonard Stokes
1912-14 Sir Reginald Blomfield
1914-17 Ernest Newton
1917-19 Henry Thomas Hare
1919-21 Sir John William Simpson
1921-23 Paul Waterhouse
1923-25 J. Alfred Gotch
1925-27 Sir Guy Dawber
1927-29 Sir Walter Tapper
1929-31 Sir Banister Fletcher
1931-33 Sir Raymond Unwin
1933-35 Sir Giles Gilbert Scott
1935-37 Sir Percy Thomas
1937-39 H.S. Goodhart-Rendel
1939-40 E. Stanley Hall
1940-43 W.H. Ansell
1943-46 Sir Percy Thomas
1946-48 Sir Lancelot Keay
1948-50 Michael T. Waterhouse
1950-52 A. Graham Henderson
1952-54 Sir Howard Robertson
1954-56 C.H. Aslin
1956-58 Kenneth M.B. Cross
1958-60 Sir Basil Spence
1960-62 The Lord Holford
1962-64 Sir Robert Matthew
1964-65 Sir Donald Gibson
1965-67 The Viscount Esher
1967-69 Sir Hugh Wilson
1969-71 Sir Peter Shepheard
1971-73 Sir Alex Gordon
1973-75 F.B. Pooley
1975-77 Eric Lyons
1977-79 Gordon Graham
1979-81 Bryan Jefferson
1981-83 Owen Luder
1983-85 Michael Manser
1985-87 Larry Rolland
1987-89 Rod Hackney
1989-91 Max Hutchinson
1991-93 Richard C. MacCormac
1993-95 Frank Duffy
1995-97 Owen Luder
1997-99 David Rock
1999-01 Marco Goldschmied
2002-03 Paul Hyett
2003-05 George Ferguson

Source: Royal Institute of British Architects

Presidents of the Society of Architectural Historians

1941-42	Turpin C. Bannister
1943-44	Rexford Newcomb
1945-47	Kenneth John Conant
1948-49	Carroll L.V. Meeks
1950	Buford L. Pickens
1951	Charles E. Peterson
1952-53	Henry-Russell Hitchcock
1954	Agnes Addison Gilchrist
1955-56	James G. Van Derpool
1957-58	Carroll L. V. Meeks
1959	Walter L. Creese
1960-61	Barbara Wriston
1962-63	John D. Forbes
1964-65	H. Allen Brooks
1966-67	George B. Tatum
1968-69	Henry A. Millon
1970-71	James F. O'Gorman
1972-74	Alan W. Gowans
1975-76	Spiro Kostof
1976-78	Marian C. Donnelly
1978-80	Adolph K. Placzek
1982-84	Damie Stillman
1984-86	Carol Herselle Krinsky
1986-88	Osmund Overby
1988-90	Richard J. Betts
1990-93	Elisabeth Blair MacDougall
1993-94	Franklin Toker
1994-96	Keith N. Morgan
1996-98	Patricia Waddy
1998-00	Richard Longstreth
2000-02	Christopher Mead
2002-04	Diane Favro

Source: Society of Architectural Historians

The idea of permanence has been, until recently, an important idea in architecture. If you visit the ruins of Acropolis you learn that it once housed many paintings. Those works of art have all disappeared. But the stones have survived—they stand as a testament of history. You see so much architecture today that has lost this sense of permanence. Many of our structures and even roads are built to survive 20 to 30 years. After one generation they are demolished. They ask to be demolished because they're so terrible. We have to be aware that buildings should survive us. They form our heritage.

Santiago Calatrava

4 Records, Rankings & Achievements

Aquariums, sports stadiums, the world's tallest buildings, the largest architecture firms in each city, and the list of architecturally significant American art museums are just some of the notable accomplishments covered in this chapter. Numerous other rankings and ratings are available for professional reference and diversion. The results of the annual Most Visited Historic House Museums survey can be found in the Design & Historic Preservation chapter on page 462, and the 5th annual rankings of architecture and interior design programs are located in the Design Education chapter on pages 554 and 555.

Aquariums

The opening of Boston's New England Aquarium in 1969 ushered in a new age for aquariums. It combined the traditional ideas found in the classic aquariums of the early twentieth-century with new technology and revised educational and research commitments. Some have called it "the first modern public aquarium." Since that time, aquariums have proliferated across the United States. Below is a list of the major free-standing aquariums currently operating in the United States along with their requisite architectural statistics.

In 2000, The South Carolina Aquarium received the Preservation Society of Charleston's (S.C.) Carolopolis Award, an annual recognition for preserved, restored, or newly constructed buildings that add to the beauty of Charleston. *Photo courtesy of the South Carolina Aquarium.*

Aquariums

Aquarium	Location	Architect
Alaska SeaLife Center	Seward, AK	Cambridge Seven Associates with Livingston Slone
Aquarium of the Bay	San Francisco, CA	Esherick Homsey Dodge and Davis (EHDD)
Aquarium of the Pacific	Long Beach, CA	A joint venture of Hellmuth, Obata & Kassabaum (HOK) and Esherick Homsey Dodge and Davis (EHDD)
Audobon Aquarium of Americas	New Orleans, LA	The Bienville Group: a joint venture of The Mathes Group, Eskew + Architects, Billes/Manning Architects, Hewitt & Washington, Concordia
Belle Isle Aquarium	Royal Oak, MI	Albert J. Kahn
Birch Aquarium at Scripps Institution of Oceanography, UCSD	La Jolla, CA	Wheeler Wimer Blackman & Associates
Colorado's Ocean Journey	Denver, CO	Odyssea: a joint venture of RNL Design and Anderson Mason Dale
Florida Aquarium	Tampa, FL	Hellmuth, Obata & Kassabaum (HOK) and Esherick Homsey Dodge and Davis (EHDD)
Great Lakes Aquarium	Duluth, MN	Hammel, Green and Abrahamson, Inc.
John G. Shedd Aquarium	Chicago, IL	Graham Anderson, Probst, and White (Lohan and Associates, 1991 addition)
Maritime Aquarium at Norwalk	Norwalk, CT	Graham Gund Architects (original building and 2001 addition)
Monterey Bay Aquarium	Monterey, CA	Esherick Homsey Dodge and Davis (original building and 1996 addition)
Mystic Aquarium	Mystic, CT	Flynn, Dalton and Van Dijk (Cesar Pelli & Associates, 1999 expansion)
National Aquarium	Washington, DC	York & Sawyer Architects
National Aquarium in Baltimore	Baltimore, MD	Cambridge Seven Associates (Grieves & Associates, 1990 addition)
New England Aquarium	Boston, MA	Cambridge Seven Associates (Schwartz/Silver Architects, 1998 addition; E. Verner Johnson and Associates, Inc., 2001 expansion)
New Jersey State Aquarium	Camden, NJ	The Hillier Group
New York Aquarium at Coney Island	Brooklyn, NY	n/a
Newport Aquarium	Newport, KY	GBBN Architects

Compl. Yr.	Cost	Total square ft. (original/current)	Tank capacity (original/current, in gallons)
1998	$56 M	115,000	400,000
1996	$38 M	48,000	707,000
1998	$117 M	156,735	900,000
1990	$42 M	110,000	1.19 M
1904	$175,000	10,000	32,000
1992	$14 M	34,000	150,000
1999	$94 M	107,000	1 M
1994	$84 M	152,000	1 M
2000	$34 M	62,382	170,000
1930	$ 3.25 M ($45 M addition)	225,000/395,000	1.5 M/3 M
1988	$11.5 M ($9 M addition)	102,000/135,000	150,000
1984	$55 M ($57 M addition)	216,000/307,000	900,000/1.9 M
1973	$1.74 M ($52 M expansion)	76,000/137,000	1.6 M/2.3 M
1931	n/a	13,500	32,000
1981	$21.3 M ($35 M addition)	209,000/115,000	1 M/1.5 M
1969	$8 M ($20.9 M 1998 addition; $19.3 M 2001 expansion)	75,000/1,082,400	1 M
1992	$52 M	120,000	1 M
1957	n/a	150,000	1.8 M
1999	$40 M	100,000	1 M

Aquariums

Aquarium	Location	Architect
North Carolina Aquarium at Fort Fisher	Kure Beach, NC	Cambridge Seven Associates (BMS Architects, 2002 expansion)
North Carolina Aquarium on Roanoke Island	Manteo, NC	Lyles, Bissett, Carlisle and Wolff Associates of North Carolina Inc. with Cambridge Seven Associates (BMS Architects, 2002 expansion)
Oklahoma Aquarium	Tulsa, OK	SPARKS
Oregon Coast Aquarium	Newport, OR	SRG Architects
Ripley's Aquarium	Myrtle Beach, SC	Enartec
Ripley's Aquarium of the Smokies	Gatlinburg, TN	Helman Hurley Charvat Peacock Architects/Inc. (HHCP)
Seattle Aquarium	Seattle, WA	Fred Bassetti & Co.
South Carolina Aquarium	Charleston, SC	Eskew + Architects with Clark and Menefee Architects
Steinhart Aquarium	San Francisco, CA	Lewis P. Hobart
Tennessee Aquarium	Chattanooga, TN	Cambridge Seven Associates
Texas State Aquarium	Corpus Christi, TX	Phelps, Bomberger, and Garza (Corpus Christi Design Associates, 2003 addition)
Virginia Marine Science Museum	Virginia Beach, VA	E. Verner Johnson and Associates (original building and 1996 expansion)
Waikiki Aquarium	Honolulu, HI	Hart Wood and Edwin A. Weed with Ossipoff, Snyder, and Rowland
Wonders of Wildlife at the American National Fish and Wildlife Museum	Springfield, MO	Cambridge Seven Associates

Source: Counsel House Research

Compl. Yr.	Cost	Total square ft. (original/current)	Tank capacity (original/current, in gallons)
1976	$1.5 M ($17.5 M expansion)	30,000/84,000	77,000/455,000
1976	$1.6 M ($16 M expansion)	34,000/68,000	5,000/400,000
2003	$15 M	71,600	500,000
1992	$25.5 M	51,000	1.4 M
1997	$40 M	87,000	1.3 M
2000	$49 M	115,000	1.3 M
1977	n/a	68,000	753,000
2000	$69 M	93,000	1 M
1923	n/a	22,566	300,000
1992	$45 M	130,000	450,000
1990	$31 M ($14 M addition)	43,000/73,800	325,000/725,000
1986	$7.5 M ($35 M expansion)	41,500/120,000	100,000/700,000
1955	$400,000	19,000	152,000
2001	$34 M	92,000	500,000

Firm Anniversaries

The following currently practicing architecture firms were founded in 1904, 1929, 1954, and 1979 respectively.

Firms Celebrating their 100th Anniversary

Boynton Rothschild Rowland Architects PC, Richmond, VA
URS, San Francisco, CA

Firms Celebrating their 75th Anniversary

A. M. Kinney, Inc., Cincinnati, OH
BLDD Architects, Inc., Decatur, IL
Kingscott Associates, Inc., Kalamazoo, MI

Firms Celebrating their 50th Anniversary

Allen & Associates Architect, Inc., Detroit, MI
BGR Architects-Engineers, Lubbock, TX
Botesch Nash & Hall Architects, PS, Everett, WA
Burris & Behne Architects, Inc., Marion, OH
Byers Gunn & Hart Architects, Kansas City, KS
CMB Architecture & Planning, Seattle, WA
Coblin/Porter & Associates, Frankfort, KY
Craddock-Cunningham Architectural Partners PC, Lynchburg, VA
David M. Crawley Associates Inc., Plymouth, MA
Dickson & Associates Architects, Clarksdale, MS
DMJMH+N, Arlington, VA
Dudley L. Flotte, AIA, CCS, NCARB, Gulf Shores, AL
Francis Cauffman Foley Hoffmann, Architects Ltd., Philadelphia, PA
Hanney & Associates Architects, Wichita, KS
Haynes Lieneck & Smith Inc., Ashby, MA
Hollis-Crocker Architects, PC, Spartanburg, SC
Jacobs and Maciejewski and Associates Architects, PC, South Holland, IL
James M. Hartley, Architects, Hollywood, FL
Jinright, Ryan, & Lynn, Architects & Planners, Thomasville, GA
Lamborghini Feibelman Ltd., Providence, RI
MBT Architecture, San Francisco, CA
MCB Architects, PC, Denver, CO
Nelson Howden & Associates, Inc., American Fork, UT
Paul F. Stewart, Architect, Ltd., Monroe, LA
Phillips Swager Associates, Peoria, IL
Rawlings Wilson & Associates, PC, Richmond, VA
Reese Lower Patrick & Scott, Ltd., Lancaster, PA
Robert P. Madison International, Cleveland, OH
RQAW Corporation, Indianapolis, IN
SAS Architects & Planners, Northbrook, IL
Shiver-Megert & Associates, Amarillo, TX
Street Dixon Rick Architecture PLC, Nashville, TN
Tomsik-Tomsik Architects/Planners, Ltd., Cleveland, OH
WRA Architects, Inc., Dallas, TX

Firms Celebrating their 25th Anniversary

Adele Naude Santos and Associates, San Francisco, CA
Andrew W. Booth & Associates, Inc., Salisbury, MD
Ankeny Kell Architects, PA, St. Paul, MN
Ann M. Dunning, AIA, Inc., Chagrin Falls, OH
Architect Larry LaDelfa, St. Petersburg, FL
Architects Plus, Inc., Cincinnati, OH
ARCON Associates, Lombard, IL
Ausland Architects, Austin, TX
Barnard Associates, Austin, TX
Batheja & Associates, Inc., Omaha, NE
Baudry Architects Inc., Roswell, GA
Ben V. Mammina, Architect, Downers Grove, IL
Bibb & Associates Inc., Overland Park, KS
Bowman & Bowman Architects, PC, Greenwood, MS

Firm Anniversaries

Brandstetter Carroll Inc., Lexington, KY
Brent Bowman & Associates, Architects, PA, Manhattan, KS
Broweleit Peterson Architects PS, Lynnwood, WA
Buck Simpers Architect + Associates, Inc., Wilmington, DE
Butler Rogers Baskett Architects PC, New York, NY
Canova Associates Architecture, Mechanicsville, VA
CCA, LLC, Bedford, MA
Century A&E of Louisiana Inc., Shreveport, LA
Chamberlin Architects, PC, Grand Junction, CO
Charles Willis & Associates Inc., Arlington, TX
Chelsea Architects, Houston, TX
Cho Benn Holback Associates, Baltimore, MD
Cole and Goyette, Architects and Planners, Cambridge, MA
Concepts Enterprise, White Plains, NY
Connolly Architects, Austin, TX
Coombs Architecture & Planning, Inc., Santee, CA
Cooper, Robertson & Partners, New York, NY
Crawford & Stearns, Architects and Preservation Planners, Syracuse, NY
Croslin & Associates, Inc., Austin, TX
Crowner/King Architects, Erie, PA
David Lawrence Gray AIA Architects, Santa Monica, CA
David Robert Crawford, AIA, Architect, Mount Laurel, NJ
Davis Rexrode Architects Inc., San Antonio, TX
Davison Smith Certo Architects, Westlake, OH
DCA, Stockton, CA
Design Associates Inc., Cambridge, MA
Design Collaborative, Inc., Wilmington, DE
Design Plus Inc., Grand Rapids, MI
Designery Architecture, Stillwater, MN
Doug Walter Architects, Denver, CO
Dougherty + Dougherty Architects LLP, Costa Mesa, CA
Duca Huder & Kumlin, Moorestown, NJ
Dunn and Associates, Inc., Pittsburgh, PA
Durand-Hollis Rupe Architects, San Antonio, TX
Edward L. Blanks, Architect, Williamsburg, VA
Edward Meinert, AIA - Architect, Pittsburgh, PA
Engan Associates Architects, Engineers, Interior Designers, PA, Willmar, MN
Environ, Inc., Chicago, IL
F. Douglas Adams & Associates, Architects Inc., Belmont, MA
Fortinberry Associates Architects, PC, Birmingham, AL
Francis C. Klein & Associates, Montclair, NJ
Fritzlen Pierce Architects, Vail, CO
Gary B. Phillips Associates, Inc., Highland Park, IL
Gates Hafen Cochrane Architects, Boulder, CO
Glover Smith Bode, Inc., Oklahoma City, OK
Gonzalez|Goodale Architects, Pasadena, CA
Green Associates Architects, Inc., Evanston, IL
Gresham, Smith and Partners, Birmingham, AL
Group II Architects PA, Marshall, MN
Hanbury Evans Wright Vlattas & Company, Norfolk, VA
Hayashida Architects, Emeryville, CA
Heights Venture Architects LLP, Houston, TX
Heiser Development Corporation, Austin, TX
Hidell Associates Architects, Carrollton, TX
Hnedak Bobo Group, Inc., Memphis, TN
Hogg & Mythen, San Francisco, CA
Howard Kulp Architects, PC, Allentown, PA
Jack D. Wilkins & Associates, Kearney, NE
Jack R. Tucker Associates Architects, Memphis, TN
John M. Senkarik & Associates, Pensacola, FL
John Senhauser Architects, Cincinnati, OH
Judith L. Kelly Architect, Lake Worth, FL
Kloiber & Associates, Green Bay, WI
KTH Architects, DuBois, PA

Firm Anniversaries

L. Craig Roberts, AIA, Architect, Mobile, AL
Lane & Associates, Inc., Fort Smith, AR
Lee & Sakahara Architects, Inc., Irvine, CA
Lien & Peterson Architects, Inc., Eau Claire, WI
LMN Architects, Seattle, WA
Logan Hopper Associates, Architects, Oakland, CA
Louis E. Barbieri, AIA, Architect-Planner, Denville, NJ
M. Mense Architects, Anchorage, AK
Manausa Lewis & Dodson Architects, Inc., Tallahassee, FL
Mark D. Lipton Associates, Architects & Designers, Staten Island, NY
Meyer-Greeson-Paullin, PA, Charlotte, NC
Michael J. Pado AIA Architect, Ltd., Chicago, IL
Mogas & Associates Architects Inc., San Antonio, TX
Mogavero Notestine Associates, Sacramento, CA
Moretta & Sheehy Architects, Evanston, IL
Mullins-Sherman, Architects, Sanford, NC
Norris R. Guthrie, AIA/NCARB, Architect, Bristol, VA
O. Douglas Boyce Jr. AIA, Architect, Charleston, SC
OPN Architects, Inc., Cedar Rapids, IA
Pascal Arquitectos, Mexico City, Mexico
Pate Associates Architects/Planners Inc., Midland, TX
Patrick Architectural, Lisle, IL
PBK Architects, Inc., Houston, TX
Perkowitz + Ruth Architects, Long Beach, CA
Platt/Whitelaw Architects, Inc., San Diego, CA
Present Architects, Kansas City, MO
Pulver Architects, Rochester, NY
R. S. Bickford & Company, Overland Park, KS
RDM Architecture, Kansas City, MO
Renner Architects LLC, Milwaukee, WI
Richard A. Bittmann Architect, Tacoma, WA
Richard B. Hudgens, Architect, Selma, AL
Richard Gardner & Associates, Inc., American Fork, UT
Richard Larsen Associates, Detroit Lakes, MN
Richard N. Manns, Architect, PC, Homestead, PA
Richard Neumann Architect, Petoskey, MI
Ripley Architects, Oakland, CA
Rizo Carreno & Partners, Inc., Coral Gables, FL
Robert E. Taylor, AIA, Architect, PA, Palatka, FL
Rust, Orling and Neale, Architects, Inc., Alexandria, VA
Salmon Bay Design Group, Seattle, WA
Salmon Falls Architecture, Biddeford, ME
Sherman-Carter-Barnhart Architects, PSC, St. Louis, MO
Sizeler Architects, New Orleans, LA
Smallwood, Reynolds, Stewart, Stewart & Associates, Inc., Atlanta, GA
Staley McDermet Associates, Salem, MA
Station 19 Architects Inc., Minneapolis, MN
Stecklein and Brungardt PA Architects, Hays, KS
Stephen Lasar, AIA, Architects, New Milford, CT
Stephen Russell and Associates, Ltd., Mount Pleasant, SC
Steven Lombardi Architect, San Diego, CA
Stevenson Design, Miles City, MT
Tappe Associates, Inc., Boston, MA
Taylor & Associates Architects, Newport Beach, CA
TC Designs, Architecture Unlimited, Inc., San Diego, CA
TEA 2 Architects, Inc., Minneapolis, MN
Tecton Architects, PC, Hartford, CT
Teter Consultants, LLP, Fresno, CA
The Albert Group Architects, Culver City, CA
The Colyer Freeman Group LLP, San Francisco, CA
The Design Cooperative, Grayslake, IL
The Design Partnership, San Francisco, CA
The Ives Group, Architects/Planners, Fair Lawn, NJ
The Johnson Partnership, Seattle, WA
The Phillips Group, New York, NY
The Spriggs Group, PC, Savannah, GA
Thomas A. Douthat Jr., Architect, Pulaski, VA
Thomas Brown Architects, Stevens Point, WI

Firm Anniversaries

Thomas Hamilton & Associates, Richmond, VA
Tushie Montgomery & Associates, Inc., Minneapolis, MN
Vandergriff Group Architects, Midland, TX
Voelter Associates Inc., Georgetown, TX
W. S. Ledbetter Incorporated, Architects & Engineers, St. Simons Island, GA
Ward Jewell and Associates, Santa Monica, CA
Watkins Hamilton Ross Architects, Inc., Houston, TX
Weatherl & Associates, Abilene, TX
Weber & Associates, Stamford, CT
Wells & Company, Spokane, WA
William E. Epp & Associates Inc., San Antonio, TX
William F. Burch Architects, Incorporated, Manhattan Beach, CA
William L. Burgin Architects, Inc., Newport, RI
William Morris Associates Architects, Augusta, KS
Wynn Associates, McAlester, OK

Source: Counsel House Research

Firm Statistics: Architecture

	Number of Establishments[1]	Annual Payroll ($1,000)	Paid Employees[2]
Alabama	230	76,253	1,664
Alaska	51	22,299	357
Arizona	552	184,870	3,912
Arkansas	147	59,078	1,402
California	3,265	1,618,818	27,546
Colorado	726	251,849	4,626
Connecticut	333	132,288	2,250
Delaware	41	14,820	292
District of Columbia	143	D	f
Florida	1,576	480,052	9,725
Georgia	575	313,492	5,684
Hawaii	182	55,501	1,083
Idaho	126	32,394	775
Illinois	1,113	494,206	8,963
Indiana	301	123,014	2,627
Iowa	116	42,178	857
Kansas	169	66,165	1,406
Kentucky	172	53,723	1,153
Louisiana	271	69,727	1,714
Maine	98	34,694	744
Maryland	399	171,707	3,216
Massachusetts	743	618,876	10,171
Michigan	589	275,074	5,129
Minnesota	412	260,784	5,028
Mississippi	113	31,606	742
Missouri	406	227,580	4,353
Montana	100	25,974	658
Nebraska	109	63,994	1,298

Firm Statistics: Architecture

	Number of Establishments[1]	Annual Payroll ($1,000)	Employees[2]
Nevada	145	81,590	1,556
New Hampshire	70	21,139	390
New Jersey	678	237,069	4,282
New Mexico	157	40,079	1,035
New York	1,860	968,601	16,929
North Carolina	579	238,696	5,074
North Dakota	38	11,456	271
Ohio	677	315,880	6,608
Oklahoma	179	65,419	1,409
Oregon	325	128,634	2,593
Pennsylvania	720	420,824	8,118
Rhode Island	88	17,878	391
South Carolina	255	92,007	1,818
South Dakota	41	D	d
Tennessee	301	155,268	2,916
Texas	1,432	711,158	13,002
Utah	192	56,587	1,359
Vermont	85	23,461	521
Virginia	519	271,682	5,337
Washington	707	308,096	6,125
West Virginia	45	12,089	275
Wisconsin	275	120,851	2,534
Wyoming	42	9,267	225
U.S. Total	**22,468**	**10,108,747**	**190,143**

[1] All numbers are 2001.
[2] Paid employees for the pay period including March 12, 2001.
d: 250-499 employees
f: 2,500-4,999 employees
D: Witheld to avoid disclosing data of individual companies.

Source: U.S. Census Bureau

STATES WITH MOST FIRMS
(Top 10 shown)

Architecture

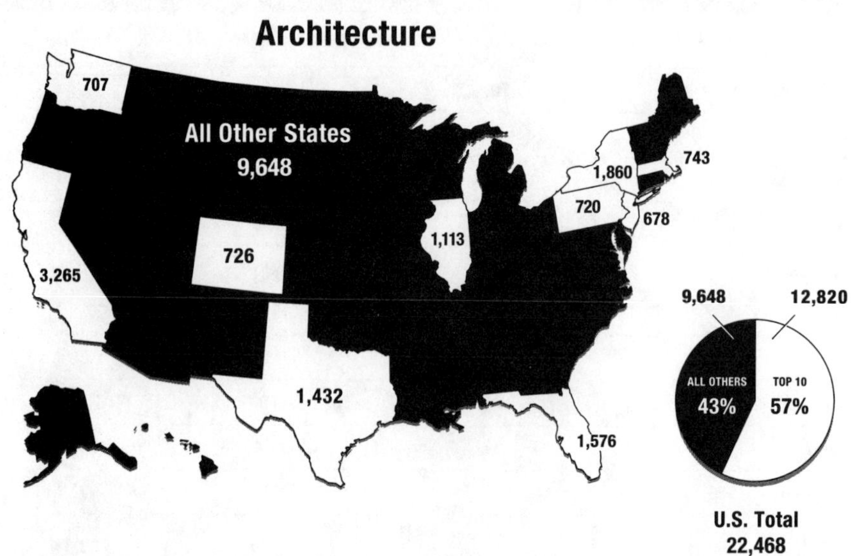

Industrial Design

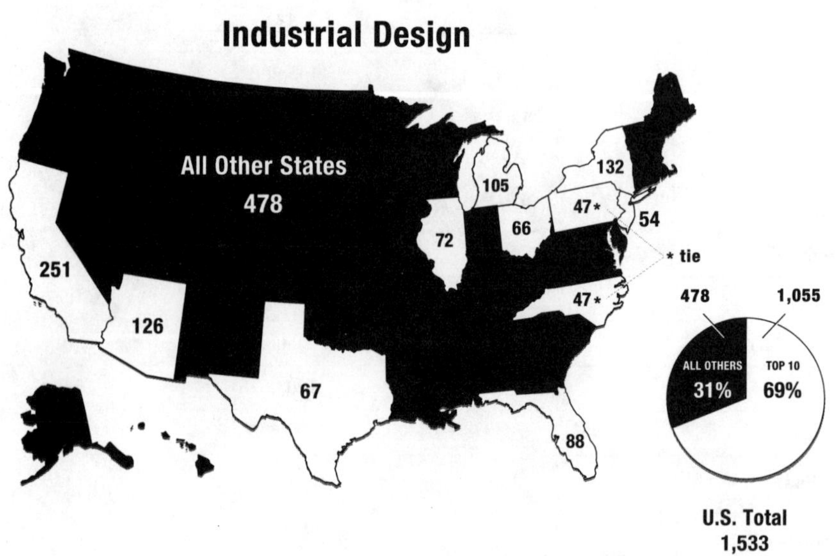

Source: Counsel House Research

Firm Statistics: Industrial Design

	Number of Establishments[1]	Annual Payroll ($1,000)	Paid Employees[2]
Alabama	7	D	b
Alaska	2	D	a
Arizona	126	7,437	21
Arkansas	4	D	a
California	251	124,350	2,223
Colorado	33	7,838	170
Connecticut	23	7,786	145
Delaware	5	13,892	218
District of Columbia	n/a	n/a	n/a
Florida	88	D	d
Georgia	39	8,227	226
Hawaii	2	D	a
Idaho	9	D	b
Illinois	72	18,059	406
Indiana	20	D	c
Iowa	5	D	c
Kansas	14	D	b
Kentucky	7	D	a
Louisiana	3	42	4
Maine	2	D	a
Maryland	27	D	d
Massachusetts	42	20,433	363
Michigan	105	69,066	1,483
Minnesota	37	D	d
Mississippi	3	D	a
Missouri	16	7,813	180
Montana	2	D	b
Nebraska	4	D	a

Firm Statistics: Industrial Design

	Number of Establishments[1]	Annual Payroll ($1,000)	Employees[2]
Nevada	7	D	a
New Hampshire	8	4,289	78
New Jersey	54	22,023	382
New Mexico	5	D	b
New York	132	42,932	794
North Carolina	47	6,539	129
North Dakota	n/a	n/a	n/a
Ohio	66	40,235	917
Oklahoma	4	D	b
Oregon	23	50,365	781
Pennsylvania	47	79,121	2,025
Rhode Island	8	D	b
South Carolina	6	D	c
South Dakota	3	D	a
Tennessee	16	D	c
Texas	67	28,402	841
Utah	9	1,210	41
Vermont	1	D	a
Virginia	20	9,971	172
Washington	27	D	c
West Virginia	3	D	b
Wisconsin	29	12,035	293
Wyoming	3	D	b
U.S. Total	**1,533**	**582,065**	**11,892**

[1] All numbers are 2001.
[2] Paid employees for the pay period including March 12, 2001.
a: 0-19 employees
b: 20-99 employees
c: 100-249 employees
d: 250-499 employees
D: Witheld to avoid disclosing data of individual companies.
Source: U.S. Census Bureau

Firm Statistics: Interior Design

	Number of Establishments[1]	Annual Payroll ($1,000)	Paid Employees[2]
Alabama	112	D	d
Alaska	14	D	b
Arizona	1,091	30,391	202
Arkansas	43	D	c
California	1,443	306,033	7,098
Colorado	327	42,509	1,136
Connecticut	155	26,705	576
Delaware	32	D	c
District of Columbia	50	40,214	670
Florida	1,259	144,675	4,820
Georgia	409	69,663	1,735
Hawaii	34	D	c
Idaho	37	2,353	96
Illinois	593	89,931	2,192
Indiana	191	D	e
Iowa	59	D	c
Kansas	68	5,204	243
Kentucky	95	D	d
Louisiana	99	11,087	508
Maine	23	D	b
Maryland	218	D	e
Massachusetts	276	50,064	1,148
Michigan	295	36,191	1,100
Minnesota	204	26,875	889
Mississippi	45	D	c
Missouri	168	20,833	692
Montana	31	D	b
Nebraska	42	D	c
Nevada	93	17,060	407

Firm Statistics: Interior Design

	Number of Establishments[1]	Annual Payroll ($1,000)	Paid Employees[2]
New Hampshire	35	D	c
New Jersey	309	43,073	1,158
New Mexico	29	2,913	100
New York	982	210,124	3,954
North Carolina	352	31,827	1,194
North Dakota	10	D	c
Ohio	307	57,869	2,298
Oklahoma	96	D	d
Oregon	110	D	d
Pennsylvania	287	50,442	1,450
Rhode Island	38	D	c
South Carolina	137	9,984	449
South Dakota	13	D	b
Tennessee	141	D	e
Texas	700	211,450	4,021
Utah	87	8,565	278
Vermont	21	D	c
Virginia	275	30,678	993
Washington	193	D	e
West Virginia	21	D	b
Wisconsin	120	15,555	560
Wyoming	9	D	b
U.S. Total	**11,778**	**1,592,268**	**39,967**

[1] All numbers are 2001.
[2] Paid employees for the pay period including March 12, 2001.
b: 20-99 employees
c: 100-249 employees
d: 250-499 employees
e: 500-999 employees
D: Witheld to avoid disclosing data of individual companies.

Source: U.S. Census Bureau

STATES WITH MOST FIRMS

(Top 10 shown)

Interior Design

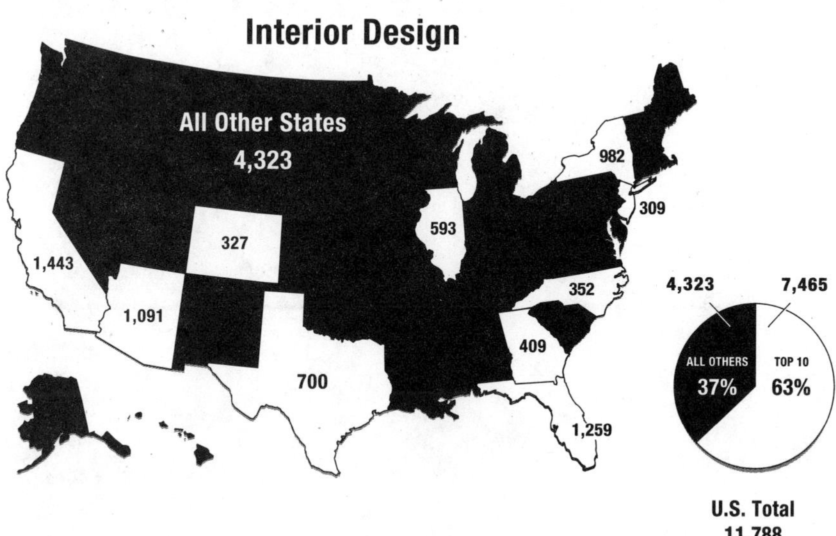

Landscape Architecture

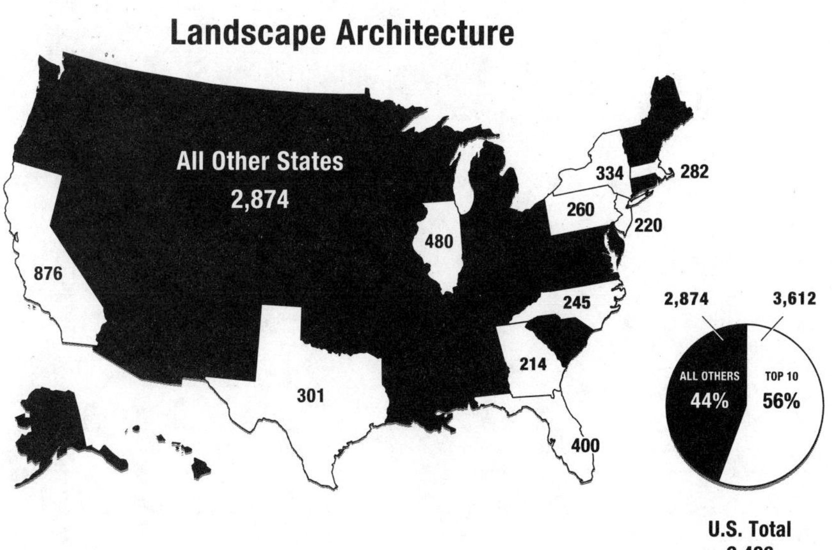

Source: Counsel House Research

Firm Statistics: Landscape Architecture

	Number of Establishments[1]	Annual Payroll ($1,000)	Paid Employees[2]
Alabama	68	13,323	531
Alaska	8	D	b
Arizona	138	36,331	1,185
Arkansas	34	D	c
California	876	281,324	8,210
Colorado	171	53,999	1,249
Connecticut	114	23,239	498
Delaware	24	4,198	134
District of Columbia	12	D	c
Florida	400	98,957	2,834
Georgia	214	39,468	1,451
Hawaii	35	13,875	426
Idaho	30	3,241	162
Illinois	480	88,944	2,054
Indiana	83	9,199	296
Iowa	49	9,116	252
Kansas	29	6,528	243
Kentucky	41	6,840	256
Louisiana	59	4,771	246
Maine	43	4,421	139
Maryland	138	27,329	802
Massachusetts	282	51,788	1,126
Michigan	206	48,372	1,164
Minnesota	97	15,968	448
Mississippi	48	7,093	348
Missouri	91	11,756	417
Montana	27	D	b
Nebraska	39	3,797	141
Nevada	42	9,796	306

Firm Statistics: Landscape Architecture

	Number of Establishments[1]	Annual Payroll ($1,000)	Paid Employees[2]
New Hampshire	45	6,127	174
New Jersey	220	37,162	928
New Mexico	42	5,596	177
New York	334	60,471	1,384
North Carolina	245	32,914	1,176
North Dakota	10	D	a
Ohio	143	24,640	728
Oklahoma	46	5,213	223
Oregon	89	15,003	531
Pennsylvania	260	44,529	1,163
Rhode Island	23	D	b
South Carolina	140	16,693	736
South Dakota	18	D	b
Tennessee	110	16,993	759
Texas	301	101,983	2,929
Utah	56	4,100	174
Vermont	31	D	b
Virginia	163	32,711	1,279
Washington	184	23,400	697
West Virginia	17	D	b
Wisconsin	113	29,260	866
Wyoming	18	D	b
U.S. Total	**6,486**	**1,330,468**	**38,842**

[1] All numbers are 2001.

[2] Paid employees for the pay period including March 12, 2001.

a: 0-19 employees

b: 20-99 employees

c: 100-249 employees

D: Witheld to avoid disclosing data of individual companies.

Source: U.S. Census Bureau

Largest Architecture Firms by City

The following architecture firms are the top ten largest in ten of America's largest cities. The rankings are based on staff size as reported by the firms themselves and gathered by Counsel House Research in the fall of 2002.

Atlanta

1. Heery International
2. Thompson, Ventulett, Stainback & Associates
3. Rosser International
4. Niles Bolton Associates
4. Perkins & Will
6. Smallwood, Reynolds, Stewart, Stewart & Associates, Inc.
7. Cooper Cary
8. Lord, Aeck & Sargent
9. CDH Partners, Inc.
10. Greenberg, Farrow Architecture, Inc.

Baltimore

1. RTKL Associates, Inc.
2. Cochran, Stephenson & Donkervoet Inc.
3. Design Collective
4. Ayers/Saint/Gross
5. Development Design Group Inc.
6. Kann and Associates Architects
7. Hord Coplan Macht, Inc.
8. Bignell Watkins Hasser Architects
8. Gaudreau Inc.
10. Marshall Craft Associates, Inc.

Boston

1. Einhorn Yaffee Prescott Architecture & Engineering
2. TRO/The Ritchie Organization
3. Sasaki Associates, Inc.
4. Shepley Bulfinch Richardson and Abbott
5. Symmes, Maini & McKee Associates, Inc.
5. CBT/Childs Bertman Tseckares, Inc.
7. Elkus/Manfredi Architects, Ltd.
8. Payette Associates, Inc.
9. HNTB Corporation
10. ADD, Inc.

Chicago

1. A. Epstein & Sons, International Inc.
2. O'Donnell Wicklund Pigozzi & Peterson
3. Teng & Associates
4. McClier
5. Skidmore, Owings & Merrill LLP
6. Perkins & Will
7. VOA Associates Incorporated
8. Solomon Coldwell Buenz & Associates
9. DeStefano and Partners
10. The Environments Group

Dallas/Ft. Worth

1. Carter Burgess
1. HKS
3. The BECK Group
4. Corgan Associates
5. RTKL Associates, Inc.
6. HDR Architecture
7. Perkins & Will | CRA
8. PageSoutherlandPage
9. Good Fulton & Farrell Architects
10. Leo A Daly

Los Angeles

1. DMJM + DMJM/Rottet
2. Gensler
3. Fields Devereaux Architects & Engineers
4. Nadel Architects
5. NTD Architects
6. Perkowitz + Ruth Architects
7. The Jerde Partnership
8. Langdon Wilson
9. RTKL Associates, Inc.
10. AC Martin Partners, Inc.

Largest Architecture Firms by City

New York

1. Skidmore, Owings & Merrill LLP
2. Gensler
3. HLW International
4. Perkins Eastman Architects
5. Kohn Pedersen Fox Associates
6. Swanke Hayden Connell Architects
7. Beyer Blinder Belle Architects & Planners
8. Mancini Duffy
8. Polshek Partnershp Architects
8. Robert A.M. Stern Architects
8. The Phillips Group

Philidelphia

1. Kling Lindquist
2. Ewing Cole Cherry Brott
3. Ballinger
4. Granary Associates
5. Francis Cauffman Foley Hoffman Architects, Ltd.
6. Wallace Roberts & Todd
7. Bower Lewis Thrower Architects
8. Robert D. Lynn Associates
9. H2L2 Architects/Planners LLP
10. Venturi, Scott Brown and Associates, Inc.

San Francisco

1. Skidmore, Owings & Merrill LLP
2. Gensler
3. Anshen + Allen Architects
4. Kaplan McLaughlin Diaz
5. Dowler Gruman Architects
6. ATI Architects and Engineers
7. MBH Architects
8. DES Architects + Engineers
8. Gordon H. Chong and Partners
10. HOK

Washington, D.C.

1. DMJMH+N
1. SmithGroup
3. Gensler
4. HNTB
5. RTKL Associates, Inc.
6. URS Greiner Woodward Clyde
7. Einhorn Yaffee Prescott Architecture & Engineering, P.C.
8. Ai
9. Ellerbe Becket
10. Leo A Daly

Source: Counsel House Research

Most Admired Poll

In the fall of 2001, *DesignIntelligence* assembled a jury of architects to rank various aspects of the built world, including cities, colleges and universities, and airports. In their consideration of cities–both in North America and the rest of the world–the jury ranked those most admired for their architecture and urban design merit. Cities of all sizes were considered, no other criteria were used. The jury also deliberated on airports and colleges & universities, which were ranked for their architectural merit, including aesthetics, functionality, and contribution to the built environment.

Most Admired Cities—North America

1. Chicago
2. Vancouver
3. Savannah
4. Toronto
5. San Francisco
6. Boston
7. Denver
8. Columbus (IN)
9. Minneapolis
10. Quebec

Most Admired Cities—Outside North America

1. Paris
2. Barcelona
3. Stockholm
4. Rome
5. Copenhagen
6. London
7. Sydney
8. Vienna
9. Venice
10. Berlin

Most Admired Airports

1. Ronald Reagan National Airport (Washington, DC)
2. Denver International Airport
3. Dulles International Airport (Chantilly, VA)
4. Chek Lap Kok International Airport (Hong Kong)
5. Kansai International Airport (Osaka, Japan)
6. Charles de Gaulle Airport (Paris, France)
7. United Terminal, O'Hare International Airport (Chicago)
8. Inchon International Airport (Seoul, Korea)
9. Copenhagen Airport (Denmark)
10. Orlando International Airport

Most Admired College and University Campuses

1. University of Virginia
2. Oxford University
3. Yale University
4. United States Air Force Academy
5. Cranbrook Academy of Art
6. Stanford University
7. Oberlin College
8. University of California, Santa Cruz
9. Harvard University
10. Cornell University

Jury

James P. Cramer, Greenway (Chair)
Friedl Bohm, NBBJ
Arlo Braun, Arlo Braun & Associates
Fernando Castillo, Pavlik Design Team
Georgio Cavaglieri, Castro-Blanco Piscion
Chuck Davis, Esherick Homsey Dodge and Davis
Robert Deering, IA, Dallas
William Eberhard, Oliver Design Group
Guy Geier, The Hillier Group
James M. Herman, Herman Gibans Fodor, Inc.
Hugh Jacobsen, Hugh Newell Jacobsen Architects
Charles Knight, Perkins & Will
Ryc Loope, Durrant
Alan Roush, HKS Architects
Scott Simpson, The Stubbins Associates
Bernard Smith, Langdon Wilson
David Standard, MSTSD Inc.
Stanley Tigerman, Tigerman McCurry Architects
Ron Van der Veen, Mithun

Source: DesignIntelligence

Most Popular U.S. Buildings

The following rankings provide a glimpse into the minds of architects (and, in one case, architecture critics) as they they reflected at various points in history on the question of what are America's best buildings.

1885 Poll conducted by the *American Architect & Building News*:

1. Trinity Church, Boston, MA
   H.H. Richardson, 1877
2. U.S. Capitol, Washington, DC
   William Thornton, Benjamin Henry Latrobe, Charles Bulfinch, 1793-1829
3. Vanderbilt House, New York, NY
   Richard Morris Hunt, 1883
4. Trinity Church, New York, NY
   Richard Upjohn, 1846
5. Jefferson Market Courthouse, New York, NY
   Frederick Withers & Calvert Vaux, 1877
6. Connecticut State Capitol, Hartford, CT
   Richard Upjohn, 1879
7. City Hall, Albany, NY
   H.H. Richardson, 1883
8. Sever Hall, Harvard University, Cambridge, MA
   H.H. Richardson, 1880
9. New York State Capitol, Albany, NY
   H.H. Richardson, 1886
10. Town Hall, North Easton, MA
    H.H. Richardson, 1881

Source: American Architect & Building News

1986 Poll conducted by The American Institute of Architects:

1. Fallingwater, Mill Run, PA
   Frank Lloyd Wright, 1936
2. Seagram Building, New York, NY
   Ludwig Mies van der Rohe, 1954-58
3. Dulles Airport, Chantilly, VA
   Eero Saarinen, 1962
4. University of Virginia, Charlottesville, VA
   Thomas Jefferson, 1826
5. Robie House, Chicago, IL
   Frank Lloyd Wright, 1909
6. Trinity Church, Boston, MA
   H.H. Richardson, 1877
7. East Wing, National Gallery, Washington, DC
   I.M. Pei & Partners, 1978
8. Rockefeller Center, New York, NY
   Raymond Hood, 1940
9. S. C. Johnson & Son Admin. Building, Racine, WI
   Frank Lloyd Wright, 1936
10. Monticello, Charlottesville, VA
    Thomas Jefferson, 1769-84; 1796-1809

Source: The American Institute of Architects

2000 Building of the Century Poll conducted at the 2000 AIA Convention in Philadelphia:

1. Fallingwater, Mill Run, PA
   Frank Lloyd Wright,1936
2. Chrysler Building, New York, NY
   William Van Alen, 1930
3. Seagram Building, New York, NY
   Ludwig Mies van der Rohe, 1958
4. Thorncrown Chapel, Eureka, AR
   E. Fay Jones, 1980
5. Dulles Airport, Chantilly, VA
   Eero Saarinen, 1962
6. Salk Institute, La Jolla, CA
   Louis I. Kahn, 1966
7. Vietnam Veterans Memorial, Washington, DC
   Maya Lin, 1982
8. Robie House, Chicago, IL
   Frank Lloyd Wright, 1909
9. Guggenheim Museum, New York, NY
   Frank Lloyd Wright, 1959
10. East Wing, National Gallery, Washington, DC
    I.M. Pei, 1978
11. S. C. Johnson & Son Admin. Building, Racine, WI
    Frank Lloyd Wright, 1939

Source: The American Institute of Architects

Most Popular U.S. Buildings

2001 Architecture Critics' Poll of the Top Rated Buildings:

1. Brooklyn Bridge, New York, NY
   John Augustus Roebling, 1883
2. Grand Central Station, New York, NY
   Warren & Wetmore, Reed & Stem, 1913
3. Chrysler Building, New York, NY
   William Van Alen, 1930
4. Monticello, Charlottesville, VA
   Thomas Jefferson, 1769-84; 1796-1809
5. University of Virginia, Charlottesville, VA
   Thomas Jefferson, 1826
6. Robie House, Chicago, IL
   Frank Lloyd Wright, 1909
7. Carson Pirie Scott Building, Chicago, IL
   Louis Sullivan, 1904
8. Empire State Building, New York, NY
   Shreve, Lamb & Harmon, 1931
9. S. C. Johnson & Son Admin. Building, Racine, WI
   Frank Lloyd Wright, 1939
10. Unity Temple, Oak Park, IL
    Frank Lloyd Wright, 1907

Source: The Architecture Critic, *National Arts Journalism Program, Columbia University*

Great Architectural Works of the 21st Century:

1. Rose Center for Earth and Space
   New York, NY
   Polshek Partnership Architects
2. Quadracci Pavilion, Milwaukee Art Museum
   Milwaukee, WI
   Santiago Calatrava with Kahler Slater Architects
3. Sandra Day O'Connor U.S. Courthouse
   Phoenix, AZ
   Richard Meier & Partners
4. 3Com Midwest Headquarters
   Rolling Meadows, IL
   Valerio Dewalt Train
5. Westside Light Rail Corridor
   Portland, OR
   Zimmer Gunsul Frasca Partnership

Source: USA Weekend

National Historic Planning Landmarks

Every year the American Institute of Certified Planners (AICP), the American Planning Association's (APA) professional and educational arm, grants National Historic Planning Landmark status to up to three historically significant projects. To be eligible, projects must be 25 years old, have initiated a new direction in planning, made a significant contribution to the community, and be available for public use and viewing. Newly designated sites are indicated in bold.

For additional information about National Historic Planning Landmarks, contact the AICP at (202) 872-0611 or visit them on the Web at *www.planning.org*.

Arizona
The Salt River Project (1911)

California
Bay Conservation and Development Commission and Creation of the San Francisco Bay Plan (1965-69)
East Bay Regional Park District, San Francisco (1934)
Los Angeles Co. "Master Plan of Highways" (1940) and "Freeways for the Region" (1943)
Napa County Agricultural Preserve (1968)
Petaluma Plan (1971-72)
San Francisco Zoning Ordinance (1867)

Colorado
The Denver Parks and Parkway System (1906+)
Speer Boulevard, Denver

Connecticut
The Nine Square Plan of New Haven (1638)

District of Columbia
Eucid v. Ambler, US Supreme Court (1926)
First National Conference on City Planning (1909)
The McMillan Commission Plan for Washington, D.C. (1901)
National Resources Planning Board (1933-43)
Plan of Washington, DC (1791)

Georgia
Plan of Savannah (1733)

Hawaii
Hawaii's State Land Use Law (1961)

Illinois
The American Society of Planning Officials (ASPO) (1934)
The Chicago Lakefront (1909+)
"Local Planning Administration" (1941)
Merriam Center, Chicago (1930+)
Plan of Chicago (1909)
Plan of Park Forest (1948)
Plan of Riverside (1869)

Indiana
New Harmony (1814-27)

Kentucky
Lexington Urban Service Area (1958)

Louisiana
Plan of the Vieux Carre, New Orleans (1721)

Maryland
Columbia (1967+)
Greenbelt (A Greenbelt Town, 1935+)
Plan of Annapolis (1695)

Massachusetts
"Emerald Necklace" Parks, Boston (1875+)
Founding of the Harvard University Graduate Planning Program (1929)

National Historic Planning Landmarks

Michigan
Kalamazoo Mall (1956)

Missouri
Country Club Plaza, Kansas City (1922)
Founding of the American City Planning Institute (ACPI, 1917)
Kansas City Parks Plan (1893)

Montana
Yellowstone National Park (1872)

New Jersey
"Radburn" at Fair Lawn (1928-29)
Society for the Establishment of Useful Manufactures Plan for Paterson (1791-92)
Southern Burlington County (NJ) NAACP v Township of Mount Laurel (1975)
Yorkship Village, Camden (1918)

New Mexico
The Laws of the Indies (1573; 1681)

New York
Bronx River Parkway and the Westchester County Parkway System (1907+)
Central Park, New York City (1857)
First Houses, New York City (1935-36)
Forest Hills Gardens (1911+)
Founding of the American City Planning Institute (ACPI, 1917)
Grand Central Terminal, New York City (1903-13)
Long Island Parkways (1885) and Parks (1920s)
New York City Zoning Code (1916)
New York State Adirondack Preserve & Park
New York State Commission of Housing and Regional Planning (1923-26)
Regional Plan of New York & Environs (1929)
Second Regional Plan of the Regional Plan Association of New York (1968)
Sunnyside Gardens (1924+)
University Settlement House and the Settlement House Movement (1886)

North Carolina
Blue Ridge Parkway (1935+)

Ohio
Cincinnati Plan of 1925
Cleveland Group Plan (1903)
Cleveland Policy Plan (1974)
Founding of Ohio Planning Conference (1919)
Greenhills (A Greenbelt Town, 1935+)
The Miami Valley Region's Fair Share Housing Plan of 1970
The Plan of Mariemont (1922)

Oregon
Oregon's Statewide Program for Land Use (1973)

Pennsylvania
Plan of Philadelphia (1683)

Rhode Island
College Hill Demonstration of Historic Renewal, Providence (1959)

South Carolina
First American Historic District, Charleston (1931)

Tennessee
Plan of Metro Government, Nashville/Davidson County (1956)
Tennessee Valley Authority (1933+)
Town of Norris (1933)

Texas
"A Greater Fort Worth Tomorrow" (1956)
Paseo del Rio, San Antonio (1939-41)

Utah
Plat of the City of Zion (1833)

National Historic Planning Landmarks

Virginia

Blue Ridge Parkway (1935+)
Jeffersonian Precinct, University of Virginia (1817)
Monument Avenue Historic District, Richmond (1888)
The new town of Reston (1962)
Roanoke Plans (1907; 1928)

West Virginia

Appalachian Trail (1921+)

Wisconsin

Greendale (A Greenbelt Town, 1935+)
Wisconsin Planning Enabling Act (1909)

Wyoming

Yellowstone National Park (1872)

Source: American Institute of Certified Planners

National Historic Planning Pioneers

Every year the American Institute of Certified Planners (AICP), the American Planning Association's (APA) professional and educational arm, selects up to three National Historic Planning Pioneers for their significant contributions to and innovations in American planning. Recipients have impacted planning practice, education, and/or theory on a national scale with long-term beneficial results. Their contributions must have occurred no less than 25 years ago. New inductees are indicated in bold.

For additional information about National Planning Pioneers, contact the American Institute of Certified Planners at (202) 872-0611 or visit them on the Internet at *www.planning.org*.

Charles Abrams
Frederick J. Adams
Thomas Adams
Edmund N. Bacon
Harland Bartholomew
Edward M. Bassett
Catherine (Wurster) Bauer
Edward H. Bennett
Alfred Bettman
Walter H. Blucher
Ernest John Bohn
Daniel Hudson Burnham
F. Stuart Chapin Jr.
Charles H. Cheney
Paul Davidoff
Frederic Adrian Delano
Earle S. Draper
Simon Eisner
Carl Feiss
George Burdett Ford
Paul Goodman
Percival Goodman
Aelred Joseph Gray
Frederick Gutheim
S. Herbert Hare
Sid J. Hare
Elisabeth Herlihy
John Tasker Howard
Henry Vincent Hubbard
Theodora Kimball Hubbard
Harlean James
T.J. Kent Jr.
George Edward Kessler
Pierre Charles L'Enfant
Kevin Lynch
Benton MacKaye
Ian Lennox McHarg
Albert Mayer
Harold V. Miller
Corwin R. Mocine
Arthur Ernest Morgan
Robert Moses
Lewis Mumford
Jesse Clyde Nichols
John Nolen Sr.
Charles Dyer Norton
Charles McKim Norton
Frederick Law Olmsted Sr.
Frederick Law Olmsted Jr.
Lawrence M. Orton
"Outdoor Circle, The"
Harvey S. Perloff
Clarence Arthur Perry
Gifford Pinchot
Planners for Equal Opportunity, 1964-1974
John Reps
Jacob August Riis
Charles Mulford Robinson
James W. Rouse
Charlotte Rumbold

National Historic Planning Pioneers

Mel Scott
Ladislas Segoe
Flavel Shurtleff
Mary K. Simkhovitch
Robert E. Simon Jr.
William E. Spangle
Clarence S. Stein
Telesis, 1939-1953
Rexford Guy Tugwell
Lawrence T. Veiller
Francis Violich
Charles Henry Wacker
Lillian Wald
Gordon Whitnall
Donald Wolbrink
Edith Elmer Wood
Henry Wright

Source: American Institute of Certified Planners

Number of Licensed Landscape Architects by State

Licensed landscape architects in each state are divided into two catagories: resident and reciprocal, or non-residential, registrants. Based on current population levels, the chart below also provides the per capita number of resident landscape architects in each state. Note that some states do not maintain a breakdown between resident and non-resident registrants. The following information is compiled by the Council of Landscape Architectural Registration Board, to which not all state licensing boards report their data.

State	Resident Land. Arch.	Reciprocal Land. Arch.	Total	Population[1]	Per capita # of Resident L.A. (per 100,000)
Alabama	104	97	201	4,447,100	2.3
Alaska	12	–	12	626,932	1.9
Arizona	253	364	617	5,130,632	4.9
Arkansas	–	–	–	2,673,400	–
California	2,752	377	3,129	33,871,648	8.1
Colorado	–	–	–	4,301,261	–
Connecticut	196	202	398	3,405,565	5.8
D.C.	–	–	–	572,059	–
Delaware	42	50	92	783,600	5.4
Florida	1,262		1,262	15,982,378	7.9
Georgia	–	–	–	8,186,453	–
Hawaii	93	40	133	1,211,537	7.7
Idaho	82	78	160	1,293,953	6.3
Illinois	–	–	–	12,419,293	–
Indiana	247	108	355	6,080,485	4.1
Iowa	116	70	186	2,926,324	4
Kansas	143	268	411	2,688,418	5.3
Kentucky	132	102	234	4,041,769	3.3
Louisiana	190	151	341	4,468,976	4.3
Maine	55	68	123	1,274,923	4.3
Maryland	–	–	–	5,296,486	–
Massachusetts	–	–	–	6,349,097	–
Michigan	393	175	568	9,938,444	4
Minnesota	251	92	343	4,919,479	5.1
Mississippi	88	83	171	2,844,658	3.1

Number of Licensed Landscape Architects by State

State	Resident Land. Arch.	Reciprocal Land. Arch.	Total	Population[1]	Per capita # of Resident L.A. (per 100,000)
Missouri	118	92	210	5,595,211	2.1
Montana	43	54	97	902,195	4.8
Nebraska	42	34	76	1,711,263	2.5
Nevada	62	172	234	1,998,257	3.1
New Hampshire	–	–	–	1,235,786	–
New Jersey	323	153	476	8,414,350	3.8
New Mexico	101	63	164	1,819,046	5.6
New York	571	267	838	18,976,457	3
North Carolina	349	142	491	8,049,313	4.3
North Dakota	–	–	–	642,200	–
Ohio	370	188	558	11,353,140	3.3
Oklahoma	57	48	105	3,450,654	1.7
Oregon	275	125	400	3,421,399	8
Pennsylvania	726	–	726	12,281,054	5.9
Rhode Island	87	163	250	1,048,319	8.3
South Carolina	159	278	437	4,012,012	4
South Dakota	8	10	18	754,844	1.1
Tennessee	143	121	264	5,689,283	2.5
Texas	879	304	1,183	20,851,820	4.2
Utah	–	–	–	2,233,169	–
Vermont	–	–	–	608,827	–
Virginia	–	–	–	7,078,515	–
Washington	385	91	476	5,894,121	6.5
West Virginia	46	122	168	1,808,344	2.5
Wisconsin	–	–	–	5,363,675	–
Wyoming	18	54	72	493,782	3.6
Totals	**11,173**	**4,806**	**15,979**	**281,421,906**	**4**

1 2000 population estimate from the U.S. Census Bureau

Note: Colorado, Washington, D.C., New Hampshire, North Dakota, and Vermont currently do not have a Landscape Architecture licensure program.

Source: Council of Landscape Architectural Registration Boards

Number of Registered Architects by State

Registered architects in each state are divided into two categories: resident and reciprocal, or non-resident, registrants. Based on current population levels, the chart below also calculates the per capita number of resident architects in each state. The following information is from the National Council of Architectural Registration Boards' 2003 survey.

State	Resident Architects	Reciprocal Registrations	Total	Population[1]	Per capita # of Resident Architects (per 100,000)
Alabama	755	1,409	2,164	4,447,100	17
Alaska	220	297	517	626,932	35
Arizona	1,907	3,945	5,852	5,130,632	37
Arkansas	463	865	1,328	2,673,400	17
California	16,809	4,628	21,437	33,871,648	50
Colorado	2,909	3,562	6,471	4,301,261	68
Connecticut	1,537	3,972	5,509	3,405,565	45
Delaware	145	1,169	1,314	783,600	19
D.C.	770	1,845	2,615	572,059	135
Florida	3,996	2,818	6,814	15,982,378	25
Georgia	2,572	3,068	5,640	8,186,453	31
Hawaii	904	950	1,854	1,211,537	75
Idaho	479	1,054	1,533	1,293,953	37
Illinois	5,345	3,551	8,896	12,419,293	43
Indiana	1,064	2,596	3,660	6,080,485	17
Iowa	445	1,027	1,472	2,926,324	15
Kansas	913	1,639	2,552	2,688,418	34
Kentucky	659	1,596	2,255	4,041,769	16
Louisiana	1,073	1,498	2,571	4,468,976	24
Maine	362	955	1,317	1,274,923	28
Maryland	1,733	3,301	5,034	5,296,486	33
Massachusetts	4,305	5,572	9,877	6,349,097	68
Michigan	2,674	2,862	5,536	9,938,444	27
Minnesota	1,714	1,429	3,143	4,919,479	35
Mississippi	310	1,127	1,437	2,844,658	11
Missouri	1,893	2,697	4,590	5,595,211	34
Montana	351	822	1,173	902,195	39
Nebraska	531	1,023	1,554	1,711,263	31

of Registered Architects

(Top 10 Shown)

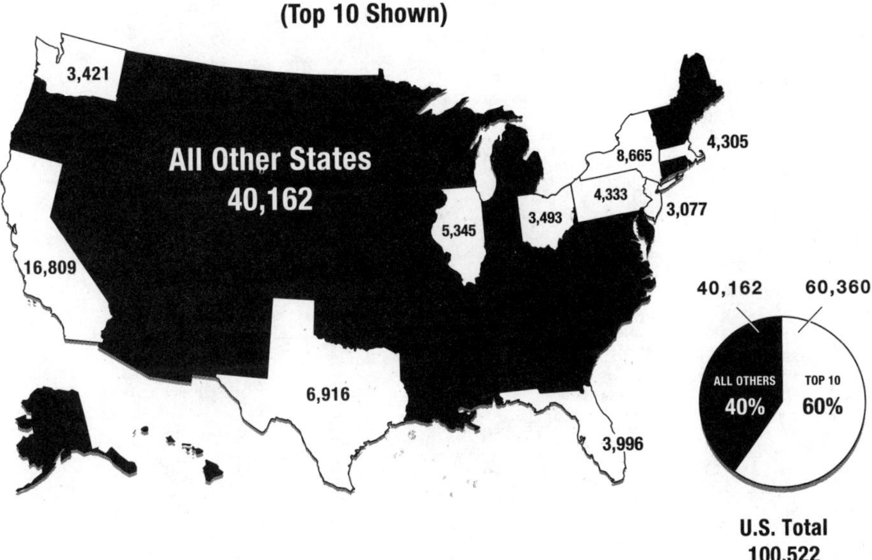

Source: Counsel House Research

Number of Registered Architects by State

State	Resident Architects	Reciprocal Registrations	Total	Population[1]	Per capita # of Resident Architects (per 100,000)
Nevada	504	1,950	2,454	1,998,257	25
New Hampshire	287	1259	1,546	1,235,786	23
New Jersey	3,077	5,264	8,341	8,414,350	37
New Mexico	722	1,316	2,038	1,819,046	40
New York	8,665	5,864	14,529	18,976,457	46
North Carolina	1,971	2,808	4,779	8,049,313	24
North Dakota	127	487	614	642,200	20
Ohio	3,493	3,304	6,797	11,353,140	31
Oklahoma	800	1,302	2,102	3,450,654	23
Oregon	1,376	1,073	2,449	3,421,399	40
Pennsylvania	4,333	3,967	8,300	12,281,054	35
Rhode Island	276	1,107	1,383	1,048,319	26
South Carolina	982	2,329	3,311	4,012,012	24
South Dakota	97	504	601	754,844	13
Tennessee	1,345	1,959	3,304	5,689,283	24
Texas	6,916	3,528	10,444	20,851,820	33
Utah	650	1,301	1,951	2,233,169	29
Vermont	248	609	857	608,827	41
Virginia	2,595	3,512	6,107	7,078,515	37
Washington	3,421	1,840	5,261	5,894,121	58
West Virginia	116	990	1,106	1,808,344	6
Wisconsin	1,565	3,020	4,585	5,363,675	29
Wyoming	118	787	905	493,782	24
Totals	**100,522**	**111,357**	**211,879**	**281,421,906**	**36**

[1] 2000 population estimate from the U.S. Census Bureau

Source: National Council of Architectural Registration Boards

Oldest Practicing Architecture Firms in the United States

The following firms were founded prior to 1900 (their specific founding dates indicated below) and are still operational today.

1827 The Mason & Hanger Group, Inc., Lexington, KY
1832 Lockwood Greene, Spartanburg, SC
1853 Luckett & Farley Architects, Engineers and Construction Managers, Inc., Louisville, KY
1853 SmithGroup, Detroit, MI
1862 FreemanWhite, Inc., Raleigh, NC
1868 Jensen and Halstead Ltd., Chicago, IL
1868 King & King Architects, Manlius, NY
1870 Harriman Associates, Auburn, ME
1871 Scholtz-Gowey-Gere-Marolf Architects & Interior Designers, PC, Davenport, IA
1872 Brunner & Brunner Architects & Engineers, St. Joseph, MO
1873 Graham Anderson Probst & White, Chicago, IL
1874 Chandler, Palmer & King, Norwich, CT
1874 Shepley Bulfinch Richardson and Abbott Inc., Boston, MA
1878 The Austin Company, Kansas City, MO
1878 Ballinger, Philadelphia, PA
1880 Beatty Harvey & Associates, Architects, New York, NY
1880 Green Nelson Weaver, Inc., Minneapolis, MN
1880 Holabird & Root LLP, Chicago, IL
1880 Zeidler Roberts Partnership, Inc., Toronto, Canada
1881 Keffer/Overton Architects, Des Moines, IA
1883 Ritterbush-Ellig-Hulsing PC, Bismarck, ND
1883 SMRT Architecture Engineering Planning, Portland, ME
1885 Cromwell Architects Engineers, Little Rock, AR
1885 HLW International LLP, New York, NY
1887 Bradley & Bradley, Rockford, IL
1888 Reid & Stuhldreher, Inc., Pittsburgh, PA
1889 Architectural Design West Inc., Salt Lake City, UT
1889 CSHQA Architects/Engineers/ Planners, Boise, ID
1889 MacLachlan, Cornelius & Filoni, Inc., Pittsburgh, PA
1889 Wank Adams Slavin Associates, New York, New York
1890 Kendall, Taylor & Company, Inc., Billerica, MA
1890 The Mathes Group PC, New Orleans, LA
1890 Plunkett Raysich Architects, Milwaukee, WI
1891 Shive/Spinelli/Perantoni & Associates, Somerville, NJ
1891 Wilkins Wood Goforth Mace Associates Ltd., Florence, SC
1892 Bauer Stark + Lashbrook, Inc., Toledo, OH
1893 Foor & Associates, Elmira, NY
1893 Wright, Porteous & Lowe/Bonar, Indianapolis, IN
1894 Colgan Perry Lawler Architects, Nyack, NY
1894 Freese and Nichols, Inc., Fort Worth, TX
1894 Parkinson Field Associates, Austin, TX
1895 Brooks Borg Skiles Architecture Engineering LLP, Des Moines, IA
1895 Albert Kahn Associates, Inc., Detroit, MI
1896 Hummel Architects, PA, Boise, ID
1896 Kessels DiBoll Kessels & Associates, New Orleans, LA
1896 Lehman Architectural Partnership, Roseland, NJ
1897 Baskerville & Son, Richmond, VA
1897 L_H_R_S Architects, Inc., Huntington, IN
1898 Beardsley Design Associates, Auburn, NY
1898 Berners/Schober Associates, Inc., Green Bay, WI
1898 Bottelli Associates, Summit, NJ
1898 Burns & McDonnell, Kansas City, MO
1898 Eckles Architecture, New Castle, PA
1898 Emery Roth Associates, New York, NY
1898 Foss Associates, Fargo, ND & Moorhead, MN
1898 PageSoutherlandPage, Austin, TX
1899 William B. Ittner, Inc., St. Louis, MO

Source: Counsel House Research

Above: Rafael Moneo connected the New Studios Building to the south wing of Michigan's Cranbrook Academy of Art to extend the linear progression of Eliel Saarinen's original 1941 building. *Photo © Balthazar Korab/Cranbrook, courtesy of the Cranbrook Academy of Art.* *Below*: Buffalo architect Edward B. Green modeled the Dayton Art Institute after the Villa d'Este, near Rome, and the Villa Farnese in Caprarola, Italy, both examples of sixteenth-century Italian Renaissance architecture. Today it is listed in the National Register of Historic Places. *Photo courtesy of The Dayton Art Institute.*

100 American Art Museums and their Architects

It has been estimated that there are over 16,000 different museums in the United States. While the collections they hold are often priceless, the facilities that contain them are also significant and lasting. As an example, a look at a list of U.S. art museums reveals some of the century's finest buildings. And, a recent museum building and renovation boom among world-class architects ensures that perhaps no other class of architecture, whether civil or public, similarly produces the quality of design. (Please note that some museums have had a nomadic history, and the buildings listed are not always the first buildings they occupied. Information about significant additions and expansions is included. However, renovations and minor alterations are not included nor any additions that have been demolished.)

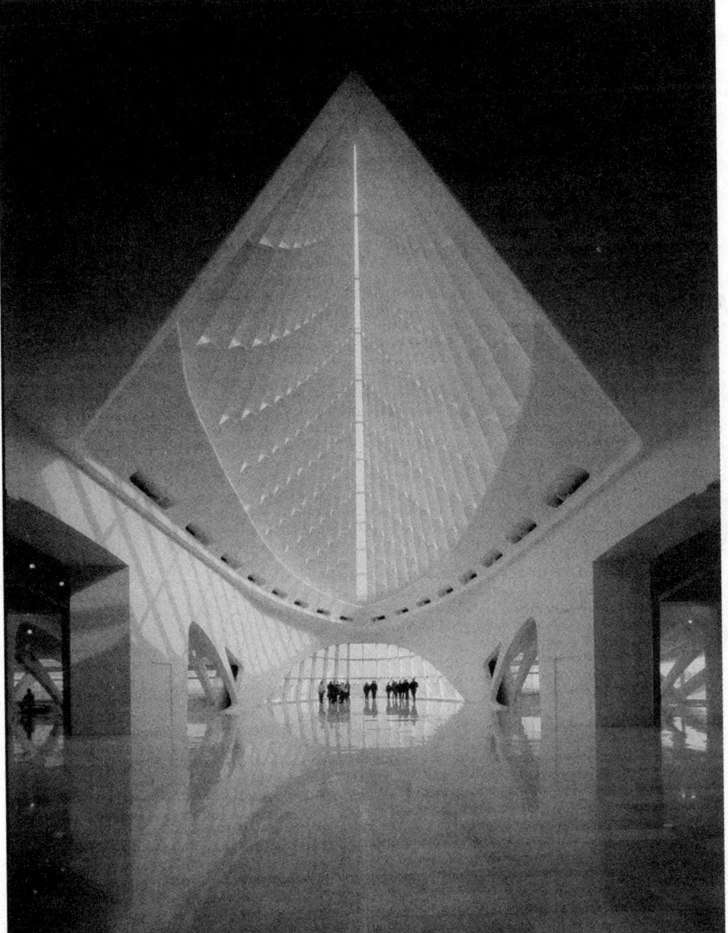

The Milwaukee Art Museum's new Quadracci Pavilion, the first Santiago Calatrava-designed building in the United States, features a 90-foot high glass-walled reception hall enclosed by the Burke Brise Soleil, a sunscreen that can be raised or lowered creating a unique moving sculpture. *Photo by Timothy Hursley, courtesy of the Milwaukee Art Museum.*

100 American Art Museums and their Architects

Museum	Location	Originally Opened
Albright-Knox Art Gallery	Buffalo, NY	1905
Allen Memorial Art Museum	Oberlin, OH	1917
American Folk Art Museum	New York, NY	2001
Amon Carter Museum	Ft. Worth, TX	1961
Anchorage Museum of History and Art	Anchorage, AK	1968
Art Institute of Chicago	Chicago, IL	1893
Arthur M. Sackler Museum	Cambridge, MA	1985
Asian Art Museum	San Francisco, CA	2003
Baltimore Museum of Art	Baltimore, MD	1929
Barnes Foundation	Merion, PA	1925
Bass Museum of Art	Miami, FL	1964
Berkeley Art Museum + Pacific Film Archive	Berkeley, CA	1970
Birmingham Museum of Art	Birmingham, AL	1959
Brooklyn Museum of Art	Brooklyn, NY	1897-1927
Butler Institute of American Art	Youngstown, OH	1919
Cincinnati Art Museum	Cincinnati, OH	1886

Original Architect	Expansion/Addition Architects
Edward B. Green	Skimore, Owings & Merrill, 1961 addition
Cass Gilbert	Venturi, Scott Brown, and Associates, 1977 addition
Tod Williams/Billie Tsien + Associates	
Philip Johnson	Johnson/Burgee, 1977 expansion; Philip Johnson/Alan Ritchie Architects, 2001 expansion
Kirk, Wallace, and McKinley with Schultz/Maynard Mitchell/Giurgola Architects with Maynard and Partch, 1986 addition	Kenneth Maynard Associates, 1974 addition;
Shepley, Rutan, and Coolidge	Skidmore, Owings and Merrill, 1977 Arthur Rubloff Building; Hammond, Beebe and Babka, 1988 Daniel F. and Ada L. Rice Building
James Stirling	
Gae Aulenti with HOK, LDA Architects, and Robert Wong Architects (adapted the 1917 main library by George Kelham)	
John Russell Pope	John Russell Pope, 1937 Jacobs Wing; Wrenn, Lewis & Jancks, 1950 May Wing, 1956 Woodward Wing and 1957 Cone Wing; Bower Lewis & Thrower Architects, 1994 West Wing for Contemporary Art
Paul Philippe Cret	
B. Robert Swartburg (adapted the 1930 Miami Beach Library by Russell Pancoast)	Arata Isozaki with Spillis Candela DJMJ, 2002 expansion
Mario J. Ciampi & Associates	
Warren, Knight and Davis	Warren, Knight and Davis, 1965 west wing, 1967 east wing, 1974 expansion, 1979 addition, and 1980 expansion; Edward Larrabee Barnes, 1993 expansion
McKim, Mead, and White	Prentice & Chan, Ohlhausen, 1978 addition; Arata Isozaki & Associates and James Stewart Polshek & Partners, 1991 Iris and B. Gerald Cantor Auditorium
McKim, Mead and White	Paul Boucherie, 1931 north and south wings; C. Robert Buchanan & Associates, 1967 addition; Buchanan, Ricciuti & Associates, 1986 west wing addition
James McLaughlin	Daniel H. Burnham, 1907 Schmidlapp Wing; Garber and Woodward, 1910 Ropes Wing and 1930 Emery, Hanna & French Wings; Rendigs, Panzer and Martin, 1937 Alms Wing; Potter, Tyler, Martin and Roth, 1965 Adams-Emery Wing

100 American Art Museums and their Architects

Museum	Location	Originally Opened
Cleveland Museum of Art	Cleveland, OH	1916
Colorado Springs Fine Arts Center	Colorado Springs, CO	1936
Columbus Museum of Art	Columbus, OH	1931
Contemporary Art Museum St. Louis	St. Louis, MO	2003
Contemporary Arts Museum, Houston	Houston, TX	1972
Corcoran Gallery of Art	Washington, DC	1897
Cranbrook Art Museum	Cranbrook, MI	1941
Dallas Museum of Art	Dallas, TX	1984
Dayton Art Institute	Dayton, OH	1930
Denver Art Museum	Denver, CO	1971
Des Moines Art Center	Des Moines, IA	1948
Detroit Institute of Arts	Detroit, MI	1888
Elvehjem Museum of Art	Madison, WI	1970
Everson Museum of Art	Syracuse, NY	1968
Fogg Art Museum	Cambridge, MA	1927
Frances Lehman Loeb Art Center	Poughkeepsie, NY	1993
Frederick R. Weisman Art Museum	Minneapolis, MN	1993
Freer Gallery Art	Washington, DC	1923
Frist Center for the Visual Arts	Nashville, TN	2001
Frye Art Museum	Seattle, WA	1952
Herbert F. Johnson Museum of Art	Ithaca, NY	1973

Original Architect	Expansion/Addition Architects
Benjamin Hubbell and W. Dominick Benes	J. Byers Hays and Paul C. Ruth, 1958 addition; Marcel Breuer and Hamilton Smith, 1971 addition; Dalton, van Dijk, Johnson & Partners, 1984 addition
John Gaw Meem	
Richards, McCarty and Bulford	Van Buren and Firestone, Architects, Inc., 1974 addition
Allied Works Architecture	
Gunnar Birkerts & Associates	
Ernest Flagg	Charles Adams Platt, 1927 expansion
Eliel Saarinen	Rafael Moneo, 2002 addition
Edward Larrabee Barnes	Edward Larrabee Barnes, 1985 decorative arts wing and 1991 Nancy and Jake L. Hamon Building
Edward B. Green	Levin Porter Associates, Inc., 1997 expansion
Gio Ponti with James Sudler Associates	
Eliel Saarinen	I.M. Pei & Associates, 1968 addition; Richard Meier & Partners, 1985 addition
James Balfour	Cret, Zantzinger, Borie and Medary, 1927 addition; Harley, Ellington, Cowin and Stirton, with Gunnar Birkerts, 1966 south wings; Harley, Ellington, Cowin and Stirton, 1966 north wing
Harry Weese	
I.M. Pei & Associates	
Coolidge, Shepley, Bulfinch, and Abbott	
Cesar Pelli & Associates	
Frank O. Gehry and Associates	
Charles Adams Platt	
Tuck Hinton Architects (adapted the 1934 U.S. Post Office by Marr and Holman Architects)	
Paul Albert Thiry	Olson Sundberg Kundig Allen Architects, 1997 expansion
I.M. Pei & Partners	

100 American Art Museums and their Architects

Museum	Location	Originally Opened
High Museum of Art	Atlanta, GA	1983
Hirshhorn Museum and Sculpture Garden	Washington, DC	1974
Hood Museum of Art	Hanover, NH	1983
Indiana University Art Museum	Bloomington, IN	1982
Indianapolis Museum of Art	Indianapolis, IN	1970
Iris & B. Gerald Cantor Center for Visual Arts	Stanford, CA	1894
J. Paul Getty Museum	Los Angeles, CA	1997
Joslyn Art Museum	Omaha, NE	1931
Kemper Museum of Contemporary Art and Design	Kansas City, MO	1994
Kimbell Art Museum	Fort Worth, TX	1972
Kreeger Museum	Washington, DC	1967
Lois & Richard Rosenthal Center for Contemporary Art	Cincinnati, OH	2003
Mead Art Museum	Amherst, MA	1949
Memphis Brooks Museum of Art	Memphis, TN	1916
Menil Collection	Houston, TX	1987
Metropolitan Museum of Art	New York, NY	1880
Milwaukee Art Museum	Milwaukee, WI	1957
Minneapolis Institute of Arts	Minneapolis, MN	1915
Modern Art Museum of Ft. Worth	Ft. Worth, TX	2002

Original Architect	Expansion/Addition Architects
Richard Meier & Partners	
Skidmore, Owings & Merrill	
Charles Moore and Centerbrook Architects	
I.M. Pei & Partners	
Richardson, Severns, Scheeler and Associates	Edward Larrabee Barnes and John M.Y. Lee, 1990 Mary Fendrich Hulman Pavilion
Percy & Hamilton Architects with Ernest J. Ransome	Polshek Partnership, 1999 addition
Richard Meier	
John and Alan McDonald	Norman Foster, 1994 Walter and Suzanne Scott Pavilion
Gunnar Birkerts & Associates	
Louis I. Kahn	
Philip Johnson with Richard Foster	
Zaha Hadid Architects with KZF Design	
McKim, Mead and White	
James Gamble Rogers with Carl Gutherz	Walk Jones and Francis Mah, 1973 addition; Skidmore, Owings & Merrill with Askew, Nixon, Ferguson & Wolf, 1989 expansion
Renzo Piano with Richard Fitzgerald & Partners	
Calvert Vaux and J. Wrey Mould	Theodore Weston, 1888 SW wing; Richard Morris Hunt and Richard Howland Hunt, 1902 Central Fifth Avenue facade; McKim, Mead, and White, 1906, side wings along Fifth Avenue; Brown, Lawford & Forbes, 1965 Thomas J. Watson Library; Kevin Roche John Dinkeloo & Associates, 1975 Lehman Wing, 1979 Sackler Wing, 1980 American Wing, 1981 Michael C. Rockefeller Wing for Primitive Art, 1988 European Sculpture and Decorative Art Wing
Eero Saarinen with Maynard Meyer	Kahler, Fitzhugh and Scott, 1975 addition; Santiago Calatrava, 2001 Quadracci Pavilion
McKim, Mead and White	Kenzo Tange, 1974 addition
Tadao Ando	

100 American Art Museums and their Architects

Museum	Location	Originally Opened
Munson-Williams-Proctor Arts Institute	Utica, NY	1960
Museum of Contemporary Art, Chicago	Chicago, IL	1996
Museum of Contemporary Art, Los Angeles (at California Plaza)	Los Angeles, CA	1986
Museum of Contemporary Art, San Diego	La Jolla, CA	1941
Museum of Fine Arts, Boston	Boston, MA	1909
Museum of Fine Arts, Houston	Houston, TX	1924
Museum of Modern Art	New York, NY	1939
Nasher Sculpture Center	Dallas, TX	2003
National Gallery of Art, East Building	Washington, DC	1978
National Gallery of Art, West Building	Washington, DC	1941
National Portrait Gallery and American Art Museum	Washington, DC	1968
Nelson Fine Arts Center	Tempe, AZ	1989
Nelson-Atkins Museum of Art	Kansas City, MO	1933
Nevada Museum of Art	Reno, NV	2003
New Orleans Museum of Art	New Orleans, LA	1911
Norman Rockwell Museum	Stockbridge, MA	1993
Oakland Museum of California	Oakland, CA	1969
Parrish Art Museum	Southampton, NY	1897
Pennsylvania Academy of the Fine Arts	Philadelphia, PA	1876

Original Architect	Expansion/Addition Architects
Philip Johnson	Lund McGee Sharpe Architecture, 1995 Education Wing
Josef Paul Kleihues	
Arata Isozaki	
Irving Gill (originally designed as a residence in 1916)	Mosher & Drew, 1950 transition to museum; Mosher & Drew, 1959 Sherwood Auditorium; Venturi, Scott Brown and Associates, 1996 expansion and renovation
Guy Lowell	Guy Lowell, 1915 Robert Dawson Evans Wing and 1928 Decorative Arts Wing; Hugh Stubbins Associates, 1968 Forsyth Wickes Galleries and George Robert White Wing; I.M. Pei & Partners, 1981 West Wing
William Ward Watkin	William Ward Watkin, 1926 addition; Kenneth Franzheim, 1953 Robert Lee Blaffer Memorial Wing; Mies van der Rohe, 1958 Cullinan Hall; Rafael Moneo, 2000 Audrey Jones Beck Building
Philip L. Goodwin and Edward Durrell Stone	Philip Johnson, 1964 east wing; Cesar Pelli & Associates, 1984 west wing
Renzo Piano	
I.M. Pei & Partners	
John Russell Pope	
Faulkner, Stenhouse, Fryer (adapted the 1836-67 Old Patent Office Building by Robert Mills)	
Antoine Predock	
Wight and Wight	
Will Bruder	
Samuel Marx	August Perez with Arthur Feitel, 1971 Wisner Education Wing, City Wing, and Stern Auditorium; Eskew Filson Architects with Billes/Manning Architects, 1993 expansion
Robert A. M. Stern Architects	
Kevin Roche John Dinkeloo & Associates	
Grosvenor Atterbury	Grosvenor Atterbury, 1902 and 1913 wings
Frank Furness and George W. Hewitt	

100 American Art Museums and their Architects

Museum	Location	Originally Opened
Philadelphia Museum of Art	Philadelphia, PA	1928
Phoenix Art Museum	Phoenix, AZ	1959
Portland Art Museum	Portland, OR	1932
Portland Museum of Art	Portland, ME	1911
Princeton University Art Museum	Princeton, NJ	1922
Pulitzer Foundation for the Arts	St. Louis, MO	2001
Renwick Gallery	Washington, DC	1859
Rodin Museum	Philadelphia, PA	1929
Saint Louis Art Museum	St. Louis, MO	1903
San Diego Museum of Art	San Diego, CA	1926
San Francisco Museum of Modern Art	San Francisco, CA	1995
Santa Barbara Museum of Art	Santa Barbara, CA	1941
Seattle Art Museum	Seattle, WA	1991
Sheldon Memorial Art Gallery	Lincoln, NE	1963
Solomon R. Guggenheim Museum	New York, NY	1959
Speed Art Museum	Louisville, KY	1927
Tacoma Art Museum	Tacoma, WA	2003
Terra Museum of American Art	Chicago, IL	1987
Toledo Museum of Art	Toledo, OH	1912

Original Architect	Expansion/Addition Architects
Horace Trumbauer with Zantzinger, Borie, and Medary	
Alden B. Dow	Alden B. Dow, 1965 east wing; Tod Williams/Billie Tsien + Associates, 1996 expansion
Pietro Belluschi	Pietro Belluschi, 1939 Hirsch Wing; Pietro Belluschi, with Wolff, Zimmer, Gunsul, Frasca, and Ritter, 1970 Hoffman Wing; Ann Beha Associates, 2000 expansion
John Calvin Stevens	I.M. Pei & Partners, 1983 Charles Shipman Payson Building
Ralph Adams Cram	Steinman and Cain, 1966 expansion; Mitchell/Giurgola Architects, 1989 Mitchell Wolfson Jr. Wing
Tadao Ando	
James Renwick Jr.	John Carl Warnecke and Hugh Newell Jacobsen, 1971 restoration
Paul Philippe Cret and Jacques Gréber	
Cass Gilbert	
William Templeton Johnson with Robert W. Snyder	Robert Mosher & Roy Drew, Architects, 1966 west wing; Mosher, Drew, Watson & Associates with William Ferguson, 1974 east wing
Mario Botta	
David Adler (adapted the 1914 Old Post Office designed by Francis Wilson)	Chester Carjola, 1942 Katherine Dexter McCormick Wing; Arendt/Mosher/Grants Architects, 1961 Preston Morton Wing and 1962 Sterling Morton Wing; Paul Gray, 1985 Alice Keck Park Wing; Edwards & Pitman, 1998 Peck Wing
Venturi, Scott Brown and Associates	
Philip Johnson	
Frank Lloyd Wright	Gwathmey Siegel & Associates, 1992 addition
Arthur Loomis	Nevin and Morgan, 1954 Preston Pope Satterwhite Wing; Brenner, Danforth, and Rockwell, 1973 north wing; Robert Geddes, 1983 South wing
Antoine Predock with Olson Sundberg Kundig Allen	
Booth Hansen Associates	
Green & Wicks with Harry W. Wachter	Edward B. Green and Sons, 1926 wing and 1933 expansion; Frank O. Gehry and Associates, 1992 Center for the Visual Arts addition

100 American Art Museums and their Architects

Museum	Location	Originally Opened
UCLA Hammer Museum of Art	Los Angeles, CA	1990
Wadsworth Atheneum Museum of Art	Hartford, CT	1844
Walker Art Center	Minneapolis, MN	1971
Wexner Center for the Arts	Columbus, OH	1989
Whitney Museum of American Art	New York, NY	1966
Yale University Art Gallery	New Haven, CT	1953

Source: Counsel House Research

Original Architect	Expansion/Addition Architects
Edward Larrabee Barnes	
Ithiel Town and Alexander Jackson Davis	Benjamin Wistar Morris, 1910 Colt Memorial and 1915 Morgan Memorial; Morris & O'Connor, 1934 Avery Memorial; Huntington, Darbee & Dollard, Architects, 1969 Goodwin Wing
Edward Larrabee Barnes	
Peter Eisenman	
Marcel Breuer	Gluckman Mayner Architects, 1998 expansion
Louis I. Kahn	

The American Airlines Center is the centerpiece of a 70-acre urban development north of Dallas' historic West End and is integral to the revitalization of downtown. It also contains over $3 million of public art in its floors, plazas, and exterior friezes. *Photo courtesy of David M. Schwarz/Architectural Services, Inc.*

Sports Stadiums

From classic ballparks to cutting-edge arenas and stadiums, the following charts provide major statistics and architectural information for all major league baseball, basketball, football, and hockey venues in the United States. All cost and architectural information refers to the stadiums as they were originally built and does not include any subsequent additions, renovations, or expansions. Capacity figures are the current numbers for the respective sports.

Detroit's historic Hudson warehouse was renovated and merged with a new stadium to create Ford Field. Two different general contractors were utilized–one responsible for construction of the new stadium and the other for the renovation and addition to the warehouse–all using the same subcontractors and suppliers. *Photo by Justin Maconochie, courtesy of SmithGroup.*

Sports Stadiums: Baseball

BASEBALL	Stadium Name	Location	Opened
AMERICAN LEAGUE			
Anaheim Angels	Edison International Field	Anaheim, CA	1966
Baltimore Orioles	Oriole Park at Camden Yards	Baltimore, MD	1992
Boston Red Sox	Fenway Park	Boston, MA	1912
Chicago White Sox	U.S. Cellular Field	Chicago, IL	1991
Cleveland Indians	Jacobs Field	Cleveland, OH	1994
Detroit Tigers	Comerica Park	Detroit, MI	2000
Kansas City Royals	Kauffman Stadium	Kansas City, MO	1973
Minnesota Twins	Hubert H. Humphrey Metrodome	Minneapolis, MN	1982
New York Yankees	Yankee Stadium	Bronx, NY	1923
Oakland Athletics	Network Associates Coliseum	Oakland, CA	1966
Seattle Mariners	Safeco Field	Seattle, WA	1999
Tampa Bay Devil Rays	Tropicana Field	St. Petersburg, FL	1990
Texas Rangers	The Ballpark at Arlington	Arlington, TX	1994
Toronto Blue Jays	SkyDome	Toronto, ON, Canada	1989

Architect (original)	Cost (original)	Capacity (current)	Roof Type	Surface	Naming Rights (amt. and expiration)
HOK Sports Facilities Group; Robert A.M. Stern Architects	$25 M	45,050	Open-Air	Bluegrass	$50 M (20 yrs.)
HOK with RTKL	$210 M	48,876	Open-Air	Grass	
Osborn Engineering	$365,000	33,871	Open-Air	Bluegrass	
HOK Sport	$150 M	44,321	Open-Air	Bluegrass	$68 M (20 yrs.)
HOK Sport	$173 M	43,345	Open-Air	Kentucky Bluegrass	$13.9 M (20 yrs.)
HOK Sport; SHG Inc.	$300 M	40,637	Open-Air	Grass	$66 M (30 yrs.)
HNTB	$50.45 M	40,625	Open-Air	Grass	
Skidmore, Owings & Merrill	$75 M	55,883	Dome	Astroturf	
Osborne Engineering Company	$3.1 M	57,545	Open-Air	Merion Bluegrass	
Skidmore, Owings & Merrill	$25.5 M	48,219	Open-Air	Bluegrass	$6 M (5 yrs.)
NBBJ	$517.6 M	46,621	Retractable	Grass	$40 M (20 yrs.)
HOK Sport; Lescher & Mahoney Sports; Criswell, Blizzard & Blouin Architects	$138 M	45,360	Dome	FieldTurf with dirt infield	$30 M (30 yrs.)
David M. Schwarz Architectural Services, Inc.; HKS, Inc.	$190 M	49,115	Open-Air	Bermuda Tifway 419 Grass	
Rod Robbie and Michael Allen	$442 M	50,516	Retractable	Astroturf	

Sports Stadiums: Baseball

BASEBALL	Stadium Name	Location	Opened
NATIONAL LEAGUE			
Arizona Diamondbacks	Bank One Ballpark	Phoenix, AZ	1998
Atlanta Braves	Turner Field	Atlanta, GA	1997
Chicago Cubs	Wrigley Field	Chicago, IL	1914
Cincinnati Reds	Great American Ball Park	Cincinnati, OH	2003
Colorado Rockies	Coors Field	Denver, CO	1995
Florida Marlins	Pro Player Stadium	Miami, FL	1987
Houston Astros	Minute Maid Park	Houston, TX	2000
Los Angeles Dodgers	Dodger Stadium	Los Angeles, CA	1962
Milwaukee Brewers	Miller Park	Milwaukee, WI	2001
Montreal Expos	Olympic Stadium	Montreal, QC, Canada	1977
New York Mets	Shea Stadium	Flushing, NY	1964
Philadelphia Phillies	Veterans Stadium	Philadelphia, PA	1971
Pittsburgh Pirates	PNC Park	Pittsburgh, PA	2001
San Diego Padres	Qualcomm Stadium	San Diego, CA	1967
San Francisco Giants	Pacific Bell Park	San Francisco, CA	2000
St. Louis Cardinals	Busch Stadium	St. Louis, MO	1966

Architect (original)	Cost (original)	Capacity (current)	Roof Type	Surface	Naming Rights (amt. and expiration)
Ellerbe Becket, with Bill Johnson	$355 M	49,033	Convertible	Kentucky Bluegrass	$33.1 M (30 yrs.)
Heery International, Inc., Williams-Russell and Johnson, Inc., and Ellerbe Becket, Inc.	$250 M	49,831	Open-Air	GN-1 Bermuda Grass	
Zachary Taylor Davis	$250,000	38,765	Open-Air	Merion Bluegrass and Clover	
HOK Sport + Venue + Event	$290 M	42,053	Open-Air	Grass	$75 M (30 yrs.)
HOK Sport	$215 M	50,445	Open-Air	Grass	$15 M (indefinite)
HOK Sports Facilities Group	$125 M	47,662	Open-Air	Tifway 419 Bermuda Grass	$20 M (10 yrs.)
HOK Sport	$248.1 M	40,950	Retractable	Grass	$170 M (28 yrs.)
Emil Praeger	$24.47 M	56,000	Open-Air	Santa Ana Bermuda Grass	
HKS with NBBJ and Eppstein Uhen Architects	$399.4 M	42,500	Retractable	Grass	$41 M (20 yrs.)
Roger Taillibert	$770 M	46,500	Retractable (inoperable)	Astroturf	
Praeger-Kavanaugh-Waterbury	$24 M	55,601	Open-Air	Bluegrass	
Hugh Stubbins & Associates	$50 M	62,382	Open-Air	NeXturf	
HOK Sports, L.D. Astorino Companies	$262 M	38,000	Open-Air	Grass	$30 M (20 yrs.)
Frank L. Hope and Associates	$27.75 M	56,133	Open-Air	Santa Ana Bermuda Grass	$18 M (20 yrs.)
HOK Sports	$345 M	40,800	Open-Air	Sports Turf	$50 M (24 yrs.)
Sverdrup & Parcel and Associates, Edward Durell Stone, Schwarz & Van Hoefen, Associated	$24 M	49,676	Open-Air	Grass	

Sports Stadiums: Basketball

BASKETBALL	Stadium Name	Location	Opened
EASTERN CONFERENCE			
ATLANTIC			
Boston Celtics	Fleet Center	Boston, MA	1995
Miami Heat	American Airlines Arena	Miami, FL	1998
New Jersey Nets	Continental Airlines Arena	East Rutherford, NJ	1981
New York Knicks	Madison Square Garden	New York, NY	1968
Orlando Magic	TD Waterhouse Centre	Orlando, FL	1989
Philadelphia 76ers	Wachovia Center	Philadelphia, PA	1996
Washington Wizards	MCI Center	Washington, DC	1997
CENTRAL			
Atlanta Hawks	Philips Arena	Atlanta, GA	1999
Chicago Bulls	United Center	Chicago, IL	1994
Cleveland Cavaliers	The Gund Arena	Cleveland, OH	1994
Detroit Pistons	The Palace of Auburn Hills	Auburn Hills, MI	1988
Indiana Pacers	Conseco Fieldhouse	Indianapolis, IN	1999
Milwaukee Bucks	The Bradley Center	Milwaukee, WI	1988
New Orleans Hornets	New Orleans Arena	New Orleans, LA	1999
Toronto Raptors	Air Canada Centre	Toronto, ON, Canada	1999

Architect (original)	Cost (current)	Capacity (original)	Naming Rights (amt. and expiration)
Ellerbe Becket	18,624	$160 M	$30 M (15 yrs.)
Arquitectonica	19,600	$175 M	$42 M (20 yrs.)
Grad Partnership; DiLullo, Clauss, Ostroski & Partners	19,040	$85 M	$29 M (12 yrs.)
Charles Luckman	19,763	$116 M	
Lloyd Jones Philpot; Cambridge Seven	17,248	$98 M	$7.8 M (5 yrs.)
Ellerbe Becket	20,444	$206 M	$40 M (29 yrs.)
Ellerbe Becket	20,674	$260 M	$44 M (13 years)
HOK, Arquitectonica	20,300	$213.5 M	$180 M (20 yrs.)
HOK Sport; Marmon Mok; W.E. Simpson Company	21,711	$175 M	$25 M (20 yrs.)
Ellerbe Becket	20,562	$152 M	$14 M (20 yrs.)
Rossetti Associates/Architects Planners	21,454	$70 M	
Ellerbe Becket	18,345	$183 M	$40 M (20 yrs.)
HOK	18,717	$90 M	
Arthur Q. Davis, FAIA & Partners	18,500	$112 M	
HOK Sport; Brisbin, Brook and Benyon	19,800	C$265 M	C$40 M (20 yrs.)

Sports Stadiums: Basketball

BASKETBALL	Stadium Name	Location	Opened
WESTERN CONFERENCE			
MIDWEST			
Dallas Mavericks	American Airlines Center	Dallas, TX	2001
Denver Nuggets	Pepsi Center	Denver, CO	1999
Houston Rockets	Toyota Center	Houston, TX	2003
Memphis Grizzlies	The Memphis Pyramid	Memphis, TN	1991
Minnesota Timberwolves	The Target Center	Minneapolis, MN	1990
San Antonio Spurs	SBC Center	San Antonio, TX	2002
Utah Jazz	The Delta Center	Salt Lake City, UT	1991
PACIFIC			
Golden State Warriors	The New Arena in Oakland	Oakland, CA	1966
Los Angeles Clippers	Staples Center	Los Angeles, CA	1999
Los Angeles Lakers	Staples Center	Los Angeles, CA	1999
Phoenix Suns	America West Arena	Phoenix, AZ	1992
Portland Trail Blazers	The Rose Garden	Portland, OR	1995
Sacramento Kings	Arco Arena	Sacramento, CA	1988
Seattle SuperSonics	Key Arena	Seattle, WA	1983

Architect (original)	Capacity (current)	Cost (original)	Naming Rights (amt. and expiration)
David M. Schwarz Architectural Services, Inc. with HKS Inc.	19,200	$420 M	$40 M (20 yrs.)
HOK Sports Facilities Group	19,309	$160 M	$68 M (20 yrs.)
HOK Sport + Venue + Event	18,300	$175 M	Undisclosed
Rosser International	21,000	$65 M	
KMR Architects	19,006	$104 M	$18.75 M (15 yrs.)
Ellerbe Becket with Lake/Flato Architects and Kelly Munoz	18,500	$86 M	$85 M (20 yrs.)
FFKR Architecture	19,911	$94 M	$25 M (20 yrs.)
HNTB	19,200	n/a	
NBBJ	20,000	$330 M	$100 M (20 yrs.)
NBBJ	20,000	$330 M	$100 M (20 yrs.)
Ellerbe Becket	19,023	$90 M	$26 M (30 yrs.)
Ellerbe Becket	21,538	$262 M	
Rann Haight	17,317	$40 M	$7 M (10 yrs.)
NBBJ	17,072	$67 M	$15.1 M (15 yrs.)

Sports Stadiums: Football

FOOTBALL	Stadium Name	Location	Opened	Cost (original)
AFC EAST				
Buffalo Bills	Ralph Wilson Stadium	Orchard Park, NY	1973	$22 M
Miami Dolphins	Pro Player Stadium	Miami, FL	1987	$125 M
New England Patriots	Gillette Stadium	Foxboro, MA	2002	$325 M
New York Jets	Giants Stadium	E. Rutherford, NJ	1976	$75 M
AFC NORTH				
Baltimore Ravens	M&T Bank	Baltimore, MD	1998	$220 M
Cincinnati Bengals	Paul Brown Stadium	Cincinnati, OH	2000	$400 M
Cleveland Browns	Cleveland Browns Stadium	Cleveland, OH	1999	$283 M
Pittsburgh Steelers	Heinz Field	Pittsburgh, PA	2001	$281 M
AFC SOUTH				
Houston Texans	Reliant Stadium	Houston, TX	2002	$325 M
Indianapolis Colts	RCA Dome	Indianapolis, IN	1984	$82 M
Jacksonville Jaguars	Alltel Stadium	Jacksonville, FL	1995	$138 M
Tennessee Titans	The Coliseum	Nashville, TN	1999	$290 M
AFC WEST				
Denver Broncos	Invesco Field at Mile High Stadium	Denver, CO	2001	$400.8 M
Kansas City Chiefs	Arrowhead Stadium	Kansas City, MO	1972	$43 M
Oakland Raiders	Network Associates Coliseum	Oakland, CA	1966	$25.5 M
San Diego Chargers	Qualcomm Stadium	San Diego, CA	1967	$27 M

Architect (original)	Capacity (current)	Roof Type	Surface	Naming Rights (amt. and expiration)
HNTB	73,800	Open-Air	AstroTurf-12	
HOK Sports Facilities Group	74,916	Open-Air	Grass	$20 M (10 yrs.)
HOK Sport + Venue + Event	68,000	Open-Air	Grass	Undisclosed
HOK Sports Facilities Group	79,670	Open-Air	Grass	
HOK Sports Facilities Group	69,084	Open-Air	Grass	$75 M (15 yrs.)
NBBJ	65,535	Open-Air	Grass	Undisclosed
HOK Sports Facilities Group	73,200	Open-Air	Grass	
HOK Sport + Venue + Event with WTW Architects	64,440	Open-Air	Bluegrass blend	$58 M (20 yrs.)
HOK Sport + Venue + Event	69,500	Retractable	Grass	$300 M (30 yrs.)
HNTB	60,127	Dome	AstroTurf-12	$10 M (10 yrs.)
HOK Sports Facilities Group	73,000	Open-Air	Grass	$6.2 M (10 yrs.)
HOK Sports Facilities Group	67,000	Open-Air	Grass	
HNTB Sports Architects with Fentress Bradburn Architects and Bertram A. Burton and Associates	76,125	Open-Air	Grass	$120 M (20 yrs.)
Kivett and Meyers	79,409	Open-Air	Grass	
Skidmore, Owings & Merrill	62,026	Suspension (fixed)	Bluegrass	$6 M (5 yrs.)
Frank L. Hope and Associates	71,294	Open-Air	Grass	$18 M (20 yrs.)

Sports Stadiums: Football

FOOTBALL	Stadium Name	Location	Opened	Cost (original)
NFC EAST				
Dallas Cowboys	Texas Stadium	Irving, TX	1971	$35 M
New York Giants	Giants Stadium	E. Rutherford, NJ	1976	$75 M
Philadelphia Eagles	Lincoln Financial Field	Philadelphia, PA	2003	$320 M
Washington Redskins	FedEx Field	Landover, MD	1996	$250.5 M
NFC NORTH				
Chicago Bears	Soldier Field	Chicago, IL	1924	$10 M
Detroit Lions	Ford Field	Allen Park, MI	2002	$500 M
Green Bay Packers	Lambeau Field	Green Bay, WI	1957	$960,000
Minnesota Vikings	Hubert H. Humphrey Metrodome	Minneapolis, MN	1982	$55 M
NFC SOUTH				
Atlanta Falcons	Georgia Dome	Atlanta, GA	1992	$214 M
Carolina Panthers	Ericsson Stadium	Charlotte, NC	1996	$248 M
New Orleans Saints	Louisiana Superdome	New Orleans, LA	1975	$134 M
Tampa Bay Buccaneers	Raymond James Stadium	Tampa, FL	1998	$168.5 M
NFC WEST				
Arizona Cardinals	Sun Devil Stadium	Tempe, AZ	1958	$1 M
San Francisco 49ers	Candlestick Park	San Francisco, CA	1960	$24.6 M
Seattle Seahawks	Seahawks Stadium	Seattle, WA	2002	$360 M
St. Louis Rams	Edward Jones Dome	St. Louis, MO	1995	$280 M

Architect (original)	Capacity (current)	Roof Type	Surface	Naming Rights (amt. and expiration)
Warren Morey	65,846	Partial Roof	Artificial	
HOK Sports Facilities Group	79,670	Open-Air	Grass	
NBBJ	66,000	Open-Air	Grass	$139.6 M (20 yrs.)
HOK Sports Facilities Group	80,116	Open-Air	Grass	$205 M (27 yrs.)
Holabird and Roche	66,944	Open-Air	Grass	
SmithGroup	64,355	Dome	FieldTurf	$40 M (40 yrs.)
John Somerville	60,890	Open-Air	Grass	
Skidmore, Owings & Merrill	64,121	Dome	Artificial Turf	
Heery International	71,149	Dome	Artificial Turf	
HOK Sports Facilities Group	73,258	Open-Air	Grass	$20 M (10 yrs.)
Curtis & Davis Architects	69,065	Dome	Artificial Turf	
HOK Sports Facilities Group	66,000	Open-Air	Grass	$32.5 M (13 yrs.)
Edward L. Varney	74,186	Open-Air	Grass	
John & Bolles	69,843	Open-Air	Grass	
Ellerbe Becket with Loschky Marquardt & Nesholm, assoc. archts.	67,000	Partial Roof	FieldTurf	
HOK Sports Facilities Group	66,000	Dome	Astroturf	$31.8 M (12 yrs.)

Sports Stadiums: Hockey

HOCKEY	Stadium Name	Location	Opened
EASTERN CONFERENCE			
ATLANTIC DIVISION			
New Jersey Devils	Continental Airlines Arena	East Rutherford, NJ	1981
New York Islanders	Nassau Veterans Memorial Coliseum	Uniondale, NY	1972
New York Rangers	Madison Square Garden	New York, NY	1968
Philadelphia Flyers	Wachovia Center	Philadelphia, PA	1996
Pittsburgh Penguins	Mellon Arena	Pittsburgh, PA	1961
NORTHEAST DIVISION			
Boston Bruins	Fleet Center	Boston, MA	1995
Buffalo Sabres	HSBC Arena	Buffalo, NY	1996
Montreal Canadiens	Le Centre Bell	Montreal, QC, Canada	1996
Ottawa Senators	The Corel Centre	Kanata, ON, Canada	1996
Toronto Maple Leafs	Air Canada Centre	Toronto, ON, Canada	1999
SOUTHEAST DIVISION			
Atlanta Thrashers	Philips Arena	Atlanta, GA	1999
Carolina Hurricanes	RBC Center	Raleigh, NC	1999
Florida Panthers	Office Depot Center	Sunrise, FL	1998
Tampa Bay Lightning	St. Pete Times Forum	Tampa, FL	1996
Washington Capitals	MCI Center	Washington, DC	1997

Architect (original)	Capacity (current)	Cost (original)	Naming Rights (amt. and expiration)
Grad Partnership; DiLullo, Clauss, Ostroski & Partners	19,040	$85 M	$29 M (12 yrs.)
Welton Becket	16,297	$31 M	
Charles Luckman	18,200	$116 M	
Ellerbe Becket	18,168	$206 M	$40 M (29 yrs.)
Mitchell and Ritchie	17,323	$22 M	$18 M (10 yrs.)
Ellerbe Becket	17,565	$160 M	$30 M (15 yrs.)
Ellerbe Becket	18,595	$127.5 M	$24 M (30 yrs.)
Consortium of Quebec Architects	21,273	C$280 M	$100 M (20 yrs.)
Rossetti Associates Architects	18,500	C$200 M	C$26 M (20 yrs.)
HOK Sport; Brisbin, Brook and Benyon	18,800	C$265 M	C$40 M (20 yrs.)
HOK, Arquitectonica	18,750	$213.5 M	$180 M (20 yrs.)
Odell & Associates	18,176	$158 M	$80 M (20 yrs.)
Ellerbe Becket	19,452	$212 M	$14 M (10 yrs.)
Ellerbe Becket	19,500	$139 M	$25 M (12 yrs.)
Ellerbe Becket	19,700	$260 M	$44 M (13 yrs.)

Sports Stadiums: Hockey

HOCKEY	Stadium Name	Location	Opened
WESTERN CONFERENCE			
CENTRAL DIVISION			
Chicago Blackhawks	United Center	Chicago, IL	1994
Columbus Blue Jackets	Nationwide Arena	Columbus, OH	2000
Detroit Red Wings	Joe Louis Arena	Detroit, MI	1979
Nashville Predators	Gaylord Entertainment Center	Nashville, TN	1997
St. Louis Blues	Savvis Center	St. Louis, MO	1994
NORTHWEST DIVISION			
Calgary Flames	Pengrowth Saddledome	Calgary, AB, Canada	1983
Colorado Avalanche	Pepsi Center	Denver, CO	1999
Edmonton Oilers	Skyreach Centre	Edmonton, AB, Canada	1974
Minnesota Wild	Xcel Energy Center	Saint Paul, MN	2000
Vancouver Canucks	General Motors Place	Vancouver, BC, Canada	1995
PACIFIC DIVISION			
Anaheim Mighty Ducks	The Arrowhead Pond of Anaheim	Anaheim, CA	1993
Dallas Stars	American Airlines Center	Dallas, TX	2001
Los Angeles Kings	Staples Center	Los Angeles, CA	1999
Phoenix Coyotes	America West Arena	Phoenix, AZ	1992
San Jose Sharks	HP Pavilion	San Jose, CA	1993

Source: Counsel House Research

Architect (original)	Capacity (current)	Cost (original)	Naming Rights (amt. and expiration)
HOK Sport; Marmon Mok; W.E. Simpson Company	20,500	$175 M	$25 M (20 yrs.)
Heinlein & Schrock, Inc.; NBBJ	18,500	$150 M	$135 M (indefinite)
Smith, Hinchmen and Grylls Associates	18,785	$57 M	
HOK	17,500	$144 M	$80 M (20 yrs.)
Ellerbe Becket	19,260	$170 M	$70 M (20 yrs.)
Graham Edmunds/Graham McCourt	20,140	C$176 M	C$20 M (20 yrs.)
HOK	18,129	$160 M	$68 M (20 yrs.)
Phillips, Barrett, Hillier, Jones & Partners w/ Wynn, Forbes, Lord, Feldberg & Schmidt	16,900	C$22.5 M	$3.307 (5 yrs.)
HOK Sport	18,064	$130 M	$75 M (25 yrs.)
Brisbin, Brook and Beynon	18,422	C$160 M	C$18.5 M (20 yrs.)
HOK Sport	17,174	$120 M	$15 M (10 yrs.)
David M. Schwarz Architectural Services, Inc. with HKS Inc.	18,000	$420 M	$40 M (20 yrs.)
NBBJ	18,500	$330 M	$100 M (20 yrs.)
Ellerbe Becket	16,210	$90 M	$26 M (30 yrs.)
Sink Combs Dethlefs	17,483	$162.5 M	$55.8 M (18 yrs.)

State Capitols

The architect(s) of each U.S. state capitol and the national Capitol is listed below. When available, the contractor(s) is also listed immediately below the architect in italics.

Alabama
Montgomery, 1851
Barachias Holt

Alaska
Juneau, 1931
Treasury Department architects with James A. Wetmore, supervising architect
N.P. Severin Company

Arizona
Phoenix, 1900
James Riley Gordon
Tom Lovell

Arkansas
Little Rock, 1911-1915
George R. Mann; Cass Gilbert
Caldwell and Drake; William Miller & Sons

California
Sacramento, 1874
Miner F. Butler; Ruben Clark and G. Parker Cummings

Colorado
Denver, 1894-1908
Elijah E. Myers, Frank E. Edbrooke

Connecticut
Hartford, 1779
Richard M. Upjohn
James G. Batterson

Delaware
Dover, 1933
William Martin

Florida
Tallahassee, 1977
Edward Durell Stone with Reynolds, Smith and Hills

Georgia
Atlanta, 1889
Edbrooke & Burnham
Miles and Horne

Hawaii
Honolulu, 1969
John Carl Warnecke with Belt, Lemman and Lo
Reed and Martin

Idaho
Boise, 1912-1920
John E. Tourtellotte
Stewart and Company with Herbert Quigley, construction supervisor

Illinois
Springfield, 1877-87
J. C. Cochrane with Alfred H. Piquenard; W. W. Boyington

Indiana
Indianapolis, 1888
Edwin May; Adolf Scherrer
Kanmacher and Dengi; Elias F. Gobel and Columbus Cummings

Iowa
Des Moines, 1884-86
J. C. Cochrane and Alfred H. Piquenard; M.E. Bell and W. F. Hackney

Kansas
Topeka, 1873-1906
John G. Haskell; E.T. Carr and George Ropes
D. J. Silver & Son; Bogart and Babcock; William Tweeddale and Company

Kentucky
Frankfort, 1910
Frank Mills Andrews

State Capitols

Louisiana
Baton Rouge, 1931
Weiss, Dryfous and Seiferth
Kenneth McDonald

Maine
Augusta, 1832
Charles Bulfinch; John C. Spofford, 1891 rear wing addition; G. Henri Desmond, 1911 expansion

Maryland
Annapolis, 1779
Joseph Horatio Anderson and Joseph Clark, interior architect; Baldwin and Pennington, 1905 rear annex
Charles Wallace; Thomas Wallace

Massachusetts
Boston, 1798
Charles Bulfinch; Charles Brigham, 1895 rear addition; R. Clipson, William Chapman, and Robert Agnew, 1917 side wing additions

Michigan
Lansing, 1878-79
Elijah E. Myers
N. Osborne & Co.

Minnesota
St. Paul, 1905
Cass Gilbert

Mississippi
Jackson, 1903
Theodore C. Link; George R. Mann, dome
Wells Brothers Company

Missouri
Jefferson City, 1917
Tracy and Swartwout
T.H. Johnson; A. Anderson & Company; John Gill & Sons

Montana
Helena, 1902
Bell and Kent; Frank Mills Andrews and Link & Hare, 1912 east and west wing addition

Nebraska
Lincoln, 1932
Bertram Grosvenor Goodhue
W.J. Assenmacher Company; J.H. Wiese Company; Peter Kewittand Sons; Metz Construction Co.

Nevada
Carson City, 1871
Joseph Gosling; Frederic J. Delongchamps and C.G. Sellman, 1913 addition
Peter Cavanough and Son

New Hampshire
Concord, 1819
Stuart James Park; Gridley J. F. Bryant and David Bryce, 1866 addition; Peabody and Stearns, 1909 addition

New Jersey
Trenton, 1792
Jonathan Doane; John Notman, 1845 expansion and renovation; Samuel Sloan, 1872 expansion; Lewis Broome and James Moylan, c.1885 renovations; Karr Poole and Lum, 1900 expansion; Arnold Moses, 1903 Senate wing renovations

New Mexico
Santa Fe, 1966
W. C. Kruger & Associates with John Gaw Meem, design consultant
Robert E. McKee General Contractor, Inc.

New York
Albany, 1879-99
Thomas Fuller; Leopold Eidlitz, Frederick Law Olmsted, Henry Hobson Richardson; Isaac G. Perry

North Carolina
Raleigh, 1840
Town and Davis, David Paton

North Dakota
Bismarck, 1934
Holabird & Root with Joseph B. DeRemer and William F. Kirke
Lundoff and Bicknell

State Capitols

Ohio
Columbus, 1857-1861
Henry Walter; William R. West; Nathan B. Kelly

Oklahoma
Oklahoma City, 1917
Layton and Smith

Oregon
Salem, 1938
Francis Keally of Trowbridge and Livingston

Pennsylvania
Harrisburg, 1906
Joseph M. Huston
George F. Payne Company

Rhode Island
Providence, 1904
McKim, Mead and White
Norcross Brothers Construction

South Carolina
Columbia, 1854-1907
John Rudolph Niernsee, 1854-85; J. Crawford Neilson, 1885-88; Frank Niernsee, 1888-91; Frank P. Milburn, 1900-04; Charles Coker Wilson, 1904-07

South Dakota
Pierre, 1911
C.E. Bell and M.S. Detwiler
O.H. Olsen with Samuel H. Lea, state engineer and construction supervisor

Tennessee
Nashville, 1859
William Strickland
A.G. Payne

Texas
Austin, 1888
Elijah E. Myers
Mattheas Schnell; Taylor, Babcock & Co. with Abner Taylore

Utah
Salt Lake City, 1915-16
Richard K. A. Kletting
James Stewart & Company

Vermont
Montpelier, 1859
Thomas W. Silloway; Joseph R. Richards

Virginia
Richmond, 1789
Thomas Jefferson with Charles-Louis Clérisseau; J. Kevin Peebles, Frye & Chesterman, 1906 wings

Washington
Olympia, 1928
Walter R. Wilder and Harry K. White

West Virginia
Charleston, 1932
Cass Gilbert
George H. Fuller Company; James Baird Company

Wisconsin
Madison, 1909-1915
George B. Post & Sons

Wyoming
Cheyenne, 1890
David W. Gibbs; William Dubois, 1915 extension
Adam Feick & Brother; Moses P. Keefe, 1890 wings; John W. Howard, 1915 extension

U.S. Capitol
Washington, DC, 1800-1829
William Thornton, 1793; Benjamin Henry Latrobe, 1803-11, 1815-17; Charles Bulfinch, 1818-29; Thomas Ustick Walter, 1851-65; Edward Clark, 1865-1902; Elliot Woods, 1902-23; David Lynn, 1923-54; J. George Stewart, 1954-70; George Malcolm White, FAIA, 1971-95; Alan M. Hantman, AIA, 1997-present

Source: Counsel House Research

Tallest Buildings in the World

The following list ranks the world's 100 tallest buildings. Each building's architect, number of stories, height, location, and completion year are also provided. Buildings which have reached their full height but are still under construction are deemed eligible and are indicated with a "UC" in the year category along with the anticipated completion date, if known. For the purposes of this list, heights are rounded to the nearest full unit of measurement.

For additional resources about tall buildings, visit the Council on Tall Buildings and Urban Habitat on the Internet at *www.ctbuh.org* and *www.skyscrapers.com.*

Rank	Building	Year	City/Country	Height (ft./m.)	Height (# stories)	Architect
1	Taipei 101	UC04	Taipei, Taiwan	1667/508	101	C.Y. Lee and Partners
2	Petronas Tower 1	1998	Kuala Lumpur, Malaysia	1483/452	88	Cesar Pelli & Associates
3	Petronas Tower 2	1998	Kuala Lumpur, Malaysia	1483/452	88	Cesar Pelli & Associates
4	Sears Tower	1974	Chicago, U.S.	1450/442	110	Skidmore, Owings & Merrill
5	Jin Mao Building	1999	Shanghai, China	1381/421	88	Skidmore, Owings & Merrill
6	Two International Finance Center	2003	Hong Kong, China	1352/412	88	Cesar Pelli & Associates
7	CITIC Plaza	1996	Guangzhou, China	1283/391	80	Dennis Lau & Ng Chun Man & Associates
8	Shun Hing Square	1996	Shenzhen, China	1260/384	69	K.Y. Cheung Design Associates
9	Empire State Building	1931	New York, U.S.	1250/381	102	Shreve, Lamb & Harmon
10	Central Plaza	1992	Hong Kong, China	1227/374	78	Ng Chun Man & Associates
11	Bank of China	1989	Hong Kong, China	1209/369	70	I.M. Pei & Partners
12	Emirates Tower One	1999	Dubai, U.A.E.	1165/355	55	NORR Group Consultants
13	T & C Tower	1997	Kaohsiung, Taiwan	1140/348	85	C.Y. Lee/Hellmuth, Obata & Kassabaum
14	Aon Centre	1973	Chicago, U.S.	1136/346	80	Edward D. Stone
15	The Center	1998	Hong Kong, China	1135/346	79	Dennis Lau & Ng Chun Man & Associates

Tallest Buildings in the World

Rank	Building	Year	City/Country	Height (ft./m.)	Height (# stories)	Architect
16	John Hancock Center	1969	Chicago, U.S.	1127/344	100	Skidmore, Owings & Merrill
17	Burj al Arab Hotel	1999	Dubai, U.A.E.	1053/321	60	W. S. Atkins & Partners
18	Chrysler Building	1930	New York, U.S.	1046/319	77	William van Alen
19	Bank of America Plaza	1993	Atlanta, U.S.	1023/312	55	Kevin Roche, John Dinkeloo & Associates
20	Library Tower	1990	Los Angeles, U.S.	1018/310	75	Pei Cobb Freed & Partners
21	Telekom Malaysia Headquarters	1999	Kuala Lumpur, Malaysia	1017/310	55	Daewoo & Partners
22	Emirates Tower Two	2000	Dubai, U.A.E	1014/309	56	NORR Group Consultants
23	AT&T Corporate Center	1989	Chicago, U.S.	1007/307	60	Skidmore, Owings & Merrill
24	JP Morgan Chase Tower	1982	Houston, U.S.	1002/305	75	I.M. Pei & Partners
25	Baiyoke Tower II	1997	Bangkok, Thailand	997/304	85	Plan Architects Co.
26	Two Prudential Plaza	1990	Chicago, U.S.	995/303	64	Leobl Schlossman Dart & Hackl
27	Kingdom Centre	2001	Riyadh, Saudi Arabia	992/302	30	Ellerbe Becket and Omrania
28	Pyugyong Hotel	1995	Pyongyang, North Korea	984/300	105	Baikdoosan Architects & Engineers
29	First Canadian Place	1975	Toronto, Canada	978/298	72	Bregman + Hamann Architects
30	Wells Fargo Plaza	1983	Houston, U.S.	972/296	71	Skidmore, Owings & Merrill
31	Landmark Tower	1993	Yokohama, Japan	971/296	70	Stubbins Associates
32	Bank of America Center	1984	Seattle, U.S.	967/295	76	Chester Lindsey Architects
33	311 S. Wacker Drive	1990	Chicago, U.S.	961/293	65	Kohn Pedersen Fox Associates
34	SEG Plaza	2000	Shenzen, China	957/292	72	Hua Yi Design
35	American International Building	1932	New York, U.S.	952/290	67	Clinton & Russell
36	Cheung Kong Centre	1999	Hong Kong, China	951/290	70	Cesar Pelli & Associates, Leo A. Daly
37	Key Tower	1991	Cleveland, U.S.	947/289	57	Cesar Pelli & Associates
38	Plaza 66	2001	Shanghai, China	945/288	62	Kohn Pedersen Fox Associates with East China Architecture and Design Institute (ECADI) and Frank C. Y. Feng Architects & Associates

Tallest Buildings in the World

Rank	Building	Year	City/Country	Height (ft./m.)	Height (# stories)	Architect
39	One Liberty Place	1987	Philadelphia, U.S.	945/288	61	Murphy/Jahn
40	Sunjoy Tomorrow Square	2003	Shanghai, China	934/285	59	John Portman and Associates
41	The Trump Building	1930	New York, U.S.	927/283	72	H. Craig Severance
42	Bank of America Plaza	1985	Dallas, U.S.	921/281	72	JPJ Architects
43	Overseas Union Bank Plaza	1986	Singapore	919/280	66	Kenzo Tange Associates
44	Union Overseas Bank Plaza	1992	Singapore	919/280	66	Kenzo Tange Associates
45	Republic Plaza	1995	Singapore	919/280	66	Kisho Kurokawa
46	Citicorp Center	1977	New York, U.S.	915/279	59	The Stubbins Associates
47	Hong Kong New World Building	2001	Shanghai, China	913/278	58	Bregman + Hamann Architects
48	Scotia Plaza	1989	Toronto, Canada	902/275	68	The Webb Zerafa Menkes Housden Partnership
49	Williams Tower	1983	Houston, U.S.	901/275	64	Johnson/Burgee Architects
50	Renaissance Tower	1975	Dallas, U.S.	886/270	56	Skidmore, Owings & Merrill
51	Dapeng International Plaza	UC03	Guangzhou, China	883/269	56	Guangzhou Design Institute
52	21st Century Tower	UC03	Dubai, U.A.E.	883/269	55	WS Atkins & Partners
53	Al Faisaliah Center	2000	Riyadh, Saudi Arabia	876/267	30	Sir Norman Foster & Partners
54	900 N. Michigan Ave.	1989	Chicago, U.S.	871/265	66	Kohn Pedersen Fox Associates
55	Bank of America Center	1992	Charlotte, U.S.	871/265	60	Cesar Pelli & Associates
56	SunTrust Plaza	1992	Atlanta, U.S.	871/265	60	John Portman & Associates
57	Shenzhen Special Zone Daily Tower	1998	Shenzhen, China	866/264	42	n/a
58	Trump World Tower	2001	New York, U.S.	861/262	72	Costas Kondylis & Partners LLP Architects
59	Water Tower Place	1976	Chicago, U.S.	859/262	74	Loebl Schlossman Dart & Hackl
60	Aon Center	1974	Los Angeles, U.S.	858/262	62	Charles Luckman & Associates
61	BCE Place-Canada Trust Tower	1990	Toronto, Canada	856/261	53	Skidmore, Owings & Merrill; Bregman + Hamann

Tallest Buildings in the World

Rank	Building	Year	City/Country	Height (ft./m.)	Height (# stories)	Architect
62	Post & Telecommunication Hub	2002	Guangzhou, China	853/260	66	n/a
63	Transamerica Pyramid	1972	San Francisco, U.S.	853/260	48	William Pereira
64	G. E. Building, Rockefeller Center	1933	New York, U.S.	850/259	70	Raymond Hood
65	Bank One Plaza	1969	Chicago, U.S.	850/259	60	C.F. Murphy
66	Commerzbank Tower	1997	Frankfurt, Germany	850/259	56	Sir Norman Foster & Partners
67	Two Liberty Place	1990	Philadelphia, U.S.	848/258	58	Murphy/Jahn
68	PBCOM Tower	2000	Makati, Philippines	848/258	55	Skidmore,Owings & Merrill; G.F. & Partners
69	Park Tower	2000	Chicago, U.S.	844/257	67	Lucien Lagrange Architects; HKS, Inc.
70	Messeturm	1990	Frankfurt, Germany	843/257	70	Murphy/Jahn
71	USX Tower	1970	Pittsburgh, U.S.	841/256	64	Harrison & Abramovitz
72	Sorrento 1	UC03	Hong Kong, China	840/256	75	n/a
73	Mokdong Hyperion Tower A	2003	Seoul, South Korea	840/256	69	n/a
74	Rinku Gate Tower	1996	Osaka, Japan	840/256	56	Nikken Sekkei
75	The Harbourside	UC03	Hong Kong, China	837/255	74	P & T Architects and Engineers Ltd.
76	Langham Place Office Tower	UC04	Hong Kong, China	837/255	59	Wong & Ouyang Ltd.
77	Capitol Tower	2000	Singapore	833/254	52	RSP Architects Planners & Engineers (Pte) Ltd.
78	Osaka World Trade Center	1995	Osaka, Japan	827/252	55	Nikken Sekkei
79	Rialto Tower	1985	Melbourne, Australia	823/251	63	Gerard de Preu & Partners
80	One Atlantic Center	1987	Atlanta, U.S.	820/250	50	Johnson/Burgee Architects
81	Wisma 46	1995	Jakarta, Indonesia	820/250	46	Zeidler Roberts Partnership with DP Architects
82	Korea Life Insurance Company	1985	Seoul, South Korea	817/249	60	C.M. Park with Skidmore, Owings & Merrill
83	CitySpire	1989	New York, U.S.	814/248	75	Murphy/Jahn
84	One Chase Manhattan Plaza	1961	New York, U.S.	813/248	60	Skidmore, Owings & Merrill

Rank	Building	Year	City/Country	Height (ft./m.)	Height (# stories)	Architect
85	Bank One Tower	1989	Indianapolis, U.S.	811/247	48	The Stubbins Associates
86	Royal Charoen Krung Tower	2001	Bangkok, Thailand	810/247	68	Rangsan Architecture Co., Ltd.
87	Condé Nast Building	1999	New York, U.S.	809/247	48	Fox & Fowle Architects
88	MetLife	1963	New York, U.S.	808/246	59	Emery Roth & Sons, Pietro Belluschi
89	JR Central Towers	2000	Nagoya, Japan	804/245	51	Kohn Pedersen Fox Associates
90	City Gate Tower	2001	Ramat-Gan, Israel	801/244	67	AMAV Architects
91	Shin Kong Life Tower	1993	Taipei, Taiwan	801/244	51	K.M.G. Architects & Engineers
92	Menara Maybank	1988	Kuala Lumpur, Malaysia	799/244	50	Hijjas Kasturi Associates
93	The Tower	2002	Dubai, U.A.E.	797/243	54	Khatib & Alami with Norr Group Consultants Int. Ltd.
94	Tokyo Metropolitan Government	1991	Tokyo, Japan	797/243	48	Kenzo Tange Associates
95	Dalian World Trade Center	2000	Dalian, China	794/242	55	Nadel Architects Inc.
96	Woolworth Building	1913	New York, U.S.	792/241	57	Cass Gilbert
97	Mellon Bank Center	1991	Philadelphia, U.S.	792/241	54	Kohn Pedersen Fox Associates
98	Bank of China Mansion	1999	Qingdao, China	791/241	54	Beijing Architectural Design & Research Institute
99	John Hancock Tower	1976	Boston, U.S.	788/240	60	I.M. Pei & Partners
100	Manulife Plaza	1998	Hong Kong, China	787/240	52	DLN Architects & Engineers

Source: Council on Tall Buildings and Urban Habitat, Illinois Institute of Technology

30 Best Buildings of the 20th Century

The following 30 buildings were judged by a panel of industry experts to be the Best Buildings of the 20th Century. Buildings designed and constructed during the 20th century, regardless of location, were deemed eligible. Buildings were judged based on the following: their influence on the course of 20th-century architecture, significant aesthetic contribution, promotion of design principles which have had a positive impact on the built environment, and/or a lasting impact on the history of the 20th century. The buildings below are listed alphabetically and are not ranked in any order.

Air Force Academy Chapel
Colorado Springs, CO
SOM, 1962

Chrysler Building
New York, NY
William Van Alen, 1930

Dulles Airport
Chantilly, VA
Eero Saarinen, 1962

East Wing, National Gallery
Washington, D.C.
I.M. Pei, 1978

Empire State Building
New York, NY
Shreve, Lamb and Harmon, 1931

Fallingwater
Mill Run, PA
Frank Lloyd Wright, 1936

Flatiron Building
New York, NY
Daniel Burnham, 1902

Gamble House
Pasadena, CA
Greene and Greene, 1909

Getty Center
Los Angeles, CA
Richard Meier, 1997

Glass House
New Canaan, CT
Philip Johnson, 1949

Guggenheim Museum
Bilbao, Spain
Frank Gehry, 1997

Hearst Castle
San Simeon, CA
Julia Morgan, 1927-47

Hong Kong and Shanghai Bank
Hong Kong, China
Norman Foster, 1986

Il Palazzo Hotel
Fukuota, Japan
Aldo Rossi, 1987

John Deere Headquarters
Moline, IL
Eero Saarinen, 1963

John Hancock Building
Chicago, IL
SOM, 1970

30 Best Buildings of the 20th Century

S.C. Johnson & Son Administration Building
Racine, WI
Frank Lloyd Wright, 1939

Kimbell Art Musuem
Fort Worth, TX
Louis Kahn, 1972

La Sagrada Familia
Barcelona, Spain
Antonio Gaudi, 1882-1926

National Farmers' Bank
Owatonna, MN
Louis Sullivan, 1908

Nebraska State Capitol
Lincoln, NE
Bertram Goodhue, 1924

Notre Dame-du-Haut
Ronchamp, France
Le Corbusier, 1955

Salk Institute
La Jolla, CA
Louis Kahn, 1966

Seagram Building
New York, NY
Mies van der Rohe, 1956

Stockholm City Hall
Stockholm, Sweden
Ragnar Östberg, 1923

Sydney Opera House
Sydney, Australia
Jørn Utzon, 1973

Thorncrown Chapel
Eureka Springs, AR
E. Fay Jones, 1980

Tokyo City Hall
Tokyo, Japan
Kenzo Tange, 1991

Villa Savoye
Poissy, France
Le Corbusier, 1929

Woolworth Building
New York, NY
Cass Gilbert, 1913

Source: Counsel House Research

Women in Architecture Timeline

While women still comprise less than a quarter of practicing U.S. architects, the road to attain that level of participation in the field has been bravely and most ably traversed by some genuine trailblazers. Since the late 1800s, women interested in design have been encouraged to work on domestic projects, including interior design, but to leave architecture, and particularly commercial work, to men. Less than 50 years ago, the dean of MIT's school of architecture advised women against entering the profession due to "great obstacles." Facing strong adversity, women have persevered, establishing their own firms, designing landmark buildings, and even raising families. The timeline below illustrates highlights in the continuing struggle for women in the practice and to lead in the field of architecture. For the sake of continuity, we have limited this context line to the United States.

1865 The Massachusetts Institute of Technology (MIT) is founded and along with it the United States' first architecture program, which is only open to men.

1869 Harriet Beecher Stowe (1811–1896) and her sister, domestic economist Catherine Beecher (1800–1878) write the seminal domestic tome *The American Woman's Home.* A central theme in Catherine's other publications as well, the book asserts the domestic superiority of women and celebrates their capacity for self-sacrifice. She includes designs for homes conducive to family life.

1869 Charlotte, North Carolina's Harriet Irwin (1828–1897) is the first woman to patent a dwelling plan. Although she had no formal architectural training, she will design and build at least two more houses.

1876 Mary Nolan (*dates unknown*) of Missouri exhibits a prototype house of interlocking bricks at the Philadelphia Centennial for which she won an award.

1880 Margaret Hicks' (1858–1883) is the first female graduate of the Cornell University architecture program and, according to the Cornell archives, is the first professional woman architect in the United States. Two years prior, in 1878, her sketch of a Workman's Cottage was the first by a woman to appear in an American architectural journal.

1881 At age 25, Louise Blanchard (1856–1913) sets up architectural shop in Buffalo, N.Y., with Robert Bethune. Seven years later (now married) Louise Blanchard Bethune becomes the first woman to be voted a member of The American Institute of Architects. She becomes The American Institute of Architect's first female fellow the following year when all members of the Western Association of Architects are made AIA Fellows.

1890 Sophia Hayden (1868–1953) is the first woman to graduate from the Massachusetts Institute of Technology with a four-year degree in architecture (with honors). Born in Chile, Hayden moved to the United States with her parents when she was six.

1891 Sophia Hayden wins a competition to design the Woman's Building for the 1893 World's Columbian Exposition in Chicago. She is selected for the project by the all-female Board of Lady Managers, who opened the competition to women only. Despite accolades from Richard Morris Hunt and Daniel Burnham, Ms. Hayden suffers a nervous breakdown

Women in Architecture Timeline

following an arduous two-year construction process and leaves the profession.

1894 Julia Morgan (1872–1957) is one of the first women to receive a degree in civil engineering from the University of California at Berkeley. The program now bears her name.

1894 Marion Mahony Griffin (1871–1961) is the second woman to graduate with a four-year degree from MIT's architecture program. She will become the first woman licensed to practice in the state of Illinois and will work from 1895–1909 in Frank Lloyd Wright's Oak Park office, becoming his chief draftsperson. When Wright departs for Europe in 1909, Hermann von Holst agrees to take over the Oak Park office only if Marion Mahoney will join him as a designer. Though she often acts as chief designer, most architectural drawings read "Hermann von Holst, Architect, Marion Mahoney, Associate." In 1911 she marries architect Walter Burley Griffin and dedicates herself to furthering his career, providing support and collaboration.

To date only eight women in the United States are known to have completed four-year programs in architecture.

After two years of tests, Julia Morgan becomes the first woman in the world accepted to L'Ecole de Beaux Arts in Paris. In 1902 at the age of 29, she wins four L'Ecole de Beaux Arts certification medals and becomes the first woman in the world to graduate from this prestigious institution.

1895 Pittsburgh, Pa., architect Elice Mercur (*dates unknown*) is awarded the commission for the Woman's Building at the Cotton States and International Exposition in Atlanta, Ga., by its Board of Women Managers.

1900 By 1900, 39 female graduates are known to have completed formal four-year architectural training programs in the Unites States.

1901 The Fred Harvey Company, a vendor of hospitality services in the Southwest, including the National Parks, hires teacher and California School of Design graduate Mary Jane Colter (1869–1958). A high school graduate at the age of 14, she becomes the company's chief architect and over the course of her 40-year career she is noted for her eye for detail and careful study of Native American architecture. Among her notable hotel, gift shop, and park designs are the Watchtower, Hopi House, and Hermit's Rest at the Grand Canyon National Park in Arizona. She also serves as architect and decorator for the Santa Fe Railway.

1903 Mary Rockwell Hook (1877–1978) is the first woman to enroll in the Chicago Art Institute's architecture department. In 1905, she departs for study in Paris. Upon completing her final examinations at the Atelier Auburtin, a studio of L'Ecole des Beaux Arts, she is doused with buckets of water by French male students. She returns home to Kansas City where her father purchases lots around town for her to design houses on, including the city's first home with an attached garage, the first with a swimming pool, and the first using cast-in-place concrete walls.

1909 Theodate Pope Riddle (1868–1946) designs Middlebury, Connecticut's Westover School. Cass Gilbert writes that it is "the most beautifully planned and designed...girls' school in the country."

Women in Architecture Timeline

1910 In one of the first known female partnerships, Ida Annah Ryan (1883–1960, MIT class of 1905) asks Florence Luscomb (1887–1985, MIT class of 1908) to join her Waltham, Mass., practice. Luscomb remains in the practice until 1917 when she devotes the rest of her life to social and political activism.

1910 Half of the architecture programs in the U.S. still deny entry to women.

1911 Anna Wagner Keichline (1889–1943) graduates from Cornell University's architecture program and becomes the first registered woman architect in Pennsylvania. She will later patent seven inventions, including an improved combined sink and washtub design, a kitchen design that includes sloped countertops and glass-doored cabinets, and K Brick, a hollow fireproof clay brick that was the precursor to the modern concrete block. The American Ceramic Society honored her for this invention in 1937.

1913 Lois Lilly Howe (1864–1964, MIT class of 1890) and Eleanor Manning (1884–1973, MIT class of 1906) form Howe & Manning, the first architecture firm founded by women in Boston and the second in the nation. Mary Almy (1883–1967, MIT class of 1922) joined the firm in 1926. They specialized in domestic architecture and championed the cause of urban and low-income housing. Manning designed the first public, low-income housing in Boston, and Howe focused on small, affordable housing in the suburbs. The firm dissolved in 1937 as a result of the Depression.

Mary Rockwell Hook (*dates unknown*) is selected to design the Pine Mountain Settlement School in Harlan County, Ky. Serving students in the isolated Appalachian mountains of Eastern Kentucky, the Pine Mountain School includes natural elements, such as boulders, in its designs. With no mill nearby, native, chestnut, oak, and poplar trees were cut, dried, and sawn onsite. Today the school serves as an environmental education facility.

1915 Harvard School of Architecture instructor Henry Frost and landscape architect Bremer Pond open the Cambridge School of Architecture and Landscape Architecture in Massachusetts, the first and only program of its kind exclusively for women. Frost had originally been tapped by the head of Harvard Univeristy's Landscape School, James Sturgis Pray, to tutor a woman who wanted to study drafting since Harvard did not accept women into their program. The number of women requesting lessons grew quickly, and so the Cambridge School was born. As of 1930, 83 percent of its graduates will be professionally active.

1919 William Randolph Hearst inherits a quarter million acres in San Simeon, Calif., overlooking the Pacific Ocean. His alleged conversation with Julia Morgan begins "Miss Morgan, we are tired of camping out in the open at the ranch in San Simeon, and I would like to build a little something..." Twenty years later, the Hearst Castle is done. Between 1919–1939, Morgan travels via train to the site 558 times for weekend work sessions. Her fee is estimated at $70,755.

1921 Elizabeth Martini (*dates unknown*) forms the Chicago Drafting Club, later the Women's Architectural Club. The group organizes displays for the Woman's Worlds Fairs of 1927 and 1928 and sponsors an International Exhibition of Women in Architecture and the Allied Arts at Chicago's 1933 World's Fair.

Women in Architecture Timeline

1923 One of the University of Illinois School of Architecture's first female graduates, Alberta Pfeiffer (1899–1994), graduates first in her class and is the first woman to win The American Institute of Architects' School Medal. She worked several years in New York before establishing a practice with her husband in Hadlyme, Conn. She continued to work into the mid-1970s.

1934 Housing reformer Catherine Bauer's (1905–1964) book, *Modern Housing*, espouses European social philosophies of architecture, particularly as related to low-income housing. She later helps develop the U.S. Housing Act of 1937, which provides federal funding for low-income housing.

1938 The Cambridge School of Architecture and Landscape Architecture becomes part of Smith College.

1941 *The Octagon* publishes a landmark report on public housing, prepared by Massachusetts Institute of Technology architecture program graduate Elizabeth Coit (1892–1987) from 1938–1940 under a Langley Fellowship from The American Institute of Architects. The report is revised and published in 1942 in *Architectural Record* as "Housing from the Tenant's Viewpoint." She goes on to spend her career working in public housing, including as principal project planner for the New York City Housing Authority from 1948–1962.

1942 Due to budgetary constraints, Smith College shuts down the Cambridge School of Architecture and Landscape Architecture. By this time, female architecture students can now attend Harvard University and many transfer there.

1944 At age 25, Natalie de Blois (*dates unknown*) graduates from the Columbia University School of Architecture and joins Skidmore, Owings & Merrill's New York office. Following a break when she is awarded a Fullbright Fellowship to the L'Ecole des Beaux-Arts in the 1950s, she returns to SOM and works directly with Gordon Bunshaft as a senior designer. After over 20 years in the position, she is promoted to the level of associate. She never becomes a partner.

1945 Sarah Pillsbury Harkness (*dates unknown*), a 1940 graduate of the Smith College Graduate School of Architecture, becomes a founding member, with Walter Gropius and others, of The Architects Collaborative (TAC) in Cambridge, Mass.

1946 Florence Knoll and her husband Hans form Knoll Associates (now Knoll International), offering modern furniture by well-known designers. Knoll studied closely under Eliel Saarinen at the Cranbrook Academy of Art, then at the Architectural Association in London, and the Illinois Institute of Technology under Mies van der Rohe. She also revolutionized the look and function of American office interiors, ideas that were revolutionary in the 1950s but are still widely used today. Florence Knoll Bassett was awarded the National Medal of Arts in 2002 for "profoundly influence[ing] post-World War II design."

1948 *Architectural Record* runs a two-part article entitled "A Thousand Women in Architecture." At that time, the magazine profiled 18 of the 1,119 women trained to practice architecture, according to research by the Women's Architectural Association and the deans of architecture schools across the U.S.

Women in Architecture Timeline

1948 Eleanor Raymond (1888–1989), an early graduate of the Cambridge School of Architecture and Landscape Architecture and a colleague of school founder Henry Atherton Frost from 1919–1935, designs the Dover Sun House in Dover, Mass. It is the first occupied solar-powered house in the U.S. Her career will span more that 50 years; in 1961 she is elected to The American Institute of Architects' College of Fellows.

1952 As Julia Morgan retires, she destroys her office records. During her lengthy career Morgan designed over 800 buildings.

1955 Pietro Belluschi, the dean of the Massachusett's School of Architecture writes in an essay entitled, "The Exceptional One": *"I know some women who have done well at it, but the obstacles are so great that it takes an exceptional girl to make a go of it. If she insisted upon becoming an architect I would try to dissuade her. If then she was still determined, I would give her my blessing that she could be that exceptional one."*

Jane Hall Johnson (1919–2001) graduates from Harvard with a bachelor's degree in architecture. She receives a degree in civil engineering in 1941 from the Missouri School of Mines and works as a structural engineer before deciding to return to school. She later receives her M.Arch from Harvard University. In 1970 she forms the firm of Jane C. Hall, Architect in St. Louis with her engineer husband, Benjamin Johnson. She retires in 1997.

1956 Lutah Maria Riggs (1896–1984), the first licensed female architect in California and the first woman in the state to be elected to The American Institute of Architect's College of Fellows, produces her most famous work, Santa Barbara's Vedanta Temple. She is a 1919 graduate of the University of California, Berkeley.

1958 An architect named Rose Connor, AIA (*dates unknown*), combs the records of the Architecture Examining Boards of all the states and finds a total of 320 registered women architects. This represents one percent of the total number of registered architects in the United States at this time. No women are registered in seven states.

1960 Beverly A. Willis, a native of Oklahoma whose parents left her and a brother in an orphanage during the depression, establishes Willis and Associates in San Francisco. Though she began her career as a designer in 1954, Willis never attends architecture school and does not become a licensed architect until 1966. Still, she produces many significant architecture and design projects in that city, beginning with retail store design and including many residences, community planning projects, the San Francisco Ballet Building, a master plan for the University of California at San Francisco, and the design and master planning for Yerba Buena Gardens, a 24-acre mixed-use development. She also designs the Aliamanu Valley Community for the Army Corps of Engineers, housing 11,500 people in Hawaii. In the early 1970s, her firm becomes a pioneer in the use of computer-aided design and planning.

Joan Edelman Goody marries fellow architect Marvin E. Goody, and they become partners in the Boston firm Goody, Clancy and Associates. In a 1998 interview with the *Boston Globe Magazine*, Goody says the 60+ member firm is "probably half women now. I was lucky. I married a very supportive architect husband, and I had wonderful partners."

1961 Senior editor of *Architectural Forum* magazine from 1952–1962, Jane Jacobs's seminal work *The Life & Death of Great American Cities* is published.

Women in Architecture Timeline

1962 Jane Jacobs organizes The Committee to Save the West Village and succeeds in defeating an urban renewal plan for New York's historic Greenwich Village. Many such groups were formed in the 1960s, as two pieces of legislation, The Housing Act of 1949 and the Highway Trust Act of 1956, triggered an aggressive alteration of the urban landscape. The Housing Act, promising "a decent house and suitable living environment for every American Family," also contained a provision allowing the exercise of eminent domain, allowing states to seize private property for "the public benefit." The Highway Trust Act provided 90 percent federal funding to states for their portion of the interstate highway system. As urban areas are razed for highways and developer's projects, many organizations and advocacy groups formed to challenge the institutions behind urban renewal.

1963 Ada Louise Huxtable is named the architecture critic of *The New York Times*, the first such staff position at any U.S. newspaper. Huxtable will receive the Pulitzer Prize for "distinguished criticism" in 1970.

1972 Denise Scott Brown turns down the deanship of the School of Art and Architecture at Yale University to continue her work with the firm of Venturi & Rauch, now Venturi, Scott Brown & Associates, Inc. With Robert Venturi and Steven Izenour she writes *Learning from Las Vegas*, one of the seminal texts of postmodernism, it celebrates the American commercial strip and encourages architects to broaden their acceptance of the tastes and values of ordinary people and everyday landscapes.

The American Institute of Architects establishes the Whitney M. Young Jr. Award, awarded to an individual or organization that demonstrates an outstanding commitment to expanding the profession. In 1960, Whitney M. Young Jr. was the executive director of the Urban League and urged the profession to reach out to women and minorities in an address at the AIA's national convention.

1973 Architect Beverly Willis becomes the first woman to chair the Federal Construction Council of the National Academy of Science. The Council is comprised of directors of all construction departments within the Federal government and is charged with overseeing joint agency cooperation. In 1976 she will be one of two architects selected as a member of the U.S. Delegation to the United Nations Habitat One in Vancouver, Canada.

Sharon Sutton, a classically trained French horn player with a bachelor's degree in music, receives her M.Arch. from the Columbia University Graduate School of Architecture and Planning. She will go on to become the first African-American woman to become a full professor in an accredited architecture professional degree program. Sutton pursues a distinguished career of writing and researching and is later presented with the Association of Collegiate Schools of Architecture Distinguished Professor Award in 1996.

1977 Miami, Fla., native Laurinda Spear forms the modernist architecture firm Arquitectonica in that city with Bernardo Fort-Brescia. Today, the firm has expanded to New York, Los Angeles, Paris, Hong Kong, Shanghai, Manila, Lima, Buenos Aires, and San Paulo. A fellow of The American Institute of Architects, she is the winner of the Rome Prize in Architecture and is a member of the Interior Design Hall of Fame, among other honors.

Women in Architecture Timeline

1977 Iraqi-born Zaha Hadid graduates from London's Architectural Association, the winner of its Diploma Prize, and joins Rem Koolhaas and Elia Zenghelis at the Office for Metropolitan Architecture (OMA). She opens her own office in 1979 and goes on to become one of the world's great architectural theorists. In addition to teaching, Hadid enters a multitude of research-based competitions and designs a host of theoretical projects, most unbuilt. Her varied projects include exhibits of her paintings and drawings, furniture design, stage set design (including the Pet Shop Boys World Tour 1999/2000), and museum exhibition design.

1980 M. Rosaria Piomelli becomes the first woman dean of a U.S. architecture school when she is named to head the City College of New York College of Architecture. Before forming her own New York City firm in 1974, she worked for several firms, including I.M. Pei and Partners.

Elizabeth Plater-Zyberk and Andrés Duany found the Miami, Fla., practice Duany Plater-Zyberk & Company and quickly establish themselves as unparalleled experts in New Urbanism and town planning, which they pioneered with their now famous town of Seaside, Fla.

1981 Two surveys (1974 and 1981) of women in architecture firms by The American Institute of Architects reveal a majority experience discriminatory practices in school and later at work. Despite these negative responses, seven out of ten say they would choose architecture again if they had the option of changing careers.

While still an undergraduate at Yale University, architecture student Maya Lin wins a competition to design the Vietnam Veterans Memorial on the mall in Washington D.C. She is 21 years old.

Illinois architect Carol Ross Barney founds Carol Ross Barney Architects (now Ross Barney + Jankowski Architects). Aimed squarely at the commercial market, the firm insinuates itself into the fabric of Chicago and becomes one of the city's largest woman-owned practices. In 2003, its Web site notes: "The makeup of our staff is a reflection of our belief that diversity is a desirable element in the design studio. Women compose 50 percent of our employees, ethnic minorities are approximately 30 percent (the remainder are very sensitive modern males)."

1983 The American Institute of Architects begins collecting data on the gender and race of its members.

1985 The International Archive of Women in Architecture (IAWA) is established as a joint program of the College of Architecture and Urban Studies and the University Libraries at Virginia Tech. The collection acquires, preserves, and stores the professional papers of women architects, landscape architects, designers, architectural historians and critics, urban planners, and the records of women's architectural organizations from around the world (http://spec.lib.vt.edu/iawa/).

Norma Merrick Sklarek becomes the first African-American woman in the United States to form her own firm, Siegel-Sklarek-Diamond. She is also the first African-American woman in the country to become a licensed architect and the first African-American woman to be inducted as a fellow of The American Institute of Architects. She is a graduate of Barnard College and the Columbia University School of Architecture.

1986 Collaborating since 1977, Billie Tsien and Tod Williams officially establish Tod Williams Billie Tsien & Associates in New York City. The firm will go to on to produce a body of

Women in Architecture Timeline

high profile, highly regarded projects, including Feinberg Hall at Princeton University, The Whitney Museum of American Art Downtown Branch in New York City, the Neurosciences Institute in LaJolla, Calif., and The Museum of Folk Art in New York City. With a fine arts degree from Yale and an M.Arch. from UCLA, Ms. Tsien is a design innovator, producing work that marries art and architecture in unique ways.

1987 Skidmore, Owings & Merrill elects Marilyn Jordan Taylor a partner of the firm. She joined the firm in 1971 working on urban design and transportation projects. From 1978–1985 Taylor served as director of design for the Stations Program of the Northeast Corridor Improvement Project, a $25 million Federally-funded project investing in intercity rail stations between Washington, D.C. and Boston. In 1985 she assumed leadership of an expanded Urban Design and Planning practice within the firm, which includes billions of dollars of rail, airport, waterfront, subway, ferry and land-use projects. She is twice named to *Crain's* list of Most Influential Women in New York. At the time of this writing, Taylor is the only current female partner at SOM.

1991 In Washington, D.C., architects Debra Lehman-Smith and James McLeish form Lehman-Smith + McLeish (LSM). The firm will grow to over 40 staff members with services in strategic planning, master planning, architectural design, interior design, and product design. *Contract Design* magazine names LSM as one of the 20 Best Interior or Design firms from 1975–1999.

1992 American Institute of Architect's President Cecil Steward convenes a Task Force on Diversity.

L. Jane Hastings becomes the first woman Chancellor of The American Institute of Architects' College of Fellows.

1993 Susan Maxman becomes the first female President of The American Institute of Architects.

Elizabeth Plater-Zyberk, is named dean of Florida's University of Miami School of Architecture. She establishes a master of architecture program in Suburb and Town Design.

1995 Chicago, Ill. architect Sally Lynn Levine's multi-media exhibit "ALICE (Architecture Lets in Chicks, Except) Through the Glass Ceiling," opens in San Francisco, exploring the status of women in the field of architecture. A co-founder of CARY (Chicks in Architecture Refuse to Yield), a Chicago women architects group, Levine's teaching credits include architecture, design, drawing, and digital design and animation at the School of the Art Institute of Chicago, the Massachusetts College of Art, and the University of Wisconsin, Milwaukee.

1998 Ann R. Chaintreuil becomes the first female president of the National Council of Architectural Registration Boards (NCARB).

Heralded as a "cultural visionary," Minneapolis, Minn., architect Sarah Susanka writes the bestseller *The Not So Big House.* Espousing a philosophy of better, not bigger, residential architecture, she is a guest on television shows, popular speaker, and the subject of numerous magazine and newspaper articles. *U.S. News & World Report* pronounces her an "innovator in American culture" upon the book's publication. Susanka will go on to write three more similarly themed books with a fourth due in 2004. In 2001 *Fast Company*

Women in Architecture Timeline

magazine names her to their list of "Fast 50" innovators whose achievements have helped change society, following *Newsweek* magazine's 2000 selection of Susanka as a "top newsmaker" for the year.

2000 An *Architectural Record* editorial by Robert Ivy reveals that in 1997, women comprised around 9 percent of The American Institute of Architects' membership roster and approximately 10 percent of licensed architects were women.

2001 According to the National Architectural Accrediting Board's annually survey, of the 1,038 tenured architecture school faculty members, 16 percent are female and 8 percent are ethnic minorities. Females comprise 37 percent of the architecture students, with ethnic minorities accounting for 15 percent. Of the architecture graduates, 34 percent are female and 20 percent are ethnic minorities.

Cornell University's College of Architecture, Art and Planning announces the appointment of Nasrine Seraji-Bozorgzad as chair of its Department of Architecture. Born in Tehran and trained in London, Seraji is the principal of Paris' Atelier Seraji and in addition to her visiting professorships in the U.S., exhibitions, and lectures, she is a professor at Vienna's Akademie der Bildenden Künste. She is the first woman to head a department of architecture in the Ivy League.

Following the terrorist attacks of September 11, architect Beverly Willis and *Metropolis* magazine Editor-in-Chief Susan Szenasy form Rebuild Downtown Our Town (R.Dot). Concerned with communicating a vision for the disaster site to the media, the public, and decision makers, the group is comprised of architects, lower Manhattan residents, businesses, community associations, and public officials and appointees.

Architect Sandra Mendler, vice president and sustainable design principal at HOK, is named the first recipient of the Sustainable Design Leadership Awards for her leadership and commitment to environmental issues in the design profession.

2002 Of the 102,002 licensed architects in the United States, 13 percent are women and 8 percent are ethnic minorities, according to the 2000-2002 AIA Firm Survey. Roughly 16 percent of full-time architectural faculty in U.S. colleges and universities are women. Women continue to make up 9 percent of the total AIA membership.

MIT employs 154 women on its architecture department faculty. This equates to 16 percent of the total architecture faculty of 956 members. Over the same period, the proportion of female undergraduates has risen rapidly to 42 percent.

Maya Lin is named an alumni fellow of the Yale Corporation. She is the first artist to serve on the Yale Corporation and the first Asian-American woman trustee in Yale University's history.

Toshiko Mori is named chair of the Harvard Graduate School of Design's Department of Architecture. She studied under John Hejduk at Cooper Union and later received her M.Arch. from Harvard, working first for Edward Larrabee Barnes and then opening her own practice, Toshiko Mori Architect, in 1981. She began teaching at Cooper Union in 1980 and joined the GSD staff in 1995.

Women in Architecture Timeline

2003 The 2003 AIA Firm Survey (reporting data from 2002) concludes that despite a period of economic weakness, women and minorities made significant gains over previous studies. The number of female registered architects rose to 20 percent from under 14 percent in 1999; racial and ethnic minorities comprised more than 11 percent, up from 6 percent.

The first woman ever to design an American museum, Zaha Hadid's Contemporary Arts Center in Cincinnati opens to great acclaim.

New Urbanists Elizabeth Plater-Zyberk and Andrés Duany announce the launch of The Fund for New Urbanism LLC, a real estate development company. The goal of the enterprise is to assist municipalities seeking alternatives to suburban sprawl. Partner Andrés Duany says the Fund will option and permit at least 10 New Urbanist Projects within 30 months.

Source: Counsel House Research

World's Best Skylines

This list ranks the impressiveness of the world's skylines by measuring the density and height of the skyscrapers in each city. Each building over 295 feet (90 meters) tall contributes points to its home city's score equal to the number of feet it exceeds this benchmark height. This list also provides the name of the tallest buildings in each city and its height.

An explanation of how the ranking is calculated and a ranking of more than 100 skylines can be found at *www.library.tudelft.nl/~egram/skylines.htm.*

Ranking	Points	City/Country	# Buildings over 295 feet/90 meters	Tallest Bldg. (with height)
1	99,031	Hong Kong, China	3,329	Union Square (1,555 ft, 474 m)
2	33,912	New York, U.S. (incl. Jersey City)	825	One World Trade Center* (1,368 ft, 417 m, destroyed)
3	14,207	Tokyo, Japan	434	Tokyo Metropolitan Government Bldg. (797 ft, 243 m)
4	13,629	Chicago, U.S.	312	Sears Tower (1,450 ft, 442 m)
5	12,616	Shanghai, China	358	Shangahi World Financial Center (1,620 ft, 494 m)
6	7,334	Bangkok, Thailand	234	Baiyoke Tower II (997 ft, 304 m)
7	6,411	Singapore, Singapore	246	United Overseas Bank Plaza (919 ft, 280 m)
8	6,295	Kuala Lumpur, Malaysia	174	Petronas Tower I (1,483 ft, 452 m)
9	5,785	Seoul, South Korea	153	Tower Palace 3, Tower G (866 ft, 264 m)
10	5,031	Manila, Philippines (incl. Makati, Mandaluyong, Ortigas, Quezon City)	144	PBCOM Tower (850 ft, 259 m)
11	4,681	Toronto, Canada	188	First Canadian Place (978 ft, 298 m)
12	4,460	Sydney, Australia	127	Citibank Centre (incl. spire) (797 ft, 243 m)
13	4,457	Houston, U.S.	101	JP Chase Tower (1,002 ft, 305 m)
14	4,098	Shenzhen, China	106	Shun Hing Square (1,260 ft, 384 m)
15	3,529	Guangzhou, China	77	CITIC Plaza (1,283 ft, 391 m)

World's Best Skylines

Ranking	Points	City/Country	# Buildings over 295 feet/90 meters	Tallest Bldg. (with height)
16	3,406	Osaka, Japan	88	Rinku Gate Tower (840 ft, 256 m)
17	3,404	Los Angeles, U.S.	76	Library Tower (1,018 ft, 310 m)
18	3,316	Melbourne, Australia	83	Eureka Tower (974 ft, 297 m)
19	3,074	San Francisco, U.S.	96	Transamerica Pyramid (853 ft, 260 m)
20	3,064	Sao Paulo, Brazil	183	Palacio Zarzur Kogan (620 ft, 189 m)
21	2,929	Beijing, China	96	China World Trade Center (1,082 ft, 330 m)
22	2,914	Curitiba, Brazil	119	Ecotower Tower 1 (55 fls.)
23	2,712	Dallas, U.S.	61	Bank of America Plaza (921 ft, 281 m)
24	2,671	Dubai, U.A.E.	53	Emirates Towers One (1,165 ft, 355 m)
25	2,624	Atlanta, U.S.	69	Bank of America Plaza (1,023 ft, 312 m)

* In memory of 9/11, New York's score will not be adjusted until the area has been rebuilt.

Source: Egbert Gramsbergen and Paul Kazmierczak

5

Sustainable/ Green Design

Sustainable design is a design philosophy that is increasingly becoming a mainstream practice. That our built environment has a profound impact on our natural environment, economy, health, and productivity makes this even more imperative. Recent winners of sustainable design awards–buildings, products, and leaders; organizations devoted to developing and promoting green design; guiding principles to aid designers in their approach; and a timeline of the movement can be found in this chapter. A presentation on Old and New Values in Eco Design from the 6th International Design Resource Awards can be found on page 29.

BSA Sustainable Design Awards

Every two years, the Boston Society of Architects' Architects for Social Responsibility and AIA New York's Committee on the Environment present the Sustainable Design Awards. Designers and projects from around the world are eligible with the primary criteria being that they "contribute to the creation of a sustainable world."

For more information, visit the Boston Society of Architects on the Internet at *www.architects.org* or contact them at 617-951-1433.

Honor Award for Design Excellence

2003 Winners

The Red Centre, The University of New South Wales
Kensington, Australia
Francis-Jones Morehen Thorp/MGT Sydney (Australia)

Citation for Design

International Banking Administrative Headquarters, Norddeutsche Landesbank Hannover, Germany
Behnisch, Behnisch & Partner Architekten (Germany)

Development Resource Center
Chattanooga, TN
Croxton Collaborative Architects and Artech Design Group, a joint venture (US)

Nonprofit Association Office and Training Facility
Ankeny, IA
RDG Bussard Dikis (US)

Jury

Dan Arons, Tsoi/Kobus & Associates (chair)
Jean Carroon, Goody, Clancy & Associates
Ken Fisher, Gensler
John Hess, Vanderweil Engineers
Rafael Pelli, Cesar Pelli & Associates

Source: Boston Society of Architects

> There isn't a human being on Earth who doesn't have an aesthetic response to nature, and that this response is deeply embedded in our genes. Until recently this intuitive understanding has been incorporated into and celebrated in our architecture.
>
> **Stephen Kellert**

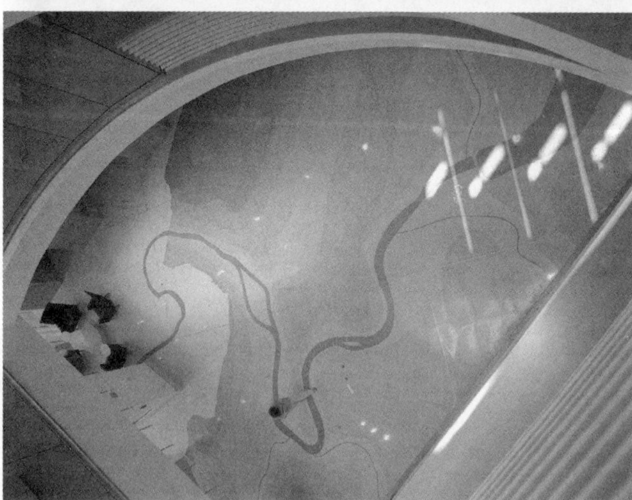

Above: The Development Resource Center, the recipient of a 2003 BSA Sustainable Design Award, is a silver-level LEED-certified building designed for the City of Chattanooga. Human well-being and productivity is enhanced through daylighting by use of deep daylighting louvers at upper windows, selective glazing, sloping ceiling geometries, and photo-dimming of electric lighting. *Bottom*: The floor in the lobby depicts the local topography, including the Tennessee River, which runs through downtown Chattanooga. *Photos by Timothy Hursley, © Croxton Collaborative Architects, PC.*

Cradle to Cradle Design Protocol

In 2002, McDonough Braungart Design Chemistry (MBDC), the private sustainable product and process design consultancy co-founded by American architect William McDonough and German chemist Michael Braungart, formed a nonprofit organization called GreenBlue to disseminate its Cradle to Cradle Design Framework. As opposed to traditional cradle to grave production processes in which materials eventually are landfilled or incinerated, Cradle to Cradle (C2C) is a model of sustainable production in which all waste materials are productively reincorporated into new production and use phases, or closed loops. This "eco-effective" method of production seeks to solve rather than to merely manage the problems currently created by industry.

The Cradle to Cradle Design Protocol assesses materials used in products and processes based on the "Intelligent Products System," designed by Michael Braungart and colleagues at the Environmental Protection Encouragement Agency (EPEA). Materials in products are inventoried and evaluated, and finally placed in one of four categories: Green, Yellow, Orange or Red, based on human health and environmental relevance criteria.

Green: Little or no risk; the chemical is acceptable.

Yellow: Low to moderate risk. The chemical is acceptable for use in the desired application until a green alternative is found.

Orange: No indication of high-risk chemical; a complete assessment is not possible due to lack of information.

Red: High risk. Red chemicals should be phased out as soon as possible and include all known or suspected carcinogens, endocrine disruptors, mutagens, reproductive toxins, and teratogens.

Following assessment, the materials in a product are optimized by selecting Green category replacements for the Red category substances as they become available.

More information about Protocol and other Cradle to Cradle initiatives, including the Chemical Profiles Knowledge Base, can be obtained through GreenBlue at *www.greenblue.org* or (434) 817-1425.

Source: GreenBlue

Declaration of Interdependence for a Sustainable Future

Adopted by the International Union of Architects (UIA) at their 1993 World Congress of Architects, the Declaration of Interdependence for a Sustainable Future was developed over the course of the event by a core group of architects, with input from the thousands of design professionals in attendance. The theme of the Congress was "Architecture at the Crossroads: Designing for a Sustainable Future." The Declaration is a statement of commitment on behalf of design professionals world-wide to "place environmental and social sustainability at the core of our practices..." with an affirmation that these professionals "adopt a world view which embraces individual and collective interdependence with the local and global environment as the basis of a New Design Paradigm of Environmental Interdependence." The Declaration was signed by both the presidents of the UIA and The American Institute of Architects, Olufemi Majekodunmi and Susan A. Maxman. To promote the realization of the Declaration's ideas, a set of principles, which are included below, and practices were also drafted as a supplement to the document.

The complete text of the Declaration can be found on the UIA's Web site at *www.uia-architectes.org*.

Principles

Principle 1

Individually and collectively the members of the Architecture Profession will advise their clients and assist with the education of the broader community on the environmental implications of development trends, strategies and policies.

Principle 2

The Architecture Profession will engage with local communities in formulating appropriate strategies and design guidelines for sustainable human settlement which are economically and environmentally appropriate to their particular culture and place.

Principle 3

Architects will, through their work seek to give full expression to a culture of interdependence with the environment.

Principle 4

Architects will advance ecologically sustainable development by contributing to and supporting appropriate designs, products, services and technologies.

Declaration of Interdependence for a Sustainable Future

Principle 5

Architects should promote the development of an ecologically sustainable future for the Planet and ensure that development strategies, design concepts and innovations which are consistent with, or improve the prospect of, ecological sustainability are made available globally, including to disadvantaged groups and nations, with appropriate mechanism to protect intellectual property.

Principle 6

In developing ecologically sustainable building and settlement practices all sources of relevant knowledge and methods, including those of indigenous people, should be considered.

Principle 7

Architects should promote healthy and environmentally responsible living and behavioural patterns and develop designs and technologies in support of such lifestyles.

Principle 8

Architects will promote development strategies and projects which anticipate the needs, and recognise the rights of present and future generations.

Principle 9

Architects will, through their practices, implement the International Conventions and Agreements for protection of the rights and well being of the Earth and its peoples, the integrity and diversity of the Cultural Heritage, Monuments and Sites, and the biodiversity, integrity and sustainability of the global ecosystem.

Principle 10

The initial education and Continuing Professional Development of Architects should recognise the need for a wide range of knowledge and insights from the Arts, Culture and Humanities, the Natural and Social Sciences, and the Technologies as a basis for understanding the behaviour and management of ecological systems, and for creating ecologically sustainable forms of production, development and settlement.

Source: International Union of Architects

Dubai International Award for Best Practices in Improving the Living Environment

The United Nations' Center for Human Settlements (HABITAT), in conjunction with the Municipality of Dubai, United Arab Emirates, biennially awards the Dubai International Award for Best Practices in Improving the Living Environment to initiatives that have made outstanding contributions to improving the quality of life in cities and communities worldwide. The first Best Practices award was presented in 1996 following an international conference on best practices held in Dubai. Each project is reviewed for its compliance with the three criteria for a best practice: impact, partnership, and sustainability. The award is open to all organizations, including governments and public and private groups. Winners receive a $30,000 prize, trophy and certificate. In addition, all entries are listed in a Best Practices database at *www.bestpractices.org* that contains over 1100 solutions to the common social, economic and environmental problems of an urbanizing world.

For additional information, contact HABITAT at (212) 963-4200, or on the Internet at *www.bestpractices.org*.

2002 Winners

Humanitarian News Agency
Argentina

Programme d'Assainissement et Protection de l'Environnement
Benin

Gender and Citizenship Programm
Santo Andre, Brazil

Livable Region Strategic Plan for Greater Vancouver
Vancouver, Canada

Action Plan for Sustainable Guangzhou
Guangzhou, China

Relocation of backyard tenants
Namibia

Women's contribution in sustainable rural development
Lebanon

Mother Centre International Network
Germany

Area-based assessment of property tax in Patna
Patna, India

Protection and rehabilitation of the heritage site of Santiago de Compostela
Spain

Jury

Hon. Rosa Russo Jervolino, honorary chair (Italy)
Dr. Sang Don Lee (Korea)
Hussain Nasser Ahmed Lootah (UAE)
Benigna Mukibi, co-chair (Uganda)
Barbara Pyle (US)
Anne Ruden (Norway)

Source: United Nations' Center for Human Settlements

Green Building Leadership Awards

The U.S. Green Building Council's (USGBC) Green Building Leadership Awards are presented in three categories: The Green Business Award honors an individual or company that has advanced the green building market through innovation; The Green Public Service Award is presented to an individual or organization for significant contributions in advancing green building through changes in policies, codes and other means; and the USGBC Leadership Award is presented to a leader in the USBBC and in the industry for advancing the mission of the Council. The leading U.S. coalition for the advancement of buildings that are environmentally responsible, profitable and healthy, the U.S. Green Building Council offers a variety of services including the industry-standard LEED Green Building Rating System™ (see page 412). Nominations for the Leadership Awards are made in August; awards are presented in November at the International Green Building Conference and Exposition.

For additional information, visit the U.S. Green Building Council's Web site at *www.usgbc.org*.

2002 Winners

Green Building Business Award

Ray Anderson, Interface, Inc.

Green Public Service Award—Non-government

Pliny Fisk, Center for Maximum Potential Building Systems

Green Public Service Award—Government

Governor George Pataki, New York

USGBC Leadership Award

Rob Watson, Natural Resources Defense Council

Source: U.S. Green Building Council

GreenBlue

GreenBlue began as a nexus of projects at McDonough Braungart Design Chemistry (MBDC), the private sustainable product and process design consultancy co-founded by American architect William McDonough and German chemist Michael Braungart in 1995. MBDC developed the Cradle to Cradle Design Protocol (see pg. 401), and established the nonprofit GreenBlue in 2002 to disseminate Cradle to Cradle information and resources. Cradle to Cradle (C2C) promotes eco-effective production, where all products are constructed from nutrients that replenish the earth (biological nutrients) or nutrients that can be infinitely recycled (technical nutrients). The name GreenBlue refers to these two types of building blocks: biological nutrients (green) and technical nutrients (blue). In addition to developing the Cradle to Cradle Design Framework, MBDC has produced C2CSpec, the Chemical Profiles Knowledge Base, and C2C Training Module. GreenBlue makes the C2C protocol available for general use.

Address

P.O. Box 2001
Charlottesville, VA 22901
Telephone: (434) 817-1424
Fax: (434) 817-1425
Internet: www.greenblue.org

> Design is the first signal of human intention.
>
> **William McDonough**

The Hannover Principles

After being selected to host the 2000 World's Fair "Humanity, Nature, and Technology," the City of Hannover, Germany commissioned renown sustainable design leader William McDonough to develop a set of guiding design principles for the event. In conjunction with Dr. Michael Braungart and the Environmental Protection Encouragement Agency in Hamburg, Germany, William McDonough Architects produced a list of issues inherent to sustainable design that has become a fundamental primer in its philosophy and practice. Universally recognized as a seminal expression on environmentally intelligent design, the Principles have inspired and influenced a wide array of works and documents, ranging from the International Union of Architects' "Declaration of Interdependence" to the U.S. General Services Administration's Guidelines for Sustainability.

The Principles conclude with the statement: "The Hannover Principles should be seen as a living document committed to the transformation and growth in the understanding of our interdependence with nature, so that they may adapt as our knowledge of the world evolves."

For the full text of the Principles, see the William McDonough + Partners Web site at *www.mcdonoughpartners.com/projects/p_hannover.html.*

1. **Insist on rights of humanity and nature to co-exist** in a healthy, supportive, diverse and sustainable condition.

2. **Recognize interdependence.** The elements of human design interact with and depend upon the natural world, with broad and diverse implications at every scale. Expand design considerations to recognize even distant effects.

3. **Respect relationships between spirit and matter.** Consider all aspects of human settlement including community, dwelling, industry, and trade in terms of existing and evolving connections between spiritual and material consciousness.

4. **Accept responsibility for the consequences of design,** decisions upon human well-being, the viability of natural systems, and their right to co-exist.

5. **Create safe objects of long-term value.** Do not burden future generations with requirements for maintenance or vigilant administration of potential design due to the careless creation of products, processes, or standards.

6. **Eliminate the concept of waste.** Evaluate and optimize the full life-cycle of products and processes to approach the state of natural systems, in which there is no waste.

7. **Rely on natural energy flows.** Human designs should, like the living world, derive their creative forces from perpetual solar income. Incorporate this energy efficiently and safely for responsible use.

The Hannover Principles

8. **Understand the limitations of design.** No human creation lasts forever and design does not solve all problems. Those who create and plan should practice humility in the face of nature. Treat nature as a model or mentor, not as an inconvenience to be evaded or controlled.

9. **Seek constant improvement by the sharing of knowledge.** Encourage direct and open communication between colleagues, patrons, manufacturers, and users to link long-term sustainable considerations with ethical responsibility, and re-establish the integral relationship between natural processes and human activity.

Source: William McDonough + Partners

Did you know...

New York City's Condé Nast Building (Fox & Fowle Architects, 1999) is the city's first green skyscraper. The buildings' photovoltaic panels and fuel cells help reduce energy costs by 20 to 30 percent annually.

International Design Resource Awards

The International Design Resource Awards (IDRA) honor products and projects which are created of sustainable or reused materials and are designed for disassembly and reuse, recycling, or composting at the end of their lifecycles. Originally created in 1994, the goal of the program was to help create new markets for recycled materials by encouraging designers to give them new life. Commercially viable examples of lighting, furniture, packaging, consumer products, clothing, building components and architecture are eligible for entry. A jury selects the first place winners and honorable mentions in both the student and professional categories. The title of the 2003-2003 competition, which was judged and celebrated in Japan, was "Design With Memory™: An Adventure in New Materials and Sustainable Design." The competition is coordinated by the Design Resource Institute in Seattle.

For additional information, visit the Design Resource Institute on the Internet at *www.designresource.org* or call (206) 789-0949. Photos of some of the winning projects and the speech given at the award ceremony in Japan on the idea of Design With Memory can be found on page 29.

2002-03 Winners

First Place, Professionals

Yolanda Collection
Gerard Minakawa (US)

Are translucent structures possible?
James Roddis (UK)

OURO
Lea Bogdan (US)

SKO Nikepark
Michael Delaney (US)

Island Wood
Mithun Architects + Designers + Planners (US)

CLIMA & TEMPO BENCH
Colin Reedy (US)

"ronde " Chained Rings
Michiaki Nakamura (Japan)

Reco Project
Nobuyuki Ishimaru (Japan)

First Place, Students

Terracell
Lemmon Michael (US)

DRIVE ON
Andreas Unterschuetz (US)

Plastic Bags Products
Karin Carter (US)

Cumulous Project
Michael McAllister (US)

Modular Hinge Sandal
Arvind Gupta (US)

PLASTIFC BAG ROBBER
Kazutoshi Tsuda, Saori Kudo, Aimi Matsuo (Japan)

Charcoal Hanger
Koji Takashi (Japan)

International Design Resource Awards

Honorable Mention, Professionals

Tectonic Plate series
James Thurman (US)

DESKTOP MEMORY PLAYER
D. Jerry Elmore (US)

Record Bowl Products
Jeff Davis (US)

Healing Resort Shimanto Eco-Lodge
Takatoshi Ishiguro (Japan)

LIGHT SHELL
Yoichiro Kishimoto (Japan)

Oyado Yoshimizu Ginza Building
Yoshimi Nakagawa (Japan)

Honorable Mention, Students

Varius
Heather Curtin (US)

GreenWare
Carlson Julia (US)

Shagbag
Peter Bristol (US)

Umbrella Skirt
Tiffany Threadgould (US)

Warm Wellies
Dominic Byrne (UK)

ECOVER
Sarah Lloyd (UK)

Bio T
Tisak Ongwattanakul (US)

Straw Links
Jacques Abelman (France)

TULIP
Tyson Atwell (US)

LINKa CARPET
Danielle Spector (US)

The Newspaper Chair
Yosuke Izaki (Japan)

Chalk Drop
Rie Akimoto (Japan)

Source: Design Resource Institute

> Human subtlety will never devise an invention more beautiful, more simple, or more direct than does Nature.
>
> **Leonardo da Vinci**

Joslyn Castle Institute for Sustainable Communities

Housed in Omaha, Nebraska's historic 1902 Joslyn Castle, the Joslyn Castle Institute for Sustainable Communities is a partnership among Nebraska state government, the Joslyn Art Museum, the University of Nebraska College of Architecture, and other public and private organizations. The Institute focuses on promoting sustainable development through outreach and education programs, as well as research. Its goal is to encourage communities to develop by balancing economic, social and environmental needs. The institute is one of 18 centers worldwide in partnership with the United Nations Centre for Human Settlement (UNCHS) in its Best Practices in Local Leadership Program (BLP).

Address

3902 Davenport Street
Omaha, NE 68131
Telephone: (402) 595-1902
Internet: www.ecospheres.com

Did you know...

On July 17, 2003, the University of California Board of Regents adopted the "Green Building Policy and Clean Energy Standard," a university-wide policy for the design of green buildings and use of clean energy, one of the first policies of its kind in the nation.

LEED™ Green Building Rating System

The LEED (Leadership in Energy and Environmental Design) Green Building Rating System™ is a voluntary national standard for developing sustainable buildings that was developed by members of the U.S. Green Building Council (USGBC). The system establishes a common system of measurement for green building and provides a framework for assessing building performance and meeting sustainability goals. LEED emphasizes state of the art strategies for sustainable site development, water savings, energy efficiency, materials selection and indoor environmental quality. Project certification, professional accreditation, training and resources are all a part of the LEED program. LEED standards are currently available for new construction and major renovation projects, existing building operations, and commercial interiors projects.

For more information on the LEED program, visit the USGBC's Web site at *www.usgbc.org* or call them at (202) 828-7422.

Did you know...

To date, the only projects to achieve platinum status are the Phillip Merrill Environmental Center for the Chesapeake Bay Foundation (Annapolis, MD, SmithGroup) and the Donald Bren School of Environmental Science & Management at the University of California, Santa Barbara (Zimmer Gunsul Frasca Partnership).

Nantucket Principles: A Policy Agenda for Architecture and Design Firms on Green and Sustainable Design

On September 28-30, 2002, 85 design firm professionals and A/E/C leaders gathered on Nantucket, Mass., for the Design Futures Council's Architects' Environment Summit. The think-tank session focused on analyzing, discussing, and debating the trends and issues that will influence green building and sustainable design over the next three years. During the event, participants developed an action agenda to equip firms and organizations of all sizes with a recommended strategy to facilitate the successful movement forward in green and sustainable design.

What follows was authored and unanimously agreed to by the Delegates of the Design Futures Council at the Architects' Environment Summit, Nantucket, September 2002.

Current practices in the design and construction of the built environment are contributing to our accelerating environmental crises. The architecture, engineering, and interior design professions and their clients are a critical part of the solutions–solutions that point to a bright, alternative future. Recognizing the fragility of our environment, design firms and clients should redefine themselves

- to engage,
- to listen,
- to learn,
- to educate, and
- to act toward a strong sustainable model.

It is time to operate under a new paradigm, a new set of values, a new set of ethics, and with new awareness of the impact of design.

Under these Nantucket Principles, design and construction organizations commit to the principles of sustainable development, including:

- environmental awareness,
- social/cultural equity,
- economic fitness,
- public policy, and
- technological ingenuity.

Design excellence shall incorporate, by definition, the meeting of sustainable principles. We believe that there is no conflict between sustainability and the art of architecture and design.

Our future and our solutions start here…today.

- It is time to redefine our conscience and look toward expansion.

Nantucket Principles: A Policy Agenda for Architecture and Design Firms on Green and Sustainable Design

- We must expand our view of the client to include tomorrow's child.
- We must expand our obligations to include the health of the public environment and the planet.
- We must expand our consideration of the community, site, and space to always include the larger systems and influences.

We will integrate these models of sustainability in our future work:

- Sustainable Development is that which meets all the needs of the present without compromising the ability of future generations to meet their own needs.*
- Design for Sustainability requires awareness of the full short and long-term consequences of any transformation of the environment. Sustainable design is the conception and realization of environmentally sensitive and responsible expression as a part of the evolving matrix of nature.**

An action agenda...the next steps for architecture and design professionals and firms:

- Lead with vision and integrity.
- Hold a sustainable conference in your office to educate and empower your employees.
- Develop a plan of action for your firm's sustainable agenda.
- Mandate firm and staff accountability toward sustainable action.
- Empower internal champions to mentor staff and external champions to guide the firm to day-to-day sustainable action.
- Build a Knowledge Base on sustainability within your firm.
- Encourage your staff and fellow principals to actively participate in organizations that support green values.
- Identify measurements of success: life cycles, issues, user success, durability, connection to the larger community.

Broaden the profession:

- Become a more responsible professional and adopt the role of sustainable design educator within your firm, with your clients, and in your community.
- Engage with design schools and listen to the students' perspectives about sustainability.
- Communicate the benefits of sustainability to the client and community at large, including research, shared knowledge and case studies.

Nantucket Principles: A Policy Agenda for Architecture and Design Firms on Green and Sustainable Design

- Connect with fellow design professionals, schools and other contributors to the industry to plan future directions toward sustainability.
- Develop a process which points to a holistic approach to sustainability that involves all disciplines (i.e. community, public sector) and seemingly unrelated or unexpected disciplines that can add value.

Redefine success goals in terms of service:
- To the users.
- To the community.
- To your clients.

Collaborate with leaders in your region to align larger development strategies that are more inline with sustainable principles, including:
- Transit/development solutions.
- Preservation of larger natural eco-systems.
- Commitment to existing urban centers.
- Reducing dependence on fossil fuel.
- Promote the development and use of ecological sustainable building products and components.

Envision your future victory and celebrate each increment of success. Sustainability is now clearly an ethical issue for us as professionals. It shall be reflected in all of our future work.

Authored and unanimously agreed to by the Delegates of the Design Futures Council at the Architects' Environment Summit, Nantucket, September 2002.

* From the U.N. Brundtland Commission, 1987.
** Part of the Hannover Principles, 1992.

Source: Design Futures Council

National Green Building Awards

The NAHB Research Center, a subsidiary of the National Association of Home Builders, presents the annual Green Building Awards in conjunction with the annual National Green Building Conference. The awards recognize leaders in the advancement of the green-home building industry and showcase resource-efficient designs. A jury of industry professions selects the winning entries except the Outstanding Green Project Award, which is selected by conference attendees as the project that has had the greatest impact on advancing the cause of resource-efficient home construction. The NAHB Research Center is the not-for-profit research arm of the National Association of Home Builders, providing product research and building process improvements, including testing and certification systems.

For more information about the National Green Building Awards or the National Green Building Conference, call the NAHB Research Center conference line at (888) 602-4663 or visit their Web site at *www.nahbrc.org*.

2003 Recipients

Green Advocate of the Year

Peter Pfeiffer, Austin, TX
Principal, Barley + Pfeiffer Architects

Green Project of the Year, Affordable Homes

Artistic Homes
Albuquerque, NM

Green Project of the Year, Production Homes

McStain Neighborhoods
Boulder, CO

Green Project of the Year, Custom Homes

Coho Construction Services, Inc.
Portland, OR

National Green Building Program of the Year, New

Built Green™
Seattle, WA

National Green Building Program of the Year, Established

Green Building Program of the Home Builders Association of Metropolitan Denver
Denver, CO

Outstanding Green Product of the Year

Bio-Based Systems
Rogers, AR

Jury

Sheila Hayter, National Renewable Energy Laboratory
Jim Hackler, EarthCraft House
John Kurowski, Kurowski Development
Kristin Shewfelt, McStain Enterprises
Pattie Glenn, GreenSmart

Source: National Association of Home Builders

Left: This year's green advocate, Peter Pfeiffer, principal at Barley + Pfeiffer Architects of Austin, Texas, is a green building pioneer and adamant believer in the benefits of passive solar design. *Bottom*: McStain Neighborhoods of Boulder, Colo., recipients of the Green Project of the Year Award for the Production Category, impressed the jury with their extensive documentation process that identifies, repairs, and tracks problems and uses this information to prevent the same problems from occurring in subsequent work. Shown here is one of their recent homes. *Photos courtesy of the NAHB Research Center.*

Sustainable Design Leadership Awards

The annual Sustainable Design Leadership Awards are presented jointly by the International Interior Design Association (IIDA), The American Institute of Architects' (AIA) Interiors Committee, and CoreNet Global in two categories. The first category honors an individual or firm who has demonstrated a commitment to environmental issues in the design profession; the second category recognizes a corporation(s) or organization(s) that has established sustainable business operations and practices which include architecture and interior design. Companies servicing the interior design and furnishings industry are not eligible.

Additional information is available on the IIDA's Web site at *www.iida.org*.

2001

Sandra F. Mendler, HOK
Ford Motor Company, Dearborn, MI

2002

Penny S. Bonda, EnvironDesignWorks
Verizon Communications, Bedminster, NJ

2003

Mithun Architects + Designers + Planners, Seattle, WA
Toyota Motor Sales, Torrance, CA
Primary Industries and Resources, South Australia (PIRSA)

Special Commendation
HOK
Fox & Fowle Architects

Source: International Interior Design Association

> There are certain fundamental laws that are inherent to the natural world that we can use as models and mentors for human designs. Ecology comes from the Greek roots Oikos and Logos, "household" and "logical discourse." Thus, it is appropriate, if not imperative, for architects to discourse about the logic of our earth household.
>
> **William McDonough**

Sustainable/Green Design Timeline

Editors at *DesignIntelligence*, the newsletter of the Design Futures Council, recently compiled a comprehensive timeline of significant moments in the development of sustainable/green design. As the effects of industrialized society are increasingly blamed for erosion of the planet's health and the quality of life for its inhabitants, the Green movement in the A/E/C industry continues to gain momentum.

1871 The Chicago Fire stimulates uniform municipal building codes and ordinances.

1890s William T. Love purchases land in New York for a proposed hydroelectric power project; a century later Love Canal becomes the poster child for hazardous waste cleanup.

1892 The Sierra Club is founded on May 28.

1893 The Colombian Exposition (Chicago World's Fair) celebrates the dawn of the Industrial Revolution.

1916 New York City passes the first ordinance for separation of land-use zones.

1936 Frank Lloyd Wright develops his concept of "Broad Acres" to accommodate the automobile.

The Urban Land Institute is founded.

1939 Shell Oil and General Motors exhibit their "City of Tomorrow" at the New York World's Fair.

1946 Henry Dreyfus exhibits his "unlimited growth" plan for Toledo, Ohio.

1947 The Levitt brothers open the first development of sub-division housing built for speculation.

1956 The U.S. Interstate Highway system is opened, justified on the basis of national defense.

1960 The Organization of the Petroleum Exporting Countries (OPEC) is formed by Iran, Iraq, Kuwait, Saudi Arabia and Venezuela.

The Pruitt Igo public housing in St. Louis, Mo., is razed after winning architectural awards.

1962 Rachel Carson publishes *Silent Spring.*

1969 The Apollo Space Program provides distant images of the whole Earth.

1970's Robert Davis inherits 80 acres of Gulf-front Florida Panhandle property from his grandfather that will eventually become Seaside.

1970 The First Earth day is celebrated on April 22.

The Nixon administration forms the Environmental Protection Agency (EPA).

The Clean Air Act establishes emission standards.

1972 The first United Nations Conference on the Human Environment is held in Stockholm, Sweden.

Sustainable/Green Design Timeline

1973 The Endangered Species Act protects plant and animal environments.

1977 President Jimmy Carter calls energy conservation "the moral equivalent of war," calling the U.S. "the most wasteful nation on Earth."

The Clean Water Act is passed.

1978 The Love Canal contamination discovered; 11 years of cleanup later, the land is declared habitable again.

1979 Portland, Ore., establishes an urban growth boundary to prevent the "ravenous" rampage of suburbia."

1980 The Superfund is established.

1982 The Energy and Environmental Building Association is formed.

1985 A team of British scientists report that there is a hole in the ozone layer over the Antarctic.

1988 The AIA Committee on the Environment is formed.

1989 The Exxon Valdez spills 11 million gallons of crude oil, resulting in a $1 billion criminal penalty.

1990 The Washington State Growth Management Act requires fast-growing areas to create comprehensive, coordinated plans for future development.

1991 Austin, Tex., starts the first organized green building program.

1992 Wendy E. Brawer creates the Green Apple Map for New York City and global effort follows (www.greenmap.org).

Environmental Building News publishes its first issue.

The U.S. Department of Energy publishes a rating system (0-100) for home energy efficiency, with 100 being a home that is completely energy-self-sufficient.

1993 The U.S. Green Building Council is formed.

The Rural Studio begins designing and building houses under the direction of Auburn University professors Samuel Mockbee and Dennis K. Ruth.

The Declaration of Interdependence for a Sustainable Future is signed by Olufemi Majekodunmi and Susan A. Maxman, presidents of the International Union of Architects and The American Institute of Architects.

1994 The EPA launches its Brownfields reclamation program.

Seattle announces a 20-year urban growth plan to limit sprawl.

1996 General Motors unveils its battery-powered EV-1 electric car.

The United Nations stages the second Habitat Conference in Istanbul and launches the global Best Practices Program for Sustainable Communities; it concurrently establishes the biennial Dubai Award.

Sustainable/Green Design Timeline

1996 William McDonough receives the Presidential Award for Sustainable Development.

The University of Virginia launches the Institute of Sustainable Design.

The Kyoto Protocol limits emissions of greenhouse gases from industrialized countries.

Architect John Hermannsson publishes the Green Building Resource Guide with cost comparison for choosing a green vs. conventional product.

The American Planning Association publishes *Best Development Practices: Doing the Right Thing and Making Money at the Same Time.*

1998 The Energy Star Commercial Buildings program begins.

The AIA Committee on the Environment grants it first annual Top 10 Green Projects awards.

The Sierra Club releases *The Dark Side of the American Dream*, listing the 20 cities most endangered by sprawl.

2000 New York becomes the first state to promote green building through tax credits.

The Phillip Merrill Environmental Center for the Chesapeake Bay Foundation (Annapolis, Md., SmithGroup) is the first project to achieve platinum status in the LEED (Leadership in Energy and Environmental Design) Green Building Rating System™.

2001 The IIDA awards first annual Sustainable Design Leadership Award.

2002 UN World Summit on Sustainable Development is held in Johannesburg, South Africa.

R.S. Means publishes the first estimating handbook for Green Building.

2003 William McDonough launches the GreenBlue organization as a means to openly share his accumulated knowledge on sustainable design.

Source: Counsel House Research

10 Greenest Designs

The 10 Greenest Designs were selected by The American Institute of Architects' (AIA) Committee on the Environment (COTE) to highlight viable architectural design solutions that protect and enhance the environment. COTE represents architects who are committed to making environmental considerations and sustainable design integral to their practice. The following projects address one or more significant environmental challenges such as energy and water conservation, use of recycled construction materials, and designs which improve indoor air quality. Responsible use of building materials, use of daylight over artificial lighting, designs that produce efficiency in heating or cooling, and overall sensitivity to local environmental issues were some of the reasons COTE selected these projects.

To view photographs and descriptions, *visit www.aia.org/pia/vote/topten* on the Internet.

2003 Greenest Designs

Argonne Child Development Center
San Francisco, CA
450 Architects

Chicago Center for Green Technology
Chicago, IL
Farr Associates Architecture and Urban Design

Colorado Court
Santa Monica, CA
Pugh Scarpa Kodama

Cusano Environmental Education Center
Philadelphia, PA
Susan Maxman & Partners, Ltd

Fisher Pavilion
Seattle, WA
Miller|Hull Partnership, LLP

Herman Miller Marketplace
Zeeland, MI
Integrated Architecture

Hidden Villa Hostel & Summer Camp
Los Altos Hills, CA
Arkin Tilt Architects

San Mateo County Sheriff's Forensic Laboratory and Coroner's Office
Redwood City, CA
Hellmuth, Obata + Kassabaum

Steinhude Sea Recreation Facility
Germany
Randall Stout Architects

Wine Creek Road Residence
Healdsburg, CA
Siegel & Strain Architects

Jury

Peter Bohlin, Bohlin Cywinski Jackson
Carol Ross Barney, Ross Barney + Jankowsky
Drury Crawley, U.S. Department of Energy
Jacqueline Rose, Environmental Protection Agency
Douglas Kelbaugh, University of Michigan

Source: The American Institute of Architects

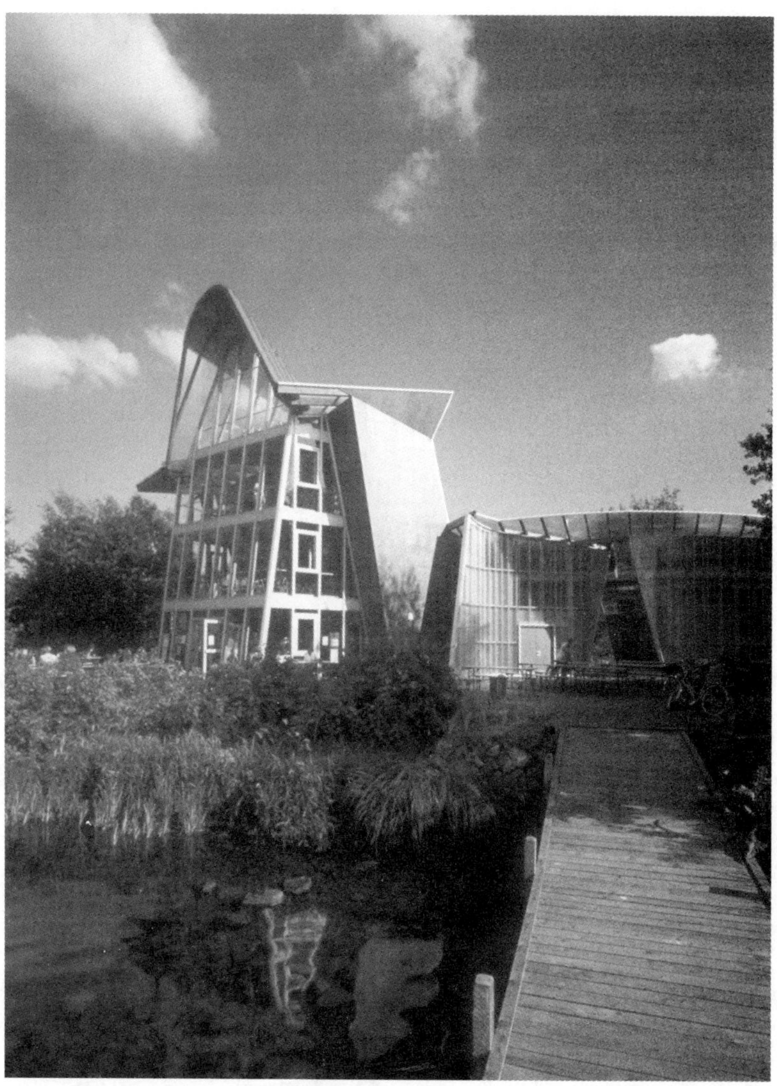

The Steinhude Sea Recreation Facility is located on an island along the north German coast. The island's sensitive ecosystem was protected during construction by off-site prefabrication of the building, which was transported to the site on a barge and assembled with a barge-mounted crane. Photovoltaic panels, solar hot water collectors, day lighting, natural ventilation, passive solar, building automation, gray water and harvested water systems, green materials, and waste reduction are just some of the sustainability practices incorporated into the design. *Photo by Peter Hübbe, courtesy of Randall Stout Architects.*

Top 10 Green Building Products of the Year

New in 2002, BuildingGreen, publisher of the *GreenSpec Directory* and *Environmental Building News (EBN)*, presents annually the Top 10 Green Building Products of the Year award. The award recognizes outstanding products added to the *GreenSpec Directory* during the past year. With over 250 new products appearing each year in the 1,700-plus product *Directory*, the Top 10 prize winners represent a wide range of materials, products and equipment that can help reduce the environmental impact of a building. Products are selected for inclusion in the *Directory* by the editors of *Environmental Building News* based on criteria the panel has developed over nearly a decade. Manufacturers do not pay to be listed in *GreenSpec* and neither *GreenSpec* nor *Environmental Building News* carries advertising. Winners will be announced each year at the Green Building Council conference and trade show.

For additional information about the awards, visit BuildingGreen on the Internet at *www.buildinggreen.com* or call (802) 257-7300.

2003 Winners

L.I.F.T. Foundation System
Pin Foundations, Inc.

FSC-Certified Tuff-Strand OSB
Roy O. Martin Lumber Company

WoodStalk Fiberboard and Underlayment
Dow BioProducts, Inc.

Fiberglass Insulation
Johns Manville Company

Kalwall R-20 with Nanogel™
Kalwall Corporation

Pittsburgh Paints Pure Performance
PPG Architectural Finishes, Inc.

Decato Office Partition Systems
Preform Manufacturing, Inc.

XLerator Electric Hand Dryer
Excel Dryer, Inc.

McDry Non-Water-Using Urinal
Duravit USA, Inc.

WatterSaver Heat Pump Water Heater
ECR International, Inc.

Source: BuildingGreen

Did you know...

According to the NAHB Research Center, over 13,000 green homes were built in 2002 alone, increasing the total number of green homes 70 percent to over 32,000.

U.S. Green Building Council

The U.S. Green Building Council (USGBC) was formed in 1993 to integrate, educate, and provide leadership for building industry leaders, environmental groups, designers, retailers, and building owners as they strive to develop and market products and services which are environmentally progressive and responsible. The Council includes more than 250 organizations worldwide with a common interest in green building practices, technologies, policies, and standards. Their most visible program, the LEED™ Green Building Rating System is a voluntary, consensus-based rating system for commercial buildings to provide a national standard on what constitutes a green building and market incentives to build "green."

Address

1015 18th St. NW, Suite 805
Washington DC 20036
Telephone: (202) 828-7422
Fax: (202) 828-5110
Internet: www.usgbc.org

Did you know...

In July 2003, the USGBC granted the Canadian Green Building Council exclusive rights to implement their LEED™ program in Canada.

6 Design & Historic Preservation

This chapter highlights many of the organizations that assist individuals, communities, and professionals with their preservation efforts as well as advocacy programs that alert the public to historic resources in imminent danger of being lost. Preservation award programs and their current winners are also included along with the results of the annual Most Visited Historic House Museums ranking.

Abbott Lowell Cummings Award

The Abbott Lowell Cummings Award is presented annually by the Vernacular Architecture Forum (VAF) to honor outstanding books published about North American vernacular architecture and landscapes. A review committee prioritizes submissions based on new information, the role of fieldwork in research, critical approach and the model provided in writing and research methods. A founder of the VAF, Abbott Lowell Cummings was a prolific researcher and writer. He is best known for his magnum opus, *The Framed Houses of Massachusetts Bay, 1625-1725* (1979).

For additional information, visit the VAF's Web site at *www.vernaculararchitectureforum.org*.

1983

"'In a Manner and Fashion Suitable to Their Degree': An Investigation of the Material Culture of Early Rural Pennsylvania," in *Working Papers from the Regional Economic History Research Center vol. 5 no. 1*, by Jack Michel

1984

No award granted

1985

Big House, Little House, Back House, Barn: The Connected Farm Buildings of New England by Thomas Hubka (University Press of New England)

1986

Hollybush by Charles Martin (University of Tennessee Press)

1987

Holy Things and Profane: Anglican Parish Churches in Colonial Virginia by Dell Upton (Architectural History Foundation)

1988

Architecture and Rural Life in Central Delaware, 1700-1900 by Bernard L. Herman (University of Tennessee Press)

1989

Study Report for Slave Quarters Reconstruction at Carter's Grove by the Colonial Williamsburg Foundation

Study Report for the Bixby House Restoration by Old Sturbridge Village

1990

Manhattan for Rent, 1785-1850 by Elizabeth Blackmar (Cornell University Press)

Building the Octagon by Orlando Rideout (The American Institute of Architects Press)

1991

Architects and Builders in North Carolina by Catherine Bishir, Charlotte Brown, Carl Lounsbury, and Ernest Wood, III (University of North Carolina Press)

1992

Alone Together: A History of New York's Early Apartments by Elizabeth Cromley (Cornell University Press)

A Place to Belong, Community, Order and Everyday Space in Calvert, Newfoundland by Gerald Pocius (University of Georgia Press)

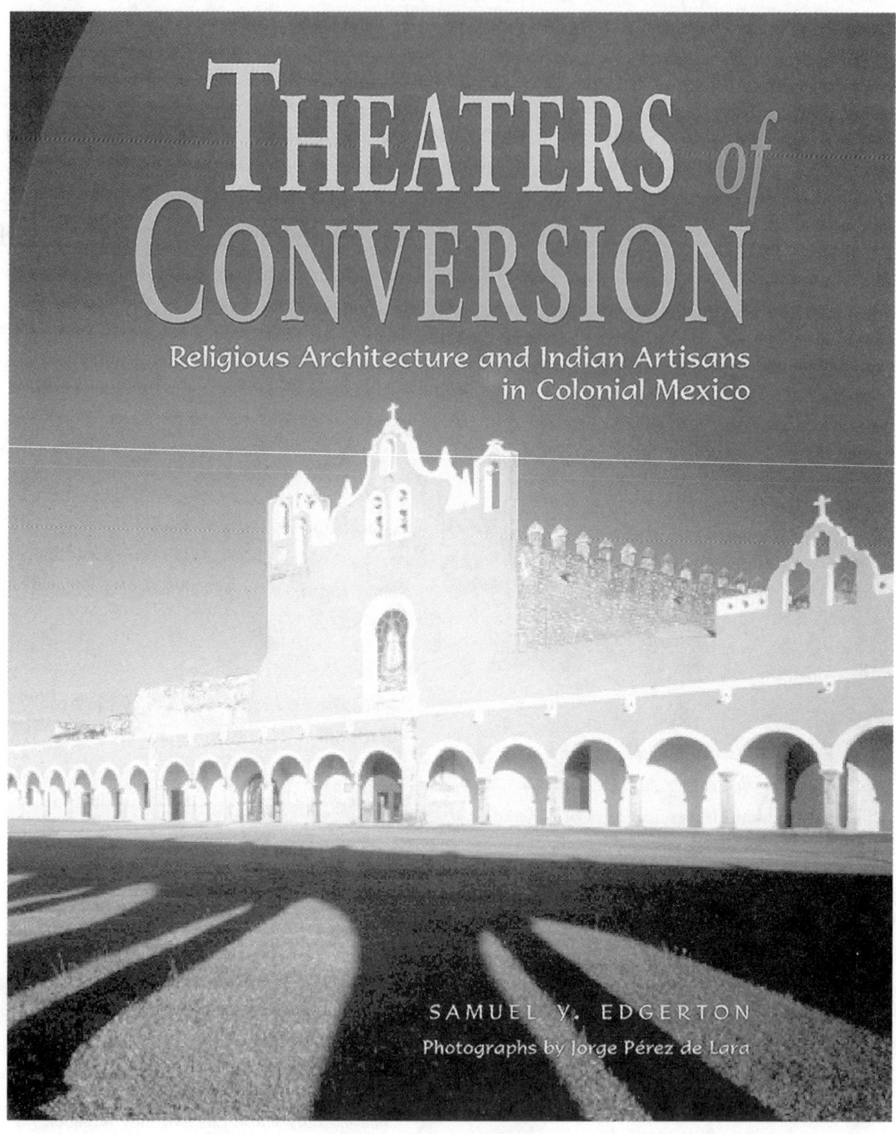
THEATERS of CONVERSION
Religious Architecture and Indian Artisans in Colonial Mexico
SAMUEL Y. EDGERTON
Photographs by Jorge Pérez de Lara

In his book *Theaters of Conversion*, Samuels Edgerton analyzes Mexico's sixteenth and seventeenth-century churches and conventos, built by Spanish friars as a means of religious conversion, for their special contribution of the spread of Italian Renaissance architecture. They were built by native Indian artisans who not only mastered European techniques and styles but added their own influence. *Photo courtesy of the University of New Mexico Press.*

Abbott Lowell Cummings Award

1993

Homeplace: The Social Use and Meaning of the Folk Dwelling in Southwestern North Carolina by Michael Ann Williams (University of Georgia Press)

The Park and the People: A History of Central Park by Roy Rosenzweig and Elizabeth Blackmar (Cornell University Press)

1994

The Stolen House by Bernard L. Herman (University Press of Virginia)

1995

Living Downtown: The History of Residential Hotels in the United States by Paul Groth (University of California Press)

1996

An Illustrated Glossary of Early Southern Architecture and Landscape by Carl Lounsbury (Oxford University Press)

1997

Unplanned Suburbs: Toronto's American Tragedy, 1900-1950 by Richard Harris (Johns Hopkins University Press)

1998

City Center to Regional Mall: Architecture, the Automobile, and Retailing in Los Angeles, 1920-1950 by Richard Longstreth (MIT Press)

1999

The Myth of Santa Fe: Creating a Modern Regional Tradition by Chris Wilson (University of New Mexico Press)

Architecture of the United States by Dell Upton (Oxford University Press)

2000

Delta Sugar: Louisiana's Vanishing Plantation Landscape by John B. Rehder (Johns Hopkins University Press)

Honorable Mentions

Cheap, Quick & Easy: Imitative Architectural Materials, 1870-1930 by Pamela H. Simpson (University of Tennessee Press)

Building Community, Keeping the Faith: German Catholic Vernacular Architecture in a Rural Minnesota Parish by Fred W. Peterson (Minnesota Historical Society Press)

2001

Vernacular Architecture by Henry Glassie (Indiana University Press)

2002

The Patina of Place: The Cultural Weathering of a New England Landscape by Kingston William Heath (University of Tennessee Press)

2003

Theaters of Conversion: Religious Architecture and Indian Artisans in Colonial Mexico, by Samuel Y. Edgerton (University of New Mexico Press)

Source: Vernacular Architecture Forum

America's 11 Most Endangered Historic Places

Every June the National Trust for Historic Preservation, in conjunction with the History Channel, compiles a list of the 11 most threatened historic sites in the United States. Since 1988, the 11 Most Endangered List has highlighted more than 160 historic buildings, sites and landscapes threatened by neglect, deterioration, insufficient funds, inappropriate development, or insensitive public policy. While being listed does not guarantee protection or financial support, in the past the attention generated by the program has brought a broader awareness to the country's diminishing historic resources and generated local support for the threatened sites.

For photos and a history of each site, visit the National Trust's Web site at *www.nationaltrust.org/11most/*.

2002 11 Most Endangered Historic Places

Urban Houses of Worship
Nationwide

Bathhouse Row
Hot Springs, AR

Little Manila
Stockton, CA

Ocmulgee Old Fields Traditional Cultural Property
Macon, GA

Michigan Boulevard Garden Apartments
Chicago, IL

East Side and Middle Schools
Decorah, IA

Amelia Earhart Memorial Bridge
Atchison, KS

U.S. Marine Hospital
Louisville, KY

Minute Man National Historical Park and environs
Concord, Lincoln, Lexington and Bedford, MA

Zuni Salt Lake and Sanctuary Zone
Catron and Cibola counties, MN

TWA Terminal at JFK International Airport
New York, NY

Source: National Trust for Historic Preservation

Did you know...

Oklahoma City's Gold Dome (1958), one of 2002's 11 Most Endangered Historic Places, is currently undergoing renovation and will open in 2004 as an Asian-American cultural center.

Top: An icon of modern design, Eero Saarinen's 1962 TWA Terminal at New York's JFK International Airport, is in danger of demolition (*Photo by Marilyn Fenollosa*). *Middle*: St. Joseph's Roman Catholic Church in Denver, one of the community and spiritual landmarks threatened nationwide (*Photo by James Baca*). *Bottom*: A nearby regional airport is negatively impacting Minute Man National Historic Park, an important American Revolution site (*Photo by Jim Lozouski*). *All photos courtesy of the National Trust for Historic Preservation.*

Antoinette Forrester Downing Award

The Society of Architectural Historians annually grants the Antoinette Forrester Downing Award to an author for an outstanding publication in the field of historic preservation. Works published in the two years prior to the award are eligible.

For more information contact the SAH at 312-573-1365 or visit their Web site at *www.sah.org*.

1987
Providence, A Citywide Survey of Historic Resources by William McKenzie Woodward and Edward F. Sanderson (Rhode Island Historic Preservation Commission)

1990
East Cambridge: A Survey of Architectural History in Cambridge by Susan E. Maycock (MIT Press)

1991
Somerset: An Architectural History by Paul Baker Touart (Maryland Historical Trust and Somerset County Historical Trust)

1994
The Buried Past: An Archaeological History of Philadelphia by John L. Cotter (University of Pennsylvania Press)

1995
Along the Seaboard Side: the Architectural History of Worcester County, Maryland by Paul Baker Touart (Worcester County)

1996
The Historic Architecture of Wake County, North Carolina by Kelly A. Lally (Wake County Government)

1997
A Guide to the National Road and The National Road by Karl B. Raitz (Johns Hopkins University Press)

1998
A Guide to the Historic Architecture of Eastern North Carolina by Catherine W. Bishir & Michael T. Southern (Chapel Hill University of N.C. Press)

1999
No award granted

2000
Boston's Changeful Times by Michael Holleran (Johns Hopkins University Press)

2001
Preserving Cultural Landscapes in America by Arnold R. Alanen and Robert Z. Melnick, editors (John Hopkins University Press)

2002
A Building History of Northern New England by James Garvin (University Press of New England)

2003
No award granted

Source: Society for Architectural Historians

> If we make out buildings and spaces right in the first place, they age well, like the trees.
>
> **Benjamin Forgey**

Crowninshield Award

The National Trust for Historic Preservation's highest honor, the Louise DuPont Crowninshield Award, recognizes an individual or organization who has demonstrated extraordinary lifetime achievement in the preservation of America's heritage. Winners are selected by the Preservation Committee of the National Trust's Board of Trustees.

For more information contact the National Trust at (800) 944-6847 or visit their Web site at *www.nationaltrust.org.*

1960	The Mount Vernon Ladies Association
1961	Henry Francis DuPont
1962	Katherine Prentis Murphy
1963	Martha Gilmore Robinson
1964	Mr. and Mrs. Bertram R. Little
1965	Charles E. Peterson
1966	Ima Hogg
	Mary Gordon Latham Kellenberger
1967	*No award granted*
1968	St. Clair Wright
1969	Mr. and Mrs. Henry N. Flynt
1970	Frank L. Horton
1971	Frances R. Edmunds
1972	Alice Winchester
1973	Dr. Ricardo E. Alegria
1974	Mr. and Mrs. Jacob H. Morrison
1975	*No award granted*
1976	Katherine U. Warren
1977	San Antonio Conservation Society
1978	Helen Duprey Bullock
1979	Old Post Office Landmark Committee
1980	William J. Murtagh
	Ernest Allen Connally
1981	Gordon C. Gray
1982	Helen Abell
1983	Historic American Buildings Survey (HABS) of the National Park Service, U.S. Department of the Interior, in cooperation with The American Institute of Architects and the Library of Congress, Washington, D.C.
1984	Leopold Adler II
1985	James Marston Fitch
1986	Antoinette Downing
1987	Frank Blair Reeves
1988	Robert Stipe
1989	Fred Rath
	Association of Junior Leagues
1990	Frederick Gutheim
1991	Robert Garvey
1992	Joan Bacchus Maynard
1993	Carl B. Westmoreland
	Arthur P. Ziegler Jr.
1994	Walter Beinecke Jr.
1995	Dana Crawford
1996	Richard H. Jenrette
1997	Marguerite Neel Williams
1998	Frederick Williamson
	Anice Barber Read
1999	Senator Daniel Patrick Moynihan
2000	National Park Service
2001	George and Cynthia Mitchell
2002	John F. Seiberling
2003	Walter Nold Mathis

Source: National Trust for Historic Preservation

DOCOMOMO

DOCOMOMO (Documentation and Conservation of Buildings, Sites and Neighborhoods of the Modern Movement) International is headquartered in France, with working parties in 40 countries. Founded in 1988, membership consists of architects, engineers, historians, and others dedicated to preserving the architectural heritage of the Modern Movement through documentation and conservation. They are also organized into specialist committees that concentrate on issues relative to registers, technology, education and theory, urbanism and landscapes, and publications. They also produce the *DOCOMOMO Journal*, published twice a year, with thematic articles and news from the individual chapters. Their technical publications focus on conservation issues related to modern structures.

Address

DOCOMOMO International
Institut français d' architecture
6 rue de Tournon
75006 Paris
FRANCE
Telephone: +33-(0)1-46 33 59 76
Fax: +33-(0)1-46 33 02 11

DOCOMOMO US
P.O. Box 230977
New York, NY 10023
Internet: www.docomomo-us.org
Email: docomomo@docomomo-us.org

All work passes out of the hands of the architect into the hands of nature, to be perfected.

Henry David Thoreau

Dozen Distinctive Destinations

The Dozen Distinctive Destinations list is compiled each year by the National Trust for Historic Preservation (NTHP), recognizing the best preserved and unique communities in the United States. Selected communities are judged on the following criteria: well-managed growth, a dynamic downtown, a commitment to historic preservation with a protected historic core and meaningful context, interesting and attractive architecture, cultural diversity, an economic base of locally owned small businesses, and walkability for residents and visitors.

For more information on the Dozen Distinctive Destinations, visit the National Trust's Web site at *www.nationaltrust.org*.

2000

San Luis Obispo, CA
Boulder, CO
Thomasville, GA
Lawrence, KS
Lowell, MA
Petoskey, MI
Cooperstown, NY
Pittman Center, TN
Fredricksburg, TX
Lexington, KY
Port Townsend, WA
Chippewa Falls, WI

2001

Eureka Springs, AR
Calistoga, CA
Silverton, CO
Madison, IN
Bonaparte, IA
Northampton, MA
Red Lodge, MT
Las Vegas, NM
Jacksonville, OR
Doylestown, PA
Beaufort, SC
Staunton, VA

2002

Asheville, NC
Butte, MT
Fernandina Beach, FL
Ferndale, CA
Frederick, MD
Holland, MI
Milan, OH
Morristown, NJ
Saratoga Springs, NY
Silver City, NM
Walla Walla, WA
Westerly, RI

2003

Burlington, VT
Coronado, CA
Edenton, NC
Galveston, TX
Georgetown, CO
Jekyll Island, GA
Keene, NH
Mackinac Island, MI
Natchez, MS
New Harmony, IN
Portland, ME
Vancouver, WA

Source: National Trust for Historic Preservation

Great American Main Street Awards

Each year the National Trust for Historic Preservation's National Main Street Center selects five communities that have demonstrated considerable success with preservation-based revitalization. These towns have all generated broad-based support from its residents and business leaders, drawn financial assistance from both public and private sources, and created innovative solutions for their unique situations. Winners each receive $5000 to be used toward further revitalization efforts, a bronze plaque, road signs, and a certificate. Since its inception, the Main Street Center has helped over 1,650 communities, which has resulted in an average of $40 in new downtown investments for every dollar spent on revitalization efforts.

For more information, visit the Main Street Center's Web site at *www.mainstreet.org* or contact them at (202) 588-6219.

1995

Clarksville, MO
Dubuque, IA
Franklin, TN
Sheboygan Falls, WI
Old Pasadena, CA

1996

Bonaparte, IA
Chippewa Falls, WI
East Carson Street Business District, Pittsburgh, PA
Saratoga Springs, NY
Wooster, OH

1997

Burlington, VT
DeLand, FL
Georgetown, TX
Holland, MI
Libertyville, IL

1998

Corning, IA
Lanesboro, MN
Morgantown, WV
Thomasville, GA
York, PA

1999

Bay City, MI
Cordell, OK
Denton, TX
Lafayette, IN
San Luis Obispo, CA

2000

Coronado, CA
Keokuk, IA
Newkirk, OK
Port Townsend, WA
St. Charles, IL

2001

Danville, KY
Elkader, IA
Enid, OK
Mansfield, OH
Walla Walla, WA

2002

Cedar Falls, IA
La Crosse, WI
Milford, NH
Okmulgee, OK
Staunton, VA

Great American Main Street Awards

2003

Greenville, SC
Littleton, NH
Manassas, VA
Rome, GA
Wenatchee, WA

Source: The National Trust Main Street Center

Did you know...
Between 1980 and 2001, 88,700 building rehabilitations resulted from the Main Street program.

Guidelines for Architectural Historians Testifying on the Historical Significance of Properties

The following guidelines were adopted by the Society of Architectural Historians (SAH) in 1986 to enhance professional standards in the preservation review process. In developing the guidelines, the SAH established a framework of acceptable conduct for those testifying as members of the discipline. The document was intended for wide circulation, to be used by the staffs and members of review bodies at the state and local levels and by all others concerned with the integrity of the review process.

Guidelines

Architectural historians engage in research into, and the dissemination of knowledge about, the evolution of the art and craft of architecture and its place in the history of civilization. The knowledge which they perpetuate, acquire, and spread is central to understanding human growth, for the buildings of any age reflect not only the visions of their designers and clients, but also the values of their era. Architectural historians have a special responsibility to the past, for their judgments as to the value of its artifacts often figure large in public and private decisions about what to preserve and what to destroy. That which is preserved nurtures the culture whose past it represents. That which is destroyed is lost forever.

Thus, the architectural historian has an awesome burden when called upon to speak to the value of a building, group of buildings, and other components of the man-made environment. It is essential to the integrity of the discipline that the architectural historian's testimony be based on sound scholarship, be an honest appraisal of all the pertinent circumstances, and be given with due regard for the gravity of its consequences.

Architectural historians testifying on the significance of historic properties before a duly constituted review board, commission, council, legislative committee, or court of law should:

- Make objective and truthful statements and eschew dissemination of untrue, unfair, or exaggerated statements regarding the significance of any property or properties;

- assess the significance of the property or properties in question according to applicable local, state, and/or federal criteria;

- express their professional opinion only when it is founded upon adequate knowledge of the facts, upon expertise in pertinent areas of scholarship, and upon honest conviction;

- state specifically the circumstances under which they are presenting testimony, including whether they are taking, or at any time have taken, a fee for work related to the case in question; and

- issue no statements on behalf of interested parties unless they indicate on whose behalf those statements are being made, the nature of any compensation related to the case, and any personal interest in the property or properties in question or in property which would be affected by the disposition of the property or properties in question.

Guidelines for Architectural Historians Testifying on the Historical Significance of Properties

Credentials

An individual who intends to testify as an expert on matters pertaining to architectural history before a duly constituted review board, commission, council, legislative committee, or court of law must have a demonstrated record of achievement in that discipline.

A full set of credentials applicable, directly and indirectly, to the case should be presented in writing for the public record.

As credentials, it is appropriate to cite institutions attended, degrees earned, research conducted, scholarly work published, pertinent consulting projects completed or in progress, and past and present employment. Professional affiliations, offices, committees, and similar forms of service related to the discipline may be included, but it must be made explicit that all testimony presented reflects solely that individual's opinion unless he or she has been duly authorized by an organization, agency, or firm to speak on its behalf.

All parties involved in a given case should understand that architectural historians are not certified, registered, or licensed according to a uniform set of standards comparable to those employed in professions such as law, medicine, or architecture. Moreover, it should be understood that no one form of academic program is acknowledged to be the sole means by which an individual can become an architectural historian. Advanced degrees in art and architectural history form the primary bases for entering the discipline; nevertheless, comparable preparation in other fields such as American history, American studies, geography, archaeology, and folk-life also may provide expertise in assessing aspects of the built environment in their historic context. Furthermore, architects, landscape architects, and others practicing in professional design and planning fields may have expertise in facets of architectural history. Finally, it is possible for a person to acquire such expertise with little or no formal education in the field.

From a legal standpoint, expert testimony must be based on specialized knowledge of a particular subject, surpassing that which might be acquired by the average, well-informed layperson. Therefore, in all the above cases, a demonstrated record of achievement related to the historical subjects in question, rather than training or professional practice per se, should be considered the essential basis for one's qualifications to testify as an expert on matters pertaining to architectural history in a given case. Moreover, simply having an interest in old buildings or being involved with efforts to preserve them should not be considered an adequate basis for such testimony.

In presenting qualifications, architectural historians should be specific in enumerating their areas of expertise with respect to the case. Working in architectural history, or even in the sphere of North American architecture, does not always render an individual fully qualified to address all pertinent topical areas with authority. For example, a scholar of eighteenth-century North American architecture may not necessarily be well equipped to assess the significance of properties dating from later periods. Moreover, it is doubtful whether someone who knows little or nothing about the architecture of a given locale is in a good position to assess the local significance of a property or properties in that place.

Guidelines for Architectural Historians Testifying on the Historical Significance of Properties

Research

A foremost responsibility of an architectural historian intending to testify on the significance of a property or properties is to familiarize himself or herself with that work to the fullest extent possible. Under all circumstances, this effort should include onsite study. Interiors also should be examined whenever feasible, and must be scrutinized when all or a portion of them are being considered in the case.

Furthermore, the architectural historian intending to testify should gain familiarity with as much additional information as possible concerning the property or properties. Of at least equal importance is knowledge of the context within which the property's significance may be evaluated. Such contextual frameworks include, but are not necessarily limited to: other work of the period(s), type(s), and designer(s) involved; work employing similar materials, construction techniques, or systems; work commissioned by the same or comparable clients, occupied by the same or comparable clients or occupied by the same or analogous groups; and the physical setting in both its historic and current dimensions. In cases involving one or more properties within a designated historic district, or a precinct that has the potential to become a historic district, the full nature of the contribution of the property or properties to that district should be carefully considered.

In some instances, the necessary research may already have been conducted for a case. The architectural historian intending to testify then has the responsibility to examine this material carefully, making sure that it is complete and accurate, prior to preparing his or her scholarly evaluation. In other instances, additional research may be needed, and the architectural historian intending to testify either should undertake this work or wait until it is completed by another responsible party before preparing an assessment. Whenever possible, architectural historians intending to testify should also seek consultation from colleagues known for their research in specialized subject areas pertinent to the case.

It should be realized that many such subject areas have received little or no scholarly attention and that the absence of this research should not necessarily preclude responsible efforts to save significant properties. It further should be recognized that many cases cannot be researched in a definitive manner when such an undertaking would require far more time than can be allocated even under favorable circumstances. Nevertheless, in all cases, an architectural historian intending to testify should exercise his or her best professional judgment in determining whether adequate information is available and determining that no available information is being concealed from consideration.

Moreover, the architectural historian offering testimony should be explicit regarding the degree to which his or her statements are based on his or her own research or on the work of others. Under no circumstances should an architectural historian convey the impression that an assessment is his or her own when it has in fact been wholly or substantially prepared by another party.

Guidelines for Architectural Historians Testifying on the Historical Significance of Properties

Criteria for Evaluation

Architectural historians intending to testify should be thoroughly familiar with applicable local, state, and federal criteria for evaluation and gain a full understanding of the issues relating to significance that the testimony is intended to resolve. The criteria for the National Register of Historic Places and for most, if not all, local landmark and historic district ordinances specify that properties may be designated on the basis of local significance as well as by virtue of their significance to a state or the nation.

However, the concept of local significance is often ignored or distorted in testimony and thus deserves special consideration here. A given work may not rank among the finest designed by a distinguished architect, for example, but this does not necessarily undermine its significance for the locality in question. Similarly, comparative analysis of examples of a building type in different geographic regions does not necessarily provide insight on the local significance of examples in any one of those regions.

Furthermore, local significance should not be interpreted as meaning only the earliest, oldest surviving, best, or most unusual examples unless the applicable criteria for evaluation so state. The objective of national preservation legislation and most local ordinances is to foster a comprehensive plan for protecting historic properties. Indeed, significance often may be fully understood only after it is studied in relation to the local context. Failure to assess a property's or properties' significance in any of the above ways will undermine the credibility of the testimony and run counter to the intent of the national historic preservation program.

Fees

Taking a fee for testimony is legal under most circumstances and should not, in itself, be construed as diminishing the value of testimony. At the same time, an architectural historian who even unintentionally conveys the impression that his or her testimony is in any way affected by monetary compensation or personal reasons contrary to those of sound scholarship blemishes both preservation efforts and the discipline's integrity. Indeed, the entire basis for scholarship, along with its public reputation, rests on its independence.

Therefore, architectural historians should make every reasonable effort to demonstrate that their testimony is motivated solely by honest conviction, understanding of all relevant material, and scholarly expertise. In every instance, architectural historians testifying should state explicitly whether they are taking a fee for that testimony; whether they are taking, or at any time have taken, a fee for work related to the case; and the source or sources for same fees. They should further explicitly state all the circumstances under which they are presenting testimony in that case. In contractual agreements which will, or may at some later date, include testimony, that agreement should stipulate that the underlying aim of the architectural historian's work is to arrive at an objective evaluation of the significance of the property or properties in question. The contracted fee should be structured according to the nature of the work undertaken for

Guidelines for Architectural Historians Testifying on the Historical Significance of Properties

research, analysis, and preparation of findings in a report or other appropriate form, and not according to the real or potential monetary value of the property or properties in question. Under some circumstances, it may be prudent to perform such work incrementally; that is, prepare preliminary findings, and, should the contracting parties so agree, then proceed with an in-depth study.

The contractual agreement should specifically preclude the contractor's later excerpting portions of the study in a manner that distorts the overall findings of that study. Furthermore, architectural historians should never agree "for monetary compensation or otherwise" to prepare a study that merely makes an argument pro or con without weighing all pertinent information and performing a full scholarly assessment.

No uniform set of standards should be established for such studies any more than for other forms of scholarly endeavor. Architectural historians should be guided by the same standards that are considered exemplary for other work in their discipline. A study too quickly prepared, lacking careful consideration of all aspects contributing to complete historical analysis, should be viewed as a serious breach of personal and professional integrity.

Summary

Architectural historians should regard testimony as a public service and as a constructive means of advocating the retention of significant components of the man-made environment in accordance with applicable local, state, and federal laws. All work done to prepare for testimony, as well as the testimony itself, also should reflect high scholarly standards and should not suggest personal gain of any sort acquired at the expense of these objectives.

The Society of Architectural Historians is the leading scholarly organization that promotes the study and preservation of the built environment world wide. For more information about the Society, please visit their website at www.sah.org.

Guidelines for the Treatment of Cultural Landscapes

The Secretary of the Interior is responsible for establishing professional standards and providing advice on the preservation of cultural resources listed or eligible for listing on the National Register of Historic Places. As the definition and scope of preservation has continued to broaden, the Secretary of the Interior developed the Guidelines for the Treatment of Cultural Landscapes to provide expert guidance when planning and implementing work involving cultural landscapes. A cultural landscape is defined as "a geographic area, including both cultural and natural resources and the wildlife or domestic animals therein, associated with a historic event, activity, or person or exhibiting other cultural or aesthetic values."

For more information about cultural landscapes and their preservation, visit the National Park Service's Web site at *www2.cr.nps.gov/hli/introguid.htm.*

1. Before undertaking project work, research of a cultural landscape is essential. Research findings help to identify a landscape's historic period(s) of ownership, occupancy and development, and bring greater understanding of the associations that make them significant. Research findings also provide a foundation to make educated decisions for project treatment, and can guide management, maintenance, and interpretation. In addition, research findings may be useful in satisfying compliance reviews (e.g. Section 106 of the National Historic Preservation Act as amended).

2. Although there is no single way to inventory a landscape, the goal of documentation is to provide a record of the landscape as it exists at the present time, thus providing a baseline from which to operate. All component landscapes and features (see definitions below) that contribute to the landscape's historic character should be recorded. The level of documentation needed depends on the nature and the significance of the resource. For example, plant material documentation may ideally include botanical name or species, common name and size. To ensure full representation of existing herbaceous plants, care should be taken to document the landscape in different seasons. This level of research may most often be the ideal goal for smaller properties, but may prove impractical for large, vernacular landscapes.

3. Assessing a landscape as a continuum through history is critical in assessing cultural and historic value. By analyzing the landscape, change over time–the chronological and physical "layers" of the landscape–can be understood. Based on analysis, individual features may be attributed to a discrete period of introduction, their presence or absence substantiated to a given date and, therefore the landscape's significance and integrity evaluated. In addition, analysis allows the property to be viewed within the context of other cultural landscapes.

Guidelines for the Treatment of Cultural Landscapes

4. In order for the landscape to be considered significant, character-defining features that convey its significance in history must not only be present, but they also must possess historic integrity. Location, setting, design, materials, workmanship, feeling and association should be considered in determining whether a landscape and its character-defining features possess historic integrity.

5. Preservation planning for cultural landscapes involves a broad array of dynamic variables. Adopting comprehensive treatment and management plans, in concert with a preservation maintenance strategy, acknowledges a cultural landscape's ever-changing nature and the interrelationship of treatment, management and maintenance.

Source: Department of the Interior, National Park Service

Did you know...

In the March/April 2003 issue, *Utne* magazine named the 10 Most Enlightened Suburbs based on civic spirit and livability: Montgomery County, MD; Tempe, AZ; Suisin, CA; Shaker Heights, OH; Royal Oak, MI; Hammond/Whiting/Gary, IN; Burlingame/San Mateo, CA; Delray Beach, FL; Markham, ON, Canada; and Naperville, IL.

Historic American Buildings Survey

The Historic American Buildings Survey (HABS) operates as part of the National Park Service and is dedicated to recording America's historic buildings through measured drawings, written histories, and large-format photographs. The program was started in 1933 as a Civil Works Administration project using unemployed architects to make permanent records of historic American architecture. Following a drop-off in activity after World War II, the program was restored in the early 1950s with student architects providing the research, a practice that continues to the present day. In 1969, the Historic American Engineering Record (HAER) was established as a companion program focusing on America's technological heritage. Records of the over 37,000 historic structures and sites are available to the public through the Prints and Photographs Division of the Library of Congress.

Address

National Park Service
HABS/HAER Division
1849 "C" Street, NW, Room NC300
Washington, D.C. 20240
Telephone: (202) 343-9625
Internet: www.cr.nps.gov/habshaer/

For information on the HABS/HAER archives, contact:
Prints and Photographs Reading Room
Library of Congress
James Madison Building, Room LM-337
1st & Independence Ave. SE
Washington, DC 20540-4730
Telephone: (202) 707-6394
Internet: www.loc.gov/rr/print

Did you know...
According to the National Park Service, as of 2003, 95 percent of the country's 2,342 National Historic Landmarks were deemed to be in good condition, up from 94 percent in 1999.

Historic Landscape Initiative

The Historic Landscape Initiative promotes responsible preservation practices to protect America's irreplaceable cultural landscapes, the result of which can lead to an improved quality of life, a sense of place, and identity for future generations, as well as scenic, economic, ecological, recreational, social and educational opportunities. As with historic properties, America's historic landscapes are threatened by loss and change through inappropriate uses, insensitive development, vandalism, and natural forces. The Initiative provides guidance on sound preservation practices for a variety of landscapes, including parks, gardens, rural villages, industrial sites, and agricultural landscapes. Through their workshops, publications, technical assistance, and national policy advisement, the Initiative serves as a clearinghouse for information related to cultural landscapes and their preservation.

Address

Heritage Preservation Services
National Park Service
1849 C Street NW NC330
Washington, D.C. 20240
Telephone: (202) 343-9597
Internet: www2.cr.nps.gov/hli/

Historic Preservation Book Prize

Sponsored by the Center for Historic Preservation at Mary Washington College in Fredericksburg, Virginia, the Historic Preservation Book Prize each year honors a book judged to have made the most significant contribution to the field of historic preservation in the United States. A jury of preservation professionals from the University and other organizations focuses on books that break new ground or contribute to the intellectual vitality of the preservation movement. Entries are accepted from any discipline that relates to the theory or practice of historic preservation. Nominations may come from any source. Winners receive a $500 cash prize and are invited to deliver a lecture at Mary Washington College.

More information is available on the Center for Historic Preservation's Web site, *www.mwc.edu/chp/events_awards_news/*, or by calling (540) 654-1356.

1989

The Past is a Foreign Country by David Lowenthal (Cambridge University Press)

1990

Saving America's Countryside: A Guide to Rural Conservation by Samuel N. Stokes and A. Elizabeth Watson, et al. (Johns Hopkins University Press)

Imagining the Past: East Hampton Histories by T. H. Breen (University of Georgia Press)

1991

Architects and Builders in North Carolina: A History of the Practice of Building by Catherine W. Bishir, Charlotte V. Brown, Carl R. Lounsbury and Ernest H. Wood (University of North Carolina Press)

1992

Constructing Chicago by Daniel Bluestone (Yale University Press)

1993

The Park and the People: A History of Central Park by Roy Rosenzweig and Elizabeth Blackmar (Cornell University Press)

1994

The Politics of Public Memory: Tourism, History, and Ethnicity in Monterey, California by Martha K. Norkunas (State University of New York Press)

1995

An Illustrated Glossary of Early Southern Architecture and Landscape by Carl R. Lounsbury (Oxford University Press)

1996

Gender, Class, and Shelter: Perspectives in Vernacular Architecture by Elizabeth Collins Cromley and Carter Hudgins (University of Tennessee Press)

1997

Mickey Mouse History and Other Essays on American Memory by Mike Wallace (Temple Univ. Press)

1998

Shadowed Ground: America's Landscapes of Violence and Tragedy by Kenneth E. Foote (University of Texas Press)

1999

The Presence of the Past: Popular Uses of History in American Life by Roy R. Rosenzweig (Columbia University Press)

A MODERN ARCADIA
Frederick Law Olmsted Jr. and the Plan
for Forest Hills Gardens
SUSAN L. KLAUS

In *A Modern Arcadia: Frederick Law Olmsted Jr.*, Susan Klaus chronicles the history of Forest Hills Gardens, a 142-acre a middle-class housing development in New York that has long been recognized as one of the most influential planned communities in the United States, from its inception in 1909 through its first two decades. The book pays particular attention to Frederick Law Olmsted Jr., who served as planner and landscape architect for the project. *Image courtesy of the University of Massachusetts Press.*

Historic Preservation Book Prize

2000

The Drive-In, The Supermarket, and The Transformation of Commercial Space in Los Angeles, 1914-1941 by Richard Longstreth (MIT Press)

2001

Houses from Books: Treatises, Pattern Books, and Catalogs in American Architecture, 1738-1950 by Daniel Reiff (Pennsylvania State University Press)

2002

From Cottage to Bungalow: Houses and the Working Class in Metropolitan Chicago 1869-1929 by Joseph C. Bigott (University of Chicago Press)

2003

A Modern Arcadia: Frederick Law Olmsted Jr. and the Plan for Forest Hills Gardens by Susan L. Klaus (University of Massachusetts Press)

Source: Center for Historic Preservation, Mary Washington College

> Preservation is about more than making things look pretty. Its ultimate purpose is to make life better for the people who live in a community.
>
> **Mills B. Lane IV**

Historic Preservation Timeline

Evolving from isolated, private initiatives to a full-scale national movement, the history of preservation in the United States is comprised of grassroots efforts, landmark court cases, and numerous laws and economic incentives. This timeline marks some of those moments, as the heroic efforts of pioneers has led to an organized and mature movement. Today even the concept of endangered places has broadened to include not only historic buildings but entire neighborhoods, landscapes, and vernacular buildings.

1791 The Massachusetts Historical Society, the first statewide organization to collect and preserve resources for the study of American history, is established.

1812 The first national historical organization, the American Antiquarian Society, is founded in Worcester, Mass.

1816 Considered one of the first acts of preservation, Philadelphia purchases Independence Hall (the Philadelphia State House, 1732) to rescue it from demolition.

1828 The Touro Synagogue (1765) in Newport, R.I., is the nation's first recorded restoration.

1850 The New York legislature purchases the Hasbrouck House (1750), George Washington's headquarters in Newburgh, and opens it to the public as the nation's first historic house museum.

1853 Ann Pamela Cunningham founds the Mount Vernon Ladies' Association of the Union, the first private preservation organization of any kind in the U.S., to save George Washington's Mount Vernon from eventual destruction by neglect.

1857 Philadelphia's Carpenter's Hall (1744), site of the First Continental Congress, is restored and presented to the public as the first privately-owned American building that is also a historic monument.

1872 Congress sets aside Yellowstone as a national park, the first such designation in America and the world.

1876 One of the first instances of preservation in an urban setting, Boston's Old South Meeting House (1729) is rescued from demolition.

1889 The Association for the Preservation of Virginia Antiquities is formed as the nation's first statewide preservation organization.

Congress provides $2,000 for preservation of the Casa Grande ruin in Arizona, the first instance of federal spending on preservation.

1890 Congress passes the first piece of legislation to authorize the preservation of an American battlefield–the Chickamauga and Chattanooga Battlefield in Georgia and Tennessee.

1896 In United States *v.* Gettysburg Electric Railway Company, the first preservation case to go before the U.S. Supreme Court, the condemnation of private property for a national memorial is upheld.

1906 The Antiquities Act, the first major federal preservation legislation, is passed, granting the President the power to designate national monuments and enacting penalties for destroying historic and cultural resources on federal land.

Historic Preservation Timeline

1910 The incorporation of the Society for the Preservation of New England Antiquities, America's first regional preservation organization, marks a broadening in preservation theory from preserving buildings with heroic associations to buildings that are "architecturally beautiful or unique."

1916 President Woodrow Wilson approves legislation establishing the National Park Service within the U.S. Department of the Interior as the administrative agency responsible for sites designated as national park areas.

1925 The Vieux Carre Commission, the first historic preservation commission in the U.S., is established to protect New Orleans' historic French Quarter, laid out in 1721. However, it is not until a 1936 state constitutional amendment passes that the commission is granted true enforcement powers.

1926 Henry Ford begins assembling old buildings and artifacts, which trace 300 years of technological and cultural history, at his Dearborn, Mich., Greenfield Village.

John D. Rockefeller Jr. begins funding the restoration and reconstruction of Williamsburg, Va., the first attempt to restore an entire community.

1931 America's first municipal preservation ordinance to establish a historic district with regulatory control is passed in Charleston, S.C., to protect the city's quickly vanishing heritage.

1933 The Historic American Buildings Survey (HABS) is established to document historic buildings through measured drawings, photographs, and written descriptions.

1935 Congress passes the National Historic Sites Act, the first law to establish historic preservation as a national policy, and with it creates the National Historic Landmarks program.

1944 *This Is Charleston* is published in Charleston, S.C., the country's first citywide inventory of public buildings.

1946 Robert Moses proposes the Vieux Carre Expressway, an elevated riverfront highway passing through the architecturally significant historic French Quarter in New Orleans. The proposal is finally defeated in 1969.

1947 The National Council for Historic Sites and Buildings, the first nationwide private preservation organization and predecessor of the National Trust (into which it merges in 1954), is formed.

The first U.S. preservation conference is held in Washington, D.C.

1949 Congress charters the National Trust for Historic Preservation to lead private-sector preservation efforts.

1951 Woodlawn Plantation (1805) in Alexandria, Va., becomes the first of 23 historic properties currently operated by the National Trust for Historic Preservation (as of 2003).

1952 *Historic Preservation* (now *Preservation*), the nation's first nationwide preservation magazine, is launched.

Historic Preservation Timeline

1959 The first urban renewal study to address preservation concerns, *College Hill, A Demonstration Study of Historic Area Renewal for Providence, R.I.,* becomes a national model for using historic preservation as a means of community renewal.

President Eisenhower approves a six-year, $650 million urban renewal appropriation that removes rather than rehabilitates old buildings and leaves a legacy of torn neighborhoods and discontinuity.

1960 The Mount Vernon Ladies' Association of the Union is named the first recipient of the National Trust's Crowninshield Award, which honors a lifetime of achievement in the field of historic preservation.

1961 Jane Jacobs publishes *The Death and Life of Great American Cities,* a commentary on the increasing demise of America's urban environments, which that is still relevant to today's issues of sprawl and rebounding from the legacy of urban renewal.

1962 At their invitation, architect John Carl Warnecke meets with President Kennedy and the First Lady to save Washington, D.C.'s historic Lafayette Square from demolition, a collaboration that restores the square's nineteenth-century townhouses and the Renwick Gallery (1859). Warnecke also utilizes a pioneering context-sensitive approach in his design of the required federal buildings, which he inserts behind the restored townhouses.

1963 Despite widespread public outcry, the demolition of New York's Pennsylvania Station begins, a loss which galvanizes the preservation movement.

1964 Columbia University's School of Architecture offers the first graduate-level course in historic preservation.

William Matson Roth purchases the 1893 Ghirardelli Square, a former San Francisco chocolate factory, to save it from demolition. He restores the building and turns it into a retail center, one of the first successful adaptive use projects in the country.

1965 The International Council on Monuments and Sites (ICOMOS) is created to establish international standards for the preservation, restoration, and management of the cultural environment.

1966 *With Heritage So Rich* is published, a seminal historic preservation book documenting American cultural resources and chronicling the preservation movement.

Congress passes the National Historic Preservation Act, a watershed for the preservation movement. It establishes the National Register of Historic Places and an Advisory Council on Historic Places; calls for broader federal funding of preservation activities and individual state historic preservation programs; encourages the creation of local historic districts; and provides, through its Section 106, for the protection of preservation-worthy sites and properties threatened by federal activities.

Historic Preservation Timeline

1966 The Department of Transportation Act prohibits the destruction or adverse use of historic sites (as well as parklands) by transportation projects unless there is no feasible and prudent alternative.

1967 The first state historic preservation officers and the first keeper of the National Register are appointed.

1968 The Association for Preservation Technology is founded as an interdisciplinary clearinghouse for information and research about preservation techniques for historic structures.

New York City enacts the nation's first ordinance allowing the transfer of development rights, providing a tool to assist in the preservation of historic buildings.

1969 The National Environmental Policy Act requires federal agencies to prepare impact statements for projects that may affect cultural, as well as natural, resources.

The Historic American Engineering Record is established as a sister program to HABS to document and record engineering and industrial sites.

1971 Executive Order 11593 requires federal agencies to inventory their lands for cultural and historic sites and to nominate places to the National Register.

The National Trust for Historic Preservation begins its annual Preservation Honor Awards program to recognize individuals, organizations and projects that represent the best in preservation.

1972 Through the Surplus Real Property Act, Congress authorizes the transfer of surplus historic federal property to local public agencies for preservation.

The World Heritage List is founded by UNESCO to record cultural and natural properties with outstanding universal value.

1973 *Old House Journal* is launched as a newsletter for Brooklyn brownstoners and quickly expands its editorial and readership nationwide. By 2003 it has over 130,000 readers.

The first National Historic Preservation Week is celebrated, an annual event held in May.

The City of New York amends its Landmarks Preservation Law to authorize the Landmarks Commission to designate interior landmarks.

1974 Preservation Action is formed and to date is the only national preservation lobby in the U.S.

1976 The Tax Reform Act of 1976 provides the first major preservation tax incentives for the rehabilitation of certified historic income-producing properties in the form of a 60-month amortization of rehabilitation costs.

The Public Buildings Cooperative Use Act encourages restoration and adaptive use of historic buildings for federal use by requiring federal government to obtain and rehabilitate, where possible, historic buildings for use as federal office space.

Historic Preservation Timeline

1976 The Historic Preservation Fund, funded by Outer Continental Shelf mineral receipts, is established to provide preservation grants to the states.

1977 The National Trust's Main Street Project, forerunner of today's National Main Street Center, is launched in Galesburg, Ill.; Hot Springs, S.D.; and Madison, Ind., to demonstrate the value of preservation as a tool for downtown revitalization. Twenty-five years later the program boasts the participation of more than 1,650 communities, a total reinvestment in these communities of $16 billion, the creation of 226,900 new jobs, and 88,700 building rehabilitation projects.

1978 In Penn Central Transportation Co. *v.* City of New York, one of preservation's landmark rulings, the U.S. Supreme Court upholds the right of the city to block construction over Grand Central Terminal, thus affirming the legitimacy of preservation ordinances and local governments' power to enforce such ordinances.

The Secretary of the Interior's Standards for Historic Preservation are released as the first professional standards for work on historic resources.

The Revenue Act of 1978 creates a 10 percent tax credit for the rehabilitation of older commercial properties.

Eero Saarinen's Dulles International Airport Terminal (Loudon County, Va.) is deemed eligible for the National Register in 1978, only 16 years after its construction, breaking the Register's typical 50-year rule.

1979 With the largest concentration of 1920s and 1930s resort architecture in the United States, Miami Beach becomes the first National Register Historic District comprised entirely of 20th-century buildings.

This Old House debuts on Boston Public Television and will eventually become one of the most popular PBS and home improvement shows in history, reaching more than 3.9 million viewers weekly.

1980 Amendments to the National Historic Preservation Act are passed that direct federal agencies to nominate and protect historic federal properties, broaden participation of local governments and require owner consent for National Register listing.

The Vernacular Architecture Forum is founded to encourage the study and preservation of traditional structures and landscapes.

1981 The Economic Recovery Tax Act expands the rehabilitation tax credit program, offering a 25 percent credit for renovating certified historic properties, and prompts a surge in rehab nationwide. It also abolishes the tax incentive for demolishing historic properties.

1982 The zero preservation funding proposed by the Regan administration is fought and funding is restored after an intensive nationwide campaign.

1983 After a zealous preservation protest, Congress approves a $48 million plan to restore the west front of the U.S. Capitol rather than the planned $73 million addition that would have obscured the historic facade.

Historic Preservation Timeline

1985 McDonald's announces plans to restore the first roadside stand built by Ray Kroc in 1955 in Des Plaines, Ill.

1986 After a nationwide campaign to save the rehabilitation tax credits, the Tax Reform Act of 1986 is passed; although the credits are reduced from the 1981 level.

1988 Manassas National Battlefield Park in Virginia is saved from a 1.2 million-square-foot shopping mall development. The park will face another battle in 1993 when Disney proposes a historic theme park, Disney's America, three miles from the Battlefield Park. After tremendous national outcry over concerns about the effect of the associated sprawl on the battlefield, Disney withdraws their proposal.

The National Trust issues its first 11 Most Endangered Historic Places List to bring attention to threatened historic sites and to generate local support. In 15 years only one of the over 160 listed sites has been destroyed.

DOCOMOMO (Documentation and Conservation of Buildings, Sites, Neighborhoods of the Modern Movement) is founded in The Netherlands in response to the increasing demolition of Modern architecture, documenting and advocating the preservation of the Modern heritage.

1991 The passage of the Intermodal Surface Transportation Efficiency Act (ISTEA) provides a significant source of federal funding for preservation projects.

1995 The World Monuments Fund establishes their biennial World Monuments Watch list of 100 worldwide cultural sites in urgent need of intervention.

1996 In response to looming development, the National Trust purchases the land directly across the Ashley River from its 1738 Drayton Hall plantation (Charleston, S.C.) in order to preserve the site's natural vistas and historic character.

1997 The state of Texas becomes a pioneer in the digitizing of preservation records with its launch of the Texas Historic Sites Atlas (http://atlas.thc.state.tx.us/), an online database of 238,000 historic and archeological site records documenting Texas history with integrated mapping software for locating the resources.

1998 Save America's Treasures, a public-private partnership, is founded to identify and rescue the enduring symbols of America and raise public awareness and support for their preservation.

The first 20th-century vernacular structure less than 50 years old, the 1959 Ralph Sr. and Sunny Wilson House in Temple, Texas, built for the founder of Wilsonart International, is listed in the National Register of Historic Places.

The 1966 appropriation providing federal funding for the National Trust is terminated. The Trust has since relied on private-sector contributions.

Historic Preservation Timeline

1998 Arapahoe Acres in Englewood, Colo., is the first post-World War II residential subdivision listed as a historic district in the National Register of Historic Places.

2001 By 2001, historic buildings provide approximately one-fourth of The General Services Administration's federally-owned space.

2003 The National Trust is the first non-profit group to receive the National Humanities Medal.

New York city passes contextual zoning regulations in a number of neighborhoods to encourage sympathetically-scaled new buildings within historic districts.

Source: Counsel House Research

International Centre for the Study of the Preservation and Restoration of Cultural Property

Founded by the United Nations' Educational, Scientific and Cultural Organization (UNESCO) in 1956, the International Centre for the Study of the Preservation and Restoration of Cultural Property (ICCROM) is an intergovernmental organization dedicated to the conservation of heritage of all types. It is funded by contributions from its over 100 Member States, plus donors and sponsors. ICCROM provides members with information, publications and training; offers technical assistance and sponsors workshops; performs ongoing research and archives findings; and serves as an advocate for preservation. The group maintains one of the largest conservation libraries in the world.

Address

13, Via di San Michele
I-00153 Rome, Italy
Telephone: +39 06 585531
Internet: www.iccrom.org

International Council on Monuments and Sites

Dedicated to the conservation of the world's historic monuments and sites, the International Council on Monuments and Sites (ICOMOS) is an international, non-governmental organization with National Committees in over 107 countries. The group is the United Nations' Educational, Scientific and Cultural Organization's (UNESCO) principal advisor on matters concerning the conservation of monuments and sites. With the World Conservation Union (IUCN), ICOMOS advises the World Heritage Committee and UNESCO on the nomination of new sites to the World Heritage List. The group also works to establish international standards for the preservation, restoration and management of the cultural environment. ICOMOS members are professional architects, archaeologists, urban planners, engineers, heritage administrators, art historians, and archivists. All members join ICOMOS through the National Committee of their respective countries.

Address

49-51 rue de la Fédération
75015 Paris, France
Telephone: +33 (0) 1 45 67 67 70
Internet: www.icomos.org

Landslide Landscapes

The Cultural Landscape Foundation (CLF) compiles a semi-annual list of 10 Landslide Landscapes, consisting of endangered cultural landscapes of a certain age and use type. The list is intended to rally public support at the local, state and national level and to provide links to the groups that are working to preserve these important parts of our national heritage. Nominations for the Landslide Landscapes list are accepted from local groups or individuals, professionals, government officials, and other interested parties. The 2002 Landslide Landscapes list focused on masterworks of landscape architecture designed in the past 250 years. The 2004 program is concerned with "working landscapes," which may include any endangered historic rural or vernacular landscape where people worked the land: farms and ranches, shipyards, logging camps, railroad yards, fishing villages, etc.

For photos, site histories, biographies, and status updates, visit the CLF Web site at *www.tclf.org* or call (202) 483-0553.

Landslide Landscapes 2002: Modern Designed Landscapes

1. East Plaza, U.S. Capitol Grounds, 1874-1892
   Washington, DC
   Frederick Law Olmsted

2. Seneca Park, 1888
   Rochester, NY
   Frederick Law Olmsted

3. Three works by Lawrence Halprin:
   Virginia Museum of Fine Arts, Richmond, VA, 1976
   Skyline Park, Denver, CO, 1973
   Heritage Park, Ft. Worth, TX, 1976

4. River Road Estates, 1875-1938
   Louisville, KY
   Frederick Law Olmsted, Carrere and Hastings, Bryant Fleming, Marian Coffin, and others

5. Stan Hywet Hall and Gardens, 1910s
   Akron, OH
   Warren Manning

6. The Indiana Landscapes of Dan Kiley:
   Concordia Seminary, Fort Wayne, IN, 1958
   North Christian Church, Columbus, IN, 1964

7. Val Verde, 1915
   Montecito, CA
   Lockwood de Forest

8. Christopher Columbus Park, 1974-1976
   Boston, MA
   Sasaki Associates

9. The City of Savannah, 1733
   Savannah, GA
   General James Oglethorpe

10. America's College Campuses, across the USA, including such pioneering nineteenth and early twentieth-century landscape architects as Frederick Law Olmsted (Stanford Univ., CA) Warren Manning (Amherst College, MA) and Beatrix Farrand (Princeton Univ., NJ) as well as innovative modernist landscape architects as Sasaki-Walker Associates (Foothills College, Los Altos, CA), Ralph Cornell (Univ. of California at Los Angeles), Thomas Church (Univ. of California at Santa Cruz) and Harriett Wimmer (Univ. of California, San Diego).

Source: Cultural Landscape Foundation

Most Visited Historic House Museums in the United States

Every year Counsel House Research, in conjunction with the *Almanac of Architecture & Design*, polls America's historic house museums to determine which are the most popular destinations. For the purposes of this study, "house museum" is defined as a historic house that is currently exhibited and interpreted as a dwelling place. The following houses are this year's most visited historic house museums.

1. Biltmore Estate, Asheville, NC
   Richard Morris Hunt, 1895
2. Mount Vernon, Mount Vernon, VA
   George Washington, 1785-86
3. Hearst Castle, San Simeon, CA
   Julia Morgan, 1927-1947
4. Graceland, Memphis, TN
   Furbringer & Ehrman, 1939
5. Monticello, Home of Thomas Jefferson, Charlottesville, VA
   Thomas Jefferson, 1768-79, 1793-1809
6. Arlington House, The Robert E. Lee Memorial, Arlington, VA
   George Hadfield, 1817
7. Vanderbilt Mansion, Hyde Park, NY
   McKim, Mead and White, 1898
8. The Breakers, Newport, RI
   Richard Morris Hunt, 1895
9. The Edison and Ford Winter Estates, Fort Myers, FL
   Thomas Edison, 1886 (Edison home)
   Architect unknown, 1911 (Ford home)
10. Betsy Ross House, Philadelphia, PA
    Architect unknown, 1740
11. Paul Revere House, Boston, MA
    Architect unknown, c.1680
12. Carter's Grove, Williamsburg, VA
    John Wheatley, c. 1750-55
13. Lincoln Home, Springfield, IL
    Architect unknown, 1839
14. The Hermitage: Home of President Andrew Jackson, Hermitage, TN
    David Morrison, Joseph Ruff, William Hume, 1819-1837
15. Boldt Castle, Alexandria Bay, NY
    Hewitt, Stevens & Paist, 1900-04
16. Marble House, Newport, RI
    Richard Morris Hunt, 1892
17. Fairlane–The Henry Ford Estate, Dearborn, MI
    William H. Van Tine, 1915
18. Viscaya, Miami, FL
    Burrall Hoffman, 1916
19. Laura: A Creole Plantation, Vacherie, LA
    Architect unknown, 1805
20. The Elms, Newport, RI
    Horace Trumbauer, 1901
21. Home of Franklin D. Roosevelt, Hyde Park, NY
    Architect unknown, c. 1800-1826
    Hoppin, Coen and Brown, 1915
22. Magnolia Plantation, Charleston, SC
    Architect unknown, 1730
23. House of the Seven Gables, Salem, MA
    Architect unknown, 1668
24. Taliesen West, Scottsdale, AZ
    Frank Lloyd Wright, 1937
25. Rosecliff, Newport, RI
    Stanford White, 1902

Source: Counsel House Research

National Center for Preservation Technology and Training

The National Center for Preservation Technology and Training (NCPTT) promotes and enhances the preservation and conservation of prehistoric and historic resources in the United States through the advancement and dissemination of preservation technology and training. Created by Congress, the NCPTT is an interdisciplinary program of the National Park Service intended to advance the art, craft and science of historic preservation in the fields of archeology, historic architecture, historic landscapes, objects, materials conservation, and interpretation through research, education and information management. The Center also administers the Preservation Technology and Training Grants Program, one of the few preservation and conservation grants programs devoted to training, technology and basic research issues.

Address

Northwestern State University
Box 5682
Natchitoches, LA 71497
Telephone: (318) 357-6464
Internet: www. ncptt.nps.gov

National Heritage Areas

Since 1984, the United States Congress has designated 23 National Heritage Areas, which are managed by partnerships among federal, state and local governments and the private sector. This distinction is awarded in an effort to preserve areas where "natural, cultural, historic, and scenic resources combine to form a cohesive, nationally distinctive landscape arising from patterns of human activity shaped by geography." The National Park Service provides technical as well as financial assistance for a limited number of years following initial designation. Though Heritage Areas often remain in private hands, activities such as tours, museums and festivals take place through voluntary efforts.

For additional information, including maps, visit ParkNet, the Web site of the National Park Service, at *www.cr.nps.gov/heritageareas/*.

National Heritage Areas

America's Agricultural Heritage Partnership (Silos & Smokestacks National Heritage Area), IA
Augusta Canal National Heritage Area, GA
Automobile National Heritage Area, MI
Cache La Poudre National Heritage Area, CO
Cane River National Heritage Area, LA
Delaware & Lehigh National Heritage Corridor, PA
Erie Canalway National Corridor, NY
Essex National Heritage Area, MA
Hudson River Valley National Heritage Area, NY
Illinois and Michigan Canal National Heritage Corridor, IL
John H. Chafee Blackstone River Valley National Heritage Corridor, RI
Lackawanna Valley National Heritage Area, PA
National Coal Heritage Area, WV
Ohio and Erie Canal National Heritage Corridor, OH
Quinebaug and Shetucket Rivers Valley National Heritage Corridor, CT
Rivers of Steel National Heritage Area, PA
Schuylkill River Valley National Heritage Area, PA
Shenandoah Valley Battlefields National Historic District Commission, VA
South Carolina National Heritage Corridor, SC
Southwestern Pennsylvania Heritage Preservation Commission (Path of Progress National Heritage Tour Route), PA
Tennessee Civil War Heritage Area, TN
Wheeling National Heritage Area, WV
Yuma Crossing National Heritage Area, AZ

Source: National Park Service

Did you know...
Heritage tourists spend an average of $30 per day more than other travelers and stay longer than other tourists.

National Main Street Leadership Awards

New in 2002, the National Trust for Historic Preservation's National Main Street Leadership Awards identify and honor key leaders in the commercial district revitalization movement. In conjunction with their Main Street Awards, the National Trust annually recognizes exceptional accomplishments in the revitalization of America's downtowns and neighborhood commercial districts. The National Main Street Leadership Awards are presented in three categories: the Civic Leadership Award recognizing an elected official, government staff person, public agency or nonprofit organization; the Business Leadership award recognizing a small business, an industry, or a corporation; and The Main Street Heroes Award for outstanding contribution by an individual toward the revitalization of a commercial district.

Applications, past winners and eligibility requirements are available online at *www.mainstreet.org.*

2003

The Civic Leadership Award
Savannah College of Art and Design
Savannah, GA

The Business Leadership Award
Tom Kiefaber
Baltimore, MD

The Main Street Heroes Award
Renee L. Hanson, Esq.
Georgetown, TX

Source: National Trust for Historic Preservation

> Communities can be shaped by choice or by chance. We can keep accepting the kind of communities we get, or we can insist on getting the kind of communities we want.
>
> **Richard Moe**

National Preservation Awards

Each year the National Trust for Historic Preservation recognizes citizens, organizations, and public and private entities that demonstrate a high level of dedication and support of the ideals and benefits of historic preservation through its National Preservation Awards program. A jury of preservation professionals and representatives selects winners based on their positive effect on the community, pioneering nature, quality, and degree of difficulty. Special interest is also placed on those undertakings that utilize historic preservation as a method of revitalization.

For more information, contact the National Trust at (800) 944-6847 or visit their Web site at *www.nationaltrust.org*.

2003 Award Winners

Atlantic City Convention Hall
Atlantic City, NJ

Beaumont Hotel
Ouray, CO

Fair Park
Dallas, TX

Ferry Building
San Francisco, CA

Hidalgo Pumphouse
Hidalgo, TX

Indiana Cotton Mill
Cannelton, IN

John (Jack) Shannahan
Hartford, CT

Kit Carson Carousel
Stratton, CO

Light House Preservation Act
Nationwide

Market Hall
Charleston, SC

Massachusetts State House
Boston, MA

Michigan Volunteers
Grand Teton National Park, WY

Porcupine House/Ute Mt. Tribal Park
Towaoc, CO

Portland Museum of Art
Portland, ME

Stone Avenue Temple
Tucson, AZ

Source: National Trust for Historic Preservation

Top: Known as the "flagship hotel of the western slope" when it first opened in 1886, the Beaumont Hotel in Ouray, Colo., has undergone a $4 million restoration and has spurred other community restoration projects (*Photo by Kathleen Norris Cook*). *Middle*: The City of Charleston's museum-quality restoration of the 1841 Market Hall has returned it to its Civil War appearance after extensive damage suffered during Hurricane Hugo. *Bottom*: A cultural icon located on Atlantic City's world-famous Boardwalk, the Atlantic City Convention Hall has regained its glamour after a five-year, $99 million tax-credit rehabilitation. *All photos courtesy of the National Trust for Historic Preservation.*

National Preservation Institute

The National Preservation Institute (NPI) is a non-profit organization dedicated to the management, development, and preservation of historic, cultural, and environmental resources. Toward this end, NPI offers specialized information, continuing education, and, upon request, professional training tailored to the sponsor's needs. Many preservation-related services are available from NPI, including authentication of historic reproductions and historic real estate. NPI is also registered with The American Institute of Architects' continuing education program.

Address

P.O. Box 1702
Alexandria, VA 22313
Telephone: (703) 765-0100
Internet: www.npi.org

National Trust for Historic Preservation

Since its founding in 1949, the National Trust for Historic Preservation (NTHP) has worked to preserve historic buildings and neighborhoods. Through educational programs, publications, financial assistance and government advocacy, the National Trust has been successful in revitalizing communities across the country. This private, non-profit organization operates six regional offices, 23 historic sites, publishes the award winning *Preservation* magazine, hosts the nation's largest annual preservation conference and works with thousands of local community groups nationwide to preserve their history and buildings.

Address

1785 Massachusetts Avenue, NW
Washington, DC 20036
Telephone: (202) 588-6000
www.nationaltrust.org

Did you know...

To coincide with National Preservation Week in May 2003, the Ad Council and the National Trust for Historic Preservation launched a public service advertising campaign, "History Is in Our Hands," to help preserve America's heritage.

NTHP/HUD Secretary's Award for Excellence in Historic Preservation

Each year, as part of its Preservation Conference, the National Trust for Historic Preservation (NTHP) confers several awards for preservation, including the HUD Secretary's Award for Excellence in Historic Preservation. This award specifically honors preservation projects which also provide affordable housing and/or expanded economic opportunities for low- and moderate-income families and individuals. The criteria for the award includes the project's impact on the community, quality and degree of difficulty, unusual or pioneering nature, affordable housing/economic development opportunities, and ability to fit into an overall community redevelopment plan.

For additional information and to request an application, call HUD USER at (800) 245-2691 and select "Secretary's Awards" when prompted, or visit the HUD Web site at *www.huduser.org/research/secaward.html.*

1998

A.T. Lewis and Rio Grande Lofts
Denver, CO

1999

Belle Shore Apartments
Chicago, IL

2000

The city of Covington (KY)

2001

Notre Dame Academy
Cleveland, OH

2002

Hamilton Hotel
Laredo, TX

2003

Ziegler Estate/La Casita Verde
Los Angeles, CA

Source: National Trust for Historic Preservation

Presidents of the National Trust for Historic Preservation

1949-1956	Frederick L. Rath Jr.
1956-1960	Richard H. Howland
1960-1967	Robert R. Garvey Jr.
1968-1980	James Biddle
1980-1984	Michael L. Ainslie
1984-1992	J. Jackson Walter
1992–	Richard Moe

Source: National Trust for Historic Preservation

Did you know...

National Trust president Richard Moe was named an honorary member of The American Institute of Architects in 2003 for his leadership in making the Trust "a nationally recognized and effective advocate for controlling sprawl and encouraging smart growth throughout the country."

Rural Heritage Program

The Rural Heritage Program (RHP), a part of the National Trust for Historic Preservation, is dedicated to the recognition and preservation of rural historic and cultural resources. Through their educational programs, publications, and technical assistance, the RHP supports the efforts of rural communities across the United States to both preserve and live with their heritage. The program works with communities on such topics as farmland preservation, scenic byways, heritage areas and parks, historic roads, and sprawl.

Address

1785 Massachusetts Avenue, NW
Washington, DC 20036
Telephone: (202) 588-6279
Internet: www.ruralheritage.org

A country with no regard for its past will do little worth remembering in the future.

Abraham Lincoln

Save America's Treasures

Launched in May 1998, Save America's Treasures is a public-private initiative between the White House Millennium Council and the National Trust for Historic Preservation dedicated to identifying and rescuing the enduring symbols of America and to raising public awareness and support for their preservation. This national effort to protect America's threatened cultural treasures includes significant documents, works of art, maps, journals, and historic structures that document and illuminate the history and culture of the United States. Applications to be designated an official project are accepted on an ongoing basis from non-profit organizations and federal, state, and local agencies that are involved in the preservation, restoration, or conservation of historic buildings, sites, documents, artifacts, objects, or related educational activities. Becoming an official project is the first step toward eligibility for Save America's Treasures grants and, in and of itself, often generates local support. In the two years since its founding, Save America's Treasures has designated over 800 official projects (a list of which is available on their Web site) and raised over $100 million in public-private funds to support preservation efforts.

Address

1785 Massachusetts Avenue, N.W.
Washington, D.C. 20036
Telephone: (202) 588-6202
Internet: www.saveamericastreasures.org

Secretary of the Interior's Standards for Rehabilitation

The Secretary of the Interior's Standards for Rehabilitation were developed to help protect our nation's irreplaceable cultural resources by promoting consistent preservation practices. The Standards recognize the need to alter or add to a historic property in order to meet continuing or changing uses. Following the Standards helps to preserve the distinctive character of a historic building and its site while accommodating new uses. The Standards (36 CFR Part 67) apply to historic buildings of all periods, styles, types, materials, and sizes, as well as to both the exterior and the interior of historic buildings. The Standards also encompass related landscape features and the building's site and environment as well as attached, adjacent, or related new construction. In addition, in order for a rehabilitation project to be eligible for the 20% rehabilitation tax credit, the Standards must be followed.

For more information about how to apply these Standards to restoration projects and tax credits, visit the National Park Service's Web site at *www2.cr.nps.gov/tps/tax/rehabstandards.htm.*

1. A property shall be used for its historic purpose or be placed in a new use that requires minimal change to the defining characteristics of the building and its site and environment.

2. The historic character of a property shall be retained and preserved. The removal of historic materials or alteration of features and spaces that characterize a property shall be avoided.

3. Each property shall be recognized as a physical record of its time, place, and use. Changes that create a false sense of historical development, such as adding conjectural features or architectural elements from other buildings, shall not be undertaken.

4. Most properties change over time; those changes that have acquired historic significance in their own right shall be retained and preserved.

5. Distinctive features, finishes, and construction techniques or examples of craftsmanship that characterize a historic property shall be preserved.

6. Deteriorated historic features shall be repaired rather than replaced. Where the severity of deterioration requires replacement of a distinctive feature, the new feature shall match the old in design, color, texture, and other visual qualities and, where possible, materials. Replacement of missing features shall be substantiated by documentary, physical, or pictorial evidence.

7. Chemical or physical treatments, such as sandblasting, that cause damage to historic materials shall not be used. The surface cleaning of structures, if appropriate, shall be undertaken using the gentlest means possible.

Secretary of the Interior's Standards for Rehabilitation

8. Significant archeological resources affected by a project shall be protected and preserved. If such resources must be disturbed, mitigation measures shall be undertaken.

9. New additions, exterior alterations, or related new construction shall not destroy historic materials that characterize the property. The new work shall be differentiated from the old and shall be compatible with the massing, size, scale, and architectural features to protect the historic integrity of the property and its environment.

10. New additions and adjacent or related new construction shall be undertaken in such a manner that if removed in the future, the essential form and integrity of the historic property and its environment would be unimpaired.

Source: Department of the Interior, National Park Service

Threatened National Historic Landmarks

National Historic Landmarks are buildings, sites, districts, structures, and objects determined by the Secretary of the Interior to possess national significance to American history and culture and are deemed worthy of preservation. Every two years, out of the almost 2,500 National Historic Landmarks, the National Park Service compiles a list of those that are in eminent danger of destruction due to deterioration, incompatible new construction, demolition, erosion, vandalism, and looting. The purpose of this list is to alert the Federal government and the American people of this potential loss of their heritage.

For additional information about the National Historic Landmarks program or the Threatened List, visit the National Park's web site at *www.cr.nps.gov/landmarks.htm* or contact Heritage Preservation Services at (202) 343-9583.

2002 Threatened Buildings and Historic Districts

Alaska
Fort Glenn, Fort Glenn
Holy Assumption Orthodox Church, Kenai
Seal Island Historic District, Pribilof Islands

Arizona
Fort Huachuca, Fort Huachuca
Old Oraibi, Oraibi
Yuma Crossing & Associated Sites, Yuma

Arkansas
Bathhouse Row, Hot Springs

California
Mare Island Naval Shipyard, Vallejo
Warner's Ranch, Warner Springs

Colorado
Central City/Black Hawk Historic District, Central City
Cripple Creek Historic District, Cripple Creek

Delaware
Eleutherian Mills, Wilmington

District of Columbia
Terrell (Mary Church) House

Georgia
Savannah Historic District, Savannah

Hawaii
Kalaupapa Leprosy Settlement, Kalaupapa Peninsula, Moloka'I Island
United States Naval Base, Pearl Harbor, Pearl City

Illinois
Grant Park Stadium, Chicago
Pullman Historic District, Chicago

Indiana
Bailly (Joseph) Homestead, Porter County

Iowa
Fort Des Moines Provisional Army Officer Training School, Des Moines

Louisiana
Courthouse (The) and Lawyers' Row, Clinton

Massachusetts
Boston Naval Shipyard, Boston
Fenway Studios, Boston
Lowell Locks & Canal Historic District, Lowell
Nantucket Historic District, Nantucket
Springfield Armory, Springfield

Threatened National Historic Landmarks

Michigan
Calumet Historic District, Calumet
Highland Park Ford Plant, Highland Park
Quincy Mining Company Historic District, Hancock

Minnesota
Fort Snelling, Minneapolis/St. Paul

Mississippi
Champion Hill Battlefield, Bolton
Siege and Battle of Corinth Sites, Corinth

Missouri
Patee House, St. Joseph

Montana
Butte Historic District, Butte
Great Northern Railway Buildings, Glacier National Park
Virginia City Historic District, Virginia City

Nevada
Virginia City Historic District, Virginia City

New Jersey
Monmouth Battlefield, Freehold
Whitman (Walt) House, Camden

New Mexico
Acoma Pueblo, Casa Blanca
Lincoln Historic District, Lincoln
National Park Service Region III Headquarters Building, Santa Fe
San Francisco De Assisi Mission Church, Ranchos de Taos
Seton Village, Santa Fe
Watrous (La Junta), Watrous
Zuni-Cibola Complex, Zuni

New York
Edna St. Vincent Millay House & Garden, Austerlitz
New York Botanical Gardens, New York

Ohio
McKinley (William) Tomb, Canton
Ohio and Erie Canal, Valley View Village
Stan Hywet Hall, Akron

Oklahoma
Fort Gibson, Fort Gibson
Wheelock Academy, Durant

Pennsylvania
Bedford Springs Hotel Historic District, Bedford
Bomberger's Distillery, New Manstown
East Broad Top Railroad, Rockhill Furnace
Eastern State Penitentiary, Philadelphia
Gallatin (Albert) House, Point Marion
Harrisburg Station and Train Shed, Harrisburg
Honey Hollow Watershed, New Hope
Meason (Isaac) House, Dunbar Township
United States Naval Asylum, Philadelphia
Woodlands, Philadelphia

South Dakota
Frawley Ranch Historic District, Spearfish

Tennessee
Beale Street Historic District, Memphis
Franklin (Isaac) Plantation, Gallatin

Texas
Fort Brown, Brownsville

Vermont
Robbins and Lawrence Armory and Machine Shop, Windsor

Virginia
Bacon's Castle, Surry County
Jackson Ward Historic District, Richmond
Saint Luke's Church, Smithfield

Threatened National Historic Landmarks

West Virginia
Elkins Coal and Coke, Bretz

Wisconsin
Taliesin East, Spring Green

Wyoming
Swan Land and Cattle Company Headquarters, Chugwater

Source: National Park Service

Did you know...
In the past two years, 30 National Landmarks have been removed from the Threatened list.

UNESCO Asia-Pacific Heritage Awards for Culture Heritage Conservation

As a part of the United Nations' Educational, Scientific and Cultural Organization's (UNESCO) culture heritage program in Asia and the Pacific, the Awards for Culture Heritage Conservation are presented each year to individuals and organizations within the private sector for superior conservation and restoration of structures over 50 years old. The projects must have been restored within the past 10 years and must also be privately leased or owned. One entry will be selected for an Award of Excellence, while two projects will be honored with an Award of Distinction. Awards of Merit and Honorable Mentions will be awarded at the jury's discretion.

Regulations and entry forms can be found online at *www.unescobkk.org/culture/heritageawards/*.

2003 Awards

Award of Excellence

Guangyu Ancestral Hall
Conghua City, Guangdong Province, China

Award of Distinction

Water Towns of the Yangtze River
Jiangsu and Zhejiang Provinces, China
(Zhouzhuang, Tongli, Luzhi, Nanxun, Wuzheng, Xitang)

Astana of Syed Mir Muhammad
Ghanche District, Baltistan, Pakistan

Award of Merit

Canqiao Historical Street
Shaoxing City, Zhejiang Province, China

The Medina Grand Adelaide Treasury
Adelaide, Australia

Virtuous Bridge
Medan, Indonesia

Honorable Mention

Gota de Leche
Manila, Philippines

Catholic Cathedral of the Immaculate Conception
Hong Kong SAR, China

Dalongdong Baoan Temple
Taipei, China

Source: United Nations' Educational, Scientific and Cultural Organization (UNESCO)

Vernacular Architecture Forum

Devoted to the "ordinary" architecture of North America, the Vernacular Architecture Forum (VAF) was formed in 1980 to encourage the study and preservation of traditional structures and landscapes. These include agricultural buildings, industrial and commercial structures, twentieth-century suburban houses, settlement patterns and cultural landscapes, and areas historically overlooked by scholars. The VAF embraces multidisciplinary interaction. Historians, designers, archaeologists, folklorists, architectural historians, geographers, museum curators and historic preservationists contribute to the organization. The VAF holds its conference every spring with part of the agenda focusing on the vernacular architecture of that region. Every few years papers are selected from past conferences and published in the series *Perspectives in Vernacular Architecture*, now in its ninth volume. The VAF presents two annual awards: the Abbott Lowell Cummings Award for the best book published on North American vernacular architecture and cultural landscapes, and the Paul E. Buchanan Award for the best non-published work on North American vernacular architecture.

Address

P.O. Box 1511
Harrisonburg, VA 22803-1511
Internet: www.vernaculararchitectureforum.org

Did you know...

The Monterey Trailer Park (c. 1920s), the oldest trailer park in Los Angeles, earned landmark status from the city in November 2002, making it the nation's only trailer park listed on a historic registry.

World Heritage List

Since 1972 the World Heritage Committee has placed more than 750 properties in 125 countries on the World Heritage List. Established under terms of The Convention Concerning the Protection of the World Cultural and Natural Heritage, the World Heritage List was adopted in November 1972 at the 17th General Conference of the United Nations Educational, Scientific, and Cultural Organization (UNESCO). The Convention states that a World Heritage Committee "will establish, keep up-to-date and publish" a World Heritage List of cultural and natural properties, submitted by the States Parties and considered to be of outstanding universal value. One of the main responsibilities of this Committee is to provide technical cooperation under the World Heritage Fund for the safeguarding of World Heritage properties to States Parties whose resources are insufficient. Assistance with the nomination process, training, grants, and loans is also available.

For a complete listing of all the World Heritage properties with detailed descriptions and photographs, visit their Web site at *www.unesco.org/whc.*

Historic Cities and Towns

Algeria

Kasbah of Algiers
M'Zab Valley

Austria

City of Graz – Historic Centre
Hallstatt-Dachstein Salzkammergut Cultural Landscape
Historic Centre of the City of Salzburg
Historic Centre of Vienna

Azerbaijan

Walled City of Baku with the Shirvanshah's Palace and Maiden Tower*

Belgium

Grand-Place, Brussels
Historic Centre of Brugge

Bolivia

City of Potosi
Historic City of Sucre

Brazil

Brasilia
Historic Centre of Salvador de Bahia
Historic Centre of São Luis
Historic Centre of the Town of Diamantina
Historic Centre of the Town of Goiás
Historic Centre of the Town of Olinda
Historic Town of Ouro Preto

Bulgaria

Ancient City of Nessebar

Canada

Lunenburg Old Town
Quebec (Historic Area)

China

Ancient City of Ping Yao
Old Town of Lijiang

Colombia

Historic Centre of Santa Cruz de Mompox
Port, Fortresses and Group of Monuments, Cartagena

World Heritage List

Croatia

Historic City of Trogir

Historical Complex of Split with the Palace of Diocletian

Old City of Dubrovnik

Cuba

Old Havana and its Fortifications

Trinidad and the Valley de los Ingenios

Czech Republic

Cathedral of Our Lady at Sedlec

Historic Centre of Cesky Krumlov

Historic Centre of Prague

Historic Centre of Telc

Holasovice Historical Village Reservation

Kutná Hora: Historical Town Centre with the Church of St Barbara and the Cathedral of Our Lady at Sedlec

Dominican Republic

Colonial City of Santo Domingo

Ecuador

City of Quito

Historic Centre of Santa Ana de los Ríos de Cuenca

Egypt

Abu Mena*

Islamic Cairo

Estonia

Historic Centre (Old Town) of Tallinn

Finland

Old Rauma

Former Yugoslav Republic of Macedonia

Ohrid Region with its Cultural and Historical Aspect and its Natural Environment

France

Historic Centre of Avignon

Historic Fortified City of Carcassonne

Historic Site of Lyons

Mont-Saint-Michel and its Bay

Paris, Banks of the Seine

Place Stanislas, Place de la Carrière and Place d'Alliance in Nancy

Provins, Town of Medieval Fairs

Roman and Romanesque Monuments of Arles

Grande Ile, Strasbourg

Germany

Classical Weimar

Collegiate Church, Castle, and Old Town of Quedlinburg

Hanseatic City of Lübeck

Historic Centres of Stralsund and Wismar

Mines of Rammelsberg and Historic Town of Goslar

Palaces and Parks of Potsdam and Berlin

Town of Bamberg

Greece

Historic Centre (Chorá) with the Monastery of Saint John "the Theologian" and the Cave of the Apocalypse on the Island of Pátmos

Medieval City of Rhodes

Guatemala

Antigua Guatemala

Holy See

Vatican City

Holy See/Italy

Historic Centre of Rome, the Properties of the Holy See in that City Enjoying Extraterritorial Rights and San Paolo Fuori le Mura

Hungary

Budapest, the Banks of the Danube and the Buda Castle Quarter

World Heritage List

Iran
Meidan Emam, Esfahan

Israel
Old City of Acre

Italy
Assisi, the Basilica of San Francesco and Other Franciscan Sites
Cathedral, Torre Civica and Piazza Grande, Modena
City of Verona
City of Vicenza and the Palladian Villas of the Veneto
Costiera Amalfitana
Crespi d'Adda
Ferrara, City of the Renaissance and its Po Delta
Historic Centre of the City of Pienza
Historic Centre of Florence
Historic Centre of Naples
Historic Centre of San Gimignano
Historic Centre of Siena
Historic Centre of Urbino
I Sassi di Matera
Late Baroque Towns of the Val di Noto (South-Eastern Sicily)
Portovenere, Cinque Terre, and the Islands (Palmaria, Tino and Tinetto)
Venice and its Lagoon

Japan
Historic Monuments of Ancient Kyoto (Kyoto, Uji and Otsu Cities)
Historic Monuments of Ancient Nara
Historic Villages of Shirakawa-go and Gokayama

Jerusalem
Old City of Jerusalem and its Walls*

Lao People's Democratic Republic
Town of Luang Prabang

Latvia
Historic Centre of Riga

Lebanon
Byblos

Libyan Arab Jamahiriya
Old Town of Ghadames

Lithuania
Vilnius Historic Centre

Luxembourg
City of Luxembourg: its Old Quarters and Fortifications

Mali
Old Towns of Djenné
Timbuktu

Malta
City of Valletta

Mauritania
Ancient Ksour of Ouadane, Chinguetti, Tichitt and Oualata

Mexico
Historic Centre of Mexico City and Xochimilco
Historic Centre of Morelia
Historic Centre of Oaxaca and Archaeological Site of Monte Alban
Historic Centre of Puebla
Historic Centre of Zacatecas
Historic Fortified Town of Campeche
Historic Monuments Zone of Querétaro
Historic Monuments Zone of Tlacotalpan
Historic Town of Guanajuato and Adjacent Mines

Morocco
Historic City of Meknes
Ksar of Ait-Ben-Haddou
Medina of Essaouira (formerly Mogador)
Medina of Fez
Medina of Marrakesh
Medina of Tétouan (formerly known as Titawin)

World Heritage List

Mozambique
Island of Mozambique

Nepal
Kathmandu Valley*

Netherlands
Historic Area of Willemstad, Inner City and Harbour, Netherlands Antilles
Droogmakerij de Beemster (Beemster Polder)

Norway
Bryggen
Røros

Oman
Frankincense Trail

Panama
Historic District of Panamá, with the Salón Bolivar

Peru
City of Cuzco
Historic Centre of Lima
Historical Centre of the City of Arequipa

Philippines
Historic Town of Vigan

Poland
Cracow's Historic Centre
Historic Centre of Warsaw
Medieval Town of Torun
Old City of Zamosc

Portugal
Central Zone of the Town of Angra do Heroismo in the Azores
Cultural Landscape of Sintra
Historic Centre of Evora
Historic Centre of Guimarães
Historic Centre of Oporto

Republic of Korea
Kyongju Historic Areas

Romania
Historic Centre of Sighisoara
Villages with Fortified Churches in Transylvania

Russian Federation
Historic and Architectural Complex of the Kazan Kremlin
Historic Centre of Saint Petersburg and Related Groups of Monuments
Historic Monuments of Novgorod and Surroundings
Kremlin and Red Square, Moscow

Senegal
Island of Saint-Louis

Slovakia
Banska Stiavnica
Bardejov Town Conservation Reserve

Spain
Alhambra, Generalife and Albayzin, Granada
Archaeological Ensemble of Mérida
Historic Centre of Cordoba
Historic City of Toledo
Historic Walled Town of Cuenca
Ibiza, biodiversity and culture
Monuments of Oviedo and the Kingdom of the Asturias
Old City of Salamanca
Old Town of Avila with its Extra-Muros Churches
Old Town of Caceres
Old Town of Segovia and its Aqueduct
San Cristóbal de La Laguna
Santiago de Compostela (Old town)
University and Historic Precinct of Alcalá de Henares

Sri Lanka
Old Town of Galle and its Fortifications
Sacred City of Kandy

World Heritage List

Suriname
Historic Inner City of Paramaribo

Sweden
Church Village of Gammelstad, Luleå
Hanseatic Town of Visby
Naval Port of Karlskrona

Switzerland
Old City of Berne

Syrian Arab Republic
Ancient City of Aleppo
Ancient City of Bosra
Ancient City of Damascus

Tunisia
Kairouan
Medina of Sousse
Medina of Tunis

Turkey
City of Safranbolu
Historic Areas of Istanbul

Ukraine
L'viv – the Ensemble of the Historic Centre

United Kingdom of Great Britain and Northern Ireland
City of Bath
Historic Town of St George and Related Fortifications, Bermuda
New Lanark
Old and New Towns of Edinburgh
Saltaire

United Republic of Tanzania
Stone Town of Zanzibar

United States of America
La Fortaleza and San Juan Historic Site in Puerto Rico

Uruguay
Historic Quarter of the City of Colonia del Sacramento

Uzbekistan
Itchan Kala
Historic Centre of Bukhara
Historic Centre of Shakhrisyabz
Samarkand – Crossroads of Culture

Venezuela
Coro and its Port

Viet Nam
Complex of Hué Monuments
Hoi An Ancient Town

Yemen
Historic Town of Zabid*
Old City of Sana'a
Old Walled City of Shibam

Yugoslavia
Natural and Culturo-Historical Region of Kotor

** Indicates the site is also on the World Heritage in Danger list as determined by the World Heritage Committee.*

Source: UNESCO, World Heritage Committee

World's 100 Most Endangered Sites

The World Monuments Fund's biennial list of the 100 Most Endangered Sites contains those cultural sites most in danger of destruction, either by natural or man-made causes. For many sites, inclusion on this list is their only hope for survival. Initial nominations are solicited from governments, heritage conservation organizations, and concerned individuals. Each site must have the support of a sponsoring institution, substantial cultural significance, an urgent need for intervention, and a viable intervention plan. The final selection committee is comprised of a panel of international experts. Limited financial support is also available from the World Monuments Watch Fund and is awarded on a competitive basis to selected sites. The World Monuments Fund is a private, non-profit organization created in 1965 with the purpose of fostering a greater awareness of the world's cultural, artistic, and historic resources; facilitating preservation and conservation efforts; and generating private financial assistance.

For information and photos on each site, visit the World Monuments Fund's Web site at *www.wmf.org* or contact them at (646) 424-9594.

2004 Most Endangered Sites

Afghanistan
Ghazni Minarets, Ghazni

Albania
Voskopojë Churches, Korcë

Antarctica
Sir Ernest Shackleton's Expedition Hut, Cape Royds, Ross Island

Argentina
Jesuit Guaraní Missions, San Ignacio Miní

Australia
Dampier Rock Art Complex, Dampier Archipelago

Bolivia
Vallegrande Rock Art Sites, Vallegrande and Saipina

Brazil
Convent of San Francisco, Olinda
Jesuit Guaraní Missions, São Nicolau

Bulgaria
Vidin Synagogue, Vidin

Canada
St. John's Anglican Church, Lunenburg, Nova Scotia

Chile
Humberstone & Santa Laura Industrial Complex, Iquique

China
Cockcrow Postal Town, Hebei Province
Great Wall of China Cultural Landscape, Beijing
Ohel Rachel Synagogue, Shanghai
Puning Temple Statues, Chengde, Hebei Province
Tianshui Traditional Houses, Tianshui, Gansu Province

Cuba
Calzada del Cerro, Havana

World's 100 Most Endangered Sites

Czech Republic

Chotesov Monastery, Chotesov
St. Anne's Church, Prague

Ecuador

Bolivar Theater, Quito
Las Peñas, Guayaquil

Egypt

Khasekhemwy at Hierakonpolis, Edfu
Mortuary Temple of Amenhotep III, Luxor
Sabil Ruqayya Dudu, Cairo

El Salvador

San Miguel Arcangel & Santa Cruz de Roma Churches, Panchimalco and Huizucar

Finland

Helsinki-Malmi Airport, Helsinki

Georgia

Timotesubani Virgin Church, Timotesubani Village, Borjomi Region

Greece

Helike Archaeological Site, Rizomylos and Eliki, Achaia
Palaikastro Archaeological site, Palaikastro, Crete

Guatemala

Usumacinta River Cultural Landscape, Petén

Hungary

Turony Church, Turony

India

Bhuj Darbargadh, Bhuj, Gujarat
Dalhousie Square, Calcutta
Osmania University College for Women, Hyderabad, Andhra Pradesh
Quila Mubarak, Patiala, Punjab

Indonesia

Omo Hada, Hilinawalö Mazingo, Nias
Tamansari Water Castle, Yogyakarta

Iraq

Erbil Citadel, Erbil
Nineveh and Nimrud Palaces, near Mosul

Ireland

Athassel Abbey, Athassel
Headfort House, Kells

Israel

Apollonia-Arsuf, Herzliya

Italy

Port of Trajan Archaeological Park, Fiumicino
Tuff-Towns and Vie Cave, Pitigliano, Sorano, Manciano, Tuscany

Jamaica

Falmouth Historic Town, Falmouth

Japan

Tomo Port Town, Fukuyama

Jordan

'Ain Ghazal, Amman

Kenya

Mtwapa Heritage Site, Kilifi, Mtwapa

Lebanon

Iskaudarouna-Naqoura Cultural Landscape, Oumm el' Amed, Naqoura

Mali

Bandiagara Escarpment Cultural Landscape, Bandiagara

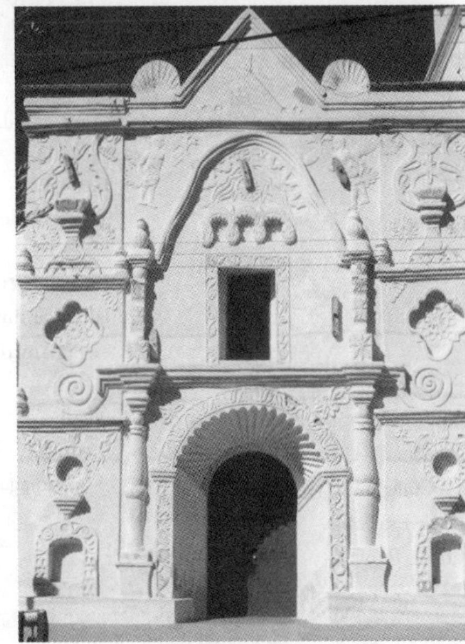

Top, Tianshui Traditional Houses, China (*Photo: WMF/Xu Wang*); *middle*, Quila Mubarak, India (*Photo: WMF/CRCI Gurmeet Rai*); *bottom*, Pimeria Alta Missions, Mexico (*Photo: WMF/Renata Schneider G.*). *All photos courtesy of the World Monuments Fund.*

World's 100 Most Endangered Sites

Mexico

Usumacinta River Cultural Landscape, Chiapas
Oxtotitlán Paintings, Chilapa, Guerrero
Pimería Alta Missions, Sonora
Quetzalcoatl Temple, Teotihuacán Mexico
San Francisco de Tzintzuntzan Convent, Tzintzuntzan, Michoacán
La Tercena, Metztitlán

Mongolia

Geser Sum Monastery, Ulaanbaatar

Morocco

Sahrij & Sbaiyin Madrassa Complex, Fez

Nigeria

Benin City Earthworks, Benin City

Palestinian Territories

Al-Qasem Palace, Beit Wazan
Tell Balatah (Shechem or Ancient Nablus), Nablus

Panama

Panama Canal Area, Panama and Colon Provinces

Paraguay

Jesuit Guaraní Missions, La Santísima Trinidad de Parana
Paraguay Railway System, Asuncion to Sapucay

Peru

Angasmarca Temple, Angasmarca, La Libertad
Our Lady of Guadalupe Monastery, Guadalupe, La Libertad
Kuelap Fortress, Kuelap, Amazonas
Túcume Archaeological Complex, Lambayeque

Poland

Old Lublin Theater, Lublin

Portugal

Roman Villa of Rabaçal, Rabaçal

Russia

Narcomfin Building, Moscow
The Chinese Palace at Oranienbaum, Lomonosov
Perm-36, Perm Region

Slovakia

Three Greek Catholic Churches, Bodruzal, Lukov-Venecia, Topola

Slovenia

Lanthieri Manor, Vipava

South Africa

Richtersveld Cultural Landscape, Richtersveld, Northern Cape Province

Spain

Pazo de San Miguel das Peñas, Monterroso

Syria

Amrit Archaeological Site, Amrit
Bosra Ancient City, Bosra

Taiwan

Jungshe Village, Penghu, Wangan

Trinidad & Tobago

Banwarie Trace Archaeological Site, Ward of Siparia

Turkey

Central Izmir Synagogues, Izmir
Ephesus Archaeological Site, Selçuk
Kariye Museum, Istanbul
Little Hagia Sophia Mosque (Küçük Ayasofya Camii), Istanbul
Temple of Augustus, Ankara

Turkmenistan

Old Nisa, Bagir Settlement

Uganda

Kampala Historic Buildings, Kampala

Top, Lanthieri Manor, Slovenia (*Photo: WMF/M. Krosec*); *middle*, Strawberry Hill, United Kingdom (*Photo: WMF/Richard Holttum Photography*); *bottom*, Ennis Brown House, United States (*Photo: WMF/John Stubbs*). *All photos courtesy of the World Monuments Fund.*

World's 100 Most Endangered Sites

Ukraine

Panticapaeum Ancient City, Kerch, Crimea
Tyras-Belgorod Fortress, Belgorod-Dnestrovsky

United Kingdom

Battersea Power Station, London, England
St. Vincent's Street Church, Glasgow, Scotland
Stowe House, Stowe, England
Strawberry Hill, London, England

United States

Ennis Brown House, Los Angeles, CA
Historic Lower Manhattan, New York, NY
North Family Shaker Site, Mount Lebanon, NY
Plum Orchard Historic District, Cumberland Island, GA
Iglesia San Jose, San Juan, Puerto Rico
St. Ann and the Holy Trinity Church, Brooklyn, NY

Venezuela

La Guaira Historic City, Vargas
Real Fuerza de Santiago de Arroyo, Araya

Yugoslavia

Prizren Historic Center, Prizren, Kosovo

Source: World Monument Fund

Did you know...

To date the World Monuments Fund has worked with local communities and partners to stem the loss of more than 400 irreplaceable sites in more than 80 countries.

1 Design Education

Current and future design students will find this chapter of particular interest and use, with entries ranging from student award programs and associations to a comprehensive listing of design degree programs and the fifth annual ranking of the top schools for architecture and interior design. Of related interest are award-winning student essays found in the Speeches & Essays chapter beginning on page 1.

ACSA Distinguished Professor Award

The Association of Collegiate Schools of Architecture's (ACSA) Distinguished Professor Award is presented annually for "sustained creative achievement" in the field of architectural education, whether through teaching, design, scholarship, research, or service. Eligible candidates must be living faculty of an ACSA member school for a minimum of 10 years or be otherwise allied with architectural education at an ACSA member school. Students or faculty of an ACSA member school may make nominations. Each year, the awards committee recommends a maximum of five candidates to the ACSA Board. Winners are entitled to use the title 'ACSA Distinguished Professor' for life.

For additional information about the ACSA Distinguished Professor Award, contact the Association at (202) 785-2324, or visit their Web site at *www.acsa-arch.org*.

1984-85

Alfred Caldwell, Illinois Institute of Technology
Robert S. Harris, Univ. of Southern Calif.
Fay Jones, Univ. of Arkansas
Charles Moore, Univ. of Texas at Austin
Ralph Rapson, Univ. of Minnesota

1985-86

James Marston Fitch, Columbia Univ.
Leslie J. Laskey, Washington Univ.
Harlan McClure, Clemson Univ.
Edward Romieniec, Texas A & M Univ.
Richard A. Williams, U. of Illinois, Urbana-Champaign

1986-87

Christopher Alexander, Univ. of California, Berkeley
Harwell Hamilton Harris, North Carolina State Univ.
Stanislawa Nowicki, Univ. of Pennsylvania
Douglas Shadbolt, Univ. of British Columbia
Jerzy Soltan, Harvard Univ.

1987-88

Harold Cooledge, Jr., Clemson Univ.
Bernd Foerster, Kansas State Univ.
Romaldo Giurgola, Columbia Univ.
Joseph Passonneau, Washington Univ.
John G. Willams, Univ. of Arkansas

1988-89

Peter R. Lee, Jr., Clemson Univ.
E. Keith McPheeters, Auburn Univ.
Stanley Salzman, Pratt Institute
Calvin C. Straub, Arizona State Univ.
Blanche Lemco van Ginkel, Univ. of Toronto

1989-90

Gunnar Birkerts, Univ. of Michigan
Olivio C. Ferrari, Virginia Polytechnic Institute
George C. Means, Jr., Clemson Univ.
Malcolm Quantrill, Texas A & M Univ.

1990-91

Denise Scott Brown, Univ. of Pennsylvania
Panos Koulermos, Univ. of Southern Calif.
William McMinn, Cornell Univ.
Forrest Wilson, The Catholic Univ. of America
David Woodcock, Texas A & M Univ.

1991-92

M. David Egan, Clemson Univ.
Robert D. Dripps, Univ. of Virginia
Richard C. Peters, Univ. of California, Berkeley
David L. Niland, Univ. of Cincinnati

1992-93

Stanley W. Crawley, Univ. of Utah
Don P. Schlegel, Univ. of New Mexico
Thomas L. Schumacher, Univ. of Maryland

ACSA Distinguished Professor Award

1993-94

George Anselevicius, Univ. of New Mexico
John Harold "Hal" Box, Univ. of Texas at Austin
Peter McCleary, Univ. of Pennsylvania
Douglas Rhyn, Univ. of Wisconsin-Milwaukee
Alan Stacell, Texas A & M Univ.

1994-95

Blake Alexander, Univ. of Texas at Austin
Robert Burns, North Carolina State Univ.
Robert Heck, Louisiana State Univ.
Ralph Knowles, Univ. of Southern California

1995-96

James Barker, Clemson Univ.
Mui Ho, Univ. of California, Berkley
Patricia O'Leary, Univ. of Colorado
Sharon Sutton, Univ. of Minnesota
Peter Waldman, Univ. of Virginia

1996-97

Colin H. Davidson, Universite de Montreal
Michael Fazio, Mississippi State Univ.
Ben J. Refuerzo, Univ. of Calif., Los Angeles
Max Underwood, Arizona State Univ.
J. Stroud Watson, Univ. of Tennessee

1997-98

Roger H. Clark, North Carolina State Univ.
Bob E. Heatly, Oklahoma State Univ.
John S. Reynolds, Univ. of Oregon
Marvin E. Rosenman, Ball State Univ.
Anne Taylor, Univ. of New Mexico

1998-99

Ralph Bennett, Univ. of Maryland
Diane Ghirardo, Univ. of Southern California
Robert Greenstreet, Univ. of Wisconsin-Milwaukee
Thomas Kass, Univ. of Utah
Norbert Schoenauer, McGill Univ.
Jan Wampler, Massachusetts Inst. of Tech.

1999-2000

Maelee Thomson Foster, Univ. of Florida
Louis Inserra, Pennsylvania State Univ.
Henry Sanoff, North Carolina State Univ.

2000-01

Ikhlas Sabouni, Prairie View A&M University
Raymond J. Cole, University of British Columbia

2001-02

Steven Paul Badanes, University of Washington
Raymond Lifchez, University of California, Berkeley
Marvin John Malecha, North Carolina State Univ.
Enrique Vivoni Farage, Universidad de Puerto Rico
James P. Warfield, Univ. of Ill., Urbana-Champaign

2002-03

Sherry Ahrentzen, Univ. of Wisconsin-Milwaukee
Lance Jay Brown, City College of the City Univ. of New York
David Crane, Univ. of South Florida
Lars Lerup, Rice University
Edward Steinfeld, Univ. at Buffalo, The State Univ. of New York

Source: Association of Collegiate Schools of Architecture

ACSP Distinguished Educator Award

The ACSP Distinguished Educator Award is presented biennially by the Association of Collegiate Schools of Planning (ACSP) in appreciation of distinguished service to planning education and practice. Nominations are welcomed from chairs and faculty members of ACSP member schools and are reviewed by the award committee. Recipients are chosen for their scholarly contributions, teaching excellence, service to the profession, and significant contributions to planning education and/or practice.

For additional information about the Distinguished Educator Award, visit ACSP's Web site at *www.acsp.org*.

1983	Harvey Perloff University of California, Los Angeles
1984	John Reps Cornell University
1986	F. Stuart Chapin Jr. University of North Carolina at Chapel Hill
1987	John Friedmann University of California, Los Angeles
1989	John Dyckman Johns Hopkins University
1990	Barclay Gibbs Jones Cornell University
1991	Britton Harris University of Pennsylvania
1992	Melville Branch University of Southern California
1993	Ann Strong University of Pennsylvania
1994	John A. Parker University of North Carolina at Chapel Hill
1995	Alan Feldt University of Michigan
1996	Martin Meyerson University of Pennsylvania
1997	Lloyd Rodwin Massachusetts Institute of Technology
1998	Michael Teitz University of California, Berkeley
1999	Lisa Redfield Peattie Massachusetts Institute of Technology
2000	Melvin M. Webber University of Calfornia, Berkeley
2002	David R. Godschalk University of North Carolina at Chapel Hill
2003	Paul Niebanck University of Washington

Source: Association of Collegiate Schools of Planning

AIA Education Honor Awards

The annual American Institute of Architects' (AIA) Education Honor Awards program is designed to recognize the achievement of outstanding teachers and to increase awareness of educational excellence in the classroom, laboratory, studio, or community-based educational environment. An independent jury selects the winners based on their development of exceptional, innovative, and intellectually challenging courses that address broad issues and contribute to the advancement of architectural education and practice.

For more information, contact the AIA at (202) 626-7417 or visit their Web site at *www.aia.org*.

2003 Winners

Honor Award

Dialogic Reciprocity: Binding Form-making to Practice in First-year Design
Christopher Monson, Mississippi State University

Honorable Mention

Awakening Consciousness Observing Great Practice
Max Underwood, Arizona State University

Building Communities
Jan Wampler, Massachusetts Institute of Technology

Jury

Jeanine Gunderson, AIAS
Laura Lee, Carnegie Mellon University
John McRae, RTKL
Bob Selby, University of Illinois, Urbana-Champaign

Source: The American Institute of Architects

Did you know...
Toshiko Mori, chair of Harvard's architecture department, is the first woman to hold this position.

AICP Outstanding Student Award

The American Institute of Certified Planners (AICP) each year presents its Outstanding Student Awards to recognize outstanding graduating students in accredited university planning programs, both at the undergraduate and graduate levels. Awarded students have been selected for the honor by their school's department head and colleagues who establish criteria with an emphasis on quality of work in the student's courses in planning and likelihood of success as a professional planner.

Additional information can be found on the American Planning Association Web site at *www.planning.org* or by calling the Washington, D.C. office of the American Planning Association at (202) 872-0611.

2003 Winners

Bachelor's Degree

Krista-Ann Staley, Ball State University
Reema Shraka, California State Polytechnic University, Pomona
Inge Lundegaard, California Polytechnic State University, San Luis Obispo
Peter Stavenger, Iowa State University
Remi Racine, University of Montreal
Dana Lucille Coelho, University of Virginia

Master's Degree

Jill Sprague, Ball State University
Tabe Vanderzwaag, California State Polytechnic University, Pomona
Quincy Struve, California Polytechnic State University, San Luis Obispo
Hope M. Hasty, Clemson University
Tracy Hegler, Florida State University
Obregon Hartleben, Georgia Institute of Technology
Arden Sokolow, Hunter College, City University of New York
Holly Killmer, Iowa State University
Craig Olwert, Ohio State University
Lauren Gallagher, Pratt Institute
Megan Lang, Rutgers University
Ana Ruiz, San Jose State University
Jennifer Leigh Flanery, Texas A&M University
Kathleen Norris, University of Florida
David Harkins, University of Iowa
Brian Pedrotti, University of Kansas
Adriane R. Aul, University of Maryland
Samantha B. Brown, University of Maryland
Monica Jeanne Murphy, University of Maryland
Chris Watson, University of Memphis
Hongliang Zhang, University of Minnesota
Juan Jose Torres Michel, University of Montreal
Bonnie Hilger, University of Nebraska
Tucker Bartlett, University of North Carolina
Robyn J. Scofield, University of Oregon
Ana P. Semedo, University of Rhode Island
Margret B. Tulloch, University of Virginia
Susan Shanks, University of Washington
William Robert Obermann, University of Wisconsin, Madison
Andrew Cross, University of Wisconsin, Milwaukee

Source: American Institute of Certified Planners

AICP Outstanding Student Project Award

Recognizing outstanding achievements that contribute to advances in the field of planning, the American Institute of Certified Planners (AICP) presents the Outstanding Student Project Award each year at the National Planning Conference. Students or groups of students in an accredited planning curriculum may enter a paper or class project; no more than three awards will be given. Award categories include the project that best demonstrates the contribution of planning to contemporary issues and the project best applying the planning process.

Student Project Award nomination packets are available by calling (202) 872-0611.

2003 Winners

Applying the Planning Process

Market Almaden Neighborhood Improvement Plan
San Jose State University
Dayana Salazar (chair), Ngozi Ajawara, Craig Araki, Karli Eschwey, Nazih Fino, Juvencio Flores, Corey Hall, Ted Heyd, Tanusri Jagtap, Nana Koranteng, Aaron Laurel, Irene Liestiawati, Eugene Maeda, Tina Mandawe, Joy Neas, Marion Payet, Debbie Pedro, Vincent Rivero, David Roemer, Jason Romes, Ana Ruiz, Brad Sedin, Darcy Smith, Keith Stamps, Todd Taylor, Yen Trinh, Phil Trom, Fleur Voute, Zhong Zheng

Demonstrating the Contribution of Planning to Contemporary Issues

Recommendations for the West Side Neighborhood of Saratoga Springs, NY
University of Albany, State University of New York
Ray Bromley (chair), Ruchi Agarwal, Hannah Blake, Christopher D. Eastman, Todd Gardner, Nadine N. Hardy, Jim Horton, Kenneth Kovalchik, Christian Leo, Robert Leslie, Kate Maynard, Aruna S. Reddy, Lori A. Shirley, Yilun Tseng, Dehui Wei, John-David Wood, Blaine T. Yatabe, Yongzhen Zhang

Source: American Institute of Certified Planners

> The best places always make you feel like all is well with the world.
>
> **Andrei Codrescu**

Alpha Rho Chi

Alpha Rho Chi is a national coeducational professional fraternity for students and professionals of architecture and the allied arts, which was founded in 1914 when the Arcus Society of the University of Illinois and Sigma Upsilon of the University of Michigan united. The organization remains dedicated to "promoting the artistic, scientific and practical proficiency of its membership and the profession." For membership information, contact your local Alpha Rho Chi chapter.

Contact

Additional information about Alpha Rho Chi, including a list of chapters and their contacts, can be found online at *www.alpharhochi.org*.

> Aspiring to design a building which can add to the educational experience of architecture is comparable to the problem of a brain surgeon operating on his own brain.
>
> **Steven Holl,** whose College of Architecture and Landscape Architecture building at the University of Minnesota opened in 2003

Alpha Rho Chi Bronze Medal

Alpha Rho Chi, a national professional coeducational fraternity for students in architecture and the allied arts, selects its annual Bronze Medal recipients from over 100 schools of architecture. The award was established in 1931 by the Grand Council of Alpha Rho Chi to "encourage professional leadership by regarding student accomplishment, promote the ideals of professional service by acknowledging distinctive individual contributions to social life, and stimulate professional merit by commending qualities in the student not necessarily pertaining to scholarship." Winners, which are selected by each schools' faculty, are graduating seniors who best exemplify the aforementioned qualities.

Additional information may be found on the fraternity's Web site: *www.alpharhochi.org*.

2003 Recipients

Rebekah Sperbeck, Andrews University
Chad Schwartz, Arizona State University
David B. Smith, Auburn University
David Barry, California College of Arts & Crafts
Kimberly D. Brown, California Polytechnic State University, San Luis Obispo
Mable W. Chung, California State Polytechnic University
Mark T. Rosen, Carlton University
Andrew C. Lee, Carnegie Mellon
Katherine A. Bojsza, Carnegie Mellon
Stephanie M. Roselle, Catholic University of America
James B. Garland, Clemson University
Christopher Barker, Columbia University
Purvi B. Gandhi, Cooper Union
Hilary K. Scruggs, Cornell University
Peter Osborne, Dalhousie University
Jackie Ford, Drexel University
Joseph M. Allen, Drury University
Rebecca Irvin, Florida A&M University
Raina E. Tilden, Georgia Institute of Technology
Sylvia O. Coffie, Hampton University
Carlos Arnaiz, Harvard University
Suzannah Y. Codlin, Howard University
M. Jessie Bowman, Iowa State University
Christina M. Strimple, Kansas State University
Matthew D. Roeder, Kansas State University
Vaillant Julie, Laval Universite
Tara R. Bradford, Louisiana State University
Misty Scroggs, Louisiana Tech
Britta E. Butler, Mass. Institute of Technology
Maria Durana, McGill University
Kristina E. Gerard, Miami University
Malika A. Kirkling, Miami University
Jerry L. Friley III, Mississippi State University
Kerry Merkel, Montana State University
Benjamin P. Bakas, New Jersey Institute of Tech.
Paul Wong, New York Institute of Technology
Jessica N. Johnson, North Carolina State University
Christopher J. Knorr, North Dakota State University
Jeffrey T. Cassianis, Norwich University
Aleksandr Daskalov, Ohio State University
Jonathan S. Slagle, Oklahoma State University
Coby J. Linton, Parsons School of Design
Kimberly A. Zoeckler, Pennsylvania State University
Erika Y. Anderson, Prairie View A&M University
Claire H. Johnson, Princeton University
Nicholas J. Caruso, Rensselaer Polytechnic Institute
David Constable, Rhode Island School of Design
Harry Lowd, Rhode Island School of Design
Jessica A. Spiegel, Rice University
Cynthia L. Gibson, Roger Williams University
Alejandra Holguin, Savannah College of Art & Design
Thomas J. Jensen, Savannah College of Art & Design

Alpha Rho Chi Bronze Medal

Kara Block, Southern Calif. Institute of Architecture
Mark D. Ferrari, State Univ. of New York at Buffalo
Casey E. Boss, Syracuse University
Michael A. Bevivino, Syracuse University
Charles R. Hawley, Temple University
Antonio Valdivia, Texas A&M University
Eden D. Livingstone, Texas Tech University
Blaise H. Durio, Tulane University
Carina A. Bien-Willner, University of Arizona
Carolyn A. Pike, University of Arkansas
John G. Vose, University of British Columbia
Paul Norris, University of Calgary
Alexandre Souto, University of California at Berkeley
Jeffrey Adams, University of Calif. at Los Angeles
Daniel W. Craig, University of Colorado
Christina Conetta, University of Florida
Wendy K. Meguro, University of Hawaii at Manoa
Jack A. Hensley, University of Houston
Laila A. Kinnunen, University of Idaho
Marcus A. Cross, University of Illinois at Champaign-Urbana
Colin G. Morgan, University of Illinois at Chicago
Lindsey N. Piant, University of Kansas
Stephanie L. King, University of Kentucky
Andre N. Bourque, Univ. of Louisiana-Lafayette
Gavin Kraemer, University of Manitoba
David P. Mogensen, University of Maryland
James T. Solomon, University of Memphis
Brian Scandariato, University of Miami
Kathryn A. Slattery, University of Michigan
Destin J. Nygard, University of Minnesota
Lindsey A. Ellsworth, Univ. of Nebraska-Lincoln
Diana Reising, University of Notre Dame
Laura Lake, University of South Florida
Jason E. Hill, University of Tennessee-Knoxville
Casey B. Carlton, University of Texas at Arlington
Hannah S. Vaughn, University of Texas at Austin
Kathryn Seymour, University of Toronto
Joseph S. Milillo, University of Utah
Melanie K. Shields, University of Virginia
Paula A. Patterson, University of Washington
Karen Smith, University of Waterloo
Jessica Brettbach, Univ. of Wisconsin-Milwaukee
David P. Pollard, Virginia Tech
Matthew J. Whitish, Washington State University
Christopher D. Eberly, Wentworth Institute of Tech.
Nicholas D. Ficaro, Wentworth Institute of Tech.
Jason D. Panneton, Woodbury University
Andrew Benner, Yale University

Source: Alpha Rho Chi

American Institute of Architecture Students

The American Institute of Architecture Students (AIAS) is a non-profit, independent, student-run organization that seeks to promote excellence in architecture education, training and practice, as well as to organize architecture students and promote the practice of architecture. The AIAS was formed in 1956 and today serves over 7,500 undergraduate and graduate architecture students. More than 150 chapters at U.S. and Canadian colleges and universities support members with professional development seminars, community projects, curriculum advisory committees, guest speakers and many other programs.

Address

1735 New York Avenue, NW
Washington, DC 20006
Telephone: (202) 626-7472
Internet: www.aiasnatl.org

> Architecture is to a degree an art, and I feel fundamentally that it's the business of art to always question, to always turn everything upside down so that one sees it anew.
>
> **Paul Rudolph**

Architecture Student Demographics

Based on a study conducted by the National Architectural Accrediting Board (NAAB), the following information outlines demographic information about NAAB accredited architecture degree programs at U.S. colleges and universities.

	1994/95	1995/96	1996/97	1997/98	1998/99	1999/00	2000/01	2001/02*
Pre-professional Undergrad. Programs								
Full-time students	10,790	9,655	12,130	11,789	12,062	13,391	13,610	12,824
Part-time students	1,577	1,494	1,602	1,524	1,386	1,782	1,856	1,651
Women students	3,895	3,432	4,317	4,419	4,495	5,314	5,836	5,094
African-American students	723	496	660	682	641	789	830	842
American Indian students	59	80	62	67	78	77	135	87
Asian/Pacific Isle students	1,010	807	1,112	1,065	1,042	1,106	1,079	855
Hispanic students	967	750	991	955	929	1,368	1,337	1,514
Total Graduates	2,369	2,154	2,324	2,199	2,397	2,716	2,791	2,191
Women graduates	708	603	746	807	774	1,044	1,127	761
African-American graduates	75	74	83	81	85	96	91	74
American Indian graduates	7	6	10	9	12	11	36	54
Asian/Pacific Isle graduates	219	198	225	233	226	244	272	301
Hispanic graduates	147	101	157	162	157	229	215	205
Accredited B. Arch Programs								
Full-time students	16,500	16,424	16,025	16,423	15,312	14,792	16,211	13,476
Part-time students	1,500	1,364	1,178	1,377	1,606	1,568	2,196	1,667
Women students	5,107	5,155	5,046	5,413	5,201	5,789	6,302	5,212
African-American students	1,174	1,247	1,122	1,165	1,243	1,342	1,156	923
American Indian students	143	195	163	138	151	129	116	99
Asian/Pacific Isle students	1,735	1,665	1,591	1,497	1,425	1,552	1,670	1,187
Hispanic students	1,466	1,436	1,340	1,249	1,184	1,400	2,090	1,797
Total Graduates	2,837	2,948	3,028	2,710	2,617	2,825	2,773	2,253
Women graduates	775	742	849	762	754	749	910	779
African-American graduates	144	148	131	111	131	137	153	129
American Indian graduates	16	14	14	8	13	19	26	43
Asian/Pacific Isle graduates	277	276	307	294	239	276	276	240
Hispanic graduates	185	215	223	222	198	212	206	147

Architecture Student Demographics

	1994/95	1995/96	1996/97	1997/98	1998/99	1999/00	2000/01	2001/02*
Accredited M. Arch Programs								
Full-time students	4,664	5,196	5,252	5,461	5,769	6,302	6,524	5,322
Part-time students	491	724	533	677	689	772	796	634
Women students	1,883	2,164	2,143	2,273	2,210	2,414	2,072	2,218
African-American students	121	142	133	133	119	160	143	147
American Indian students	11	21	17	20	42	16	30	24
Asian/Pacific Isle students	508	540	522	550	607	709	584	334
Hispanic students	235	267	302	301	427	595	380	361
Total Graduates	1,629	1,676	1,645	1,799	2,002	1,998	1,750	1,611
Women graduates	580	558	580	747	744	643	672	547
African-American graduates	28	26	45	32	40	41	49	28
American Indian graduates	3	5	3	9	10	4	5	9
Asian/Pacific Isle graduates	169	140	156	164	197	252	219	173
Hispanic graduates	87	83	82	92	104	113	116	105

** Not all schools participated in the 2001/02 survey.*

Source: National Architectural Accrediting Board

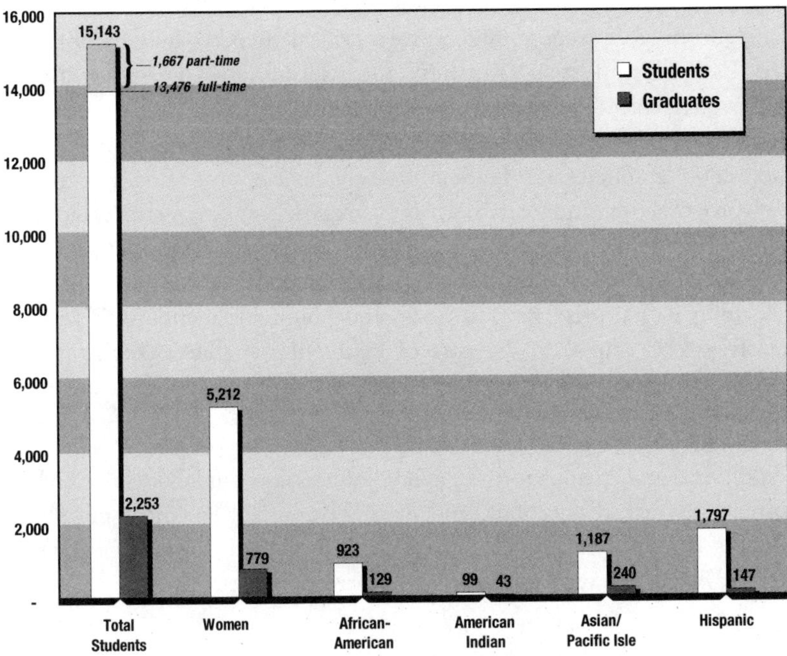

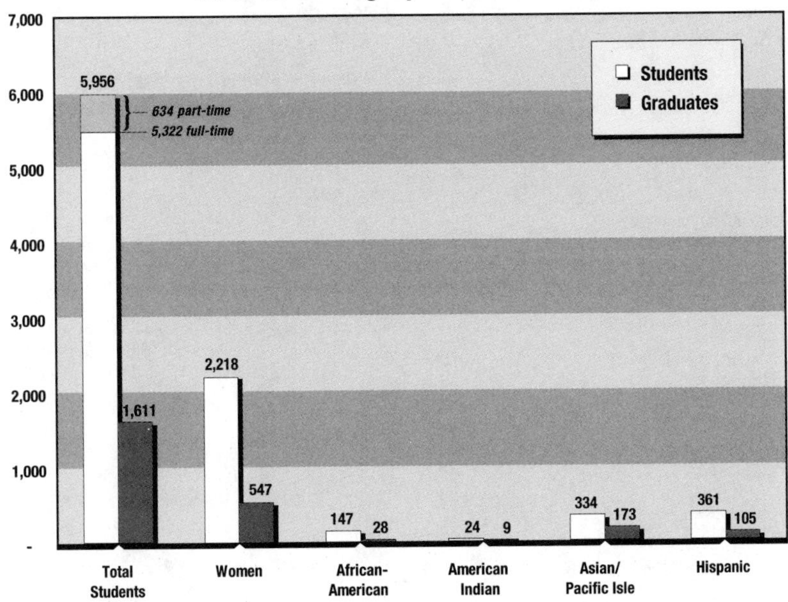

Source: Counsel House Research

ArchVoices Essay Competition

Intended to encourage, promote, and reward critical thinking and writing, the new ArchVoices Essay Competition was developed specifically for young architecture professionals. ArchVoices is an independent, nonprofit think tank on architectural education and internships. The competition is open to interns, non-registered architects, architecture school graduates and graduating students. Entrants initially prepare a 500-word essay proposal reflecting on their daily experiences as interns. Selected semi-finalists further explore their ideas from their first submission, developing a 2,500 word essay. A jury of educators and professionals vote on the finalists, conferring multiple honors, including a first prize, second prize, and honorable mentions. The first prize winner receives $981, equal to the cost of taking the Architect Registration Exam (ARE). The second place winner receives a Macintosh iPod, compliments of Architosh.

The competition is conducted online at *www.archvoices.org/competition.* The Web site contains additional information on eligibility, submission guidelines, the competition calendar, frequently asked questions, and writing resources. For more information on the ArchVoices Essay Competition, contact them by email at *info@archvoices.org* or by calling (510) 757-6213. To read this year's first prize essay, see page 13.

2003 Winners

First Prize

J. Brantley Hightower
Lake/Flato Architects Inc.

Second Prize

Jeff Ponitz
University of Michigan

Honorable Mention

Kara Byrn
Ratio Architects, Inc.

Fouad Khalil
SMBW Architects

Maria Sutter
Unemployed

Christopher Yost
Murphy Burnham Buttrick Architects

Source: ArchVoices

ASLA National Student Design Competition

The American Society of Landscape Architects annually conducts a competition to identify and recognize outstanding works of design and research from landscape architecture students. Any landscape architecture student, undergraduate or graduate, in the United States or Canada is eligible to enter. Awards are granted by the jury at their discretion. Winners receive a certificate, and first place winners receive a complimentary conference registration. All winning entries are displayed at the ASLA's annual conference.

For additional information about the Competition, contact the ASLA at (202) 898-2444 or *www.asla.org*.

2003 Research Category Winners

Undergraduate First Place, Individual

Station Area Redevelopment for Rural Communities
Jennifer K. Margison
University of Nevada, Las Vegas

Undergraduate Commendation, Individual

A Redevelopment of Cuban Memorial Boulevard and the Latin Quarter
Manuel Arencibia; University of Florida

Undergraduate First Place, Team

I Sassi Di Matera: A Landscape Interpreted
Ryan R. Binkowski and Aaron Feldman-Grosse
The Pennsylvania State University

Undergraduate Commendation, Team

Principles of Urban Spatial Design - Piazza della Rotunda
Michele Schuster, Brooke Ingram, Nicolette Slagle, Rebecca Mitchell, and Emily Volgstadt
The Pennsylvania State University

Graduate First Place, Individual

The Thickness of Landscape, horizontally and vertically considered
George Hazelrigg
Virginia Polytechnic Institute and State University

Graduate Commendation, Individual

User Dynamics in Two Neighborhood Parks, Bombay, India
Nandita Godbole
University of Illinois at Urbana-Champaign

Restorative Environments & Landscape Architecture in Healthcare Settings
Jeff Maxwell
University of Florida

Spirit Island Native American Holocaust Memorial
Sivaya Parasivam
University of Minnesota

Straighter is Not Always Better
Kelly Alison Pugh
University of Texas at Arlington

Process: A Strategy for Developing Place Attachment and Community Life
Kimberly L. Rennick
Virginia Polytechnic Institute and State University

Sidewalk Living Rooms
Steven Rasmussen Cancian
University of California, Berkeley

ASLA National Student Design Competition

The Creativity Experience
Lori L. Pullman
California Polytechnic State University, Pomona

Graduate First Place, Team
Revealing the Japanese Garden
Sadahisa Kato and Stanley J. Szwalek III
University of Michigan

Graduate, Second Professional Degree First Place, Individual
Inevitable Emergence
Steve Roelof
University of Oregon

An Artist's Garden
Claire Dorlac-Leach
University of Oregon

2003 Design Category Winners

Undergraduate First Place
Integrating Bird Habitat with Golf Course Design
Jen Degidts
University of Guelph

Green Roofs: Second Nature
Kristina White
University of Guelph

Pavonine Park: A Residential Park at 14th and U St., Washington, DC
Laura Thompson
Ball State University

Undergraduate Commendation, Individual
The Philosophy of Design
Emily Mann
University of Guelph

Redesigning Naturalistic Zoo Habitats for Animal Comfort and Visibility
Jeph Brown
University of Guelph

Uncommon Ground: Revelation of the Urban Experience
Jeff Schurek
University of Guelph

The New Face of Urban Agriculture
Holly Purvis
University of Guelph

Revealing the Flow of the City
Saya Nakano
University of Guelph

Mojave Plaza
Elizabeth A. Scott
University of Nevada, Las Vegas

Nokhu Crags Resort, Colorado
B. Cannon Ivers
Colorado State University

Undergraduate First Place, Team
Tierra Segunda
Ken Gibson and Brock Reimer
Kansas State University

Undergraduate Commendation, Team
Active Discovery Education
Shawn Balon, Patrick Kelly, Mark Stuermann, and Laura Voelz
Clemson University

ASLA National Student Design Competition

Echo
Shannon Lee Mohr and Timothy John Norder
Michigan State University

A Sound Experience
Melissa Gumbis and Tonya Hunter
Michigan State University

Cincinnati Central Riverfront Park
Kevin Burch and Jonathan Nutt
West Virginia University

Phoenix Rio Salado Multi-Cultural Pathway
Joshua Turnbull and Travis Webb
Arizona State University

Applebrook
Josh Metzger, Anne McKisson, and Amy Groner
Ohio State University

Designing the High Line: The Synergy of Nature and Culture
Joseph Charles and April Dewart
Rutgers University

Graduate First Place, Individual

Urban Revitalization Through Green Infrastructure at Allapattah Neighborhood, Miami
Sansern Kiatsupaibul
University of Florida

Graduate Commendation, Individual

High Water Line
Anne Samuel
University of Virginia

Threshold
Robin Carmichael
University of Virginia

La Carlota: Plotting the Hidden City
Huilai Shi
University of Pennsylvania

Getaway
Patricia Sharpe
University of Toronto

Stormwater: The Flow from Liability to Asset
Pallavi Shashank Shinde
University of Georgia

Graduate First Place, Team

Borderlands
Scott Chastain, Matthew Edwards and Bradley L. Martin
Auburn University

Native American Music Garden
Susan E. Atkinson and Kuo-Liang Liao
University of Texas at Arlington

Graduate Commendation, Team

Urban Meridian: Panama City Waterfront Restoration
Fan Wang and Monica Lynne Mahoney
University of Arizona

Developing a New Suburbanism
John Fishback and Josh Segal
California Polytechnic State University, Pomona

Graduate, Second Professional Degree First Place, Individual

Taylor Yard Master Plan
David Fletcher
Harvard University

Source: American Society of Landscape Architects

Association Student Chapters

The following national design associations offer student memberships, often at reduced rates, as well as operate student chapters at many U.S. colleges and universities. Student newsletters, leadership opportunities, networking, job postings, discounts, and many other member benefits are typically available to students. More information about specific benefits and a current listing of the active student chapters are available from the organizations and their Web sites. Profiles of the associations can be found in the Organizations chapter. As the American Institute of Architecture Students is independent of any association, although partially funded by The American Institute of Architects, detailed information about its programs and benefits can be found on page 504.

American Planning Association (APA)

www.planning.org/students/

American Society of Interior Designers (ASID)

www.asid.org/students/benefits.asp

American Society of Landscape Architects (ASLA)

www.asla.org/nonmembers/student_news

International Interior Design Association (IIDA)

www.iida.org

Industrial Designers Society of America (IDSA)

www.idsa.org

Berkeley Prize

The Berkeley Undergraduate Prize for Architectural Design Excellence, an annual online essay competition and the centerpiece of the Berkeley Prize Endowment, was established in 1996 at the Department of Architecture, University of California Berkeley. The Endowment aspires to encourage students to embrace social ideals as fundamental to making buildings of worth and to recognize, through the lessons of past examples, how contemporary architecture may serve social needs. Each year students submit essays in response to a question developed around the theme of architecture as a social art. Submissions are encouraged from undergraduate architecture students from around the world and must be in English.

For further information, including a history of the Berkeley Prize, past winning entries, or for details about entering the Prize, visit *www.berkeleyprize.org* on the Internet. To read one of this year's winning essays, see page 45.

2000

First Place

Nathan Koren, Arizona State University (US)

Second Place

Andres Stebelski, Cornell University (US)

Third Place

Abbie Janette de Leon, University of Southern California (US)

Charles Fadem, Cornell University (US)

2001

First Place

Christopher Holmes, Dalhousie University (Canada)

Second Place

Ashley Paine, Queensland University of Technology (Australia)

Third Place

Alix Ogilvie, Ball State University (US)

Honorable Mention

David Foxe, Massachusetts Institute of Tech. (US)

John Sharpe, Queensland, University of Technology (Australia)

Sara Stevens, Rice University (US)

2002

First Place

Thomas-Bernard Kenniff, Univ. of Waterloo (Canada)

Honorable Mention

Ray Harli, Univ. of Witwatersrand (South Africa)

Trevor Lewis, University of Oregon (US)

Nadia Watson, Queensland University of Technology (Australia)

2003

First Prize

Philip Tidwell, Washington University (US)

Second Prize

Karen Weise, Yale University (US)

Third Prize

Ema Bonifacic, Architectural Association School of Architecture (UK)

Priyanka Shah, Rizvi College of Architecture (India)

Finalists

Virginia Bernard, Savannah College of Art and Design (US)

Swasti Bhattarai, Institute of Engineering (Nepal)

Sara Hayden, University of California, Berkeley (US)

Colin Rose, Cambridge University (UK)

Source: The Berkeley Prize Endowment

Charles E. Peterson Prize

A student competition of measured drawings, the Charles E. Peterson Prize is presented jointly by The Historic American Buildings Survey (HABS) of the National Park Service, The Athenaeum of Philadelphia and The American Institute of Architects (AIA). The annual competition honors Charles E. Peterson, FAIA, founder of the HABS program, and is intended to heighten awareness about U.S. historic buildings and to add to the permanent HABS collection of measured drawings at the Library of Congress. In addition to generating over 4,000 drawings for the collection to date, the competition presents awards totaling $7,000 to winning students. These have included those studying architecture, architectural history, interior design, and American studies. Drawings must be of a building that has not been recorded by HABS through measured drawings or be an addendum to existing HABS drawings that makes a substantial contribution to the understanding of the significant features of the building.

Additional information is available on the Internet at *www.cr.nps.gov/habshaer/joco/pete/*.

2003 Winners

First Place

Old Oakville Jail (1867)
Oakville, Live Oak County, TX
School of Architecture, University of Texas at San Antonio: Sue Ann Pemberton-Haugh (leader), Cheryl Davani, Julia Dunks, Wanira Oliveira

Second Place

Hotel Palomar Courts (1937-38)
Shreveport, Caddo Parish, LA
School of Architecture, College of Liberal Arts, Louisiana Tech University: Guy W. Carwile (leader), Michael Blake, Becky Carson, Billisha Johnson, Jay Langham, Benjamin Rath, Raymond I. Zabala III

Third Place

Brawner Farmhouse (1841)
Manassas National Battlefield Park, Manassas, Prince William County, VA
Historic Preservation Certificate Program, Department of Social Sciences, Bucks County Community College: Kathryn Ann Auerbach (leader), David Corliss, Bernice Graeter-Reardon, R. Stephen Gray, Richard L. Green, Vanessa Zeoli

Fourth Place

Bastrop State Park (1937)
Bastrop, Bastrop County, TX
School of Architecture, University of Texas at Austin: Dan Leary (leader), Sarah Benson, A. Elizabeth Butman, Laura Caffrey, Adrienne Vaughan Campbell, Ely Marheb-Emanuelli, Terri Asendorf Ruiz, Aparna S. Surte

Honorable Mention

New York Life Building (1887-91)
Kansas City, Jackson County, MO
School of Architecture & Urban Design, University of Kansas: Steve Padget (leader), Benjamin Audrain, Richard Todd Cowger, Jonathan Emert, Doug Hurt, Keri Jacobs, Ryan Knock, Kamali Marsh, Katherine Nichols, Hilary Padget, Jon Peterson, Ashleigh Self, Robert Smith, Christy Thorpe, Jonathan Tramba, Jerry Wright

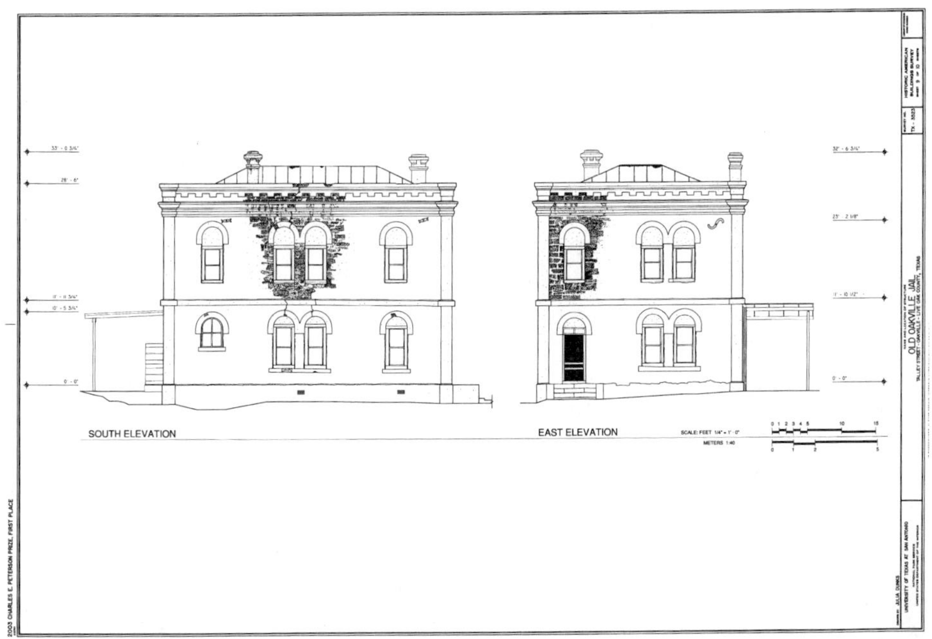

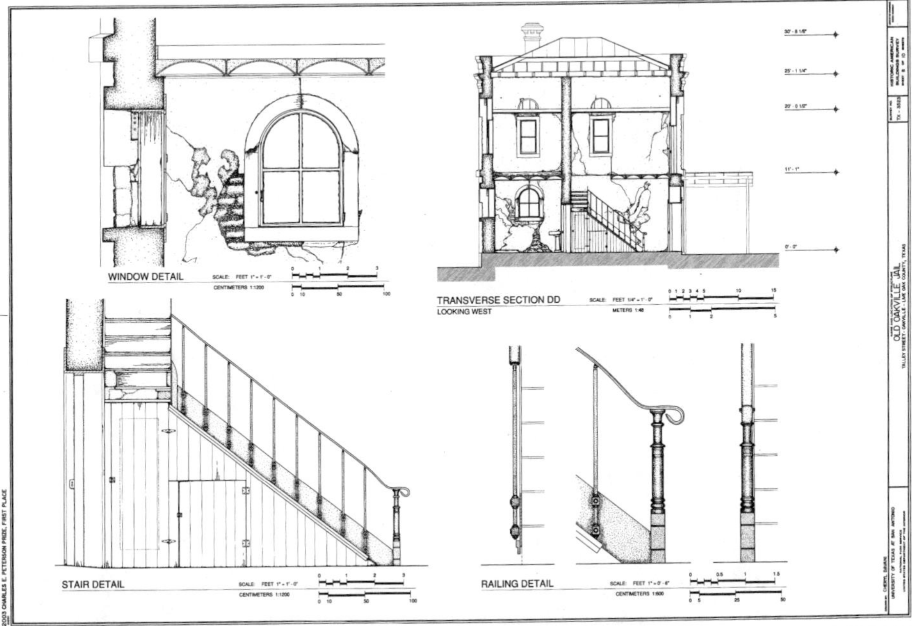

The first-place winning team produced ink-on-Mylar drawings of the Old Oakville Jail located in Oakville, Texas. The Old Jail Building is all that remains of a town that once served as the seat of Live Oak County. From 1867 to 1919 the jail was Live Oak's third and most sophisticated detention facility. The jail recalls not only a once thriving town but also an era of construction whose significance has been all but lost. *Images courtesy of the Historic American Buildings Survey, National Park Service.*

Charles E. Peterson Prize

St. Paul Episcopal Church of East Cleveland (1845-60)
East Cleveland, Cuyahoga County, OH
School of Architecture & Environmental Design, Kent State University: Elizabeth Corbin Murphy (leader), Nicole Baden, Aaron Brooker, Stacey Contoveros, Chad Kocher, Lucas Kraft, Chris Malensek, Katharine Morris, Victoria Myers, Benjamin Rantilla, Eric Sauer, Douglas Shaulis, Tim Swartz, Elizabeth Timmerman, Amanda Tromczynski

Source: Historic American Buildings Survey

Did you know...
Although it looks like stone, the dome of the United States Capitol is constructed with 8,909,200 pounds of iron.

Design Degree Programs

The following chart outlines the schools across the United States that offer design and design related degrees, including associates (A), certificate (C), professional (P), bachelor's (B), and master's (M). All the architecture, interior design, landscape architecture, and planning programs indicated below are accredited by the disciplines' respective accrediting bodies: National Architectural Accrediting Board (NAAB), Foundation for Interior Design Education Research (FIDER), Landscape Architectural Accrediting Board (LAAB), and Planning Accreditation Board (PAB). For degree programs not listed and accredited by other bodies and students seeking Ph.D. programs, consult the individual schools.

School	City	Web Address	Architecture	Architecture History	Historic Preservation	Industrial Design	Interior Design	Landscape Architecture	Planning
ALABAMA									
Alabama A&M University	Normal	aamu.edu							B M
Auburn University	Auburn	auburn.edu	B			B M	B	M	
Samford University	Birmingham	samford.edu					B		
Tuskegee University	Tuskegee	tusk.edu	B						
University of Alabama	Tuscaloosa	ua.edu					B		
ARIZONA									
Arizona State University	Tempe	asu.edu	M			B M	B	B	B M
Frank Lloyd Wright School of Architecture	Scottsdale	taliesin.edu	M						
University of Arizona	Tucson	arizona.edu	B					M	M
ARKANSAS									
University of Arkansas	Fayetteville	uark.edu	B				B	B	
CALIFORNIA									
Academy of Art College	San Francisco	academyart.edu				B M	B		
American InterContinental University	Los Angeles	aiula.edu					B		
Art Center College of Design	Pasadena	artcenter.edu				B M			
Brooks College	Long Beach	brookscollege.edu					A		
California College of the Arts	San Francisco	cca.edu	B			B M	B		

Design Degree Programs

School	City	Web Address	Architecture	Architecture History	Historic Preservation	Industrial Design	Interior Design	Landscape Architecture	Planning
California Polytechnic State University	San Luis Obispo	calpoly.edu	B					B M	B M
California State Polytechnic University	Pomona	csupomona.edu	B M					B M	B M
California State University, Fresno	Fresno	csufresno.edu					B		
California State University, Long Beach	Long Beach	csulb.edu				B M			
California State University, Northridge	Northridge	csun.edu					B		
California State University, Sacramento	Sacramento	csus.edu					B		
College of the Redwoods	Eureka	redwoods.cc.ca.us			C				
Design Institute of San Diego	San Diego	disd.edu					B		
Fashion Institute of Design and Merchandising	Los Angeles	fidm.edu					A		
Interior Designers Institute	Newport Beach	idi.edu					B		
Newschool of Architecture	San Diego	newschoolarch.edu	B M						
San Diego Mesa College	San Diego	sdmesa.sdccd .cc.ca.us				A			
San Francisco State University	San Francisco	sfsu.edu				B M			
San Jose State University	San Jose	sjsu.edu				B			M
Southern California Institute of Architecture	Los Angeles	sciarc.edu	B M						
University of California, Berkeley	Berkeley	berkeley.edu	M	M				M	M
University of California, Berkeley Extension	Berkeley	unex.berkeley.edu					C		
University of California at Davis	Davis	ucdavis.edu						B	

Design Degree Programs

School	City	Web Address	Architecture	Architecture History	Historic Preservation	Industrial Design	Interior Design	Landscape Architecture	Planning
University of California at Irvine	Irvine	uci.edu							M
University of California at Los Angeles	Los Angeles	ucla.edu	M	M					M
University of California at Los Angeles Extension	Los Angeles	uclaextension.edu					P		
University of California at Santa Barbara	Santa Barbara	ucsb.edu		M					
University of Southern California	Los Angeles	usc.edu	B						M
West Valley College	Saratoga	westvalley.edu					C		
Woodbury University	Burbank	woodbury.edu	B				B		
COLORADO									
Art Institute of Colorado	Denver	cia.aii.edu				B			
Colorado State University	Fort Collins	colostate.edu					B	B	
Metropolitan State College of Denver	Denver	mscd.edu				B			
Rocky Mnt. College of Art & Design	Denver	rmcad.edu					B		
University of Colorado at Denver/Boulder	Denver	cudenver.edu	M	M				M	M
CONNECTICUT									
University of Bridgeport	Bridgeport	bridgeport.edu				B			
University of Connecticut	Storrs	uconn.edu						B	
University of Hartford	Hartford	hartford.edu	M[1]						
Yale University	New Haven	yale.edu	M						
DELAWARE									
University of Delaware	Newark	udel.edu		M					
DISTRICT OF COLUMBIA									
Catholic University of America	Washington	cua.edu	B M						

Design Degree Programs

School	City	Web Address	Architecture	Architecture History	Historic Preservation	Industrial Design	Interior Design	Landscape Architecture	Planning
George Washington University	Washington	gwu.edu		M			B M		
George Washington Univ. at Mount Vernon College	Washington	mvc.gwu.edu					B		
Howard University	Washington	howard.edu	B						
FLORIDA									
AI Miami International University	Miami	aimiu.artinstitutes .edu					A		
Art Institute of Fort Lauderdale	Fort Lauderdale	aifl.edu				B			
Florida A&M University	Tallahassee	famu.edu	B M						
Florida Atlantic University	Fort Lauderdale	fau.edu	B						M
Florida International University	Miami	fiu.edu	M					M	
Florida State University	Tallahassee	fsu.edu		M			B		M
International Academy of Design, Tampa	Tampa	academy.edu					B		
Ringling School of Art and Design	Sarasota	rsad.edu					B		
Seminole Community College	Sanford	scc-fl.edu					A		
University of Florida	Gainesville	ufl.edu	M				B	B M	M
University of Miami	Miami	miami.edu	B M						
University of South Florida	Tampa	usf.edu	M						
GEORGIA									
American Intercontinental University	Atlanta	aiuniv.edu					B		
Art Institute of Atlanta	Dunwoody	aia.aii.edu					B		
Brenau University	Gainesville	brenau.edu					B		
Georgia Institute of Technology	Atlanta	gatech.edu	M	M		B M			M

Design Degree Programs

School	City	Web Address	Architecture	Architecture History	Historic Preservation	Industrial Design	Interior Design	Landscape Architecture	Planning
Georgia Southern University	Statesboro	gasou.edu					B		
Georgia State University	Atlanta	gsu.edu			M				
Savannah College of Art and Design	Savannah	scad.edu	M	M	M				
Southern Polytechnic State University	Marietta	spsu.edu	B						
University of Georgia	Athens	uga.edu			C M		B	B M	
HAWAII									
University of Hawaii at Manoa	Honolulu	hawaii.edu	B M						M
IDAHO									
Brigham Young University	Rexburg	byui.edu					B		
University of Idaho	Moscow	uidaho.edu	M					B	
ILLINOIS									
Art Institute of Chicago	Chicago	artic.edu			M				
Harrington Institute of Interior Design, Chicago	Chicago	interiordesign.edu					B		
Illinois Institute of Art at Chicago	Chicago	ilic.artinstitutes.edu					B		
Illinois Institute of Art at Schaumburg	Schaumburg	ilis.artinstitutes.edu					B		
Illinois Institute of Technology	Chicago	iit.edu	B M						
Illinois State University	Normal	ilstu.edu					B		
International Academy of Merchandising and Design, Chicago	Chicago	iadtchicago.edu					B		
Judson College	Elgin	judson-il.edu	M[1]						
Southern Illinois University at Carbondale	Carbondale	siu.edu				B	B		
University of Chicago	Chicago	uchicago.edu		M					

Design Degree Programs

School	City	Web Address	Architecture	Architecture History	Historic Preservation	Industrial Design	Interior Design	Landscape Architecture	Planning
University of Illinois at Chicago	Chicago	uic.edu	B M	M		B M			M
University of Illinois at Urbana-Champaign	Urbana-Champaign	uiuc.edu	M	M		B M		B M	B M
INDIANA									
Ball State University	Muncie	bsu.edu	B		M			B M	B M
Indiana University	Bloomington	indiana.edu					B		
ITT Technical Institute	Fort Wayne	itt-tech.edu				B			
Purdue University	Lafayette	purdue.edu				B M	B	B	
University of Notre Dame	South Bend	nd.edu	B M			B M			
IOWA									
Iowa State University	Ames	iastate.edu	B M				B	B	B M
University of Iowa	Iowa City	uiowa.edu		M					M
KANSAS									
Kansas State University	Manhattan	ksu.edu	B				B	B M	M
University of Kansas	Lawrence	ukans.edu	B M			B M			M
KENTUCKY									
University of Kentucky	Lexington	uky.edu	B		M		B	B	
University of Louisville	Louisville	louisville.edu		M			B		
LOUISIANA									
Louisiana State University	Baton Rouge	lsu.edu	B M[1]				B	B M	
Louisiana Tech University	Ruston	latech.edu	B				B		
Southern University A&M College	Baton Rouge	subr.edu	B						
Tulane University	New Orleans	tulane.edu	M		C M				
University of Louisiana at Lafayette	Lafayette	louisiana.edu	B			B	B		
University of New Orleans	New Orleans	uno.edu							M

Design Degree Programs

School	City	Web Address	Architecture	Architecture History	Historic Preservation	Industrial Design	Interior Design	Landscape Architecture	Planning
MARYLAND									
Goucher College	Baltimore	goucher.edu			B M				
Morgan State University	Baltimore	morgan.edu	M					M	M
University of Maryland	College Park	umd.edu	M		C M			B	M
MASSACHUSETTS									
Boston Architectural Center	Boston	the-bac.edu	B M						
Boston University	Boston	bu.edu		M	M		B M		
Endicott College	Beverly	endicott.edu					B		
Harvard University	Cambridge	harvard.edu	M					M	M
Massachusetts College of Art	Boston	massart.edu				B M			
Massachusetts Institute of Technology	Cambridge	mit.edu	M	M					M
Mount Ida College	Newton	mountida.edu					B		
Newbury College	Brookline	newbury.edu					A		
New England School of Art & Design at Suffolk University	Boston	suffolk.edu/nesad					B M		
Northeastern University	Boston	northeastern.edu	M						
Tufts University	Medford	tufts.edu							M
University of Massachusetts/Amherst	Amherst	umass.edu	M[1]					B M	M
Wentworth Institute of Technology	Boston	wit.edu	B			B	B		
MICHIGAN									
Andrews University	Berrien Springs	andrews.edu	B						
College for Creative Studies	Detriot	ccscad.edu				B			
Cranbrook Academy of Art	Bloomfield Hills	cranbrookart.edu				M			

Design Degree Programs

School	City	Web Address	Architecture	Architecture History	Historic Preservation	Industrial Design	Interior Design	Landscape Architecture	Planning
Eastern Michigan University	Ypsilanti	emich.edu			C M		B		B
Kendall College of Art and Design	Grand Rapids	kcad.edu				B	B		
Lawrence Technological University	Southfield	ltu.edu	M				B		
Michigan State University	East Lansing	msu.edu					B	B	B M
University of Detroit Mercy	Detroit	udmercy.edu	B						
University of Michigan	Ann Arbor	umich.edu	M			B M		M	M
Wayne State University	Detriot	wayne.edu							M
Western Michigan University	Kalamazoo	wmich.edu				B	B		
MINNESOTA									
Alexandria Technical College	Alexandria	atc.tec.mn.us					A		
Dakota County Technical College	Rosemount	dctc.mnscu.edu					A		
University of Minnesota	St. Paul/Mpls.	umn.edu	B M				B	M	M
MISSISSIPPI									
Mississippi State University	Mississippi State	msstate.edu	B				B	B	
University of Southern Mississippi	Hattiesburg	usm.edu					B		
MISSOURI									
Drury University	Springfield	drury.edu	B						
Maryville University of St. Louis	St. Louis	maryville.edu					B		
Southeast Missouri State University	Cape Girardeau	semo.edu			B M				
University of Missouri, Columbia	Columbia	missouri.edu		M			B		

Design Degree Programs

School	City	Web Address	Architecture	Architecture History	Historic Preservation	Industrial Design	Interior Design	Landscape Architecture	Planning
Washington University in St. Louis	St. Louis	wustl.edu	M						
MONTANA									
Montana State University	Bozeman	montana.edu	M						
NEBRASKA									
University of Nebraska	Lincoln	unl.edu	M				B		M
NEVADA									
University of Nevada, Las Vegas	Las Vegas	unlv.edu	M				B	B	
NEW JERSEY									
Berkeley College	Paramus	berkeleycollege.edu					A		
Kean University	Union	kean.edu					B		
New Jersey Institute of Technology	Newark	njit.edu	B M						
Princeton University	Princeton	princeton.edu	M						
Rutgers, The State University of New Jersey	New Brunswick	rutgers.edu		M				B	M
NEW MEXICO									
University of New Mexico	Albuquerque	unm.edu	M	M				M	M
NEW YORK									
Binghamton University, SUNY	Binghamton	binghamton.edu		M					
Buffalo State College, SUNY	Buffalo	buffalostate.edu					B		
City College of New York, CUNY	New York	ccny.cuny.edu	B					B	
College of Environmental Science and Forestry, SUNY	Syracuse	esf.edu						B M	
Columbia University	New York	columbia.edu	M	M	M				M
Cooper Union	New York	cooper.edu	B						
Cornell University	Ithaca	cornell.edu	B	M	M		B	B M	M

Design Degree Programs

School	City	Web Address	Architecture	Architecture History	Historic Preservation	Industrial Design	Interior Design	Landscape Architecture	Planning
Fashion Institute of Technology, SUNY	New York	fitnyc.suny.edu					B		
Hunter College, CUNY	New York	hunter.cuny.edu							M
New York Institute of Technology	various	nyit.edu	B				B		
New York School of Interior Design	New York	nysid.edu					B		
New York University	New York	nyu.edu		M					M
Parsons School of Design	New York	parsons.edu	M			B			
Pratt Institute	Brooklyn	pratt.edu	B		M	B M	B		M
Rensselaer Polytechnic Institute	Troy	rpi.edu	B M						
Rochester Institute of Technology	Rochester	rit.edu				B M	B		
School of Visual Arts	New York	schoolofvisualarts.edu					B		
Suffolk County Community College, SUNY	Riverhead	sunysuffolk.edu					A		
Syracuse University	Syracuse	syr.edu	B M	M		B M	B		
University at Albany, SUNY	Albany	albany.edu							M
University at Buffalo, SUNY	Buffalo	buffalo.edu	M						M
Villa Maria College of Buffalo	Buffalo	villa.edu					A		
NORTH CAROLINA									
East Carolina University	Greenville	ecu.edu					B		B
Meredith College	Raleigh	meredith.edu					B		
North Carolina A&T State University	Greensboro	ncat.edu						B	
North Carolina State University	Raleigh	ncsu.edu	B M			B M		B M	

Design Degree Programs

School	City	Web Address	Architecture	Architecture History	Historic Preservation	Industrial Design	Interior Design	Landscape Architecture	Planning
University of North Carolina at Chapel Hill	Chapel Hill	unc.edu							M
University of North Carolina at Charlotte	Charlotte	uncc.edu	B M						
University of North Carolina at Greensboro	Greensboro	uncg.edu					B		
Western Carolina University	Cullowhee	wcu.edu					B		
NORTH DAKOTA									
North Dakota State University	Fargo	ndsu.nodak.edu	B				B	B	
OHIO									
Belmont Technical College	St. Clairsville	belmont.cc.oh.us			A				
Cleveland Institute of Art	Cleveland	cia.edu				B			
Cleveland State University	Cleveland	csuohio.edu							M
Columbus College of Art & Design	Columbus	ccad.edu				B	B		
Kent State University	Kent	kent.edu	B				B		
Miami University	Oxford	muohio.edu	M				B		
Ohio State University	Columbus	osu.edu	M	M		B M	B	B M	M
Ohio University	Athens	ohiou.edu					B		
University of Akron	Akron	uakron.edu					B		
University of Cincinnati	Cincinnati	uc.edu	B M			B M	B		B M
Ursuline College	Pepper Pike	ursuline.edu			B				
OKLAHOMA									
Oklahoma State University	Stillwater	okstate.edu	B				B	B	
University of Oklahoma	Norman	ou.edu	B M				B	M	M
OREGON									
Portland State University	Portland	pdx.edu							M
University of Oregon	Eugene	uoregon.edu	B M	M	M		B M	B	M

Design Degree Programs

School	City	Web Address	Architecture	Architecture History	Historic Preservation	Industrial Design	Interior Design	Landscape Architecture	Planning
PENNSYLVANIA									
Bucks County Community College	Newtown	bucks.edu			C				
Carnegie Mellon University	Pittsburgh	cmu.edu	B			B M			
Drexel University	Philadelphia	drexel.edu	B				B		
La Roche College	Pittsburgh	laroche.edu					B		
Moore College of Art and Design	Philadelphia	moore.edu					B		
Pennsylvania State University	State College	psu.edu	B	M				B	
Philadelphia University	Philadelphia	philau.edu	B			B	B		
Temple University	Philadelphia	temple.edu	B					B	
University of Pennsylvania	Philadelphia	upenn.edu	M	M	C M			M	M
University of Pittsburgh	Pittsburgh	pitt.edu		M					
University of the Arts	Philadelphia	uarts.edu				B M			
RHODE ISLAND									
Brown University	Providence	brown.edu		M					
Rhode Island School of Design	Providence	risd.edu	B M			B M		B M	
Roger Williams University	Bristol	rwu.edu	B M		B				
Salve Regina University	Newport Beach	salve.edu			B				
University of Rhode Island	Kingston	uri.edu						B	M
SOUTH CAROLINA									
Clemson University	Clemson	clemson.edu	M					B	M
College of Charleston	Charleston	cofc.edu			B				
Winthrop University	Rock Hill	winthrop.edu					B		
TENNESSEE									
Middle Tennessee State University	Murfreesboro	mtsu.edu			M		B		
O'More College of Design	Franklin	omorecollege.edu					B		

Design Degree Programs

School	City	Web Address	Architecture	Architecture History	Historic Preservation	Industrial Design	Interior Design	Landscape Architecture	Planning
University of Memphis	Memphis	memphis.edu					B		M
University of Tennessee, Chattanooga	Chattanooga	utc.edu					B		
University of Tennessee, Knoxville	Knoxville	utk.edu	B M				B		M
Watkins College of Art & Design	Nashville	watkins.edu					A		
TEXAS									
El Centro College	Dallas	ecc.dcccd.edu					C		
Houston Community College/ Central College	Houston	ccollege.hccs.cc.tx.us					A		
Prairie View A&M University	Prairie View	pvamu.edu	B M						
Rice University	Houston	rice.edu	B M						
Stephen F. Austin State University	Nacogdoches	sfasu.edu					B		
Texas A&M University	College Station	tamu.edu	M					B M	M
Texas Christian University	Fort Worth	tcu.edu					B		
Texas State University, San Marcos	San Marcos	txstate.edu					B		
Texas Tech University	Lubbock	ttu.edu	M				B	B	
University of Houston	Houston	uh.edu	B M						
University of North Texas	Denton	unt.edu					B		
University of Texas at Arlington	Arlington	uta.edu	M				B	M	M
University of Texas at Austin	Austin	utexas.edu	B M	M	C M		B		M
University of Texas at San Antonio	San Antonio	utsa.edu	M				B		
UTAH									
Brigham Young University	Provo	byui.edu				B			
University of Utah	Salt Lake City	utah.edu	M						
Utah State University	Logan	usu.edu					B	B M	

Design Degree Programs

School	City	Web Address	Architecture	Architecture History	Historic Preservation	Industrial Design	Interior Design	Landscape Architecture	Planning
VERMONT									
Norwich University	Northfield	norwich.edu	B M						
University of Vermont	Burlington	uvm.edu			M				
VIRGINIA									
Hampton University	Hampton	hamptonu.edu	B						
James Madison University	Harrisonburg	jmu.edu					B		
Marymount University	Arlington	marymount.edu					B		
Mary Washington College	Fredericksburg	mwc.edu			B				
University of Virginia	Charlottesville	virginia.edu	M	M				M	B M
Virginia Commonwealth University	Richmond	vcu.edu		M			B		M
Virginia Polytechnic Institute and State University	Blacksburg	vt.edu	B M			B M	B	B M	M
WASHINGTON									
Eastern Washington University	Spokane	ewu.edu							B M
Washington State University	Pullman	wsu.edu	B				B	B	
Western Washington University	Bellingham	wwu.edu				B			
University of Washington	Seattle	washington.edu	M	M		B M		B M	M
WEST VIRGINIA									
West Virginia University	Morgantown	wvu.edu					B	B	
WISCONSIN									
Milwaukee Institute of Art & Design	Milwaukee	miad.edu				B			
Mount Mary College	Milwaukee	mtmary.edu					B		
University of Wisconsin, Madison	Madison	wisc.edu		M			B	B	M
University of Wisconsin, Milwaukee	Milwaukee	uwm.edu	M						M

Design Degree Programs

School	City	Web Address	Architecture	Architecture History	Historic Preservation	Industrial Design	Interior Design	Landscape Architecture	Planning
University of Wisconsin, Stevens Point	Stevens Point	uwsp.edu					B		
University of Wisconsin, Stout	Menomonie	uwstout.edu				B	B		

[1] This program is currently in candidate status for National Architectural Accreditation Board (NAAB) accreditation.

Source: Counsel House Research and Foundation for Interior Design Education Research, Industrial Designers Society of America, Landscape Architectural Accrediting Board, National Architectural Accrediting Board, National Council for Preservation Education, Planning Accreditation Board, and Society of Architectural Historians

Did you know...

According to the Design-Build Institute of America, five schools now offer design–build master's degrees: Georgia Institute of Technology, Stanford University, University of Oklahoma, Washington State University, and Worchester Polytechnic Institute.

Doctorate Programs in Architecture and Design

The following schools offer Doctorate and Ph.D. degrees in architecture and design. Detailed information about entrance requirements and the programs' field of study is available from the individual schools.

Architecture

Arizona State University (Tempe)
Carnegie Mellon University (Pittsburgh, PA)
Columbia University (New York, NY)
Georgia Institute of Technology (Atlanta)
Harvard University (Cambridge, MA)
Illinois Institute of Technology (Chicago)
Massachusetts Institute of Technology (Cambridge)
Princeton University (Princeton, NJ)
Rice University (Houston, TX)
Texas A&M University (College Station)
Texas Tech University (Lubbock)
University of California, Berkeley
University of California, Los Angeles
University of Colorado (Denver)
University of Florida (Gainesville)
University of Hawaii (Honolulu)
University of Michigan (Ann Arbor)
University of Nebraska-Lincoln
University of Pennsylvania (Philadelphia)
University of Texas at Austin
University of Wisconsin, Milwaukee
Virginia Polytechnic Institute (Blacksburg)

Architectural History

The Society of Architectural Historians' Web site, www.sah.org, *in addition to the individual schools, offers detailed information about each program, including their areas of focus, faculty data, and statistics.*

Brown University (Providence, RI)
City University of New York (New York)
Columbia University (New York, NY)
Cornell University (Ithaca, NY)
Florida State University (Tallahassee)
George Washington University (Washington, DC)
Georgia Institute of Technology (Atlanta)
Harvard University (Cambridge, MA)
Massachusetts Institute of Technology (Cambridge)
New York University (New York)
Northwestern University (Evanston, IL)
Ohio State University (Columbus)
Pennsylvania State University (State College)
Princeton University (Princeton, NJ)
Rutgers University (New Brunswick, NJ)
Stanford University (Stanford, CA)
State University of New York at Binghamton
University of California at Berkeley
University of California at Los Angeles
University of California at Santa Barbara
University of Chicago (IL)
University of Delaware (Newark)
University of Colorado (Denver)
University of Illinois at Chicago
University of Illinois at Urbana-Champaign
University of Iowa (Iowa City)
University of Louisville (KY)
University of Missouri-Columbia
University of New Mexico (Albuquerque)
University of Oregon (Eugene)
University of Pennsylvania (Philadelphia)
University of Pittsburgh (PA)
University of Texas at Austin
University of Virginia (Charlottesville)
University of Washington (Seattle)
University of Wisconsin-Madison
Virginia Commonwealth University (Richmond)
Yale University (New Haven, CT)

Historic Preservation

Cornell University (Ithaca, NY)
University of Texas at Austin

Industrial Design

Carnegie Mellon University (Pittsburgh, PA)

Doctorate Programs in Architecture and Design

Interior Design

Arizona State University (Tempe)
Bard Graduate Center for Studies in the Decorative Arts, Design and Culture (New York, NY)
Michigan State University (East Lansing)
Oregon State University (Eugene)
Texas Tech University (Lubbock)
Virginia Polytechnic Institute and State University (Blacksburg)
University of Minnesota (St. Paul/Minneapolis)
University of Missouri-Columbia

Landscape Architecture

In addition to landscape architecture, other schools offer related Ph.D. degrees that may be of interest with such titles as environmental design and land use planning.

Harvard University (Cambridge, MA)
University of Illinois at Urbana-Champaign
University of Michigan (Ann Arbor)

Planning

Arizona State University (Tempe)
Cleveland State University (OH)
Columbia University (New York, NY)
Cornell University (Ithaca, NY)
Florida State University (Tallahassee)
Georgia Institute of Technology (Atlanta)
Harvard University (Cambridge, MA)
Massachusetts Institute of Technology (Cambridge)
Ohio State University (Columbus)
Portland State University (OR)
Princeton University (Princeton, NJ)
Rutgers, The State University of New Jersey (New Brunswick)
Texas A&M University (College Station)
University of Akron (OH)
University of California, Berkeley
University of California, Irvine
University of California, Los Angeles
University of Colorado (Boulder)
University of Illinois at Chicago
University of Illinois at Urbana-Champaign
University of Massachusetts (Amherst)
University of Michigan (Ann Arbor)
University of New Orleans (LA)
University of North Carolina at Chapel Hill
University of Pennsylvania (Philadelphia)
University of Southern California (Los Angeles)
University of Texas at Austin
University of Washington (Seattle)
University of Wisconsin-Madison
Virginia Polytechnic Institute and State University (Blacksburg)
Washington State University (Pullman)

Source: Association of Collegiate Schools of Architecture (ACSA); Society of Architectural Historians (SAH); National Council for Preservation Education (NCPE); Industrial Designers Society of America (IDSA); Interior Design Educators Council (IDEC); Association of Collegiate Schools of Planning (ACSP); American Society of Landscape Architects (ASLA)

Educational Resources

In addition to the individuals schools, the following organizations can provide information about design education.

Architecture

Association of Collegiate Schools of Architecture (ACSA)
1735 New York Avenue, NW
Washington, DC 20006
Tel: (202) 785-2324
Internet: www.acsa-arch.org

National Architectural Accrediting Board (NAAB)
1735 New York Avenue, NW
Washington, DC 20006
Telephone: (202) 783-2007
Internet: www.naab.org

Architecture History

Society of Architectural Historians (SAH)
1365 North Astor Street
Chicago, Illinois 60610
Telephone: (312) 573-1365
Internet: www.sah.org

Historic Preservation

National Council for Preservation Education (NCPE)
University of Vermont
Burlington, VT 05405
Telephone: (802) 656-0577
Internet: www.uvm.edu/histpres/ncpe/

Industrial Design

Industrial Designers Society of America (IDSA)
45195 Business Center #250
Dulles, VA 20166
Telephone: (703) 707-6000
Fax: (703) 787-8501
Internet: www.idsa.org

Interior Design

Foundation for Interior Design Education Research (FIDER)
146 Monroe Center NW, Suite 1318
Grand Rapids, MI 49503-2822
Telephone: (616) 458-0400
Internet: www.fider.org

Interior Design Educators Council (IDEC)
9202 North Meridian Street, Ste. 200
Indianapolis, IN 46260-1810
Telephone: (317) 816-6261
Internet: www.idec.org

Landscape Architecture

Council of Educators in Landscape Architecture (CELA)
1800 Canyon Park Circle, Suite 403
Edmond, OK 73013
Telephone: (405) 341-3631
Internet: www.ssc.msu.edu/~la/cela/

Landscape Architectural Accreditation Board (LAAB)
Internet: www.asla.org/nonmembers/accredited_programs.cfm

Planning

Association of Collegiate Schools of Planning (ACSP)
6311 Mallard Trace
Tallahassee, FL 32312
Telephone: (850) 385-2054
Internet: www.acsp.org

Planning Accreditation Board (PAB)
Merle Hay Tower, Ste. 302
3850 Merle Hay Road
Des Moines, IA 50310
Telephone: (515) 252-0729
Internet: http://showcase.netins.net/web/pab_fi66/

Henry Adams Medal

Each year The American Institute of Architects and The American Architectural Foundation award an engraved medal and certificate of merit to the top-ranking graduating student from each architecture program accredited by the National Architectural Accrediting Board (NAAB). A certificate of merit is also awarded to the second-ranking graduating student. Recipients are chosen by the architecture faculty at each school based on their scholastic standings. Graduating students in bachelor's and master's programs are eligible. Formerly called "The School Medal," the program began in 1914 and, to date, has honored approximately 8,800 students. The top-ranking student(s) is listed below first followed by the second-ranked student(s). In some cases, only the first-rank student was honored. Not all schools participate each year.

For more information about the Medal, contact the individual schools' architecture department or Mary Felber at The American Architectural Foundation at (202) 626-7511.

2003 Undergraduate Recipients

Andrews University
Trent Bell
Andrew Van Lente

Arizona State University
Stephen Thomas Webster
Chad J. Schwartz

Auburn University
Kathryn Bryan
Matthew Christopher

California College of Arts and Crafts
Heather Levine-Chesler
Kimberly Naumann

California Polytechnic State University, San Luis Obispo
Aaron D. Walker
Frank E. Mahan

Carleton University
Ana Lukas
Chiara Camposilvan

Carnegie Mellon University
Sze Wee Chen; Dwight Yee

Clemson University
Daniel Ryan Culbertson
Kelley Lynn Hubbard

Cooper Union
Sony Devabhaktuni
Maria Elena Fanna; Michael A. LaFreniere

Cornell University
Aaron E. Zalneraitis
Alfred Huang

Drexel University
Dani Leiman
Joshua Dourte; William Stichter

Drury University
Ruth Esther Wetteroff
Darcia Elizabeth Thomas

Florida A&M University
Rebecca Irvin
Neil Campbell

Henry Adams Medal

Georgia Institute of Technology
Joseph Smith Claghorn
Susan Leigh Pryor

Howard University
Katryna Carter
Suzannah Codlin

Illinois Institute of Technology
Kelby Phillips
Yunseok Oscar Kang

Kansas State University
Lacy A. Brittingham
Nathan J. Schutte

Louisiana State University
Laura Morris; Lloyd Shenefelt
Stephanie Skinner; Raymond Scriber

Louisiana Tech University
Thomas Bradley Deal
Michael Connan Blake

Mississippi State University
Daniel S. Oakley
Paul W. Kirkpatrick

Montana State University
Matt Christensen
Boone Lennon; Keith Redfern

Morgan State University
Radhika Tambe
Jane Amin Boone

New Jersey Institute of Technology
Wai Lung Choi
Alexandra Shull

New York Institute of Technology
Christine Caine
Keun Sook Suk

Norwich University
Dana M. Dahlin
Elizabeth A. Wheatley

Oklahoma State University
Brian M. Winterscheidt
Katherine Atherton; Sarah Guion

Parsons School of Design/New School University
Lucas Cascardo
Robin Blodgett

Pennsylvania State University
Christine Aiken
Kyle Hollick

Philadelphia University
Laura Beck
Ryan Fennell

Polytechnic University of Puerto Rico
Pedro E. Claudio Montalvo
Romualdo Martínez

Rensselaer Polytechnic Institute
Brendan Harnett
Nicholas Caruso

Rhode Island School of Design
Sandra Beer
Amy Thornton

Rice University
David Jefferis
Parrish Kyle

Roger Williams University
Michelle Hartwell
Cynthia Lynne Gibson

Savannah College of Art and Design
Svetlana Legiteć
Daniela Moebius

Henry Adams Medal

Southern California Institute of Architecture
Selva Gurdogan
Francisco J. Sanchez

Southern University
Tchernavina R. McMickens
Sahaja R. Pitre

Syracuse University
Allen Wyatt Williams; Nicholas Saponara
Ronald Pelusio; Sarah A. Mossien

Temple University
Timothy Isak Wanaselja
Anthony J. Mancuso

Texas Tech University
Aaron Nathanael Benefiel
Jared Ethan Wright

Tulane University
Constanza Andre Marcheselli
James William Carse Jr.

Tuskegee University
Patrice Alicia Musaib-Ali
Melissa Cyrila Mattel

Université Laval
Stéphanie Migneault
Trycie Jolicoeur

University of Arizona
Laura Elizabeth Ennis
Siriporn Junn Beidler

University of Arkansas
Melissa J. Harlan
Iova Dineva

University of Calgary
Scott Pickles
Patric Langevin

University of California at Berkeley
Nicholas Papaefthimiou
Ryan Smith

University of California at Los Angeles
David Garnett
Daniel Wickline

University of Colorado at Denver/Boulder
John David Graham
Kangyoung Choi

University of Florida
Richard D. Pickler
Renwick Daelo

University of Hawaii at Manoa
Wendy Meguro
Jill Miyata

University of Houston
Laszlo Pallagi
Wing Yan Wong

University of Idaho
Darrin Griechen
Jerrod Wallgren

University of Illinois at Chicago
Tracie Cote
Karla Sierralta

University of Illinois at Urbana-Champaign
Brian S. Faulkner
Todd M. Watzel

University of Kansas
Lindsey Nicole Erickson
Mecayla Deanne Bruns

Henry Adams Medal

University of Kentucky
George Haviland Argo III
Dennis Jason Crowder

University of Louisiana at Lafayette
Talal A. AlModhayan
Zari S. Aljuwaisri

University of Miami
Ellen C. Buckley
Marcia Charles

University of Michigan
Carrie P. Johnson
Gregory Adam Pinter

University of North Carolina at Charlotte
William J. Scales; Michael E. Romot
Scott M. Cryer; Rebecca M. Joy

University of Notre Dame
Andrew Wilson
Jeffrey Schwaiger

University of Pennsylvania
Benjamin Robert Stough
Matthew Everett Herman

University of South Florida
Laura Lake

University of Southern California
Charles Callahan
Susan Cutler

University of Tennessee, Knoxville
Erica Leigh Walczak
Chung Fai Yang; Megan E. Nielsen-Hegstad

University of Texas at Arlington
Richard S. Atchison
John Robert Watkins

University of Texas at Austin
Beckie Lynn Dennis
Eve Maureen Trester-Wilson

University of Virginia
Breck August Gastinger
Andrew Eben Burdick

University of Waterloo
Danielle Wiley
Karen Smith

University of Wisconsin-Milwaukee
Chad Griswold
Jennifer Fletcher

Virginia Polytechnic Institute and State University
Roselie Mesina Enriquez
Marianne Virginia Parsons

Washington State University
Irena N. Korenkova
Peter James Kanyer

Woodbury University
Michael P. Paluso
Lisa C. You

Yale University
William L. Tims
William Todd Reisz

Henry Adams Medal

2003 Graduate Recipients

Catholic University of America

Katie D. Poindexter (*one and a half year program*); Adis Rodriguez (*two year program*); Paul R. Powers (*three year program*); Lisa A. Pallo (*fast track*)

Charles F. McGrath (*one and a half year program*); Deborah L. Lerner (*two year program*); James R. Sanderson (*three year program*)

Columbia University

Ian Dunn
Jason Stoikoff

Dalhousie University

Kevin Loewen
Tina Nicole Smith

Florida A&M University

Calvin Pemberton
William Santiago

Harvard University

Bryan Young
Yenche Tioanda

Illinois Institute of Technology

Jin-Hoon Lee; David Osivnik

McGill University

Lisa-Marie Fortin
Mr. Francis Moss

Miami University

Manole Voroneanu
Chad Knight

New Jersey Institute of Technology

Lori V. Shoyer
Carrie Ann Zegarski

North Carolina State University

Rodney Chadwick Everhart
Jessica Nicole Johnson

Ohio State University

Tamara Hilmey
Michael Denison

Princeton University

Susan Kathleen Nelson
Claire Hilary Johnson

Rensselaer Polytechnic Institute

Alsi Erdem
Thomas Bursey

Southern California Institute of Architecture

Jonathan Haruo Garnett
Paul Wysocan

Texas A&M University

Amey Bhan
Marc Frame

Tulane University

Wendy Weatherall Kerrigan
Jennifer Lynn Kaltwasser

Université Laval

Geneviève Beaulieu
Rémi Hovington Jr.

University at Buffalo

Anirban Adhya
Elizabeth Perreault

University of British Columbia

Martin Peter

Henry Adams Medal

University of Hawaii at Manoa
Olivier Pennetier

University of Houston
Chula Sanchez
William R. Wooton

University of Kansas
Christina Assmann
Christine E. Prescott

University of Louisiana at Lafayette
Andre N. Bourque

University of Manitoba
Gavin Kraemer
Scott Neish

University of Maryland
Keif Samulski
Anne Dutton

University of Miami
Gorata Madigele
Mikhail Webster

University of Nebraska
John Francis Manning
Sakura Hino

University of Tennessee, Knoxville
Jonathan David Cothern
Barbara B. Laurent

University of Texas at Austin
Cameron Wilson Cooper
Erik Jon Haden

University of Toronto
Jose Uribe Pabon
Tarisha Dolyniuk

University of Utah
Cecilia Parera
Derrick Larm

University of Washington
Virginia Rose Franey
Kevin Michael Armstrong

Virginia Polytechnic Institute and State University
Derek Hudson
George Blume; Jon Zellweger

Source: The American Architectural Foundation

IDSA Education Award

The Industrial Designers Society of America (IDSA) grants the Education Award to recognize excellence in industrial design education. Educators are presented this award in honor of their significant and distinguished contributions.

For additional information, visit IDSA on the Internet at *www.idsa.org*.

1988 Arthur J. Pulos
Syracuse University

1989 Robert Lepper
Carnegie Mellon University

1990 Edward Zagorski
University of Illinois, Urbana-Champaign

1991 James M. Alexander
Art Center College of Design

1992 Strother MacMinn
Art Center College of Design

Robert Redmann
University of Bridgeport

1993 Vincent Foote
North Carolina State University

Herbert Tyrnauer
California State University at Long Beach

1994 Hin Bredendieck
Georgia Institute of Technology

Joseph Koncelik
Ohio State University

1996 Toby Thompson
Rochester Institute of Technology

1997 Marc Harrison
Rhode Island School of Design

1998 Bruce Hannah
Pratt Institute

1999 Michael Nielsen
Arizona State University

2000 Katherine McCoy
Illinois Institute of Technology

Michael McCoy
Illinois Institute of Technology

2001 Jim Pirkl
Syracuse University

2002 Steven Skov Holt
California College of Arts and Crafts

2003 *No award granted*

Source: Industrial Designers Society of America

Design is a method of action.

Ray and Charles Eames

Jot D. Carpenter Medal

The American Society of Landscape Architects (ASLA) bestows the Jot D. Carpenter Prize and Medal upon a university educator who has made a sustained and significant teaching contribution to a landscape architecture program at a school with an official ASLA Student Chapter. The award, consisting of a medal and a cash prize, began in 2000 to honor the memory of Ohio State Professor Jot D. Carpenter and his significant contributions to landscape architecture education and the profession. Nominations for the award may be made by an ASLA member or an ASLA student chapter member.

For additional information, call (202) 216-2338 or visit *www.asla.org* on the Web.

2000 Roy H. DeBoer
Rutgers University

2002 Alton A. Barnes Jr.
Kansas State University

2003 Craig W. Johnson
Utah State University

Source: American Society of Landscape Architects

Craig Johnson received the Jot D. Carpenter Medal for his sustained and significant contribution to landscape architecture education. In addition to serving on the faculty of the Department of Landscape Architecture and Environmental Planning at Utah State University for 37 years, he has been named Teacher of the Year eight times, Department Advisor of the Year twice, and Utah State University College of Humanities, Arts, and Social Science Teacher of the Year in 1984, 1996, and 1999. *Photo by USU Photography, courtesy of the American Society of Landscape Architects.*

Michael Tatum Educator of the Year Award

The Michael Tatum Excellence in Education Award was created by the International Interior Design Association (IIDA) to honor outstanding interior design educators. The Award also celebrates the life and career of Michael Tatum, an outstanding educator and IIDA member who passed away in 1998. When reviewing the nominations, the awards committee considers excellence in teaching, innovative teaching techniques, student mentoring, contributions to the profession, creative scholarship, including the publication of scholarly research, and leadership in interior design education within the community. Nominees must be full-time faculty at FIDER-accredited schools. Recipients are awarded a $5,500 cash prize and are invited to present a scholarly paper to the IIDA membership.

For more information about the Tatum Award, contact IIDA at (312) 467-1950 or visit them on the Internet at *www.iida.org*.

1999 Joy Dohr
University of Wisconsin at Madison

2000 Henry P. Hildebrandt
University of Cincinnati

2001 Stephen Marc Klein
Pratt Institute

2002 Denise Guerin
University of Minnesota

JoAnn Asher Thompson
Washington State University

2003 *No award granted*

Source: International Interior Design Association

NCARB Prize for Creative Integration of Practice and Education in the Academy

The National Council of Architectural Registration Boards (NCARB) presents its annual NCARB Prize for Creative Integration of Practice and Education in the Academy to recognize accredited academic programs that best emphasize the continuum between practice and education. A jury consisting of the five members of the NCARB Practice Education Task Force and one dean from a school in each of the six NCARB regions selects the winners. Six cash awards are presented: one grand prize award of $25,000 and five awards of $7,500 each. The Prize was inspired by the 1996 Carnegie Foundation report, Building Community: A New Future for Architectural Education and Practice, written by Lee D. Mitgang and the late Ernest L. Boyer.

For additional information or to request an entry packet, contact NCARB at (202) 879-0535, or visit the NCARB Web site at *www.ncarb.org*.

2003 Winners

Grand Prize

Studio 804, Inc.
University of Kansas

Prize Winners

"Upper-Concord Street Neighborhood"
Clemson University

"Dialogic reciprocity: Binding form making to practice in first-year design"
Mississippi State University

"American Indian Housing Initiative"
Pennsylvania State University and University of Washington

"Building Connections...Building Practice"
University of Maryland

"The Art of Integration/The Science of Building"
Virginia Polytechnic Institute and State University

Honorable Mentions

"Yale Building Project"
Yale University

"Re-building the City through Community Design"
University of Puerto Rico

Source: National Council of Architectural Registration Boards

> Creativity has to do more with the elimination of the inessential than inventing something new.
>
> **Helmut Jahn**

Polsky Academic Achievement Award

In order to recognize outstanding design research or a thesis project by an undergraduate or graduate student, the American Society of Interior Designers (ASID) presents the ASID Educational Foundation/Joel Polsky Academic Achievement Award. Winning entries should address the needs of the public, designers and students on topics related to design business, education, process, research, behavioral science, theory or other technical subjects. Recipients receive a $1,000 prize.

More information is available on ASID's Web site, *www.asid.org*, or by calling the ASID Educational Foundation at (202) 546-3480.

1988

Open Office Programming: Assessment of the Workstation Game, Nancy C. Canestaro

1989

Restroom Usage in Selected Public Buildings and Facilities: A Comparison of Males and Females, Sandra K. Rawls

1990

Preference, Mystery and Visual Attributes of Interiors: A Study of Relationships, Suzanne Benedict Scott

1991

The History of the Railroad of New Jersey Maritime Terminal in Jersey City, New Jersey, Commemorating its Centennial 1889-1989, Sharon K. Sommerlad Keenan

1992

Design for a Residential Facility for the Elderly in Combination with a Child Care Facility, Marida A. Stearns

1993

View to Nature: Effects on Attentional Capacity, Carolyn Marie Gilker

1994

WAYFINDING – You are Here/You are There, Jacqueline Gommel

1995

Home Builders' and Remodelers' Role in the Adoption and Diffusion of Universally Designed Housing, Beatriz E. Blanco

Honorable Mention

Impact on the Campus Physical Environment on Older Adult Learners, Maurine Moore

1996

Impact of Interior Design on the Dining Disabilities of the Elderly Residents in Assisted Living and Nursing Homes, Elizabeth Rylan

Honorable Mention

Computers in the Design Process: Comparing Creativity Ratings of Interior Design Solutions Using Pencil Based Design Methods in Schematic Development, Lynn Brandon

1997

A Comparison of Spatial Interpretations of NASA's Payload Operations Control Center, Marshall Space Flight Center, Using Real World and Virtual Reality Observations, Patricia F. Lindsey

La Bottega D'Artigianato Regionale in the Palazzo Massimo alle Colonne, Rome, Italy: A Story of Adaptive Reuse, Cigdem T. Bulut

Polsky Academic Achievement Award

1998

Residential Interior Environments of Retired Government Employees in Thailand, Benjamas Kutintara

Physical and Social Attributes Influencing Mobile Workers' Sense of Place, Jacquelyn Purintan

1999

Interior Design for Alzheimer Care Facilities: Investigating Established Design Recommendations, Kathleen L. Cackowski

Graduate Education Research and the Interior Design Profession, Patti Lawlor

2000

A Comparison of Career Preparation and Development Between Two-year and Four-Year Interior Design Graduates, Barbara Marini

2001

Universal Design Standards for Single-Family Housing, Nancy L. Wolford

2002

Environmental Quality and Healing Environments: A Study of Flooring Materials In a Healthcare Telemetry Unit, Debra Harris

2003

An Exploration of Critical Factors for Accessibility and Wayfinding for Adults with Mental Retardation, Patricia Salmi

Honorable Mention

Bridging the Gap Between Graduation and Registered Professional Practice in Interior Design, Sooz Klinkhammer

Source: American Society of Interior Designers

Presidents of the American Institute of Architecture Students

1956-57 James R. Barry
Rice Univ.

1957-58 Robert Harris
Princeton Univ.

1958-59 Paul Ricciutti
Case Western Reserve Univ.

1959-60 Charles Jones
Univ. of Arizona

1960-61 Ray Gaio
Univ. of Notre Dame

1961-62 Donald Williams
Univ. of Illinois at Urbana-Champaign

1962-63 Carl Schubert
California State Polytechnic Univ.

1964-65 Joseph Morse
Howard Univ.

1965-66 Kenneth Alexander
Pratt Institute

1966-67 Jack Worth III
Georgia Institute of Technology

1967-68 Morten Awes
Univ. of Idaho

1968-69 Edward Mathes
Univ. of Southwestern Louisiana

1969-70 Taylor Culver
Howard Univ.

1970-71 Michael Interbartolo
Boston Architectural Center

1971-72 Joseph Siff
Rice Univ.

1972-73 Fay D'Avignon
Boston Architectural Center

1973-74 Fay D'Avignon
Boston Architectural Center

1974-75 Patric Davis
Boston Architectural Center

1975-76 Ella Hall
North Carolina State Univ.

1976-77 Jerry Compton
Southern California Inst. of Arch.

1977-78 Charles Guerin
Univ. of Houston

1978-79 John Maudlin-Jeronimo
Univ. of Miami

1979-80 Richard Martini
Boston Architectural Center

1980-81 Alejandro Barbarena
Univ. of Houston

1981-82 Bill Plimpton
Univ. of California at Berkeley

1982-83 Robert Klancher
Univ. of Cincinnati

1983-84 Robert Fox
Temple Univ.

1984-85 Thomas Fowler IV
NYIT–Old Westbury

1985-86 Scott Norberg
Univ. of Nebraska

1986-87 Scott Norberg
Univ. of Nebraska

1987-88 Kent Davidson
Univ. of Nebraska

1988-89 Matthew W. Gilbertson
Univ. of Minnesota

1989-90 Douglas A. Bailey
Montana State Univ.

1990-91 Alan D.S. Paradis
Roger Williams College

1991-92 Lynn N. Simon
Univ. of Washington

1992-93 Courtney E. Miller
Univ. of Maryland

1993-94 Garen D. Miller
Drury College

1994-95 Dee Christy Briggs
City College of New York

1995-96 Robert J. Rowan
Washington State Univ.

1996-97 Raymond H. Dehn
Univ. of Minnesota

Presidents of the American Institute of Architecture Students

1997-98	Robert L. Morgan Clemson Univ.
1998-99	Jay M. Palu Univ. of Nebraska
1999-00	Melissa Mileff Univ. of Oklahoma
2000-01	Scott Baldermann Univ. of Nebraska
2001-02	Matt Herb University of Maryland
2002-03	Lawrence Fabbroni Carnegie Mellon University
2003-04	Wayne Mortenson Univ. of Nebraska

Source: American Institute of Architects Students

It is the relationship of all things that creates value.

Frank Lloyd Wright

SOM Foundation Traveling Fellowship Program

Each year, the SOM Foundation invites accredited schools of architecture, design, engineering, and urban design to nominate their most promising students for traveling fellowships in their fields. The SOM Foundation Traveling Fellowship Program fulfills the Foundation's mission to help young architects broaden their education and take an enlightened view of society's need to improve the built and natural environments. The program recognizes the importance of travel to a designer's education, that when immersed in another place and culture can transform an architect's work and, ultimately, the field itself. The programs of the SOM Foundation, established in 1980, are funded by an endowment established by the partners of Skidmore, Owings & Merrill LLP.

For more information, contact the SOM Foundation at (312) 427-4202, or email *somfoundation@som.com.*

2003 Recipients

Architecture Bachelor Degree Traveling Fellowship

Che Wei Wang, Pratt Institute

Architecture Master Degree Traveling Fellowship

Ramiro Diazgranados, University of California at Los Angeles

Interior Architecture Traveling Fellowship

Kyle Reynolds, University of Wisconsin at Milwaukee

Structural Engineering Traveling Fellowship

Forest Flager, Massachusetts Institute ofTechnology

Urban Design Traveling Fellowship

Jan Leenknegt, Columbia University

Architecture Jury

Peter Ellis, Skidmore, Owings & Merrill LLP (chair)
George Schipporeit, Illinois Institute of Technology
Doug Garofalo, University of Illinois at Chicago and Garofalo Architects
Anders Nereim, The School of the Art Institute of Chicago

Interior Architecture Jury

Jaime Velez, Skidmore, Owings & Merrill LLP (chair)
Cindy Coleman, Frankel + Coleman
Gary Wheeler, Perkins & Will

Structural Engineering Jury

Mark Sarkisian, Skidmore, Owings & Merrill LLP (chair)
Greg Cosko, Hathaway Dinwiddie Construction Co.
Mark Ketchum, OPAC Engineers
John King, San Francisco Chronicle
Stanley Saitowitz, Stanley Saitowitz Architecture

Urban Design Jury

Philip Enquist, Skidmore, Owings & Merrill LLP (chair)
Linda Searl, Searl & Associates
Joseph Valerio, Valerio DeWalt Train Associates

Source: SOM Foundation

Top, left to right: George Schipporeit, Hilary Sample (finalist), Peter Ellis, Lisa Westerfield, Che Wei Wang (winner), Duy Ho (finalist), Ramiro Diazgranados, Anders Nereim. Not pictured: Doug Garofalo. *Bottom, left to right*: Lisa Westerfield, Gary Wheeler, Jennifer Silbert (finalist), Kyle Reynolds (winner), Cindy Coleman, Jaime Velez.

Student Sustainable Design Competition

The International Interior Design Association (IIDA) and DuPont™ Antron® partner to present the annual Student Sustainable Design Competition. Inaugurated in 2003, the contest awards outstanding sustainable design by students enrolled in post-secondary interior design programs. Designs are judged for innovative character of the overall design, responsible use of materials, practical application, visual comfort and sustainable material application. Projects should be between 1,000–30,000 square feet. Award prizes include: $3,500 for the grand prize; $1,500 for the first prize; and a gift certificate for the honorable mention.

Additional information and entry forms are available online at *www.iida.org* or by contacting the IIDA at (312) 467-1950.

2003 Winners

Grand Prize

"Linden Village"
Nadia Orawski
Ryerson University

First Prize

"Greenpeace Headquarters"
Krisztina Schuszter
Fashion Institute of Technology

Honorable Mention

"Law Firm"
Mandy Calloway
University of North Texas

Source: International Interior Design Association

Tau Sigma Delta

Formed in 1913 at the University of Michigan, Tau Sigma Delta is an honor society for Architecture and the Allied Arts. University juniors and seniors who are majoring in architecture, architectural engineering, architectural design, landscape architecture, painting, sculpting, planning, decorative design, interior design and all allied arts are eligible for membership. To date, over 65 chapters have been organized at schools across the United States, each administered by the universities' Schools of Architecture. In addition, the honor society presents both a Gold Medal to honor a professional and a Bronze medal to honor an outstanding student, each year.

Contact

Additional information about Tau Sigma Delta, including a list of chapters and their contacts, can be found online at *www.ttu.edu/~tsd/*.

Did you know...

When Chicago's $130 million University Center by VOA and Antunovich Associates is completed in the fall 2004, it will be the largest dormitory in the United States, housing students from DePaul, Roosevelt, and Columbia Universities.

Top 15 Colleges and Universities of Interior Design

Each year the *Almanac of Architecture & Design*, in conjunction with *DesignIntelligence* and Counsel House Research, conducts a survey to determine the best schools and colleges for interior design in the United States. The only study of its kind, we contact leading firms in varying market sectors throughout the country and ask them to indicate which FIDER-accredited (Foundation for Interior Design Education Research) programs produce graduates most prepared for professional practice. Based on their hiring practices in the past five years, the following information reflects what institutions top firms felt prepared graduates for real-world practice.

While the information below can be helpful to current and prospective interior design students, it is recommended that schools be analyzed from many different perspectives. For instance, what is a program's job placement record? Its focus of study? What are faculty members' areas of specialization? What is the availability and caliber of a school's internship program? Are there international study options? The information below is intended to comprise one of the many factors influencing the decision-making process.

1. University of Cincinnati
2. Pratt Institute
3. Cornell University
4. Kansas State University
5. University of Oregon
6. California College the Arts
7. Arizona State University
8. Virginia Polytechnic Institute and State University
9. Auburn University
10. Syracuse University
11. Iowa State University
12. Fashion Institute of Technology State University of New York
    Kent State University
    Woodbury University
15. University of Florida

* This survey combined Kansas State University's Interior Architecture and Interior Design programs and Syracuse University's Environmental Design/Interior and Interior Design programs.

Source: DesignIntelligence and Counsel House Research

Top 15 Schools and Colleges of Architecture

Each year the *Almanac of Architecture & Design*, in conjunction with *DesignIntelligence* and Counsel House Research, conducts a survey to determine the best schools and colleges for architecture in the United States. The only study of its kind, we contact leading architecture firms in varying market sectors throughout the country and ask them to indicate which NAAB-accredited (National Architectural Accrediting Board) programs produce graduates most prepared for professional practice. Based on their hiring practices in the past five years, the following information reflects what institutions top firms felt prepared graduates for real-world practice. For the first time, undergraduate and graduate programs are ranked separately.

While the information below can be helpful to current and prospective architecture students, it is recommended that schools be analyzed from many different perspectives. For instance, what is a program's job placement record? Its focus of study? What are faculty members' areas of specialization? What is the availability and caliber of a school's internship program? Are there international study options? The information below is intended to comprise one of the many factors influencing the decision-making process.

Undergraduate Programs

1. University of Cincinnati
2. Cornell University
3. California Polytechnic State University, San Luis Obispo
4. Rhode Island School of Design
   Rice University
   Syracuse University
   Virginia Polytechnic Institute and State University
8. Kansas State University
9. University of Notre Dame
10. University of Texas at Austin
11. Iowa State University
    University of Oregon
13. Ball State University
    Carnegie Mellon University
    Illinois Institute of Technology

Graduate Programs

1. Harvard University
2. Yale University
3. Columbia University
4. University of Cincinnati
5. Massachusetts Institute of Technology
6. Princeton University
7. University of Michigan
   University of Pennsylvania
9. University of Virginia
10. University of Illinois at Urbana-Champaign
11. Rice University
12. University of California, Berkeley
    Washington University in St. Louis
14. Arizona State University
    Rhode Island School of Design

Source: DesignIntelligence *and Counsel House Research*

TOPAZ Medallion

The TOPAZ Medallion is awarded jointly by The American Institute of Architects (AIA) and the American Collegiate Schools of Architecture (ACSA) to honor individuals who have made an outstanding contribution to the field of architectural education. Candidates may be nominated by colleagues, students and former students. Recipients have made a significant impact on the field of architecture, expanded into fields beyond their specialty, and affected a lasting impact on their students.

For additional information about this award program, visit the AIA's Web site at *www.aia.org*.

1976 Jean Labatut
Princeton University

1977 Henry Kamphoefner
North Carolina State University

1978 Lawrence Anderson
Massachusetts Inst. of Technology

1979 G. Holmes Perkins
University of Pennsylvania

1980 Serge Chermayeff
Yale University

1981 Marcel Breuer
Harvard University

1982 Joseph Esherick
University of California, Berkeley

1983 Charles E. Burchard
Virginia Polytechnic University

1984 Robert Geddes
Princeton University

1985 Colin Rowe
Cornell University

1986 Vincent Scully Jr.
Yale University

1987 Ralph Rapson
University of Minnesota

1988 John Hejduk
Cooper Union

1989 Charles Moore
University of California, Berkeley

1990 Raymond L. Kappe
Southern California Institute of Arch.

1991 Kenneth B. Frampton
Columbia University

1992 Spiro Kostof*
University of California, Berkeley

1993 Mario Salvadori
Columbia University

1994 Harlan E. McClure
Clemson University

1995 Henry N. Cobb
Harvard University

1996 Denise Scott Brown
University of Pennsylvania

1997 Donlyn Lyndon
University of California, Berkeley

1998 Werner Seligmann
Syracuse University

1999 W. Cecil Steward
University of Nebraska

2000 Alan H. Balfour
Rensselaer Polytechnic Institute

2001 Lee G. Copeland
Washington College and Univ. of Penn.

2002 Jerzy Soltan
Harvard University

2003 Marvin J. Malecha
North Carolina State University

* honored posthumously

Source: The American Institute of Architects

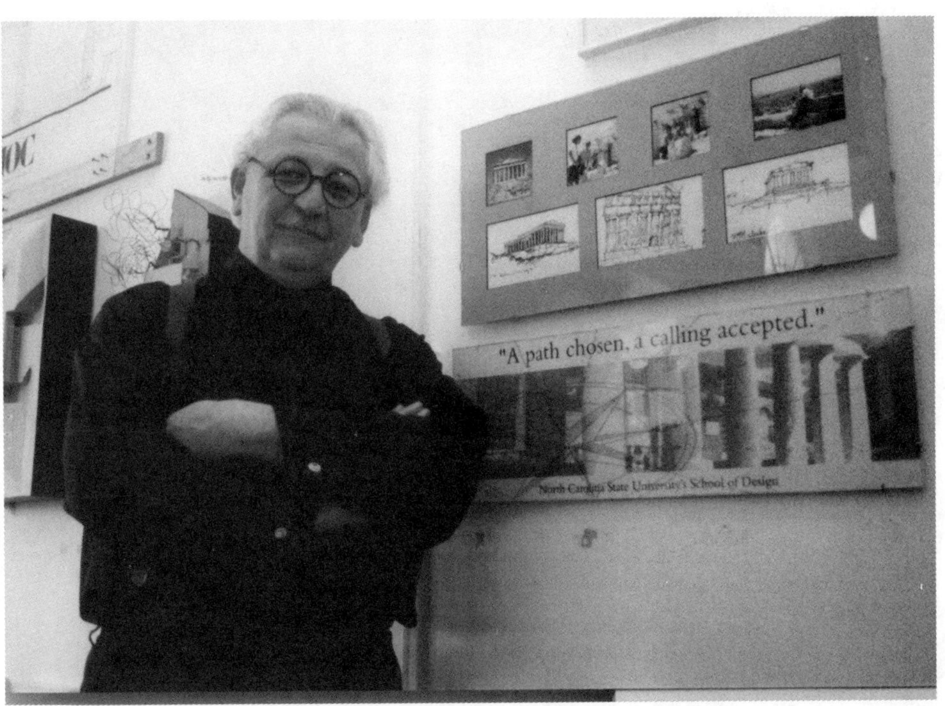

In selecting Marvin Malecha for the 2003 TOPAZ Medallion, the jury commented: "Marvin Malecha has gained significant peer recognition and his efforts are supported by architecture school deans. He championed the practice of using drawing as a method of instruction, and his case studies approach has bridged academia with practice. Marvin manages to keep all areas of education in perspective, and his global bridging is noteworthy. He understands the intrinsic value of international studies and he has displayed vision in that regard." *Photo by Catherine Lazorko, courtesy of North Carolina State University.*

8 Organizations

The history, purpose, and membership benefits of the major national and international design associations can be found in this chapter, with a summary listing of numerous design and building-related organizations and government agencies available beginning on page 574. Other organizations related to sustainable design (pg. 397), historic preservation (pg. 427), and design education (pg. 493) can be found in their respective chapters.

American Architectural Foundation

AAF

Headquartered in America's oldest museum devoted to architecture, Washington, DC's Octagon, the American Architectural Foundation (AAF) is dedicated to furthering the public's understanding of architecture and the human experience. The non-profit AAF sponsors education and outreach programs which foster public participation in the design process, encourages public stewardship of America's architectural heritage, and promotes alliances between architects and their communities. It is also a repository for a growing architectural archive of over 60,000 drawings and 30,000 photographs.

Address

1735 New York, Avenue NW
Washington, DC 20006
Telephone: (202) 626-7500
Fax: (202) 626-7420
Internet: www.archfoundation.org

Mission Statement

The American Architectural Foundation is a national resource for those who want our communities to be centers of civilization and our children to inherit a wholesome physical environment that uplifts the spirit. The AAF is a national resource that seeks to educate people about the value of architecture and design as a resource to enrich lives and transform communities.

American Council of Engineering Companies

ACEC

The American Council of Engineering Companies (ACEC) represents private engineering firms in the United States by promoting their interests and providing educational opportunities to members. Specifically, the goals of the group are to help members achieve higher business standards, serve as an information clearinghouse, advise on legislation, and to support the advancement of engineering. The ACEC was formed by the union of the American Institute of Consulting Engineers and the Consulting Engineers Council in 1973. Today it is the largest national organization of consulting engineers. Fifty-one state and regional Member Organizations represent more than 5,800 engineering firms. These firms employ more than 309,000 engineers, architects, land surveyors, scientists, technicians and other professionals who design approximately $100 billion of private and public works annually.

Address

1015 15th St., NW, 8th Fl.
Washington, DC 20005
Telephone: (202) 347-7474
Fax: (202) 898-0068
Internet: www.acec.org

Mission Statement

The American Council of Engineering Companies is the business association of America's engineering industry, representing approximately 6,000 independent engineering companies throughout the United States engaged in the development of America's transportation, environmental, industrial, and other infrastructure. Founded in 1910 and headquartered in Washington, DC ACEC is a national federation of 51 state and regional organizations.

American Institute of Architects

AIA

Representing the professional interests of America's architects since 1857, The American Institute of Architects (AIA) provides education, government advocacy, community redevelopment and public outreach activities with and for its 62,000 members. With over 300 local and state AIA organizations, the Institute closely monitors legislative and regulatory actions at all levels of government. It provides professional development opportunities, industry standard contract documents, information services, and a comprehensive awards program.

Address

1735 New York Ave., NW
Washington, DC 20006
Telephone: (202) 626-7300 or (800) AIA-3837
Fax: (202) 626-7547
Internet: www.aia.org

Mission Statement

The American Institute of Architects is the voice of the architecture profession dedicated to: serving its members, advancing their value, and improving the quality of the built environment.

American Institute of Graphic Arts (AIGA)

AIGA

Billing itself as the oldest and largest membership association for professionals engaged in the discipline, practice and culture of visual communication and graphic design, the AIGA (American Institute of Graphic Arts) was founded in 1914 and now represents more than 15,000 designers. Members of AIGA include professional designers, educators and students engaged in type and book design, editorial design, communications and corporate design, posters, interface and web design, and new media and motion graphics design. AIGA serves as a hub of information and activity within the design community through conferences, competitions, exhibitions, publications, educational activities and its Web site.

Address

164 Fifth Avenue
New York, NY 10010
Telephone: (212) 807-1990
Fax: (212) 807-1799
Internet: www.aiga.org

Mission Statement

The purpose of the American Institute of Graphic Arts is to further excellence in communication design as a broadly defined discipline, strategic tool for business and cultural force. AIGA is the place design professionals turn to first to exchange ideas and information, participate in critical analysis and research and advance education and ethical practice.

American Planning Association

APA

The American Planning Association (APA) represents 30,000 planners, officials and citizens involved with urban and rural planning issues. Sixty-five percent of APA's members are employed by state and local government agencies. The mission of the organization is to encourage planning that will contribute to public well-being by developing communities and environments that meet the needs of people and society more effectively. APA is headquartered in Washington, D.C. and operates local chapters across the country. The American Institute of Certified Planners (AICP) is APA's professional and educational arm, certifying planners who meet specific criteria. The group also has research, publications, conference, and education components.

Address

1776 Massachusetts Ave., NW
Washington, DC 20036
Telephone: (202) 872-0611
Fax: (202) 872-0643
Internet: www.planning.org

Mission Statement

The American Planning Association is a nonprofit public interest and research organization committed to urban, suburban, regional, and rural planning. APA and its professional institute, the American Institute of Certified Planners, advance the art and science of planning to meet the needs of people and society.

American Society of Interior Designers

ASID

The American Society of Interior Designers (ASID) was formed in 1975 by the consolidation of the American Institute of Designers (AID) and the National Society of Interior Designers (NSID). It serves over 30,000 members with continuing education, government affairs, conferences, publications, online services, and more. Members include residential and commercial designers; 3,500 manufacturers of design-related products and services, also known as Industry Partners; and 7,500 interior design students. ASID operates 48 local chapters throughout the United States.

Address

608 Massachusetts Avenue, NE
Washington, DC 20002-6006
Telephone: (202) 546-3480
Fax: (202) 546-3240
Internet: www.asid.org

Mission Statement

To advance the interior design profession through knowledge generation and sharing, advocacy of interior designers' right to practice, professional and public education, and expansion of interior design markets.

American Society of Landscape Architects

ASLA

Representing the landscape architecture profession in the United States since 1899, the American Society of Landscape Architects (ASLA) currently serves over 13,500 members through 48 chapters across the country. The ASLA's goal is to advance knowledge, education, and skill in the art and science of landscape architecture. The benefits of membership include a national annual meeting, *Landscape Architecture* magazine, continuing education credits, seminars and workshops, professional interest groups, government advocacy, and award programs. In addition, the U.S. Department of Education has authorized the Landscape Architectural Accreditation Board (LAAB) of the ASLA as the accrediting agency for landscape architecture programs at U.S. colleges and universities.

Address

636 Eye Street, NW
Washington, DC 20001-3736
Telephone: (202) 898-2444
Fax: (202) 898-1185
Internet: www.asla.org

Mission Statement

The mission of the American Society of Landscape Architects is to lead, to educate and to participate in the careful stewardship, wise planning and artful design of our cultural and natural environments.

Design Futures Council

DFC

The Design Futures Council (DFC) is a think-tank of design and building industry leaders who collaborate through a series of regular meetings, Summits, and *DesignIntelligence*, a monthly newsletter. The group shares information among its members on best practices and new trends in the design community in order to help member organizations anticipate change and increase competitive fitness. Recent Summit topics have included sustainable/green design and creativity (with the Salk Institute). Members include leading architecture and design firms; dynamic manufacturers; service providers; and small, forward-thinking A/E/C companies taking an active interest in their future.

Address

30 Technology Parkway South, Ste. 200
Atlanta, GA 30092
Telephone: (800) 726-8603
Internet: www.di.net

Mission Statement

The Design Futures Council is a think-tank with the mission to explore trends, changes, and new opportunities in design, architecture, engineering, and building technology for the purpose of fostering innovation and improving the performance of member organizations.

Industrial Designers Society of America

IDSA

Founded in 1965, the Industrial Designers Society of America (IDSA) is a professional association of industrial designers, educators and students dedicated to the promotion of the profession. By fostering innovation and high standards of design, IDSA communicates the value of design to the public and mentors young designers in their professional career development. IDSA serves its constituency through the professional journal *Innovation*, award programs, an annual conference, research sponsorship and collection, networking opportunities and promotion of the practice at all levels of government.

Address

45195 Business Court
Suite 250
Dulles, VA 20166
Telephone: (703) 707-6000
Fax: (703) 707-8501
Internet: www.idsa.org

Mission Statement

The Industrial Designers Society of America is dedicated to communicating the value of industrial design to society, business and government. IDSA provides leadership to and promotes dialog between practice and education. As a professional association, it serves its diverse membership by recognizing excellence, promoting the exchange of information and fostering innovation.

International Interior Design Association (IIDA)

IIDA

The International Interior Design Association (IIDA) provides a variety of services and benefits to its over 10,000 members through eight specialty forums, nine regions, and more than 30 Chapters around the world. This professional networking and educational association promotes the interior design practice to the public and serves its members as a clearinghouse for industry information. IIDA was founded in 1994 as the result of a merger of the Institute of Business Designers (IBD), the International Society of Interior Designers (ISID), and the Council of Federal Interior Designers (CFID). The goal of the merger was to create an international association with a united mission that would represent interior designers worldwide.

Address

13-122 Merchandise Mart
Chicago, IL 60654-1104
Telephone: (312) 467-1950
Fax: (312) 467-0779
Internet: www.iida.org

Mission Statement

The International Interior Design Association is committed to enhancing the quality of life through excellence in interior design and advancing interior design through knowledge. IIDA advocates for interior design excellence; provides superior industry information; nurtures a global interior design community; maintains educational standards; and responds to trends in business and design.

Society of Architectural Historians

SAH

Since its founding in 1940, the Society of Architectural Historians (SAH) has sought to promote the history of architecture. The membership of SAH ranges from professionals such as architects, planners, preservationists, and academics to those simply interested in architecture. The Society produces a quarterly journal and monthly newsletter and organizes study tours and an annual conference. There are also a number of associated, although independent, local chapters. The SAH's national headquarters is located in the architecturally significant Charnley-Persky House which was designed in 1891 by the firm of Dankmar Adler and Louis Sullivan. Guided tours of the house are offered.

Address

1365 North Astor Street
Chicago, IL 60610-2144
Telephone: (312) 573-1365
Fax: (312) 573-1141
Internet: www.sah.org

Mission Statement

The mission of the Society of Architectural Historians is to advance knowledge and understanding of the history of architecture, design, landscape, and urbanism worldwide.

Society for Environmental Graphic Design

SEGD

The Society for Environmental Graphic Design (SEGD) is a non-profit organization formed in 1973 to promote public awareness of and professional development in environmental graphic design. This interdisciplinary field encompasses the talents of many design professionals, including graphic designers, architects, landscape architects, product designers, planners, interior designers, and exhibition designers in the planning and design of graphic elements that shape our built and natural environments. Practitioners in this field design graphic elements to help identify, direct, inform, interpret, and visually enhance our surroundings. From wayfinding systems and mapping to exhibit design and themed environments, environmental graphic design impacts our experiences everywhere. SEGD offers its members an interdisciplinary network to support and enhance their efforts in this growing discipline, a bi-monthly newsletter, annual conference, design award program, technical bulletins, job bank listings, and many other formal and informal resources.

Address

1000 Vermont Ave., Suite 400
Washington, DC 20001
Telephone: (202) 638-5555
Fax: (202) 638-0891
Internet: www. segd.org

Mission Statement

The Society for Environmental Graphic Design is an international non-profit educational organization providing resources for design specialists in the field of environmental graphic design, architecture, and landscape, interior, and industrial design.

Urban Land Institute

ULI

Formed in 1936 as a research arm of the National Association of Real Estate Boards (now the National Association of Realtors), the Urban Land Institute (ULI) is an independent organization for those engaged in the entrepreneurial and collaborative process of real estate development and land use policy-making. ULI now has 18,000 members working in the public and private sectors, a staff of 100 in Washington, D.C., and a $27 million operating budget. ULI members are the people that plan, develop and redevelop neighborhoods, business districts and communities across the U.S. and around the world, working in private enterprise and public service. The Institute's activities include research, forums and task forces, awards, education, and publishing.

Address

1025 Thomas Jefferson Street, NW
Suite 500 West
Washington, DC 20007
Telephone: (202) 624-7000
Fax: (202) 624-7140
Internet: www.uli.org

Mission Statement

The mission of the Urban Land Institute is to provide responsible leadership in the use of land in order to enhance the total environment. ULI's strategic direction is to extend its industry leadership to: bring together the people able to influence the outcome of important issues related to land use and the built environment; communicate who we are and what we-our members and our Institute-have learned about land use to increase ULI's influence on land use policy and practice; and continue to provide relevant and current information about land use and real estate development to all our members and stakeholders.

Design & Building Related Organizations

The following associations, organizations, and government agencies offer a variety ofinformation and support for the design and construction industry.

Associations & Organizations

Acoustical Society of America
2 Huntington Quadrangle, Suite 1NO1
Melville, NY 11747-4052
Tel: (516) 576-2360
Fax: (516) 576-2377
Internet: http://asa.aip.org

Air-Conditioning & Refrigeration Institute
4100 North Fairfax Dr. #200
Arlington, VA 22203
Tel: (703) 524-8800
Fax: (703) 528-3816
Internet: www.ari.org

Air Conditioning Contractors of America, Inc.
2800 Shirlington Road #300
Arlington, VA 22206
Tel: (703) 575-4477
Fax: (703) 575-4449
Internet: www.acca.org

Alliance to Save Energy
1200 18th St. NW #900
Washington, DC 20036
Tel: (202) 857-0666
Fax: (202) 331-9588
Internet: www.ase.org

American Arbitration Association
335 Madison Ave. 10th Floor
New York, NY 10017-4605
Tel: (212) 716-5800
Fax: (212) 716-5905
Internet: www.adr.org

American Architectural Manufacturers Association
1827 Walden Office Square #550
Schaumburg, IL 60173-4268
Tel: (847) 303-5664
Fax: (847) 303-5774
Internet: www.aamanet.org

American Center for Design
325 West Huron, Suite 711
Chicago, IL 60610
Tel: (312) 787-2018
Fax: (312) 649-9518
Internet: www.ac4d.org

American Concrete Institute
PO Box 9094
38800 Country Club Drive
Farmington Hills, MI 48331
Tel: (248) 848-3700
Fax: (248) 848-3701
Internet: www.aci-int.org

American Forest Foundation
1111 19th Street, NW, #780
Washington, DC 20036
Tel: (202) 463-2462
Fax: (202) 463-2461
Internet: www.affoundation.org

American Gas Association
400 North Capitol St. NW
Washington, DC 20001
Tel: (202) 824-7000
Fax: (202) 824-7115
Internet: www.aga.org

Design & Building Related Organizations

American Hardware Manufacturers Association
801 North Plaza Drive
Schaumburg, IL 60173-4977
Tel: (847) 605-1025
Fax: (847) 605-1030
Internet: www.ahma.org

American Horticultural Society
7931 East Boulevard Drive
Alexandria VA 22308
Tel: (703) 768-5700
Fax: (703) 768-8700
Internet: www.ahs.org

American Institute of Building Design
2505 Main Street #209-B
Stratford, CT 06615
Tel: (800) 366-2423
Fax: (203) 378-3568
Internet: www.aibd.org

American Institute of Steel Construction
One East Wacker Dr. #3100
Chicago, IL 60601-2001
Tel: (312) 670-2400
Fax: (312) 670-5403
Internet: www.aisc.org

American Lighting Association
P.O. Box 420288
Dallas, TX 75342-0288
Tel: (800) 274-4484
Internet: www.americanlightingassoc.com

American National Standards Institute
1819 L Street NW Sixth Floor
Washington, DC 20036
Tel: (202) 293-8020
Fax: (202) 293-9287
Internet: www.ansi.org

American Nursery & Landscape Association
1000 Vermont Avenue, NW #300
Washington, DC 20005-4914
Tel: (202) 789-2900
Fax: (202) 789-1893
Internet: www.anla.org

American Resort Development Association
1220 L Street N.W. Suite 400
Washington, DC 20005-2842
Tel: (202) 371-6700
Fax: (202) 289-8544
Internet: www.arda.org

American Society for Horticulture Science
113 South West Street, Suite 200
Alexandria, VA 22314-2851
Tel: (703) 836-4606
Fax: (703) 836-2024
Internet: www.ashs.org

American Society for Testing & Materials
100 Barr Harbor Dr.
West Conshohocken, PA 19428-2959
Tel: (610) 832-9585
Fax: (610) 832-9555
Internet: www.astm.org

American Society of Civil Engineers
1801 Alexander Bell Dr.
Reston, VA 20191-4400
Tel: (703) 295-6300
Fax: (703) 295-6222
Internet: www.asce.org

Design & Building Related Organizations

American Society of Consulting Arborists
15245 Shady Grove Road, Suite 130
Rockville, MD 20850
Tel: (301) 947-0483
Fax: (301) 990-9771
Internet: www. asca-consultants.org

American Society of Golf Course Architects
111 East Wacker Drive, 18th Floor
Chicago, IL 60601
Tel: (312) 372-7090
Fax: (312) 372-6160
Internet: www.golfdesign.org

American Society of Heating, Refrigerating & Air-Conditioning Engineers
1791 Tullie Circle NE
Atlanta, GA 30329
Tel: (404) 636-8400
Fax: (404) 321-5478
Internet: www.ashrae.org

American Society of Mechanical Engineers
Three Park Ave.
New York, NY 10016-5990
Tel: (212) 591-7722
Fax: (212) 591-7674
Internet: www.asme.org

American Society of Plumbing Engineers
8614 W. Catalpa Avenue #1007
Chicago, IL 60656-1116
Tel: (773) 693-2773
Fax: (773) 695-9007
Internet: www.aspe.org

American Society of Professional Estimators
11141 Georgia Ave. #412
Wheaton, MD 20902
Tel: (301) 929-8848
Fax: (301) 929-0231
Internet: www.aspenational.com

American Subcontractors Association, Inc.
1004 Duke Street
Alexandria, VA 22314-3588
Tel: (703) 684-3450
Fax: (703) 836-3482
Internet: asaonline.com

American Textile Manufacturers Institute
1130 Connecticut Ave., NW, Suite 1200
Washington, DC 20036-3954
Tel: 202-862-0500
Fax: 202-862-0570
Internet: www.atmi.org

APA - The Engineered Wood Association
P.O. Box 11700
Tacoma, WA 98411-0700
Tel: (253) 565-6600
Fax: (253) 565-7265
Internet: www.apawood.org

Architectural Woodwork Institute
1952 Isaac Newton Square
Reston, VA 20190
Tel: (703) 733-0600
Fax: (703) 733-0584
Internet: www.awinet.org

ASFE
8811 Colesville Rd. #G106
Silver Spring, MD 20910
Tel: (301) 565-2733
Fax: (301) 589-2017
Internet: www.asfe.org

Design & Building Related Organizations

Asphalt Roofing Manufacturers Association
1156 – 15th Street, NW, #900
Washington, DC 20005
Tel: (202) 207-0917
Fax: (202) 223-9741
Internet: www.asphaltroofing.org

Associated Builders & Contractors
1300 North 17th St. #800
Rosslyn, VA 22209
Tel: (703) 812-2000
Fax: (703) 812-8200
Internet: www.abc.org

Associated General Contractors of America
333 John Carlyle St. #200
Alexandria, VA 22314
Tel: (703) 548-3118
Fax: (703) 548-3119
Internet: www.agc.org

Associated Owners & Developers
PO Box 4163
McLean, VA 22103-4163
Tel: (703) 734-2397
Fax: (703) 734-2908
Internet: www.constructionchannel.net

Associated Landscape Contractors of America
150 Elden Street, Suite 270
Herndon, VA 20170
Tel: (703) 736-9666
Fax:(703) 736-9668
Internet: www.alca.org

Association for Contract Textiles
P.O. Box 101981
Fort Worth, TX 76185
Tel: (817) 924-8050
Internet: www.contract-textiles.com

Association for Facilities Engineering
8160 Corporate Park Dr. #125
Cincinnati, OH 45242
Tel: (513) 489-2473
Fax: (513) 247-7422
Internet: www.afe.org

Association for the Advancement of Cost Engineering
209 Prairie Ave. #100
Morgantown, WV 26501
Tel: (304) 296-8444
Fax: (304) 291-5728
Internet: www.aacei.org

Association of Energy Engineers
4025 Pleasantdale Rd. #420
Atlanta, GA 30340
Tel: (770) 447-5083
Fax: (770) 446-3969
Internet: www.aeecenter.org

Association of Higher Education Facilities Officers
1643 Prince St.
Alexandria, VA 22314-2818
Tel: (703) 684-1446
Fax: (703) 549-2772
Internet: www.appa.org

Association of the Wall & Ceiling Industries
803 West Broad St. #600
Falls Church, VA 22046
Tel: (703) 534-8300
Fax: (703) 534-8307
Internet: www.awci.org

Brick Industry Association
11490 Commerce Park Drive
Reston, VA 20191-1525
Tel: (703) 620-0010
Fax: (703) 620-3928
Internet: www.bia.org

Design & Building Related Organizations

Building Codes Assistance Project
1200 18th St. NW #900
Washington, DC 20036
Tel: (202) 857-0666
Fax: (202) 331-9588
Internet: www.ase.org

Building Futures Council
2131 K Street NW #700
Washington, DC 20037-1810
Tel: (202) 785-6420
Fax: (202) 833-2604
Internet: www.thebfc.com

Building Owners & Managers Association International
1201 New York Ave. NW #300
Washington, DC 20005
Tel: (202) 408-2662
Fax: (202) 371-0181
Internet: www.boma.org

Building Stone Institute
P.O. Box 507
Purdys, NY 10578
Tel: (914) 232-5725
Fax: (914) 232-5259
Internet: www.buildingstone.org

California Redwood Association
405 Enfrente Drive, #200
Novato, CA 94946
Tel: (415) 382-0662
Fax: (415) 382-8531
Internet: www.calredwood.org

Carpet and Rug Institute
P.O. Box 2048
Dalton, GA 30722
Tel: (706) 278-3176
Internet: www.carpet-rug.com

Cedar Shake and Shingle Bureau
P.O. Box 1178
Sumas, WA 98295-1178
Tel: (604) 820-7700
Fax: (604) 820-0266
Internet: www.cedarbureau.org

Center for Environmental Education and Information
P.O. Box 1778
Sun Valley, ID 83353
Tel: (208) 788-1731
Fax: (208) 727-1713
Internet: www.wcei.org

Center for Health Design
3478 Buskirk Avenue #1000
Pleasant Hill, CA 94523
Tel: (925) 746-7188
Fax: (925) 746-7101
Internet: www.healthdesign.org

Color Association of the United States
315 West 39th Street, Studio 507
New York, NY 10018
Tel: (212) 947-7774
Fax: (212) 594-6987
Internet: www.colorassociation.com

Composite Panel Association/ Composite Wood Council
18922 Premiere Court
Gaithersburg, MD 20879-1574
Tel: (301) 670-0604
Fax: (301) 840-1252
Internet: www.pbmdf.com

Construction Management Association of America
7918 Jones Branch Dr. #540
McLean, VA 22102-3307
Tel: (703) 356-2622
Fax: (703) 356-6388
Internet: www.cmaanet.org

Design & Building Related Organizations

Construction Specifications Institute
99 Canal Center Plaza, #300
Alexandria, VA 22314
Telephone: (800) 689-2900
Fax: (703) 684-8436
Internet: www.csinet.org

Copper Development Association
260 Madison Avenue
New York, NY 10016
Tel: (212) 251-7200
Fax: (212) 251-7234
Internet: www.copper.org

Council of Professional Surveyors
1015 15th St. NW 8th Floor
Washington, DC 20005-2605
Tel: (202) 347-7474
Fax: (202) 898-0068
Internet: www.acec.org/about/cops.cfm

Council on Tall Buildings and Urban Habitat
Illinois Institute of Technology
S.R. Crown Hall
3360 South State Street
Chicago, IL 60616-3793
Telephone: (312) 909-0253
Fax: (610) 419-0014

Deep Foundations Institute
326 Lafayette Avenue
Hawthorne, NJ 07506
Tel: (973) 423-4030
Fax: (973) 423-4031
Internet: www.dfi.org

Design-Build Institute of America
1010 Massachusetts Avenue, NW
Third Floor
Washington, DC 20001-5402
Telephone: (202) 682-0110
Fax: (202) 682-5877
Internet: www.dbia.org

Design Management Institute
29 Temple Place, 2nd Floor
Boston, MA 02111-1350
Telephone: (617) 338-6380
Fax: (617) 338-6570
Internet: www.dmi.org

Door & Hardware Institute
14150 Newbrook Dr. #200
Chantilly, VA 20151-2223
Tel: (703) 222-2010
Fax: (703) 222-2410
Internet: www.dhi.org

Edison Electric Institute
701 Pennsylvania Ave. NW
Washington, DC 20004-2696
Tel: (202) 508-5000
Fax: (202) 508-5360
Internet: www.eei.org

EIFS Industry Members Association
3000 Corporate Center Dr. #270
Morrow, GA 30260
Tel: (770) 968-7945
Fax: (770) 968-5818
Internet: www.eima.com

Electrical Power Research Institute
3412 Hillview Ave.
Palo Alto, CA 94304
Tel: (800) 313-3774
Internet: www.epri.com

Gas Technology Institute
1700 S. Mount Prospect Road
Des Plaines, IL 60018-1804
Tel: (847) 768-0500
Fax: (847) 768-0501
Internet: www.gastechnology.org

Design & Building Related Organizations

Glass Association of North America
2945 SW Wanamaker Dr. #A
Topeka, KS 66614-5321
Tel: (785) 271-0208
Fax: (785) 271-0166
Internet: www.glasswebsite.org

Hardwood Plywood & Veneer Association
P.O. Box 2789
Reston, VA 20195
Tel: (703) 435-2900
Fax: (703) 435-2537
Internet: www.hpva.org

Hearth, Patio & Barbecue Association
1601 North Kent St. #1001
Arlington, VA 22209
Tel: (703) 522-0086
Fax: (703) 522-0548
Internet: www.hpba.org

Human Factors and Ergonomics Society
P.O. Box 1369
Santa Monica. CA 90406-1369
Tel: (310) 394-1811
Fax: (310) 394-2410
Internet: www.hfes.org

Illuminating Engineering Society of North America
120 Wall St. 17th Floor
New York, NY 10005
Tel: (212) 248-5000
Fax: (212) 248-5017
Internet: www.iesna.org

Initiative for Architectural Research
c/o ACSA
1735 New York Avenue, NW
Washington, DC 20006
Telephone: (202) 785-2324
Fax: (202) 628-0448
Internet: www.iaronline.org

Institute of Electrical & Electronics Engineers Inc.
3 Park Ave. 17th Floor
New York, NY 10016-5997
Tel: (212) 419-7900
Fax: (212) 752-4929
Internet: www.ieee.org

Institute of Store Planners
25 North Broadway
Tarrytown, NY 10591
Tel: (800) 379-9912
Fax: (914) 332-1541
Internet: www.ispo.org

International Association of Lighting Designers
The Merchandise Mart
Suite 9-104
Chicago, IL 60654
Tel: (312) 527-3677
Fax: (312) 527-3680
Internet: www.iald.org

International Code Council
5203 Leesburg Pike, Suite 600
Falls Church, VA 22041
Tel: (703) 931-4533
Fax: (703) 379-1546
Internet: www.iccsafe.org

International Conference of Building Code Officials
5360 Workman Mill Rd.
Whittier, CA 90601-2298
Tel: (800) 423-6587
Fax: (562) 692-3853
Internet: www.icbo.org

Design & Building Related Organizations

International Facility Management Association
1 East Greenway Plaza #1100
Houston, TX 77046-0194
Tel: (713) 623-4362
Fax: (713) 623-6124
Internet: www.ifma.org

International Furnishings and Design Association
191 Clarksville Road
Princeton, NJ 08550
Tel: (609) 799-3423
Fax: (609) 799-7032
Internet: www.ifda.com

International Society of Arboriculture
P.O. Box 3129
Champaign, IL 61826-3129
Tel: (217) 355-9411
Fax: (217) 355-9516
www2.champaign.isa-arbor.com

International Wood Products Association
4214 King Street, West
Alexandria, VA 22302
Tel: (703) 820-6696
Fax: (703) 820-8550
Internet: www.iwpawood.org

Irrigation Association
6540 Arlington Boulevard
Falls Church, VA 22042-6638
Tel: (703) 536-7080
Fax: (703) 536-7019
Internet: www.irrigation.org

ISA–The Instrumentation, Systems, and Automation Society
67 Alexander Dr.
Research Triangle Park, NC 27709
Tel: (919) 549-8411
Fax: (919) 549-8288
Internet: www.isa.org

Light Gauge Steel Engineers Association
1201 15th Street NW #320
Washington, DC 20005
Tel: (202) 263-4488
Fax: (202) 785-3856
Internet: www.lgsea.com

Maple Flooring Manufacturers Association
60 Revere Drive, #500
Northbrook, IL 60062
Tel: (847) 480-9138
Fax: (847) 480-9282
Internet: www.maplefloor.org

Marble Institute of America
28901 Clemens Road #100
Westlake, OH 44145
Tel: (440) 250-9222
Fax: (440) 250-9223
Internet: www.marble-institute.com

Metal Building Manufacturers Association
1300 Sumner Ave.
Cleveland, OH 44115-2851
Tel: (216) 241-7333
Fax: (216) 241-0105
Internet: www.mbma.com

National Arborist Association, Inc.
3 Perimeter Road, Unit 1
Manchester, NH 03103
Tel: (603) 314-5380
Fax: (603) 314-5386
Internet: www.natlarb.com

National Association of Environmental Professionals
P.O. Box 2086
Bowie, MD 20718
Tel: (301) 860-1140
Fax: (301) 860-1141
Internet: www.naep.org

Design & Building Related Organizations

National Association of Home Builders
1201 15th Street, NW
Washington, DC 20005
Tel: (202) 266-8200
Fax: (202) 266-8559
Internet: www.nahb.com

National Clearinghouse for Educational Facilities
1090 Vermont Ave. NW #700
Washington, DC 20005-4905
Tel: (202) 289-7800
Fax: (202) 289-1092
Internet: www.edfacilities.org

National Concrete Masonry Association
13750 Sunrise Valley Drive
Herndon, VA 20171-4662
Tel: (703) 713-1900
Fax: (703) 713-1910
Internet: www.ncma.org

National Conference of States on Building Codes & Standards, Inc.
505 Huntmar Park Dr. #210
Herndon, VA 20170
Tel: (703) 437-0100
Fax: (703) 481-3596
Internet: www.ncsbcs.org

National Council of Acoustical Consultants
66 Morris Ave. #1A
Springfield, NJ 07081-1409
Tel: (973) 564-5859
Fax: (973) 564-7480
Internet: www.ncac.com

National Electrical Contractors Association
3 Bethesda Metro Center #1100
Bethesda, MD 20814
Tel: (301) 657-3110
Fax: (301) 215-4500
Internet: www.necanet.org

National Electrical Manufacturers Association
1300 North 17th St. #1847
Rosslyn, VA 22209
Tel: (703) 841-3200
Fax: (703) 841-5900
Internet: www.nema.org

National Fire Protection Association
1 Batterymarch Park
PO Box 9101
Quincy, MA 02169-7471
Tel: (617) 770-3000
Fax: (617) 770-0700
Internet: www.nfpa.org

National Fire Sprinkler Association
40 Jon Barrett Rd.
PO Box 1000
Patterson, NY 12563
Tel: (845) 878-4200
Fax: (845) 878-4215
Internet: www.nfsa.org

National Glass Association
8200 Greensboro Drive, #302
McLean, VA 22102-3881
Tel: (866) 342-5642
Fax: (703) 442-0630
Internet: www.glass.org

National Institute of Building Sciences
1090 Vermont Avenue, NW, Suite 700
Washington, DC 20005-4905
Telephone: (202) 289-7800
Fax: (202) 289-1092
Internet: www.nibs.org

Design & Building Related Organizations

National Lighting Bureau
8811 Colesville Road, Suite G106
Silver Spring, MD 20910
Tel: (301) 587-9572
Fax: (301) 589-2017
Internet: www.nlb.org

National Kitchen & Bath Association
687 Willow Grove Street
Hackettstown, NJ 07840
Tel: (877) NKBA-PRO
Fax: (908) 852-1695
Internet: www.nkba.org

National Oak Flooring Manufacturers Association
P.O. Box 3009
Memphis, TN 38173-0009
Tel: (901) 526-5016
Fax: (901) 526-7022
Internet: www.nofma.org

National Organization of Minority Architects
c/o School of Architecture and Design
College of Engineering, Architecture and Computer Sciences
Howard University
2366 6th Street, NW Room 100
Washington, DC 20059
Telephone: (323) 298-0534
Internet: www.noma.net

National Paint & Coatings Association
1500 Rhode Island Ave., NW
Washington, DC 20005
Tel: (202) 462-6272
Fax: (202) 462-8549
Internet: www.paint.org

National Society of Professional Engineers
1420 King St.
Alexandria, VA 22314-2794
Tel: (703) 684-2800
Fax: (703) 836-4875
Internet: www.nspe.org

National Spa and Pool Institute
2111 Eisenhower Avenue
Alexandria, VA 22314
Tel: (703) 838-0083
Fax: (703) 549-0493
Internet: www.nspi.org

National Sunroom Association
2945 SW Wanamaker Dr. #A
Topeka, KS 66614-5321
Tel: (785) 271-0208
Fax: (785) 261-0166
Internet: www.nationalsunroom.org

National Wood Flooring Association
16388 Westwoods Business Park
Ellisville, MO 63021
Tel: (800) 422-4556
Fax: (636) 391-6137
Internet: www.woodfloors.org

New Buildings Institute Codes & Standards Office
142 E. Jewett Blvd.
White Salmon, WA 98672
Tel: (509) 493-4468
Fax: (509) 493-4078
Internet: www.newbuildings.org

North American Insulation Manufacturers Association
44 Canal Center Plaza #310
Alexandria, VA 22314
Tel: (703) 684-0084
Fax: (703) 684-0427
Internet: www.naima.org

Design & Building Related Organizations

North American Steel Framing Alliance
1201 15th Street, NW #320
Washington, DC 20005
Tel: (202) 785-2022
Fax: (202) 785-3856
Internet: www.steelframingalliance.com

NSSN: A National Resource for Global Standards
25 West 43rd Street
New York, NY 10036
Tel: (212) 642-4980
Fax: (212) 302-1286
Internet: www.nssn.org

Oak Flooring Institute/National Oak Flooring Manufacturers Association
P.O. Box 3009
Memphis, TN 38173-0009
Tel: (901) 526-5016
Fax: (901) 526-7022

Plumbing Manufacturers Institute
1340 Remington Rd. #A
Schaumburg, IL 60173
Tel: (847) 884-9764
Fax: (847) 884-9775
Internet: www.pmihome.org

Portland Cement Association
5420 Old Orchard Road
Skokie, IL 60077
Tel: (847) 966-6200
Fax: (847) 966-8389
Internet: portcement.org

Precast/Prestressed Concrete Institute
209 W. Jackson Blvd. #500
Chicago, IL 60606-6938
Tel: (312) 786-0300
Fax: (312) 786-0353
Internet: www.pci.org

Preservation Trades Network, Inc.
PO Box 10236
Rockville, MD 20849-0236
Tel: (866) 853-9335
Fax: (866) 853-9336
Internet: www.ptn.org

Professional Construction Estimators Association of America
PO Box 680336
Charlotte, NC 28216
Tel: (704) 987-9978
Fax: (704) 987-9979
Internet: www.pcea.org

Rocky Mountain Institute
1739 Snowmass Creek Road
Snowmass, CO 81654-9199
Tel: (970) 927-3851
Internet: rmi.org

Society of Fire Protection Engineers
7315 Wisconsin Ave. #1225 W
Bethesda, MD 20814
Tel: (301) 718-2910
Fax: (301) 718-2242
Internet: www.sfpe.org

Society for Marketing Professional Services
99 Canal Center Plaza, Suite 330
Alexandria, VA 22314
Telephone: (800) 292-7677
Fax: (703) 549-2498
Internet: www.smps.org

Tile Council of America
100 Clemson Research Boulevard
Anderson, SC 29625
Tel: (864) 646-8453
Fax: (864) 646-281
Internet: www.tileusa.com

Design & Building Related Organizations

Underwriters Laboratories Inc.
333 Pfingsten Rd.
Northbrook, IL 60062-2096
Tel: (847) 272-8800
Fax: (847) 272-8129
Internet: www.ul.com

United Nations Centre for Human Settlements
P.O. Box 30030
Nairobi, Kenya
Telephone: (254-2) 623120
Fax: (254-2) 623477
Internet: www.unchs.org

Waterfront Center
1622 Wisconsin Avenue, N.W.
Washington, DC 20007
Tel: (202) 337-0356
Fax: (202) 625-1654
Internet: www.waterfrontcenter.org

Western Red Cedar Lumber Association
1501-700 West Pender Street
Pender Place 1, Business Building
Vancouver BC
Canada V6C 1G8
Tel: (604) 684-0266
Fax: (604) 687-4930
Internet: www.wrcla.org

Window & Door Manufacturers Association
1400 East Touhy Ave. #450
Des Plaines, IL 60018-3337
Tel: (847) 299-5200
Fax: (847) 299-1286
Internet: www.nwwda.org

Government Agencies

The Access Board
1331 F St. NW #1000
Washington, DC 20004-1111
Tel: (202) 272-0080
Fas: (202) 272-0081
Internet: www.access-board.gov

Army Corps of Engineers
441 G Street NW
Washington, DC 20314
Tel: (202) 761-0660
Internet: www.usace.army.mil

Bureau of Land Management
Office of Public Affairs
1849 C Street, Room 406-LS
Washington, DC 20240
Tel: (202) 452-5125
Fax: (202) 452-5124
Internet: www.blm.gov

Census Bureau Manufacturing, Mining, and Construction Statistics
Washington, DC 20233-6900
Tel: (301) 457-4100
Fax: (301) 457-4714
Internet: www.census.gov/const/www

Department of Agriculture
1400 Independence Ave., SW
Washington, DC 20250
Tel: (202) 720-2791
Fax: (202) 720-2166
Internet: www.usda.gov

Department of Energy
Forrestal Bldg.
1000 Independence Ave. SW
Washington, DC 20585
Tel: (800) 342-5363
Fax: (202) 586-4403
Internet: www.energy.gov

Design & Building Related Organizations

Department of Labor Occupational Safety & Health Administration
200 Constitution Ave. NW
Frances Perkins Building
Washington, DC 20210
Tel: (202) 693-1999
Internet: www.dol.gov

Department of the Interior
1849 C St. NW
Washington, DC 20240
Tel: (202) 208-3100
Internet: www.doi.gov

Department of Transportation
400 7th Street SW
Washington, DC 20590
Tel: (202) 366-4000
Internet: www.dot.gov

Environmental Protection Agency
1200 Pennsylvania Avenue, NW
Ariel Rios Building
Washington, DC 20460
Tel: (202) 260-2090
Internet: www.epa.gov

Federal Emergency Management Agency
500 C Street, SW
Washington, DC 20472
Tel: (202) 566-1600
Internet: www.fema.gov

General Services Administration
1800 F Street, NW
Washington, DC 20405
Tel: (202) 208-3100
Internet: www.gsa.gov

National Institute of Standards & Technology
100 Bureau Dr. Stop 3460
Gaithersburg, MD 20899-3460
Tel: (301) 975-8295
Internet: www.nist.gov

International Organizations

Architects' Council of Europe
Rue Paul Emile Janson, 29
B-1050
Brussels, Belgium
Telephone: 32 2 543 11 40
Fax: 32 2 543 11 41
Internet: www.ace-cae.org

Architecture Institute of Japan
26-20, Shiba 5-chome, Minato-ku
Tokyo 108-8414 Japan
Telephone: +81-3-3456-2051
Fax: +81-3-3456-2058
Internet: www.aij.or.jp

International Council of Societies of Industrial Design
Erottajankatu 11 A 18
00130 Helsinki
Finland
Telephone: +358 9 696 22 90
Fax: +358 9 696 22 910
Internet: www.icsid.org

International Federation of Interior Architects/Designers
P.O. Box 91640
Auckland Park
Johannesburg, 2006
South Africa
Telephone: +27 11 8888212
Internet: www.ifi.co.za

Design & Building Related Organizations

International Federation of Landscape Architects
4 rue Hardy
F-78009 Versailles
France
Telephone: +33 1 39 51 84 39
Fax: +33 1 39 53 53 16
Internet: www.iflaonline.org

International Union of Architects
51, rue Raynouard
75016 Paris, France
Telephone: 33 (1) 45 24 36 88
Fax: 33 (1) 45 24 02 78
Internet: www.uia-architectes.org

Japan Institute of Architects
Kenchikuka Kaikan
2-3-18 Jingumae
Shibuya-ku
Tokyo 150 Japan
Telephone: +81-3-3408-7125
Fax: +81-3-3408-7129
Internet: www.jia.or.jp

Royal Architecture Institute of Canada
330-55 Murray Street
Ottawa, Ontario, K1N 5M3
Canada
Telephone: (613) 241-3600
Fax: (613) 241-5750
Internet: www.raic.org

Royal Australian Institute of Architects
2a Mugga Way
Red Hill ACT 2603
MNUKA ACT 2603
Australia
Telephone: (02) 6273 1548
Fax: (02) 6273 1953
Internet: www.architecture.com.au

Royal Institute of British Architects
66 Portland Place
London W1B 1AD
United Kingdom
Telephone: +44 (0) 20 7580 5533
Fax: +44 (0) 20 7255 1541
Internet: www.riba.org

Source: Counsel House Research

9

Design Resources

This chapter contains a variety of concise, informative entries from the fully updated 2004 Salary and Compensation Guide for architects, registration and licensure laws, guidelines for hiring an architect or interior designer to lists of design-oriented bookstores, journals & magazines and museums.

Bookstores

The following is a list of bookstores in the United States focused on architecture and design including rare and out-of-print dealers that specialize in design titles.

ARIZONA

Builder's Book Depot
1033 E. Jefferson, Suite 500
Phoenix, AZ 85034
(800) 284-3434
www.buildersbookdepot.com

CALIFORNIA

Art Haus Books, Inc.
5828 Wilshire Blvd.
Los Angeles, CA 90036
(323) 930-1170

Builders Booksource
1817 Fourth Street
Berkeley, CA 94710
(510) 845-6874
www.buildersbooksite.com

J.B. Muns Fine Arts Books
1162 Shattuck Avenue
Berkeley, CA 94707
(510) 525-2420

Moe's Art & Antiquarian Books
2476 Telegraph Avenue
Berkeley, CA 94704
(510) 849-2133
www.moesbooks.com

Builder's Book
8001 Canoga Avenue
Canoga Park, CA 91304
(800) 273-7375
www.buildersbook.com

Builders Booksource
Ghirardelli Square
900 North Point
San Francisco, CA 94109
(415) 440-5773
www.buildersbooksite.com

William Stout Architectural Books
804 Montgomery Street
San Francisco, CA 94133
(415) 391-6757
www.stoutbooks.com

Sullivan Goss Books and Prints Ltd.
7 E. Anapamu Street
Santa Barbara, CA 93101
(805)730-1460
www.sullivangoss.com

Hennessey & Ingalls Art and Architecture Books
1254 Third Street Promenade
Santa Monica, CA 90401
(310) 458-9074
www.hennesseyingalls.com

COLORADO

Tattered Cover Bookstore
1628 16th Street
Denver, CO 80202
(303) 436-1070
www.tatteredcover.com

Tattered Cover Bookstore
2955 East First Avenue
Denver, CO 80206
(303) 322-7727
www.tatteredcover.com

DISTRICT OF COLUMBIA

AIA Bookstore
The American Institute of Architects
1735 New York Avenue NW
Washington, DC 20006
(202) 626-7475
www.aia.org/books

Franz Bader Bookstore
1911 I Street NW
Washington, DC 20006
(202) 337-5440

Bookstores

National Building Museum Shop
401 F Street NW
Washington, DC 20001
(202) 272-7706
www.nbm.org/shop

GEORGIA

Architectural Book Center
231 Peachtree Street NE Suite B-4
Atlanta, GA 30303
(404) 222-9920
www.aiaga.org/aia/bookstore

ILLINOIS

Chicago Architecture Foundation Bookstore
224 S. Michigan Avenue
Chicago, IL 60604
(312) 922-3432
www.architecture.org

Chicago Architecture Foundation Bookstore
John Hancock Center
875 N. Michigan Avenue
Chicago, IL 60611
(312) 751-1380
www.architecture.org

Prairie Avenue Bookshop
418 S. Wabash Avenue
Chicago, IL 60605-1209
(312) 922-8311
www.pabook.com

INDIANA

Architectural Center Bookstore
Indiana Society of Architects
47 S. Pennsylvania Street, Suite 110
Indianapolis, IN 46204
(317) 634-3871

MASSACHUSETTS

Ars Libri
500 Harrison Avenue
Boston, MA 02118
(617) 357-5212
www.arslibri.com

Cambridge Architectural Books
12 Bow Street
Cambridge, MA 02138
(617) 354-5300
www.archbook.com

Charles B. Wood III Antiquarian Booksellers
P.O. Box 2369
Cambridge, MA 02238
(617) 868-1711

F.A. Bernett
144 Lincoln Street
Boston, MA 02111
(617) 350-7778
www.fabernett.com

MARYLAND

Baltimore AIA Bookstore
11 ½ Chase Street
Baltimore, MD 21201
(410) 625-2585
www.aiabalt.com

MISSOURI

St. Louis AIA Bookstore
911 Washington Avenue, Suite 100
St. Louis, MO 63101
(314) 621-3484
www.aia-stlouis.org

NEW YORK

Archivia: The Decorative Arts Bookshop
1063 Madison Ave., 2nd Floor
New York, NY 10028
(212) 439-9194
www.archivia.com

Argosy Bookstore
116 E. 59th Street
New York, NY 10022
(212) 753-4455
www.argosybooks.com

Bookstores

Cooper-Hewitt Museum Bookstore
2 East 91st St
New York, NY 10128
(212) 849-8355

Hacker Art Books
45 W. 57th Street
New York, NY 10019
(212) 688-7600
www.hackerartbooks.com

Perimeter Books
21 Cleveland Place
New York, NY 10012
(212) 334-6559

Rizzoli Bookstore
31 W. 57th Street
New York, NY 10019
(212) 759-2424

Royoung Bookseller
564 Ashford Avenue
Ardsley, NY 10502
(914) 693-6116
www.royoung.com

Strand Book Store
828 Broadway
New York, NY 10003
(212) 473-1452
www.strandbooks.com

Urban Center Books
Villard Houses
457 Madison Avenue
New York, NY 10022
(212) 935-3592
www.urbancenterbooks.com

Ursus Books
981 Madison Avenue
New York, NY 10021
(212) 772-8787
www.ursusbooks.com

Ursus Books
132 W. 21st Street
New York, NY 10011
(212) 627-5370
www.ursusbooks.com

OHIO

Wexner Center Bookstore
1871 N. High Street
Columbus, OH 43210-1105
(614) 292-1807

OREGON

David Morrison Books
530 NW 12th Street
Portland, OR 97209
(503) 295-6882
www.morrisonbooks.com

PENNSYLVANIA

AIA Bookstore & Design Center
117 South 17th Street
Philadelphia, PA 19103
(215) 569-3188
www.aiaphila.org

TEXAS

Brazos Bookstore
2421 Bissonnet Street
Houston, TX 77005
(713) 523-0701
www.brazosbookstore.com

WASHINGTON

Peter Miller Architecture and Design Books
1930 First Avenue
Seattle, WA 98101
(206) 441-4114
www.petermiller.com

Source: Counsel House Research

How to Hire an Architect

The information provided below was prepared by The American Institute of Architects (AIA) to assist the public with the architect selection process. The AIA Web site has a wealth of information about the profession and additional resources to guide you through the process of selecting an architect. This includes a list of 20 suggested questions to ask an architect during the interview process and an online searchable database of architects, all available at *www.aia.org*.

Finding an Architect

Each architect has an individual style, approach to design and a method of work, so, it's important to find an architect who is compatible with your style and needs.

Ask around. Find out who designed projects in your community that you like. Get recommendations from friends, relatives and acquaintances who have worked with architects. Check to see if the architect is a member of The American Institute of Architects (AIA). Membership in the AIA means that the architect subscribes to a high professional purpose to advance standards of practice and service to society. This includes having a code of ethics and access to a variety of professional and technical resources.

The Architect Finder (*www.aia.org/consumer/profile/profile_search.asp*), available on the AIA's Web site, can help you find AIA architects interested in your type of project. Call your local AIA chapter for details on firms that interest you, or to see examples of the firms' work. Many AIA chapters have directories containing details of local architecture firms and photos of completed projects.

Call each firm on your short list and describe your project. Ask if they are available to accomplish it, and if so, request literature that outlines the firm's qualifications and experience. If the office is unable to handle your project, ask if they can recommend another firm. Interviewing a firm gives you a chance to meet the people who will design your project and to learn if the chemistry between you is right. Allow at least an hour for the interview, preferably at the architect's office where you can see where the work will be done. Some architects charge for the interview; ask if there is a fee.

During the interview, ask questions. How busy is the firm? Does it have the capacity to take on your work? Who will handle the job? Insist on meeting the person who will actually design your project. What is the firm's design philosophy? Talk about a project budget and the range of fees that the architect anticipates for your project. Before you select an architect, ask to be taken to at least one completed project. Also, ask for references from past clients. These are invaluable. In addition, obtain an Architect's Qualification Statement (B431) from your local AIA chapter. This standardized document may be used to verify an architect's credentials and other information prior to selecting an architect for a project. The right architect will be the one who can provide the judgment, technical expertise, and creative skills–at a reasonable cost–to help you realize a project that fits your practical needs as well as your dreams.

How to Hire an Architect

Why an AIA Architect?

Like doctors and lawyers, architects are licensed professionals. The title "Architect" may be used only by an individual who possesses a state license to practice architecture. They are ethically bound to represent you, the building owner.

Professional qualifications generally include:

- College degree from an accredited school of architecture
- Three years of internship under the supervision of licensed architects
- Passage of a rigorous five-day examination

Only those professionals who have fulfilled these requirements, or other requirements as stipulated by each individual state, may legally call themselves architects and practice architecture in the jurisdiction granting the license.

Look for the AIA initials after the name of any architect you consider for your project. AIA architects remain current with professional standards through continuing education and subscribe to a code of ethics and professional conduct that assure clients, the public and colleagues of their dedication to high standards in professional practice.

The Architect's Fee

There is no set fee arrangement for a particular type of project. Fees are established in a number of ways, depending on the type of project plus the extent and nature of services required from an architect.

Common methods of compensation include: hourly rates, a stipulated sum based on the architect's compensation proposal, a stipulated sum per unit of what's to be built (i.e., the number of square feet or rooms), a percentage of construction costs, or a combination of these methods. Your architect will explain how a fee is to be established. Then, the basis for the fee, the amount and the payment schedule are issues for you and your architect to work out together.

The 1998 Means Square Footage Cost Data survey indicates that fees for architectural services on a custom house can range from 5 to 15 percent of the total cost of construction. Factors that affect the fees include the scope of the project, the level of quality and detail, and economic conditions. The architect's fee is usually a relatively small part of the cost of the entire building project, including the estimated construction cost (on which the fee is computed), the furnishings and equipment, and the interest paid on the mortgage.

Get It in Writing: AIA Contract Documents

The AIA Contract Documents Program, the oldest and most comprehensive program of its kind in the world, develops standardized contract forms and administrative procedures for the building industry. AIA contract documents provide the basis for nationwide uniformity for contractual relationships in the design and construction process. They represent the state of the

How to Hire an Architect

law regarding construction industry practices and new legal developments. Most important they assure fairness to all parties–owners, architects, engineers, builders, and contractors–and contribute to successful projects.

Any project will benefit from the use of AIA contract documents. Contact your local AIA chapter or discuss AIA contract documents with an AIA architect.

How to Hire an Interior Designer

The following information has been prepared by the American Society of Interior Designers (ASID) to assist the public in making an informed choice about hiring and working with an interior designer. More information about the interior design profession is available from ASID on the Web at *www.asid.org*. An online searchable database of interior designers can be found at *www.interiors.org*.

What Is My Role In the Design Process?

Before contacting an interior designer, take some time to think about what you want and what you need. **The first step in this process** is to consider some questions that an interior designer will ask regarding your project:

For whom is the space being designed?
What activities will take place there?
How long do you plan to occupy the space?
What is your time frame?
What is your budget?

If you're feeling overwhelmed, don't worry. Your interior designer will lead you through the process. Keep in mind the more information you provide, the more successful your designer will be in meeting your needs and expectations. You may want to reference other visual images (photos, postcards, corporate logos, magazine photographs) or environments that reflect your aesthetic and functional criteria.

The second step is to interview designers. Interview several designers to become familiar with differences in personality, style and business methods. Take this opportunity to acquaint the designer with your project ideas. Ask to see the designer's portfolio and request a list of relevant experience and client references. During an interview, you may want to:

Inquire about the designer's education, experience, and other credentials.
Ask about other services the designer can provide.
Ask what can be done to help you optimize your understanding of the cost of the project.
Discuss project duration or deadlines.
Establish parameters for ongoing communication between you and the interior designer.
Discuss the designer's fee structure.

The third step is to hire the designer. Once you've interviewed several designers, take time to compare their estimates. Don't base your decision on price alone. Keep in mind that differences in each proposal reflect variables such as level of service and quality of merchandise. After the designer is hired, you need to address specific project needs and goals. You will share ideas and the designer will lend insights and observations to your ideas to identify the overall scope of the project. During this process, your design professional will:

How to Hire an Interior Designer

Communicate concepts and help you understand the design process.
Articulate your ideas, and help you to visualize the finished product.

Are Contracts Important?

Contracts are very important because they allow both you and the designer to define the scope of your project. A contract allows you to specify who will be responsible for what, how long the project will last and what the budget limits will be. It is in your best interest to have a signed contract before any work begins or any money is exchanged.

How Much Is This Going to Cost?

It depends on what you want. There are many variables including the size of the project (one room or whole house?), quality of products selected (custom or prefabricated cabinets?), and the timeframe in which the project needs to be completed (two weeks or two months?). Developing the budget is a partnership between the client and the designer. A professional designer assesses your needs and helps you determine where to spend and where to save, prioritizing expenses while creating an interior that is within your budget. Also, remember that not everything has to be completed at once. Your designer can develop a long-range plan, consult with you to establish a list of priorities and determine a time line for accomplishing your project.

How Interior Designers Charge for Their Services

Designers work with a variety of fee structures, and as with other professions, base their fees on variables such as complexity of the project, its geographical location, and the expertise of the designer. Most designers will work in one of the following methods, or combine methods to suit a client's particular needs:

Fixed fee (or flat fee)–The designer identifies a specific sum to cover costs, exclusive of reimbursement for expenses. One total fee applies to the complete range of services, from conceptual development through layouts, specifications and final installation.

Hourly fee–Compensation is based on actual time expended by the designer on a project or specific service.

Percentage fee–Compensation is computed as a percentage of construction/ project costs.

Cost plus–A designer purchases materials, furnishings and services (e.g., carpentry, drapery workrooms, picture framing, etc.) at cost and sells to the client at the designer's cost plus a specified percentage agreed to with the client.

Retail–The designer sells furnishings, furniture and all other goods to the client at retail rates to cover the designer's fee and services. This is most applicable to retail establishments offering design services.

How to Hire an Interior Designer

Per square foot–The designer charges fees based on the area of the project as might be calculated for large commercial properties.

In addition to the fee structures outlined above, designers may require a retainer before beginning a design project. A retainer is an amount of money paid by the client to the designer and applied to the balance due at the termination of the project. The retainer is customarily paid upon signing the contractual agreement in advance of design services.

Source: ©2003 American Society of Interior Designers. Reprinted with permission.

Journals & Magazines

The following is a list of major architecture and design journals and magazines from around the world, ranging from the most popular to the cutting edge. Whether looking for periodicals which take a less traditional approach or for exposure to the most recent projects and design news, it is hoped this list will provide an opportunity to explore new ideas and perspectives about design and expand your knowledge about the profession.

U.S. Publications

Architectural Digest
6300 Wilshire Boulevard
Los Angeles, CA 90048
(800) 365-8032
www.archdigest.com
Published monthly by Condé Nast Publications, Inc.

Architectural Record
Two Penn Plaza
New York, NY 10121-2298
(212) 904-2594
www.architecturalrecord.com
The official magazine of the AIA, published monthly by the McGraw-Hill Companies.

Architecture
770 Broadway
New York, NY 10003
(212) 536-6221
www.architecturemag.com
Published monthly by VNU Business Media, Inc.

ASID ICON
608 Massachusetts Ave. NE
Washington, D.C. 20002-6006
(202) 546-3480
www.asid.org
The magazine of the American Society of Interior Designers, published quarterly.

Contract
770 Broadway, 4th Fl.
New York, NY 10003-9595
(646) 654-4500
www.contractmagazine.com
Published monthly by Bill Communications.

Communication Arts
110 Constitution Drive
Menlo Park, CA 94025
(650) 326-6040
www.commarts.com
Published 8 times per year.

Dwell
99 Osgood Place
San Francisco, CA 94133
(415) 743-9990
www.dwellmag.com
Published bi-monthly by Pixie Communications.

Engineering News Record
Two Penn Plaza
9th Floor
New York, NY 10121
(212) 904-3507
www.enr.com
Published by McGraw-Hill Construction Information Group.

Faith & FORM
P.O. Box 1253
State College, PA 16804-1253
(814) 364-2449
www.faithnform.org
The journal of the Interfaith Forum on Religion, Art and Architecture (IFRAA), a Professional Interest Area of the AIA, published three times a year.

Journals & Magazines

Fine Homebuilding
Taunton Press
63 S. Main St.
P.O. Box 5506
Newtown, CT 06470-5506
(203) 426-8171
www.taunton.com/fh/
Published bi-monthly by Taunton Press.

Harvard Design Magazine
48 Quincy St.
Cambridge, MA 02138
(617) 495-7814
www.gsd.harvard.edu
Published 2 times a year by the Harvard University Graduate School of Design.

I.D.
116 East 27th St. Floor 6
New York, NY 10016
(212) 447-1400
www.idonline.com
Published 8 times per year.

Innovation
45195 Business Center
Suite 250
Dulles, VA 20166
(703) 707-6000
www.idsa.org
Quarterly journal of the Industrial Designers Society of America.

Interior Design
360 Park Ave. South
New York, NY 10010
(646) 746-7265
www.Interiordesign.net
Published 15 times a year by Reed Business Information.

Interiors & Sources
840 U.S. Hwy. One, Suite 330
North Palm Beach, FL 33408
(561) 627-3393
www.isdesignet.com
Published 8 times per year.

Journal of Architectural Education (JAE)
Association of Collegiate Schools of Architecture
1735 New York Avenue, NW
Washington, DC 20006
(202) 785-2324
www.acsa-arch.org
Published quarterly by MIT Press for the ACSA.

Journal of Interior Design
Interior Design Educators Council, Inc.
9202 North Meridian Street, Suite 200
Indianapolis, IN 46260-1810
(317) 816-6261
www.ejid.org
Published bi-annually by the Interior Design Educators Council.

Journal of the American Planning Association
122 S. Michigan Ave.
Suite 1600
Chicago, IL 60603-6107
(312) 431-9100
www.planning.org
Published quarterly.

Journal of the Society of Architectural Historians
1365 N. Astor St.
Chicago, IL 60610
(312) 573-1365
www.sah.org
Published quarterly by the Society of Architectural Historians.

Journals & Magazines

Landscape Architecture
636 Eye St. NW
Washington, DC 20001-3736
(202) 898-2444
www.asla.org
Published monthly by the American Society of Landscape Architects.

Metropolis
61 W. 23rd St., 4th Floor
New York, NY 10010
(212) 627-9977
www.metropolismag.com
Published 11 times a year.

Nest
P.O. Box 2446
Lenox Hill Station
New York, NY 10021
(888) 321-6378
www.nestmagazine.com
Published quarterly.

Old House Journal
1000 Potomac Street NW
Suite 102
Washington, DC 20007
(202) 399-0744
www.oldhousejournal.com
Published bimonthly.

Perspective
13-122 Merchandise Mart
Chicago, IL 60654-1104
(312) 467-1950
www.iida.org
The International Magazine of the International Interior Design Association, published quarterly.

Places
Center for Environmental Design Research
University of California
390 Wurster Hall
Berkeley, CA 94720
(510) 642-2896
www.cedr.berkeley.edu
Published 3 times a year by the Design History Foundation.

Preservation
1785 Massachusetts Ave. NW
Washington, DC 20036
(202) 588-6000
www.nthp.org
Published bimonthly by the National Trust for Historic Preservation.

International Publications

Abitare
Via Ventura, 5
Milano, 20134
Italy
+39 022 1058 1
www.abitare.it
Monthly magazine in Italian and English.

AD (Architectural Design)
1 Oaklands Way
Bognor Regis
West Sussex 22 9 SA
U.K.
+ 44 01243 843 272
Published bi-monthly by Wiley-Academy.

AJ (Architects' Journal)
151 Rosebery Avenue
33 39 Bowling Green Lane
London, EC1R 4GB
U.K.
+44 020 7505 6709
www.ajplus.co.uk
Published by EMAP Construct.

Journals & Magazines

l'Arca
Via Valcava 6
Milano, 20155
Italy
+39 02 325246
www.arcadata.com
Published 11 times a year.

Archis
Stichting Artimo
Gijs Stork
Fokke Simonszstraat 8
1017 TG Amsterdam
The Netherlands
+31 20-330 2511
www.archis.org
Bilingual magazine published 6 times each year by Stichting Artimo in association with the Netherlands Architecture Institute (NAI).

Architectural History: The Journal of the Society of Architectural Historians of Great Britain
Pixham Mill, Pixham Lane
Dorking, Surrey, RH14 1PQ
U.K.
www.sahgb.org.uk
Published annually.

Architectural Review
151 Rosebery Avenue
London, EC1R 4GB
U.K.
+44 020 7505 6725
www.arplus.com
Published by EMAP Construct.

Architecture Australia
4 Princes Street
Level 3
Port Melbourne, Victoria 3207
Australia
+61 (03) 9646 4760
www.archmedia.com.au/aa/aa.htm
Official magazine of the RAIA.

l'Architecture d'Aujourd'hui
6, rue Lhomond
Paris, F-75005
France
+33 1 44320590
www.architecture-aujourdhui.presse.fr
Published 6 times a year in French and English.

Arkitektur
SE-102
4296 66 Stockholm
Sweden
+46 8 702 7850
www.arkitektur.se
Published 8 times yearly; with English summaries.

a+u magazine
2-30-8, Yushima, Bunkyo-ku
Tokyo, 113-0034
Japan
+81 33816-2935
www.japan-architect.co.jp
Published monthly in Japanese and English by A+U Publishing Co., Ltd.

Blueprint
Sadlers House
2 Legg Street
Chelmsford Essex CM1 1AH
U.K.
+ 44 0245 4917 17
Published monthly by ETP Ltd.

Canadian Architect
1450 Don Mills Road
Don Mills, Ontario, M3B 2X7
Canada
(416) 510-6854
www.canadianarchitect.com
Published monthly by Business Information Group, a division of Hollinger Canadian Newspapers, LP

Journals & Magazines

Casabella
D. Trentacoste 7
Milan, 20134
Italy
+39 02 66 81 43 63
Published monthly in Italian with an English summary.

El Croquis
Av. De los Reyes Catolicos 9
Madrid, E-28280 El Escorial
Spain
+34 918969410
www.elcroquis.es
Published 5 times a year in Spanish and English.

Daidalos
Redaktion Daidalos
Littenstra Be 106/107
Berlin, D-10179
Germany
+49 30246575
Published quarterly in English by The Gordon and Breach Publishing Group.

Domus
Via Achille Grandi 5/7
Rozzano
Milan, 20089
Italy
+39 0282472276
www.domus.edidomus.it
Published monthly in Italian and English.

Hinge
2/F West, Sincere Insurance Building
6 Hennessy Road
Wanchai
Hong Kong, PRC
+852 2520 2468
www.hingenet.com
Published monthly.

Japan Architect
2-30-8 Yushima, Bunkyo-ku
Tokyo, 113-0034
Japan
+81 33811-7101
www.japan-architect.co.jp
Published quarterly in Japanese and English.

Journal of Architecture
11 New Fetter Lane
London, EC4P 4EE
U.K.
+44 (0) 20 7842 2001
www.tandf.co.uk/journals/routledge/
Published 4 times a year by Taylor & Francis Journals for the RIBA.

Journal of Urban Design
Institute of Urban Planning
University of Nottingham
University Park
Nottingham, NG7 2RD
U.K.
+44 115 951 4873
www.carfax.co.uk
Published 3 times a year by Carfax Publishing Limited for the Institute of Urban Planning.

Ottagono
Via Stalingrado, 97/2
Bologna, 40128
Italy
+39 051 3540 111
www.ottagono.com
Published bimonthly in Italian and English.

Rassegna
Via Stalingrado 97-2
Bologna, 40128
Italy
+39 51 3540 111
www.compositori.it
Published quarterly in Italian and English by Editrice Compositori.

Journals & Magazines

Wallpaper
Brettenham House, 5th Floor
Lancaster Place
London, WC2E7TL
U.K.
+44 2073221177
www.wallpaper.com
Published 10 times a year.

World of Interiors
Vogue House
Hanover Square
London W1S 1JU
U.K.
+44 020 7499 9080
www.worldofinteriors.co.uk
Published monthly by Condé Nast.

Source: Counsel House Research

Museums

There are many museums around the world devoted solely to architecture and design, and many major museums that maintain strong design collections and regularly host architecture and design related exhibits. Below is a listing of those museums, along with their contact information.

A+D Architecture and Design Museum
Bradbury Building
304 South Broadway
Los Angeles, CA 90013
(213) 620-9961
www.aplusd.org

Alvar Aalto Museum
Alver Aallon katu 7
Jyväskylä, Finland
+358 (0) 14 624 809
www.alvaraalto.fi

Architektur Zentrum Wien
Museumsplatz 1, im MQ
A-1070 Vienna
Austria
+43 522 31 15 23
www.azw.at

Architekturmuseum Basel
Pfluggässlein 3
Postfach 911
CH-4001 Basel
Switzerland
+41 61 261 1413
www.architekturmuseum.ch

Art Institute of Chicago, Department of Architecture
111 South Michigan Avenue
Chicago, Illinois 60603
(312) 443-3949
www.artic.edu/aic/

Athenaeum of Philadelphia
219 S. Sixth Street
Philadelphia, PA 19106-3794
(215) 925-2688
www.PhilaAthenaeum.org

Atlanta International Museum of Art and Design
Marquis II Office Tower
285 Peachtree Center Avenue
Atlanta, GA 30303-1229
(404) 688-2467
www.atlantainternationalmuseum.org

Bauhaus Archive/Museum of Design
Klingelhöferstraße 14
D – 10785 Berlin
Germany
+49 (0) 30 254 00 20
www.bauhaus.de

Canadian Centre for Architecture
1920 Baile Street
Montrél, Québec
Canada H3H 2S6
(514) 939-7026
www.cca.qc.ca

Cooper-Hewitt, National Design Museum, Smithsonian Institution
2 East 91st Street
New York, NY 10128
(212) 849-8400
www.ndm.si.edu

Danish Center for Architecture, Gammel Dok
Strandgade 27B
1401 Copenhagen K
Denmark
+45 32 57 19 30
www.gammeldok.dk

Danish Design Center
H C Andersens Boulevard 27
1553 Copenhagen V, Denmark
+45 33 69 33 69
www.ddc.dk

Museums

Design Museum
28 Shad Thames
London
SE1 2YD
United Kingdom
+44 (0) 20 7940 8790
www.designmuseum.org

Heinz Architectural Center, Carnegie Museum of Art
4400 Forbes Avenue
Pittsburgh, PA 15213-4080
(412) 622-3131
www.cmoa.org

The Lighthouse: Scotland's Centre for Architecture, Design & the City
11 Mitchell Lane
Glasgow, G1 3LX
United Kingdom
+44 (0) 141 221 6362
www.thelighthouse.co.uk

MAK Center for Art & Architecture L.A. Schindler House
835 North Kings Road
West Hollywood, CA 90069-5409
(323) 651-1510
www.makcenter.org

Museum of Contemporary Art, Los Angeles
MOCA at California Plaza
250 South Grand Avenue
Los Angeles, CA 90012
(213) 626-6222
www.moca-la.org

Museum of Finnish Architecture
Kasarmikatu 24, 00130
Helsinki, Finland
+358 9 8567 5100
www.mfa.fi

Museum of Modern Art
11 West 53rd Street
New York, NY 10019
(212) 708-9400
www.moma.org

National Building Museum
401 F Street NW
Washington, DC 20001
(202) 272-2448
www.nbm.org

Netherlands Architecture Institute
Museumpark 25
3015 CB Rotterdam
Netherlands
+31 (0) 10-4401200
www.nai.nl

Norwegian Museum of Architecture
Kongens gate 4, N-0153
Oslo, Norway
+47 22 42 40 80
www.museumsnett.no/arkitekturmuseet/

The Octagon
1799 New York Avenue, NW
Washington, DC 20006
(202) 638-3221
www.theoctagon.org

RIBA Architecture Gallery
66 Portland Square
London W1N 4AD UK
+44 (0) 171 580 5533
www.architecture.com

San Francisco Museum of Modern Art
151 Third Street
San Francisco, CA 94103-3159
(415) 357-4000
www.sfmoma.org

Museums

Skyscraper Museum
39 Battery Place
New York, NY 10281
(212) 968-1961
www.skyscraper.org

Swedish Museum of Architecture
Skeppsholmen, SE-111 49
Stockholm, Sweden
+46 8 587 270 00
www.arkitekturmuseet.se

Vitra Design Museum
Charles-Eames-Str. 1
D-79576 Weil am Rhein
Germany
+49 7621 702 32 00
www.design-museum.de/weil.php

Vitra Design Museum Berlin
Kopenhagener Straße 58
D-10437 Berlin
Germany
+49 30 473 777 0
www.design-museum.de/berlin.php

Zurich Museum of Design
Ausstellungsstr. 60
CH-8005, Zürich
Switzerland
+411 446 22 11
www.museum-gestaltung.ch

Source: Counsel House Research

Registration Laws: Architecture

The following information provides a brief overview of the major components of initial licensure requirements for architects, including work experience, degree requirements, and the Architectural Registration Exam (ARE). Complete information regarding registration requirements, renewal procedures, interstate registration, and corporate practice guidelines is available from the individual state boards at the phone numbers listed below. Due to the complex and changing nature of the requirements, it is recommended that the state licensing board(s) be contacted to receive the most up-to-date information. The National Council of Architectural Registration Boards (NCARB) also maintains information about registration on their Web site at *www.ncarb.org*.

States and State Boards	Type of Law		Initial Requirements			Ongoing Requir.
	Title Act	Practice Act	College Degree Required	Internship Required	ARE Exam Required	Continuing Education Required
Alabama (334) 242-4179	❍	❍	❍	❍	❍	❍
Alaska (907) 465-1676	❍	❍	❍	❍	❍	
Arizona (602) 364-4937	❍	❍	❍		❍	
Arkansas (501) 682-3171	❍	❍	❍	❍	❍	❍
California (916) 445-3394	❍	❍	❍	P	❍	
Colorado (303) 894-7801	❍	❍	CB	❍	❍	
Connecticut (860) 713-6145	❍	❍	❍	❍	❍	
Delaware (302) 744-4505	❍	❍	❍	❍	❍	P
District of Columbia (202) 442-4461	❍	❍	❍	❍	❍	P
Florida (850) 487-1395	❍	❍	❍	❍	❍	❍
Georgia (478) 207-1400	❍	❍	❍	❍	❍	❍
Hawaii (808) 586-2702	❍	❍	❍	❍	❍	
Idaho (208) 334-3233	❍	❍	❍	❍	❍	
Illinois (217) 785-0877	❍	❍	❍	❍	❍	❍

Registration Laws: Architecture

States and State Boards	Type of Law		Initial Requirements			Ongoing Requir.
	Title Act	Practice Act	College Degree Required	Internship Required	ARE Exam Required	Continuing Education Required
Indiana (317) 232-3931	❍	❍	❍	❍	❍	
Iowa (515) 281-7362	❍	❍	❍	❍	❍	❍
Kansas (785) 296-3053	❍	❍	❍	❍	❍	❍
Kentucky (859) 246-2069	❍	❍	❍	❍	❍	❍
Louisiana (225) 925-4802	❍	❍	❍	❍	❍	❍
Maine (207) 624-8522	❍	❍	CB	❍	❍	
Maryland (410) 230-6262	❍	❍		❍	❍	
Massachusetts (617) 727-3072	❍	❍	CB	❍	❍	
Michigan (517) 241-9253	❍	❍	❍	❍	❍	P
Minnesota (651) 296-2388	❍	❍	❍	❍	❍	❍
Mississippi (601) 899-9071	❍	❍	❍	❍	❍	
Missouri (573) 751-0047	❍	❍	❍	❍	❍	
Montana (406) 841-2367	❍	❍	❍	❍	❍	P
Nebraska (402) 471-2021	❍	❍	❍	❍	❍	❍
Nevada (702) 486-7300	❍	❍	❍	❍	❍	P
New Hampshire (603) 271-2219	❍	❍	❍	❍	❍	
New Jersey (973) 504-6385	❍	❍	❍	❍	❍	❍
New Mexico (505) 476-1103	❍	❍	❍	❍	❍	❍
New York (518) 474-3817 x110	❍	❍	❍	❍	❍	❍
North Carolina (919) 733-9544	❍	❍	❍	❍	❍	❍

Registration Laws: Architecture

States and State Boards	Type of Law		Initial Requirements			Ongoing Requir.
	Title Act	Practice Act	College Degree Required	Internship Required	ARE Exam Required	Continuing Education Required
North Carolina (919) 733-9544	❍	❍	❍	❍	❍	❍
North Dakota (701) 223-3184	❍	❍	❍	❍	❍	
Ohio (614) 466-2316	❍	❍	❍	❍	❍	
Oklahoma (405) 949-2383	❍	❍	❍	❍	❍	❍
Oregon (503) 378-4270	❍	❍	❍	❍	❍	❍
Pennsylvania (717) 783-3397	❍	❍	❍	❍	❍	
Rhode Island (401) 222-2565	❍	❍	❍	❍	❍	❍
South Carolina (803) 896-4412	❍	❍		❍	❍	❍
South Dakota (605) 394-2510	❍	❍	❍	❍	❍	❍
Tennessee (615) 741-3221	❍	❍	❍	❍	❍	❍
Texas (512) 305-8535	❍	❍	CB	❍	❍	❍
Utah (801) 530-6403	❍	❍	❍	❍	❍	P
Vermont (802) 828-2373	❍	❍	❍	❍	❍	❍
Virginia (804) 367-8512	❍	❍	❍	❍	❍	
Washington (360) 664-1388	❍	❍		❍	❍	
West Virginia (304) 528-5825	❍	❍	❍	❍	❍	❍
Wisconsin (608) 261-7096	❍	❍	❍	❍	❍	
Wyoming (307) 777-7788	❍	❍	❍	❍	❍	❍

P = There is current legislation pending regarding this requirement.
CB = Contact Board

Source: National Council of Architectural Registration Boards

Registration Laws: Interior Design

The following information provides a brief overview of the major components of initial registration requirements for interior designers, including work experience, degree requirements and the National Council for Interior Design Qualification (NCIDQ) exam. More specific details about these requirements are available from the individual state boards reachable at the phone numbers listed below. Due to the complex and changing nature of registration laws, it is recommended that the state licensing board(s) be contacted for the most up-to-date information. The American Society of Interior Designers (ASID) also maintains information about registration on their Web site at *www.asid.org*. Note that not all states regulate the interior design profession at this time.

States and State Board Phone Numbers	Type of Law		Initial Requirements			Ongoing Requir.
	Title Act	Practice Act	Post-HS Education Required	Work Experience Required	NCIDQ Exam Required	Continuing Education Required
Alabama (205) 879-6785	❍	❍	❍	❍	❍	❍
Arkansas (870) 226-6875	❍		❍	❍	❍	❍
California (760) 761-4734	*			❍	❍	❍
Colorado (303) 894-7801	**		❍	❍	❍	
Connecticut (860) 713-6135	❍		❍	❍	❍	
Florida (850) 487-1395	❍	❍	❍	❍	❍	❍
Georgia (478) 207-1400	❍		❍		❍	❍
Illinois (217) 785-0813	❍		❍	❍	❍	
Kentucky (859) 246-2069	❍		❍	❍	❍	❍
Louisiana (225) 298-1283	❍	❍	❍	❍	❍	❍
Maine (207) 624-8603	❍		❍	❍	❍	
Maryland (410) 333-6322	❍		❍	❍	❍	❍
Minnesota (651) 296-2388	❍		❍	❍	❍	❍
Missouri (573) 522-4683	❍		❍	❍	❍	❍

Registration Laws: Interior Design

States and State Board Phone Numbers	Type of Law		Initial Requirements			Ongoing Requir.
	Title Act	Practice Act	Post-HS Education Required	Work Experience Required	NCIDQ Exam Required	Continuing Education Required
Nevada (702) 486-7300	❍	❍	❍	❍	❍	
New Jersey (973) 504-6385	❍		❍	❍	❍	❍
New Mexico (505) 476-7077	❍		❍	❍	❍	❍
New York (518) 474-3846	❍		❍	❍	❍	
Tennessee (615) 741-3221	❍		❍	❍	❍	❍
Texas (512) 305-8539	❍		❍	❍	❍	❍
Virginia (804) 367-8514	❍		❍	❍	❍	
Washington, D.C. (202) 442-4330	❍	❍	❍	❍	❍	❍
Wisconsin (608) 266-5439	❍		❍	❍	❍	❍

* Self-Certification Act
** Permitting Statute

Source: American Society of Interior Designers

Registration Laws: Landscape Architecture

The following matrix provides a brief overview of the major components of initial licensure for landscape architects, including if non-LAAB-accredited programsand/or work experience are accepted. Complete information regarding licensing requirements, renewal procedures, and reciprocity is available from the individual state boards, at the phone numbers listed below. Due to the complex and changing nature of the regulations, it is recommended that the state licensing board(s) be contacted for the most up-to-date information. The Council of Landscape Architectural Registration Boards (CLARB) and the American Society of Landscape Architects (ASLA) also maintain information about licensure on their Web sites at *www.clarb.org* and *www.asla.org*, respectively.

States and State Board Phone Numbers	Type of Law		Initial Requirements				Ongoing Requir.
	Title Act	**Practice Act**	**Non-LAAB accredited degree accepted**	**Non-LA degree with exp. accepted**	**Experience only accepted**	**LARE Exam Required**	**Continuing Ed. Requir.**
Alabama (334) 262-1351		❍	❍	❍	❍	❍	❍
Alaska (907) 465-2540		❍	❍	CB	❍	❍	
Arizona (602) 362-4930		❍	❍	❍	❍	❍	
Arkansas (501) 682-3171		❍	❍	❍	❍	❍	❍
California (916) 445-4954		❍	❍			❍	
Connecticut (860) 713-6145		❍			❍	❍	❍
Delaware (302) 744-4504		❍	❍		❍	❍	❍
Florida (850) 487-1395		❍			❍	❍	❍
Georgia (478) 207-1400		❍				❍	❍
Hawaii (808) 586-2702		❍	❍	❍	❍	❍	
Idaho (208) 334-3233		❍			❍	❍	
Illinois (217) 782-8556	❍					❍	
Indiana (317) 232-2980		❍			❍	❍	
Iowa (515) 281-5596			❍	❍	❍	❍	❍

Registration Laws: Landscape Architecture

States and State Board Phone Numbers	Type of Law		Initial Requirements				Ongoing Requir.
	Title Act	Practice Act	Non-LAAB accredited degree accepted	Non-LA degree with exp. accepted	Experience only accepted	LARE Exam Required	Continuing Ed. Requir.
Kansas (785) 296-3053		❍				❍	❍
Kentucky (859) 246-2753		❍				❍	❍
Louisiana (225) 952-8100		❍		❍	❍	❍	
Maine (207) 624-8522	❍		CB	CB	CB	❍	
Maryland (410) 230-6322		❍			❍	❍	
Massachusetts (617) 727-3072	❍				❍	❍	
Michigan (517) 241-9201	❍				❍	❍	
Minnesota (651) 296-2388		❍	❍	❍	❍	❍	❍
Mississippi (601) 899-9071		❍	❍	❍	❍	❍	❍
Missouri (573) 751-0047		❍				❍	
Montana (406) 841-2386		❍				❍	
Nebraska (402) 471-2407		❍			❍	❍	❍
Nevada (775) 688-1316		❍	❍	❍	❍	❍	
New Jersey (973) 504-6385	❍		CB			❍	❍
New Mexico (505) 476-7077		❍	❍	❍	❍	❍	❍
New York (518) 474-3817		❍	❍	❍	❍	❍	
North Carolina (919) 850-9088		❍	❍	❍	❍	❍	❍
Ohio (614) 466-2316		❍				❍	
Oklahoma (405) 949-2383		❍				❍	❍
Oregon (503) 589-0093		❍		❍	❍	❍	

Registration Laws: Landscape Architecture

States and State Board Phone Numbers	Type of Law		Initial Requirements				Ongoing Requir.
	Title Act	Practice Act	Non-LAAB accredited degree accepted	Non-LA degree with exp. accepted	Experience only accepted	LARE Exam Required	Continuing Ed. Requir.
Pennsylvania (717) 772-8528		❍			❍	❍	❍
Rhode Island (401) 222-2565		❍	CB	CB	❍	❍	
South Carolina (803) 734-9131		❍			❍	❍	
South Dakota (605) 394-2510		❍				❍	❍
Tennessee (615) 741-3221		❍				❍	❍
Texas (512) 305-8519		❍				❍	❍
Utah (801) 530-6403		❍			❍	❍	
Virginia (804) 367-8514	❍		❍	❍	❍	❍	
Washington (360) 664-1388	❍		❍	❍	❍	❍	
West Virginia (304) 293-9304	❍				❍	❍	
Wisconsin (608) 266-5511	❍		CB			❍	
Wyoming (307) 777-7788		❍			❍	❍	❍

Note: Colorado, Washington, D.C., New Hampshire, and Vermont currently do not have a Landscape Architecture licensure program. The North Dakota law is effective 1/1/2005; specific eligibility requirements are to be determined.

CB: Contact Board

Source: Council of Landscape Architectural Registration Boards and American Society of Landscape Architects

Salary and Compensation Guide

Each year as part of its ongoing research agenda, Counsel House Research tracks the hiring of design professionals and reviews compensation packages for marketplace comparisons. Below are the results from their 2003 study on salary ranges and national averages for a select category of positions within the design professions. Please use caution in drawing any quick or precise conclusions from this broad survey, as there can be significant variations depending on geographic location and micro-economic fluctuations within certain building types. Information from the U.S. Department of Labor, Bureau of Labor Statistics' *Occupational Outlook Handbook, 2002-2003* is also included.

ARCHITECTURE

U.S. Department of Labor, Bureau of Labor Statistics
Median: $52,510
Median range: $41,060 – $67,720

Intern Architect
National Average: $36,500
Range: $32,000 – $44,000

Architect–5 years experience
National Average: $48,200
Range: $41,000 – $60,300

Architect–10 years experience
National Average: $55,800
Range: $43,500 – $74,000

Architect–15 Years experience
National Average: $62,200
Range: $49,500 – $93,500

Architect/Engineer–Project Manager, 10+ years experience
National Average: $76,500
Range: $48,000 – $111,250

Design Technology Supervisor (responsibility for all hardware and software systems)
National Average: $67,500
Range: $42,800 – $110,000

Executive Architect–private sector work in corporate settings, significant span of responsibility
National Average: $135,000
Range: $52,000 – $350,000+

Managing Principal/President–medium size firm (10 to 50 employees)
National Average: $128,000
Range: $78,000 – $350,000+

Owner/Principal–small sole proprietorship (under 10 employees)
National Average: $84,500
Range: $47,500 – $203,000

Owner/Principal–large full-service firm, may include A/E and design-build services (50 to 225 employees)
National Average: $147,250
Range: $95,500 – $1,000,000+

CEO/President–large multi-national firm (over 225 employees)
National Average: $235,000
Range: $155,000 – $1,000,000+

Marketing Director–Architecture, Interior Design, Engineering
National Average: $69,000
Range: $45,000 – $115,000

Salary and Compensation Guide

University Architecture and Design Faculty and Administration
Dean, Architecture: $142,000
Dean, Engineering: $153,000
Chief Facilities Architect: $107,000
Professor: $78,500
Associate Professor: $55,800
Assistant Professor: $47,000

INDUSTRIAL DESIGN

U.S. Department of Labor, Bureau of Labor Statistics
Median: $48,780 – $64,120
Median range: $23,580 – $42,570
1–2 years experience: $36,500
5 years experience: $45,000
8 years experience: $64,000
Managers/Executives: $80,000 – $180,000

Industrial/Product Designer–Private Practice
National Average: N/A
Range: $53,000 – $91,000

Principal/President
National Average: N/A
Range: $90,000 – $300,000+

INTERIOR DESIGN

U.S. Department of Labor, Bureau of Labor Statistics
Median: $36,540
Median range: $26,800 – $51,140

Interior Designer–10 to 15 years experience
National Average: $62,500
Range: $35,000 – $102,000

Owner/Principal of small firm (under 10 employees)
National Average: N/A
Range: $45,000 – $225,000+

Owner/Principal, 10+ employees (may also include architectural services)
National Average: $83,500
Range: $46,500 – $300,000

LANDSCAPE ARCHITECTURE

U.S. Department of Labor, Bureau of Labor Statistics
Median: $43,540
Median range: $32,990 – $59,490
Federal employees (all levels), median: $62,824

Principal/Owner, 10 to 50 employees
National Average: $88,000
Range: $63,000 – $165,000

URBAN AND REGIONAL PLANNING

U.S. Department of Labor, Bureau of Labor Statistics
Median: $46,500
Median range: $36,510 – $57,900
Local government employees, median: $45,300

Sources: Greenway Consulting, DesignIntelligence, The American Institute of Architects, International Interior Design Association, Industrial Designers Society of America, Chronicle of Higher Education, *American Society of Interior Designers,* Occupational Outlook Handbook *(U.S. Department of Labor, Bureau of Labor Statistics)*

Obituaries

This chapter is in memory of the design and preservation leaders and patrons who died between Oct. 1, 2002 and Aug. 31, 2003.

Jody Kingrey Albergo, 84

Pioneering Chicago interior designer Jody Kingrey Albergo died June 11, 2003. With Kitty Baldwin Weese, wife of architect Harry Weese, Albergo formed the home and office interiors company Baldwin-Kingrey in 1947. Offering design services and selling modernist furnishings from a Michigan Avenue store, Baldwin-Kingrey was the first retailer in Chicago to import Finnish designer Alvar Aalto's furniture, before traditional furniture retailers offered modern designs. A book about the firm, *Baldwin-Kingrey: 1947-1957 Mid-Century Design*, is forthcoming from Kitty Weese. Albergo, a native of Minnesota, moved to Chicago after World War II and, though she had a degree in art, pursued a career in interior design. After Baldwin-Kingrey, she operated her own firm, Jody Kingrey Inc., more than 45 years.

Mae Babitz, 91

Artist Mae Babitz, who preserved the legacy of Los Angeles' long-lost Victorian architecture by sketching it, died January 11, 2003. Born Lily Mae Laviolette in Crowley, La., she moved to Los Angeles during the depression and worked as a secretary until marrying Sol Babitz, a contract violinist at 20th Century Fox. In addition to their civic contributions to the city's music community, the Babitz' were members of the Committee for Simon Rodia's Towers in Watts from its inception in 1958. Babitz was a board member until 1998, selling her sketches of the towers to raise money for their preservation. A self-taught artist, she sketched 40 of L.A.'s historic landmarks, including the Pico House, Bradbury Building, Hollywood Hotel, and many views of Bunker Hill in its heyday with a host of expensive Victorian homes. Her work has been displayed in galleries, festivals, buildings, and exhibits. Twenty-seven pieces were hung in Mayor Tom Bradley's office. John Dreyfus, the then-architecture critic of the Los Angeles Times, wrote of her work, "This 70-year-old artist's light touch isolates and captures the essence of Los Angeles' old residential architecture."

Geoffrey Bawa, 83

Sri Lankan architect Geoffrey Bawa died May 27, 2003. A 2002 recipient of the Aga Khan Chairman's Award for Lifetime Achievement, Bawa synthesized a style of architecture that merged Western modernism with traditional Sri Lankan designs. More than any other concern, Bawa addressed the relationship between building and landscape and integrated his designs with their surroundings with a minimum of environmental damage and disruption. A London-trained lawyer, Bawa practiced in his native Sri Lanka for two years before his mother died. He then departed for lengthy travels across Europe, Asia and the U.S. Becoming enamored of Italy's architecture and gardens, Bawa returned to Sri Lanka and apprenticed under the architect H.H. Reid. When Reid died in 1952, Bawa went to London to study at the Architectural Association, qualifying to practice in 1957 at the age of 38. He returned home and assumed what was left of Reid's practice. Bawa began assembling a portfolio of work that included religious, educational, governmental, commercial, and residential projects, each with a unique blend of influences that introduced a new aesthetic. His most famous projects include his own house, the Lunuganga Estate, as well as the 1962 home of artist Ena de Silva, which features rooms oriented toward a central courtyard. He also designed some of Sri Lanka's most prominent resort hotels, including the Bentota Beach Hotel, the Triton Hotel, and the Lighthouse. He constructed the Kandalama Hotel without earthmoving equipment in order not to disrupt the ancient Sinhalese Buddhist cave temples nearby. In 1979 he was commissioned to design Sri Lanka's Parliament building. For this project, Bawa created the illusion of a group of copper-topped pavilions emerging from a sheet of water. Following a debilitating stroke in 1998 that left him paralyzed and unable to speak, Bawa continued to supervise designs from his bedside.

Ward Bennett, 85

Famed New York designer Ward Bennett died August 13, 2003. His lengthy career included window dressing, costume design, product design, interior design, furniture design, and much more–from Sterling flatware for Tiffany to offices for Rolling Stone magazine. His American modern aesthetic blended

Ward Bennett, 85

sophisticated style with industrial functionalism. His own studio apartment in Manhattan's Dakota building was hailed as "the most exciting modern apartment in New York," in a 1964 New York Times Magazine. The son of a vaudeville actor, Bennett began working in New York's garment district at the age of 13. In addition to costume design, Bennett branched out into ceramics, jewelry design and, in the mid-1940s, interior design. Several of his 1970s vases and flatware designs for Brickel Associates, a New York furniture company, are in the permanent design collection at the Museum of Modern Art. He was once credited by The American Institute of Architects as "treasured for having transformed industrial hardware into sublime objects," and for "creating a new vocabulary for the whole design profession," Bennett was also a member of the Interior Design Magazine Hall of Fame.

Leslie Boney Jr., 83

Lifelong North Carolina resident and architect Leslie Boney Jr., FAIA, died June 19, 2003. Following military service during World War II, Boney joined his father in the firm of Leslie N. Boney, Architect, in Wilmington, where he worked for the rest of his career. Though he designed hundreds of public buildings, Boney is also remembered as a tireless advocate for the profession through his teaching, writing, preservation efforts, and community service. He was named a fellow in The American Institute of Architects in 1966 and received its Kemper Award in 1982, granted to one architect each year for their significant contribution of service to the profession. In 2000, the AIA College of Fellows created the Leslie N. Boney Jr. Spirit of Fellowship Award and selected its namesake as the initial recipient. Over the years, Boney served the regional and local chapters of the AIA in numerous capacities, including director of the AIA South Atlantic Region and Chancellor of the AIA College of Fellows. His many book projects include collaborating on *The Lincoln Memorial and Its Architect, Henry Bacon*; coordinating *The AIA Gold Medal*; and editing *The History of the AIA in North Carolina: 1913–1999*; *Harnett Hooper and Howe: Revolutionary Leaders in the Lower Cape Fear*; and *Let There Be Light: God's Story Through Stained Glass.*

Andrew Briger, 82

Andrew Briger, a former deputy lord mayor of Sydney, Australia, and a progressive urban reformer, died in June 2003. Raised in Europe by Russian immigrant parents, Briger brought a vision of parks, pedestrian-friendly malls, and tree-lined sidewalks to Australia. He was elected to the Sydney City Council in 1969 and became chairman of the City Development Planning Committee, a position he held until he was elected deputy lord mayor in 1975. Under his leadership, the Council established its first planning department and developed a series of strategic plans for the city. As a result, Martin Place, Circular Quay, and Dixon Street (Chinatown) were converted into pedestrian malls, and Woolloomooloo underwent significant urban revitalization. Briger also helped save Sydney's Queen Victoria Building and initiated the Pitt Street Mall. In 1977, he was awarded the Order of Australia and in 1981 the Sidney Luker Memorial Medal, the highest honor bestowed by the Royal Australian Planning Institute.

Andrew Daniel Bryant, 72

Longtime Washington, D.C. architect Andrew Daniel Bryant died November 3, 2002. He founded and operated the firm Bryant Associates from 1966 until his retirement in August 2002. A native of the nation's Capital, Bryant designed many projects there, including schools, libraries, housing for seniors, shopping centers, metro stops, and bridges. He also designed the Philadelphia national headquarters of the Kappa Alpha Psi social fraternity, of which he was a member. Bryant was a former president of the D.C. Chamber of Commerce and a director of The American Institute of Architects as well as the National Organization of Minority Architects.

Col. Wilfred C. Burdick, 91

Civil engineer and retired Air Force Col. Wilfred C. Burdick died August 27, 2003. He oversaw the construction of some of Chicago's most prominent buildings, including the Prudential Building, the IBM Building, the Dirksen Federal Building, and McDonald's Hamburger University. Between serving in World War II and the Korean War and again starting in 1953, Col.

Col. Wilfred C. Burdick, 91

Burdick worked for Chicago's C.F. Murphy Associates, an architectural firm specializing in skyscrapers, as their architectural superintendent. He retired in 1984.

Pedro Casariego, 75

Spanish architect Pedro Casariego H. Vaquero died September 8, 2002. He designed several of Madrid's most prominent skyscrapers, including the Windsor Tower, Trieste, and Edificio Centro. One of his most famous projects, the Monky instant coffee factory, was demolished in the early 1990s, despite a large public outcry. Built in 1960, it had been a landmark on the airport highway, as large glass spans allowed passersby to see the large cylinder inside where coffee was processed. Casariego won a Europa Nostra architecture award for a public housing project in the city of Alicante, and he also restored the nineteen-century Teatro Campoamor opera house in his birth city of Oviedo.

Achille Castiglioni, 84

Italian designer Achille Castiglioni died December 2, 2002. Before there was a Philippe Starck or a Michael Graves, there was Achille Castiglioni, an architect who turned to product design as commissions became scarce around the time of World War II. Working both with his brother, Pier Giacomo, and alone, Castiglioni designed over 200 household products, including lamps, vacuum cleaners, cameras, and shelving. The Castiglionis led a pack of designers who produced the work that gave Italy its post-war reputation as a hotbed of inspired modern design. Castiglioni's best-known design is probably that of the Arco lamp, an arc-shaped stainless steel floor lamp supported by a marble base at one end and capped by a bulbous chrome shade at the other. This 1962 design, designed with his brother, is still in production. Many of their other lamp designs endure, including the Toio lamp, a floor fixture featuring a car reflector light and a transformer which doubles as its base. They also designed the Mezzadro (Sharecropper's Stool), with its plain bent metal tractor seat atop a sleek base. Following the death of Pier Giacomo in 1968, Achille Castiglioni continued to produce trend-setting lamps and household objects. He was the subject of a 1997 exhibit at the Museum of Modern Art in New York.

William Brooks Cavin Jr., 88

Architect William Brooks Cavin Jr., FAIA, died December 19, 2002. Most of his career was spent in Minneapolis where he designed many prominent buildings including the Veterans Service Building at the Capitol. He was hired by Ralph Rapson, dean of the University of Minnesota's school of architecture, in 1954, where he taught for 20 years. He had also been an active preservationist, heading a committee to save the old federal courthouse in St. Paul, now the Landmark Center. He also helped preserve working-class homes on Milwaukee Avenue, the Grove Street Flats on Nicollet Island, and Louis Sullivan's Owatonna, Minn., bank building. Cavin studied under Walter Gropius at Harvard University, earning a master's degree in architecture. He then worked for Eero Saarinen in Washington, D.C. He moved to Minneapolis in 1946 when he won an international design competition for the Veterans Service Building. In 1959 he formed a partnership with Clayton Page, which lasted until Page's death in 1969. He partnered with John Rova forming Cavin/Rova in 1980. He retired in 1986. His body of work encompasses museums, restorations, schools, apartment buildings, senior housing, and many private residences. He led the 1981 renovation of the Minnesota State Capitol. He was elected to the College of Fellows of The American Institute of Architects in 1975.

Alphonse Chapanis, 85

A founder of what is today referred to as "ergonomics," Alphonse Chapanis died October 4, 2002. He began his career in the Army, where he discovered poor placement of instruments in B-17 bombers was responsible for a string of runway crashes. After receiving his Ph.D. in psychology from Yale University in 1943, Chapanis joined the faculty of Johns Hopkins University. He taught psychology and industrial engineering there, and in 1949, he and colleagues Wendell Garner and Clifford Morgan published the first ergonomics textbook, Applied Experimental Psychology: Human Factors in Engineering Design. During his years at Johns Hopkins and following his retirement in 1982, Chapanis was a leading industry consultant. He aided in the development of the keypad for push-button telephones, as well as teleconferencing and voice mail, and the improvement of oil exploration techniques and commercial shipping operations. He published an autobiography in 1999 entitled *The Chapanis Chronicles.*

Robertson E. Collins, 81

Oregon preservation leader Robertson Collins died May 23, 2003 in Singapore where he resided. During the 1960s and 1970s Collins led the fight to restore and preserve Jacksonville, Ore., a declining 1850s gold-rush town. Upon moving to Jacksonville in 1962, he spearheaded opposition to a four-lane highway slated to cut through the community and destroy some of its historic buildings. He then began restoring many of those buildings himself, protecting them with architectural easements, "a tool he pioneered," according to *Preservation* magazine. In 1966, thanks in large part to his efforts, the entire town was designated a National Historic Landmark and more than 100 buildings in Jacksonville were listed in the National Register of Historic Places. He later moved to Southeast Asia where he worked to preserve some of the area's most famous sites while developing them for tourism. He was a trustee of the National Trust for Historic Preservation from 1971 to 1982 and served on the boards of the Southern Oregon Historical Society and the Historic Preservation League of Oregon. In 1980 the University of Oregon honored him for his preservation work with its Distinguished Service Award. He also received the Distinguished Preservation Award from Oregon's governor.

Hugh Neville Conder, 81

British architect Neville Conder died June 20, 2003. He was a partner in the firm Casson, Conder & Partners along with Hugh Casson, who died in 1999. Conder first worked with Casson, whose career as an architect, educator, journalist and painter included organizing the 1951 Festival of Britain and teaching watercolor painting to the Prince of Wales. They first collaborated on exhibition design before becoming partners. For 30 years, the firm would produced high profile architecture in and around London, including the arts faculty buildings at the University of Cambridge, buildings for Birmingham University, the Elephant and Rhinoceros Pavilion at the London Zoo, the regional headquarters of the National Westminster Bank in Manchester, the Derby Civic Centre, the Wyvern Theater in Swindon, and the Ismaili Centre, South Kensington. Conder also authored the 1949 *An Introduction to Modern Architecture.*

Lawrence M. Cox, 90

Lawrence M. Cox, head of the Norfolk, Va., Redevelopment and Housing Authority for over 25 years, died November 7, 2002. From 1941 to 1969 he directed the Norfolk Housing Authority, leaving in 1969 to become assistant secretary of the U.S. Department of Housing and Urban Development (HUD) under President Richard Nixon. Though critics charged that his program created ghettos, Cox helped shape the Federal Housing Act of 1949, calling for "a decent home and suitable living environment for every American family."

Curt Dale, 57

Denver, Colo., architect Curt Dale, FAIA, died February 22, 2003. A partner in the firm Anderson Mason Dale, Dale was an outdoor enthusiast who was killed in an avalanche while on a weekend backcountry ski trip. He had climbed all of Colorado's "fourteeners" as well as Mount McKinley and Mount Rainier. Called the workhorse of the firm, Dale's organization helped design Colorado's Ocean Journey, as well as a $40 million, 10-year reconstruction of the entrance to Mount Rushmore and its visitor center. Anderson Mason Dale also designed the nearly completed $75 million addition to the federal courthouse in Denver. Dale had been recently elected to The American Institute of Architects' College of Fellows.

Kenneth Dayton, 80

Minneapolis department store magnate Kenneth Dayton died July 19. 2003. A driving force behind some of the best architecture in Minneapolis, he was the last of five brothers, all grandsons of the chain's founder, to run the Dayton Hudson Corporation (now Target Corporation). In 1946 he introduced a corporate giving program that committed Dayton Hudson to contribute five percent of its pre-tax profits to worthy organizations. These programs helped fund Minneapolis' Orchestra Hall, the University of Minnesota's Design Center for the American Urban Landscape, and projects at the Walker Art Center and Guthrie Theater. A modern architecture enthusiast, Dayton built two private homes of merit. The first, on Minnesota's Lake Minnetonka, was designed by Romaldo Giurgoa in the late 1960s. When they decided to sell that house

Kenneth Dayton, 80

and move into the city in 1994, the Daytons visited with 27 architects from around the world before selecting Minneapolis architect Vince James. When the developers of the IDS Center in Minneapolis approached Dayton Hudson in the 1960s about becoming anchor tenants in their planned marquee building, Dayton required they retain a first-class architect for the job. He vetoed a traditional historic design by Edward Durell Stone and instead approved the hiring of Philip Johnson. When approached in the mid-1980s by Harrison Fraker, dean of the University of Minnesota architecture school, about funding a design center in the city, Dayton's Dayton-Hudson Foundation donated $1.3 million for its startup. Asked to assist with the building of Los Angeles' Getty Center, he helped select Richard Meier as the architect and later served as a trustee of the Center. In addition to many corporate directorships, Dayton served on the boards of a number of civic organizations, including the National Endowment for the Arts, the J. Paul Getty Trust, the Rockefeller Foundation, as well as a founding chairman of Public Radio International.

Philip W. Dinsmore, 60

Former American Institute of Architects Secretary Philip Dinsmore, FAIA, died January 28, 2003. He served a four-year term as secretary in addition to holding numerous positions with the AIA on the local, state, and national levels. He had been regional director on the AIA Board from the Western Mountain Region as well as chair of the Board of Trustees of the AIA Trust. He was elected to the AIA's College of Fellows in 1986. Dinsmore was managing principal for The Durrant Group's Tucson, Ariz., office and was renown for his school architecture. In addition to the University of Arizona Electrical and Computer Engineering Building, he designed libraries at Arizona State University and Northern Arizona University as well as many Tucson schools and office buildings. Before joining Durrant, Dinsmore was vice president and principal-in-charge of Architecture One Ltd., Tucson and Phoenix. He had also worked for CNWC Architects in Tucson and William L. Pereira & Associates in Los Angeles.

Gilbert Fein, 83

Miami architect Gilbert Fein died March 9, 2003. His influential tailfin designs helped define the look and character of North Miami Beach in the 1940s and 1950s. Through the years his brand of Miami Modernism (or "MiMo") has become a celebrated architectural movement. Today the New York Municipal Art Society includes MiMo among its list of architectural genres. Preservationists in South Florida monitor the status of his designs, and recently the Miami Design Preservation League began monthly tours of MiMo architecture featuring the buildings from 60th to 72nd Streets. Fein designed hundreds of buildings, including the Washington Federal Savings and Loan on Meridian Avenue and Temple Menorah on 75th St. in Miami Beach. He moved to the area from New York after honeymooning there with wife Beverly in 1947.

James Deforest Ferris, 77

Chicago architect James Deforest Ferris, FAIA, a student of Mies van der Rohe and a contributing designer on many of the city's landmark buildings, died December 25, 2002. During tenures with Chicago firms, including Skidmore, Owings & Merrill; C.F. Murphy Associates; Bertrand Goldberg; and Graham Anderson Probst & White, Ferris worked on the CNA Center, the Northern Trust restoration and addition, and the First National Bank building. Following military service during World War II, Ferris studied at the Pratt Institute in New York and then at the Illinois Institute of Technology, where he worked with Mies. Ferris attributed the red exterior of the CNA Center to Mies. On a visit to the site when the building was in its early stages and still black, Mies admired the color of the building as it reflected the setting sun. And so it became permanently red. In the 1970s, Ferris began his own architecture firm that produced projects across the Midwest.

Tony Fitzpatrick, 52

Renowned civil engineer Tony Fitzpatrick died July 26, 2003. He was chairman of the Americas Division of the Arup Group, an international engineering consulting company. Perhaps most famous for taking the wobble out of London's Millennium Footbridge, Fitzpatrick worked on many high profile projects, including Sir Norman Foster's Century Tower in Tokyo and his Hong Kong and Shanghai Banking Corp. headquarters in Hong

Tony Fitzpatrick, 52

Kong. He also worked with Sir Richard Rogers on the Reuters Building in London, and Jean Nouvel on the unbuilt 1,378-foot Tour San Fin planned for Paris. A native of London, Fitzpatrick joined Arup upon his graduation from England's Leeds University in 1972, the same year he won the Holst Prize for civil engineering. He worked for the firm's London, Newcastle, and Tehran offices before being named to the Arup board of directors in 1986. Fitzpatrick moved to San Francisco, Calif., in 2001 to head Arup's Americas group.

Roy W. Forrey, Jr., 55

Roy W. Forrey, an expert on Chicago's landmark buildings, died May 12, 2003. He served as deputy director of the Commission on Chicago Landmarks from 1974 to 1993. A native Chicagoian, Forrey was an enthusiast and expert on the city's buildings and neighborhoods. Under his direction, the Commission spent 12 years researching and compiling a list of Chicago's potential landmarks, which contains over 17,000 structures. A contributor to The American Institute of Architects' Guide to Chicago, Forrey also assisted in the editing of the third edition of Chicago's Famous Buildings, published in 1980 by University of Chicago Press.

Richard T. Foster, 83

Modern architect Richard Foster, a collaborator for many years with Philip Johnson, died September 13, 2002. From 1950 until 1962 and on several New York University projects in the early 1970s, Foster partnered with Johnson to produce a portfolio of landmark projects that include the New York State Pavilion at the 1964 World's Fair; the David Lloyd Kreeger house in Washington, D.C., now the Kreeger Museum; and the Kline Biology Tower at Yale University. For NYU, the pair designed the Elmer Holmes Bobst Library, Tisch Hall, and the Hagop Kevorkian Center. Following graduation as valedictorian of his 1950 Pratt Institute class, Foster was hired by Johnson, his former instructor. In 1962 he established his own firm, Richard Foster Associates. Another of his noteworthy projects was his own Greenwich, Conn. house–a revolving, glass-walled structure built in 1968. The house can revolve forward and backward and make a complete revolution in a span of 45 minutes to four hours.

James F. Fulton, 73

Former Industrial Designers Society of America (IDSA) president James F. Fulton died in late summer 2003. He was instrumental in keeping *I.D.* Magazine alive in the mid-1970s and served as a chairman of the board at New York's Pratt Institute, his alma mater, from 1991 to 2001. During his term as IDSA president, from 1975 to 1978, he established a small full-time staff for the organization. He bought the majority share of a floundering *I.D.* Magazine in 1977 and prevented its demise. Following graduation from Pratt in 1951, Fulton worked in the office of Harley Earl and then for Raymond Loewy at the Loewy/Snaith offices in Paris and New York. He then established Fulton & Partners, which served as a design consultant for Owings Corning for over 25 years. In the late 1980s, Fulton raised over $30,000 to buy the Raymond Loewy archives for donation to the Library of Congress. He was also a former trustee of the Worldesign Foundation and a member of the IDSA Academy of Fellows.

Curt Green, 77

A founder of one of Minnesota's leading architecture firms, Curt Green, FAIA, died November 3, 2002. With friend Dick Hammel, he founded Hammel, Green and Abrahamson of Minneapolis in 1953. Today the firm employs 550 people in six offices nationwide and is well known for its school and church portfolio. In December 2002, HGA won four of ten Honor Awards granted at the American Institute of Architects' Minnesota convention. Green worked on many noteworthy projects, including the executing Hardy Holzman and Pfeiffer' design for the Minneapolis Orchestra Hall. His other projects included the arts center at Gustavus Adolphus College in St. Peter, Minn., O'Shaughnessy Auditorium at the College of St. Catherine in St. Paul, Minn., and the Benedicta Arts Center at the college of St. Benedict in St. Joseph, Minn.

Sir George Grenfell-Baines, 95

British architect and town planner George Grenfell-Baines died May 9, 2003. He was the founding chairman of the Building Design Partnership (BDP), which is the largest multi-professional design organization in Britain. He founded the Grenfell Baines Group in 1938, which grew through the post-war years to include 15 different practice groups. In 1961, he changed the firm's name to BDP to reflect his management ethos: that creating complex buildings required a firm with many types of professionals, each responsible for contributing to the firm, that are rewarded and recognized for their contributions. The firm's many commissions included master plans for Bradford and Surrey universities, Belfast city, Aldershot military town, the Bank of England in Leeds, the Halifax Building Society headquarters, the Queen's Medical Centre, Nottingham, and the Leeds General Infirmary. Grenfell-Baines was a Royal Institute of British Architects (RIBA) vice president in 1967. He was named an honorary fellow of The American Institute of Architects (AIA) in 1981 and of the Russian International Academy of Architecture in 1990. A supporter and architectural education enthusiast, Grenfell-Baines left BDP in 1974 to become a professor of architecture at Sheffield University. Upon retiring in 1978 he was knighted for his services to architecture.

Armand H. Gustaferro, 79

Concrete expert and Chicago-area civil engineer Armand "Gus" Gustaferro died August 3, 2003. An early advocate and researcher of prestressed concrete, he developed procedures for making all types of concrete more fire-resistant. His concepts were incorporated into the then regional, now national, model building codes governing construction. Gustaferro received his bachelor's degree from Ohio State and his master's degree from Yale University, both in civil engineering. He joined the Chicago office of the Portland Cement Association in 1954 and later worked in its fire research laboratory in Skokie, Ill. He joined the Consulting Engineers Group of Mt. Prospect, Ill., in 1970 and consulted on hundreds of projects in the U.S. and overseas. For 29 years, Gustaferro lectured at the annual World of Concrete trade show and exhibition and also taught seminars for the American Concrete Institute.

Patrick Gwynne, 90

British modernist architect Patrick Gwynne died May 3, 2003. His own house, The Homewood (Esher, UK), was donated to the National Trust in England and is only one of two pre-war modern houses the National Trust has acquired with "continuity of occupant and contents," according to London's The Guardian newspaper, along with Erno Goldfinger's house in Willow Road, Hampstead. Originally designed for his parents, The Homewood is one of Gwynne's earliest projects. Upon seeing Amyas Connell's English modern house High and Over as a schoolboy, Gwynne became an unabashed modern design enthusiast. He became an apprentice to the architect John Coleridge before working in the office of Wells Coates. While there he designed The Homewood and later moved both his office and his residence to the house. Gwynne also designed other modern U.K. homes, featuring connecting rooms that could be opened up for entertaining, and later, curvilinear and geometric forms. He is equally renown for his restaurant designs, including the Dell Restaurant in Hyde Park, which has been listed as a historically significant site.

Robert Mitchell Hanna, 67

Robert Mitchell Hanna, FASLA, a professor of landscape architecture at the University of Pennsylvania for over 30 years, died March 8, 2003. He was also a principal in the Philadelphia firm Hanna/Olin Ltd., which he founded in 1976 with Laurie Olin. A specialist in shaping urban open spaces, Hanna contributed to the master plan for Battery Park City in New York and the Westlake Square revitalization in downtown Seattle. In 1962, he worked with Richard Haag on the transformation of the grounds of the 1962 Seattle World's Fair into a park. He joined the faculty of the University of Pennsylvania in 1969 and was named its first chairman of environmental design in 1974. In 1995 Hanna/Olin Ltd. divided into RM Hanna Landscape Architects and the Olin Partnership.

William Hartmann, 86

William Hartmann, FAIA, an early partner with the international architecture firm Skidmore, Owings & Merrill (SOM) and head of their Chicago office from 1947 until his retirement in 1981, died March 4, 2003. Though he helped lead the firm during a period that included the design of Chicago's iconic John Hancock Center and Sears Tower buildings, Hartmann is best remembered for persuading the artist Pablo Picasso to create a sculpture for that city's Daley Center Plaza. Active in Chicago civic and cultural affairs, Hartmann began courting Picasso in 1963, making several trips to the artist's home in the South of France. Eventually the artist agreed to the project, presenting his 50-foot, 162-ton Corten steel sculpture as a gift to the people of the City of Chicago in 1967. Hartmann also persuaded the artists Alexander Calder and Joan Miró to contribute works to other SOM buildings in the Midwest. He served on the boards of the Art Institute of Chicago and of the Illinois Institute of Technology and was elected to The American Institute of Architects' College of Fellows in 1963.

Judith Arango Henderson, 75

Judith Arango Henderson died July 12, 2003. Her unerring eye and enthusiasm for good design made her Miami store, Arango, internationally known and admired. She and her first husband, architect Jorge Arango, opened the eponymous Arango in 1959 next to Miami's art-house movie theater. Though it moved in the mid-1960s to the new Dadeland Mall, the store's consummate adherence to an aesthetic of functional, non-trendy design has remained unwavering for nearly 45 years. From Finnish glass and flatware to Italian lighting, Arango continues to stock classic modern furniture and accessories. A graduate of Wellesley College, Henderson organized the Arango Design Foundation in 1977 to exhibit themed work by both famous and unknown designers. The Foundation sponsors an annual design award program and, in 1998, instituted the annual Design and Architecture Day.

Donald C. Hensman, 78

Donald Hensman, FAIA, one of the original Case Study Program architects, died December 9, 2002. The designer of hundreds of contemporary homes in and around Los Angeles, Hensman was a modernist with a risk-taking approach to architecture. This made him ideal for inclusion in the Case Study Program, sponsored by *Arts & Architecture* magazine to spur design of modern, affordable houses following World War II. Hensman designed two homes in the Program, No. 20 and No. 28. Other Program architects included Charles and Ray Eames, Pierre Koenig, Richard Neutra, Eero Saarinen, and Craig Ellwood. Hensman spent many years in collaboration with architects Conrad Buff III and, later, Calvin C. Straub. He and Buff were partners in the firm Buff Smith & Hensman and had attended the University of Southern California together. While students there, the pair designed more than 600 tract and model homes near Long Beach. Hensman went on to teach at USC with Buff where their students included Frank Gehry and Jon Jerde.

Benjamin H. Janda, 82

Chicago contractor Benjamin H. Janda died January 28, 2003. His company, B.H. Janda Construction, helped build Chicago's CNA Building, John Hancock Center, and the Ferguson Wing of the Art Institute of Chicago. His company was the sole contractor on the construction of the administrative offices of United Airlines, AT&T, and Ameritech, all in Chicago, and it built the award-winning Jardine Water Purification Plant near Chicago's Navy Pier. Janda received a degree in civil engineering from the University of Illinois at Urbana-Champaign.

Richard "Peter" Norman Johnson, 79

Australian architect and educator Richard "Peter" Norman Johnson died in May 2003. He was a past president of the Royal Australian Institute of Architects and head of the school of architecture at the University of Sydney from 1968–1986. He then spent 10 years, from 1988–1998, as chancellor at the University of Technology, Sydney. Following graduation from

Richard "Peter" Norman Johnson, 79

the University of Sydney, Johnson formed the partnership of McConnel Smith and Johnson, designers of many prominent public buildings in Sydney, including the Law Courts, Queens Square, the Sydney Water Board headquarters, and the University of Sydney's law school and faculty of architecture buildings. In 1964, Johnson's own home received the Wilkinson award for excellence in domestic architecture. He was a 1985 recipient of the Royal Australian Institute of Architects' Gold Medal.

Thomas W. Kellogg, 71

Industrial designer Thomas Kellogg, most famous for his work on the Avanti sports car under Raymond Loewy, died August 14, 2003. Kellogg had an opportunity to show his work to Loewy when he visited the Art Center College of Design in Pasadena, Calif. A 1955 graduate of the school, Kellogg was called upon to work on the Avanti design as a member of a three-man team that included John Ebstein and Robert Andrews, under Loewy's direction. Their mandate was a heady one: to design a sports car that would compete with the Ford Thunderbird and right the financially ailing Studebaker-Packard Corporation, and have the car be ready in one year. The designers, working from a rented Palm Springs home, produced a model of the car within two weeks and the Avanti debuted at the New York Auto Show in April 1962 to great acclaim. It was not, however, enough to save Studebaker, which closed its last plant in 1966. The popularity of the sculptural coupe continues, however, and collectors and car clubs often invited Kellogg to speak. During his career, he also worked on exterior designs for Rolls-Royce, Porsche, and recreational vehicles. He designed a line of dinnerware for Wedgewood and the shuttle craft for the original Star Trek television series.

William H. Kessler, 77

Called "the dean of Detroit's architectural community," by the Detroit Free Press, William H. Kessler, FAIA, died November 16, 2002. A consistent and unapologetic modernist, Kessler founded William Kessler and Associates in Detroit, Mich. (now Kessler Francis Cardoza) in the 1950s. Harvard educated and a one-time collaborator with Walter Gropius and Minoru Yamasaki, he began designing modernist houses around the city. His work peaked in the 1970s with designs for the Detroit Receiving Hospital, the original Detroit Science Center, and the College for Creative Studies (Detroit). In the late 1990s, Kessler designed the Delphi Automotive Systems World Headquarters in Troy, Mich. An outspoken advocate of human-scale design, Kessler was awarded the Gold Medal from The American Institute of Architect's Michigan chapter, among many honors.

Vlastimil Koubek, 75

Noted Washington, D.C.-based architect Vlastimil Koubek died February 15, 2003. He designed many notable projects in and around the nation's capital, including the headquarters of the National Bank of Washington, American Security Bank, Union Labor Life Insurance Co., American Automobile Association, and U.S. Postal Service. His nearly 100 office, hotel, and multi-family housing projects earned him a designation by Washingtonian magazine in 1985 as one of 20 notable Washingtonians "who in the past 20 years had the greatest impact on the way we live and who forever altered the look of Washington." Koubek was the lead architect for L'Enfant Plaza's east building, the International Square building, and the renovation of the Willard Inter-Continental hotel and office building in the mid-1980s. He also designed Baltimore's 40-story U.S. Fidelity and Guaranty Life Insurance Co. headquarters, as well as the Richmond, Va., headquarters for Virginia Electric and Power Co. A native of Czechoslovakia, Koubek came to the U.S. in 1952 and opened his own firm, Koubek Architects, in Washington in 1957.

Denis Lawrence Kurutz, 61

Award-winning landscape architect Denis L. Kurutz died February 12, 2003. He re-created the gardens of a Roman villa destroyed by the eruption of Mt. Vesuvius in AD 79 for the original J. Paul Getty Museum in Malibu, Calif. His meticulous research for the project ranged from travels to Italy to study native plants to examination of a fresco from the garden room of the villa Livia Drusilla, the wife of Emperor Augustus, housed in the National Museum of Rome. He also studied the writings of historian Pliny the Younger and of pharmacologist Pedanius Dioscorides, both of whom kept detailed notes on plants and gardens of the period. When the Getty Villa opened in 1974, Kurutz and his firm, Emmet L. Wemple and Associates of Los Angeles, received a national landscape award for their work. As vice president of the firm, he led the 1987 landscaping of the Getty Museum in Brentwood, Calif. His other projects included the U.S. Embassy in Japan, the King Fahad National Park in Saudi Arabia, and the MGM Grand Hotel in Las Vegas. He formed his own firm in the late 1980s, Denis L. Kurutz and Associates. Kurutz received awards from the American Society of Landscape Architects for his work on several projects, including the restoration of the historic Workman-Temple Homestead in City of Industry, Calif., the Einstein estate in Brentwood, Calif., and Camp Snoopy for the Mall of America in Minnesota.

Samuel Jackson LeFrak, 85

New York City developer and champion of middle-income housing, Samuel LeFrak, died April 16, 2003. LeFrak assumed leadership of the family business, the Lefrak Organization, a private building firm, in 1948. LeFrak is known for his commitment to affordable housing and responsible community development. Well-known projects include Lefrak City in Queens, home to 15,000 residents, built on 40 acres of the former William Waldorf Astor estate. The company is also responsible for the ongoing Newport development on the Hudson River in Jersey City, N.J. Upon completion, the $10 billion residential and commercial project is expected to house 35,000 people. In the 1980s Lefrak built 1,800 apartments at Gateway Plaza in Manhattan's Battery Park City. Other projects include University Gardens in Flushing, Queens; College Park in Rego Park, Queens: and the Hollywood Park in Sheepshead Bay, Brooklyn. Samuel LeFrak spelled his name differently than his father and grandfather, adopting the spelling common in the family's native country of France.

Chester Lindsey, 76

Chester Lindsey, designer of Seattle's tallest building, died August 16, 2002. Then known as the Columbia Seafirst Center, the 76-story Bank of America Center was completed in 1984 and is currently ranked number 32 by the Council on Tall Buildings and Urban Habitats. Lindsey, whose firm Chester Lindsey Architects mentored many of Seattle's prominent architects, also designed many other significant projects in and around the city. With developer Martin Selig, he planned nearly a dozen shopping centers. He also designed office buildings on lower Queen Anne Hill and high-rises at Fourth and Vine, Fourth and Blanchard, and Fourth and Battery streets.

Robert Macleod, 70

Architect and author Robert Macleod died in March 2003. He was raised in Vancouver, Canada but spent much of his career in England. As a teacher and author, he espoused a theory of moral architecture that had as its goals fine craftsmanship and usefulness, much like the arts and crafts movement. He was the author of *Charles Rennie Mackintosh Architect* in 1968 and Style and Society in 1971. In England, Macleod worked for the London firm of Howell, Killick, Partridge & Amis before embarking on a teaching career. He held teaching positions at Cambridge University, the Institute of Advanced Architectural Studies, Bristol University, and the then Brighton Polytechnic in the U.K. In Canada, he had been the head of the school of architecture at the University of British Columbia from 1974–1979.

Lane Marshall, 65

Former dean of the Kansas State University College of Architecture and Design, Lane Marshall, FASLA, died in June 2003. He also served as president of the American Society of Landscape Architects from 1978 to 1980 and received the ASLA President's Medal in 1981. Marshall practiced landscape architecture in Florida for 20 years before he returned to school and received a MLA from the University of Illinois. He then became head of the department of landscape architecture at Texas A&M University from 1981 to 1988. He joined Kansas State in 1989 and served as dean until 1995. From 1996 until his death, Marshall was a member of the school's landscape architecture faculty. He received the first Distinguished Alumnus Award from the department of landscape architecture at the University of Florida, his undergraduate alma mater.

Philip J. Meathe, 76

Former chairman and CEO of the SmithGroup, Philip Meathe, FAIA, died September 17, 2002. Meathe joined the Detroit-based architecture firm, formerly known as Smith, Hinchman & Grylls, in 1969 as executive vice president. He became president in 1971 and chairman and chief executive in 1974, a position which he held until his retirement in 1992. Under his leadership, SmithGroup designed the Kmart Corporation headquarters in Troy, Mich., and the Central Intelligence Agency headquarters expansion in Langley, Va., among many other high profile projects. Meathe had previously worked for Leinweber, Yamasaki and Hellmuth of Detroit and then as a partner in Meathe, Kessler & Associates. His many awards included the Gold Medal from The American Institute of Architects' Detroit chapter in 1967, a Gold Medal from the Michigan Society of Architects in 1969, and the University of Michigan Architecture & Urban Planning Alumni Society Award for Distinguished Service.

Doug Michels, 59

Architect and installation designer Doug Michels died June 12, 2003, while climbing to a whale observation point near Sydney, Australia, where he was consulting on a movie about whales. Michels may be best known for the 1974 "Cadillac Ranch" public art piece in Texas, which was conceived of by Ant Farm, a counterculture art collective he cofounded. With its array of 10 vintage Cadillacs buried nose down, fins up, along Route 66, Cadillac Ranch has become world famous. A 1967 graduate of the Yale University School of Architecture, Michels founded Ant Farm in San Francisco with partners Chip Lord, Hudson Marquez, and Curtis Schreirer. The group's other projects include the American Culture Time Capsule exhibition for the 1969 Paris Biennale; 1972s House of the Century, a "visionary homespace" in Texas; and the 1975 Media Burn media presentation. The group eventually disbanded in 1978, and Michels became a senior designer for Philip Johnson from 1979–1982. In 1988, Michels established his own firm, Doug Michels Studio. Working for an array of clients, Michels' lengthy list of design projects included physical structures, monuments, multimedia presentations, nightclubs, museums, toys, and fashion products. In 1999, he directed the University of Houston's architecture college FutureLab design studio for a year. He had also held teaching positions through the years at Rice University, Texas A&M University, and the University of California.

Tanya Moiseiwitsch, 88

Tanya Moiseiwitsch, a theater designer who revolutionized the shape of modern theater stages, died February 18, 2003. She had an established career in Europe before designing a stage for the Stratford Festival of Canada that deviated from the traditional proscenium-arch or "picture frame" theater, returning to the "thrust" style stage on which Shakespeare's own company played. Her 1953 design has been widely imitated, transforming the look of theater stages in the United States, Canada, and Europe. She created her own variations on the design for the Guthrie Theater in Minneapolis and the Crucible Theatre in England. A designer of sets and costumes, Moiseiwitsch worked on more than 40 Stratford Festival productions, as well as for the Royal Shakespeare Company, the National Theatre in England,

Tanya Moiseiwitsch, 88

the Metropolitan Opera, London's West End, and many others. She was awarded honorary doctorates for her work by the University of Toronto in 1988 and the University of Minnesota in 1994. She had also recently been named an Honorary Officer of the Order of Canada.

Jennifer Moulton, 53

Denver, Colorado's longtime planning director, Jennifer Moulton, FAIA, died July 28, 2003. She was hand-picked in 1992 by then Denver Mayor Wellington Webb for the job. At news of Moulton's passing, he told the Denver Post, "I had the best planning director in the country." After earning an architecture degree from the University of Colorado at Denver, Moulton focused her career on historic renovation. She served from 1989–1992 as president of Historic Denver Inc., a group dedicated to preserving Denver's historic architecture. As planning director, she directed Denver's redevelopment of the Central Platte Valley, Stapleton Airport, and Lowry Air Force Base. Moulton was Mayor Webb's inspiration for committing to downtown redevelopment. He named her to lead the newly consolidated Community Planning and Development Agency in 1998. A leading voice for the selection of marquee architect Daniel Libeskind to design the new wing of the Denver Art Museum, Moulton advocated good design in all urban architecture and worked to save relatively unpopular but significant modern architecture in the city.

Charles Morris Mount, 60

Restaurant designer Charles Morris Mount, an Alabama native who built his career in Manhattan, died November 18, 2002. He worked briefly in New York for furniture designer George Nelson before opening his own firm in the early 1970s. Known for dramatic looks and pragmatic approaches to his projects, Mount designed over 300 restaurants, including Manhattan's Gloucester House, the American Café chain, Bistro Bistro restaurants, and, most recently, the largest McDonald's in the United States. The 17,500 sq. ft. McDonald's near Times Square features real theatrical lighting, plasma televisions, and Broadway memorabilia.

Sen. Daniel Patrick Moynihan, 76

Former U.S. senator, ambassador, and educator Daniel Patrick Moynihan died March 26, 2003. A tireless advocate for architecture, Moynihan is credited with tenaciously promoting the relationship between government buildings and good design. During his 40-year tenure as a public servant, he led the redesign of Washington, D.C.'s Pennsylvania Avenue between the Capitol and the White House. In New York, he spearheaded the effort to move Penn Station into the former James A. Farley Post Office Building, a project scheduled for completion in 2008. Immediately upon his death, officials announced the new transportation hub would be named the Daniel Patrick Moynihan Station. Though best known as a four-term Democratic senator, Moynihan began his political career in 1953, working on the mayoral campaign of New York's Robert F. Wagner. He received a Ph.D. in international relations from Syracuse University in 1961, and moved to Washington to join the Labor Department. Early in his career as assistant labor secretary, Moynihan authored "Guiding Principles of Federal Architecture." This document was the forerunner to the U.S. General Service Administration's Design Excellence program, and for 40 years it helped shape government design policy. Moynihan was first elected to the U.S. Senate from New York in 1976. A former Fullbright Scholar, Sen. Moynihan used his power to save historic buildings and influence the course of new buildings. His work on Pennsylvania Avenue culminated in the 1996 completion of the Washington's Federal Triangle with Pei Cobb Freed's Ronald Reagan Building and International Trade Center. In New York City he was instrumental in restoring the U.S. Customs House in Battery Park City. In Buffalo, N.Y., he saved Louis Sullivan's 1896 Guaranty Building and then moved his upstate headquarters into the building. The American Institute of Architects named him an honorary member in 1984 and in 1992 bestowed their first Thomas Jefferson Award, which honors champions of public architecture, to him along with George White and James Ingo Freed.

Courtland Paul, 75

California landscape architect Courtland Paul, FASLA, died January 28, 2003. One of California's first licensed landscape architects, he founded a landscape architecture firm now called the Peridian Group, more than 50 years ago in Newport Beach, Calif. Their projects include the Euro Disney theme park as well as scores of golf courses, hotels, and planned communities in Southern California. In 1955 he was a founding member of the American Institute of Landscape Architects and served as its director for five years. He had also been president of the California Council of Landscape Architects and served four years on the state's Board of Landscape Architects. Infamous for his saddle shoes and ever-present bow tie, Paul was an innovator in his field. In the 1970s, his concept for hillside development in Newport Beach's Harbor Ridge community prompted most California cities to revise their grading ordinances.

George Clayton Pearl, 79

Though not a native of New Mexico, architect George Clayton Pearl, FAIA, adopted it as his home and his muse. His designs are a blend of traditional pueblo-style vernacular architecture and modernism. His preservation work around Albuquerque was also extensive. He died August 16, 2003. Pearl moved to Albuquerque from Texas in 1949 and spent his 40-plus year career as the principal designer for Stevens Mallory Pearl & Campbell, now known as SMPC Architects. His design for the Albuquerque Civic Auditorium drew praise from Frank Lloyd Wright during a 1956 visit. He also designed the Albuquerque Public Library, the library and National Radio Astronomy Observatory on the New Mexico Tech campus in Socorro, the Simms Fine Arts Center at Albuquerque Academy, and the theater and college of business building at Eastern New Mexico University in Portales. A dedicated preservationist, Pearl was a founding member and served on the boards of the New Mexico Heritage Preservation Alliance and the Albuquerque Conservation Association. He also served on the Albuquerque Landmarks and Urban Conservation Commission board.

John L. Petrarca, 51

New York architect John Petrarca died May 9, 2003. Petrarca has received attention recently for his work designing and developing the first spec townhouses in lower Manhattan in 150 years. A leading advocate of low-toxic, environmentally sound design, his five Tribeca homes also pioneered the use of geothermal heating and cooling in the city. These houses have been detailed in many media outlets, including *The New York Times* and *Dwell* magazine. The five-story, 7,000+ sq. ft. townhomes were developed on lots around Petrarca's longtime home in Tribeca. One of the five was designed for his own family. In addition to geothermal HVAC systems that draw on a 1,250-foot-deep well, the houses featured foot-thick insulated concrete walls to reduce noise, air purifiers, and non-toxic finishes. Petrarca joined Gwathmey Siegel & Associates in New York in 1981 and in 1984 formed Architecture Plus Furniture. With Robin Guenther he formed the firm Guenther Petrarca in 1991, and in 2001 he established his own practice, Studio Petrarca, on the ground floor of his house. During his career, Petrarca's other projects ranged from MTV's Times Square offices to intensive care units for Columbia Presbyterian Hospital to the residential conversion of the Franklin Tower office building in lower Manhattan.

Eleanore Pettersen, 86

Eleanore Pettersen, FAIA, one of the first practicing female architects in New Jersey and a former apprentice of Frank Lloyd Wright, died January 15, 2003. Licensed to practice in 1950, Pettersen was the first woman in the New Jersey to open her own firm. She was also the first woman to serve as president and regional director of The American Institute of Architects' New Jersey chapter and as president of the New Jersey State Board of Architects. Though she designed both commercial and residential buildings, her best-known project is a house which became the post-presidency home of Richard Nixon. The 15-room house in Saddle River, N.J., complete with tennis court and swimming pool, was originally designed in 1971 for businessman John Alford, who sold it to the former president in 1981. Following graduation from Cooper Union in 1941, Pettersen apprenticed for Wright in Arizona and Wisconsin until joining the Tennessee Valley Authority in 1946.

Abel "John Henry" Brown Pierce Jr., 93

Houston architect and artist Abel "John Henry" Brown Pierce Jr. died July 3, 2003. In addition to helping design some of Houston's signature buildings, Pierce was an accomplished watercolorist whose work was exhibited at the Rice Institute, the Houston Museum of Fine Art, and the Art League of Houston. A graduate of the University of Pennsylvania, Pierce helped design ships during World War II, including the craft used in the Normandy landing. With George F. Pierce, no relation, he started the practice Pierce and Pierce. Their many Houston projects included the master plan and two terminal buildings at Bush International Airport, six buildings on the campus at Rice University, and the Houston Museum of Natural Science. Before the war, he worked for Nunn and McGinty Architects in Houston and helped design the River Oaks Shopping Center and the Cuney Homes and Kelley Courts housing projects.

Sir Philip Powell, 82

British architect Sir Philip Powell, who founded a leading U.K. architectural partnership with Hidalgo Moya in 1946, died May 5, 2003. In 1974, Powell and Moya were presented the Royal Institute of British Architects' Gold Medal; in 1975 Philip was knighted; and in 1984 he was the first architect to be appointed a Companion of Honour. The first commission Philip and Moya completed was for a housing estate at Churchill Gardens on the north bank of the Thames. Like most of their projects, this was a modern design that drew both lavish praise and blunt criticism. Years later, seated next to then Prime Minister Margaret Thatcher at a dinner, Powell recalled that she was quite vocal in her dislike for his firm's design of the modern Queen Elizabeth Conference Hall opposite Westminster Abbey. This didn't stop Powell and Moya from completing a number of noteworthy projects during their career, including the Skylon tower for the 1951 Festival of Britain, the Princess Margaret Hospital in Swindon, and the Mayfield School in Putney. They also designed undergraduate dormitories for Brasenose College, Oxford University, and the Festival Theatre at Chinchester, a hexagonal building featuring an apron stage, where seats are arranged on three sides of the auditorium. Many commissions followed, including Sir Philip's favorite, the Christ Church Picture Gallery (Oxford), sunk into a garden so the height of the building is even with that of the garden wall. They also designed the futuristic Expo '70 British Pavilion in Osaka, Japan.

Cedric John Price, 68

British designer and architectural theorist Cedric Price died August 10, 2003. Though most of his concepts were never built, his theories influenced a generation of architects including Norman Foster, Will Alsop, Archigram, and especially Richard Rogers and Renzo Piano in their design for the Pompidou Centre in Paris. A socialist who believed in function-specific, temporary architecture that served all classes equally, Price envisioned structures that could be changed, reconfigured, or demolished to suit a present need. He was the only architect to be a fully qualified member of the National Institute of Demolition Contractors. He once persuaded English Heritage not to list one of his built projects, preferring instead that it be torn down so something more appropriate could be constructed in its place. The best known of his built projects is the aviary at the London Zoo; its modern mesh and steel girder architecture is still fresh today. During his career he also proposed a Pop-up Parliament to replace the Houses of Parliament.

Harvey Probber, 80

Mid-century modern furniture designer Harvey Probber died February 16, 2003. In a 1958 interview, Probber articulated the "quality of aging gracefully" as "design's fourth dimension." His own elegant designs have enjoyed a recent resurgence in popularity as collectors now seek his work along with that of contemporaries such as Charles and Ray Eames, Paul McCobb, George Nelson, and T.H. Robsjohn-Gibbings. Largely self-taught, Probber sold his first design before finishing high school. He learned furniture production while working at Trade Upholstery in New York, and formed his own company, Harvey Probber Inc., in 1945. He pioneered the design of modular seating in the 1940s and continued to manufacture his own designs through 1986, when he closed his manufacturing business. Probber's designs were based in modernism though he augmented pieces with decorative elements and/or bright colors, believing the severity of academic modernism would fail to hold his customers' interest.

Else Regensteiner, 96

Modernist textile innovator Else Regensteiner died January 18, 2003. A native of Munich, Germany, Regensteiner studied at the University of Munich and was an accomplished textile artist by the time she emigrated to the United States with her husband in 1936. She was experimental and, with a creative eye for color and materials, adapted the Bauhaus aesthetic to her design and weaving. She joined the staff of The School of the Art Institute of Chicago in 1945 and was a professor there for more than 25 years. Around the time the joined the school's faculty she also formed reg/wick with Julia McVicker. The small textiles studio supplied commissioned fabric to interior designers, architects, and industrial designers such as Raymond Loewy, Ludwig Mies van der Rohe, and Henry Glass. Her work has been included in more than 75 solo and group exhibitions.

Willard G. Rouse III, 60

Willard Goldsmith Rouse III, founder and former CEO of Liberty Property Trust, one of the largest real estate property trusts in the United States, died May 27, 2003. Though his father and uncle founded the Rouse Company and developed Boston's Faneuil Hall Marketplace and Manhattan's South Street Seaport, among other shopping malls, the younger Rouse elected not to join the family business. He graduated from the University of Virginia in 1966 with a degree in English before joining the Great Southwest Corporation of Texas. In 1972 he and three associates formed the development company Rouse & Associates. In the mid-1990s, the company reorganized into Liberty Property Trust, an REIT which the New York Times reported in May 2003 was one of the country's 20 largest public real estate businesses. "As of the first of the year [2003] it owned 652 properties, with more than 50 million square feet of industrial and office space," said the Times. In May 2002, Rouse commissioned Robert A.M. Stern to design an office building in Philadelphia called 1 Pennsylvania Plaza. The new $360 million building will have 1.23 million square feet of rentable space.

Nancy Halverson Schless

Nancy Halverson Schless, architectural historian, author, and educator, died November 6, 2002. She was a former member of the board of directors of the Society of Architectural Historian and endowed the Harry Halverson Memorial Lectureship in American Architecture in the Art Department at Wellesley College. The fellowship was named for her father, who had been an architect. Schless was a past president of the Philadelphia Chapter of the SAH, and an avid researcher and writer, especially on the topics of Anglo-American Neo-Classicism and the work of Philadelphia's William Strickland. She gave the first William Strickland Memorial Lecture at the Athenaeum of Philadelphia in 1988. Among her noted writings were pieces on the Governor's Palace at Williamsburg (JSAH, 1969) and the Touro Synagogue at Newport (Winterthur Portfolio, 1973).

William M. Schoenfeld, 78

William M. Schoenfeld, the former head of Los Angeles International Airport's architecture, planning, and engineering for nearly 25 years, died January 11, 2003. As a former deputy executive of Los Angeles World Airports, Schoenfeld directed the transformation of the airport in the late 1970s and early 1980s into what was dubbed "The New LAX." The effort, designed to accommodate an unprecedented increase in air passengers, included the building of the Tom Bradley International Terminal, domestic Terminal 1, the second level for the central terminal roadway, four new parking structures, and several air cargo terminals. For these projects, Schoenfeld was awarded the Distinguished Community Service Achievement Award from the Institute for the Advancement of Engineering in 1989. Following his graduation from the University of Southern California School of Architecture in 1950, he served three years on the school's faculty before joining the Southern California architectural and engineering firm Charles Luckman Associates. While there, Schoenfeld directed the planning and construction of military facilities in Spain, arenas, shopping centers, and many airline terminal facilities at LAX. He joined the then Los Angeles Department of Airports in 1970, retiring in 1994.

Harwood Knox Smith, 89

HKS Inc, founder Harwood Knox Smith, FAIA, died December 8, 2002. During his lifetime, he built his one-man Dallas firm into one of the largest in the United States, with currently over 500 architects and projects in 35 states and abroad. A graduate of what is now Texas A&M University, Smith began practicing in 1939 with a focus on residential projects, eventually diversifying into education, industrial, banking, and healthcare. HKS designs include many Texas landmarks such as the Texas Scottish Rite Hospital for Children (Dallas), the School of Architecture building at Texas A&M University (College Station), and Moody Coliseum at Southern Methodist University (Dallas). Smith served as a president of Dallas chapter of The American Institute of Architects in 1972 and chairman of the Dallas Planning Commission. He received a Dallas AIA Lifetime Achievement Award and a national AIA presidential citation. He was elected to the AIA College of Fellows in 1984. An accomplished painter, Smith's work has been exhibited nationwide.

Peter Denham Smithson, 79

British architect Peter Smithson died March 3, 2003. Along with his late wife and architectural partner Alison Smithson, Peter Smithson wrote, taught, and designed, espousing an approach to architecture around promoting social interaction. The Smithsons are best known not only for the success of some of their commissions but for the failure of one major project, the Robin Hood Gardens housing project in east London. With its poured concrete walls and balconies spaced to simulate a socially successful street pattern, the 214-unit project produced complaints from tenants at 20 times the normal rate for the Greater London Council who built it, mostly from water leakage and burglary. Because Smithson wrote and lectured with so much enthusiasm on the social mission of architecture, the failure of this project marred what is largely considered to be a career of influence and distinction. One of the Smithson's first commissions came in 1949 for the Hunstanton School in Norfolk. Widely acclaimed as England's first example of Brutalist design, the secondary school launched the couple's career. Perhaps their best-known building is the Economist building in London, comprised of three buildings centered on a

Peter Denham Smithson, 79

pedestrian piazza. Containing a bank, apartments, and the offices of the *Economist* magazine, the 1964 project was well received at the time and is aging gracefully. Smithson was a visiting professor at Bath University from 1978–1990; during the 1980s, the school commissioned five buildings from the architect. Together, the Smithsons were published widely, including the collection Changing the Art of Inhabitation (1999). Following the death of his wife in 1993, Smithson continued to lecture and write, completing *The Charged Void: Architecture* (2002) shortly before his death.

Whitney Snow Stoddard, 90

Architectural historian Whitney Snow Stoddard died April 2, 2003. A longtime member of the Williams College faculty, he was the Amos Lawrence Professor of Art Emeritus as well as an accomplished researcher and author. His primary areas of interest were modern and medieval sculpture and architecture. He found many common denominators between works of the two periods–mostly in the power of form as the main tenet of design. His books include *The West Portals of Saint-Denis and Chartres*, published in 1952 by Harvard University Press; *Adventure in Architecture*, published in 1958 by Wesleyan University Press; and *Monastery and Cathedral in France*, published in 1966 by Wesleyan University Press. The later was the work that established him as a preeminent scholar and historian. In addition to writing, in 1970 Stoddard initiated and directed the excavation of the monastery at Psalmodi in southern France, which has continued for over three decades. He was a member of the editorial board of the 1982 Macmillan Encyclopedia of Architects and was a founding member of the International Center of Medieval Art.

John Storrs, 83

Credited with defining and practicing a strictly Northwestern U.S. style of regional architecture, John Storrs died August 31, 2003. He designed Oregon's Salishan Lodge (Gleneden Beach), described by The Oregonian newspaper as "one of the state's most enduring architectural icons." His body of work includes many symbols of Northwestern culture, including the World Forestry Center, Catlin Gabel School, and the Oregon College of Art & Craft, all in Portland. Inspired by a lecture by Portland architect Pietro Belluschi, Storrs moved to Oregon after he finished his master of architecture degree work at Yale University. His first commission, a modernist home for the Portland Garden Club, led to commissions for more than 80 homes as well as commercial projects. His other works include the 1959 Forestry Pavilion for the Oregon Centennial (destroyed by a storm in 1962), Lakeridge High School in Lake Oswego, Sokol-Blosser Winery (Dundee), and Congregation Ahavath Achim (Portland). A determined visionary, Storrs often worked on site with few drawings. During the construction of Salishan, he slept in a tent on-site. On many of his projects, including Salishan, he worked with developer John Gray and landscape architect Barbara Fealy.

Dennis Strah, 57

Colorado landscape architect Dennis Strah died in July 2003. He was the national director of federal recreation for HNTB Corporation. Before joining that firm, Strah had been co-owner of the Landplan Design Group and a senior landscape architect and team captain in the National Park Service. While with the Park Service, Strah worked on The Comprehensive Design Plan for the White House and President's Park in Washington, D.C.; Sitka Gateway Community Planning in Sitka, Alaska; and Timucuan Ecological and Historic Preserve in Jacksonville, Florida, among many projects.

Frank Weise, 84

Philadelphia architect and activist Frank Weise died January 31, 2003. A designer of clean, modern rowhouses, he helped define the look of the city. He also led the fight to place Interstate 95 below ground in front of Penn's Landing in an effort to boost the waterfront development's potential. An elevated highway had been planned for the area, so Weise organized a group of architects and citizens into the Gateway Committee and produced a detailed plan for burying a stretch of the road, ultimately persuading federal officials. Weise designed dozens of houses in Washington Square West, Rittenhouse Square, Fairmount, Roxborough, and Philadelphia's suburbs. Though his rowhouses had a mid-century modern façade, Weise disliked flat surfaces, so his homes contain many curving walls and arches. His designs were renowned for the way they blended seamlessly with their surroundings. Weise also won national acclaim for his work renovating Head House Square.

Ira Yellin, 62

A champion of downtown Los Angeles, civic leader, and attorney Ira Yellin was credited for much of that city's improvement. He died in September 2002. Yellin left a successful career as a lawyer and real estate developer to concentrate on revitalizing historic downtown Los Angeles. While he is best known for his restoration of Grand Central Market, Yellin and a group of investors also bought and restored the landmark Bradbury Building, the Million Dollar Theater, and the old Metropolitan Water District headquarters, among others. He also led the restoration of L.A.'s Union Station. With business partner Dan Rosenfeld, Yellin had recently led the effort to bring quality new architecture to Los Angeles. He encouraged Cardinal Roger M. Mahony to launch an international competition to select an architect for the design of the new Cathedral of Our Lady of the Angels, which was designed by Rafael Moneo. His firm also worked with Morphosis and Arquitectonica on commercial and mixed-use projects. Nicolai Ouroussoff, architecture critic of the Los Angeles Times, wrote of Yellin, "...his stubborn desire to push his work beyond the boundaries of conventional development was an invaluable asset in the struggle over the city's urban future."

Abraham Zabludovsky, 78

Mexican modernist architect Abraham Zabludovsky died April 9, 2003. He designed and built more than 200 buildings. His most famous works include a renovation of the National Auditorium, the design of the Rufino Tamayo Museum, the National Education University, and the Mexican Library, all in Mexico City. He also designed the Mexican Embassy in Brasilia, Brazil. A native of Poland, Zabludovsky moved to Mexico City as a young child and became a naturalized Mexican citizen in 1941. He was a recipient of the Mexican National Arts Prize in 1982 and also the gold medal at the World Architecture Biennial in Sofia, Bulgaria.

Name Index

NOTE: Pages in italics refer to illustrations. Please see the Site Index on page 711 for architectural projects, sites and works.

A

Name Index

Architectural Photography Competition, 78–79
Architectural Record, 104, 600
Architectural Review, 81, 603
Architectural Woodwork Institute, 576
Architecture, 159, 600
Architecture Australia, 603
l'Architecture d'Aujourd'hui, 603
Architecture Firm Award, 35–37, 80
Architecture Institute of Japan, 586
Architecture One Ltd., 631
Architecture Plus Furniture, 648
Architecture Resource Center, 67
Architektur Zentrum Wien, 606
Architekturmuseum Basel, 606
Archivia: The Decorative Arts Bookshop, 592
ArchVoices Essay Competition, 13, 508
ARCON Associates, 312
ar+d award, 81–83, *82*
Ardiles-Arce, Jaime, 288
Arehart, Robert A., 261
Arencibia, Manuel, 509
Arendt/Mosher/Grants Architects, 353
Arfaa, Peter F., 232
Argo, George Haviland, III, 538
Argosy Bookstore, 592
Arguelles, Carlos D., 277
Arizona Republic, 215
Arizona State University
  degree programs, 517, 532, 533
  rankings, 554, 555
  staff, 295, 495, 496, 498, 541
  students/alumni, 502, 511, 513, 535
Arkin Tilt Architects, 422
Arkitektur, 603
Armajani, Siah, 66
Armbruster, David S., 264
Armour Institue. *See* Illinois Institute of Technology
Armstrong, Eric, 222
Armstrong, Kevin Michael, 540
Armstrong Workd Industries, 271
Arnaiz, Carlos, 502
Arnaud, Leopold, 294
Arneill, Bruce P., 232
Arnett, Warren G., 261
Arnold, C. Adrian, 227
Arnold, Chris, 232
Arnold, Christopher C., 232
Arnold, Henry F., 264
Arnold, Philip J., 284
Arnold W. Brunner Memorial Prize, 84, *85*
Arnott, Gordon R., 277, 300
Aron, Trudy, 280
Arons, Dan, 399
Aronson, Joseph H., 223
Arquitectonica, 363, 371, 389, 656
Arrigoni, Robert V., 232
Ars Libri, 592
Art Center College of Design, 517, 541, 639
Art Conservation Associates, 120
Art Haus Books, Inc., 591
Art Insititute of Chicago, 385
Art Institute of Atlanta, 520
Art Institute of Chicago, 66, 391, 519, 521, 606, 651
Art Institute of Fort Lauderdale, 520
Artech Design Group, 399
Arthur, Eric R., 169
Arthur Q. Davis, FAIA & Partners, 363
Artunc, Sadik C., 264
Arup, 113, 632
Arup, Ove, 177
ASFE, 576
Asher-Stubbins, Hugh, 225
Ashley, J. Tom, III, 232
Ashley, Ludd, 280
Ashley, Roy O., 264
Ashton, Raymond J., 291
Ashton Raggatt McDougall Pty Ltd., 138
Ashworth, Henry Ingham, 301
ASID ICON, 600
Asken, Yvonne W., 232
Askew, Laurin B., 232
Askew, Lee Hewlett, III, 232
Askew, Nixon, Ferguson & Wolf, 349
ASLA Design Medal, 86, *87*
ASLA Firm Award, 88, *89*
ASLA Medal, 90, *91*
ASLA National Student Design Competition, 509–511
ASLA Professional Awards, 92–95, *93*
Aslin, C. H., 302
Asphalt Roofing Manufacturers Association, 577
Aspinwall Clouston Pte. Ltd., 201
Assadi, Felipe, 83
Assmann, Christina, 540
Associated Builders & Contractors, 577
Associated General Contractors of America, 577
Associated Landscape Contractors of America, 577
Associated Owners & Developers, 577
Association for Contract Textiles, 577
Association for Facilities Engineering, 577
Association for Preservation Technology, 455
Association for the Advancement of Cost Engineering, 577
Association for the Preservation of Virginia Antiquities, 66, 452
Association of Bay Area Governments, 105
Association of Collegiate Schools of Architecture, 294–295, 495–497534
Association of Collegiate Schools of Planning, 534
Association of Energy Engineers, 577
Association of Higher Education Facilities Officers, 577
Association of Junior Leagues, 435
Association of the Wall & Ceiling Industries, 577
Astle, Neil L., 232
Astorino, Louis D., 232
ASYL Design Inc., 126
Atchison, Richard S., 538
Atelier Auburtin, 385
Atelier Seraji, 392
Aten, D. Lyle, 264
Athenaeum of Philadelphia, 514, 606
Atherton, Charles H., 232
Atherton, Katherine, 536
ATI Architects and Engineers, 327
Atkin, Tony, 232
Atkins, James B., 232
Atkins, John L., 232
Atkinson, Susan E., 511
Atlanta International Museum of Art and Design, 606
Atlanta Journal-Constitution, 215
Atterbury, Grosvenor, 351
Atwell, Tyson, 410
a+u magazine, 603
Aubock, Carl, 277
Aubry, Eugene E., 232
Auburn University, 420, 495, 502, 511, 517, 535, 554
Auerbach, Kathryn Ann, 514
Auerbach, Seymour, 232
Aufiero, Frederick G., 227
Augspurger, Quent, 227
Auguste Perret Prize, 96
Augustin Product Development, 129
Aul, Adriane R., 499
Aulenti, Gae(tana), 162, 345
Ausland Architects, 312
Austin, Donald B., 264
Austin, Don, 227
Austin, Douglas H., 232
Austin, Marsha, 77
Austin, Texas, 420
Austin American-Standard, 215
Austin Company, 341
Austin Veum Robbins Parshalle, 170
Austrian Frederick and Lillian Kiesler Private Foundation, 97
Austrian Frederick Kiesler Prize for Architecture and the Arts, 97
Available Light, 145
Avant Architects, 76
AVCA/Alberici Joint Venture, 155
Avchen, Daniel, 232
Avia, Robin Klehr, 274
Avin, Uri P., 257
Awes, Morten, 548
Axon, Donald C., 232
Axon, Janice, 280
Aydelott, Alfred L., 232
Ayers, Richard W., 220
Ayers/Saint/Gross, Architects & Planners, 326
Aymonino, Carlo, 277

B

B3 Architects, a Berkus Design Studio, 68
Babcock, William M., 280
Babey, Pamela, 287
Babitz, Mae, 623
Baca, Elmo, 223
Bach, Alfons, 272
Bachman, William, 219
Bachrach, Julia Sniderman, 95
Backen, Howard J., 232
Backman, Kenneth J., 264
Bacon, Edmond, 194, 257
Bacon, Edmund N., 64, 77, 188, 232, 334
Bacon, Henry, 59
Badanes, Steven Paul, 496
Baden, Nicole, 516
Badgeley, Clarence Dale, 220
Baer, David C., 110, 232
Baer, George, 286
Baer, Morley, 223
Baesel, Stuart, 232
Baetjer, E. Bruce, 222
Baft-e-Shahr Consulting Architects and Urban Planners, 57
Bahr, Deon F., 232
Baikdoosan Architects & Engineers, 378

Name Index

Beidler, Siriporn Junn, 537
Beijing Architectural Design & Research
Institute, 381
Beinecke, Walter, Jr., 435
Bektas, Cengiz, 57
Belcher, John, 175, 302
Bell, Byron, 233
Bell, Frederic, 233
Bell, James G., 227
Bell, James R., 257, 264
Bell, M. E., 374
Bell, M. Wayne, 233
Bell, Richard C., 222, 264
Bell, Theodore T., 227
Bell, Trent, 535
Bell and Kent, 375
Bellafiore, Vincent J., 264, 293
Belle, John, 233
Belluschi, Anthony, 233
Belluschi, Pietro
anecdote/quote, 388, 655
awards/honors, 59, 157, 194, 197, 353, 381
Belmont Technical College, 527
Belt, Lemman and Lo, 374
Belzner Holmes Architektur Licht Bühne, 145
Ben V. Mammina, Architect, 312
Bender, Ralph C., 233
Benedek, Armand, 264
Benefiel, Aaron Nathaniel, 537
Benepe, Barry, 233
Benes, W. Dominick, 347
Benjamin Thompson & Associates, 80
Bennet, H, 188
Bennett, Claire R., 264, 293
Bennett, Daniel D., 233
Bennett, David J., 233
Bennett, Edward H., 334
Bennett, Ralph, 496
Bennett, Stephen M., 280
Bennett, Ward, 65, 287, 624–625
Bennett, Wells, 294
Benoit, Gerard, 277
Benson, John, 64, 163
Benson, Sarah, 514
Bentel, Carol Rusche, 233
Bentel, Frederick R., 233
Bentel, Maria A., 233
Bentel, Paul Louis, 233
Bentel & Bentel, Architects/Planners, 62
Bentsen, Kenneth E., 233
Bentz, Frederick J., 233
Benya Lighting Design, 147
Benyrus, Janine, 31
Beranek, Leo L., 280
Berenson, Bertram, 294
Bereuter, Hon. Douglas, 284
Berg, Karl A., 233
Berg, Raymond, 168, 301
Berg, Shary Page, 264
Bergdoll, Barry, 160
Bergen Record, 215
Bergman, Elaine, 280
Bergman, Teree L., 257
Bergmann, Paul A., 257
Bergmann, Richard R., 233
Bergquist, Lloyd F., 233
Bergson, Maria, 287
Bergstedt, Milton V., 205
Bergstrom, Edwin, 291
Berke, Deborah, 287
Berkebile, Robert J., 233, 271
Berkeley College, 525
Berkeley Prize, 45–48, 513
Berkoff, Marlene J., 233
Berlage, Hendrik Petrus, 177
Bernard, Virginia, 513
Bernard Tschumi Architects, 60
Berners, Edgar H., 299
Berners/Schober Associates, Inc., 341
Bernhardt, Richard C., 257
Bernheim, Anthony N., 233
Bernstein, Phillip, 233, 271
Berry, Barbara, 287
Berry, Frank Lee, 261
Berry, K. Norman, 233
Berry, Karl, 264
Bertman, Richard J., 233
Bertone, Ronald P., 233
Bertram, Frederic A., 233
Bertram, James, 257
Bertram A. Burton and Associates, 367
Bertrand Goldberg, 632
Bertsch, Dale F., 257
Berube, Claude, 274
Bess, Dave E., 257
Best, Melvin H., 272
Best in American Living Award, 98–99
Best of Seniors' Housing Award, 100–103, *101*
Bethune, Louise Blanchard, 384
Bethune, Robert, 384
Bettman, Alfred, 334
Betts, Hobart, 233
Betts, Richard J., 303
Bevins, William, 233, 299
Bevivino, Michael A., 503
Beyer Blinder Belle, 80, 163, 327
BGR Architects-Engineers, 312
B.H. Janda Construction, 638
Bhalla, Jai Rattan, 277, 298
Bhan, Amey, 539
Bhattarai, Swasti, 513
Biallas, Randall, 284
Bibb & Associates Inc., 312
Bickel, John H., 233
Biddle, James, 280, 471
Bidwill, J., 280
Biebesheimer, Frederick C., III, 233
Bien-Willner, Carina A., 503
Bienville Group, 308
Bierman, Bruce, 287
Big-D Construction Corporation, Inc., 119
Bigger, William I., 227
Biggs, T. J., 233
Bignell Watkins Hasser Architects, 326
Bigott, Joseph C., 451
Billani, John Carlos, 215
Billes Manning Architects, 308, 351
Binder, Rebecca L., 233
Binger, Wilson V., 227
Binghamton University, SUNY, 525, 532
Binkley, James, 233
Binkowski, Ryan R., 509
Birch, Eugenie Ladner, 257
Birchfield, Hal F. B., 261
Bird, Daniel, 257
Bird, Lance L., 233
Birge, John R., 233
Birk, Sherry, 280
Birkerts, Gunnar, 84, 194, 233, 347, 495
Birnbaum, Charles A., 223, 264
Bischoff, Dan, 217
Bishir, Catherine W., 429, 434, 449
Bishop, Calvin T., 264, 293
Bishop, James A., 233
Bishop, Merle H., 257
Bissell, George, 233
Bitter, Adriana, 261
Bitter, Edwin, 261
Bizios, Georgia, 233
BJ Krivanek Art + Design, 186
Black, Alan, 257
Black, J. Sinclair, 233
Black, Shirley, 286
Blackburn, Walter S., 233
Blackett, William Arthur, 301
Blackford, Leonard D., 233
Blackmar, Elizabeth, 429, 431, 449
Blackmer, Bruce E., 233
Blackmon, Jan Gaede, 233
Blackner, Boyd A., 233
Blackwell, Marlon, 81
Blackwood, Michael, 66
Blaich, Robert I., 272
Blair, Lachlan F., 257
Blake, David K., 227
Blake, Hannah, 500
Blake, Michael Connan, 514, 536
Blake, Peter, 233
Blanc, Luis, 125
Blanchard, Howard T., 299
Blanchard, Louise, 384
Blanco, Beatriz E., 546
Bland, Frederick A., 233
Bland, John, 169
Blanski, William A., 209
Blau, David H., 264
Blau, Eve, 73, 160, 190
Blayney, John A., 257
BLDD Architects, Inc., 312
Blegvad, Jacob, 277
Blehle, Frederick, 220
Blessing, Charles A., 64
Blessing, Wilfred E., 233
Blind, Kerry, 264
Blinder, Richard L., 233
Bliss, Anna Campbell, 223
Bliss, Richard L., 233
Bliss, Robert L., 233, 294
Blitch, Ronald B., 233
Block, Herbert Lawrence, 225
Block, Kara, 503
Blodgett, Robin, 536
Blomfield, Sir Arthur, 175
Blomfield, Sir Reginald, 175, 302
Blondheim, Charles A., Jr., 299
Blonkvist, Timothy Brent, 233
Bloodgood, John D., 234
Bloodgood Sharp Buster, 100, 102
Bloomenthal, Martin, 234
Blouin, Patrick, 300
Blucher, Walter H., 334
Blueprint, 603
Bluestone, Daniel, 449
Blum, Sigmund F., 234
Blumberg, Charles, 274, 286
Blume, George, 540
Blumenauer, Earl, 284
Blumenfeld, Alfred M., 272
Blumenfeld, Hans, 188
Blumentals, Susan, 234

Name Index

Brockway, A. L., 299
Brockway, William R., 234
Brodie, M. J. "Jay," 195, 234
Brody, Samuel, 84
Bromley, R. Scott, 287
Bromley, Ray, 500
Bronet, Frances, 295
Brooke, Steven, 65, 223
Brooker, Aaron, 516
Brooks, Arthur N., 227
Brooks, H. Allen, 72, 276, 303
Brooks, H. Gordon, II, 234
Brooks, Hon. Jack, 195, 280
Brooks, James, 175
Brooks, Jane S., 257
Brooks, Turner, 220
Brooks Borg Skiles Architecture Engineering, 341
Brooks College, 517
Broome, John W., 234
Broome, Lewis, 375
Broshar, Robert C., 234, 291
Bross, Jeffrey M., 227
Brotman, David J., 234
Broweleit Peterson Architects, 313
Brower, David J., 257
Brown, A. B., 280
Brown, Andrea Clark, 220
Brown, C. Dudley, 261
Brown, Charlotte Vestal, 280, 429, 449
Brown, Chilton, 286
Brown, David R., 300
Brown, Everett, 109, 261
Brown, F. Bruce, 300
Brown, George D., Jr., 234
Brown, J. Carter, 152, 161
Brown, J. N., 280
Brown, Jennie Sue, 234
Brown, Jeph, 510
Brown, John Seely, 271
Brown, Joseph E., 264
Brown, Joseph L., 227
Brown, Kenneth F., 140, 234
Brown, Kimberly D., 502
Brown, Lance Jay, 234, 496
Brown, Lawford & Forbes, 349
Brown, Nancy Benziger, 257
Brown, Paul B., 234
Brown, Peter Hoyt, 234
Brown, R. Michael, 261
Brown, Randy G., 209
Brown, Robert F., Jr., 234
Brown, Robert L., Jr., 234
Brown, Samantha B., 499
Brown, Terrance, 234
Brown, Theodore L., 220
Brown, Walton E., 261
Brown, Wayne H., 227
Brown, William A., Sr., 280
Brown, Woodlief, 234
Brown University, 528, 532
Brownell, Charles, 160
Browning, William D., 280
Brownlee, David, 72, 160
Brubaker, C. William, 219, 234
Bruce, Barry B., 234
Bruce, Bonnie, 274
Bruce, Jeffrey L., 264
Bruder, William, 74, 220, 351
Bruegmann, Robert, 190
Brugger, Benno, 189
Bruner, Van B., Jr., 205, 234
Bruner Foundation, 179
Brunner & Brunner Architects & Engineers, 341
Bruno, Harry A., 234
Bruno, Martin, 257
Bruns, Mecayla Deanne, 537
Bruton, Larry S., 234
Bruton, Robert O., 227
BRW, Inc., 164
Bryan, Harvey, 234
Bryan, John M., 280
Bryan, Kathryn, 535
Bryan, Mary A., 261
Bryan, Ross, 227
Bryant, Andrew Daniel, 626
Bryant, Gridley J. F., 375
Bryant, John H., 234
Bryce, David, 375
Brydone, Eleanor, 261
BSA Sustainable Design Award, 399, *400*
BTA Architects Inc., 199
Buatta, Mario, 287
Bubenik, Jackie Karl, 264
Bublys, Algimantas V., 234
Buchanan, Colin, 188
Buchanan, Marvin H., 220, 234
Buchanan, Ricciuti & Associates, 345
Buchanan, Robert T., 222
Buck Simpers Architect + Associates, 313
Buckingham, Margaret, 286
Buckley, Ellen C., 538
Buckley, James W., 234
Buckley, Michael P., 234
Bucknam, Paul C., Jr., 227
Bucks County Community College, 514, 528
Budlong, Dudley W., 227
Budrevics, Alexander, 264
Budz, Robert S., 264
Buehrer, Huber H., 234
Buenz, John B., 234
Buettner, Dennis R., 264
Buff, Conrad, III, 638
Buff, Glenn A., 235
Buff Smith & Hensman, 638
Buffalo State College, SUNY, 496, 503, 525, 526, 539
Buggenhagen, Wayne L., 264
Builder's Book, 591
Builder's Book Depot, 591
Builders Booksource, 591
Building Codes Assistance Project, 578
Building Design Partnership, 635
Building Futures Council, 578
Building Owners & Managers Association International, 578
Building Stone Institute, 578
BuildingGreen, 424
Buley, Nancy Callister, 284
Bulfinch, Charles, 329, 375, 376
Bull, Henrik H., 235
Bullock, Ellis W., Jr., 219, 235
Bullock, Helen Duprey, 435
Bullock, Thomas A., Sr., 235
Bullock, W. Glenn, 235
Bullock, William, 272
Bulut, Cigdem T., 546
Bumpers, Hon. Dale, 284
Bunch, Franklin S., 235
Bundy, Richard S., 235
Bunshaft, Gordon, 75, 84, 165, 387
Burby, Raymond, 257
Burch, Kevin, 511
Burchard, Charles E., 294, 556
Burck, Richard, 222
Burdick, Andrew Eben, 538
Burdick, Col. Wilfred C., 626–627
Burdifilek, 117
Bureau Mijksenaar, 186
Burgee, John H., 235
Burgess, Charles E., 235
Burggraf, Frank, Jr., 264
Burgun, J. Armand, 235
Burke, Bob, 257
Burke, Edmund, 227
Burke, Edward M., 235
Burke, Robert H., Jr., 299
Burke-Jones, Joyce A., 261, 292
Burkhardt, Robert G., 227
Burlage, James E., 235
Burley, Jon Bryan, 94
Burley, Robert, 235
Burnet, Sir John James, 177
Burnham, Daniel Hudson, 42, 291, 334, 345, 382
Burns, Arthur L., 235
Burns, John A., 235
Burns, Norma DeCamp, 235
Burns, Robert P., 235, 294, 496
Burns & McDonnell, 341
Buro Happold, 81
Burris & Behne Architects, 312
Bursey, Thomas, 539
Burson, Rodger E., 235
Burton, William S., 264
Busby, J. Scott, 209
Busby, John A., Jr., 219, 235, 291
Business Week, 104, 129
Business Week/Architectural Record Awards, 104
Buskuhl, C. Joe, 235
Bussard, H. Kennard, 235
Butler, Britta E., 502
Butler, Charles, 299
Butler, David M., 261
Butler, Miner F., 374
Butler, Russell L, II, 264
Butler, Theodore R., 235
Butler Rogers Baskett Architects, 313
Butman, A. Elizabeth, 514
Butner, Fred W., 235
Butt, Eric Graham, 301
Butt, Thomas K., 235
Butterfield, William, 175
Butterworth, Richard, 168
Buttrick, Harold, 235
BY IV Design Associates, Inc., 133
Byard, Paul Spencer, 235
Bye, Arthur E. "Ed," Jr., 90, 264
Byers Gunn & Hart Architects, 312
Byrd, Willard C., 264
Byrn, Kara, 508
Byrne, Dominic, 410
Byrne, Jeanne, 235
Bystrom, Arne, 235

C

C. Robert Buchanan & Associates, 345
Cackowski, Kathleen L., 547

Name Index

Caddell Construction Company, Inc., 119
Cadwalader, Burns, 235
Cadwell, Michael B., 223
Caffrey, Laura, 514
Cafritz, Morris, 152
Cahill, Dennis, 286
Cahill, Timothy G., 235
Cain, Raymond F., 264
Cain, Walker O., 220
Caine, Christine, 536
Calatrava, Santiago, 96, 113, 303, 330, 343, 349
Calder, Rus, 274
Caldwell, Alfred, 495
Caldwell and Drake, 374
Calhoun, Harold, 235
California College of Arts and Crafts, 502, 535, 541, 554. *See also* California College of the Arts
California College of the Arts, 517. *See also* California College of Arts and Crafts
California Design Community & Environment, 105
California Institute of Architecture, 503
California Polytechnic State University, 499, 502, 510, 511, 518, 535, 555
California Redwood Association, 578
California State Polytechnic University, 295, 499, 502, 518, 548
California State University, Fresno, 518
California State University, Long Beach, 518, 541
California State University, Northridge, 518
California State University, Sacramento, 518
Callahan, Charles, 538
Callans, Robert A., 264
Callaway, William B., 265
Callies, David Lee, 257
Callmeyer, Ferenc, 277
Calloway, Mandy, 552
Caloger, Ion, 227
Calvo, Santiago A., 277
Cama, Rosalyn, 261, 292
Cambridge Architectural Books, 592
Cambridge School of Architecture and Landscape Architecture, 386, 387, 388
Cambridge Seven Associates Inc., 80, 114, 308, 310, 363
Cambridge University, 513
Campaglia, Muriel, 280
Campagna, Barbara, 209
Campbell, Adrienne Vaughan, 514
Campbell, Barbara J., 108, 261
Campbell, C. Robert, 235, 299
Campbell, Craig S., 265
Campbell, Leroy M., 205
Campbell, Neil, 535
Campbell, Paschall, 265
Campbell, R. Neal, 227
Campbell, Robert, 64, 167, 215, 225, 235
Campbell, Wendell J., 64, 205, 235
Camposilvan, Chiara, 535
Canadian Architect, 603
Canadian Centre for Architecture, 66, 606
Canadian Green Building Council, 425
Canaves, Jaime, 235
Cancian, Steven Rasmussen, 509
Candela, Felix, 96, 277
Candela, H. F., 235
Canestaro, Nancy C., 546
Canina, Luigi, 175
Canizaro, Robert H., 235
Cannady, William T., 235
Cannon, Jamie, 235
Cannon, Roger, 235
Cannon Design, 121
Canova Associates Architecture, 313
Cantor, Marvin J., 235
Cantrell, Horace S., Jr., 235
Canty, Donald, 65, 280
Caparn, Harold A., 293
Capelin, Joan, 280
Caplan, Aubrey, 227
Caplan, Ralph, 285
Caples Jeffers Architects, 60
Capsule, 130
Cardasis, Dean, 265
Carde, Richard Scott, 235
Cardinal, Douglas, 169
Cardoso, J., 96
Cardoza, Robert R., 265
Cardwell, Kenneth Harvey, 235
Cardwell Architects, 143
Cares, Charles, 265
Carjola, Chester, 353
Carl, Peter, 220
Carleton University, 535
Carlhian, Jean P., 110, 235
Carlisle, William A., 235
Carlo, Giancarlo de, 177, 206
Carlough, Edward, 280
Carlson, Bryan D., 265
Carlson, DeVon M., 235
Carlson, Donald Edwin, 235
Carlson, Richard, 274, 287
Carlton, Casey B., 503
Carlton University, 502
Carman, John Leslie, 265
Carmichael, Dennis B., 265
Carmichael, Robin, 511
Carnegie Mellon University
  degree programs, 528, 532
  rankings, 555
  staff, 294, 541
  students/alumni, 121, 502, 535, 549
Carnegie Museum of Art, 607
Carol Ross Barney Architects, 390
Carolin, Paulette, 257
Carpenter, Clyde R., 235
Carpenter, Derr A., 265
Carpenter, Jack A., 235
Carpenter, James Fraser, 66, 153
Carpenter, James W., 227
Carpenter, Jot D., 265, 293, 542
Carpenter, William J., 209, 235
Carpenter/Norris Consulting, 145
Carpet and Rug Institute, 578
Carpo, Mario, 190, 191
Carr, Charles D., 227
Carr, E. T., 374
Carr, Eugene E., 257
Carr, Oliver T., Jr., 152
Carr, Orville V., 261
Carrere and Hastings, 461
Carriero, Joseph, 272
Carrino, Dominic B., 227
Carroll, Edwin Winford, 235
Carroll, Jefferson Roy, Jr., 219, 291
Carroll, M. E., 235
Carroll, Marley, 235
Carruth, David B., 265
Carry, Cooper, 201
Carry, Walter T., 235, 299
Carson, Becky, 514
Carson, Chris, 235
Carson, Daniel M., 227
Carson, Heather, 223
Carson, Rachel, 419
Carter, Brian, 130
Carter, Donald K., 235, 265
Carter, Eugene H., 265
Carter, Hugh C., 227
Carter, Karin, 409
Carter, Katryna, 536
Carter, Pres. James Earl, Jr., 284, 420
Carter, Virgil R., 235
Carter & Burgess, Inc., 326
Cartnal, David R., 235
Caruso, Nicholas J., 502, 536
Carwile, Guy W., 514
CARY (Chicks in Architecture Refuse to Yield), 391
Casabella, 604
Casai, Timothy A., 235
Casariego, Pedro, 627
Casbarian, John J., 223, 235
Cascardo, Lucas, 536
Cascieri, A., 235
Case Western Reserve University, 548
Casella, Sam, 257
Casendino, Anthony B., 265
Cashio, Carlos J., 265
Caskey, Donald W., 235
Cass, Gilbert, 385
Cass, Heather W., 235
Casserly, Joseph W., 235
Cassianis, Jeffrey T., 502
Casson, Conder & Partners, 629
Casson, Hugh, 629
Cassway, Robert L., 78
Castellana, John J., 235
Castellanos, Particia Gutierrez, 274
Castellanos, Stephan, 235
Castiglioni, Achille, 285, 627
Castleman, Elizabeth M., 261
Castles, John Stanley, 301
Castor, Daniel, 220
Castro-Blanco, David, 205
Catanese, Anthony James, 257
Cathedral Church of St. John the Divine, 65
Catholic University of America, 495, 502, 519, 539
Catlin, Juliana M., 261, 292
Catlin, Robert A., 257
Caton, Robert J., 227
Catroux, Francois, 287
Caudill, Samuel J., 235
Caudill, William Wayne, 59, 194
Caudill Rowlett Scott, 80
Caufield, Robert Lindsay, 301
Cavaglieri, Giorgio, 235
Cavanaugh, M. Steve, Jr., 227
Cavin, W. Brooks, Jr., 235, 628
Cavin/Rova, 628
Cawley, Charles M., 280
C2CSpec, 406
C2C Training Module, 406
CBT/Childs Bertman Tseckares Inc., 326
CCA, LLC, 313
CDH Partners, Inc., 326

Name Index

Cochran, Jack R., 265
Cochran, Stephenson & Donkervoet Inc., 326
Cochrane, J. C., 374
Cockerell, Charles Robert, 175, 302
Codlin, Suzannah Y., 502, 536
Codrescu, Andrei, 500
Coe, Christopher W., 209
Coe, Jon Charles, 265
Coe, Theodore Irving, 110
Coelho, Dana Lucille, 499
Coen, Shane, 159
Coen + Partners, 159
Coffee, R. F., 236
Coffey, Daniel P., 236
Coffie, Sylvia O., 502
Coffin, Beatriz de Winthuysen, 265
Coffin, David, 70
Coffin, Laurence E., Jr., 265
Coffin, Marian, 461
Cogan, Arnold, 257
Cogela, 201
Cohagen, Chandler C., 299
Cohen, Adrian O., 236
Cohen, Andrew S., 236
Cohen, Edward, 227
Cohen, Eustace Gresley, 277, 301
Cohen, Jack C., 236
Cohen, Martin H., 236
Cohen, Stuart, 236
Coho Construction Services, Inc., 416
Coia, Jack Antonio, 177
Coit, Elizabeth, 387
Coker, Coleman, 220
Cole, Doris, 236
Cole, Raymond J., 496
Cole and Goyette, Architects and Planners, 313
Coleman, Cindy, *551*
Coleman, Susan, 274
Coleridge, John, 636
Coles, Robert Traynham, 205, 219, 236
Colgan Perry Lawler Architects, 341
Collard, Max Ernest, 301
Collcutt, Thomas Edward, 175, 302
College for Creative Studies, 523
College of Charleston, 528
College of Environmental Science and Forestry, SUNY, 525
College of the Redwoods, 518
Collignon, Fred, 257
Collins, Brad, 257
Collins, Brian Clay, 261
Collins, David S., 236
Collins, Donald C., 265
Collins, John F., 265
Collins, Robertson E., 629
Collins, William J., Jr., 227
Colliton, Dennis C., 265
Colonial Williamsburg Foundation, 429
Color Association of the United States, 578
Colorado Department of Transportation, 163
Colorado State University, 510, 519
Colter, Mary Jane, 385
Columbia University
  degree programs, 525, 532, 533
  degrees/programs, 454
  rankings, 555
  staff, 225, 294, 495, 556
  students/alumni, 387, 389, 390, 502, 539, 550
Columbus College of Art & Design, 527
The Colyer Freeman Group, 314
COMEX, 137
Committee for the Preservation of Architectural Records, 64
Commoner, Barry, 64
Communication Arts, 600
Communication Arts, Inc., 271
Composite Panel Association/Composite Wood Council, 578
Compton, Jerry, 548
Comstock, Donald, 236
Conant, Kenneth John, 70, 303
Conant, Richard, 265
Concepts Enterprise, 313
Concordia, 308
Conder, Hugh Neville, 629
Conetta, Christina, 503
Congress for the New Urbanism, 105
Conklin, William T., 236
Connally, Ernest Allen, 280, 435
Connolly Architects, 313
Connor, Rose, 388
Conrad, Max Z., 265
Conrad, Paul E., 227
Conrad, Richard T., 236
Conrad, W. M., 236
Conron, John P., 236, 261
Conroy, J. J., 236
Conroy, S. B., 280
Conservation Trust of Puerto Rico, 66
Consortium of Quebec Architects, 371
Constable, David, 502
Constant, Caroline B., 220
Construction Management Association of America, 578
Construction Market Data Group, 271
Construction Specifications Institute, 579
Consulting Engineers Group, 635
Contovernos, Stacey, 516
Contract, 76, 121, 600
Cook, Eugene E., 236
Cook, George Glenn, 265
Cook, Lawrence D., 236
Cook, Linda J., 222
Cook, Peter, 137
Cook, Richard B., 236
Cook, Walter, 291
Cook, William H., 236
Cooke, David, 274
Cooke, Thomas, 257
Cooke, William H., Jr., 227
Cooledge, Harold, Jr., 495
Coolidge, Frederic S., 220
Coolidge, Shepley, Bulfinch and Abbott, 347
Coolman, Charles Douglas, 265
Coombs Architecture & Planning, Inc., 313
Coon, Burwell R., 300
Cooper, Alexander, 236
Cooper, Cameron Wilson, 540
Cooper, Celeste, 287
Cooper, Connie B., 257
Cooper, Douglas, 67
Cooper, Jerome M., 236
Cooper, Robertson & Partners, 313
Cooper, Sir Edwin, 177
Cooper, W. Kent, 236
Cooper Cary, 326
Cooper-Hewitt Museum, 65, 153, 181, 606
Cooper-Hewitt Museum Bookstore, 593
Cooper Union, 392, 502, 525, 535, 556, 648
Coover, Christopher, 236
Cope, Gerald M., 236
Copeland, Lee G., 236, 556
Copeland, Rolaine V., 280
Copper Development Association, 579
Corberó, Xavier, 148, 149
Corbett, Harrison & MacMurray, 197
Cordes, Loverne C., 261
Cordier, Herbert, 261
CoreNet Global, 418
Corgan, C. Jack, 236
Corgan, Jack M., 236
Corgan Associates, 326
Corkle, Eleanor, 274
Corlett, William, 236
Corlew, Philip M., 227
Corlin, Len, 286
Corliss, David, 514
Cornell, Ralph, 461
Cornell University
  degree programs, 525, 532, 533
  rankings, 554, 555
  staff, 294, 295, 392, 495, 497, 556
  students/alumni, 384, 386, 502, 513, 535
Corning Incorporated, 66
Cornish, Bob, 257
Corona Martin, Ramon, 298
Corpus Christi Design Associates, 310
Correa, Charles M., 162, 177, 189, 200, 226, 277
Correale, Fred J., 265
Corrigan, Peter, 168
Cossutta, Araldo A., 236
Costa, Lucio, 188
Costas Kondylis & Partners LLC Architects, 379
Costello, Jini, 261
Cote, Leahy and Associates, 201
Cote, Tracie, 537
Cothern, Jonathan David, 540
Cothran, James Robert, 265
Cott, Leland, 236
Cotter, John L., 434
Cottier, Keith, 168
Cottingham, J. Richard, 227
Cotton, John O., 236
Cotton, W. Philip, Jr., 236
Coulter, Kenneth R., 265
Council of Education Facility Planners International, 116
Council of Educators in Landscape Architecture, 534
Council of Landscape Architectural Registration Boards, 336, 614
Council of Professional Surveyors, 579
Council on Tall Buildings and Urban Habitat, 377, 579
Counsel House Research, 326, 462, 554, 555, 617
Courtenay, Virginia W., 261
Courtland, Paul, 647
Cousins, Morison S., 223
Cowell, C. H., 236
Cowger, Richard Todd, 514
Cowgill, Clinton H., 299
Cowling, Dan C., 236
Cox, David C., 236
Cox, Frederic H., 236
Cox, Lawrence M., 630

D

Name Index

E

Name Index

Edmunds, James R., Jr., 291
Edward B. Green and Sons, 353
Edward C. Kemper Award, 110
Edward L. Banks, Architect, 313
Edward Larrabee Barnes Associates, 80, 198, 225, 349, 355. *See also* Barnes, Edward Larrabee
Edward Meinert Architect, 313
Edwards, Arthur A., 228
Edwards, David A., 238
Edwards, David W., 277, 300
Edwards, Jared I., 238
Edwards, Judy A., 281
Edwards, Matthew, 511
Edwards & Pitman, 353
Effenberger, Don, 218
Efron, Albert, 238
EGA P.C., 102
Egan, M. David, 281, 495
Eggers, David L., 238
Ehrenkrantz, Ezra D., 238
Ehrenkrantz Eckstut and Kuhn Architects, 115
Ehrig, John P., 238
Ehrlich, Joseph, 238
Ehrlich, Steven D., 238
E.I. Du Pont de Nemours & Company, 108
Eichbaum, Thomas N., 238
Eid, Yehya M., 277
Eiden, Carl, 228
Eidlitz, Leopold, 375
Eifler, John A., 238
EIFS Industry Members Association, 579
Einhorn, Steven L., 238
Einhorn Yaffee Prescott Architecture & Engineering, 120, 326, 327
Einsweiler, Robert C., 258
Eisen, David, 215
Eisenman, Peter D., 8, 84, 194, 225, 238, 355
Eisenman Architects, 159, 225
Eisenshtat, Sidney H., 238
Eisner, Michael D., 152
Eisner, Richard Karl, 238
Eisner, Simon, 334
El Centro College, 529
El-Hakim, Mahmoud, 57
El Wakil, Abdel W., 277
Elam, Merrill, 74
Elbasani, Barry P., 238
Eldon Beck and Associates, 201
Eldred, Brian E., 300
Eldredge, Joseph L., 238
Electrical Power Research Institute, 579
Eley, Charles N., 238
Elinoff, Martin, 261
Eliot, Charles W., II, 90
Elizondo, Juan Gil, 188
Elkerton, Stanley D., 228
Elkus, Howard F., 238
Elkus/Manfredi Architects, Ltd., 182, 201, 326
Ellenzweig, Harry, 238
Ellerbe Becket
  awards/honors, 150
  organizational profile/information, 327
  works/projects, 361, 363, 369, 371, 373, 378
Ellerthorpe, Robin M., 238
Ellickson, Dale R., 238
Ellinoff, Martin, 292
Elliott, Benjamin P., 238
Elliott, Rand L., 238
Elliott + Associates Architects, 60, 62, 63, 76
Ellis, James R., 281
Ellis, John M., 238
Ellis, Margaret Holben, 223
Ellis, Peter, 550, *551*
Ellison, James E., 238
Ellsworth, Lindsey A., 503
Elmer, Frank L., 238
Elmo, John, 261
Elmore, D. Jerry, 410
Elmore, James W., 238
Emerson, Jon Stidger, 222, 265
Emerson, Ralph Waldo, 172
Emerson, Sir William, 294, 302
Emert, Jonathan, 514
Emery, Katherine G., 265
Emery, Sherman R., 288
Emery Roth & Sons, 341, 381
Emmet L. Wemple and Associates, 641
Emmons, Frederick E., 238
Emmons, Terrel M., 195, 238
Enartec, 310
End, Henry, 287
Endangered Species Act, 420
Endicott College, 523
Endo, Shuhei, 138, 139
Energy and Environmental Building Association, 420
Energy Star Commercial Buildings, 421
Eng, Henry, 258
Eng, William, 238
Engan Associates Architects, Engineers, Interior Designers, 313
Engebretson, Douglas K., 238
Engelbrecht, Mark C., 238
Engineering Excellence Awards, 112–113
Engineering News Record, 600
Engstrom Design Group, 183
Ennis, Laura Elizabeth, 537
Enquist, Philip J., 238, 271, 550
Enriquez, Roselie Mesina, 538
Ensign, Donald H., 265
Ensign, William L., 238
Entenza, John D., 64, 281
Environ, Inc., 313
EnvironDesignWorks, 418
Environmental Building News, 420, 424
Environmental Protection Agency. *See* US Environmental Protection Agency
Environmental Protection Encouragement Agency, 401, 407
Enyart, Lawrence, 238
Eplan, Leon S., 258
Epling, John W., 258
Eppstein-Uhen Architects Inc., 361
Epstein, Herbert, 110, 238
Erber, Ernest, 258
Erdem, Alsi, 539
Ergas, Joel M., 261
Erickson, Arthur C., 59, 96, 169, 194, 277
Erickson, Lindsey Nicole, 537
Erickson, Mark, 217
Erickson, Sammye J., 261
Ericsen, Rudy P., 300
Ericson, Elizabeth S., 238
Ernest J. Kump Associates, 80
Ernst, Jerome R., 238
Erskine, Ralph, 169, 177, 203, 206
Ertegun, Mica, 287
Eschwey, Karli, 500
Eshbach, William W., 110
Esher, Lord, 277, 302
Esherick, Joseph, 59, 194, 556
Esherick Homsey Dodge & Davis, 80, 308
Eshima, Takane, 78
Eskew, R. Allen, 238
Eskew + Architects, 62, 308, 310
Eskew + Dumez + Ripple, 170
Eskew Filson Architects, 351
Esocoff, Philip A., 238
Esten, Harold Lionel, 238
Estern, Neil, 163
Estes/Twombly Architects, 68, 173
Estrada, Steve, 265
Etherington, A. B., 238
Etlin, Richard, 73
Etter, Carolyn B., 284
Etter, Don D., 284
Euforia Design, 130
Eva Maddox Branded Environments, 76
Evans, Deane M., Jr., 238
Evans, J. Handel, 238
Evans, James Matthew, 265
Evans, Morgan "Bill," 90, 265
Evans, Ralph F., 238
Evans, Robert J., 238
Evans, Robert Ward, 220
Evans, Robin, 190
Evans, Sally Kitredge, 72
Evans, Sir Arthur John, 175
Evans, William S., 238
Evanson, Clifford E., 228, 290
Evenson, Norma, 72
Everett, C. Richard, 238
Everett, L. Susan, 265
Everhart, Rodney Chadwick, 539
Everton, Gary, 238
Ewing Cole Cherry Brott, 327
Excel Dryer, Inc., 424
Excellence on the Waterfront Awards, 114–115
Exhibition of School Architecture Awards, 116
Exner, Inger, 277
Exner, Johannes, 277
Eyerman, Thomas J., 238

F

F. Douglas Adams & Associates, Architects Inc., 313
F.A. Bernett, 592
Fabbroni, Lawrence, 549
Faber, Tobias, 277
Fabos, Julius Gy., 90, 265
Facilides, Otto Reichert, 238
Fadem, Charles, 513
Faga, Barbara, 265
Fain, William H., Jr., 223, 238
Fainsilber, Adien, 96
Faison, Gilbert L., 228
Faith & FORM, 170, 600
Fajardo, Francisco B., 277
Falick, James, 238
Fallon, Kristine K., 238
Fanna, Maria Elena, 535
Fanning, Oliver M., 265
Fanning Howey Associates, Inc., 116

Name Index

Forbes, John D., 281, 303
Forbes, Peter, 239
Forbes, Rob, 181
Ford, George Burdett, 334
Ford, Henry, 453
Ford, Jackie, 502
Ford, John G., 261
Ford, O'Neil, 194
Ford, Robert M., 239
Ford Motor Company, 418
Forester, Russell, 239
Forgey, Benjamin, 66, 218, 434
Forkenbrock, David J., 258
Forrest, Deborah Lloyd, 262
Forrey, Roy W., Jr., 633
Forsythe + MacAllen Design Associates, 81
Fort, William S., 281
Fort-Brescia, Bernardo, 239, 287, 389
Fortin, Lisa-Marie, 539
Fortinberry Associates Architects, 313
Foss Associates, 341
Foster, James R., 239
Foster, John H., 228, 290
Foster, Maelee Thomson, 496
Foster, Mark M., 220
Foster, Richard, 239, 349, 633
Foster, Sir Norman Robert. *See also* Foster & Associates; Sir Norman Foster & Partners
  awards/honors, 59, 84, 96, 162, 165, 177, 203, 226, 278, 382
  influences on, 650
  works/projects, 8, 349
Foster & Associates, 226
Fougeron Architecture, 150
Foundation for Architecture, Philadelphia, 66
Foundation for Interior Design Education Research, 287, 517, 534, 554
450 Architects, 422
Fowell, Joseph Charles, 168
Fowle, Bruce S., 239
Fowler, Bob J., 239
Fowler, Charles A., 278, 300
Fowler, Thomas, IV, 548
Fowles, Dorothy L., 262, 274
Fowlkes, Marion L., 239
Fox, Arthur J., Jr., 281
Fox, Catherine, 215
Fox, Donald Mark, 266
Fox, Kathleen M., 266
Fox, Robert, 548
Fox, Sheldon, 239
Fox & Fowle Architects, 381, 400, 407, 418
Foxe, David, 513
Fraker, Harrison, 239, 271, 631
Frame, Marc, 539
Frampton, Kenneth B., 65, 194, 225, 556
Francis, Billy W., 287
Francis, Edward D., 239
Francis, Mark, 266
Francis C. Klein & Associates, 313
Francis Cauffman Foley Hoffman Architects, Ltd., 312, 327
Francis-Jones Morehen Thorp, 399
Franey, Virginia Rose, 540
Frank, Jay E., 239
Frank, Morton, 239
Frank, Richard C., 239
Frank, Thomas, 262
Frank C. Y. Feng Architects & Associates, 378
Frank L. Hope and Associates, 361, 367
Frank Lloyd Wright School of Architecture, 517
Frank O. Gehry and Associates, Inc., 347, 353
Frankel, Neil P., 239, 271, 274, 287, 297
Frankel + Coleman, 271
Franklin, Carol L., 266
Franklin, Daniel B., 266
Franklin, James R., 110, 239
Franta, Gregory, 239
Franz Bader Bookstore, 591
Franzen, John P., 239
Franzen, Ulrich J., 84, 239
Frasca, Robert J., 239
Fraser, Charles E., 284
Frazer, Robert L., 266
Fred Bassetti & Co., 310
Fred Harvey Company, 385
Fredericks, Marshall M., 284
Freed, James Ingo, 84, 157, 195, 239
Freedman, Doris C., 281
Freelon, Philip G., 239
Freeman, Beverly L., 239
Freeman, Raymond L., 90, 293
Freeman, William C., 228
Freeman, William W., 239
FreemanWhite Inc., 341
Freese and Nichols, Inc., 341
Fregonese Calthorpe Associates, 202
French, Jeffrey S., 239
French, Jere S., 266
Frey, Angela, 274
Frey, John W., 266
Fridstein, Thomas K., 239
Friedberg, M. Paul, 64, 266
Friedlaender, Stephen, 239
Friedman, Daniel S., 239
Friedman, David, 73
Friedman, Hans A., 239
Friedman, Mildred "Mickey," 66, 281
Friedman, Rodney F., 239
Friedmann, Arnold, 289
Friedmann, John, 497
Friedrichs, Edward, 239
Friend, Sandra C., 262
Friends of Post Office Square, 66
Frier, Sid, 299
Friley, Jerry L., III, 502
Fritzlen Pierce Architects, 313
frog design inc., 130
Frost, Henry, 386, 388
Frost, Patsy L., 281
Frostic, Gwen, 284
Fry, E. Maxwell, 177
Fry, Louis E., 239
Fry, Louis E., Jr., 239
Fry, Richard E., 239
Fry, Roger, 201
Frye & Chesterman, 376
Fucik, E. M., 228
Fujikawa, Joseph Y., 239
Fujiki, Randall K., 239
Fuksas, Massimiliano, 278
Fukuda, Lester, 228
Fulford, Eric Reid, 222
Fuller, Albert B., Jr., 239
Fuller, David R., 228
Fuller, Frank L., IV, 239
Fuller, Richard Buckminster, 35, 59, 75, 177, 271, 285
Fuller, Ruth, 281
Fuller, Thomas, 375
Fulton, Duncan T., 239
Fulton, James F., 272, 296, 634
Fulton & Partners, 634
Fund for New Urbanism, 393
Fung, Hsin-Ming, 74, 223
Funk, Roger, 272
Furbinger & Ehrman, 462
Furlani, Walter, 272
Furlong, John F., 266
Furman, David F., 239
Furman, Thomas D., Jr., 228
Furness, Frank, 351
Furr, James E., 239
fuseproject, inc., 129, 130

G

Ga.A Architects, 159
Gabel-Luddy, Emily J., 266
Gabellini, Michael, 287
Gaede, Robert C., 239
Gage, Elliot H., 228
Gaio, Ray, 548
Gaither, E. B. "Bas," 228
Gale, Fulton G., III, 239
Gallagher, Herbert K., 239
Gallagher, John, 216
Gallagher, Lauren, 499
Gallery-Dilworth, Leslie M., 239
Gambaro, E. James, 110
Gamble House, 66
Gamboa de Buen, Jorge, 278
Gammon Pte. Ltd., 201
Gandhi, Purvi B., 502
Gandy, Charles D., 109, 262, 274, 292
Gandy, Matthew, 190, 191
Ganser, Karl, 188
Gantt, Harvey B., 194, 239
Gantz, Carroll M., 127, 272, 296
Gapp, Paul, 167, 281
Garber and Woodward, 345
Gardescu, Paul, 266
Gardiner, Marion, 262
Gardner, D. E., 281
Gardner, John W., 158
Gardner, Todd, 500
Garduque, Theodore, 239
Gargett, Peter Robertson, 301
Gargett, Thomas Brenan, 301
Garland, James B., 502
Garland, Robert D., Jr., 239
Garner, Wendell, 628
Garnett, David, 537
Garnett, Jonathan Haruo, 539
Garnham, Harry L., 266
Garnier, Charles, 175
Garofalo, Douglas A., 239
Garrison, Charles E., 239, 299
Garrison, Truitt B., 239
Garrison Architects, 119
Garvan, Anthony, 70
Garvey, Robert R., Jr., 435, 471
Garvin, James, 434
Gary, Benjamin W., Jr., 266, 293
Gary B. Phillips Associates, Inc., 313
Gas Technology Institute, 579
Gass, Alan G., 239
Gast, Fred C., Jr., 239

Gastinger, Breck August, 538
Gastinger, Kirk A., 239
Gates, Martha M., 239
Gates Hafen Cochrane Architects, 313
Gatje, Robert F., 239
Gatsch, James A., 239
Gatton, James B., 239
Gaudi, Antonio, 383
Gaudreau Inc., 326
Gaulden, F. E., 239
Gaunt, John C., 239
Gavasci, Alberto Paolo, 289
GBBN Architects, 308
G.C. Wallace, Inc., 202
GCT Venture, 163
Geck, Francis J., 262
Geddes, Robert, 239, 353, 556
Geddes Brecher Qualls Cunningham, 80
Geddis, Barbara L., 239
Geddis, William J., 239, 299
Geering, Robert J., 239
Gehl, Jan, 188
Gehry, Frank O.
anecdote, 169
awards/honors, 59, 75, 84, 97, 157, 162, 165, 169, 177, 206, 225, 239, 287, 382
Bilbao effect, 5–6
Geiger, David H., 65
Geise, Carolyn D., 239
Gelber, Martin B., 239
Gelsomino, Gerald, 274
Genecki, Paul, 281
General Motors Co., 419, 420
Gensler, 80, 104, 271, 326, 327
Gensler, M. Arthur, Jr., 192, 239, 271, 274, 287
Gentile, George G., 266
George, David W., 239
George, F. Vreeland, Jr., 228
George, Frank Dan, 239
George, Reagan W., 239
George, Robert S., 239
George, Sir Ernest, 175, 302
George, Stephen A., 239
George B. Post & Sons, 376
George F. Payne Company, 376
George H. Fuller Company, 376
George Sexton Associates, 145
George Washington University, 520, 532
George Washington University at Mount Vernon College, 520
Georgia Institute of Technology
degree programs, 520, 531, 532, 533
staff, 541
students/alumni, 499, 502, 536, 548
Georgia Southern University, 521
Georgia State University, 521
Gerard, Kristina E., 502
Gerard de Preu & Partners, 380
Gerckens, Laurance Conway, 258
Geren, Preston M., 239
Gerfen, Thomas B., 239
Gerou, Phillip H., 239
G.F. & Partners, 380
Ghirardo, Diane, 295, 496
Giacomo, Pier, 627
Gianninoto, Franceco, 272
Gianotti, Frank B., III, 228
Giattina, Joseph P., Jr., 239, 299
Gibans, James D., 239
Gibbons, Richard George, 266
Gibbs, Dale L., 239
Gibbs, David W., 376
Gibson, C. D., 281
Gibson, Cynthia L., 502, 536
Gibson, John, 175
Gibson, Ken, 510
Gibson, Robin Findlay, 168
Gibson, Sir Donald, 302
Gideon, Randall C., 239
Gilbert, Cass
AIA Presidency, 291
awards/honors, 75
works/projects, 345, 353, 374, 375, 381, 383
Gilbert, Ralph W., Jr., 228
Gilbert, Sidney P., 239
Gilbertson, Matthew W., 548
Gilbertson, Victor C., 239
Gilchrist, Agnes Addison, 303
Gilker, Carolyn Marie, 546
Gill, Brendan, 281
Gill, Irving, 351
Gill, Louis J., 299
Gilland, Wilmot G., 239, 294
Giller, Norman M., 239
Gilling, Ronald Andrew, 168, 301
Gilmore, Bruce L., 228
Gilpin, W. Douglas, 239
Gimpel, James S., 239
Gindroz, Raymond L., 240
Ginsberg, David L., 240
Giordano, Jeanne, 223
Gipe, Albert B., 228
Girard, Alexander, 194, 262
Girault, Charles Louis, 175
Girod, Judy, 262
Girvigian, Raymond, 240
Giuliani, Joseph Carl, 240
Giurgola, Romaldo, 59, 84, 168, 240, 495, 630
Gladding, McBean & Company, 65
Glanville Associates, 202
Glaser, Milton, 66, 262
Glaser, Richard E., 240
Glass, Henry P., 272
Glass, William R., 240
Glass Association of America, 580
Glasser, David Evan, 240
Glassie, Henry, 431
Glatting Jackson Kercher Anglin Lopez Rinehart, Inc., 105
Glavin, James E., 266
Glendening, E. A., 240
Glick, D. Newton, 266
Glitsch, Val, 240
Glover, William J., Jr., 228
Glover Smith Bode, Inc., 313
Gluckman, Richard J., 240, 287
Gluckman Mayner Architects, 355
Glucksman, Harold D., 240
Glusberg, Jorge, 137, 281
Glymph, James M., 240
Gobbel, Tina M., 281
Gobbell, Ronald V., 240
Gobel, Elias F., 374
Godbole, Nandita, 509
Goddard, Stephen G., 228, 290
Godfrey, William Purves Race, 168, 301
Godi, Donald H., 266
Godschalk, David R., 258, 497
Godwin, George, 175
Godwin, James B., 266
Goettsch, James, 240
Goetz, Ellin, 266
Goetz, Lewis J., 240, 274, 297
Goetz, Robert E., 266
Goff, Bruce, 198
Going, E. Jackson, 228
Gold Key Awards for Excellence in Hospitality Design, 117, *118*
Goldberg, Alan E., 240
Goldberg, Alfred, 281
Goldberg, Donald T., 228
Goldberg, Howard G., 281
Goldberg, Jeff, 67
Goldberg, Steven M., 240
Goldberger, Paul, *2,* 3–10, 65, 167, 217, 271, 281
Golden, William T., 181
Golder, Robert M., 220
Goldfinger, M. H., 240
Goldman, Andrew, 78
Goldman, Ron, 240
Goldschmidt, Carl, 258
Goldschmied, Marco, 302
Goldsmith, Goldwin, 294
Goldsmith, Nicholas, 240
Goldsmith, William, 127, 272, 296
Goldstein, Stanley J., 240
Goldstone, Harmon H., 240
Golemon, Albert S., 219
Gomez, Mariette Himes, 287
Gommel, Jacqueline, 546
Gonzales, Bennie M., 240
Gonzalez, Armando L., 240
Gonzalez, Juan, 278
Gonzalez/Goodale Architects, 313
Goo, Donald W. Y., 240
Good, R. L., 240
Good, Robert Wilson, 266
Good, Wayne L., 240
Good Fulton & Farrell Architects, 143, 326
Goodhart-Rendel, H. S., 302
Goodhue, Bertram Grosvenor, 59, 375, 383
Goodhue, D. B., 240
Goodman, Cary C., 240
Goodman, Jeremiah, 289
Goodman, John P., 240
Goodman, Paul, 334
Goodman, Percival, 334
Goodwin, Michael K., 240
Goodwin, Philip L., 351
Goodwin, Warren N., 240
Goody, Clancy & Associates, 105, 388
Goody, Joan Edelman, 240, 388
Goody, Marvin E., 388
Goorevich, Michael L., 220
Gordon, Dennis Andrew, 258
Gordon, Douglas E., 281
Gordon, Eric, 223
Gordon, Ezra, 240
Gordon, Harry T., 240
Gordon, James Riley, 374
Gordon, Sir Alex, 302
Gordon H. Chong and Partners, 327
Gores, H. B., 281
Gorlin, Alexander C., 220
Gorman, Robert, 266

Name Index

Gornick, Naomi, 132
Gorski, Eleanor Esser, 223
Gorski, Gilbert, 67, 125
Gosling, Joseph, 375
Gotch, J. Alfred, 302
Gote, Diane, 262
Gottesdiener, T. J., 240
Goucher College, 523
Gould, Amy L., 240
Gould, Robert E., 240
Gould, Whitney, 216
Gould Evans Goodman Associates, 120
Gourley, Ronald, 240
Gowans, Alan W., 70, 276, 303
Grabowski, Thomas C., 262
Gracey, Brian, 240
Grad, Bernard J., 240
Grad Partnership, 363, 371
Graef, Anhalt, Schloemer and Associates, 112
Graef, Luther, 228
Graeter-Reardon, Bernice, 514
Gragg, Randy, 217
Graham, Bruce J., 240
Graham, Carol S., 274
Graham, D. R., 281
Graham, Gary L., 240
Graham, Gordon, 302
Graham, J. Patrick, IV, 266
Graham, John David, 537
Graham, Lori, 286
Graham, Philip H., Jr., 266
Graham, Robert, 163
Graham, Roy E., 240
Graham, Theodora Kim, 262
Graham Anderson Probst & White, 308, 341, 632
Graham Gund Architects, Inc., 308
Gramann, Robert E., 240
Gran, Warren Wolf, 240
Granary Associates, 150, 327
Grange, Jacques, 287
Grant, Bradford C., 295
Grant, Margo, 287
Grassli, Leonard, 266
Grasso, Anthony J., 228
Gratz, Roberta, 281
Grava, Sigurd, 258
Graven, Paul H., 299
Graves, Charles P., 240
Graves, Clifford W., 258
Graves, Dean W., 240
Graves, Ginny W., 281
Graves, Michael
 awards/honors, 59, 84, 157, 181, 194, 220, 240, 287
Gray, Aelred Joseph, 334
Gray, Ann E., 67, 240
Gray, Barbara, 281
Gray, Brian L., 228
Gray, David Lawrence, 240
Gray, Gordon C., 435
Gray, James W., Jr., 266
Gray, John, 655
Gray, Paul, 353
Gray, R. Stephen, 514
Gray, Thomas A., 240
Graziani, Lyn E., 240
Greager, Robert E., 240
Great American Main Street Awards, 438–439
Gréber, Jacques, 353
Grebner, Dennis W., 240
Greeley, Mellen C., 299
Green, Aaron G., 240
Green, Cecil H., 281
Green, Curt, 634
Green, Curtis H., 240
Green, Edward B., 342, 345, 347
Green, Richard J., 240
Green, Richard L., 514
Green, Thomas G., 240
Green, William Curtis, 177
Green & Wicks, 353
Green Apple Map, 420
Green Associates Architects, Inc., 313
Green Building Leadership Awards, 405
Green Building Resource Guide, 421
Green Nelson Weaver, Inc., 341
Greenberg, Aubrey, 240
Greenberg, Farrow Architecture, Inc., 326
Greenberg, Mike, 217
Greenberger, Stephen, 262
GreenBlue, 401, 406, 421
Greene, Bradford M., 266
Greene, Isabelle Clara, 266
Greene, James A., 240
Greene and Greene, 382
Greenfield, Sanford R., 240, 294
Greenhorne & O'Mara, 113
Greenleaf, James L., 293
GreenSpec Directory, 424
Greenstreet, Robert, 295, 496
Greenwald, Jody, 262
Greenwald, Susan, 240
Greer, John O., 240
Gregan, E. Robert, 266
Gregg, Glenn H., 240
Gregga, Bruce, 287
Gregory, Jules, 110
Grenader, Nonya, 240
Grenald, Raymond, 240
Grenfell-Baines, Sir George, 635
Gresham, James A., 220, 240
Gresham, Smith and Partners, 313
Grey, Earl de, 302
Gridley, William C., 240
Griebel, K., 188
Griechen, Darrin, 537
Grieve, L. Duane, 240
Grieves, James R., 240
Grieves & Associates, 308
Griffin, Brand Norman, 220
Griffin, Marion Mahony, 385
Griffin, Roberta S., 262
Griffin, Walter Burley, 385
Griffith, Thomas, 281
Grimes, Robert F., 228
Grimm + Parker Architects, 116
Grinberg, Donald I., 240
Griselle, Sherman, 258
Grissim, John N., 266
Griswold, Chad, 538
Griswold, John S., 272
Griswold, Ralph E., 222
Grochowiak, Edward A., 240
Groner, Amy, 511
Gropius, Walter Adolf, 59, 177, 387, 628
Gropp, Louis Oliver, 289
Gross, Kaplin Coviensky, 201
Grossi, Olindo, 220, 240, 294
Groth, Paul, 431
Ground Zero plans, 7–10
Grounds, Sir Roy, 168
Group II Architects, 313
Group 91 Architects, 188
Grover, William H., 240
Grube, J. C., 240
Gruber, Michael, 220
Gruen, Robert, 272
Gruen Associates, 163
Grunley Construction Company, Inc., 119
Grunsfeld, Ernest A., 240
Gruzen, Jordan L., 240
GSA Design Awards, 119–120
Guangzhou Design Institute, 379
Gueft, Olga, 262, 289
Guenther, John C., 240
Guenther, Karen, 274, 297
Guenther, Robin, 648
Guenther Petrarca, 648
Guerin, Charles, 548
Guerin, Denise, 544
Guertin, Paul D., 228
Guest, Rita C., 262
Gueze, Adriaan, 203
Guffey, Francis A., II, 240
Guffey, Roberta J., 281
Guggenheim, Charles, 65
Guillot, Frank M., 299
Guion, Sarah, 536
Gumbinger, Paul J., 240
Gumbis, Melissa, 511
Gund, Graham, 240
Gunn, Clare A., 266
Gunnar Birkerts & Associates, 347, 349
Gunsul, Brooks R., 240
Gunts, Edward, 215
Gupta, Arvind, 130, 409
Guran, Michael, 220
Gurdogan, Selva, 537
Gurland, Gerald, 240
Gurney, Robert M., 68, 173, 240
Gustaferro, Armand "Gus" H., 635
Gustafson, William R., 240
Gustavson, Dean L., 240, 299
Gutbrod, Rolf, 96
Guth, John J., 228
Gutheim, Frederick, 64, 334, 435
Gutherz, Carl, 349
Gutman, Robert, 281
Guttenburg, Albert, 258
Guzman, Dianne, 258
Guzzardo, Anthony M., 266
Gwathmey, Cabell, 240
Gwathmey, Charles, 8, 84, 240, 287
Gwathmey Siegel & Associates Architects, 80, 353, 648
Gwilliam, Willard E., 240
Gwynne, Patrick, 636
Gyrus ENT. LLC, 130

H

Haag, E. Keith, 240
Haag, Edgar C., 222
Haag, Richard, 90, *91,* 266, 281, 636
Haas, Lester C., 240
Haas, Richard, 64
Haas, Wallace L., Jr., 240

HABITAT. *See* United Nations Centre for Human Settlements
Habitat for Humanity, 205
Hacker Art Books, 592
Hackl, Donald J., 240, 291
Hackler, John B., 240
Hackney, Roderick P., 189, 278, 298, 302
Hackney, W. F., 374
Haden, Erik Jon, 540
Hadfield, George, 462
Hadid, Zaha, 148, 278, 390, 393
Hadley, Albert, 287
Hagan, Stephen R., 240
Haggstrom, Olle E., 272
Hahnfeld, L. R., 240
Haines, Frank S., 240
Haire, William H., 240
Hakim, Besim S., 258
Halasz, Imre, 240
Halback, Frederick Edward, 266
Haley & Aldrich Inc., 67
Hall, Anthony, 287
Hall, Corey, 500
Hall, David W., 262
Hall, Donald J., 281
Hall, E. Stanley, 302
Hall, Ella, 548
Hall, Gaines B., 240
Hall, John C., 266
Hall, Mark W., 240
Hall, Robert Darwin, 301
Hall, William A., 240
Hall, William L., 281
Hallen, H. H., 278
Hallenbeck, Donalee, 281
Hallenbeck, Harry C., 110, 240
Hallet, Stanley I., 240
Hallissy, Gerald, 241
Halpin, Anna M., 241
Halprin, Lawrence
    awards/honors, 86, *87*, 90, 157, 163, 194
    memberships, 225, 262, 266
    works/projects, 461
Halsband, Frances, 241
Halverson, James M., 262
Hambleton, David H., 300
Hamby, William, 241
Hamer, Hardt Walther, 189
Hamill, Robert L., Jr., 241
Hamilton, Calvin S., 266
Hamilton, D. K., 241
Hamilton, E. G., Jr., 241, 299
Hamilton, Mel, 287
Hamilton, William D., 262
Hamlin, Talbot, 70
Hammel, Dick, 634
Hammel, Green and Abrahamson, Inc. (HGA), 170, 271, 308, 634
Hammell, Robert P., 241
Hammer, P., 281
Hammer, Theodore S., 241
Hammond, Beebe and Babka, 345
Hammond, Charles H., 291
Hammond, Gerald S., 241
Hammond, John Hyatt, 241
Hammond, Shirley, 262
Hammond, Wilton N., 228
Hamner, W. Easley, 241
Hampson, Alice, 83
Hampton, A. Niolon, 262
Hampton, Mark G., 241, 287
Hampton, Philip M., 228
Hampton University, 295, 502, 530
Hanamoto, Asa, 266
Hanbury, John Paul C., 241
Hanbury Evans Wright Vlattas & Company, 313
Hancock, Marga Rose, 281
Hand, Irving, 258
Hand, Peter H., 241
Hangen, Richard E., 228
Hanke, Byron R., 266
Hanna, Karen C., 266
Hanna, Robert Mitchell, 222, 266, 636
Hanna/Olin Ltd., 636
Hannah, Bruce, 541
Hanney & Associates Architects, 312
Hannover Principles, 407–408
Hansen, J. Paul, 241
Hansen, James G., 272
Hansen, Marilyn, 262
Hansen, Richard F., 241
Hansen, Robert E., 241
Hanson, Becca, 266
Hanson, Brian L., 228
Hanson, Mary L., 284
Hanson, Renee L., 465
Hanson, Walter E., 228
Hantman, Alan M., 241, 376
Hara, John M., 241
Harboe, P. Thomas M., 209
Harbour, Antony, 287
Harby, Steven, 220
Hardee, Joseph E., 228
Harder, Dellas H., 241
Hardesty, Nancy M., 266
Hardison, Donald L., 219, 241
Hardwick, Philip, 175
Hardwood Plywood & Veneer Association, 580
Hardy, Hugh, 84, 241, 287
Hardy, Nadine N., 500
Hardy, Tom, 163
Hardy Holzman Pfeiffer Associates, 62, 63, 80, 634
Hare, Henry Thomas, 302
Hare, S. Herbert, 293, 334
Hare, Sid J., 334
Hargreaves, George, 266
Harkins, David, 499
Harkness, John C., 241
Harkness, Sarah Pillsbury, 241, 387
Harkness, Terence G., 266
Harlan, Meliss J., 537
Harley, Ellington, Cowin and Stirton, 347
Harli, Ray, 513
Harmon, Frank, 241
Harmon, Harry W., 110, 241
Harmon-Vaughan, Beth, 274, 297
Harnett, Brendan, 536
Haro, John C., 241
Harper, Angela N., 258
Harper, Charles F., 110, 241
Harper, David M., 241
Harper, Robert L., 241
Harrell, James W., 241
Harrell, Thomas B., Jr., 228
Harriman Associates, 341
Harrington Institute of Interior Design, 521
Harris, Britton, 258, 497
Harris, Charles W., 266
Harris, Cyril M., 64
Harris, David A., 241
Harris, Debra, 547
Harris, Donald M., 284
Harris, Edwin F., Jr., 241
Harris, Emanuel Vincent, 177
Harris, Harwell Hamilton, 495
Harris, James Martin, 241
Harris, John, 160
Harris, Richard, 431
Harris, Robert S., 241, 294, 495, 548
Harris, Samuel Y., 241
Harris, William M., Sr., 258
Harrison, Marc, 541
Harrison, Michael S., 258
Harrison, Partrick K., 281
Harrison, Robert V. M., 241
Harrison, Wallace Kirkman, 59
Harrison & Abramovitz, 380
Harrover, Roy P., 241
Harry Weese & Associates, 80, 163
Hart, Arthur A., 281
Hart, Dianne, 281
Hartigan, Michael J., 228
Hartleben, Obregon, 499
Hartman, Craig W., 241
Hartman, Douglas C., 241
Hartman, George E., 220, 241
Hartman, Morton, 241
Hartman-Cox Architects, 80, 143, 144
Hartmann, William E., 241, 637
Hartray, Jack, 60
Hartray, John F., Jr., 110, 241
Hartung, Arthur F., 228
Hartung, Timothy, 241
Hartwell, Michelle, 536
Hartzog, George B., Jr., 284
Harvard Design Magazine, 601
Harvard University
    awards/honors given by, 203
    degree programs, 331, 523, 532, 533
    rankings, 555
    staff, 226, 386, 392, 495, 498, 556
    students/alumni, 388, 392, 502, 511, 539, 628, 640
Harvey, Eugene C., 228
Harvey, Patricia, 262
Harvey, Robert R., 266
Harvey Probbber Inc., 650
Harwood, Buie, 262
Hasbrouck, Wilbert R., 241
Haskell, Dennis E., 64, 241
Haskell, John G., 374
Haskins, Albert L., Jr., 241
Haslam, Wilfried Thomas, 301
Hass, Dr. F. Otto, 281
Hasselman, Peter M., 241
Hassid, Sami, 241
Hasslein, George J., 241
Hastings, Hubert de Cronin, 177
Hastings, James M., 228
Hastings, Judith, 274, 297
Hastings, L. Jane, 219, 241, 391
Hastings, Robert F., 291
Hastings, Thomas, 177
Hasty, Hope M., 499
Hatami, Marvin, 241
Hatchell, Susan M., 266
Hattery, Donald, 228

Name Index

Hauf, Harold D., 241
Haugerud, Amy J., 228
Haus, Stephen C., 222
Hauschild-Baron, Beverly E., 281
Hauser, Inc., 130
Hauser, Jon W., 272
Hauser, Stephen G., 272
Hausner, Robert O., 241
Hautau, Richard G., 266
Havekost, Daniel J., 241
Havens, William H., 266
Haviland, David S., 66
Haviland, Perry A., 241
Hawes, Velpeau E., Jr., 241
Hawkins, Dale H., 222
Hawkins, H. Ralph, 241
Hawkins, Jasper Stillwell, 241
Hawkins, William J., III, 241
Hawkinson, Laurie, 84
Hawks, Richard S., 266
Hawley, Charles R., 503
Hawley, William R., 241
Haworth, Dennis, 262
Hawtin, Bruce A., 241
Hayashi, Shoji, 278
Hayashida Architects, 313
Hayden, Richard S., 241
Hayden, Sara, 513
Hayden, Sophia, 384
Hayes, J. Byers, 347
Hayes, J. F., 241
Hayes, John Freeman, 241
Hayes, Seay, Mattern & Mattern, Inc., 113
Haynes, Irving B., 241
Haynes Lieneck & Smith Inc., 312
Hays, Steve M., 228
Haysom, Edward Robert, 301
Hazelgrove, A. J., 300
Hazelhurst, Franklin Hamilton, 72
Hazelrigg, George, 509
HDR Architecture, 119, 326
Healey, Edward H., 241
Healthcare Environment Award, 121–122
Hearn, Michael M., 241
Hearst, William Randolph, 386
Hearth, Patio & Barbecue Association, 580
Heath, Kingston William, 431
Heatly, Bob E., 496
Heck, Robert, 496
Hecksher, A., 281
Hedefine, Alfred, 228
Hedrich, Jack, 289
Hedrick, Roger K., 258
Heery, George T., 241
Heery International, Inc., 326, 361, 369
Hegler, Tracy, 499
Heights Venture Architects, 313
Heikkinen-Komonen Architects, 57
Heilenman, Diane, 216
Heilig, Robert Graham, 266
Heimbaugh, John D., Jr., 220
Heimsath, Clovis, 241
Heineman, Paul L., 228
Heinfeld, Dan, 241
Heinlein & Schrock, Inc., 373
Heinz, Jo, 274
Heinz Architectural Center, Carnegie Museum of Art, 607
Heiser Development Corporation, 313
Heiskell, Andrew, 281
Hejduk, John, 84, 241, 392, 556
Helfand, Margaret, 220, 241
Helfeld, Edward, 258
Heller, Barbara, 241
Hellmann, Maxwell Boone, 241
Hellmuth, George F., 241
Hellmuth, Obata & Kassabaum, Inc. (HOK)
  awards/honors, 120, 150, 418, 422
  company profile/rankings, 327
  HOK Sport, 63, 202, 359, 361, 363, 371, 373
  HOK Sport + Venue + Event, 361, 365, 367
  HOK Sport Facilities Group, 359, 361, 365, 367, 369
  staff, 271, 392
  works/projects, 308, 345, 359, 363, 371, 373, 377
Helman, A. C., 241
Helman Hurley Charvat Peacock Architects/Inc., 310
Helmer, Dorothy G., 262
Helpern, David P., 241
Helphand, Kenneth I., 95, 266
Hemphill, James C., Jr., 241
Henderson, A. Graham, 302
Henderson, Arn, 241
Henderson, Brenda, 281
Henderson, Edith H., 266
Henderson, Judith Arango, 637
Henderson, Philip C., 241
Henderson, Richard, 84
Hendricks, James L., 241
Hendrix, Glenn O., 266
Heney, Joseph E., 228
Henner, Edna, 274
Hennessey & Ingalls Art and Architecture Books, 591
Hennessy, John F., III, 228
Henry, Mary Lou, 258
Henry, Vernon G., 258
Henry, William R., 241
Henry Adams Medal, 535–541
Henry C. Turner Prize for Innovation in Construction Technology, 123, *124*
Hensel Phelps Construction Company, 155
Henshell, Justin, 241
Hensley, Jack A., 503
Hensley, Marble J., Sr., 228
Hensman, Donald C., 241, 638
Herb, Matt, 549
Herbert, Albert E., 262
Herbert, Charles, 241
Herbert, Glendon M., Jr., 266
Herbert Lewis Kruse Blunck Architecture, 63, 80
Herbst LaZar Bell, 129, 130
Herlihy, Elisabeth, 334
Herman, Bernard L., 429, 431
Herman, Matthew Everett, 538
Herman, Robert G., 241
Herman & Coliver, 172
Herman Miller Inc., 65
Hermann, Elizabeth Dean, 222
Hermannsson, John, 421
Herrin, William W., 241
Herring, Ricardo C., 241
Herring, Robert, 262
Herron, John, 274
Hershberger, Robert G., 241
Hershey, Fred B., 262
Hershfang, Amy, 281
Herson, Albert, 258
Herzog, Jacques, 165, 278
Herzog, Thomas, 96
Hess, Alan, 218, 241
Hesse, Richard J., 228
Hester, Randolph T., 266
Heuer, Charles R., 241
Hewitt, D. M., 241
Hewitt, George W., 351
Hewitt, Stevens & Paist, 462
Hewitt & Washington, 308
Hewlett-Packard, 132
Heyd, Ted, 500
Heylman, Warren Cummings, 241
HGA. *See* Hammel, Green and Abrahamson, Inc.
Hickman, Robert E., 228
Hicks, David, 287
Hicks, Margaret, 384
Hicks, Mason S., 241
Hidell Associates Architects, 313
Hight, Charles C., 241, 294
Hightower, J. Brantley, *12,* 13–18, 508
Hijjas Kasturi Associates, 381
Hildebrandt, Henry P., 544
Hilderbrand, Gary R., 222, 266
Hilderbrandt, Donald F., 266
Hilfinger, Dean F., 110, 241
Hilger, Bonnie, 499
Hill, Eric, 241
Hill, Jason E., 503
Hill, John W., 241
Hill Partnership Inc., 102
Hillier, J. Robert, 241
Hillier Group, 308
Hills, Arthur W., 266
Hills, Edith Mansfield, 287
Hills, Gilbertson & Hays, 197
Hilmey, Tamara, 539
Himmel, Richard, 287
Hinds, George A., 220
Hines, Gerald D., 136, 152, 281
Hinge, 604
Hino, Sakura, 540
Hinojosa, Jesus H., 258
Hinshaw, Mark L., 241, 258
Hinton, Kem G., 241
Hird, Lyle F., 228
Hirsch, Howard, 287
Hirsch Bedner Associates, 117
Hirten, John E., 258
Hisaka, Don M., 241
Hise, Gregory, 190
Hispanic American Construction Industry Association, 205
Historic American Buildings Survey, 64, 435, 447, 453, 514
Historic American Engineering Record, 447, 455
Historic Denver, Inc., 645
Historic Landscape Initiative, 448
Historic New Harmony, Inc., 65
Historic Preservation Book Prize, 449–451, *450*
Historic Preservation Fund, 456
Historic Savannah Foundation, 66
History Channel, 432
Hitchcock, Henry-Russell, 70, 303

Hite, Charles L., 281
Hittorf, Jacques Ignace, 175
Hixon, Allen W., Jr., 266
HKS Inc., 326, 359, 361, 365, 373, 380, 653
HLW International, 327, 341
Hnedak, Gregory O., 241
Hnedak Bobo Group,, Inc., 313
HNTB Corporation
awards/honors, 112, 155
rankings, 326, 327
staff, 655
works/projects, 359, 365, 367
Ho, Duy, *551*
Ho, Mui, 496
Ho, Tao, 278
Hoag, Paul S., 242
Hobart, Lewis P., 310
Hobbs, Jerry, 271
Hobbs, Richard W., 242
Hobin, Barry J., 278, 300
Hockaday, Peter S., 242
Hodgell, Murlin R., 242
Hodges, Allan A., 258
Hodgetts, Craig, 74
Hodgins, William, 109, 287
Hodne, Thomas H., 242
Hoedemaker, David C., 242
Hoenack, August F., 242
Hoffman, Burrall, 462
Hoffman, David H., 242
Hoffman, David L., 242
Hoffman, Douglas, 172
Hoffman, Stanley R., 258
Hoffman Corporation, 155
Hoffmann, John J., 242
Hogan, Robert E., 228, 290
Hogg, Ima, 435
Hogg & Mythen, 313
Hoglund, J. David, 242
HOK. *See* Hellmuth, Obata & Kassabaum, Inc.
Holabird, John A., 242
Holabird & Root, 80, 341, 375
Holabird and Roche, 369
Holden, Charles Henry, 177
Holden, Edward A., 258
Holder, L. M., 242
Holford, Lord, 177, 302
Holguin, Alejandra, 502
Holl, Steven, 8, 84, 153, *154,* 225, 501
Holland, A. W., 228
Holland, Major L., 242
Hollein, Hans, 165, 278
Holleran, Michael, 142, 434
Hollerith, Richard, 272, 296
Hollick, Kyle, 536
Hollingsworth, Fred T., 300
Hollis-Crocker Architects, 312
Hollmén, Saija, 83
Holloway, Benjamin D., 289
Holman, Joseph W., 299
Holmes, Christopher, 513
Holmes, Dwight E., 242
Holmes, Jess, 242
Holmes, Nicholas H., Jr., 242
Holmquist, Darrel V., 228
Holroyd, Harry J., 242
Holt, Barachias, 374
Holt, Stephen A., 228
Holt, Steven Skov, 541
Holtz, David A., 242
Holway, William N., 228, 290
Holzbauer, Wilhelm, 278
Holzman, Malcolm, 84, 194, 242, 287
Homan Square Community Center Foundation, 202
Home Builders Association of Denver, 416
Homsey, George W., 242
Hong Kong Housing Department, 189
Hongkong Land Property Company, Ltd., 201
Hood, Bobbie S., 242
Hood, Raymond, 329, 380
Hood, Vance R., 284
Hood, Walter, 222
Hood & Fouilhoux, 197
Hook, Alfred Samuel, 168, 301
Hook, Mary Rockwell, 385, 386
Hooker, Van D., 242
Hooper, Vicki L., 209
Hoover, G. N., 242
Hoover, George, 242
Hoover, Ray C., III, 242
Hope, A. J. B. Beresford, 302
Hope, Frank L., Jr., 242
Hope Liturgical Works, 172
Hopkins, Alden, 222
Hopkins, Eugene C., 242, 291
Hopkins, Lady Patricia, 177, 278
Hopkins, Lewis D., 258
Hopkins, Sir Michael, 177, 278
Hopper, Leonard J., 266, 293
Hoppin, Coen & Brown, 462
Hopprier, Peter, 220
Horan, Joseph P., 262
Hord, Edward M., 242
Hord Coplan Macht, Inc., 326
Horii, Howard N., 242
Horn, Gerald, 242
Horns, Miller, 223
Horsbrugh, Patrick, 242, 284
Horsky, Charles A., 152
Horton, Frank L., 435
Horton, Jim, 500
Horty, T., 242
Hose, Robert H., 272, 296
Hospitality Design, 117
Hotel & Motel Management, 117
House, Steven, 78
Houseman, William, 281
Houser, Donald E., 229
Houston Community College/Central College, 529
Housworth, Marvin C., 242
Hoversten, Mark Elison, 266
Hovey, David C., 242
Hoving, Thomas P., 281
Hovington, Rémi, Jr., 539
Howard, Elizabeth B., 262, 292
Howard, J. Murray, 242
Howard, John Tasker, 334
Howard, John W., 376
Howard, Perry, 266
Howard, William S., 229, 290
Howard Hughes Corporation, 202
Howard Kulp Architects, 313
Howard University, 502, 520, 536, 548
Howarth, Thomas, 70, 278
Howe, Deborah A., 258
Howe, Lois Lilly, 386
Howe & Manning, 386
Howell Killick Partridge & Amis, 642
Hower, Donovan E., 266
Howerton, Hart, 92
Howey, John, 242
Howland, Richard W., 276, 471
Howorth, Thomas Sommerville, 209, 242
Hoyt, Charles K., 242
Hozumi, Nobuo, 278
Hricak, Michael M., Jr., 242
H&S International, 98
Hsiung, Robert Y., 242
H2L2 Architects/Planners LLP, 327
Hua Yi Design, 378
Huang, Alfred, 535
Hubacek, Karel, 96
Hubbard, Charles A., 242
Hubbard, Henry Vincent, 293, 334
Hubbard, Kelley Lynn, 535
Hubbard, Theodora Kimball, 334
Hubbell, Benjamin, 347
Hubbell, Kent, 295
Huberman, Jeffrey A., 242
Hubka, Thomas, 429
Hudak, Joseph, 266
Huddleston, Sam L., 266
Hudgins, Carter, 449
Hudson, Derek, 540
Huefner, Robert P., 258
Huey, J. Michael, 281
Huff, Linda L., 229
Huffman, Richard W., 242
Hugh Ferriss Memorial Prize, 125
Hugh Stubbins & Associates, 80, 351, 361
Hughes, Harold E., 229
Hughes, Mary V., 266
Hughes, Nina, 262
Hughes, Robert S. F., 225
Hughes, Sanford, 242
Huh, Stephan S., 242
Hull, Robert E., 35–37, *36,* 242
Hulme, Graham Alan, 301
Human Factors and Egronomics Society, 580
Humanitarian News Agency, 404
Hume, William, 462
Hummel, Charles F., 242
Hummel Architects, 341
Humphries, Graham, 301
Humstone, Elizabeth, 220
Hunderman, Harry J., 242
Hunner, Mark B., 266
Hunt, Gregory, 242
Hunt, Richard Howland, 349
Hunt, Richard Morris, 175, 291, 329, 349, 462
Hunter, Dorian, 262
Hunter, Robert, 258
Hunter, Tonya, 511
Hunter College, CUNY, 499, 526
Huntington, Darbee & Dollard, Architects, 355
Huppert, Frances P., 242
Hurand, Fred, 258
Hursley, Timothy, 66
Hurst, Sam T., 242
Hurt, Doug, 514
Husain, Syed V., 242
Hustoles, Edward J., 258
Huston, Joseph M., 376
Hutchins, Mary Alice, 242

Name Index

Hutchins, Robert S., 219
Hutchinson, Max, 302
Hutchinson, Philip A., 281
Hutchirs, Frederick, 274
Huxtable, Ada Louise, 137, 167, 218, 225, 281, 389
Huygens, Remmert W., 242
Hvale, James L., 272
Hwang, Il-in, 278
Hyatt Foundation, 165
Hyde, Bryden B., 242
Hyett, Paul, 302
Hylton, Thomas, 284
Hyman, Isabelle, 73
Hynek, Fred J., 242
Hynes, J. P., 300

I

IBM Corp., 130, 132, 152
I.D., 126, 601, 634
I.D. Annual Design Review, 126
IDEA, Inc., 202
IDEO, 129, 130
IDSA Education Award, 541
IDSA Personal Recognition Award, 127–129, *128*
II BY IV Design Associates, 76
Iliescu, Sanda D., 220
Illingworth, Dean, 242
Illinois Institute of Art at Schaumburg, 521
Illinois Institute of Technology
  degree programs, 521, 532
  rankings, 555
  staff, 495, 541
  students/alumni, 387, 536, 539, 632
Illinois State University, 521
Illuminating Engineering Society of North America, 580
I.M. Pei & Partners. *See also* Pei, I. M.
  awards/honors, 80, 329, 382
  staff, 390
  works/projects, 347, 349, 351, 353, 377, 378
Immenschuh, David, 274
Indiana University, 522
Industrial Design Excellence Awards, 130–132, *131*
Industrial Designers Society of America
  awards/honors given by, 127–132, 541
  Fellows, 272–273
  Honorary Members, 285
  organizational information, 534, 569
  Presidents, 296
  student chapters, 512
Ingenhoven Overdiek & Partner, 81
Ingraham, Elizabeth W., 242
Ingram, Brooke, 509
Initiative for Architectural Research, 580
Inner Harbor Development of the City of Baltimore, 65
Innovation, 569, 601
Inouye, Lester Hikoji, 266
Inserra, Louis, 496
Institute for Architecture & Urban Studies, 64, 65
Institute of Electrical & Electronics Engineers Inc., 580
Institute of Engineering, 513
Institute of Store Planners, 580
Integrated Architecture, 422
Interface, Inc., 193, 271, 405
Interfaith Forum on Religion, Art and Architecture, 170
Interior Design, 133, 287, 601
Interior Design Competition, 133
Interior Design Educators Council, 534
Interior Designers Institute, 518
Interiors & Sources, 601
International Academy of Design, Tampa, 520
International Academy of Merchandising and Design, 521
International Archive of Women in Architecture, 390
International Association of Lighting Designers, 145, 580
International Centre for the Study of Preservation and Restoration of Cultural Property, 459
International Code Council, 580
International Conference of Building Code Officials, 580
International Council of Societies of Industrial Design, 586
International Council on Monuments and Sites, 454, 460
International Design Conference, 108
International Design Resource Awards, 29, 409–410
International Facility Management Association, 581
International Federation of Interior Architects/Designers, 586
International Federation of Landscape Architects, 587
International Furnishings and Design Association, 581
International Interior Design Association
  awards/honors given by, 133, 192, 418, 421, 544, 552
  Fellows, 274–275
  Honorary Members, 286
  organizational profile, 570
  Presidents, 297
  student chapters, 512
International Society of Arboriculture, 581
International Union of Architects
  awards/honors given by, 96, 137, 188, 189, 200
  organizational information, 587
  Presidents, 298
  sustainable future principles, 402–403, 420
International Wood Products Association, 581
Intrawest Corporation, 201
Iowa State University, 294, 499, 502, 522, 554, 555
Iranian Cultural Heritage Organization, 57
Ireys, Alice R., 266
Irrigation Association, 581
Irvin, Rebecca, 502, 535
Irving, Robert Grant, 72
Irwin, Harriet, 384
Irwin, James Campbell, 301
ISA-The Instrumentation, Systems and Automation Society, 581
Isais, Geraldine Forbes, 295
Iselin, Donald G., 281
Ishimaru, Nobuyuki, 409
Isley, William A., 242
Isozaki, Arata, 84, 177, 278, 345, 351
Israel, Franklin D., 74, 220, 287
Israeli Association of Landscape Architects, 95
Ito, Toyo, 84, 278
ITT Technical Institute, Indiana, 522
Ittner, H. Curtis, 242
Iu, Carolyn, 287
Ivers, B. Cannon, 510
Iversen, Erling F., 220
Iverson, Wayne D., 266
The Ives Group, Architects/Planners, 314
Ivester, H. Cliff, 262
Ivy, Robert, 242, 392
Izaki, Yosuke, 410
Izenour, Steven, 389
Izumita, Ronald M., 266

J

J. Mayer H. Architects, 81
J.A. Brennan Associates, 114
Jack D. Wilkins & Associates, 313
Jack R. Tucker Associates Architects, 313
Jackman, Dianne, 286
Jackson, Daryl Sanders, 168, 278
Jackson, H. Rowland, 266
Jackson, Huson, 242
Jackson, John B., 65
Jackson, Kathy C., 281
Jackson, Mike, 242
Jackson, R. Graham, 242
Jackson, Ralph T., 242
Jackson, Roland David, 278, 301
Jackson, Sir Thomas Graham, 175
Jacob, Bernard, 242
Jacob, David J., 220
Jacobs, Allan B., 220
Jacobs, Barbara L., 262
Jacobs, Bernard, 266
Jacobs, Harry M., 242
Jacobs, Jane, 169, 204, 388, 389, 454
Jacobs, Keri, 514
Jacobs, Peter D. A., 267
Jacobs, Stephen B., 242
Jacobs and Maciejewski and Associates Architects, 312
Jacobs Civil Inc., 112
Jacobsen, Arne, 273
Jacobsen, Hugh Newell, 242, 353
Jacobson, Phillip L., 242
Jacobson, Roger L., 229
Jacobson, Susan L. B., 267, 293
Jacobson, Victoria Tatna, 209
Jacoby, J. P., 242
Jaeger, Dale G. M., 267
Jafar Tukan & Partners, 57
Jaffe, Dr. Christopher, 67
Jagtap, Tanusri, 500
Jahn, Graham, 301
Jahn, Helmut, 84, 242, 545
James, Dr. Frank D., 222
James, Harlean, 334
James, Vincent, 74, 631
James Baird Company, 376
James Beard Foundation, 134
James Beard Restaurant Design Award, 134, *135*
James M. Hartley, Architects, 312

James Madison University, 530
James Stewart & Company, 376
James Stewart Polshek and Partners, 80, 345
James Sudler Associates, 347
Jameson-Gibson Construction Company, Inc., 202
Jamieson, Douglas E., 125
Jamieson, Timm, 242
Janda, Benjamin H., 638
Jandl, Henry A., 242
Jane C. Hall, Architect, 388
Japan Architect, 604
Japan Art Association, 162
Japan Institute of Architects, 587
Jarmusch, Ann, 218
Jarratt, William Robert, 219, 242
Jarrett, James R., 220
Jarvis, Frederick D., 267
Jary, Lloyd, 242
JASMAX Limited, 104
Jáuregui, Jorge Mario, 203
J.B. Muns Fine Arts Books, 591
J.C. Nichols Prize for Visionary Urban Development, 136
Jean Tschumi Prize, 137
Jeanneret-Gris, Charles Edouard. *See* Le Corbusier
Jefferis, David, 536
Jefferson, Bryan, 302
Jefferson, Peter, 242
Jefferson, Thomas, 59, 329, 330, 376, 462
Jelks, Jordan O., 242
Jellicoe, Sir Geoffrey, 90
Jenkins, J. Edward, 229
Jenkins, Leerie T., Jr., 267
Jenkins, Sarah B., 262
Jennewein, J. J., 242
Jennings, Richard W., 242
Jenrette, Richard H., 435
Jensen, Bruce H., 242
Jensen, Charlotte, 262
Jensen, David R., 267
Jensen, Robert, 223
Jensen, Thomas J., 502
Jensen & Skodvin, 83
Jensen and Halstead Ltd., 341
Jepson, David, 242
Jerde, Jon Adams, 242
The Jerde Partnership, 326
Jervolino, Hon. Rosa Russo, 404
Jester, Thomas L., 229
Jet Propulsion Laboratory, 163
Jeter, Cook and Jepson Architects, Inc., 116
Jewell, Linda Lee, 267
J.H. Wiese Company, 375
Jickling, John W., 242
Jinright, Ryan & Lynn, Architects & Planners, 312
Jiricna, Eva, 287
J.M. Kaplan Fund, 66
Joaquim de Meio Siza, Alvaro, 278
Jody Kingrey Inc., 623
Johannes, Connie, 262
Johansen, John M., 84, 242
John & Bolles, 369
John Dinkeloo & Associates, 378
John Gill & Sons, 375
John M. Senkarik & Associates, 313
John Portman and Associates, Inc., 379
John Senhauser Architects, 313
Johns, Anthony N., Jr., 242
Johns, Barry, 278
Johns Hopkins University, 497, 628
Johns Manville Company, 424
Johnson, Arthur D., 242
Johnson, Benjamin, 388
Johnson, Bill, 361
Johnson, Billisha, 514
Johnson, Carl D., 90, 267
Johnson, Carol R., 90, 267
Johnson, Carrie P., 538
Johnson, Cary D., 274, 297
Johnson, Christina, 274
Johnson, Claire H., 502, 539
Johnson, Clifford W., 229
Johnson, Craig W., 542, *543*
Johnson, Danie, 242
Johnson, Dean A., 222, 267
Johnson, Derrell E., 229
Johnson, Dr. Joseph E., 281
Johnson, Edmund G., 229
Johnson, Edwin J., 242
Johnson, Eric B., 242
Johnson, Floyd Elmer, 242
Johnson, J. B., 281
Johnson, James A., 152
Johnson, James H., 242
Johnson, Jane Hall, 388
Johnson, Jed, 287
Johnson, Jed V., 242
Johnson, Jessica N., 502, 539
Johnson, Lady Bird, 64, 152, 281
Johnson, Mark Robert, 242
Johnson, Mark W., 267
Johnson, Morris E., 258
Johnson, P. N., 278
Johnson, Philip C. *See also* Philip Johnson Architects
  awards/honors, 59, 75, 165, 197, 225, 382
  quote, 68, 103
  works/projects, 345, 349, 351, 353, 631
Johnson, Pres. Lyndon B., 284
Johnson, Ralph E., 242
Johnson, Reginald D., 197
Johnson, Richard "Peter" Norman, 168, 301, 638–639
Johnson, Scott, 242
Johnson, T. H., 375
Johnson, Tom, *28,* 29–35
Johnson, Walker C., 242
Johnson, William J., 90, 267
Johnson, William Templeton, 353
Johnson, Yandell, 242
Johnson Bros. Corporation, 155
Johnson/Burgee Architects, 345, 379, 380
The Johnson Partnership, 314
Johnston, Norman J., 242
Johnstone, B. Kenneth, 294
Jolicoeur, Trycie, 537
Jolley, Dr. Harley, 284
Jonason, Wallace R., 262, 292
Jonassen, James O., 242
Jones, Arthur E., 243
Jones, Barclay Gibbs, 497
Jones, Bernard I., 243
Jones, Carol, 274, 297
Jones, Charles L., 272, 548
Jones, E. Fay, 59, 194, 220, 243, 329, 383, 495
Jones, Gerre, 281
Jones, Grant R., 89, 267
Jones, Ilze, 89, 267
Jones, J. Delaine, 243
Jones, Jack B., 243
Jones, Johnpaul, 243
Jones, Margo, 274
Jones, Marnie, 272
Jones, Mary Margaret, 222
Jones, Melvin E., 229
Jones, Owen, 175
Jones, Paul Duane, 243
Jones, Renis, 243
Jones, Richard W., 262, 292
Jones, Robert Lawton, 243
Jones, Robert Trent, Sr., 267
Jones, Roy Childs, 294
Jones, Rudard Artaban, 243
Jones, Sir Horace, 302
Jones, Walk, 349
Jones, Warren D., 267
Jones, Wesley, 220
Jones & Emmons, 80
Jones & Jones, 88, *89*
Jong, Bendrew G., 243
Jongejan, Dirk, 267
Jordan, Henry, 262
Jordan, Joe J., 243
Jordan, June Meyer, 223
Jordan, Lewis H., 300
Jordan, V., Jr., 281
Jordani, David A., 243
Jordy, William H., 65
Jorge Mario Jáuregui Architects, 203
Jorgensen, Roberta W., 243
Joseph, Wendy Evans, 220, 243
Joseph Passonneau & Partners, 163
Joslyn Art Museum, 411
Joslyn Castle Institute, 271, 411
Jot D. Carpenter Medal, 542, *543*
Journal of Architectural Education, 601
Journal of Architecture, 604
Journal of Interior Design, 601
Journal of the American Planning Association, 601
Journal of the Society of Architectural Historians, 601
Journal of Urban Design, 604
Jova, Henri B., 220, 243, 262
Joy, Rebecca M., 538
Joy, Rick, 74
JPJ Architects, 379
JPRA Architects, 183
Judd, Bruce D., 243
Judd, H. A., 281
Judith L. Kelly Architect, 313
Judson, Franklin S., 262
Judson College, 521
Jules Fisher & Paul Marantz, Inc., 65
Julia, Carlson, 410
Julie, Vaillant, 502
Jumsai, Sumet, 278
Jung, Yu Sing, 243
Junius, Ralph W., Jr., 229
Juster, Howard H., 243
Juster, Robert J., 258
Justice, Lorraine, 272

K

Kaelber, Carl F., Jr., 243
Kaeyer, Richard E., 243

Name Index

Kagan, Gerald, 243
Kagermeier, Jeffry Lee, 209
Kahan, Richard A., 195
Kahane, Melanie, 288
Kahler, David T., 243
Kahler, Fitzhugh and Scott, 349
Kahler Slater Architects, 113, 121, 330
Kahn, Albert J., 308
Kahn, Charles H., 243
Kahn, Louis I.
  awards/honors, 59, 75, 84, 177, 197, 198, 271, 329, 383
  quote, 299
  works/projects, 349, 355
Kahn, Robert, 221
Kahn, Vivian, 258
Kainlauri, Eino O., 243
Kaiser, C. Hayden, Jr., 229
Kaiser, Edward, 258
Kaiser, Lloyd, 281
Kalamar, Andrej, 83
Kale, Harry, 243
Kalin, Mark, 243
Kallmann, Gerhard Michael, 225, 243
Kallmann, McKinnell & Wood Architects , 63, 80, 119, 225
Kalman, Tibor, 45, 46, 48
Kaltwasser, Jennifer Lynn, 539
Kamber, Dennis, 229
Kamin, Blair, 67, 167, 215
Kamphoefner, Henry, 294, 556
Kanalstein Danton Associates, 102
Kane, Janet E., 262
Kang, Yunseok Oscar, 536
Kanmacher and Dengi, 374
Kann and Associates Architects, 326
Kanner, Stephen H., 243
Kansas State College, 294
Kansas State University
  degree programs, 522
  rankings, 554, 555
  staff, 495, 542, 643
  students/alumni, 502, 510, 536
Kanvinde, Achyut P., 278
Kanyer, Peter James, 538
Kaplan, Gary Y., 243
Kaplan, Richard H., 243
Kaplan, Wendy, 223
Kaplan McLaughlin Diaz, 327
Kappe, Raymond L., 243, 556
Kappe, Shelly, 281
Kapsch, Robert J., 281
Karfik, Vladimir, 278
Karlsberger Companies, 133
Karn Charuhas Chapman & Twohey, 120
Karner, Gary E., 267
Karr, Joseph P., 267
Karr Poole and Lum, 375
Kaskey, Raymond J., 243
Kass, Spence, 221
Kass, Thomas, 496
Kassabaum, George Edward, 219, 291
Kassner, John J., 229
Kast, Miller I., 299
Kato, Sadahisa, 510
Katz, Joel, 222
Kauffman, Jerome L., 258
Kaufman, Donald, 67
Kaufman, Edward, 160
Kaufmann, Edgar, Jr., 285
Kautz, Barbara, 258
Kavanagh, Jean Stephans, 267
Kawaguchi, Stanley K., 229, 290
Kawahigashi, Theodore S., 229
Kawasaki, Frank H., 267
KCE Structural Engineers, 113
Keahey, Kirby M., 243
Keally, Francis, 376
Kean University, 525
Keane, Gustave R., 243
Keane, Jan, 243
Keating, Richard C., 243
Keay, Sir Lancelot, 302
Keefe, Lloyd, 258
Keefe, Moses P., 376
Keenan, Sharon K. Sommerlad, 546
Keenberg, Ronald, 300
Keeter, James E., 267
Keffer/Overton Architects, 341
Kehm, Walter H., 267
Kehrt, Allan, 243
Keichline, Anna Wagner, 386
Kelbaugh, Douglas S., 243
Kelham, George, 345
Kell, Duane A., 243
Kell, John H., 243
Kellenberger, Mary Gordon Latham, 435
Kellenyi, Bernard, 243
Keller, Charles W., 229
Keller, Genevieve Pace, 284
Keller, J. Timothy, 267
Keller, John, 258
Keller, Larry J., 243
Keller, Suzanne, 281
Kellert, Stephen, 399
Kelley-Markham Architecture and Planning, 105
Kellogg, Thomas W., 639
Kelly, Eric Damian, 258
Kelly, Frank S., 243
Kelly, Nathan B., 376
Kelly, Patrick, 510
Kelly, Philip E., 289
Kelman, Paul B., 258
Kelsey, Chester C., 229
Kelsey, F. L., 243
Kemnitzer, Ron, 272
Kemp, Diane Legge, 243
Kemper, Edward C., 110
Kendall, Edward H., 291
Kendall, Henry H., 291
Kendall, Taylor & Company, Inc., 341
Kendall, William D., 243
Kendall College of Art and Design, 524
Kender, Dorothy, 281
Kennard, Robert, 205
Kennedy, David D., 229
Kennedy, Raymond, 292
Kennedy, Robert N., 243, 274
Kennedy, Roger G., 281
Kennedy and Violich Architecture Ltd., 143
Kennedy/Jenks Consultants, 113
Kenner, Todd J., 229
Kenneth F. Brown Asia Pacific Culture & Architecture Design Award, 138–140, *139*
Kenneth Maynard Associates, 345
Kenniff, Thomas-Bernard, 513
Kennon, Kevin, 8
Kent, T. J., Jr., 334
Kent State University, 516, 527, 554
Kenzo Tange Associates, 379, 381
Kerbis, Gertrude L., 243
Kerns, Thomas L., 243
Kerr, Leslie A., 267
Kerrigan, Wendy Weatherall, 539
Kerry Hill Architects, 57, 138
Kertland, D. F., 300
Kesler, Gary B., 267
Kessels DiBoll Kessels & Associates, 341
Kessler, George Edward, 334
Kessler, William H., 243, 640
Kessler Francis Cardoza, 640
Ketcham, Herbert A., 243
Ketchum, Morris, Jr., 219, 291
Keune, Russell V., 243
Kevin Roche John Dinkeloo & Associates, 80, 198, 349, 351
Keyes, A. H., Jr., 243
Keystone Award, 141
Khalil, Fouad, 508
Khan, Fazlur, 65
Khatib & Alami, 381
KHR AS Arkitekten, 83, 96
KI, 129
Kiatsupaibul, Sansern, 511
Kidder, Bradley P., 110
Kiefaber, Tom, 465
Kieran, Stephen J., 221, 243
Kiesler, Frederick, 97
Kihl, Mary R., 258
Kiil, Leevi, 243
Kikutake, Kiyonori, 278
Kilbourn, Lee F., 243
Kilcullen, Justin, 189
Kiley, Daniel Urban, 84, 153, *154*, 157, 461
Killebrew, James R., 243
Killingsworth, Edward A., 243
Killmer, Holly, 499
Kim, Jihea, 186
Kim, Tai Soo, 243
Kimball, Thomas R., 291
Kime, Sidney R., Jr., 267
Kimm, Jong S., 243
Kimsey, J. Windom, 209
King, David R. H., 243
King, Dennis M., 243
King, Donald, 243
King, Frederick D. A., Jr., 229
King, Gordon L., 243
King, J. Bertram, 243
King, John, 167, 218
King, Jonathan, 281
King, Leland, 243
King, Ronette, 288
King, Sol, 243
King, Stephanie L., 503
King, Steven G., 267
King & King Architects, 341
Kingscott Associates, Inc., 312
Kingston, M. Ray, 243
Kinner, Edward B., 229
Kinnison, Paul, Jr., 243
Kinnunen, Laila A., 503
Kinoshita, Masao, 267
Kinstlinger, Jack, 229
Kips Bay Decorator Show House, 289
Kirchoff, Roger C., 299
Kirgis, George, 229
Kirjassoff, Gordon L., 229

L

Name Index

Lamantia, James R., 221
Lamb, Albert R., III, 222
Lamb, Charles E., 244
Lambert, Phyllis, 169, 226, 278
Lambeth, James L., 221, 244
Lamborghihi Feilbelman Ltd., 312
Lammers, James I., 244
Lamont, William, Jr., 258
Lamson, Kyle, 126
Lancaster, David P., 282
Lanchester, Henry Vaughan, 177
Lanciani, Rodolfo Amadeo, 175
Landahl, Gregory W., 244
Landon, Peter H., 244
Landry, D. E., 244
Landry, Jane, 244
Landscape Architectural Accreditation Board, 517, 534, 567
Landscape Architecture, 567, 602
Landslide Landscapes, 461
Lane, Barbara Miller, 72
Lane, Mills B., IV, 451
Lane & Associates, Inc., 314
Lang, Megan, 499
Langdon-Wilson, 326
Langenbach, Randolph, 223
Langevin. Patric, 537
Langham, Jay, 514
Langran, Joe W., 267
Lanier, Lucille Chenery, 267
l'Anson, Edward, 302
Lanzillotta, Mary Katherine, 209
Laping, John M., 244
Lapp, Floyd, 258
Larm, Derrick, 540
LaRochelle, Donald R., 229
Larsen, Arnold Les, 244
Larsen, Henning, 278
Larsen, Jack Lenor, 181, 289
Larsen, Robert G., 244
Larsen Shein Ginsberg Snyder, 150
Larson, Dayl A., 244
Larson, Gary, 221
Larson, Neil A., 78
Larson, Roy F., 219
Larson, Thomas N., 221
Larson, William L., 244
Larson, William N., 244
Lasch, Mary Ann, 267
Lasdun, Sir Denys L., 177, 206, 278
Laskey, Leslie J., 495
Latham, Richard S., 272
Latimer, George, 282
Latrobe, Benjamin Henry, 329, 376
Latta, Hugh L., 109, 262
Lau, Dennis, 377
Lauesen, Warren E., 267
Laurel, Aaron, 500
Laurent, Barbara B., 540
Laurie, Michael M., 267
Laurie, William Rae, 168, 301
Laurila, Brett Keith, 209
Laval Université, 502
Law, Dennis L., 267
Law, Richard K., 267
Lawal, Mohammed, 209
Lawler, Carroll James, 110, *111,* 219, 244, 291
Lawler, Cindy, *111*
Lawlor, Drue, 262
Lawlor, Patti, 547
Lawrence, Charles E., 244
Lawrence, Ellis, 294
Lawrence, Geoffrey, 301
Lawrence, Jerry, 244
Lawrence, Robert M., 244, 291
Lawrence Technological University, 524
Lawson, David E., 244
Lawson, Edward, 222
Lawson, Elizabeth, 244
Lawson, William R., 244
Lawyer, Franklin D., 244
Lax, Michael, 223
Layard, Sir Henry, 175
Layborne-Smith, Louis, 168, 301
Layton and Smith, 376
L.D. Astorino Companies, 361
LDA Architects, 345
Le Bey, John C., 244
Le Corbusier, 51, 59, 177, 383
Le group ARCOP, 201
Le Messurier, William J., 282
Le Ricolais, Robert, 64
Lea, Samuel H., 376
Leader, Tom, 222
Leaman, Jack E., 267
Leary, Dan, 514
Leavitt, David L., 221
Lebowitz, Annie, 187
L'Ecole de Beaux Arts, 385, 387
Leczinski, Dennis W., 262
Ledbetter, Celia, 221
Leddy, William E., 244
Lederer, Donald F., 267
Ledingham, Robert, 274
Lee, Andrew C., 502
Lee, Benjamin B., 244
Lee, Donald R., 244
Lee, Elizabeth B., 244
Lee, Gary, 288
Lee, Jin-Hoon, 539
Lee, John M.Y., 244, 349
Lee, Kwang-Ro, 278
Lee, Kyung-Hoi, 278
Lee, M. David, 244
Lee, Peter R., Jr., 495
Lee, Robin, 282
Lee, Sarah Tomerlin, 288
Lee & Sakahara Architects, Inc., 314
Lee H. Solnick Architecture, 62
LEED Green Building Rating System, 412, 421, 425
Leeds University, 633
Leedy, Gene, 244
Leefe, James M., 244
Leenknegt, Jan, 550
Leers, Andrea P., 244
Leff, Naomi, 288
Lefferts, Gillet, 244
LeFrak, Samuel Jackson, 641
LeFrak Organization, 641
Legetic, Svetlana, 536
Legorreta, Ricardo, 59, 194, 200, 226
Lehman Architectural Partnership, 341
Lehman-Smith, Debra, 288, 391
Lehman-Smith + McLeish, 119, 120, 391
Lehmann, Phyllis Williams, 72
Leibrock, Cynthia, 108, 286
Leider, Charles L., 267
Leigh Whitehead Associates, 163
Leighton, Lord, 175
Leiman, Dani, 535
Leineweber, Spencer A., 244
Leinweber, Yamasaki and Hellmuth, 643
Leira, Eduardo, 188
Leis, Lawrence J., 244
Leiserowitz, Nila, 262
Leitch, Richard, 244
Leithead, William G., 300
Leiviskä, Juha Ilmari, 278
Lembcke, Herbert, 244
Lembo, Joseph, 288
Lemon, Christian, 92
LeMond, Robert, 244
Lenci, Sergio, 278
Lendrum, James T., 244
Lendrum, Peter A., 244
L'Enfant, Pierre Charles, 334
Lennon, Boone, 536
Leo, Christian, 500
Leo A Daly Architects, 116, 170, 326, 327
Leobl Schlossman Dart & Hackl, 378
Leon, Abbie Janette de, 513
Leonard, Eason H., 244
Leonard, Paul, 286
Leonardo da Vinci, 410
LePatner, Barry B., 282
Leplastrier, Richard, 168
Lepper, Robert, 541
Lepsius, C. R., 175
Lerner, Deborah L., 539
Lerner, Jaime, 189, 278, 298
Lerner, Lawrence, 288
Lerner, Ralph, 244
Lerner-Miller, Fola, 274
LeRoy, Glen S., 244, 258
Leroy Adventures, 134
Lerup, Lars, 496
Les constructions Devlor, 201
Les enterprises du Bon Ltee, 201
Lescher & Mahoney Sports, 359
Lesko, Nicholas, 244
Leslie, Donald W., 267, 293
Leslie, Robert, 500
Leslie Elkins Architecture, 170
Leslie N. Boney, Architect, 625
Lesueur, Jean-Baptiste Cicéron, 175
Lethbridge, Francis D., 244
Lettieri, Anthony, 258
Levenson, Conrad, 244
Levi, Jonathan, 244
Levin, Brenda A., 244
Levin, Jack, 274
Levin, Richard D., 244
Levin Porter Associates, Inc., 347
Levine, Aaron, 267, 282
Levine, Joe, 207
Levine, Julius S., 258
Levine, Sally Lynn, 391
Levine-Chesler, Heather, 535
Levis, Calvin E., 229
Levison, Robert H., 110
Levitas, E. H., 282
Levitt brothers, 419
Levy, Alan G., 244
Levy, Eugene P., 244
Levy, Herbert W., 244
Levy, Morton L., 244
Levy, Raoul L., 229
Levy, Toby S., 244

Lewis, Anne McCutcheon, 244
Lewis, Calvin F., 244
Lewis, David, 110, 244
Lewis, Diane, 221
Lewis, Howarth, Jr., 244
Lewis, James R., 78
Lewis, Lawrence, Jr., 282
Lewis, Michael J., 73
Lewis, Neville, 274, 288
Lewis, Paul, 221
Lewis, Philip H., Jr., 90, 267
Lewis, Richard L., 244
Lewis, Roger K., 244
Lewis, Roy W., 221
Lewis, Sally Sirkin, 288
Lewis, Tom, Jr., 244
Lewis, Trevor, 513
Lewis, Walter H., 244, 284
Lewis, William D., 229, 290
Lewis Mumford Prize, 142
LeWitt, Sol, 64
L_H_R_S Architects, Inc., 341
Li, Wei, 125
Liaigre, Christian, 288
Liang Yong, Wu, 278
Liao, Kuo-Liang, 511
Liberty Property Trust, 651
Libeskind, Daniel, 8, 9, 74
Library Buildings Awards, 143, *144*
Library of Congress, 435
Licht, George T., 221
Liddle, Alan C., 244
Lieber, J. Roland, 267
Liebhardt, Frederick, 244
Liebman, Theodore, 221, 244
Lieder, Constance, 258
Lien & Peterson Architects, Inc., 314
Liestiawati, Irene, 500
Lifchez, Raymond, 496
Liff, Bernard J., 244
Light, Pamela, 274
Light Gauge Steel Engineers Association, 581
The Lighthouse: Scotland's Centre for Architecture, Design and the City, 607
Lighting Design Awards, 145–147, *146*
Lightle, Helen M. Olson, 258
Lijewski, John A., 274, 297
Lillard, David H., 229
Lillie, Richard R., 258
Lim Ee Man, Joseph, 138
Lin, Jou Min, 83
Lin, Maya, 74, 329, 390, 392
Lin, T. Y., 65
Lincoln, Abraham, 4, 472
Lincoln, Frank L., 229
Lind, John H., 244
Lindbloom, Leon J., 229
Lindenthal, Robert S., 262
Linders, Howard D., 229
Lindhult, Mark S., 267
Lindsey, Chester, 642
Lindsey, David, 244
Lindsey, Gail A., 244
Lindsey, Patricia F., 546
Link, Theodore C., 375
Link & Hare, 375
Linley, Viscount David, 286
Linn, Charles D., 244
Linn, Karl, 267
Linnard, Lawrence G., 293
Linton, Coby J., 502
Lippincott, H. Mather, Jr., 244
Lipscomb, Joseph, 229
Liskamm, William H., 244
Lister, James M., 222
Lit, Steve, 216
Little, Bertram R., 435
Little, J. Mack, 267
Little, Mrs. Bertram R., 435
Little, Robert A., 244
Little, Susan P., 267
Littlejohn, Earl R., 267
Littleton, Charles, 274
Litton, R. Burton, Jr., 267
Littrell, John, 229
Liu, Dr. Binyi, 284
Liu, Lina, 121
Livesey, Robert S., 221, 244
Livingston, Stanley C., 244
Livingston, Thomas W., 244
Livingston, Walter R., Jr., 244
Livingston Slone, 308
Livingstone, Bruce, 229
Livingstone, Eden D., 503
Lizon, Peter, 244
Lloyd, Sarah, 410
Lloyd Jones Philpot, 363
LMN Architects, 143, 314
Loch, Emil, 299
Lockard, W. Kirby, 244
Lockett, Thomas A., 267
Lockwood, Andrews, & Newman, 113
Lockwood Greene, 341
Loeb Fellowship in Advanced Environmental Studies, 65
Loebl Schlossman Dart & Hackl, 379
Loendorf, Boyd L., 262
Loewen, Kevin, 539
Loewy, Raymond, 127, 272, 634, 639
Loewy/Snaith, 634
Loftis, James L., 244
Loftness, Vivian, 244
Logan, Donn, 244
Logan Hopper Associates, Architects, 314
Logictech, Inc., 129, 132
Lohan, Dirk, 244
Lohan Associates Inc., 308
Lollini, Thomas E., 244
Lomax, Jerrold E., 245
Lombardi, Steven, 207
Long, Nimrod W. E., III, 267
Longoria, Rafael, 295
Longstreth, Richard, 142, 190, 303, 431, 451
Loo, Kington, 278
Loomis, Arthur, 353
Looney, J. Carson, 245
Looney Ricks Kiss, 105, 202
Loope, R. Nicholas, 245
Loquasto, Santo, 289
Lorant, Gabor, 245
Lorch, Emil, 294
Lord, Aeck & Sargent, 326
Lord, Chip, 644
Lord, Larry, 245
Lord, W. H., 299
Lorenzo, Aldana E., 278
Lortz, C. Richard, 229
Los Angeles Times, 167, 216
Loschky, George H., 245
Loschky Marquardt & Nesholm, 369
Lose, David O., 267
Loss, John C., 245
Lotery, Rex, 245
Louie, William C., 245
Louis E. Barbieri, Architect-Planner, 314
Louise DuPont Crowinshield Award, 435
Louisiana State University, 496, 502, 522, 536
Louisiana Tech University, 502, 514, 522
Louisville Courier-Journal, 216
Lounsbury, Carl R., 429, 431, 449
Louvain la Neuve, 188
Love, John A., 284
Love, Michael, 262
Love, Ronald, 125
Love, William, 245, 419
Love Canal, 419, 420
Love-Stanley, Ivenue, 245
LoVecchio, Joseph, 262
Lovelace, Eldridge, 267
Lovelace, Richard, 125
Lovell, Tom, 374
Loversidge, Robert D., Jr., 245
Lovett, Wendell H., 245
Lowd, Harry, 502
Lowe, Peter E., 272
Lowe, Rick, 141
Lowell, Guy, 351
Lowenthal, David, 449
Lower Manhattan Development Corporation, 7–8
Lowery, Jack, 292
Lowrie, Charles N., 293
Lowry, Patricia, 217
Loy, LeRoy D., 229
Loza, Serapio P., 278
LPT Architects, 201
Lu, Paul C. K., 267
Lu, Weiming, 282
Lubben, Ronald, 274
Lubetkin, Berthold, 177
Lucas, Frank E., 245
Lucas, Frederick Bruce, 168, 301
Lucas, Thomas J., 245
Lucey, Lenore M., 245
Lucien Lagrange Architects, 380
Luckenbach, Carl F., 245
Luckett & Farley Architects, Engineers and Construction Managers, Inc., 341
Luckman, Charles, 363, 371
Luder, Owen, 302
Ludwig, Lucinda, 245
Lueck, Odette, 262
Luhn, Graham B., 245
Lukas, Ana, 535
Lukermann, Barbara, 258
Lumsden, Anthony J., 245
Lunar Design, 130
Lund, Kjell, 278
Lund McGee Sharp Architecture, 351
Lunde, Frithjof, 245
Lundegaard, Inge, 499
Lunden, Samuel E., 110
Lundgren, Ray, 229
Lundoff and Bicknell, 375
Lundwall, Phillip, 245
Lundy, Victor A., 245
Lupia, Major General Eugene, 282
Lurcott, Robert H., 258
Luscomb, Florence, 386

Name Index

Lutes, Donald H., 245
Lutyens, Sir Edwin Landseer, 59, 175
Lye, Eric Kumchew, 137
Lyle, John, 90
Lyles, Bissett, Carlisle and Wolff Associates of North Carolina Inc., 310
Lyman, Frederic P., 245
Lynch, Andy, 114
Lynch, Kevin, 334
Lynch, Robert Dale, 245
Lynch, Robert J., 245
Lyndon, Donlyn, 245, 294, 556
Lyndon, Maynard, 245
Lynford, Ruth K., 262, 289
Lynn, David, 376
Lynn, Greg, 8, 74
Lyons, Eric, 302

M

M. Mense Architects, 314
Maas, Jane, 282
Maas, Michael, 245
Mabe, R. Doss, 245
MacAlister, Paul, 272
MacAllister, John E., 245
Macaulay, David A., 64
MacCormac, Richard C., 302
MacDonald, Donald, 245
MacDonald, Lee, 284
MacDonald, Virginia B., 245
MacDonald, William J., 72, 73
MacDougall, E. Bruce, 284
MacDougall, Elisabeth Blair, 276, 303
MacEwen, H. A., 245
MacFadyen, John H., 221
MacFarlane, J. Les, 229, 290
Machado, Rodolfo, 74
Machado and Silvetti Associates, Inc., 60
Machida, Hiroko, 274
Mack, Linda, 216
Mack, Robert C., 245
Mack Scogin Merrill Elam Architects, 143
MacKay-Lyons, Brian, 278
MacKaye, Benton, 334
MacKenzie, Candace, 274
Mackey, Eugene J., III, 245
Mackey, Howard Hamiton, Sr., 205
MacKinlay, Ian, 245
MacLachlan, Cornelius & Filoni, Inc., 341
MacLean, Alex S., 222
Macleod, Robert, 642
MacMahon, Charles H., 245
MacMillan, Kyle, 216
MacMinn, Strother, 541
Macris, Dean L., 258
Macris, Marjorie, 258
Macsai, John, 245
Macy, J. Douglas, 267
Madawick, Tucker P., 272, 296
Maddox, Diane, 282
Maddox, Eva L., 192, 288
Mader, George G., 258
Madigan, Colin Frederick, 168
Madigele, Gorata, 540
Madison, Robert P., 205, 245
Madsen, Peter E., 245
Mae, Fannie, 152
Maeda, Eugene, 500
Maffitt, Theodore S., Jr., 245
Magaziner, Henry J., 245
Maginnis, Charles Donagh, 59, 291
Magnusson, Jon D., 282
Magnusson Klemencic Associates, 112
Maguire Thomas Partners, 66
Mah, Francis, 349
Mahaffey, Gary, 245
Mahan, A. Catherine, 267
Mahan, Frank E., 535
Mahayni, Riad G., 258
Maheux, Anne Frances, 223
Mahler, Victor C., 245
Mahlum, John E., 245
Mahlun Architects, 143
Mahoney, Monica Lynne, 511
Maiwald, C. R., 245
Majekodunmi, Olufemi, 278, 298, 402, 420
Major League Baseball, 152
MAK Center for Art & Architecture L.A. Schindler House, 607
Maki, Fumihiko
  awards/honors, 84, 162, 165, 200, 203, 206, 226, 278
Makin, Guy St. John, 301
Makinen, Matti K., 278
Makinson, Randell Lee, 282
Malacara, Rutilo, 278
Malassigné, Pascal, 272
Malcolm Pirnie, Inc., 113
Malecha, Marvin John, 111, 245, 295, 496, 556, *557*
Malefane, Motlatsi Peter, 278
Malensek, Chris, 516
Mallach, Alan, 258
Mallgrave, Harry Francis, 73
Mallory, Stephen, 288
Maloof, L. Vic, 245
Maltzan, Michael Thomas, 209
Malyn, Michael H., 267
Man, Cameron R. J., 267, 293
Manausa Lewis & Dodson Architects, Inc., 314
Mancini Duffy, 327
Mancuso, Anthony J., 537
Mandawe, Tina, 500
Manderfield, Ellen, 127
Mango, Joseph R., 272
Mangones, Albert, 278
Mangurian, Robert, 221
Mankins, Paul D., 209, *210*
Manly, William M., 262
Mann, Arthur E., 245
Mann, Emily, 510
Mann, George R., 374, 375
Mann, Lawrence, 258
Mann, Lian Hurst, 67
Mann, Michael, 245
Manning, Eleanor, 386
Manning, John Francis, 540
Manning, Warren H., 293, 461
Manny, Carter H., Jr., 245, 276
Manser, Michael, 302
Mansur, Cline L., 229
Manus, Clark D., 245
Maple Flooring Manufacturers Association, 581
Maples, Bonnie, 300
Marble Institute of America, 581
March, Nancy, 77
March, Virginia S., 245
Marcheselli, Constanza Andre, 537
Marcou, George T., 258
Marcus, Stanley, 282
Marcus Curtis Design, 126
Mardones-Restat, Hector, 298
Margerum, Roger W., 245
Margison, Jennifer K., 509
Marheb-Emanuelli, Ely, 514
Mariani, Theodore F., 110
Marines, Louis L., 282
Marini, Barbara, 547
Marino, Peter, 288
Mario J. Ciampi & Associates, 345
Mark Cavagnero Associates, 134
Mark D. Lipton Associates, Architects & Designers, 314
Markelius, Sven Gottfrid, 177, 188
Markham, Fred L., 299
Marks, Judy, 282
Markwood, Phillip T., 245
Marmon, Harvey V., Jr., 245
Marmon Mok, 363, 373
Marpillero Pollak Architects, 69, 207
Marquardt, Jud R., 245
Marquez, Hudson, 644
Marquis, Robert B., 219
Marr, Clinton, Jr., 245
Marr and Holman Architects, 347
Mars Pathfinder Mission, 163
Marschall, Albert R., 282
Marsh, Kamali, 514
Marshall, Denton Corker, 168
Marshall, Lane L., 293, 643
Marshall, Mortimer M., Jr., 245
Marshall, Richard C., 245, 267
Marshall, William "Chick," Jr., 291
Marshall Craft Associates, Inc., 326
Martens, Walter F., 299
Martin, Albert C., 245
Martin, Bradley L., 511
Martin, Charles, 429
Martin, Christopher C., 245
Martin, David C., 245
Martin, Edward C., Jr., 267
Martin, Janet, 271
Martin, Robert E., 245
Martin, Roger B., 222, 267, 293
Martin, Sir Leslie, 177
Martin, W. Mike, 245
Martin, William, 374
Martin-Vegue, Phyllis, 109
Martínez, Romualdo, 536
Martinez, Walter B., 245
Martini, Elizabeth, 386
Martini, Richard, 548
Martino, Steve, 267
Marvel, Thomas S., 245
Marvin, Robert E., 90, 267
Marx, Maureen, 282
Marx, Roberto Burle, 90
Marx, Samuel, 351
Mary Washington College, 449, 530
Marymount University, 530
Maryville University of St. Louis, 524
Marzella, Joseph V., 245
Masayoshi, Yendo, 278
Maschal, Richard, 215
Mason, George D., 299
Mason, Ronald L., 245
Mason & Hangar Group, Inc., 341

Masoner, Helen, 262
Mass, Marvin, 66
Massachusetts College of Art, 391, 523
Massachusetts Historical Society, 452
Massachusetts Institute of Technology
degree programs, 523, 532, 533
founding, 384
rankings, 555
staff, 225, 294, 392, 496, 497, 556
students/alumni, 384, 385, 386, 387, 502, 513, 550
Massey, Right Honorable Vincent, 169
Masten, Paul W., 229
Masters, Richard E., 229
Maternus, Inc., 130
Mathes, Earl L., 299
Mathes, Edward, 548
Mathes Group, 308, 341
Mathew & Ghosh Architects, 138
Mathews, Thomas F., 72
Mathis, Walter Nold, 435
Matsu, Aimi, 409
Matsumoto, George, 245
Matsumoto, Michael P., 229
Matsuzaki, Eva, 300
Mattel, Melissa Cyrila, 537
Matthei, Edward H., 245
Matthei & Colin Associates, 121
Matthew, Sir Robert, 177, 298, 302
Matthews, David R., 229
Mattox, Robert F., 245
Mattson, Robert M., 267
Matzke, Frank J., 245
Maudlin-Jeronimo, John M., 245, 548
Maufe, Sir Edward, 177
Mauk Design, 186
Maule, Tallie B., 221
Mauran, John L., 291
Maurer, Laurie M., 245
Maurer, Terri, 262, 292
Mauro, Sebastian di, 83
Maxman, Susan A., 245, 291, 391, 402, 420
Maxwell, Jeff, 509
Maxwell, Murvan M., 245
Maxwell, W. S., 300
May, Arthur, 84, 221, 245
May, Aubrey D., 229
May, Edwin, 374
May, Lewis T., 267
May, Richard, Jr., 258
Maybeck, Bernard Ralph, 59
Maycock, Susan E., 434
Mayekawa, Kunio, 96
Mayer, Albert, 334
Mayer, Jürgen, 148
Mayer, Richard E., 267
Mayer/Reed, 186
Mayer-Reed, Carol, 267
Mayernik, David, 221
Maynard, Joan Bacchus, 435
Maynard, Kate, 500
Maynard, Kenneth D., 245
Maynard and Partch, 345
Mayne, Thom, 74
Mayors' Institute on City Design, 66, 164
Mays, Vernon L., Jr., 67
Maytum, Marsha, 245
Mazzucotelli, Richard, 274
MBH Architects, 327
MBT Architecture, 312
McAfee, Charles F., 205, 245
McAfee-Mitchell, Cheryl Lynn, 245
McAllister, Michael, 409
McAndrew, John, 70
McAnelly, Michael D., 258
MCB Architects, 312
McCafferty, Charles, 245
McCagg, E. K., II, 245
McCall, Debra, 223
McCall, Joe M., 245
McCallum, Ann K., 245
McCann, Michael, 125
McCarthy, Michael A., 245
McCartney, Heather, 259
McCarty, Bruce, 245
McCleary, Peter, 496
McClellan Architects, 170
McClenaham, Mary Tyler Cheek, 282
McClendon, Bruce W., 259
McClennen, Alan, Jr., 259
McClier Corporation, 202, 326
McClintock, T. K., 223
McClure, Harlan E., 245, 294, 495, 556
McClure, Wesley A., 245
McCombs, William "Skip" H., 229
McCommons, Richard E., 245
McConihe, F. M., 282
McConnel Smith and Johnson, 639
McConnell, Jack Hobbs, 168, 301
McConnell, Patrick, 288
McConnell, Robert E., 245
McConnell, Ron, 259
McCord, Kenneth A., 229
McCormick, Mike, 259
McCoy, Dr. Robert, 282
McCoy, Esther, 65
McCoy, Katherine J., 272, 296, 541
McCoy, Margarita P., 259
McCoy, Michael, 541
McCrary, Edward D., 245
McCree, M. Allen, 245
McCue, Gerald M., 110, 245
McCullagh, Grant G., 245
McCullar, James, 245
McCulley, Earl Byron, 267
McCurry, Margaret, 109, 288
McCutcheon, Sir Osborn, 168
McDade, Phillip L., 267
McDermott, Terrence M., 282
McDermott, Vincent C., 267
McDonald, Alan, 349
McDonald, John J., 221, 349
McDonald, Kenneth, 375
McDonalds, 457
McDonough, William A., 32, 245, 401, 406, 407, 418, 421
McDonough Braungart Design Chemistry, 401, 406
McDowell, Bruce D., 259
McDowell, Stephen A., 245
McEldowney, H. Clay, 229
McEldowney, Robert, 229
McErlane, Roger B., 267
McFall, James D., 229
McFarland, Connie S., 245
McFarland, Donald, 272
McFarland, Mark E., 267
McGarry Ni Eanaigh Architects, 114
McGaughan, A. S., 245
McGill University, 496, 502, 539
McGinty, John M., 245, 291
McGinty, Milton B., 245
McGinty, Richard A., 245
McGlenn, John C., 229
McGough, John W., 246
McGowen, Sandra, 262
McGranahan, James R., 246
McGrath, Charles F., 539
McGrath, Dorn Charles, Jr., 259
McGrath, Evelyn B., 282
McGrath, Norman, 65
McGraw, Harold, 152
McGraw, Terry, 152
McGraw-Hill Companies, 152
McHarg, Ian Lennox, 21, 90, 157, 194, 267, 282, 334
McIntosh, James E., 262
McInturff, Mark, 246
McInturff Architects, 62, 174
McIntyre, Peter, 168, 278, 301
McKay, Ronald, 67
McKee, Larry A., 229
McKellar, Chris, 286
McKenzie, Robert W., 229
McKim, Charles Follen, 59, 175, 291
McKim, Herbert P., 229, 246, 299
McKim, Mead and White, 345, 349, 376, 462
McKinley, David A., 246
McKinnell, Noel Michael, 84, 225, 246
McKinney, Arthur W., 229
McKisson, Anne, 511
McKittrick, Thomas L., 246
McKnight-Thalden, Kathryn E., 267
McKown, Zack, 288
McLarand Vasquez Emsick & Partners, 99, 202
McLaughlin, Charles C., 284
McLaughlin, H. Roll, 246
McLaughlin, James, 345
McLean, C. Andrew, II, 246
McLeish, James, 391
McManus, James M., 246
McMath, George A., 246
McMickens, Tchernavina R., 537
McMinn, William G., 221, 246, 495
McMurrich, Norman H., 300
McNall, Cameron, 221
McNamara, Kevin, 288
McNaughton, E. Eean, Jr., 246
McNeal, David A., 267
McNulty, Carrell S., Jr., 246
McPheeters, E. Keith, 246, 495
McRae, John M., 246, 295
McReynolds, Charles B., 246
McSherry, Laurel, 222
McVicker, Julia, 651
Mead, Christopher , 303
Mead, Franklin, 246
Mead, William Rutherford, 75
Means, George C., Jr., 246, 495
Meathe, Kessler & Associates, 643
Meathe, Philip J., 110, 219, 246, 643
Meck, Stuart, 259
Meckel, David, 246
Medary, Milton Bennett, 59, 291
Medrano, Jose, 274
Mee, Joy, 259
Meeker & Associates, Inc., 186
Meeks, Carroll L. V., 70, 303
Meeks, Everett, 294

Name Index

Moline, Lawrence R., 268
Moline, Ronald L., 246
Molnar, Donald J., 268
Molseed, Robert B., 246
Molzan, Lynn H., 246
Molzen, Dayton, 229
Monacelli Press, 67
Moneo, Jose Rafael
awards/honors, 84, 148, 165, *176,* 177, 200
memberships, 226, 278
works/projects, *342,* 351, 656, 3347
Monical, R. Duane, 229, 290
Monson, Christopher, 498
Montalvo, Pedro E. Claudio, 536
Montana, Frank, 246
Montana State University, 502, 525, 536, 548
Montgomery, Kathy Ford, 262, 292
Montgomery, Martha Barber, 282
Montgomery Sisam Architects Inc., 207
Monticciolo, Joseph D., 110, 246
Montoya, Juan, 288
Montreal Metro System, 64
Moody, Curtis J., 205, 246
Moon, Thomas B., 246
Moore, Barry M., 246
Moore, Charles W., 59, 84, 194, 349, 495, 556
Moore, Gene, 289
Moore, Lynn A., 268
Moore, Maurine, 546
Moore, Pat, 272
Moore, Patrick C., 268
Moore, Phyllis, 262
Moore, Richard A., 268
Moore, Robert C., 229
Moore, Terry, 259
Moore, William B., Jr., 282
Moore College of Art and Design, 528
Moore Lyndon Turnbull Whitaker, 198
Moore Ruble Yudell Architects & Planners, 60, 115
Moorhead, Gerald L., 246
Morelli, Jill K., 246
Moretta & Sheehy Architects, 314
Morey, Warren, 369
Morgan, Arthur Ernest, 334
Morgan, Clifford, 628
Morgan, Colin G., 503
Morgan, Jesse O., Jr., 246
Morgan, Julia, 382, 385, 386, 388, 462
Morgan, Keith N., 303
Morgan, Robert L., 549
Morgan, Sherely, 294
Morgan, William, 67, 246
Morgan State University, 523, 536
Morgas & Associates Architects, Inc., 314
Morgensen, David P., 503
Morgridge, Howard H., 246
Mori, Toshiko, 392, 498
Moriarty, Stacy T., 222
Moris, Lamberto G., 246
Moriyama, Raymond, 169, 278
Morphett, John, 168
Morphosis, 656
awards/honors, 60, 62, 63, 74, 119, 120, 159
Morris, Benjamin Wistar, 355
Morris, John W., 282
Morris, Katharine, 516
Morris, Laura, 536
Morris, Paul F., 268, 293
Morris, Philip A., 282, 284
Morris, Robert Schofield, 177, 300
Morris, Seth I., 246
Morris & O'Connor, 355
Morrison, Darrel G., 268
Morrison, David, 462
Morrison, Hunter, 195
Morrison, Jacob H., 435
Morrison, Lionel, 246
Morrison, Mark K., 268
Morrison, Mrs. Jacob H., 435
Morrison, Murdo D., 246
Morrow, Baker H., 268
Morse, John, 246
Morse, Joseph, 548
Mortensen, Robert H., 268, 293
Mortenson, Wayne, 549
Mortlock, Harold Bryce, 168, 301
Morton, Terry B., 282
Morton, Woolridge Brown, III, 282
Moses, Arnold, 375
Moses, Robert, 334, 453
Moshe Safdie Architects Limited, 225
Mosher, Drew, Watson & Associates, 353
Mosher, Frederick K., 229
Mosher, Robert, 246, 353
Mosher & Drew, 351
Moskow, Keith, 209
Moskowitz, Harvey, 259
Moskowitz, Samuel Z., 246
Moss, Eric Owen, 74, 246
Moss, Murray, 181
Mossbarger, W. A., 229
Mossien, Sarah A., 537
Most Endangered Sites, 456, 457, 486–492
Most Visited Historic House Museums, 462
Mostafavi, Mohsen, 176
Mostoller, G. Michael, 246
Mother Centre International Network, 404
Motley, Kenneth L., 246
MOTO Development Group, 129
Motorola, 132
Motorola Consumer Experience Design, 129
Mott, John K., 246
Mott, Ralph O., 299
Mould, J. Wrey, 349
Moulder, James "Bud" E., 229
Moule & Polyzoides Architects and Urbanists, 105, 107
Moulthrop, Edward A., 246
Moulton, Jennifer T., 246, 645
Mount, Charles Morris, 645
Mount Ida College, 523
Mount Mary College, 530
Mount Vernon Ladies Association, 435, 452, 454
Mouton, Grover E., III, 221
Mox, Dana W., 272
Moya, Hidalgo, 649
Moyer, Frederic D., 246
Moylan, James, 375
Moynihan, Hon. Daniel Patrick, 136, 152, 195, 435, 646
Muchow, William C., 219, 299
Mudano, Frank R., 246
Muhly, Louis Bert, 259
Mukibi, Benigna, 404
Mularz, Theodore L., 247, 299
Mulcahy, Edward J., 229
Mulcahy, Vincent, 221
Muldawer, Paul, 247
Mulfinger, Dale, 247
Mullen, John W., III, 247
Muller, Kenneth, 274
Muller, Rosemary F., 247
Müller-Munk, Peter, 272
Mullin, John R., 259
Mullins, Margaret Ann, 268
Mullins-Sherman, Architects, 314
Mumford, Lewis, 3, 22, 122, 177, 188, 334
Munger, Harold C., 247
Munich Architecture Class, 81
Municipal Art Society of New York, 66
Munly, Anne, 221
Munoz, Kelly, 365
Muntz, Jean G., 282
Munzer, Frank W., 247
Murase, Robert K., 268
Murcutt, Glenn Marcus, 138, 165, 168
Murdoch, Norman, 259
Murdock, Richard C., 222
Murphree, Martha, 282
Murphy, Charles F., 247
Murphy, Elizabeth Corbin, 516
Murphy, Frank N., 247
Murphy, Katherine Prentis, 435
Murphy, Monica Jeanne, 499
Murphy Burnham Buttrick Architects, 508
Murphy/Jahn, Inc., 379, 380
Murray, David G., 247
Murray, Maria, 282
Murray, Padraig, 278
Murtagh, William J., 435
Musaib-Ali, Patrice Alicia, 537
Muschamp, Herbert, 167, 216
Muse, Stephen A., 247
Muse Architects, 68
Museum of Contemporary Art, Los Angeles, 607
Museum of Finnish Architecture, 607
Museum of Modern Art, 160, 607
Musho, Theodore J., 221
Musiak, Thomas A., 268
Musselman, Betty J., 282
Mutchler, Robert C., 247
Mutlow, John V., 247
Myer, Donald B., 247
Myer, John R., 247
Myerberg, Henry, 143
Myers, Barton, 169, 247
Myers, C. Stowe, 272
Myers, Denys Peter, 276
Myers, Elijah E., 374, 375, 376
Myers, Ralph E., 247
Myers, Robert William, 221
Myers, Victoria, 516

N

N. Osborne & Co., 375
Nabokov, Peter, 66
Nacht, Daniel J., 247
Nadel, Barbara, 247
Nadel, Herbert N., 247
Nadel Architects Inc., 326, 381
Nagahiro, David T., 209
Nagel, Chester Emil, 247
Nagle, James L., 247
Nagler, Florian, 148

Name Index

NAHB Research Center, 416, 424
Naidorf, Louis, 247
Najjar, Salim, 229
Nakaba, Kenneth S., 268
Nakamura, Michiaki, 409
Nakamura, Noboru, 247
Nakamura, Toshio, 67, 137, 278
Nakano, Kenichi, 268
Nakano, Saya, 510
Nakata, C. S., 247
Nall, Daniel H., 247
Nangle, James, 301
Nantucket Principles, 413–415
Nash, Diarmuid, 300
Nash, Robert Johnson, 205, 247
Nasher, Raymond D., 282
Naslund, Eric Christopher, 247
Nassauer, Joan I., 268
Nathan, Thomas M., 247
National Aeronautics and Space Administration, 163
National Arborist Association, Inc., 581
National Architectural Accrediting Board, 505, 517, 534, 535–541, 555
National Association of Environmental Professionals, 581
National Association of Home Builders, 98, 100, 416, 582
National Association of Realtors, 573
National Building Museum, 123, 152, 204, 607
National Building Museum Honor Award, 152
National Building Museum Shop, 592
National Center for Preservation Technology and Training, 463
National Clearinghouse for Educational Facilities, 582
National Concrete Masonry Association, 582
National Conference of States on Building Codes & Standards, Inc., 582
National Council for Historic Sites and Buildings, 453
National Council for Interior Design Qualification, 612
National Council for Preservation Education, 534
National Council of Acoustical Consultants, 582
National Council of Architectural Registration Boards, 299, 338, 545, 609
National Council on Seniors' Housing, 100
National Council on the Arts, 157
National Design Awards, 153, *154*
National Design-Build Awards, 155–156
National Electrical Contractors Association, 582
National Electrical Manufacturers Association, 582
National Endowment for the Arts, 64, 157, 163, 164
National Environmental Policy Act, 455
National Fire Protection Association, 582
National Fire Sprinkler Association, 582
National Football League, 152
National Gallery of Art, 225
National Glass Association, 582
National Green Building Awards, 416, *417*
National Heritage Areas, 464
National Historic Landmarks, 453, 456, 476–478
National Historic Planning Landmarks, 331–333
National Historic Planning Pioneers, 334–335
National Historic Preservaton Act, 454, 456
National Historic Sites Act, 453
National Humanities Medal, 458
National Institute of Building Sciences, 582
National Institute of Standards & Technology, 586
National Kitchen & Bath Association, 583
National Lighting Bureau, 583
National Main Street Leadership Awards, 465
National Medal of Arts, 157
National Oak Flooring Manufacturers Association, 583
National Organization of Minority Architects, 583
National Paint & Coatings Association, 583
National Park Service
  awards/honors given by, 514
  awards/honors given to, 163, 435
  establishment, 453
  programs/services, 163, 445, 447, 448, 463, 464, 476
  staff, 655
National Preservation Awards, 466, *467*
National Preservation Institute, 468
National Real Estate Investor, 156
National Register of Historic Places, 454, 455
National Resources Defense Council, 405
National Resources Planning Board, 331
National Society of Professional Engineers, 583
National Spa and Pool Institute, 583
National Sunroom Association, 583
National Trust for Historic Preservation
  awards/honors given by, 432, 435, 437–439, 454–457, 465–466, *467,* 469–470, 472–473
  awards/honors given to, 64, 458
  organizational information, 453
  Presidents, 471
National Wood Flooring Association, 583
Native American Architecture, 66
Natkin, Kenneth H., Esq., 247
Naughton, John, 221
Naumann, Kimberly, 535
NBBJ
  awards/honors, 104, 150, 184
  works/projects, 359, 361, 365, 367, 369, 373
NCARB Prize for Creative Integration of Practice and Education in the Academy, 545
Neal, Darwina L., 268, 293
Neal, James A., 247
Neas, Joy, 500
Necipoglu, Gülru, 190
Neel, Paul R., 110, 247
Neighorhood Design Center, 108
Neil Pryde Int., 129
Neilson, J. Crawford, 376
Neish, Scott, 540
Nelsen, Ibsen, 247
Nelson, Albert L., 229
Nelson, Arthur C., 259
Nelson, Doreen, 282
Nelson, Edward H., 247
Nelson, George, 127, 272
Nelson, James Richard, 247
Nelson, John A., 268
Nelson, John H., 247
Nelson, Kenneth E., 229
Nelson, Mark, 262
Nelson, Susan Kathleen, 539
Nelson, T. C., 247
Nelson, William R., Jr., 268
Nelson-Byrd Landscape Architects, 94
Nelson Chen Architects Ltd., 170
Nelson Haley Patterson and Quirk, 163
Nelson Howden & Associates, Inc., 312
Nemeti, Ede I., 247
Nenot, Henri Paul, 175
Neptune, Donald E., 247
Nereim, Andres, *551*
Nervi, Pier Luigi, 59, 177
Nes, Charles M., Jr., 291
Nesholm, John F., 247
Neski, Barbara, 247
Neski, Julian J., 247
Nest, 602
NetForm International, 271
Netherlands Architecture Institute, 607
Netsch, Walter A., 194, 247
Netzer, Dick, 259
Neubauer, Perry King, 247
Neubek, Kurt, 247
Neuhaus, J. Victor, III, 247
Neuhaus, Paul, 209, *210*
Neuhaus, William O., III, 247
Neuman, David J., 247
Neumann, Dietrich, 160
Neumann, Hans, 247
Neumann, S. Kenneth, 247
Neunschwander, Roger L., 247
Neutra, Richard Joseph, 59, 161
Nevaril, Roi C., 262
Nevelson, Louise, 64
Nevin and Morgan, 353
Nevius, Joseph N., 268
New Buildings Institute Codes & Standards Office, 583
New England School of Art & Design at Suffolk University, 523
New Jersey Institute of Technology, 295, 502, 525, 536, 539
New York, New Visions, 67
New York City Housing Authority, 153
New York City Landmarks Preservation Commission, 64, 455
New York Institute of Technology, 502, 526, 536, 548
New York Landmarks Conservancy, 67
New York Planning Commission, 64
New York School of Interior Design, 526
New York State Commission of Housing and Regional Planning, 332
The New York Times, 167, 216, 389
New York University, 225, 532
New York World's Fair, 419
New Yorker, 217, 271
Newark Star-Ledger, 217
Newbury College, 523
Newcomb, Rexford, 70, 303
Newlin, Peter, 247

Newman, Herbert S., 195, 247
Newman, Michael, 247
Newport News Daily Press, 217
Newschool of Architecture, 518
Newsom, Robert L., 247
Newton, Chartier C., 247
Newton, Ernest, 175, 302
Newton, Linda, 262
Newton, Norman T., 90, 222, 293
Newton, Sir Charles T., 175
Ng Chun Man & Associates, 377
Niall McLaughlin Architects, 81
Nicholaeff, Doreve, 247
Nicholas Grimshaw & Partners, 148
Nichols, Frederick D., 70
Nichols, James R., 229
Nichols, Jesse Clyde, 136, 334
Nichols, Karen V., 247
Nichols, Katherine, 514
Nicholson, Frank, 288
Nicklas, Michael H., 247
Nicol, Gilbert Ridgway, 168
Nicol, Robert Duncan, 247
Nicolaides, E. N., 229
Niebanck, Paul, 497
Niederkorn, Thomas P., 259
Nielsen, Michael, 541
Nielsen, Signe, 268
Nielsen-Hegstad, Megan E., 538
Nieman, Thomas J., 268
Niemeyer, Oscar, 165, 177, 226
Niernsee, Frank, 376
Niernsee, John Rudolph, 376
Nike, Inc., 132
Nike Brand Design, 186
Nike Techlab Audio Team, 126
Nikken Sekkei, 380
Nikolajevich, George Z., 247
Nikolov, Nikola I., 278
Niland, David L., 495
Niles, Edward R., 247
Niles Bolton Associates, 326
Nims, Christopher G., 247
Nishimura, George K., 229
Nishimura, Lennox K., 229
Nishita, Satoru, 268
Nishizawa, Ryue, 84
Nitsch, Judith, 230
Nix, Ivey L., 247
Nixon, Robert J., 247
Nobbs, Percy E., 300
Noble, Douglas, 247
Noblitt, Jack, 230
Noffke, W. E., 262
Noguchi, Isamu, 140, 142, 157
Nolan, Mary, 384
Noland, Frederick L., 284
Nolen, John, Sr., 334
Nonell, Juan Bassegoda, 278
Norberg, Scott, 548
Norberg-Schulz, Christian, 65, 137
Norcross Brothers Construction, 376
Nordensen, Guy, 74
Norder, Timothy John, 511
Norkunas, Martha K., 449
Norma, Rafael, 278
Norr Group Consultants Int. Ltd., 377, 378, 381
Norris, Kathleen, 499
Norris, Paul, 503
Norris R. Guthrie, Architect, 314
North American Insulation Manufacturers Association, 583
North American Steel Framing Alliance, 584
North Carolina A&T State University, 526
North Carolina State University
  degree programs, 526
  staff, 294, 495, 496, 541, 556
  students/alumni, 502, 539, 548
North Dakota State University, 502, 527
Northcurr, James, 288
Northeastern University, 523
Northwestern University, 532
Norton, Charles Dyer, 334
Norton, Charles McKim, 334
Norton, Perry, 259
Norvell, Shirley J., 282
Norwegian Museum of Architecture, 607
Norwich, John Julius, 66
Norwich University, 502, 530, 536
Notman, John, 375
Notter, George M., Jr., 247, 291
Nottingham-Spirk Design Associates, 130
Nouvel, Jean, 162, 177, 278
Novack, John M., 247
Novick, David, 230
Nowicki, Stanislawa, 64, 495
Noyes, Frederick, 247
N.P. Severin Company, 374
NSSN: A National Resource for Global Standards, 584
NTD Architects, 326
NTHP/HUD Secretary's Award, 470
Nugent, Barbara, 262, 292
Nunn, Jimmie R., 247
Nunn and McGinty Architects, 649
Nussbaum, Bruce, 285
Nussberger, Hans Jörg, 189
Nutt, Jonathan, 511
Nutter, David Alan, 301
Nuzum, Dwayne, 294
Nyfeler, John, 247
Nygard, Destin J., 503
Nype, Diantha, 289
Nyren, Carl J. A., 278

O

O. Ahlborg & Sons, Inc., 156
O. Douglas Boyce Jr., Architect, 314
Oak Flooring Institute, 584
Oakley, Charles W., 247
Oakley, Daniel S., 536
Obata, Gyo, 247, 284
Oberlander, Cornelia A., 268
Oberman, William Robert, 499
Oberste Baubenhörde, 189
Oblinger, Warren J., 268
O'Boyle, Robert L., 268
O'Brien, James W., 247
O'Brien, John "Mel," Jr., 299
O'Brien, W. L., Jr., 247
Ochsner, Jeffrey K., 247
Ockman, Joan, 67
O'Connor, Thomas, 247
The Octagon, 607
Odell, A. Gould, Jr., 291
Odell & Associates, 371
Odenwald, Neil, 268
Odermatt, Robert A., 219, 247
O'Donnell, L. J., 247
O'Donnell, Patricia M., 268
O'Donnell Wicklund Pigozzi & Peterson, 326
Odyssea, 308
Oehme, Wolfgang W., 268
Oehrlein, Mary L., 247
Oenslager, Donald, 223
Office dA, 159
Office for Metropolitan Architecture, 390
Ogawa/Depardon Architects, 134
Ogilvie, Alix, 513
Oglethorpe, General James, 461
O'Gorman, James F., 160, 303
Ohio State University
  degree programs, 527, 532, 533
  staff, 294, 541, 542
  students/alumni, 499, 502, 511, 539, 635
Ohio University, 527
Ohlhausen, Rolf H., 247
Oishi, Satoshi, 230
Ojeda-O'Neill, Pablo, 223
Okada, ShinIchi, 279
Okinaka, Chad M., 78
Oklahoma State University, 496, 502, 527, 536
Olcott, Richard M., 221, 247
Old House Journal, 455, 602
Old Post Office Landmark Committee, 435
Old Sturbridge Village, 429
Oldenburg, Claes, 64
Oldziey, Edward A., 247
O'Leary, Arthur F., 247
O'Leary, Patricia, 496
O'Leary, William A., 268
Oles, Paul Stevenson, 65, 125, 247
Olin, H. B., 247
Olin, Laurie D., 74, 222, 268, 282, 636
Olin, Peter J., 268
Olin Partnership, 92, 94, 636
Olinger, Edward J., 268
Oliveira, Wanira, 514
Olko, Stephen M., 230
Olmsted, Frederick Law, Jr., 293, 334
Olmsted, Frederick Law, Sr., 75, 90, 334, 375, 450, 461
Olmsted, John C., 293
Olsen, Donald E., 247
Olsen, O. H., 376
Olson, Don H., 222, 268
Olson, Sheri, 218
Olson Sundberg Kundig Allen Architects, 347, 353
Olumyiwa, Oluwole O., 279
Olwert, Craig, 499
Olympiad Games XXIII, 65
O'More College of Design, 528
Omrania, 378
Onblahd, G., 188
O'Neal, Paul Murff, Jr., 247
Ong, Edmund W., 195, *196*
Ongwattanakul, Tisak, 410
OPEC, 419
OPN Architects, Inc., 314
Oppenheimer, Herbert B., 247
Oppermann, Joseph K., 247
Orawski, Nadia, 552
Oregon State University, 533
Oremen, Edward L., 247
Oringdulph, Robert E., 247, 299

Name Index

Orland, Brian, 268
Orlov, Georgui M., 279, 298
Orlov, Iosif Bronislavovitch, 188
Orr, Douglas W., 197, 291
Orr, Gordon D., Jr., 247
Ortiz-Santiago, Pedro J., 230
Orton, Lawrence M., 334
Osborne, Peter, 502
Osborne Engineering Company, 359
O'Shea, Peter, 222
Osivnik, David, 539
Osler, David William, 247
Osler, Peter, 222
Oslund, Thomas R., 222, 268
Osman, Mary E., 282
Osmundson, Theodore O., 90, 268, 293
Ossipoff, Snyder, and Rowland, 310
Ossipoff, Vladimir, 219
Östberg, Ragnar, 59, 177, 383
Ostergaard, Paul, 230
Otak, Inc., 164
Otis Elevator Company, 125
Otsuji, Dennis Y., 268, 293
Ottagono, 604
Otten, Johnson, Robinson, Neff and Ragonetti, 202
Otto, Frei, 96, 206
Oudens, G. F., 247
Ouellet, J. P., 300
Ouroussoff, Nicolai, 167, 216, 656
"The Outdoor Circle," 334
Outstanding Civil Engineering Achievement Award, 113
Outstanding Planning Awards, 158
Ove Arup & Partners, 66
Over, R. Stanton, 230
Overall, Sir John Wallace, 168
Overby, Osmund, 276, 303
Overend, Acheson Best, 301
Overland Partners Architects, 143
Ovresat, Raymond C., 247
Owens, Hubert B., 90, 293
Owens, Kenneth, Jr., 247
Owings, Nathaniel Alexander, 59
Owings Corning, 634
Ownby, J. Steve, 268
OXO Intl., 128, 132

P

P/A Awards, 159
Pabon, Jose Uribe, 540
Paderewski, C. J. "Pat," III, 247, 299
Padget, Hilary, 514
Padget, Steve, 514
Padjen, Elizabeth Seward, 247
Paepcke, Elizabeth, 108
Page, Clayton, 628
Page, Forsey, 300
Page, Max, 190
PageSoutherlandPage, 326, 341
Pahlman, William, 109
Paine, A. J. C., 300
Paine, Ashley, 513
Painter, Michael, 268
Palacious, Jose Luis, 209
Palermo, Gregory, 247
Paley, Albert, 66
Palladino, Michael, 223
Palladium Company, 201
Pallagi, Laszlo, 537
Pallasmaa, Juhani, 137, 279
Pallay, Ross D., 284
Pallo, Lisa A., 539
Pallone, Rep. Frank, 282
Palm, Inc., 129
Palmer, J. Hambleton, 230
Palmer, James F., 268
Palmer, Meade, 90, 268
Palmer, Ralph J., 230
Palmer, Stewart R., 230
Palu, Jay M., 549
Paluso, Michael P., 538
Pan, Joshua J., 247
Pan, Solomon, 247
Panciera, Ronald J., 282
Pancoast, Lester C., 248
Pancoast, Russell, 345
Pangrazio, John R., 248
Panneton, Jason D., 503
Pansky, Stanley H., 221
Panton, Vernon, 109
Panushka, Donald H., 248
Paoletti, Dennis A., 248
Paoluccio, Joseph P., 230
Papachristou, Tician, 248
Papadopoulos, S. G., 230
Papaefthimiou, Nicholas, 537
Papandrew, Thomas P., 268, 293
Papanek, Victor, 127
Papp, Laszlo, 248
Pappageorge, George C., 248
Pappas, Constantine George, 248
Pappas, Nicholas A., 248
Pappas, Ted P., 248, 291
Paradis, Alan D. S., 548
Parasivam, Sivaya, 509
Paredes Pedrosa Arquitectos, 81
Parent, Claude, 137
Parera, Cecilia, 540
Parise, Charles J., 248
Parish, Mrs. Henry, II, 288
Park, C. M., 380
Park, Ki Suh, 205, 248, 259
Park, Nell H., 222
Park, Sharon C., 248
Park, Stuart James, 375
Parken, David, 301
Parker, Alfred B., 248
Parker, Andrew J., Jr., 230, 290
Parker, Cary M., 268
Parker, Derek, 248
Parker, Donald, 274
Parker, Douglas R. , 192, 262, 271, 286
Parker, Howard C., 248
Parker, J. Derrell, 274
Parker, Jan, 262
Parker, John A., 497
Parker, Leonard S., 248
Parker, William Stanley, 110
Parkes, Cobden, 168, 301
Parkin, John C., 169
Parkinson, Henry Jardine, 301
Parkinson Field Associates, 341
Parnell, Jacqueline A., 259
Parriott, Joseph M., 272, 296
Parrish, Linda, 218
Parrott, R. C., 248
Parry, Mervyn Henry, 168
Parshall, Steven A., 248
Parsons, John G., 268
Parsons, Marianne Virginia, 538
Parsons, Samuel, Jr., 293
Parsons Brinckerhoff Quade & Douglas, Inc., 112, 164
Parsons School of Design/New School University, 502, 526, 536
Parthum, Charles A., 230
Pasanella, Giovanni, 248
Pasanella+Klein Stolzman+Berg Architects, 133
Pascal, Jean Louis, 59, 175
Pascal Arquitectos, 314
Paseur, C. H., 248
Passonneau, Joseph, 67, 248, 495
Pataki, Gov. George, 405
Pate Associates Architects/Planners Inc., 314
Paterakis, Alice Boccia, 223
Paternoster, Robert J., 259
Paton, David, 375
Patri, Piero, 248
Patri, Tito, 268
Patrick, Allen L., 248
Patrick Architectural, 314
Patten, Gerald D., 268, 293
Patterson, Paula A., 503
Patterson, Suzanne, 262
Patton, Carl V., 259
Patton, George E., 222
Patton, J. L., 230
Patty, R. Bruce, 291
Paul, Courtland P., 268
Paul E. Buchanan Award, 480
Paul F. Stewart, Architect, Ltd., 312
Paul Warchol Photography, Inc., 67
Paulmann, James, 259
Paulo A. Mendes da Rocha Arquitectos Associados, 149
Paulsen, S. Glen, 248
Paulsen, Sherida Elizabeth, 248
Paulson, Merlyn J., 268
Pavlik Design Team, 182, 183
Pawley, Charles Harrison, 248
Pawlowski, Paul R. V., 222
Pawson, John, 288
Paxton, Donald D., 230
Payet, Marion, 500
Payette, Maurice, 300
Payette, Thomas M., 248
Payette Associates, Inc., 184, 326
Payne, A. G., 376
Payne, Alina A., 73
Payne, H. Morse, 248
Payne, Harry D., 110
Payne, Lee, 273
Payne, Richard W., 248
PBK Architects, Inc., 314
PDD Ltd., 129
Peabody, Arthur, 299
Peabody, Lawrence, 262
Peabody, Robert S., 291
Peabody and Stearns, 375
Pearl, George Clayton, 248, 647
Pearsall, Bryce, 248
Pearson, Charles Almond, Jr., 248
Pearson, Gene, 259
Pearson, Gerald Phillip, 268
Pearson, John L., 175
Pease, J. Norman, Jr., 248
Pease, R. B., 282

Name Index

Q

R

Name Index

Roy, Clarence, 269
Roy O. Martin Lumber Company, 424
Royal Academy of FIne Arts, 25
Royal Architectural Institute of Canada, 169, 300, 587
Royal Australian Institute of Architects, 168, 256, 301, 587
Royal Institute of British Architects, 175, 302, 587
Royoung Bookseller, 593
Royston, Robert N., 64, 90, 269
RQAQ Corporation, 312
R.S. Bickford & Company, 314
R.S. Means, 421
RSA Architects, Inc., 98
RSP Architects Planners & Engineers Ltd., 380
RTKL International, Inc., 117, 182, 326, 327, 359
Rubeling, Albert W., Jr., 250
Rubenstein, Harvey M., 269
Ruble, John, 250
Rucker, J. Ronald, 250
Rucker, Robert H., 269
Rudd, J. W., 250
Rudofsky, Bernard, 64
Rudolph, Paul, 84, 504
Rudy Bruner Award for Urban Excellence, 179, *180*
Ruehl, Gordon E., 250
Ruff, Joseph, 462
Ruffcorn, Evett J., 250
Ruga, Wayne, 108, 263, 275
Ruggiero, Janet M., 259
Ruhnau, Herman O., 250
Ruiz, Ana, 499, 500
Ruiz, Terri Asendorf, 514
Rumbold, Charlotte, 334
Rumpel, Peter L., 250
Rupe, William W., 250
Rural Heritage Program, 472
Rural Studio, 420
Russel Wright Award, 181
Russell, Beverly, 192
Russell, Earnest J., 291
Russell, J. H. G., 300
Russell, John A., 169
Russell, T. T., 250
Russell, Virginia Lockett, 269
Rust, Orling and Neale, Architect, Inc., 314
Rutes, Walter A., 250
Rutgers University, 499, 511, 525, 532, 533, 542
Ruth, Dennis K., 420
Ruth, H. Mark, 250
Ruth, Paul C., 347
Ruthazer, Jack G., 263
Rutledge, Harry R., 250
Ryan, Ida Annah, 386
Ryan, James, 273, 296
Ryan, Leslie A., 222
Ryan, Robert, 183
Ryan, Roger N., 250
Ryan, Terry Warriner, 269
Rybczynski, Witold, 271, 279
Rydeen, James E., 250
Ryder, Donald P., 250
Ryerson University, 552
Rykwert, Joseph, 73
Rylan, Elizabeth, 546

S

S/L/A/M Collaborative, 184
Saarinen, Eero, 59, 197, 329, 349, 382, 456
Saarinen, Eliel, 59, 177, 197, 342, 347, 387
Saarinen, Saarinen & Associates, 197
Sabo, Werner, 250
Sabouni, Ikhlas, 496
SADI Awards, 182–183
Sadler, George O., 230
Sadler, Harold G., 250
Safdie, Moshe, 120, 169, 194, 225, 250
Saffron, Inga, 217
Sagenkahn, Chester F., 263
Saia Barbarese Topouzanov, 207
St. Clair, Rita, 109, 263, 288, 292
St. Florian, Friedrich, 221
St. Gaul Plan, 65
St. Louis AIA Bookstore, 592
Saito, Paul M., 269
Sakata, Carol S., 250
Saksena, Raj, 250
Saladino, Charles S., II, 269
Saladino, John F., 288
Salazar, Dayana, 500
Salins, Peter D., 259
Salk, Jonas, 271
Salk Institute, 271
Salmela, David D., 250
Salmela Architect, 207
Salmi, Patricia, 547
Salmon, F. Cuthbert, 250
Salmon, Frank, 190
Salmon Bay Design Group, 314
Salmon Falls Architecture, 314
Salvadori, Mario G., 282, 556
Salvadori Educational Center of the Build Environment, 66
Salve Regina University, 528
Salvin, Anthony, 175
Salzman, Stanley, 495
Samford University, 517
Samhammer, Clair A., 273
Sample, Hilary, *551*
Sample, John, 286
Sample, Nathaniel W., 250
Samsung Electronics Co. Ltd, 129, 132
Samton, Peter, 250
Samuel, Anne, 511
Samuels, Danny M., 224, 250
Samuels, Thomas, 250
Samulski, Keif, 540
San Antonio Conservation Society, 67, 435
San Antonio Express-News, 217
San Antonio River Walk, 65
San Diego Mesa College, 518
San Diego Union-Tribune, 218
San Francisco Chronicle, 167, 218
San Francisco Museum of Modern Art, 607
San Francisco State University, 130, 518
San Jose Mercury News, 218
San Jose State University, 499, 500, 518
Sanabria, Thomas J., 279
Sanchez, Chula, 540
Sanchez, Francisco J., 537
Sanchez, Gil A., 250
Sand, Margaret, 269
Sanders, James J., 250
Sanders, Kenneth D., 250
Sanders, Linda W., 250, 295
Sanders, Walter, 294
Sanders, William D., 269
Sanderson, Edward F., 434
Sanderson, James R., 539
Sandlin, Joe Scott, 209
Sandman, Helena, 83
Sands, Stephen P., 283
Sandy, Donald, Jr., 250
Sanoff, Henry, 496
Santeramo, Joseph, 66
Santiago, William, 539
Santini, Martin G., 250
Santos, Adele N., 250
Santowasso, Leo A., 230
Sanz, Carlos R., 250
Sapers, Carl M., 283
Saponara, Nicholas, 537
Sappenfield, Charles M., 250
Saqui, Angel C., 250
Sarkisian, Mark, 550
Saroki, Victor, 250
Sartoris, Alberto, 279
SAS Architects & Planners, 312
Sasaki, Hideo, 90, 269
Sasaki Associates, Inc., 62, 94, 326, 461
Sasaki-Walker Associates, 461
Sass, George L., 269
Sauer, Eric, 516
Sauer, Louis, 250
Sauerbrey, Barbara A., 263
Saunders, Joyce, 275
Saur, Louis R., 250
Savage, Terry W., 269
Savannah College of Art and Design, 465, 502, 513, 521, 536
Save America's Treasures, 457, 473
Sawasy, Mitchell E., 275
Sawyer, Robert W., 250
Saylor, Henry H., 110, 250
SBLM Architects, 116
Scaccia, Sam, 250
Scalabrin, Joseph J., 250
Scales, William J., 538
Scandariato, Brian, 503
Scarborough, John Francis, 301
Scarpa, Lawrence, 62
Scatchard, William, 269
Scavenger Hotline, 108
Schaal, Herbert R., 269
Schach, Horst, 269
Schach, Janice Cervelli, 293
Schack, Mario L., 250
Schaefer, Kenneth M., 250
Schaefer, Robert J., 250
Schaefer, William D., 283
Schaffer, J. Gorman, 230
Schaffner, Charles E., Jr., 230
Schaible, Michael, 288
Schaller, Thomas Wells, 125
Schamu, Walter, 250
Scharoun, Hans, 96
Schatz, George F., 299
Schaudt, Peter Lindsay, 222
Schaum, Martin, 283
Schauman, Sally, 269
Scheatzle, David, 250
Scheeler, James A., 110, 250
Schell, Paul, 283
Scherer, Jeffrey Allen, 250
Scherrer, Adolf, 374

Name Index

Name Index

Stastny, Donald J., 252, 259
Station 19 Architects, Inc., 314
Stauffer, Richard G., 269
Stavenger, Peter, 499
Steadham, B. Carole, 283
Stearns, Marida A., 546
Stebelski, Andres, 513
Stecker, Russell L., 252
Stecklein and Brungardt Architects, 314
Steelcase, 132, 271
Steele, Harland, 300
Steele, Mark W., 252
Steenhagen, Robert, 269
Stefany, John E., 252
Steffian, Peter, 252
Steger, Charles W., Jr., 252
Steidl, Douglas L., 252, 291
Stein, Achva Benzinberg, 269
Stein, Carl, 252
Stein, Clarence S., 59, 197, 335
Stein, Morris A., 252
Stein, Stuart W., 259
Steinberg, Goodwin B., 252
Steinberg, Paul L., 224
Steinberg, Robert T., 252
Steinberg, Saul, 64
Steinborn, S., 283
Steinbrueck, Peter, 209
Steiner, Prof. Frederick, 223
Steinfeld, Edward, 496
Steinglass, Ralph, 252
Steinhardt, Henry, 252
Steinhauser, Karl L., 263
Steinhilber, Budd, 127, 273
Steinman, Douglas E., Jr., 252
Steinman and Cain, 353
Steinmetz, Deborah, 263
Stenhouse, James A., 252
Stephen F. Austin State University, 529
Stephen Lasar Architects, 314
Stephen Russell and Associates, Ltd., 314
Stephens, Donald J., 252
Stephenson, C. Eugene, 263
Stephenson, Karen, 271
Stephenson, Sir Arthur George, 168, 177
Stepner, Michael J., 252, 259
Stern, Robert A. M., 252, 288, 651
Stern, William F., 252
Sternfeld, Joel, 224
Steven Ehrlich Architects, 173
Steven Holl Architects, 60, 225
Steven Lombardi Architect, 314
Stevenor-Dale, Janice, 275
Stevens, Brooks, 127, 273
Stevens, John Calvin, 353
Stevens, Philip H., 273
Stevens, Preston, Jr., 252
Stevens, Sara, 513
Stevens, Saundra, 283
Stevenson, James M., 252
Stevenson, Markley, 293
Stevenson Design, 314
Steward, W. Cecil, 252, 271, 291, 391, 556
Stewart, David R., 230
Stewart, J. George, 376
Stewart, R. K., 252
Stewart, William W., 252
Stewart and Company, 374
Stichter, William, 535
Stieber, Nancy, 190
Stifter, Charles, 221
Stikes, Henry A., 230
Stilgoe, John R., 67
Stillman, Damie, 303
Stipe, Robert, 435
Stirling, Sir James, 84, 162, 165, 177, 345
Stitt, P. D., 283
Stockwell, Sherwood, 252
Stoddard, Susan, 259
Stoddard, Whitney Snow, 654
Stoddart, John Goddfrey, 269
Stoikoff, Jason, 539
Stoilov, Georgi, 298
Stokes, Leonard, 175, 302
Stokes, Samuel N., 449
Stokoe, James S., 221
Stoller, Claude, 252
Stollman, Israel, 259
Stone, Edward D., II, 293
Stone, Edward D., Jr., 90, 269
Stone, Edward Durell, 351, 361, 374, 377, 631
Stone, Edward H., II, 269
Stone, Michelle, 224
Stonehill, John J., 221
Storrs, John, 655
Stough, Benjamin Robert, 538
Stout, Randall Paul, 252
Stovall, Allen D., 269
Stowe, Harriet Beecher, 384
Stowe, Neal P., 252
Stowell, H. T., 252
Strack, Neil E., 252
Strah, Dennis, 655
Straka, Ronald A., 110, 252
Strand Book Store, 593
Stransky, Michael J., 252
Strategic Horizons LLP, 271
Strater, Blanche F., 263
Straub, Calvin C., 495, 638
Straub, Frank, 252
Strauss, Carl A., 252
Street, George Edmund, 175, 302
Street, John R., Jr., 252
Street Dixon Rick Architecture, 312
Street-Works, 201
Strickland, William, 376
Striefel, Jan, 269
Strimple, Christina M., 502
Strock, Arthur V., 252
Strom, Steven, 269
Strong, Ann, 497
Strong, Norm, 35
Stroud, Roger G., 230
Struve, Quincy, 499
Stuart Collection, 66
Stubbins, Hugh, 194, 252
Stubbins Associates, Inc., 271, 378, 379, 381
Stubbs, Sidney W., Jr., 252
Student Sustainable Design Competition, 552
Studio E Architects, 63
Studio Petrarca, 648
Stuermann, Mark, 510
Stuler, Friedrich August, 175
Stull, Donald L., 252
Stumpf, Karl W., 209
Stumpf, Willliam, 127
Sturdivant, Robert L., 259
Sturgis, R. Clipston, 291
Sturgis, Robert S., 252
STV, Incorporated, 113, 163
STX, 129
Styczinski, Rosheen Marie, 269
Su, Gin, 279
Suchecka, Rysia, 288
Sueberkrop, Erik, 252
Suer, Marvin D., 252
Suess, Douglas F., 230
Suffolk County Community College, SUNY, 526
Sugawara, Michio, 279
Sugden, John W., 252
Suisman, Douglas R., 252
Suk, Keun Sook, 536
Sullam, Edward, 252
Sullivan, Ann, 263
Sullivan, Charles, 222
Sullivan, Doris M., 269
Sullivan, Jack, 222
Sullivan, John P., 252
Sullivan, Louis Henry
  awards/honors, 59
  memberships, 571
  works/projects, *71,* 330, 383, 628, 646
  and Wright, 14–15
Sullivan, Patrick M., 252
Sullivan, William, 192
Sullivan Goss Books and Prints Ltd., 591
Sulzer, Kenneth E., 259
Summers, Gene R., 252
Summerson, Sir John, 65, 177
Sumner, Alan R., 252
Sumner, Billy T., 230, 290
Sundberg, Richard P., 252
Sunset magazine, 66
Sunshine, Donald R., 252
Superfund, 420
Surber, Eugene L., 252
Surplus Real Property Act, 455
Surte, Aparna S., 514
Susan Maxman & Partners, 422
Susanka, Sarah, 271, 391–392
Sussman, Deborah, 283
Sussman/Prejza & Company Inc., 66
Sustainable Design Leadership Awards, 418
Sutter, Maria, 508
Sutton, Charles R., 222, 252
Sutton, Sharon E., 252, 389, 496
Sutton, Thomas, Jr., 286
Sutton Suzuki Architects, 174
Suyama, George, 252
Svenson, Erik A., 222
Sverdrup & Parcel and Associates, 361
SWA Group, 92, *93,* 94
Swaback, Vernon D., 259
Swager, Anne J., 283
Swager, Eugene C., 252
Swain, William G., 90, 269, 293
Swanke Hayden Connell Architects, 327
Swanson, Betsy, 72
Swanson, Pipsan S., 283
Swartburg, B. Robert, 345
Swarts, Ernest L., 273
Swartz, David Louis, 209
Swartz, Tim, 516
Swatt, Robert M., 252
Swedish Museum of Architecture, 608
Swett, Richard, 252, 271
Swicegood, Stephen, 252
Swinburne, H. H., 252
Swink, Rodney L., 269, 293

Name Index

Switzer, Lou, 288
Swofford, Don A., 252
Sylvester, David, 125
Symmes, Maini & McKee Associates, Inc., 326
Symonds, Anne C., 230
Syracuse University, 503, 526, 537, 541, 554, 556
Syvertsen, John M., 252
Szabo, A. J., 230
Szensay, Susan, 392
Szwalek, Stanley J., III, 510

T

Tabler, William B., 253
Tafel, Edgar, 253
Taff, Marvin, 253
Tai, Lolly, 269
Taillibert, Roger, 361
Tainha, Manuel, 137
Takahashi, Edward K., 253
Takashi, Koji, 409
Takata, Ray, 253
Takeyama, Minoru, 279
Takoudes, George A., 209
Talerico, John P., 230
Taliaferro, Francis T., 253
Tambe, Radhika, 536
Tan, R. H., 253
Tanaka, Ted Tokio, 253
Tange, Kenzo, 59, 162, 165, 177, 226, 349, 383
Taniguchi, Alan, 205, 279, 294
Tanzmann, Virginia W., 253
Tao, Austin Paul, 269
Taos Pueblo, 66
Tapley, Charles R., 253
Tapp, D. Rodney, 269
Tappe, A. Anthony, 253
Tappe Associates, Inc., 314
Tapper, Sir Walter, 302
Taransky, Richard, 221
Tarantino, John, 195, 253
Target, 132
Tarleton, H. Harold, 253
Tarlow, Rose, 288
Tate, Anne, 209
Tatsuo Kawanishi Architects, 83
Tattered Cover Bookstore, 591
Tatum, George B., 276, 283, 303
Tatum, Michael, 544
Tau Sigma Delta, 194, 553
Tau Sigma Delta Gold Medal, 194
Taven, Ron, 284
Tax Reform Acts, 455, 457
Taylor, Albert D., 293
Taylor, Anne, 283, 496
Taylor, Babcock & Co., 376
Taylor, D. Coder, 253
Taylor, James, 301
Taylor, Jennifer, 137
Taylor, Katherine Fischer, 190
Taylor, Marilyn Jordan, 253, 391
Taylor, Michael, 109, 288
Taylor, Richard L., Jr., 253
Taylor, Russell C., 230
Taylor, Todd, 500
Taylor, Walter Q., 253
Taylor, Wayne, 221
Taylor & Associates Architects, 314
Taylor Culllity Lethlean, 114
Taylore, Abner, 376
TC Designs, Architecture Unlimited, Inc., 314
TEA 2 Architects, Inc., 314
Teasdale, Thomas H., 219, 253
Tecton Architects, 314
Tehrani, Nader, 74
Teitz, Michael, 497
Telesis, 335
Tellez, German, 279
Temko, Allan, 66, 167
Temple, Leslee A., 269, 503
Temple University, 528, 537, 548
Temprano, Eliseo, 300
TEN Arquitectos, 149
Ten Eyck, Christine Elizabeth, 269
10 Greenest Building Products, 424
10 Greenest Designs, 422
Tenazas, Lucille, 153, *154*
Teng & Associates, Inc., 326
Tengbom, Anders, 279
Tengbom, Ivar, 177
Tennessee Valley Authority, 332
Tepe, Jerry R., 253
Ternstrom, Clinton C., 253
Terrell, Thomas J., 230
Terrien, George B., 299
Terry, Belaunde, 188
Terry, Roland, 253
Teska, Robert B., 259
Tessier, Robert L., 253, 299
Testa, Clorindo, 96
Teter Consultants, 314
Tétreault, Paul-André, 279, 300
Texas A&M University
  degree programs, 529, 532, 533
  staff, 495, 496, 643
  students/alumni, 499, 503, 539, 653
Texas Christian University, 529
Texas Historic Sites Atlas, 457
Texas State University, San Marcos, 529
Texas Tech University, 503, 529, 532, 533, 537
Texier, Charles, 175
Thalden, Barry R., 269
Thanh-Son Cao, Andrew, 222
Tharp, B. C., 253
Thayer, Robert, Jr., 269
Theilacker, Michael, 269
Thevenot, Richard, 283
Thiry, Paul Albert, 219, 347
This Old House, 456
Thomas, Carol J., 259
Thomas, Darcia Elizabeth, 535
Thomas, Donald, 275
Thomas, Dorwin A. J., 253
Thomas, James B., 253
Thomas, James L., 253
Thomas, James R., Jr., 230, 290
Thomas, Joseph F., 253
Thomas, June Manning, 259
Thomas, Sidney F., Jr., 259
Thomas, Sir Percy, 177, 302
Thomas, Val, 253
Thomas A. Douthat Jr., Architect, 314
Thomas Brown Architects, 314
Thomas Hacker Architects, Inc., 119
Thomas Hamilton & Associates, 315
Thomas Jefferson Award for Public Architecture, 195, *196*
Thomopulos, Gregs G., 230
Thompson, Benjamin, 59, 253
Thompson, David C., 253
Thompson, Dean, 286
Thompson, Donald E., 231
Thompson, Everett S., 231, 290
Thompson, J. William, 269
Thompson, Jane, 66, 127
Thompson, JoAnn Asher, 275, 544
Thompson, Laura, 510
Thompson, Maryann, 209
Thompson, Milo H., 221, 253
Thompson, Robert L., 253
Thompson, Sharyn, 273
Thompson, Toby, 541
Thompson, Ventulett, Stainback & Associates, 80, 326
Thompson, Warren D., 253
Thompson Design Group Inc., 115
Thomsen, Charles B., 253
Thomson, Sheona, 83
Thorbeck, Duane, 221, 253
Thoreau, Henry David, 436
Thorne, Karl, 253
Thornton, Amy, 536
Thornton, April, 271
Thornton, Dr. William, 329, 376
Thornton-Tomasetti Group, 112
Thorpe, Christy, 514
Thorson, Oswald H., 253
Thorton, Jonathan, 223
Threadgould, Tiffany, 410
Thrush, George, 209
Thurman, James, 410
Thurmond, J. S., 283
Tice, John P., Jr., 253
Tickle, Evelyn, 221
Tidwell, Philip, 513
Tiedt, H. G., 188
Tigerman, Stanley, 253, 288
Tighe, Patrick J., 62
Tihany, Adam, 288
Tilden, Raina E., 502
Tile Council of America, 584
Tillett, Michael P. C., 259
Tillett, Patrick, 253
Timberlake, James H., 221, 253
Time Magazine, 225
Timme, Robert H., 221, 253
Timmerman, Elizabeth, 516
Tims, William L., 538
Tincknell, Leslie D., 253
Tioanda, Yenche, 539
Tipton, Glen A., 253
Tishler, William H., 269
Tite, Sir William, 175, 302
Tittle, James D., 219, 253
TMP Architecture, 121
Tobey, Philip E., 253
Tobey + Davis, 163
Tobin, Calvin J., 253
Tobola, Logic, II, 253
Tod Williams, Billie Tsien and Associates, 60, 63, 345, 353, 390–391
Todd, Anderson, 253
Todd, David F. M., 253
Todd, Thomas A., 253
Todd & Associates Inc., 102

Toft, Carolyn H., 283
Toft, Jan, 286
Togawa and Smith Inc., 69
Toker, Franklin, 72, 303
Toledano, Roulhac, 72
Toll Architecture, 100
Tollefson, Lee, 253
Tomassi, John, 253
Tomazinis, Anthony R., 259
Tombazis, Alexandros N., 279
Tomblinson, James E., 253
Tompkins, David D., 273, 296
Tompkins, Donald H., 269
Tomsick, Frank, 253
Tomsik-Tomsik Architects/Planners, Ltd., 312
Tomson, Bernard, 283
Tonev, Luben N., 279
TOPAZ Medallion, 556, *557*
Topelson de Grinberg, Sara, 298
Topping, Kenneth C., 260
Torley, Caroline, 263
Torrance, T. Curtiss, 231
Torrance, William A. Clevenger, 231
Torre, L. Azeo, 222, 270
Torres Michel, Juan Jose, 499
Torti, John Francis, 253
Torti Gallas & Partners-CHK, Inc., 62, 63
Tortorich, Mark Joseph, 253
Toshiko Mori Architect, 392
Touart, Paul Baker, 434
Tough, Coulson, 253
Toulan, Nohad A., 260
Tournon-Branly, Marion, 279
Tourtellotte, John E., 374
Towers, Shavaun, 270
Town, Ithiel, 355
Town and Davis, 375
Toyomura, Dennis T., 253
Toyota Motor Sales, 418
Trachtenberg, Marvin, 72, 73
Tracy and Swartwout, 375
Traendly, W. F., 283
Train, Jack D., 110, 253
Train, R. E., 283
Tramba, Jonathan, 514
Trancik, Roger T., 270
Trask, Tallman, III, 283
Traugott, Alan, 271
Travisano, Fred, 221
Treanor, Betty, 275
Treberspurg, Martin, 189
Treffinger, Karl E., Sr., 253
Tregre, Louis, 109
Treib, Marc, 160, 224
Treister, Kenneth, 253
Trester-Wilson, Eve Maureen, 538
Tri-County Metropolitan Transportation District of Oregon, 164
Tribble, Michael, 253
Trigiani, David M., 253
Trim, Donald R., 231, 290
Trinh, Yen, 500
TRO/The Richie Organization, 326
Trogdon, William H., 253
Troller, Howard E., 270
Trom, Phil, 500
Tromczynski, Amanda, 516
Trotter, Morris E., 222
Trowbridge, Peter J., 270
Trowbridge and Livingston, 376
Troyan, Marcia, 275
Troyer, Leroy, 253
Trudnak, Stephen J., 270
Truex, William H., Jr., 253
Trumbauer, Horace, 353, 462
Tsao, Calvin, 288
Tschumi, Jean, 298
Tse-Chan, Chiu Lin, 253
Tseckares, Charles N., 253
Tseng, Yilun, 500
Tsien, Billie, 84, 288, 390
Tsoi, Edward T. M., 253
Tsuda, Kazutoshi, 409
Tubbs, Ralph, 79
Tuck, Seab A., III, 253
Tuck Hinton Architects, 347
Tucker, Jack R., Jr., 253
Tucker, Robert, 271
Tucker, Thomas B., 253
Tufts University, 523
Tugwell, Rexford Guy, 335
Tulane University, 294, 503, 522, 537, 539
Tulloch, Margret B., 499
Tully, Richard L., 253
Tunnell-Splangler-Walsh, 105
Turano, Emanuel N., 253
Turnbull, John Gordon, 253
Turnbull, Joshua, 511
Turnbull, William, Jr., 221
Turnbull Griffin Haesloop, 173, 174, 207
Turner, Frank F., 260
Turner, James R., 222, 270
Turner, Jerry Mitchell, 270
Turner, John F. C., 189
Turner, Judith, 66
Turner, Paul Venable, 72
Turner, Stuart, 260
Turner, Suzanne Louise, 270
Turner, Taylor F., Jr., 231
Turner, Thomas P., Jr., 253
Turner, Tom, 95
Turner, William, 294
Turner Construction Co., 123
Tushie Montgomery & Associates, Inc., 315
Tuskegee University, 517, 537
Tusler, Wilbur H., Jr., 253
Tustian, Richard E., 260
Tuttle, Daniel, 222
Tuttle, Jack K., 231
Tuttle, Ronald W., 270
Twenty-Five Year Award, 197–199
T.Y. Lin International, 112
Tyler, Ilene R., 253
Tyler, James L., 253
Tyler, Robert, 253
Tyng, Anne G., 253
Tyrnauer, Herbert H., 273, 541
Tyznik, Anthony, 270

U

Uchii, Shozo, 279
Uecker, Raymond L., 270
Uesugi, Takeo, 270
Uhlin, Lennart, 279
Uhlir, Edward K., 253
UIA Gold Medal, 200
Umemoto, Nanako, 74
Underwood, Kenneth A., 253
Underwood, Max, 496, 498
Underwriters Laboratories Inc., 585
UNESCO, 455, 459, 460, 481
UNESCO Asia-Pacific Heritage Awards for Culture Heritage Conservation, 479
Unger, Dean F., 253
Unger, Roberta Marrano, 253
United Nations, 419
United Nations Centre for Human Settlements (HABITAT), 404, 411, 420, 585
United Nations Habitat One, 389
Universidad de Puerto Rico, 496
Universite de Montreal, 496
Université Laval, 537, 539
University of Akron, 527, 533
University of Alabama, 517
University of Albany, SUNY, 500, 526
University of Arizona, 503, 511, 517, 537, 548
University of Arkansas, 495, 503, 517, 537
University of Bridgeport, 519, 541
University of British Columbia, 495, 496, 503, 539
University of Calgary, 503, 537
University of California, system, 411
University of California, Berkeley
  Berkeley Prize, 513
  degree programs, 518, 532, 533
  rankings, 555
  staff, 225, 271, 294, 495, 496, 497, 556
  students/alumni, 385, 388, 503, 509, 513, 537, 548
University of California, Berkeley Extension, 518
University of California, Davis, 518
University of California, Irvine, 519, 533
University of California, Los Angeles
  degree programs, 519, 532, 533
  staff, 271, 496, 497
  students/alumni, 391, 503, 537, 550
University of California, Los Angeles Extension, 519
University of California, Santa Barbara, 519, 532
University of Chicago, 521, 532
University of Cincinnati, 21, 527, 544, 548, 554, 555
University of Colorado, Denver/Boulder
  degree programs, 519, 532, 533
  staff, 294, 496
  students/alumni, 503, 537, 645
University of Connecticut, 519
University of Delaware, 519, 532
University of Detriot Mercy, 524
University of Florida
  degree programs, 520, 532
  rankings, 554
  staff, 295, 496
  students/alumni, 499, 503, 509, 537, 643
University of Georgia, 511, 521
University of Greenwich, London, 95
University of Guelph, 510
University of Hartford, 519
University of Hawaii, Honolulu, 532
University of Hawaii, Manoa, 138, 503, 521, 537, 540
University of Houston, 295, 503, 529, 537, 540, 548
University of Idaho, 503, 521, 537, 548

Name Index

V

Van Siclen, Bill, 217
Van Sweden, James, 270
Van Tine, William H., 462
Van Valkenburgh, Michael R., 222, 270
Van Zanten, David, 73
Vanbourg, Mitchell, 253
Vanderfleet-Scott, Jill, 286
Vandergriff Group Architects, 315
Vanderwarker, Peter, 66
Vanderzwaag, Tabe, 499
VanDine, Harold F., Jr., 253
VanTilburg, Johannes, 253
Vaporciyan, Harutun, 253
Vargas, Marcelo E., 279
Varner, Harold R., 253
Varney, Carleton, 288
Varney, Edward L., 369
Vasquez, Pedro R., 279
Vassos, John, 127, 273
Vaughn, Hannah S., 503
Vaughn, Randall C., 209
Vaux, Calvert, 329, 349
Vazzano, Andrew A., 253
Vecsei, Eva, 279
Veiller, Lawrence T., 335
Veitzer, Leonard M., 253
Velardo, Margaret, 275
Velez, Jaime, 550, *551*
Velleco, James, 221
Velzy, Charles O., 231
Venne, Gérard, 300
Ventulett, Thomas W., 254
Venturi, Rauch and Scott Brown, 80
Venturi, Robert
anecdote/quote, 204, 389
awards/honors, 64, 84, 157, 165, 198, 204, 221, 226, 254, 288
Venturi, Scott Brown and Associates, 225, 226, 327, 345, 351, 353
Verdugo, Jorge N., 279
Verga, Mariana L., 283
Vergason, E. Michael, 222
Verges, Judith André, 263
Veri, Albert R., 270
Verizon Communications, 418
Vernacular Architecture Forum, 429, 456, 480
Vernon, Shirley J., 254
Vernon-McKeen, Kathryn C., 254
Veronica Rudge Green Prize in Urban Design, 203
Verzone, Craig P., 223
Vesnin, Victor, 177
Vicente Wolf Associates, 134
Vick, Donald D., 231
Vick, William R., 254
Vickery, Robert L., 254
Vickrey, Wilmont, 254
Vicuna, Tomas R., 279
Vidler, Anthony, 73
Viemeister, Read, 273
Viemeister, Tucker, 273
Vieux Carre Commission, 453
Vignelli, Lella, 181, 288
Vignelli, Massimo, 181, 288
Viguier, Jean-Paul, 279
Vilanova Artigas, Joao Baptista, 96, 137
Vilchis, Ricardo L., 279
Villa Maria College of Buffalo, 526
Villacortaq, Eduardo O., 279
Villanueva, Gregory D., 254
Villarrceal, Carlos C., 231
Villere, Keith J., 270
Vincent J. Scully Prize, 204
Vincent James Associates, Inc., 207
Vincent Snyder, Architect, 159
Vinci, John, 254
Vinick, Bernard, 263
Vining, Donna, 263
Viñoly, Rafael, 8, 254
Violett-le-Duc, Eugène Emmanuel, 175
Violich, Francis, 260, 335
Virginia Commenwealth University, 530, 532
Virginia Polytechnic Institute and State University
degree programs, 390, 530, 532, 533, 545
rankings, 554, 555
staff, 294, 495, 556
students/alumni, 503, 509, 538, 540
Viscovich, Roen, 275
Vitols, Austris J., 221
Vitra Design Museum, 608
Vitra Design Museum Berlin, 608
VOA Associates Incorporated, 326, 553
Voelter Associates Inc., 315
Voelz, Laura, 510
Vogel, Craig, 296
Vogel, Stephen, 254
Vogt, Noland, 273
Vogue, Marquis de, 175
Volgstadt, 509
Volk, Leonard W., II, 254
Von Bieberstein, Karl, 270
Von Brock, A. R., 254
Von Dohlen, Robert J., 254
Von Eckardt, Wolf, 283
von Ferstel, Baron, 175
von Hansen, Baron, 175
von Holst, Herman, 385
von Klenze, Leo, 175
Von Luhrte, Richard L., 254
von Schmidt, Baron, 175
Von Wodtke, Mark J., 270
Vonier, Thomas, 254
Voorhees, Alan M., 260
Voorhees, Stephen F., 291
Voorsanger, Bartholome, 254
Vosbeck, R. Randall, 254, 291
Vosbeck, William F., 254
Vose, John G., 503
Vouga, Jean-Pierre, 137
Voute, Fleur, 500
Voysey, Charles Francis Annesley, 177
Vreeland, Thomas R., 254
Vrooman, R. E., 254
V'Soske, 66

W

W Architecture & Landscape Architecture, 94
Wachs, Martin, 260
Wachter, Harry W., 353
Wacker, Charles Henry, 335
Wacker, John, 270, 293
Waddy, Patricia, 73, 303
Wade, Robert C., 231
Wagener, Hobart D., 254
Wagner, Fritz, 260
Wagner, William J., 254
Wagoner, Robert, 260
Waid, Dan E., 291
Wainwright, Sam H., 231
Waite, John G., 254
Waitkus, Robert A., 231
Walczak, Erica Leigh, 538
Wald, Lillian, 335
Waldman, Peter D., 221, 496
Waldron, Lawrence G., 254
Waley, William Richard, 292
Walker, Aaron D., 535
Walker, Bruce M., 254
Walker, Kenneth H., 254, 288
Walker, Lawrence L., 270
Walker, Peter E., 66, 270
Walker, Ralph Thomas, 59, 219, 291
Walker, Richard O., Jr., 231
Walker, Victor J., 270
Walker Art Center, 64
Walker Group/CNI Design, 182
Walkley, Gavin, 301
Wall Street Journal, 218
Wallace, Charles, 375
Wallace, Connie C., 283
Wallace, David A., 254
Wallace, David D., 254
Wallace, Donald Q., 254
Wallace, Mike, 449
Wallace, Thomas, 375
Wallace Roberts & Todd, 327
Wallach, Les, 254
Wallgren, Jerrod, 537
Walling, Larry D., 270
Wallis, Thomas H., 270
Wallpaper, 605
Walmsley, Elizabeth, 223
Walsh, Charles G., 254
Walsh, Sally, 288
Walt Disney Company, 21, 152, 457
Walt Disney Imagineering, 117
Walter, Henry, 376
Walter, J. Jackson, 471
Walter, Lloyd G., Jr., 254
Walter, Thomas Ustick, 291, 376
Walter P. Moore, Inc., 112
Walter Taylor Award, 116
Walters, Ronald M., 270
Walton, Craig H., 221
Walton, Tony, 289
Walz, Kevin, 224, 288
Wampler, Jan, 496, 498
Wanaselja, Timothy Isak, 537
Wandelmaier, W. G., 254
Wander, Sheldon D., 254
Wang, Che Wei, 550, *551*
Wang, Fan, 511
Wang, Thomas C., 270
Wank Adams Slavin Associates, 174, 341
Warburton, R. J., 254, 284
Ward, Barbara, 64
Ward, G. T., 254
Ward, Robertson, Jr., 254
Ward Jewell and Associates, 315
Ware, C. E., 254
Warfield, James P., 496
Warnecke, John Carl, 84, 254, 271, 353, 374, 454
Warner, Barry J., 270
Warner, Charles H., Jr., 254
Warner, Clyde K., Jr., 254

Name Index

Wickstead, George W., 270
Widener, Christopher, 254
Widom, Chester A., 254, 291
Wiedemann, Nichole, 222
Wiener, Michael, 263
Wierenga, Jeffrey Allen, 78
Wiese, William, II, 254, 299
Wigginton, Brooks E., 223
Wigginton, Ron, 270
Wight and Wight, 351
Wilcox, E. D., 254
Wilcox, Glenda, 275
Wilcox, Jerry Cooper, 254
Wilcox, Steve, 273
Wilde, Dudley Keith, 301
Wilder, Walter R., 376
Wildermuth, Gordon L., 254
Wiley, Charles D., 222
Wiley, Danielle, 538
Wiley, James E., 254
Wilkerson, Charles E., 254
Wilkes, Joseph A., 254
Wilkes, Michael B., 254
Wilkins Wood Goforth Mace Associates Ltd., 341
Wilkinson, Eugene R., 231
Wilkinson, Leslie, 168
Wilkinson Eyre Architects, 83, 104
Wilkoff, William L., 108, 263
Wilks, Barbara E., 254
Will, Philip, Jr., 291
Will Bruder Architects, 207
Willen, Paul, 254
WIlliam and Flora Hewlett Foundation, 202
William B. Ittner, Inc., 341
William E. Epp & Associates Inc., 315
William F. Burch Architects, Inc., 315
William L. Burgin Architects, Inc., 315
William L. Pereira & Associates, 631
William McDonough + Partners, 407
William Miller & Sons, 374
William Morris Associates Architects, 315
William Rawn Associates Architects Inc., 63
William Stout Architectural Books, 591
William Tweeddale and Company, 374
Williams, A. Richard, 254
Williams, Allen Wyatt, 537
Williams, Allison G., 255
Williams, Betsy, 207
Williams, Bunny, 288
Williams, Daniel E., 255
Williams, Donald L., 255, 548
Williams, E. Stewart, 255
Williams, Edgar I., 219
Williams, F. Carter, 110, 255
Williams, Frank, 255
Williams, Harold L., 255
Williams, Homer L., 255, 299
Williams, Jerald A., 231
Williams, John G., 255, 495
Williams, Lorenzo D., 255, 299
Williams, Marguerite Neel, 435
Williams, Mark F., 255
Williams, Michael Ann, 431
Williams, Richard A., 495
Williams, Richard L., 231
Williams, Roger B., 255
Williams, Sara Katherine, 270
Williams, Susan, 195, *196*
Williams, Terence J., 255, 279, 300
Williams, Tod C., 84, 222, 255, 288, 390
Williams, W. Gene, 255
Williams, Wayne R., 255
Williams College, 654
Williams-Russell & Johnson Inc., 361
Williamson, Frederick, 435
Williamson, Ronald A., 260
Willis, Beverly A., 255, 388, 389, 392
Willis, Daniel, 125
Willis, Michael E., 255
Willis, Rev. Robert, 175
Willis, Shelby K., 290
Willis and Associates, 388
Willwerth, Roy W. , 279, 300
Wilmot, John C., 255
Wilson, Andrew, 538
Wilson, Blair Mansfield, 301
Wilson, Charles Coker, 376
Wilson, Chris, 431
Wilson, Forrest, 495
Wilson, Frances E., 263, 275
Wilson, Francis, 353
Wilson, Harry M., 231
Wilson, Honorable Pete, 283
Wilson, Jeffrey, 255
Wilson, John E., 255
Wilson, John L., 205
Wilson, Larry T., 270
Wilson, M. Judith, 275
Wilson, Merrill & Alexander, 197
Wilson, Richard A., 270
Wilson, Richard Guy, 283
Wilson, Robert, 66
Wilson, Sir Hugh, 302
Wilson, Trisha, 288
Wilson, William D., 255
Wilsonart International, 457
Wimmer, Harriett, 461
Winchester, Alice, 435
Windman, Arnold L., 231, 290
Window & Door Manufacturers Association, 585
Windsor, Deirdre, 223
WIngfield, J. D., 260
Winkel, Steven R., 255
Winkelstein, Jon Peter, 255
Winkler, Gail Casey, 263
Winkler, John H., 255
Winslow, Paul D., 255
Winslow, William P., III, 270
Winstead, D. Geary, 275
Winter, Arch R., 255, 260
Winter, Steven, 255
Wintermute, Marjorie M., 255
Winterscheidt, Brian M., 536
Winterthur Museum and Gardens, 289
Winthrop University, 528
Wirkler, Norman E., 255
Wirth, Conrad L., 90
Wirth, Theodore J., 270, 293
Wirtz, Michael, 192, 263, 275
Wise, Gloria, 283
Wiseman, Carter, 65
Wiseman, Paul Vincent, 109
Wisner, John B., 263
Wisnewski, Joseph J., 255
Withers, Benjamin C., 260
Withers, Frederick, 329
Witherspoon, Gayland B., 255
Witsell, Charles, Jr., 255
Witte, D. C., 263
Wittenberg, Gordon G., 255
Wittkower, Rudolf, 65, 72
Wittwer, Gall, 223
W.J. Assenmacher Company, 375
Wnderlich, C. A., 279
Woehle, Fritz, 255
Woerner, Robert L., 270, 293
Wojcik, J. Daniel, 270
Wolbrink, Donald, 335
Wold, Robert L., 255
Wolf, Arnold, 273
Wolf, Dr. Ricardo, 206
Wolf, Harry C., III, 255
Wolf, Martin F., 255
Wolf, Vicente, *135*, 288
Wolf Foundation, 206
Wolf Prize for Architecture, 206
Wolfangle, Douglas G., 231
Wolfberg Alvarez and Partners, 201
Wolff, Zimmer, Gunsul, Frasca, and Ritter, 353
Wolff Lyon Architects, 174
Wolford, Arol, 271, 283
Wolford, Nancy L., 547
Women's Architecture Club, 386
Won, Chung Soo, 279
Wong, F. Michael, 67
Wong, Gin D., 255
Wong, John L., 223
Wong, Joseph O., 255
Wong, Kellogg H., 255
Wong, Paul, 502
Wong, William, Jr., 255
Wong, Wing Yan, 537
Wong & Ouyang Ltd., 380
Woo, Carolina Y., 255
Woo, Kyu S., 255
Wood, Bernard, 279, 300
Wood, Edith Elmer, 335
Wood, Edmund D., 263
Wood, Ernest, III, 429, 449
Wood, H. A., III, 255
Wood, Hart, 310
Wood, John-David, 500
Wood, Marilyn, 283
Wood, Susan, 275
Wood Design & Building, 207
Wood Design Awards, 207, *208*
Wood Le Bois, 207
Woodbridge, John M., 255
Woodbridge, Sally B., 66
Woodbury University, 295, 503, 519, 538, 554
Woodcock, David Geoffrey, 255, 495
Woodhouse, David, 255
Woodhurst, Robert S., III, 255
Woodhurst, Stanford, Jr., 255
Wooding, Peter H., 273, 296
Woodlock, Hon. Douglas P., 195
Woodring, Cooper C., 127, 273, 296
Woodroffe, Enrique, 255
Woods, Elliot, 376
Woods, Lebbeus, 66
Woodsen, Riley D., 231
Woodward, Thomas E., 255
Woodward, William McKenzie, 434
Wooldridge, Joel C., 260
Wooley, David L., 255
Woolford, Paul, 209, *210*

Name Index

X

Y

Z

Site Index

NOTE: This is an index of architectural sites, projects and works. Locations that are not an architectural site per se–for example, universities–can be found in the Name Index on page 659. Pages in italics refer to illustrations.

A

B

C

Site Index

D

E

F

Site Index

Site Index

T

U

Site Index

Site Index

Site Index

Site Index

Site Index

Site Index

Elvehjem Museum of Art (Madison), 346
Grand Avenue (Milwaukee), 183
Greendale, 333
La Crosse, 316, 438
Lambeau Field (Green Bay), 368
Lincoln Creek Design-Build Flood Control Ecological Restoration (Milwaukee), 155
Miller Park (Milwaukee), 360
Milwaukee Art Museum, 348
Milwaukee Art Museum Addition, 112
Milwaukee Art Museum Quadracci Pavilion, 113, 330, *343*
S.C. Johnson & Son Administration Building (Racine), 197, 329, 330, 383
Sheboygan Falls, 316, 438
St. Boniface Episcopal Church (Mequon), 170
State Capitol (Madison), 376
Taliesin East (Spring Green), 478

Wyoming
Riddell Residence (Wilson), 207
State Capitol (Cheyenne), 376
Swan Land and Cattle Company Headquarters (Chugwater), 478
Yellowstone National Park, 330, 333, 452

URUGUAY
Colonia del Sacramento Historic Quarter, 485

UZBEKISTAN
Bukhara Historic Centre, 485
Itchan Kala, 485
Samarkand-Crossroads of Culture, 485
Shakhrisyabz Historic Centre, 485

VENEZUELA
Coro and its Port, 485
La Guaira Historic City (Vargas), 492
Real Fuerza de Santiago de Arroyo (Araya), 492

VIET NAM
Hoi An Ancient Town, 485
Hué Monuments, 485

YEMEN
Sana'a Old City, 485
Shibam Old Walled City, 485
Zabid Historic Town, 485

YUGOSLAVIA
Kotor Natural and Culturo-Historic Region, 485
Prizren Historic Centre (Kosovo), 492

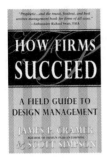

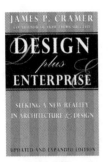

ORDER FORM

How Firms Succeed: A Field Guide to Design Management: $39

Design plus Enterprise: $29

Almanac of Architecture & Design: $49.50

America's Best Architecture & Design Schools: $29.95

DesignIntelligence (including a one-year membership to the Design Futures Council): $289 annually

Shipping: $4.95
(add $1.50 per additional title)

NOTE: Shipping is included with DesignIntelligence–there is NO additional charge

Title	Quantity	Price:
	Shipping	
	Order Total	

❑ Check ❑ Credit card

Card # Expiration Signature

Contact/Shipping Information

Name Company

Address

City State Zip

Telephone Fax

Email

Please fax this form to Greenway Communications: (770) 209-3778 or mail: Greenway Communications, 30 Technology Parkway South, Suite 200, Norcross, GA 30092. For additional information call (800) 726-8603.

COMMENT FORM

Invitation For Comments and Suggestions

Please include any ideas, comments, or suggestions for the *Almanac of Architecture & Design.*

Suggestions and Comments

Contact Information

Name

Address

City State Zip

Telephone

Fax

Email

Please return this form to:

Greenway Consulting
ATTN: Almanac
30 Technology Parkway South, Suite 200
Norcross, GA 30092
Tel 770.209.3770
Fax 770.209.3778

Or email us at almanac@greenwayconsulting.com

The Greenway Group, Inc.

The Greenway Group, Inc. is a multi-faceted firm that supports design excellence through the promotion of innovative business practices, a focus on the future, and knowledge sharing. Its consulting division, Greenway Consulting (www.greenwayconsulting.com), specializes in future-based strategic advisory services, executive coaching, mergers and acquisitions, executive recruitment, strategic planning, brand analysis, futures forecasting, and business modeling for the A/E/C industry. Counsel House Research, Greenway's research arm, supports many of Greenway Consulting's initiatives with its extensive databases and pursues customized research projects such as the annual architecture and interior design school rankings. Its communications division, Greenway Communications, publishes the annual *Almanac of Architecture & Design*, as well as many design management titles under its Östberg Library of Design Management imprint, and the Archidek series of educational, collectable architecture trading cards. Greenway also manages the non-profit think-tank, the Design Futures Council; its mission is to explore trends, changes, and new opportunities in design, architecture, engineering, and building technology to foster innovation and improve the performance of member organizations. The Council also publishes the monthly *DesignIntelligence* (www.di.net), the international design marketplace's strategic management newsletter. Greenway Group is firmly committed to helping organizations grow faster, smarter and healthier through shared knowledge and strategic insights for the future.

Counsel House Research

Counsel House Research, one of the world's oldest and most trusted research firms focused on the built environment, became affiliated with The Greenway Group in 1995. Counsel House Research identifies and analyzes emerging trends and "design futures" in the global market as well as their impact upon the business of design, construction and product manufacturing. It has worked with some of the world's leading design firms, construction companies, corporations, publications, and associations, helping them to anticipate the future. Some common service areas include market research and competitive intelligence; profession, industry and consumer-based benchmarking; brand audits and diagnostics; trends analysis and forecasting; and leadership and staff audits. All research initiatives are customized, confidential and proprietary in nature. Counsel House's years of experience and its careful mining of relevant information has produced an extensive "intelligence bank[sm]" with ready access to knowledge on a range of issues, which is the foundation of our ability to help clients understand markets and to elevate their position in the future. This investment in intelligence establishes Counsel House Research as the preeminent authority on the historical paths to success and as an innovative generator of knowledge about the future of design management. Our intelligence bank[sm] and our unique processes enable us to obtain superior results and insure a sustainable future for our clients.

James P. Cramer

James P. Cramer is the founder and chairman of The Greenway Group, Inc.; co-chair of the Washington D.C.-based think-tank, the Design Futures Council; editor-in-chief of *DesignIntelligence*, a monthly letter on trends, strategies, and changes published by the Design Futures Council; and adjunct professor of architecture at the University of Hawaii. He researches, consults, and gives seminars for leading professional firms around the world and is the author of over 135 articles and several books, including the critically acclaimed *Design + Enterprise, Seeking a New Reality in Architecture*, and co-author of *How Firms Succeed, A Field Guide to Management Solutions.* Cramer is the former chief executive of The American Institute of Architects in Washington, D.C., past president of the American Architectural Foundation, and a former publisher of *Architecture* magazine. He is also a fellow of the Western Behavioral Sciences Institute in La Jolla, Cal., and a Richard Upjohn Fellow of The American Institute of Architects.

Jennifer Evans Yankopolus

Jennifer Evans Yankopolus is the co-editor of the *Almanac of Architecture & Design* and an architectural historian. She is also the editor of the Archidek series of collectable, educational architecture trading cards and an editor for the Östberg press where she helps projects to achieve the imprint's goal of promoting design excellence. She has a master's degree in architecture history from the Georgia Institute of Technology. She also studied at Drake University, where she received her B.S. in business administration and earned a master's degree in heritage preservation from Georgia State University. As a researcher, architectural historian, and project director, she brings a historical perspective to Greenway's initiatives.

Robert Ivy

Robert Ivy, FAIA, the editor in chief of *Architectural Record*, has combined two disparate careers–that of practicing architect and editor–into a single job. During his tenure, *Record* has grown to become the world's largest professional architectural publication, encompassing both print and the Web. A frequent spokesperson for the profession, he travels extensively for the magazine and has broadened its coverage to include more international projects. Born in Mississippi, he was educated at the University of the South (BA, English) and architecture (Tulane University). His book on the architect Fay Jones was re-released in soft cover in May 2001.

östberg™

Library of Design Management

Every relationship of value requires constant care and commitment. At Östberg, we are relentless in our desire to create and bring forward only the best ideas in design, architecture, interiors, and design management. Using diverse mediums of communications, including books and the Internet, we are constantly searching for thoughtful ideas that are erudite, witty, and of lasting importance to the quality of life. Inspired by the architecture of Ragnar Östberg and the best of Scandinavian design and civility, the Östberg Library of Design Management seeks to restore the passion for creativity that makes better products, spaces, and communities. The essence of Östberg can be summed up in our quality charter to you: "Communicating concepts of leadership and design excellence."